T0074456

Argumentation
in Artificial Intelligence

Argumentation in Artificial Intelligence

Edited by

Iyad Rahwan

Guillermo R. Simari

 Springer

Editors

Dr. Iyad Rahwan
Faculty of Informatics
British University in Dubai
P.O.Box 502216, Dubai
United Arab Emirates
irahwan@acm.org

Guillermo R. Simari
Department of Computer Science &
  Engineering
Universidad Nacional del Sur
Alem 1253
(8000) Bahía Blanca - Argentina
grs@cs.uns.edu.ar

and

School of Informatics
University of Edinburgh
Edinburgh EH8 9AB, UK

ISBN 978-0-387-98196-3   e-ISBN 978-0-387-98197-0
DOI 10.1007/978-0-387-98197-0
Springer Dordrecht Heidelberg London New York

Library of Congress Control Number: 2009927013

Printed on acid-free paper

Springer is part of Springer Science+Business Media (www.springer.com)

To Zoe, for her love and support.

– I.R.

To my family with love.

– G.S.

Foreword

Argumentation is all around us. Letters to the Editor often make points of consistency, and "Why" is one of the most frequent questions in language, asking for reasons behind behaviour. And argumentation is more than 'reasoning' in the recesses of single minds, since it crucially involves interaction. It cements the coordinated social behaviour that has allowed us, in small bands of not particularly physically impressive primates, to dominate the planet, from the mammoth hunt all the way up to organized science. This volume puts argumentation on the map in the field of Artificial Intelligence. This theme has been coming for a while, and some famous pioneers are chapter authors, but we can now see a broader systematic area emerging in the sum of topics and results.

As a logician, I find this intriguing, since I see AI as 'logic continued by other means', reminding us of broader views of what my discipline is about. Logic arose originally out of reflection on many-agent practices of disputation, in Greek Antiquity, but also in India and China. And logicians like me would like to return to this broader agenda of rational agency and intelligent interaction. Of course, Aristotle also gave us a formal systems methodology that deeply influenced the field, and eventually connected up happily with mathematical proof and foundations. Thus, I see two main paradigms from Antiquity that come together in the modern study of argumentation: Platos' *Dialogues* as the paradigm of intelligent interaction, and Euclid's *Elements* as the model of rigour. Of course, some people also think that formal mathematical proof is itself the ultimate ideal of reasoning - but you may want to change your mind about reasoning's 'peak experiences' when you see top mathematicians argue interactively at a seminar.

But more themes went into the mixture of this Book. Leibniz and those after him, from Boole to Turing or McCarthy, added computation as a major category in understanding reasoning. Now, this is not necessarily congenial to argumentation: Leibniz' famous 'Calculemus' calls for replacing interactive disputation by mechanical computing. But modern computation itself is distributed and interactive, so we are in tune again.

Also relevant to understanding this Book is the emergence of 'Argumentation Theory' in the 20th century, partly in opposition to formal logic. In particular, Toulmin gave us a much richer view of actual inference than just a bleak jump from premises to conclusion, and placed it in a historical tradition of dynamic legal procedure (what he calls the 'formalities') rather than just the static mathematical form of statements. Indeed, Mathematics and Law seem two major pillars of our culture, with the latter often under-estimated as an intellectual force. This tandem seems significant to me, since it fits the Dynamic Turn I have long advocated toward logical studies of cognitive actions, and indeed multi-agent interaction. Strategic responses to others, and 'logical empathy' putting yourself in someone else's place, are keys to rational behaviour. And argumentation is one of the major processes that make this interaction happen. Thus, *pace* Toulmin, logic and argumentation theory can form happy unions after all, witness the work of colleagues like van Eemeren, Krabbe & Walton, Gabbay & Woods, etc.

And even beyond these strands, the land of rational agency is populated by other tribes, many equipped with mathematical tools. Game theorists study social mechanisms, social scientists care about social choice and decisions, and philosophers, too, have long studied rational interaction. Think of Kant's categorical imperative of treating others as an end like yourself, not just a means. This only makes sense in a society of agents.

AI lets all these strands come together: logic, mathematics, computation, and human behaviour. It has long been a sanctuary for free-thinkers about reasoning and other intelligent activities, taking a fresh look at the practice of common sense all around us. Indeed, I see the above perspective as an appropriate extension of the very concept of 'common sense', which is not just 'sense' about how single agents represent the world and make inferences about it, but equally much 'common' about how they sensibly interact with others. And once more, argumentation is a major mechanism for doing so.

The content of this rich volume is definitely not exhausted by the above. It contains methods from computer science, mathematics, philosophy, law, and economics, merging artificial with natural intelligence. Its formal methods range from logic programs to abstract argumentation systems, and from non-monotonic default logics and belief revision to classical proof theory. It also highlights multi-agent dialogue and decision making, including connections with game theory - where our rich practices of argumentation and debate pose many unsolved challenges. Just try to understand how we successfully conduct meetings, and 'play' arguments of various strengths over time! Finally, I would mention an intriguing feature in many studies of argumentation, viz. attention to fallacies and errors. Once I was taken to task by a prominent medical researcher, who claimed that the most interesting information about the human body and mind is found with patients deviating from the norm, and coping with 'disturbance' in unexpected creative ways. He did not understand why logicians would wilfully ignore the corresponding rich evidence in the case of reasoning, concentrating just on angelic correctness. I agree, and linking up with empirical psychology and cognitive science seems an attractive next step, given the suggestive material collected here.

This volume tries to stake out a new field, and hence: papers, careers, tenure. But something broader is at stake. Original visions of AI tended to emphasize hugely uninspiring, if terrifying, goals like machines emulating humans. A Dutch book with 'vision statements' by leading scientists once revealed a disturbing uniformity: all described a technological end goal for their field of which all said they hoped to be dead long before it was achieved. I myself prefer goals that I could live with. Understanding argumentation means understanding a crucial feature of ourselves, perhaps using machines to improve our performance, helping us humans be better at what we are.

I am happy that books like this are happening and I congratulate the editors and authors.

Amsterdam and Stanford, December 2008   *Johan van Benthem*

Preface

This book is about the common ground between two fields of inquiry: Argumentation Theory and Artificial Intelligence. On the one hand, formal models of argumentation are making significant and increasing contributions to Artificial Intelligence, from defining semantics of logic programs, to implementing persuasive medical diagnostic systems, to studying negotiation dialogues in multi-agent systems. On the other hand, Artificial Intelligence has also made an impact on Argumentation Theory and Practice, for example by providing formal tools for argument analysis, evaluation, and visualisation.

The field of Argumentation in Artificial Intelligence has grown significantly in the past few years resulting in a substantial body of work and well-established technical literature. A testimony to this is the appearance of several special issues in leading scientific journals in recent years, (*e.g.,* Springer's Journal of Autonomous Agents and Multiagent Systems 2006; Elsevier's Artificial Intelligence Journal 2007; IEEE Intelligent Systems 2007; Wiley's International Journal of Intelligent Systems 2007). Another evidence of the maturity of this area is the establishment of a new biannual international conference in 2006 (see www.comma-conf.org). In addition, two series of workshops have been co-located with major AI conferences: the Argumentation in Multi-Agent Systems (ArgMAS) workshop series running annually alongside AAMAS since 2004, and the Computational Models of Natural Argument (CMNA) workshop running series alongside IJCAI and ECAI since 2001. Yet, although valuable survey papers exist, there is no comprehensive presentation of the major achievements in the field. This volume is a response to a growing need for an in-depth presentation of this fast-expanding area. As such it can be seen as a confluence of deep exposition and comprehensive exploration of the underlying themes in the various areas, done by leading researchers. While no single volume on Argumentation and Artificial Intelligence could cover the entire scope of this dynamic area, these selected writings will give the reader an insightful view of a landscape of stimulating ideas that drive forward the fundamental research and the creation of applications.

This book is aimed at new and current researchers in Argumentation Theory and in Artificial Intelligence interested in exploring the rich terrain at the intersection between these two fields. In particular, the book presents an overview of key concepts in Argumentation Theory and of formal models of Argumentation in AI. After laying a strong foundation by covering the fundamentals of argumentation and formal argument modeling, the book expands its focus to more specialised topics, such as algorithmic issues, argumentation in multi-agent systems, and strategic aspects of argumentation. Finally, as a coda, the book presents some practical applications of argumentation in AI and applications of AI in argumentation.

Although the book is an edited collection, the chapters' topics and order was done carefully to produce a highly organised text containing a progressive development of intuitions, ideas and techniques, starting from philosophical backgrounds, to abstract argument systems, to computing arguments, to the appearance of applications presenting innovative results. Authors had the chance to review each others' work at various stages of writing in order to coordinate content, ensuring unified notation (when possible) and natural progression.

Readers of this book will acquire an appreciation of a wide range of topics in Argumentation and Artificial Intelligence covering, for the first time, a breadth of hot topics. Throughout the chapters the authors have provided extensive examples to ensure that readers develop the right intuitions before they move from one topic to another.

The primary audience is composed of researchers and graduate students working in Autonomous Agents, AI and Law, Logic in Computer Science, Electronic Governance, Multi-agent Systems, and the growing research represented by the interdisciplinary inquiry carried out in many areas such as Decision Support Systems. Given the scope and depth of the chapters of this book, its content provides an excellent foundation for several different graduate courses.

The book begins with an "Introduction to Argumentation Theory" by Douglas Walton, who was one of the argumentation theorists who pioneered joint work with AI researchers. The rest of the book's twenty three chapters have been organised into four parts: "Abstract Argument Systems", "Arguments with Structure", "Argumentation in Multi-Agent Systems", and "Applications". Chapters in this book have been written by researchers that have helped shape the field. As such, we are confident that this book will be an essential resource for graduate students and researchers coming to the area.

The value of this book is in the ideas it presents. Thus we gratefully acknowledge efforts by all authors who shared their ideas and deep insights of this fertile area of research in such a clear manner. Furthermore, they also acted as peer reviewers of other chapters and helped to significantly improve the quality and the flow of the book. We would also like to thank all the contributions made by the different organisations that supported the authors of this book as they individually recognise in each chapter.

We are grateful to the Springer team, and in particular Melissa Fearon and Valerie Schofield, for supporting the creation of this book from early discussions right through to final editorial work.

Last but not least, we are always grateful to our families for their endless love and support.

Dubai, Edinburgh and Bahia Blanca,   *Iyad Rahwan*
December 2008   *Guillermo Simari*

Contents

Chapter 1
Argumentation Theory: A Very Short Introduction

Douglas Walton

1 Introduction

Since the time of the ancient Greek philosophers and rhetoricians, argumentation theorists have searched for the requirements that make an argument correct, by some appropriate standard of proof, by examining the errors of reasoning we make when we try to use arguments. These errors have long been called fallacies, and the logic textbooks have for over 2000 years tried to help students to identify these fallacies, and to deal with them when they are encountered. The problem was that deductive logic did not seem to be much use for this purpose, and there seemed to be no other obvious formal structure that could usefully be applied to them. The radical approach taken by Hamblin [7] was to refashion the concept of an argument to think of it not just as an arbitrarily designated set of propositions, but as a move one party makes in a dialog to offer premises that may be acceptable to another party who doubts the conclusion of the argument. Just after Hamblin's time a school of thought called informal logic grew up that wanted to take a new practical approach to teaching students skills of critical thinking by going beyond deductive logic to seek other methods for analyzing and evaluating arguments. Around the same time, an interdisciplinary group of scholars associated with the term 'argumentation,' coming from fields like speech communication, joined with the informal logic group to help build up such practical methods and apply them to real examples of argumentation [9].

The methods that have been developed so far are still in a process of rapid evolution. More recently, improvements in them have been due to some computer scientists joining the group, and to collaborative research efforts between argumentation theorists and computer scientists. Another recent development has been the adoption of argumentation models and techniques to fields in artificial intelligence, like multi-agent systems and artificial intelligence for legal reasoning. In a short paper, it is not possible to survey all these developments. The best that can be done is to offer

Douglas Walton
University of Windsor, e-mail: dwalton@uwindsor.ca

I. Rahwan, G. R. Simari (eds.), *Argumentation in Artificial Intelligence,*
DOI 10.1007/978-0-387-98197-0_1, © Springer Science+Business Media, LLC 2009

an introduction to some of the basic concepts and methods of argumentation theory as they have evolved to the present point, and to briefly indicate some problems and limitations in them.

2 Arguments and Argumentation

There are four tasks undertaken by argumentation, or informal logic, as it is also often called: identification, analysis, evaluation and invention. The task of identification is to identify the premises and conclusion of an argument as found in a text of discourse. A part of this task is to determine whether a given argument found in a text fits a known form of argument called an argumentation scheme (more about schemes below). The task of analysis is to find implicit premises or conclusions in an argument that need to be made explicit in order to properly evaluate the argument. Arguments of the kind found in natural language texts of discourse tend to leave some premises, or in some instances the conclusion, implicit. An argument containing such missing assumptions is traditionally called an enthymeme. The task of evaluation is to determine whether an argument is weak or strong by general criteria that can be applied to it. The task of invention is to construct new arguments that can be used to prove a specific conclusion. Historically, recent work has mainly been directed to the first three tasks, but there has been a tradition of attempting to address the fourth task from time to time, based on the tradition of Aristotelian topics [1, ch. 8].

There are differences in the literature in argumentation theory on how to define an argument. Some definitions are more minimal while others are more inclusive. We start here with a minimal definition, however, that will fit the introduction to the elements of argumentation presented below. An argument is a set of statements (propositions), made up of three parts, a conclusion, a set of premises, and an inference from the premises to the conclusion. An argument can be supported by other arguments, or it can be attacked by other arguments, and by raising critical questions about it.

Argument diagramming is one of the most important tools currently in use to assist with the tasks of analyzing and evaluating arguments. An argument diagram is essentially a box and arrow representation of an argument where the boxes contain propositions that are nodes in a graph structure and where arrows are drawn from nodes to other nodes representing inferences. At least this is the most common style of representation. Another style growing in popularity is the diagram where the nodes represent arguments and the boxes represent premises and conclusions of these arguments. The distinction between a linked argument and a convergent argument is important in argumentation theory. A linked argument is one where the premises work together to support the conclusion, whereas in a convergent argument each premise represents a separate reason that supports the conclusion. Arguments fitting the form of an argumentation scheme are linked because all of the premises are needed to adequately support the conclusion. Here is an example of a convergent

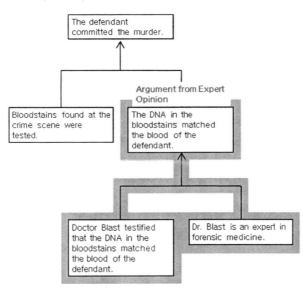

Fig. 1.1 Example of an Argument Diagram

argument: gold is malleable; it can be easily made into jewelry, and my metallurgy textbook says it is malleable. In the example shown in Figure 1.1, two linked arguments are combined in a chain of reasoning (called a serial argument).

The linked argument on the right at the bottom has a colored border and the label Argument from Expert Opinion is shown in a matching color at the top of the conclusion. This label represents a type of argument called an argumentation scheme.

Figure 1.1 was drawn with argument diagramming tool called Araucaria [14]. It assists an argument analyst using a point-and-click interface, which is saved in an Argument Markup Language based on XML [14]. The user inserts the text into Arauacaria, loads each premise or conclusion into a text box, and then inserts arrows showing which premises support which conclusions. As illustrated above, she can also can insert implicit premises or conclusions and label them. The output is an argument diagram that appears on the screen that can be added to, exported or printed (http://araucaria.computing.dundee.ac.uk/).

The other kind of format for representing arguments using visualization tools is shown in the screen shot in Figure 1.2. According to this way of representing the structure of the argument, the premises and conclusions appear as statements in the text boxes, while the nodes represent the arguments. Information about the argumentation scheme, and other information as well, is contained in a node (http://carneades.berlios.de/downloads/).

Both arguments pictured in Figure 1.2 are linked. Convergent arguments are represented as separate arguments. Another chapter in this book (see Chapter 12) shows how Carneades represents different proof standards of the kinds indicated on the lower right of the screen shot.

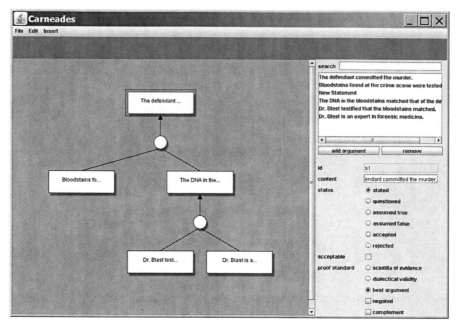

Fig. 1.2 Carneades Screen Shot of an Argument

Argument diagrams are very helpful to display premises and conclusions in an argument and to show how groups of premises support conclusions that can in turn be used as premises in adjoining arguments. Smaller arguments are chained together into longer sequences, and an argument diagram can be very useful to help an analyst keep track of the chain of reasoning in its parts. However, typical argument diagrams are made up only of statements in text boxes joined together by arrows. Such an argument diagram is of limited or less use when it comes to representing critical questions and the relationship of these questions to an argument.

The definition of 'argument' relied on so far could be called a minimal inferential definition, and the method of argument diagramming shown so far fits this minimal definition. The boxes represent propositions and the arrows represent inferences from some propositions to others.

The general approach or methodology of argumentation can be described as distinctively different from the traditional approach based on deductive logic. The traditional approach concentrated on a single inference, where the premises and conclusion are designated in advance, and applied formal models like propositional calculus and quantification theory determine whether the conclusion conclusively follows from the premises. This approach is often called monological.

In contrast, the argumentation approach is called dialogical (or dialectical) in that it looks at two sides of an argument, the pro and the contra. According to this approach, the method of evaluation is to examine how the strongest arguments for and against a particular proposition at issue interact with each other, and in particular how each argument is subject to probing critical questioning that reveals doubts about it. By this dialog process of pitting the one argument against the other, the weaknesses in each argument are revealed, and it is shown which of the two arguments is the stronger.[1]

To fill out the minimal definition enough to make it useful for the account of argumentation in the paper, however, some pragmatic elements need to be added, that indicate how arguments are used in a dialog between two (in the simplest case) parties. Argumentation is a chain of arguments, where the conclusion of one inference is a premise in the next one. There can be hypothetical arguments, where the premises are merely assumptions. But generally, the purpose of using an argument in a dialog is to settle some disputed (unsettled) issue between two parties. In the speech act of putting forward an argument, one party in the dialog has the aim of trying to get the other party to accept the conclusion by offering reasons why he should accept it, expressed in the premises. This contrasts with the purpose of using an explanation, where one party has the aim of trying to get the other party to understand some proposition that is accepted as true by both parties. The key difference is that in an argument, the proposition at issue (the conclusion) is doubted by the one party, while in an explanation, the proposition to be explained is not in doubt by either party. It is assumed to represent a factual event.

3 Argument Attack and Refutation

One way to attack an argument is to ask an appropriate critical question that raises doubt about the acceptability of the argument. When this happens, the argument temporarily defaults until the proponent can respond appropriately to the critical question. Another way to attack an argument is to question one of the premises. A third way to attack an argument is to put forward counter-argument that opposes the original argument, meaning that the conclusion of the opposing argument is the opposite (negation) of the conclusion of the original argument. There are other ways to attack an argument as well [10]. For example, one might argue that the premises are not relevant to the conclusion, or that the argument is not relevant in relation to the issue that is supposedly being discussed. One might also argue that the original argument commits a logical fallacy, like the fallacy of begging the question (arguing in a circle by taking for granted as a premise the very proposition that is to be proved). However, the three first ways cited above of attacking an argument are especially important for helping us to understand the notion of argument refutation. A refutation of an argument is an opposed argument that attacks the original argument and defeats it.

A simple way to represent a sequence of argumentation in the dialogical style is to let the nodes in a graph represent arguments and the arrows represent attacks on

---

[1] This approach has been neglected for a long time in the history of logic, but it is not new. Cicero, based on the work of his Greek predecessors in the later Platonic Academy, Arcesilaus and Carneades, adopted the method of dialectical inquiry that, by arguing for and against competing views, reveals the one that is the more plausible [16, p. 4].

arguments [5]. In this kind of argument representation, one argument is shown as attacking another. In this example, argument A1 attacks both A2 and A3. A2 attacks A6. A6 attacks A7, and A7 attacks A6. A3 attacks A4, and so forth.

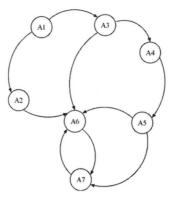

Fig. 1.3 Example of a Dung-style Argument Representation

Notice that arguments can attack each other. A6 attacks A7 and A7 also attacks A6. An example [4, p. 23] is the following pair of arguments.

Richard is a Quaker and Quakers are pacifists, so he is a pacifist. Richard is a Republican and Republicans are not pacifists, so he is a not a pacifist.

In Dung's system, the notions of argument attack are undefined primitives, but the system can be used to model criteria of argument acceptability. One such criterion is the view that an argument should be accepted only if every attack on it is attacked by an acceptable argument [3, p. 3].

There is general (but not universal) agreement in argumentation studies that there are three standards by which the success of the inference from the premises to the conclusion can be evaluated. This agreement is generally taken to mean that there are three kinds of arguments: deductive, inductive, and defeasible arguments of a kind widely thought not to be inductive (Bayesian) in nature. This third class includes arguments like 'Birds fly; Tweety is a bird; therefore Tweety flies,' where exceptions, like 'Tweety has a broken wing' are not known in advance and cannot be anticipated statistically. Many of the most common arguments in legal reasoning and everyday conversational argumentation that are of special interest to argumentation theorists fall into this class. An example would be an argument from expert opinion of this sort: Experts are generally right about things in their domain of expertise; Dr. Blast is an expert in domain D, Dr. Blast asserts that A, A is in D; therefore an inference can be drawn that A is acceptable, subject to default if any reasonable arguments to the contrary or critical questions are raised. Arguments of this sort are important, for example in legal reasoning, but before the advent of argumentation theory, useful logical tools to identify, analyze and evaluate them were not available.

4 Argumentation Schemes

Argumentation schemes are abstract argument forms commonly used in everyday conversational argumentation, and other contexts, notably legal and scientific argumentation. Most of the schemes that are of central interest in argumentation theory are forms of plausible reasoning that do not fit into the traditional deductive and inductive argument forms. Some of the most common schemes are: argument from witness testimony, argument from expert opinion, argument from popular opinion, argument from example, argument from analogy, practical reasoning (from goal to action), argument from verbal classification, argument from sign, argument from sunk costs, argument from appearance, argument from ignorance, argument from cause to effect, abductive reasoning, argument from consequences, argument from alternatives, argument from pity, argument from commitment, *ad hominem* argument, argument from bias, slippery slope argument, and argument from precedent. Each scheme has a set of critical questions matching the scheme and such a set represents standard ways of critically probing into an argument to find aspects of it that are open criticism.

A good example of a scheme is the one for argument from expert opinion, also called appeal to expert opinion in logic textbooks. In this scheme [1, p. 310], A is a proposition, E is an expert, and D is a domain of knowledge.

Major Premise: Source E is an expert in subject domain S containing proposition A.

Minor Premise: E asserts that proposition A is true (false).

Conclusion: A is true (false).

The form of argument in this scheme could be expressed in a modus ponens format where the major (first) premise is a universal conditional: If an expert says that A is true, A is true; expert E says that A is true; therefore A is true. The major premise, for practical purposes, however, is best seen as not being an absolute universal generalization of the kind familiar in deductive logic. It is best seen as a defeasible generalization, and the argument is defeasible, subject to the asking of critical questions. If the respondent asks any one of the following six critical questions [1, p. 310], the proponent must give an appropriate reply or the argument defaults.

CQ1:   Expertise Question. How credible is E as an expert source?
CQ2:   Field Question. Is E an expert in the field that A is in?
CQ3:   Opinion Question. What did E assert that implies A?
CQ4:   Trustworthiness Question. Is E personally reliable as a source?
CQ5:   Consistency Question. Is A consistent with what other experts assert?
CQ6:   Backup Evidence Question. Is E's assertion based on evidence?

Some other examples of schemes will be introduced when we come to study the example of extended argumentation in section 2.

5 Enthymemes

As indicated in the introduction, an enthymeme is an argument with an implicit premise or conclusion that needs to be made explicit before the argument can be properly understood or evaluated. The classic example is the argument: all men are mortal; therefore Socrates is mortal. As pointed out in many logic textbooks, the premise 'Socrates is a man' needs to be made explicit in order to make the argument into a deductively valid argument. Because both premises are needed to support the conclusion adequately, this argument is linked. Consider the following example of an enthymeme.

Example 1.1 ((The Free Animals)). Animals in captivity are freer than in nature because there are no natural predators to kill them.

The explicit conclusion is clearly the first statement: animals in captivity are freer than in nature. The explicit premise offered to support the conclusion is the statement that there are no natural predators to kill animals that are in captivity. There are two assumptions that play the role of implicit premises in the argument. The first is the statement that there are natural predators to kill animals that are in nature. The second is the conditional statement that if animals are in a place where there are no natural predators to kill them, they are freer than if they are in a place where there are natural predators to kill them. The first implicit premise is a matter of common knowledge. The second one, however, expresses a special way that the arguer is using the word 'free' that seems to go against common knowledge, or at any rate, does not seem to be based on it. It seems to represent the arguer's own special position on the meaning of 'freedom.'

In the argument diagram in Figure 1.4, the two premises on the right are enclosed in darkened boxes, with a broken line around the border, indicating that both are implicit premises. The one in the middle is labeled as based on common knowledge (CK) and the one on the right is labeled as based on the arguer's special commitment (COM).

The argument shown in Figure 4 is clearly a linked argument, since all three premises are required to adequately support the conclusion. They all function together in support of the conclusion, rather than being separate reasons, each of which supports the conclusion independently of the others.

In some cases of enthymemes it is fairly obvious to determine what the missing premise or conclusion should be. In such cases, an argumentation scheme can often be used to apply to the argument given in the text of discourse to see which premise is missing. In other cases, however, there can be different interpretations of the text of discourse, and different judgments about what the missing premise should be taken to be. The more general problem is to judge what an arguer's commitment is, given some evidence of what the arguer has said and how he has responded to criticisms and other moves in a dialog. If an arguer explicitly asserts a statement and does not retract it, then it is clear that he is committed to that statement. But suppose he explicitly asserts two statements, and a third statement follows from the first two by *modus ponens*. Is he then committed to the third statement? Logically, it

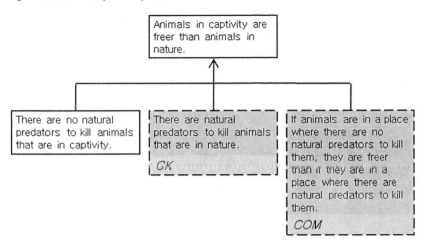

Fig. 1.4 Argument Diagram of the Free Animals Example

seems that he should be, but when he is confronted with the third statement he may deny that he is committed to it. The other party in the dialog should then challenge him to resolve the inconsistency one way or the other, by either retracting the third statement or one of the premises.

6 An Example Dialog

In the following dialog, called the smoking dialog, two participants Ann and Bob, are discussing the issue of whether governments should ban smoking. They take turns making moves, and each move after Ann's opening move appears to address the prior move of the other party. Thus the dialog has an appearance of being connected and continuous in addressing the issue by bringing forward arguments pro and con.

The Smoking Dialog:

Ann (1):   Governments should protect its citizens from harm. There is little doubt that smoking tobacco is extremely harmful to the smoker's health. Therefore governments should ban smoking.

Bob (2):   How do you know that smoking tobacco is extremely harmful to the smoker's health?

Ann (3):   Smoking leads to many other health problems, including lung cancer and heart disease. According to the American Cancer Society, 3 million people die from smoking each year.

Bob (4):   The government has a responsibility to protect its citizens, but it also has a responsibility to defend their freedom of choice. Banning smoking would be an intrusion into citizens' freedom of choice.

Ann (5):   Smoking is not a matter of freedom of choice. Nicotine is an addictive drug. Studies have shown that once smokers have begun smoking, they become addicted to nicotine. Once they become addicted they are no longer free to choose not to smoke.

Bob (6):   Governments should not stop citizens from doing things that can be extremely harmful to their health. It is legal to eat lots of fatty foods or drink alcohol excessively, and it makes no sense for governments to try to ban these activities.

Examining Ann's first argument, it is fairly straightforward to put it in a format showing that it has two premises and a conclusion.

Premise: Governments should protect its citizens from harm.
Premise: Smoking tobacco is extremely harmful to the smoker's health.
Conclusion: Therefore governments should ban smoking.

This argument looks to be an instance of the argumentation scheme for argument from negative consequences [1, p. 332]. The reason it offers to support its conclusion that governments should ban smoking is that smoking has negative consequences. An implicit premise is that being extremely harmful to health is a negative consequence, but we ignore this complication for the moment.[2]

Scheme for Argument from Negative Consequences

Premise: If A is brought about, then bad consequences will occur.
Conclusion: Therefore A should not be brought about.

The reason is that a premise in the argument claims that the practice of smoking tobacco has harmful (bad) consequences, and for this reason the conclusion advocates something that would make it so that smoking is no longer brought about.

However there is another argumentation scheme, one closely related to argument from negative consequences, that could also (even more usefully) be applied to this argument. It is called practical reasoning. The simplest version of this scheme, called practical inference in [1, p. 323] is cited below with its matching set of critical questions.

Scheme for Practical Inference

Major Premise: I have a goal G.
Minor Premise: Carrying out this action A is a means to realize G.
Conclusion: Therefore, I ought (practically speaking) to carry out this action A.

Critical Questions for Practical Inference

CQ1:   What other goals do I have that should be considered that might conflict with G?

---

[2] To more fully analyze the argument we could apply a more complex scheme called value-based practical reasoning [2].

CQ2:   What alternative actions to my bringing about *A* that would also bring about *G* should be considered?

CQ3:   Among bringing about *A* and these alternative actions, which is arguably the most efficient?

CQ4:   What grounds are there for arguing that it is practically possible for me to bring about *A*?

CQ5:   What consequences of my bringing about *A* should also be taken into account?

CQ5 asks if there are negative consequences of the action (side effects) that need to be taken into account, and it can be seen that it covers argumentation from both positive and negative consequences.

Applying the argumentation scheme for practical reasoning, we get the following reconstruction of the original argument. Premise 1: Governments have the goal of protecting their citizens from harm. Premise 2: Smoking is harmful to their citizens. Premise 3: Carrying out the action of banning smoking is a means for governments to protect their citizens from this harm. Conclusion: governments should ban smoking. This argument can be diagrammed as shown in Figure 1.5.

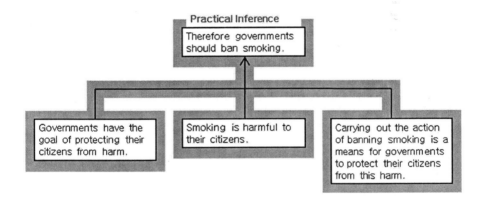

Fig. 1.5 Argument Diagram of the Smoking Example with Practical Inference

At his first move, Bob questions one of the premises of Ann's argument. He asks her to give a reason to support her assertion that smoking tobacco is extremely harmful to the smoker's health. In response to Bob's question, Ann offers two such reasons. There could be various ways to represent the structure of her additional argument. The two reasons could perhaps function together as a linked argument, or they could function as two separate reasons having the structure of a convergent argument. But there is another way to analyze her additional argumentation.

When Ann puts forward her argument, it appears that she is using her new assertion that smoking leads to many other health problems, including lung cancer and heart disease, as additional support for her previous premise that smoking tobacco is extremely harmful to the smoker's health. What about her next statement that according to the American Cancer Society, 3 million people die from smoking each year? It appears that this statement is being used to back up her previous statement that smoking leads to many other health problems, including lung cancer and heart disease. This seems to be a plausible reconstruction of her argument.

We can produce an even better analysis of her argument using the argumentation scheme for argument from expert opinion. It would appear that she is citing the American Cancer Society as an expert source on health issues relating to cancer and smoking. We could analyze her argument by inserting an implicit premise to this effect, as shown in the argument diagram in Figure 1.6.

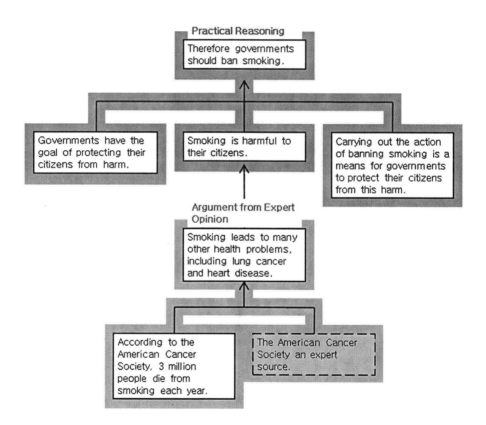

Fig. 1.6 Argument Diagram of the Smoking Example with Implicit Premise

On this analysis, the implicit premise that the American Cancer Society is an expert source is shown in the darkened box with dashed lines around it at the lower right. This premise, when taken with Ann's explicit premise shown on the left, makes up an argument from expert opinion supporting her previous claim. This example shows how an argumentation scheme can be useful in helping an argument analyst to identify an implicit premise that is not explicitly stated in the argument, but that is important for helping us to realize what the basis of the argument is.

At move 4, Bob concedes Ann's claim that the government has a responsibility to protect its citizens, but then he introduces a new argument. This argument is an interesting example of an enthymeme because the implicit statement needed to complete the argument is its conclusion.

Premise: Governments have a responsibility to defend citizens' freedom of choice.
Premise: Banning smoking would be an intrusion into citizens' freedom of choice.
Implicit Conclusion: Governments should not ban smoking.

Notice that the conclusion of this argument is the opposite of Ann's previous argument that had the conclusion that governments should ban smoking. Thus Bob's argument above is meant as a refutation of Ann's previous argument. It is easy to see that Bob's argument is connected to Ann's whole previous argumentation, and is meant to attack it. This observation is part of the evidence that the dialog to this point hangs together in the sense that each move is relevant to previous moves made by one party or the other.

There is perhaps one exception to the general pattern in the dialog that each move is connected to the prior move made by the other party. There is something that Bob should perhaps question after Ann's move 5 when she attacks Bob's assertion that banning smoking would be an intrusion into citizens' freedom of choice. She attacks his assertion by arguing that smoking is not a matter of freedom of choice, but does this attack really bear on Bob's assertion? One might reply that even though it may be true that citizens who have been smoking for a while are addicted to the habit, still, for the government to ban smoking would be an intrusion into citizens' freedom of choice. It would force them by law to take steps to cure their addiction, and it would even force them by law not to start smoking in the first place. Whether Ann's argument at move 5 really refutes Bob's prior argument at move 4 is questionable. Instead of raising these questions about the relevance of Ann's argument, Bob moves on to a different argument at his move 6. It could be suggested that he might have done better at his move 6 to attack Ann's prior argument instead of hastily moving ahead to his next argument.

7 Types of Dialog

Six basic types of dialog are fundamental to dialog theory – persuasion dialog, the inquiry, negotiation dialog, information-seeking dialog, deliberation, and eristic dialog. The properties of these six types of dialog are summarized in Table 1.

In argumentation theory, each type of dialog is used as a normative model that provides the standards for analyzing a given argument as used in a conversational setting in a given case. Each type of dialog has three stages, an opening stage, an argumentation stage and a closing stage. In a persuasion dialog, the proponent has a particular thesis to be proved, while the respondent has the role of casting doubt

Type of Dialog	Initial Situation	Participant's Goal	Goal of Dialog
Persuasion	Conflict of Opinions	Persuade Other Party	Resolve or Clarify Issue
Inquiry	Need to Have Proof	Find and Verify Evidence	Prove (Disprove) Hypothesis
Negotiation	Conflict of Interests	Get What You Most Want	Reasonable Settlement Both Can Live With
Information-Seeking	Need Information	Acquire or Give Information	Exchange Information
Deliberation	Dilemma or Practical Choice	Co-ordinate Goals and Actions	Decide Best Available Course of Action
Eristic	Personal Conflict	Verbally Hit Out at Opponent	Reveal Deeper Basis of Conflict

Table 1.1 Six Basic Types of Dialog

on that thesis or arguing for an opposed thesis. These tasks are set at the opening stage, and remain in place until the closing stage, when one party or the other fulfils its burden of persuasion. The proponent has a burden of persuasion to prove (by a set standard of proof) the proposition that is designated in advance as her ultimate thesis.[3] The respondent's role is to cast doubt on the proponent's attempts to succeed in achieving such proof. The best known normative model of the persuasion type of dialog in the argumentation literature is the critical discussion [17]. It is not a formal model, but it has a set of procedural rules that define it as a normative structure for rational argumentation.

The goal of a persuasion dialog is to reveal the strongest arguments on both sides by pitting one against the other to resolve the initial conflict posed at the opening stage. Each side tries to carry out its task of proving its ultimate thesis to the standard required to produce an argument stronger than the one produced by the other side. This burden of persuasion, as it is called [13], is set at the opening stage. Meeting one's burden of persuasion is determined by coming up with a strong enough argument using a chain of argumentation in which individual arguments in the chain are of the proper sort. To say that they are of the proper sort means that they fit argumentation schemes appropriate for the dialog. 'Winning' means producing an argument that is strong enough to discharge the burden of persuasion set at the opening stage.

In a deliberation dialog, the goal is for the participants to arrive at a decision on what to do, given the need to take action. McBurney, Hitchcock and Parsons [11] set out a formal model of deliberation dialog in which participants make proposals and counter-proposals on what to do. In this model (p. 95), the need to take action is expressed in the form of a governing question like, "How should we respond to the prospect of global warming?" Deliberation dialog may be contrasted with persuasion dialog.

---

[3] The notions of burden of persuasion and burden of proof have recently been subject to investigation [6, 13]. Here we have adopted the view that in a persuasion dialog, the burden of persuasion is set at the opening stage, while a burden of proof can also shift from one side to the other during the argumentation stage.

In the model of [11, p. 100], a deliberation dialog consists of an opening stage, a closing stage, and six other stages making up the argumentation stage.

Open: In this stage a governing question is raised about what is to be done. A governing question, like 'Where shall we go for dinner this evening?,' is a question that expresses a need for action in a given set of circumstances.

Inform: This stage includes discussion of desirable goals, constraints on possible actions that may be considered, evaluation of proposals, and consideration of relevant facts.

Propose: Proposals cite possible action-options relevant to the governing question

Consider: this stage concerns commenting on proposals from various perspectives.

Revise: goals, constraints, perspectives, and action-options can be revised in light of comments presented and information gathering as well as fact-checking.

Recommend: an option for action can be recommended for acceptance or non-acceptance by each participant.

Confirm: a participant can confirm acceptance of the recommended option, and all participants must do so before the dialog terminates.

Close: The termination of the dialog.

The initial situation of deliberation is the need for action arising out of a choice between two or more alternative courses of action that are possible in a given situation. The ultimate goal of deliberation dialog is for the participants to collectively decide on what is the best available course of action for them to take. An important property of deliberation dialog is that an action-option that is optimal for the group considered as a whole may not be optimal from the perspective of an individual participant [11, p. 98].

Both deliberation and persuasion dialogs can be about actions, and common forms of argument like practical reasoning and argument from consequences are often used in both types of dialog. There is no burden of persuasion in a deliberation dialog. Argumentation in deliberation is primarily a matter of supporting one's own proposal for its chosen action-option, and critiquing the other party's proposal for its chosen action-option. At the concluding stage one's proposal needs to be abandoned in favor of the opposed one if the reasons given against it are strong enough to show that the opposed proposal is better to solve the problem set at the opening stage. Deliberation dialog is also different from negotiation dialog, which centrally deals with competing interests set at the opening stage. In a deliberation dialog, the participants evaluate proposed courses of action according to standards that may often be contrary to their personal interests.

8 Dialectical Shifts

In dialectical shifts of the kind analyzed in [18, pp. 100-116], an argument starts out as being framed in one kind of dialog, but as the chain of argumentation proceeds, it needs to be framed in a different type of dialog. Here is an example.

Example 1.2 ((The Dam)). In a debate in a legislative assembly the decision to be made is whether to pass a bill to install a new dam. Arguments are put forward by both sides. One side argues that such a dam will cost too much, and will have bad ecological consequences. The other side argues that the dam is badly needed to produce energy. A lot of facts about the specifics of the dam and the area around it are needed to reasonably evaluate these opposed arguments. The assembly calls in experts in hydraulics engineering, ecology, economics and agriculture, to testify on these matters.

Once the testimony starts, there has been a dialectical shift from the original deliberation dialog to an information-seeking dialog that goes into issues like what the ecological consequences of installing the dam would be. But this shift is not a bad thing, if the information provided by the testimony is helpful in aiding the legislative assembly to arrive at an informed and intelligent decision on how to vote. If this is so, the goal of the first dialog, the deliberation, is supported by the advent of the second dialog, the information-seeking interval. A constructive type of shift of this sort is classified as an embedding [18, p. 102], meaning that the advent of the second dialog helps the first type of dialog along toward it goal. An embedding underlies what can be called a constructive or licit shift.

Other dialectical shifts are illicit, meaning that the advent of the second dialog interferes with the proper progress of the first toward reaching its goal [18, p. 107]. Wells and Reed [19] constructed two formal dialectical systems to help judge whether a dialectical shift from a persuasion dialog to a negotiation dialog is licit or illicit. In their model, when a participant is engaged in a persuasion dialog, and proposes to shift to a different type of dialog, he must make a request to ask if the shift is acceptable to the other party. The other party has the option of insisting on continuing with the initial dialog or agreeing to shift to the new type. Wells and Reed have designed dialog rules to allow for a licit shift from persuasion to negotiation. Their model is especially useful in studying cases where threats are used as arguments. This type of argument, called the *argumentum ad baculum* in logic, has traditionally been classified as a fallacy, presumably because making threat to the other party is not a relevant move in a persuasion dialog. What one is supposed to do in a persuasion dialog is to offer evidence to support one's contention, and making a threat does not do this, even though it may give the recipient of the threat a prudential reason to at least appear to go along the claim that the other party wants him to accept.

The study of dialectical shifts is important in the study of informal fallacies, or common errors of reasoning, of a kind studied in logic textbooks since the time of Aristotle. A good example is provided in the next section.

9 Fallacious Arguments from Negative Consequences

Argument from consequences (*argumentum ad consequentiam*) is an interesting fallacy that can be found in logic textbooks used to help students acquire critical thinking skills. The following example is quoted from Rescher [15, p. 82].

Example 1.3 ((The Mexican War)). The United States had justice on its side in waging the Mexican war of 1848. To question this is unpatriotic, and would give comfort to our enemies by promoting the cause of defeatism.

The argument from consequences in this case was classified as a fallacy for the reason that is not relevant to the issue supposedly being discussed. Rescher (p. 82) wrote that "logically speaking," it can be "entirely irrelevant that certain undesirable consequences might derive from the rejection of a thesis, or certain benefits accrue from its acceptance." It can be conjectured from the example that the context is a persuasion dialog in which the conflict of opinions is the issue of which country had justice on its side in the Mexican war of 1848. This issue is a historical or ethical one, and prudential deliberation about whether questioning whether the U.S. had justice on its side would give comfort to our enemies is not relevant to resolving it. We can analyze what has happened by saying that there has been a dialectical shift at the point where the one side argues that questioning that the U.S. was in the right would promote defeatism.

Notice that in this case there is nothing wrong in principle with using argumentation from negative consequences. As shown above, argument from the negative consequences is a legitimate argumentation scheme and any argument that fits this scheme is a reasonable argument in the sense that if the premises are acceptable, then subject to defeasible reasoning if new circumstances come to be known, the conclusion is acceptable as well. It's not the argument itself that is fallacious, or structurally wrong as an inference. The problem is the context of dialog in which these instances of argumentation from negative consequences have been used. Such an argument would be perfectly appropriate if the issue set at the opening stage was how to make a decision about how to best support the diplomatic interests of the United States. However, notice that the first sentence of the example states very clearly what the ultimate thesis to be proved is: "The United States had justice on its side in waging the Mexican war of 1848." The way that this thesis is supposed to be proved is by giving the other side reasons to come to accept it is true. Hence it seems reasonable to conjecture that the framework of the discussion is that of a persuasion dialog.

Rescher (1969, 82) classified the Mexican War example as an instance of argument from negative consequences that commits a fallacy of relevance. But what exactly is relevance? How is it to be defined? It can be defined by determining what type of dialog an argument in a given case supposedly belongs to, and then determining what the issue to be resolved is by determining what the goal of the dialog is. The goal is set at the opening stage. If during the argumentation stage, the argumentation strays off onto a different path away from the proper kind of argumentation needed to fulfill this goal, a fallacy of relevance may have been committed. Based on this analysis, it can be said that a fallacy of relevance has been committed in the Mexican War example. The dialectical shift to the prudential issue leads to a different type of dialog, a deliberation that interferes with the progress of the original persuasion dialog. The shift distracts the reader of the argument by introducing another issue, whether arguing this way is unpatriotic, and would give comfort to enemies by promoting the cause of defeatism. That may be more pressing, and it may indeed be true that arguing in this way would have brought about the negative consequences of giving comfort to enemies in promoting the cause of defeatism. Still, even though this argument from negative consequences might be quite reasonable, framed in the context of the deliberation, it is not useful to fulfill the burden of persuasion necessary to resolve the original conflict of opinions.

10 Relevance and Fallacies

Many of the traditional informal fallacies in logic are classified under the heading of fallacies of relevance [8]. In such cases, the argument may be a reasonable one that is a valid inference based on premises that can be supported, but the problem is that the argument is not relevant. One kind of fallacy of irrelevance, as shown in the Mexican War example above, is the type of case where there has been a dialectical shift from one type of dialog to another. However, there is also another type of fallacy of relevance, where there is no dialectical shift, but there still is a failure to fulfill the burden of persuasion. In this kind of fallacy, which is very common, the arguer stays within the same type of dialog, but nevertheless fails to prove the conclusion he is supposed to prove and instead goes off in a different direction.

The notion of relevance of argumentation can only be properly understood and analyzed by drawing a distinction between the opening stage of a dialog, where the burden of persuasion is set, and the argumentation stage, where arguments, linked into chains of argumentation, are brought forward by both sides. In a persuasion dialog, the burden of persuasion is set at the opening stage. Let's say, for example, that the issue being discussed is whether one type of light bulb lasts longer than another. The proponent claims that one type of bulb lasts longer than another. She has the burden of persuasion to prove that by bringing forward arguments that support it. The respondent takes the stance of doubting the proponent's claim. He does not have the burden of persuasion. His role is to cast doubt on the proponent's attempts to prove her claim. He can do this by bringing forward arguments that attack the claim that one type of bulb lasts longer than another. Suppose, however, that during the argumentation stage, he wanders off to different topic by arguing that the one type of bulb is manufactured by a company has done bad things that have led to negative consequences. This may be an emotionally exciting argument, and the claim made in it may even be accurate, but the problem is that it is irrelevant to the issue set at the opening stage.

This species of fallacy of relevance is called the red herring fallacy. It occurs where an arguer wanders off the point in a discussion, and directs a chain of argumentation towards proving some conclusion other than the one he is supposed to prove, as determined at the opening stage. The following example is a classic case of this type of fallacy cited in logics textbook [8].

Example 1.4 ((The Light Bulb)). The Consumers Digest reports that GE light bulbs last longer than Sylvania bulbs.[4] But do you realize that GE is this country's major manufacturer of nuclear weapons? The social cost of GE's irresponsible behavior has been tremendous. Among other things, we are left with thousands of tons of nuclear waste with nowhere to put it. Obviously, the Consumers Digest is wrong.

In the first sentence of the example, the arguer states the claim that he is supposed to prove (or attack) as his ultimate *probandum* in the discussion. He is supposed to be attacking the claim reported in the Consumers Digest that GE light bulbs last longer than Sylvania bulbs. How does he do this? He launches into a chain of argumentation, starting with the assertion that GE is this country's major manufacturer of nuclear weapons. This makes GE sound very bad, and it would be an emotionally exciting issue to raise. He follows up the statement with another one to the effect that the social cost of GE's irresponsible behavior has been tremendous. This is another serious allegation that would rouse the emotions of readers. Finally he uses argumentation from negative consequences by asserting that because of GE's irresponsible behavior, we are left with thousands of tons of nuclear waste with nowhere to put it. This line of argumentation is a colorful and accusatory distraction. It diverts the attention of the reader, who might easily fail to recall that the real issue is whether GE light bulbs last longer than Sylvania bulbs. Nothing in all the allegations made about GE's allegedly responsible behavior carries any probative weight for the purpose of providing evidence against the claim reported in the Consumers Digest that GE light bulbs last longer than Sylvania bulbs.

In the red herring fallacy the argumentation is directed along a path of argumentation other than one leading to proving the conclusion to be proved. The chain of argumentation goes off in a direction that is exciting and distracting for the audience to whom the argument was directed. The red herring fallacy becomes a problem in cases where the argumentation moves away from the proper chain of argument leading to the conclusion to be proved. Sometimes the path leads to the wrong conclusion (one other than the one that is supposed to be proved), but in other cases it goes nowhere. The general pattern of this type of fallacy is displayed in Figure 1.7.

Such a distraction may be harmless if there is plenty of time for discussion. But it can be a serious problem if there is not, because the real issue is not discussed. According to the burden of persuasion, the line of argumentation has as its end point a specific conclusion that needs to be proved. And if the argumentation moves away, it may not do this.

---

[4] In the 1994 edition (p. 127), the first sentence of the light bulb example is, "The Consumers Digest reports that Sylvania light bulbs last longer than GE bulbs." The example makes more sense if the two light bulb manufacturers names are reversed, and so I have presented the light bulb example this way.

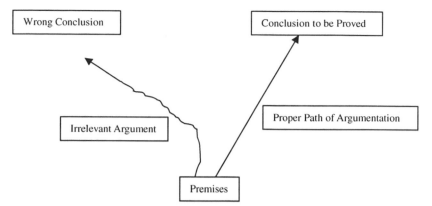

Fig. 1.7 General Pattern of the Red Herring Fallacy

11 Basic Problems to be Solved

This paper has only touched on the main concepts of argumentation theory and the main techniques used in argumentation studies. It is important to emphasize that the use of such concepts and techniques, while they have proved very valuable for teaching skills of critical thinking, have raised many problems about how to make the concepts and techniques more precise so that they can be applied more productively to realistic argumentation in natural language texts of discourse. Many of these problems arise from the fact that it can be quite difficult to interpret what is meant in a natural language text of discourse and precisely identify arguments contained in it. Ambiguity and vagueness are extremely common, and in many instances, the best one can do is to construct a hypothesis about how to interpret the argument based on the evidence given from the text of discourse. Much of the current research is indeed directed to studying how to marshal such evidence in an objective manner.

For example, applying an abstract argumentation scheme to an argument in a specific case can be very tricky. In some cases, the same argument can fit more than one scheme. A project that needs to be undertaken is to devise criteria that students of critical thinking can use to help them determine in a particular case whether a given argument correctly fits a scheme or not. Another problem is that schemes can vary contextually. For example the scheme for argument from expert opinion used in law has to be different in certain respects from the standard scheme for argument from expert opinion cited above. The reason is that in the law rules have been developed for the admissibility and evaluation of expert opinion evidence. Any argumentation scheme for argument from expert opinion suitable for use in law would have to take these legal developments into account.

Similarly, the problem of how to deal with enthymemes in a precise and objective manner has still not been solved, because we lack tools for determining what an arguer's commitments are, and what should properly be taken to constitute common knowledge, in specific cases where we are examining a text of discourse to find implicit statements. While the field has helped to develop objective methods for collecting evidence to deal with these problems in analyzing arguments, much work remains to be done in making them more precise.

Of all the types of dialog, the one that has been most carefully and systematically studied is persuasion dialog, and there are formal systems of persuasion dialog [12]. Just recently, deliberation dialog also has come to be formally modeled [11, p. 100]. There is an abundance of literature on negotiation, and there are a software tools for assisting with negotiation argumentation. Comparatively less work is noticeable on information-seeking dialog and on the inquiry model of dialog. There is a scattering of work on eristic dialog, but there appears to be no formal model of this type of dialog that has been put forward, or at least that is well known in the argumentation literature. The notion of dialectical shift needs much more work. In particular, what kinds of evidence are useful in helping an argument analyst to determine when a dialectical shift has taken place during the sequence of argumentation in discourse is a good topic for study.

The concepts of burden of proof and presumption are also central to the study of argumentation in different types of dialog. Space has prevented much discussion of these important topics, but the recent work that has been done on them raises some general questions that would be good topics for research. This work [6, 13] suggests that what is called the burden of persuasion is set at the opening stage of a persuasion dialog, and that this burden affects how a different kind of burden, often called the burden of production in law, shifts back and forth during the argumentation stage. Drawing this distinction is extremely helpful for understanding how a persuasion dialog should work, and more generally, it helps us to grasp how the critical questions should work as attacks on an argumentation scheme. But is there some comparable notion of burden of proof in the other types of dialog, for example in deliberation dialog? This unanswered question points a direction for future research in argumentation.

References

1. D. Walton, C. Reed and F. Macagno. *Argumentation Schemes*. Cambridge University Press, Cambridge, UK, 2008.
2. T. J. M. Bench-Capon. Persuasion in practical argument using value-based argumentation frameworks. *Logic and Computation*, 13:429–448, 2003.
3. T. J. M. Bench-Capon and P. E. Dunne. Argumentation and dialogue in artificial intelligence, IJCAI 2005 tutorial notes. Technical report, Department of Computer Science, University of Liverpool, 2005.
4. P. Besnard and A. Hunter. *Elements of Argumentation*. MIT Press, Cambridge MA, USA, 2008.
5. P. M. Dung. On the acceptability of arguments and its fundamental role in nonmonotonic reasoning, logic programming and n-person games. *Artificial Intelligence*, 77(2):321–358, 1995.

6. T. F. Gordon, H. Prakken, and D. Walton. The Carneades model of argument and burden of proof. *Artificial Intelligence*, 171(10–15):875–896, 2007.
7. C. L. Hamblin. *Fallacies*. Methuen, London, UK, 1970.
8. P. J. Hurley. *A Concise Introduction to Logic*. Belmont, Wadsworth, CA, USA, 1994.
9. R. H. Johnson and A. J. Blair. The current state of informal logic. *Informal Logic*, 9:147–151, 1987.
10. E. C. W. Krabbe. Nothing but objections. In H. V. Hansen and R. C. Pinto, editors, *Reason Reclaimed*. Vale Press, Newport News, Virginia, USA, 2007.
11. D. Hitchcock, P. McBurney and S. Parsons. The eightfold way of deliberation dialogue. *International Journal of Intelligent Systems*, 22(1):95–132, 2007.
12. H. Prakken. Formal systems for persuasion dialogue. *The Knowledge Engineering Review*, 21(2):163–188, 2006.
13. H. Prakken and G. Sartor. Formalising arguments about the burden of persuasion. In *Proceedings of the 11th International Conference on Artificial Intelligence and Law*, pages 97–106. ACM Press, New York NY, USA, 2007.
14. C. Reed and G. Rowe. Araucaria: Software for argument analysis. *International Journal of AI Tools*, 14(3–4):961–980, 2004.
15. N. Rescher. *Introduction to Logic*. St. Martin's Press, New York NY, USA, 1964.
16. H. Thorsrud. Cicero on his academics predecessors: the fallibilism of Arcesilaus and Carneades. *Journal of the History of Philosophy*, 40(1):1–18, 2002.
17. F. H. van Eemeren and R. F. Grootendorst. *A Systematic Theory of Argumentation*. Cambridge University Press, Cambridge, UK, 2004.
18. D. N. Walton and E. C. W. Krabbe. *Commitment in Dialogue: Basic Concepts of Interpersonal Reasoning*. SUNY Press, Albany NY, USA, 1995.
19. S. Wells and C. Reed. Knowing when to bargain: the roles of negotiation and persuasion in dialogue. In F. Grasso, R. Kibble, and C. Reed, editors, *Proceedings of the ECAI workshop on Computational Models of Natural Argument (CMNA), Riva del Garda, Italy*, 2006.

Part I
Abstract Argument Systems

Chapter 2
Semantics of Abstract Argument Systems

Pietro Baroni and Massimiliano Giacomin

1 Abstract Argument Systems

An *abstract argument system* or *argumentation framework*, as introduced in a seminal paper by Dung [13], is simply a pair $\langle A, \mathcal{R} \rangle$ consisting of a set A whose elements are called *arguments* and of a binary relation $\mathcal{R}$ on A called *attack relation*. The set A may be finite or infinite in general, however, given the introductory purpose of this chapter, we will restrict the presentation to the case of finite sets of arguments. An argumentation framework has an obvious representation as a directed graph where nodes are arguments and edges are drawn from attacking to attacked arguments. A simple example of argumentation framework $AF_{2.1} = \langle \{a,b\}, \{(b,a)\} \rangle$ is shown in Figure 2.1.

While the word *argument* may recall several intuitive meanings, like the ones of "line of reasoning leading from some premise to a conclusion" or of "utterance in a dispute", abstract argument systems are not (even implicitly or indirectly) bound to any of them: an abstract argument is not assumed to have any specific structure but, roughly speaking, an argument is anything that may attack or be attacked by another argument. Accordingly, the argumentation framework depicted in Figure 2.1 is suitable to represent many different situations. For instance, in a context of reasoning about weather, argument a may be associated with the inferential step

b $\longrightarrow$ a

Fig. 2.1 $AF_{2.1}$: a simple argumentation framework

Pietro Baroni
Dip. di Elettronica per l'Automazione, University of Brescia, Via Branze 38, 25123 Brescia, Italy
e-mail: baroni@ing.unibs.it

Massimiliano Giacomin
Dip. di Elettronica per l'Automazione, University of Brescia, Via Branze 38, 25123 Brescia, Italy
e-mail: giacomin@ing.unibs.it

I. Rahwan, G. R. Simari (eds.), *Argumentation in Artificial Intelligence*,
DOI 10.1007/978-0-387-98197-0_2, © Springer Science+Business Media, LLC 2009

"Tomorrow will rain because the national weather forecast says so", while b with "Tomorrow will not rain because the regional weather forecast says so". In a legal dispute a might be associated with a prosecutor's statement "The suspect is guilty because an eyewitness, Mr. Smith, says so" while b with the defense reply "Mr. Smith is notoriously alcohol-addicted and it is proved that he was completely drunk the night of the crime, therefore his testimony should not be taken into account". In a marriage arrangement setting (corresponding to the game-theoretic formulation of *stable marriage problem* [13]), a may be associated with "The marriage between Alice and John", while b with "The marriage between Barbara and John". Similarly, the attack relation has no specific meaning: again at a rough level, if an argument b attacks another argument a, this means that if b holds then a can not hold or, putting it in other words, that the evaluation of the status of b affects the evaluation of the status of a. In the weather example, two intrinsically conflicting conclusions are confronted and the attack relation corresponds to the fact that one conclusion is preferred to the other, e.g. because the regional forecast is considered more reliable than the national one (this kind of attack is often called *rebut* in the literature). In the legal dispute, the fact that Mr. Smith was drunk is not incompatible *per se* with the fact that the suspect is guilty, however it affects the reason why s/he should be believed to be guilty (this kind of attack has sometimes been called *undercut* in the literature, but the use of this term has not been uniform). In the stable marriage problem, the attack from b to a may simply be due to the fact that John prefers Barbara to Alice.

Abstracting away from the structure and meaning of arguments and attacks enables the study of properties which are independent of any specific aspect, and, as such, are relevant to any context that can be captured by the very terse formalization of abstract argument systems. As a counterpart of this generality, abstract argument systems feature a limited expressiveness and can hardly be adopted as a modeling formalism directly usable in application contexts. In fact the gap between a practical problem and its representation as an abstract argument system is patently too wide and requires to be filled by a less abstract formalism, dealing in particular with the construction of arguments and the conditions for an argument to attack another one. For instance, in a given formalism, attack may be identified at a purely syntactic level (e.g. the conclusion of an argument being the negation of the conclusion of another one). In another formalism, attack may not be a purely syntactic notion (e.g. the conclusions of two arguments being incompatible because they give rise to contradiction through some strict logical deduction). Only after the attack relation is defined in these "concrete" terms, it is appropriate to derive its abstract representation and exploit it for the analysis of general properties.

2 Abstract Argumentation Semantics

Given that arguments may attack each other, it is clearly the case that they can not stand all together and their status is subject to evaluation. In particular what we are usually interested in is the *justification state* of arguments: while this notion will be given a precise formal meaning[1] in the following, intuitively an argument is regarded as justified if it has some way to survive the attacks it receives, as not justified (or rejected) otherwise. In the following we will use the term *argument evaluation* to refer to a process aimed at determining the justification state of the arguments in an abstract argument system, i.e. on the basis of the attack relation only. In the case of Figure 2.1 the outcome of the evaluation process is almost undebatable: b should be justified (in particular it does not receive attacks) while a should not be justified (it has no way to survive the attack from b). The case of mutual attack of Figure 2.2 is less obvious: evident symmetry reasons suggest that the evaluation process should assign to b and a the same state, which should correspond neither to "full" justification nor to "full" rejection. An intuitive counterpart to Figure 2.2 is given by the case of two contradicting weather forecasts about rain tomorrow, coming from sources considered equally reliable.

It is important to remark that the evaluation process in abstract argument systems concerns the justification state of arguments, not of their conclusions (conclusions "do not exist" in the abstract setting). To clarify this distinction consider a new argument put forward by the prosecutor in the example of legal dispute: "The suspect is guilty because his fingerprints have been found on the crime scene". The new argument (let say c) has no attack relationships with the previous ones (in particular, the fact that the fingerprints have been found on the crime scene does not conflict with the fact that the witness was drunk that night) and, as a consequence, the corresponding abstract representation is the one given in Figure 2.3. Then a is still rejected, b is still justified and c (not receiving any attack) is justified too. Note that, at the underlying level, a and c have the same conclusion ("the suspect is guilty") and that this conclusion should now be intuitively regarded as justified. However, summarizing the justification state of conclusions is outside the scope of the abstract representation.

An *argumentation semantics* is the formal definition of a method (either declarative or procedural) ruling the argument evaluation process. Two main styles of argumentation semantics definition can be identified in the literature: *extension-based* and *labelling-based*.

In the extension-based approach a semantics definition specifies how to derive from an argumentation framework a set of *extensions*, where an extension E of an argumentation framework $\langle A, R \rangle$ is simply a subset of A, intuitively representing a set of arguments which can "survive together" or are "collectively acceptable".

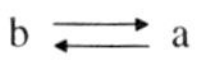

b $\rightleftharpoons$ a

Fig. 2.2 $AF_{2.2}$: a mutual attack

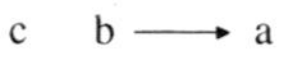

c   b $\longrightarrow$ a

Fig. 2.3 $AF_{2.3}$: presence of an isolated argument

---

[1] Actually the term "justification" is used informally and with different meanings in the literature.

Putting things in more formal terms, given an extension-based semantics S and an argumentation framework $AF = \langle A, \mathcal{R} \rangle$ we will denote the set of extensions prescribed by S for AF as $\mathcal{E}_S(AF) \subseteq 2^A$. The justification state of an argument $a \in A$ according to an extension-based semantics S is then a derived concept, defined in terms of the membership of a to the elements of $\mathcal{E}_S(AF)$.

In the labelling-based approach a semantics definition specifies how to derive from an argumentation framework a set of *labellings*, where a labelling L is the assignment to each argument in A of a label taken from a predefined set $\mathbb{L}$, which corresponds to the possible alternative states of an argument *in the context of a single labelling*. Putting things in formal terms, given a labelling-based semantics S with set of labels $\mathbb{L}$, a labelling of an argumentation framework $\langle A, \mathcal{R} \rangle$ is a mapping $L : A \to \mathbb{L}$. We denote the set of all possible labellings, i.e. of all possible mappings from A to $\mathbb{L}$, as $\mathfrak{L}(A, \mathbb{L})$, and the set of labellings prescribed by S for AF as $\mathcal{L}_S(AF) \subseteq \mathfrak{L}(A, \mathbb{L})$. Again, the justification state of an argument a according to a labelling-based semantics S turns out to be a derived concept, defined in terms of the labels assigned to a in the various elements of $\mathcal{L}_S(AF)$.

Let us exemplify the semantics definition styles with reference to the simple case of Figure 2.2. Let S_{ext}^1 be a hypothetical extension-based semantics whose underlying principle consists in identifying as extensions the largest sets of non-conflicting arguments which reply to the attacks they receive. Intuitively, both the sets $\{a\}$ and $\{b\}$ satisfy this principle, yielding $\mathcal{E}_{S_{ext}^1}(AF_{2.2}) = \{\{a\}, \{b\}\}$. Alternatively, let S_{ext}^2 be a hypothetical extension-based semantics whose underlying principle consists in identifying as extensions the sets of arguments which are unattacked. Clearly, no argument features this property in $AF_{2.2}$, yielding as unique extension the empty set: $\mathcal{E}_{S_{ext}^2}(AF_{2.2}) = \{\emptyset\}$. Let us turn to the labelling-based style and adopt the set of labels $\mathbb{L} = \{in, out, undecided\}$. Let S_{lab}^1 be a hypothetical labelling-based semantics whose underlying principle consists in labelling *in* the elements of the largest sets of non-conflicting arguments which reply to the attacks they receive and labelling *out* the arguments attacked by arguments labelled *in*. Then two labellings are prescribed: $\mathcal{L}_{S_{lab}^1}(AF_{2.2}) = \{\{(a, in), (b, out)\}, \{(a, out), (b, in)\}\}$. On the other hand, let S_{lab}^2 be a hypothetical labelling-based semantics whose underlying principle consists in labelling *in* only unattacked arguments, labelling *out* the arguments attacked by arguments labelled *in*, and labelling *undecided* all the remaining ones. Clearly this would yield $\mathcal{L}_{S_{lab}^2}(AF_{2.2}) = \{\{(a, undecided), (b, undecided)\}\}$.

As it is also evident from the above examples, for a given argumentation framework one or more extensions (labellings) may be prescribed by a given semantics. It has to be remarked that also the case where no extensions (labellings) are prescribed for an argumentation framework AF is in general possible, namely $\mathcal{E}_S(AF) = \emptyset$ ($\mathcal{L}_S(AF) = \emptyset$). This corresponds to the case where the semantics S is undefined in AF since no extensions (labellings) compliant with the definition of S exist. For extension-based semantics, note in particular that the case $\mathcal{E}_S(AF) = \emptyset$ is very different from $\mathcal{E}_S(AF) = \{\emptyset\}$. In the following we will denote as $\mathcal{D}_S$ the set of argumentation frameworks where a semantics S is defined, namely, $\mathcal{D}_S = \{AF \mid \mathcal{E}_S(AF) \neq \emptyset\}$ or $\mathcal{D}_S = \{AF \mid \mathcal{L}_S(AF) \neq \emptyset\}$. A semantics S is called *universally defined* if any argumentation framework belongs to $\mathcal{D}_S$. Further, an important terminological convention concerning the cardinality of the set of extensions (labellings) is worth introducing. If a semantics S always prescribes exactly one extension (labelling) for any argumentation framework belonging to $\mathcal{D}_S$ then S is said to belong to the *unique-status* (or *single-status*) approach, otherwise it is said to belong to the *multiple-status* approach.

While the adoption of the labelling or extension-based style is a matter of subjective preference by the proponent(s) of a given semantics, a natural question concerns the expressiveness of the two styles. It is immediate to observe that any extension-based definition can be equivalently expressed in a simple labelling-based formulation, where a set of two labels is adopted (let say $\mathbb{L} = \{in, out\}$) corresponding to extension membership. On the other hand, an arbitrary labelling can not in general be formulated in terms of extensions. It is however a matter of fact that labellings considered in the literature typically include a label called *in* which naturally corresponds to extension membership, while other labels correspond to a partition of other arguments, easily derivable from extension membership and the attack relation. As a consequence, equivalent extension-based formulations of labelling-based semantics are typically available. Given this fact and the definitely prevailing custom of adopting the extension-based style in the literature, this chapter will focus on extension-based semantics.

3 Principles for extension-based semantics

While alternative semantics proposals differ from each other by the specific notion of extension they endorse, one may wonder whether there are reasonable general properties which are shared by all (or, at least, most) existing semantics and can be regarded as evaluation principles for new semantics. We discuss these principles in the following, distinguishing between properties of individual extensions and properties of the whole set of extensions. The reader may refer to [2] for a more extensive analysis of this issue.

The first basic requirement for any extension E corresponds to the idea that E is a set of arguments which "can stand together". Consequently, if an argument a attacks another argument b, then a and b can not be included together in an extension. This corresponds to the following *conflict-free* principle, which, as to our knowledge, is satisfied by all existing semantics in the literature.

Definition 2.1. Given an argumentation framework $AF = \langle \mathcal{A}, \mathcal{R} \rangle$, a set $S \subseteq \mathcal{A}$ is *conflict-free*, denoted as $cf(S)$, if and only if $\nexists a, b \in S$ such that $a\mathcal{R}b$. A semantics S satisfies the *conflict-free principle* if and only if $\forall AF \in \mathcal{D}_S, \forall E \in \mathcal{E}_S(AF)$ E is conflict-free.

A further requirement corresponds to the idea that an extension is a set of arguments which "can stand on its own", namely is able to withstand the attacks it receives from other arguments by "replying" with other attacks. Formally, this has a counterpart in the property of *admissibility*, which lies at the heart of all semantics discussed in [13] and is shared by many more recent proposals. The definition

is based on the notions of acceptable argument and admissible set. In words, a is
acceptable wrt. (or, equivalently, *defended* by) a set S if S "counterattacks" all attackers of a and a set S is *admissible* if it is conflict-free and defends all its elements.

Definition 2.2. Given an argumentation framework $AF = \langle A, \mathcal{R} \rangle$, an argument $a \in A$ is *acceptable* wrt. a set $S \subseteq A$ if and only if $\forall b \in A \ b\mathcal{R}a \Rightarrow S\mathcal{R}b$.[2]
The function $\mathcal{F}_{AF} : 2^A \rightarrow 2^A$ which, given a set $S \subseteq A$, returns the set of the
acceptable arguments wrt. S, is called the *characteristic function* of AF.

Definition 2.3. Given an argumentation framework $AF = \langle A, \mathcal{R} \rangle$, a set $S \subseteq A$ is
admissible if and only if $cf(S)$ and $\forall a \in S \ a$ is acceptable wrt. S. The set of all the
admissible sets of AF is denoted as $\mathcal{AS}(AF)$.

Definition 2.4. A semantics $\mathcal{S}$ satisfies the *admissibility principle* if and only if
$\forall AF \in \mathcal{D}_\mathcal{S} \ \mathcal{E}_\mathcal{S}(AF) \subseteq \mathcal{AS}(AF)$, namely $\forall E \in \mathcal{E}_\mathcal{S}(AF)$ it holds that:

$$a \in E \Rightarrow (\forall b \in A, b\mathcal{R}a \Rightarrow E\mathcal{R}b). \tag{2.1}$$

The property of reinstatement is somewhat dual with respect to the notion of
defense. Intuitively, if the attackers of an argument a are in turn attacked by an extension E one may assume that they have no effect on a: then a should be, in a sense,
reinstated, therefore it should belong to E. This leads to the following *reinstatement
principle* which turns out to be the converse of the implication (2.1).

Definition 2.5. A semantics $\mathcal{S}$ satisfies the *reinstatement principle* if and only if
$\forall AF \in \mathcal{D}_\mathcal{S}, \forall E \in \mathcal{E}_\mathcal{S}(AF)$ it holds that:

$$(\forall b \in A, b\mathcal{R}a \Rightarrow E\mathcal{R}b) \Rightarrow a \in E. \tag{2.2}$$

To exemplify these properties consider the argumentation framework $AF_{2.4}$ rep-
resented in Figure 2.4. It is easy to see that $\mathcal{AS}(AF_{2.4}) = \{\emptyset, \{a\}, \{b\}, \{a,c\}\}$, in
particular c needs the "help" of a in order to be defended from the attack of b.
The set $\{b\}$ obviously satisfies the reinstatement condition (2.2), and so does $\{a,c\}$,
while the set $\{a\}$ does not, since it attacks all attackers of c, but does not include it.

Let us turn now to principles concerning sets of extensions. A first fundamental principle corresponds to the fact that the set of extensions only depends on the
attack relation between arguments while it is totally independent of any property
of arguments at the underlying language level. Formally, this principle corresponds
to the fact that argumentation frameworks which are isomorphic have the "same"
(modulo the isomorphism) extensions, as stated by the following definitions.

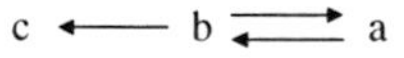

$$c \longleftarrow b \rightleftharpoons a$$

Fig. 2.4 $AF_{2.4}$: not just a mutual attack

---

[2] With a little abuse of notation we define $S\mathcal{R}b \equiv \exists a \in S : a\mathcal{R}b$. Similarly, $b\mathcal{R}S \equiv \exists a \in S : b\mathcal{R}a$.

Definition 2.6. Two argumentation frameworks $AF_1 = \langle A_1, \mathcal{R}_1 \rangle$ and $AF_2 = \langle A_2, \mathcal{R}_2 \rangle$ are isomorphic if and only if there is a bijective mapping $m : A_1 \to A_2$, such that $(a, b) \in \mathcal{R}_1$ if and only if $(m(a), m(b)) \in \mathcal{R}_2$. This is denoted as $AF_1 \stackrel{\circ}{=}_m AF_2$.

Definition 2.7. A semantics $\mathcal{S}$ satisfies the *language independence principle* if and only if $\forall AF_1 \in \mathcal{D}_\mathcal{S}, \forall AF_2 \in \mathcal{D}_\mathcal{S}$ such that $AF_1 \stackrel{\circ}{=}_m AF_2, \mathcal{E}_\mathcal{S}(AF_2) = \{M(E) \mid E \in \mathcal{E}_\mathcal{S}(AF_1)\}$, where $M(E) = \{b \mid \exists a \in E, b = m(a)\}$.

All argumentation semantics we are aware of adhere to this principle.

Another principle concerns possible inclusion relationships between extensions. Considering for instance the admissible sets of the example in Figure 2.4, the empty set is of course included in all other ones, moreover the set $\{a\}$ is included in $\{a, c\}$. In such a situation, the question arises whether an extension may be a strict subset of another one. The answer is typically negative, for reasons which are related in particular with the notion of skeptical justification, to be discussed later. Accordingly, the I-maximality principle can be introduced.

Definition 2.8. A set of extensions $\mathcal{E}$ is I-maximal if and only if $\forall E_1, E_2 \in \mathcal{E}$, if $E_1 \subseteq E_2$ then $E_1 = E_2$. A semantics $\mathcal{S}$ satisfies the *I-maximality principle* if and only if $\forall AF \in \mathcal{D}_\mathcal{S} \; \mathcal{E}_\mathcal{S}(AF)$ is I-maximal.

A further principle is related with the notion of attack which is intrinsically directional: if a attacks b this corresponds to the fact that a has the power to affect b, while not vice versa (unless, in turn, b attacks a). Generalizing this consideration, one may require the evaluation of an argument a to be only affected by its attackers, the attackers of its attackers and so on, i.e. by its ancestors in the attack relationship. In other words, an argument a may affect another argument b only if there is a directed path from a to b. For instance, in Figure 2.4 the evaluations of a and b affect each other and both affect c, while the evaluation of c should not affect those of a and b but rather depend on them. It is reasonable to require this notion of *directionality* to be reflected by the set of extensions prescribed by a semantics. This can be formalized by referring to sets of arguments not receiving attacks from outside.

Definition 2.9. Given an argumentation framework $AF = \langle A, \mathcal{R} \rangle$, a non-empty set $S \subseteq A$ is *unattacked* if and only if $\nexists a \in (A \setminus S) : a\mathcal{R}S$. The set of unattacked sets of AF is denoted as $\mathcal{US}(AF)$.

We also need to introduce the notion of restriction of an argumentation framework to a subset S of its arguments.

Definition 2.10. Let $AF = \langle A, \mathcal{R} \rangle$ be an argumentation framework. The *restriction* of AF to $S \subseteq A$ is the argumentation framework $AF \downarrow_S = \langle S, \mathcal{R} \cap (S \times S) \rangle$.

The directionality principle can then be defined by requiring an unattacked set to be unaffected by the remaining part of the argumentation framework as far as extensions are concerned.

Definition 2.11. A semantics $\mathcal{S}$ satisfies the *directionality principle* if and only if $\forall AF \in \mathcal{D}_\mathcal{S}, \forall S \in \mathcal{US}(AF), \mathcal{AE}_\mathcal{S}(AF, S) = \mathcal{E}_\mathcal{S}(AF \downarrow_S)$, where $\mathcal{AE}_\mathcal{S}(AF, S) \triangleq \{(E \cap S) \mid E \in \mathcal{E}_\mathcal{S}(AF)\} \subseteq 2^S$.

In words, the intersection of any extension prescribed by S for AF with an unattacked set S is equal to one of the extensions prescribed by S for the restriction of AF to S, and vice versa. Referring to the example of Figure 2.4, $\mathfrak{US}(AF_{2.4}) = \{\{a,b\},\{a,b,c\}\}$. Then, the restriction of $AF_{2.4}$ to its unattacked set $\{a,b\}$ coincides with $AF_{2.2}$ shown in Figure 2.2. A hypothetical semantics S_1 such that $\mathcal{E}_{S_1}(AF_{2.4}) = \{\{a,c\},\{b\}\}$ and $\mathcal{E}_{S_1}(AF_{2.2}) = \{\{a\},\{b\}\}$ would satisfy the directionality principle in this case. On the other hand, a hypothetical semantics S_2 such that $\mathcal{E}_{S_2}(AF_{2.4}) = \{\{a,c\}\}$ and $\mathcal{E}_{S_2}(AF_{2.2}) = \{\{a\},\{b\}\}$ would not.

4 The notion of justification state

At a first level, the justification state of an argument a can be conceived in terms of its extension membership. A basic classification encompasses only two possible states for an argument, namely justified or not justified. In this respect, two alternative types of justification, namely *skeptical* and *credulous* can be considered.

Definition 2.12. Given a semantics S and an argumentation framework $AF \in \mathcal{D}_S$, an argument a is:

- *skeptically justified* if and only if $\forall E \in \mathcal{E}_S(AF)\ a \in E$;
- *credulously justified* if and only if $\exists E \in \mathcal{E}_S(AF)\ a \in E$.

Clearly the two notions coincide for unique-status approaches, while, in general, credulous justification includes skeptical justification. To refine this relatively rough classification, a consolidated tradition considers three justification states.

Definition 2.13. [18] Given a semantics S and an argumentation framework $AF \in \mathcal{D}_S$, an argument a is:

- *justified* if and only if $\forall E \in \mathcal{E}_S(AF)$, $a \in E$ (this is clearly the "strongest" possible level of justification, corresponding to skeptical justification);
- *defensible* if and only if $\exists E_1, E_2 \in \mathcal{E}_S(AF) : a \in E_1, a \notin E_2$ (this is a weaker level of justification, corresponding to arguments which are credulously but not skeptically justified);
- *overruled* if and only if $\forall E \in \mathcal{E}_S(AF)$, $a \notin E$ (in this case a can not be justified in any way and should be rejected).

Some remarks are worth about the above classification, which is largely (and sometimes implicitly) adopted in the literature: on one hand, while (two) different levels of justified arguments are encompassed, no distinctions are drawn among rejected arguments; on the other hand, the attack relation plays no role in the derivation of justification state from extensions. These points are addressed by a different classification of justification states introduced by Pollock [16] in the context of a unique-status approach. Again, three cases are possible for an argument a:

- a belongs to the (unique) extension E: then it is justified, or, using Pollock's terminology, *undefeated*;

- *a* does not belong to the (unique) extension E and is attacked by (some member of) E: then, using Pollock's terminology, it is *defeated outright*, corresponding to a strong form of rejection;
- *a* does not belong to the (unique) extension E but does not receive attacks from E: then it is *provisionally defeated*, corresponding to a weaker form of rejection.

Both these classifications of justification states are unsatisfactory in some respect. It is however possible to combine the intuitions underlying both of them, obtaining a systematic classification of seven possible justification states [6]. As a starting point, considering the relationship between an argument a and a specific extension E, three main situations[3], as in Pollock's classification, can be envisaged:

- *a* is *in* E, denoted as $in(a,E)$, if $a \in E$;
- *a* is *definitely out from* E, denoted as $do(a,E)$, if $a \notin E \wedge E\mathcal{R}a$;
- *a* is *provisionally out from* E, denoted as $po(a,E)$, if $a \notin E \wedge \neg E\mathcal{R}a$.

Then, taking into account the possible existence of multiple extensions, an argument can be in any of the above three states with respect to all, some or none of the extensions. This gives rise to 27 hypothetical combinations. It is however easy to see that some of them are impossible: for instance, if an argument is in a given state with respect to all extensions this clearly excludes that it is in another state with respect to any extension. Directly applying this kind of considerations, seven possible justification states emerge.

Definition 2.14. Given an argumentation framework $AF = \langle \mathcal{A}, \mathcal{R} \rangle$ and a *non-empty* set of extensions $\mathcal{E}$ the possible justification states of an argument $a \in \mathcal{A}$ according to $\mathcal{E}$ are defined by the following mutually exclusive conditions:

- $\forall E \in \mathcal{E}\ in(a,E)$, denoted as JS_I;
- $\forall E \in \mathcal{E}\ do(a,E)$, denoted as JS_D;
- $\forall E \in \mathcal{E}\ po(a,E)$, denoted as JS_P;
- $\exists E \in \mathcal{E} : do(a,E)$, $\exists E \in \mathcal{E} : po(a,E)$, and $\nexists E \in \mathcal{E} : in(a,E)$, denoted as JS_{DP};
- $\exists E \in \mathcal{E} : in(a,E)$, $\exists E \in \mathcal{E} : po(a,E)$, and $\nexists E \in \mathcal{E} : do(a,E)$, denoted as JS_{IP};
- $\exists E \in \mathcal{E} : in(a,E)$, $\exists E \in \mathcal{E} : do(a,E)$, and $\nexists E \in \mathcal{E} : po(a,E)$, denoted as JS_{ID};
- $\exists E \in \mathcal{E} : in(a,E)$, $\exists E \in \mathcal{E} : do(a,E)$, and $\exists E \in \mathcal{E} : po(a,E)$, denoted as JS_{IDP}.

Correspondences with "traditional" definitions of justification states are easily drawn. An argument is skeptically justified if and only if it is in the JS_I state, while credulous justification corresponds to the disjunction of the states JS_I, JS_{IP}, JS_{ID}, and JS_{IDP}. As to Definition 2.13, the state of justified corresponds to JS_I, the state of overruled to the disjunction of JS_D, JS_P, and JS_{DP}, while the state of defensible to the disjunction of JS_{IP}, JS_{ID}, and JS_{IDP}. Turning to Pollock's classification, it is easy to see that in the case of a unique-status semantics only JS_I, JS_D and JS_P may hold, which correspond to the state of undefeated, defeated outright and provisionally defeated, respectively. Other meaningful ways of defining aggregated justification states are investigated in [6].

---

[3] The case $a \in E \wedge E\mathcal{R}a$ is prevented by the conflict-free principle.

5 A review of extension-based argumentation semantics

Turning from general notions to actual approaches, we now examine several argumentation semantics proposed in the literature. From a historical point of view, it is possible to distinguish between:

- four "traditional" semantics, considered in Dung's original paper [13], namely *complete*, *grounded*, *stable*, and *preferred* semantics;
- subsequent proposals introduced by various authors in the literature, often to overcome some limitation or improve some undesired behavior of a traditional approach: we consider *stage*, *semi-stable*, *ideal*, *CF*2, and *prudent* semantics.

It is important to note that while the definitions of the semantics we will describe are formulated in the context of purely abstract argumentation frameworks, the underlying intuitions have commonalities with other (somewhat more concrete) formalizations in related contexts. In fact, as already mentioned, one of the main results of Dung's paper is showing that abstract argumentation frameworks are able to capture the properties of a large variety of more specific formalisms. This means that it is possible to define mappings from entities defined in a more specific formalism into an argumentation framework. In [13] mappings of this kind are provided for *stable marriage* problems, *default theories* in Reiter's default logic, logic programs with negation as failure, and Pollock's theory of defeasible reasoning.

Let $AF = \langle \mathcal{A}, \mathcal{R} \rangle$ be an argumentation framework obtained through a mapping from a more specific formalism (e.g. a logic program). We have now two ways of deriving a "meaningful" set of subsets of $\mathcal{A}$: on one hand, we can apply a purely abstract semantics $\mathcal{S}$ to AF, obtaining the relevant set of extensions $\mathcal{E}_{\mathcal{S}}(AF)$. On the other hand, we can start from a meaningful concept in the underlying formalism (e.g. the set of models of a logic program) and then map it into a set $\mathcal{M}$ of subsets of $\mathcal{A}$ (continuing the example, by deriving the set of arguments corresponding to each model). An important question then arises: can interesting relationships be identified between $\mathcal{E}_{\mathcal{S}}(AF)$ and $\mathcal{M}$, given a suitable choice of the semantics $\mathcal{S}$? A strikingly affirmative answer is provided in [13]: it is shown that properly selecting $\mathcal{S}$ among the traditional grounded, preferred, and stable semantics one obtains sets of extensions $\mathcal{E}_{\mathcal{S}}(AF)$ which coincide with the sets of arguments corresponding to meaningful notions in the formalisms mentioned above. Specific indications about these coincidences will be given in the review of individual semantics. At a general level, they confirm that abstract argumentation semantics is a powerful analysis tool, able to focus on essential properties of a variety of formalisms and to shed light on their (possibly hidden) significant common features.

5.1 Complete semantics

We start our review by the notion of complete extension, as it lies at the heart of all traditional Dung's semantics. Actually the notion of complete extension is not associated with a notion of *complete semantics* in [13], but the term complete semantics has subsequently gained acceptance in the literature and will be used in the present analysis to refer to the properties of the set of complete extensions. Complete semantics is denoted as $\mathcal{CO}$.

The notion of complete extension is based on the principles of admissibility and reinstatement: a complete extension is a set which is able to defend itself and includes all arguments it defends, as stated by the following definition.

Definition 2.15. Given an argumentation framework $AF = \langle \mathcal{A}, \mathcal{R} \rangle$, a set $E \subseteq \mathcal{A}$ is a *complete extension* if and only if E is admissible and every argument of $\mathcal{A}$ which is acceptable wrt. E belongs to E, i.e. $E \in \mathcal{AS}(AF) \wedge \mathcal{F}_{AF}(E) \subseteq E$.

It is worth noting here that the empty set is admissible and that arguments not receiving attacks in an argumentation framework AF (called *initial arguments* and denoted as $\mathcal{IN}(AF)$ in the sequel) are acceptable wrt. the empty set (in fact $\mathcal{IN}(AF) = \mathcal{F}_{AF}(\emptyset)$). It can be shown that the following properties hold:

- $\forall AF \; \mathcal{E}_{\mathcal{CO}}(AF) \neq \emptyset$ (namely $\mathcal{CO}$ is universally defined);
- $\emptyset \in \mathcal{E}_{\mathcal{CO}}(AF)$ if and only if $\mathcal{IN}(AF) = \emptyset$;
- $\forall E \in \mathcal{E}_{\mathcal{CO}}(AF) \; \mathcal{IN}(AF) \subseteq E$.

Due to reinstatement, any complete extension not only includes the initial arguments, but also the arguments they defend, those which are in turn defended by them, and so on. More formally, for any argumentation framework $AF = \langle \mathcal{A}, \mathcal{R} \rangle$, given a set $S \subseteq \mathcal{A}$, let $\mathcal{F}^1_{AF}(S) \triangleq \mathcal{F}_{AF}(S)$ and for $i > 1$, $\mathcal{F}^i_{AF}(S) \triangleq \mathcal{F}_{AF}(\mathcal{F}^{i-1}_{AF}(S))$. Then, it turns out that $\forall AF, \forall E \in \mathcal{E}_{\mathcal{CO}}(AF), \forall i \geq 1, \mathcal{F}^i_{AF}(\emptyset) \subseteq E$.

In the example of Figure 2.1, $\{b\} = \mathcal{IN}(AF_{2.1})$ is clearly the only complete extension. Similarly in the example of Figure 2.3 the only complete extension is $\{b, c\}$. In the example of Figure 2.2 there are three complete extensions: $\emptyset$ (as there are no initial arguments), $\{a\}$, and $\{b\}$ (each one defending itself against the other). By similar considerations and the property of reinstatement it is easy to see that in the example of Figure 2.4 $\mathcal{E}_{\mathcal{CO}}(AF_{2.4}) = \{\emptyset, \{a, c\}, \{b\}\}$. The example of Figure 2.5 requires some more articulated considerations. First note that $\mathcal{IN}(AF_{2.5}) = \emptyset$ hence $\emptyset \in \mathcal{E}_{\mathcal{CO}}(AF_{2.5})$. Then note that all singletons except $\{c\}$ are admissible: to check whether they are complete extensions or not we have to resort to the reinstatement property. In particular, a defends c from b but not from d, so $\{a\}$ stands as a complete extension. On the other hand b defends d from its only attacker c, therefore $\{b, d\}$ is a complete extension, while $\{b\}$ is not. Argument d does not defend any other argument apart itself, thus $\{d\}$ is a complete extension. We have now to consider possibly larger admissible sets. It is easy to see that $\{a, c\}$ and $\{a, d\}$ are admissible (and attack all arguments they do not include). Summarizing we have $\mathcal{E}_{\mathcal{CO}}(AF_{2.5}) = \{\emptyset, \{a\}, \{d\}, \{b, d\}, \{a, c\}, \{a, d\}\}$.

We complete the treatment of $\mathcal{CO}$ by considering its ability to satisfy the properties which are not common to all semantics: we note that admissibility and reinstatement are enforced by definition, while the satisfaction of directionality is proved in

d $\rightleftarrows$ c $\longleftarrow$ b $\rightleftarrows$ a

Fig. 2.5 $AF_{2.5}$: two mutual attacks.

[2]. As the examples above abundantly show, $\mathcal{CO}$ does not satisfy I-maximality, since a complete extension E_1 may be a proper subset of a complete extension E_2.

5.2 Grounded semantics

Grounded semantics, denoted as $\mathcal{GR}$, is a traditional unique-status approach whose formulation in argumentation-based reasoning (see e.g. the one proposed by Pollock in [16]) predates the following quite technical definition given in [13].

Definition 2.16. The grounded extension of an argumentation framework AF, denoted as $GE(AF)$, is the least fixed point of its characteristic function $\mathcal{F}_{AF}$.

The underlying and preexisting informal intuition is however rather simple and can be directly put in relationship with some notions we already discussed in the context of complete semantics. The basic idea is that the (unique) grounded extension can be built incrementally starting from the initial unattacked arguments. Then the arguments attacked by them can be suppressed, resulting in a modified argumentation framework where, possibly, the set of initial arguments is larger. In turn the arguments attacked by the "new" initial arguments can be suppressed, and so on. The process stops when no new initial arguments arise after a deletion step: the set of all initial arguments identified so far is the grounded extension. An example with a graphical illustration of this incremental process is given in Figure 2.6, resulting in $\mathcal{E}_{\mathcal{GR}}(AF) = \{\{a,c\}\}$. To put it in other words, the grounded extension includes those and only those arguments whose defense is "rooted" in initial arguments (see [2] for a formal treatment of this notion, called *strong defense*). If there are no initial arguments the grounded extension is the empty set.

The reader should have noticed that the above construction corresponds to the iterated application of $\mathcal{F}_{AF}(\emptyset)$ already met in previous section: the set of arguments obtained up to each step i above coincides with $\mathcal{F}^i_{AF}(\emptyset)$ and the process stops when $\mathcal{F}^i_{AF}(\emptyset) = \mathcal{F}^{i+1}_{AF}(\emptyset)$ (i.e. a fixed point of $\mathcal{F}_{AF}$ is reached). As a counterpart to this intuitive correspondence, it is proved in [13] that:

i) the grounded extension is the least (wrt. set inclusion) complete extension: for any AF $GE(AF) \in \mathcal{E}_{\mathcal{CO}}(AF)$ and $\forall E \in \mathcal{E}_{\mathcal{CO}}(AF)$ $GE(AF) \subseteq E$;
ii) for any finite (and, more generally, finitary [13]) AF $GE(AF) = \cup_{i=1,\dots,\infty} \mathcal{F}^i_{AF}(\emptyset)$.

Given the above explanations it should be now immediate to see that $GE(AF_{2.1}) = \{b\}$, $GE(AF_{2.3}) = \{b,c\}$, $GE(AF_{2.2}) = GE(AF_{2.4}) = GE(AF_{2.5}) = \emptyset$.

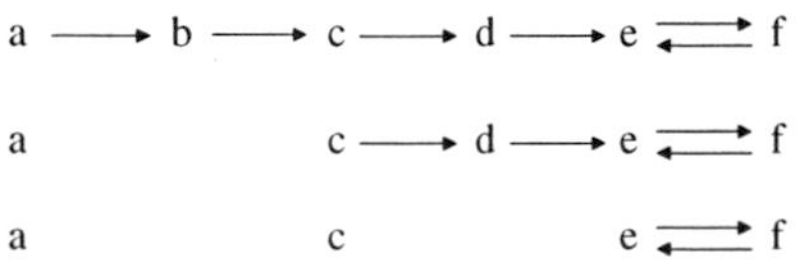

a ⟶ b ⟶ c ⟶ d ⟶ e ⇄ f

a   c ⟶ d ⟶ e ⇄ f

a   c   e ⇄ f

Fig. 2.6 $AF_{2.6}$: an example to illustrate grounded semantics

Besides the relationship with Pollock's approach [16], the grounded extension has been put in correspondence in [13] with the well-founded semantics of logic programs [20]. Turning to general semantics properties it is immediate to see that $\mathcal{GR}$ is universally defined and satisfies admissibility, reinstatement and I-maximality. It is proved in [2] that $\mathcal{GR}$ also satisfies directionality.

5.3 Stable semantics

Stable semantics, denoted as $\mathcal{ST}$, relies on a very simple (and easy to formalize) intuition: an extension should be able to attack all arguments not included in it. This leads to the notion of stable extension [13].

Definition 2.17. Given an argumentation framework $AF = \langle \mathcal{A}, \mathcal{R} \rangle$, a set $E \subseteq \mathcal{A}$ is a *stable extension* of AF if and only if E is conflict-free and $\forall a \in \mathcal{A}, a \notin E \Rightarrow E \mathcal{R} a$.

By definition, any stable extension E is also a complete extension (thus in particular $GE(AF) \subseteq E$) and a maximal conflict-free set of AF. Referring to the examples seen so far, identifying stable extensions is straightforward: $\mathcal{E}_{\mathcal{ST}}(AF_{2.1}) = \{b\}$, $\mathcal{E}_{\mathcal{ST}}(AF_{2.2}) = \{\{a\}, \{b\}\}$, $\mathcal{E}_{\mathcal{ST}}(AF_{2.3}) = \{b, c\}$, $\mathcal{E}_{\mathcal{ST}}(AF_{2.4}) = \{\{a,c\}, \{b\}\}$, $\mathcal{E}_{\mathcal{ST}}(AF_{2.5}) = \{\{a,c\}, \{a,d\}, \{b,d\}\}$, $\mathcal{E}_{\mathcal{ST}}(AF_{2.6}) = \{\{a,c,e\}, \{a,c,f\}\}$.

The simple intuition underlying stable semantics has significant counterparts in several contexts: it is proved in [13] that stable extensions can be put in correspondence with solutions of cooperative n-person games, solutions of the stable marriage problem, extensions of Reiter's default logic [19], and stable models of logic programs [15]. Stable semantics however has also a significant drawback: it is not universally defined as there are argumentation frameworks where no stable extensions exist. A simple example is provided in Figure 2.7: no conflict-free set is able to attack all other arguments in this case. While it has sometimes been claimed by supporters of stable semantics that situations where stable extensions do not exist are "pathological" in some sense, it has been shown in [13] that perfectly reasonable problems may be formalized with argumentation frameworks such that $\mathcal{E}_{\mathcal{ST}}(AF) = \emptyset$.

As to general properties, it is easy to see that I-maximality is enforced by definition and, since stable extensions are a subset of complete extensions, also admissibility and reinstatement are satisfied. $\mathcal{ST}$ is not directional, due to the fact that it is not universally defined. To see this, consider the example in Figure 2.8: we have that $\mathcal{E}_{\mathcal{ST}}(AF_{2.8}) = \{\{b\}\}$, however, considering the unattacked set $S = \{a,b\}$, we have $\mathcal{E}_{\mathcal{ST}}(AF_{2.8}\downarrow_S) = \{\{a\}, \{b\}\}$. Therefore $\mathcal{AE}_{\mathcal{ST}}(AF_{2.8}, S) = \{\{b\}\} \neq \mathcal{E}_{\mathcal{ST}}(AF_{2.8}\downarrow_S)$.

Fig. 2.7 $AF_{2.7}$: a three-length cycle

5.4 Preferred semantics

The "aggressive" requirement that an extension must attack anything outside it may be relaxed by requiring that an extension is as large as possible and able to defend itself from attacks. This is captured by the notion of preferred extension [13].

Definition 2.18. Given an argumentation framework $AF = \langle A, R \rangle$, a set $E \subseteq A$ is a *preferred extension* of AF if and only if E is a maximal (wrt. set inclusion) element of $AS(AF)$.

According to this definition every preferred extension E is also a complete extension (entailing that $GE(AF) \subseteq E$); indeed, preferred extensions may be equivalently defined as maximal complete extensions. It follows that preferred semantics, denoted as $\mathcal{PR}$, is universally defined (as complete semantics is) and that, taking into account the treatment of the examples in Section 5.1, $\mathcal{E}_{\mathcal{PR}}(AF_{2.1}) = \{\{b\}\}$, $\mathcal{E}_{\mathcal{PR}}(AF_{2.2}) = \{\{a\}, \{b\}\}$, $\mathcal{E}_{\mathcal{PR}}(AF_{2.3}) = \{\{b, c\}\}$, $\mathcal{E}_{\mathcal{PR}}(AF_{2.4}) = \{\{a, c\}, \{b\}\}$, $\mathcal{E}_{\mathcal{PR}}(AF_{2.5}) = \{\{a, c\}, \{a, d\}, \{b, d\}\}$, and $\mathcal{E}_{\mathcal{PR}}(AF_{2.6}) = \{\{a, c, e\}, \{a, c, f\}\}$. The reader may notice that in all these examples the set of preferred extensions coincides with the set of stable extensions. In general any stable extension is also a preferred extension but not vice versa. In the example of Figure 2.7 we have $\mathcal{E}_{\mathcal{PR}}(AF_{2.7}) = \{\emptyset\}$ while $\mathcal{E}_{\mathcal{ST}}(AF_{2.7}) = \emptyset$. In the example of Figure 2.8 there are two preferred extensions, namely $\{a\}$, $\{b\}$, but only one of them, namely $\{b\}$, is also stable.

The intuition underlying preferred semantics has a correspondence with preferential semantics of logic programs [12]. As to general semantics properties it is immediate to see that $\mathcal{PR}$ satisfies I-maximality, admissibility, reinstatement, while it is proved in [2] that it is directional. Given these facts, $\mathcal{PR}$ has often been regarded as the most satisfactory semantics in the context of Dung's framework.

5.5 Stage and semi-stable semantics

Stage [21] and semi-stable [8] semantics, denoted respectively as $\mathcal{STA}$ and $\mathcal{SST}$, are based on the idea of prescribing the maximization not only of the arguments included in an extension but also of those attacked by it.

Definition 2.19. Given an argumentation framework $AF = \langle A, R \rangle$ and a set $E \subseteq A$ the *range* of E is defined as $E \cup E^+$, where $E^+ \triangleq \{a \in A : ERa\}$. E is a *stage extension* if and only if E is a conflict-free set with maximal (wrt. set inclusion) range. E is a *semi-stable extension* if and only if E is a complete extension with maximal (wrt. set inclusion) range.

As evident from Definition 2.19, the two semantics differ in the requirement on the sets whose range is maximal: being conflict-free for stage semantics, complete

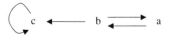

Fig. 2.8 $AF_{2.8}$: $\mathcal{ST}$ is not directional

extensions (or equivalently, admissible sets) for semi-stable semantics. Both $\mathcal{STA}$ and $\mathcal{SST}$ are clearly universally defined (differently from stable semantics), while coinciding with stable semantics (differently from preferred semantics) when stable extensions exist. In fact, for any stable extension E it holds that $E \cup E^+ = \mathcal{A}$. It follows that any complete extension (conflict-free set) which is not stable does not satisfy the range maximization requirement for argumentation frameworks where stable extensions exist, hence the coincidence of $\mathcal{ST}$ and $\mathcal{SST}$ ($\mathcal{STA}$) in these cases. If stable extensions do not exist, $\mathcal{SST}$ selects anyway as extensions some complete extensions and the maximization requirement restricts the choice to preferred extensions: $\forall AF \; \mathcal{E}_{\mathcal{SST}}(AF) \subseteq \mathcal{E}_{\mathcal{PR}}(AF)$. On the other hand, $\mathcal{STA}$ does not necessarily select admissible sets as extensions. Figure 2.9 shows an argumentation framework where $\mathcal{SST}$ and $\mathcal{STA}$ agree and do not coincide neither with $\mathcal{ST}$ nor with $\mathcal{PR}$: in fact $\mathcal{E}_{\mathcal{ST}}(AF_{2.9}) = \emptyset$, $\mathcal{E}_{\mathcal{PR}}(AF_{2.9}) = \{\{a\}, \{b\}\}$, $\mathcal{E}_{\mathcal{SST}}(AF_{2.9}) = \mathcal{E}_{\mathcal{STA}}(AF_{2.9}) = \{\{b\}\}$. On the other hand, in the case of Figure 2.7 $\mathcal{E}_{\mathcal{PR}}(AF_{2.7}) = \mathcal{E}_{\mathcal{SST}}(AF_{2.7}) = \{\emptyset\}$ while $\mathcal{E}_{\mathcal{STA}}(AF_{2.7}) = \{\{a\}, \{b\}, \{c\}\}$.

It is easy to see that both $\mathcal{SST}$ and $\mathcal{STA}$ satisfy I-maximality, while only $\mathcal{SST}$ satisfies admissibility and reinstatement. $\mathcal{SST}$ and $\mathcal{STA}$ do not satisfy directionality, as $\mathcal{ST}$ does not.

5.6 Ideal semantics

Ideal semantics [14], denoted as $\mathcal{ID}$, provides a unique-status approach allowing the acceptance of a set of arguments possibly larger than in the case of $\mathcal{GR}$.

Definition 2.20. Given an argumentation framework $AF = \langle \mathcal{A}, \mathcal{R} \rangle$ a set $S \subseteq \mathcal{A}$ is ideal if and only if S is admissible and $\forall E \in \mathcal{E}_{\mathcal{PR}}(AF) \; S \subseteq E$. The ideal extension, denoted as $\mathrm{ID}(AF)$, is the maximal (wrt. set inclusion) ideal set.

The definition of ideal set prescribes admissibility and skeptical justification under preferred semantics. From Section 5.2 we know that the grounded extension satisfies both requirements and is therefore an ideal set (this in particular implies that ideal semantics is universally defined). Ideal sets strictly larger than the grounded extension may exist, as shown by the example in Figure 2.10 where it holds that $\mathcal{E}_{\mathcal{PR}}(AF_{2.10}) = \{\{a,d\}, \{b,d\}\}$: in this case the grounded extension is empty while $\mathrm{ID}(AF_{2.10}) = \{d\}$.

By definition $\mathcal{ID}$ satisfies I-maximality and admissibility. It is proved in [2] that $\mathcal{ID}$ also satisfies reinstatement and directionality.

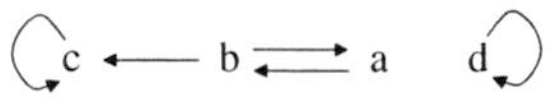

Fig. 2.9 $AF_{2.9}$: $\mathcal{SST}$ may not coincide with $\mathcal{PR}$ or $\mathcal{ST}$

5.7 *CF2 semantics*

CF2 semantics is defined in the frame of the SCC-recursive scheme [7] which is a general pattern for the definition of argumentation semantics based on the graph-theoretical notion of *strongly connected components* (SCCs) of an argumentation framework, i.e. the equivalence classes of arguments under the relation of mutual reachability via attack links. *CF2* semantics can be roughly regarded as selecting its extensions among the maximal conflict-free sets of *AF*, on the basis of some topological requirements related to the decomposition of *AF* into strongly connected components. Examining in detail the definition of *CF2* semantics is beyond the scope of this chapter: the interested reader may refer to [7].

Definition 2.21. Given an argumentation framework $AF = \langle \mathcal{A}, \mathcal{R} \rangle$, a set $E \subseteq \mathcal{A}$ is an extension of *CF2* semantics, i.e. $E \in \mathcal{E}_{CF2}(AF)$, if and only if

- $E \in \mathcal{MCF}(AF)$ if $|SCCS_{AF}| = 1$
- $\forall S \in SCCS_{AF}$ $(E \cap S) \in \mathcal{E}_{CF2}(AF \downarrow_{UP_{AF}(S,E)})$ otherwise

where $\mathcal{MCF}(AF)$ denotes the set of maximal conflict-free sets of *AF*, $SCCS_{AF}$ denotes the set of strongly connected components of *AF*, and, for any $E, S \subseteq \mathcal{A}$, $UP_{AF}(S,E) = \{a \in S \mid \nexists b \in E : b \notin S, b\mathcal{R}a\}$.

The underlying idea consists in relying only on I-maximality and the conflict-free principle within a unique strongly connected component *S*, where all arguments (if more than one) both receive and deliver at least an attack. In particular it turns out that when *AF* consists of exactly one strongly connected component, the set of extensions prescribed by *CF2* semantics exactly coincides with the set of maximal conflict-free sets of *AF*. This yields a uniform multiple-status treatment of cycles, which is not achieved by other semantics. In fact, it is easy to see that for any argumentation framework *AF* consisting of an even-length attack cycle it holds that $\mathcal{E}_{\mathcal{ST}}(AF) = \mathcal{E}_{\mathcal{PR}}(AF) = \mathcal{E}_{\mathcal{SST}}(AF) \neq \{\emptyset\}$. For instance we already know that $\mathcal{E}_{\mathcal{ST}}(AF_{2.2}) = \mathcal{E}_{\mathcal{PR}}(AF_{2.2}) = \mathcal{E}_{\mathcal{SST}}(AF_{2.2}) = \mathcal{MCF}(AF_{2.2}) = \{\{a\}, \{b\}\}$. Similarly, in the case of a four-length cycle two extensions arise, each consisting of two arguments. On the other hand, for any argumentation framework *AF* consisting of an

Fig. 2.10 $AF_{2.10}$: an example to illustrate ideal semantics

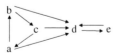

Fig. 2.11 $AF_{2.11}$: an example to illustrate *CF2* semantics

odd-length attack cycle it holds that $\mathcal{E}_{ST}(AF) = \emptyset$ and $\mathcal{E}_{PR}(AF) = \mathcal{E}_{SST}(AF) = \{\emptyset\}$. This disuniformity in the treatment of cycles gives rise to counterintuitive behaviors in some simple examples and has therefore been regarded as problematic in the literature [17]. Clearly $CF2$ semantics is able to overcome this limitation since $\mathcal{E}_{CF2}(AF) = \mathcal{MCF}(AF)$ for any argumentation framework AF consisting of an attack cycle, independently of its length. For instance, $\mathcal{E}_{CF2}(AF_{2.7}) = \{\{a\}, \{b\}, \{c\}\}$.

In a generic argumentation framework, $CF2$ extensions may be computed following the decomposition of AF into strongly connected components, which, due to a well-known graph-theoretical property, can be partially ordered according to the attack relation. Consider the example in Figure 2.11, which consists of two SCCs, namely $S_1 = \{a,b,c\}$ and $S_2 = \{d,e\}$. According to Definition 2.21 it must be the case that $E \cap S_1$ is a maximal conflict-free set of $AF_{2.11}\downarrow_{\{a,b,c\}}$. Thus we get three possible starting points for the construction of extensions, namely $\{a\}$, $\{b\}$, $\{c\}$. It has then to be noted that in any of these three cases d is attacked. Therefore in all cases $UP_{AF}(S_2, E)$ consists of the only argument e, yielding $E \cap S_2 = \{e\}$ as the only possibility. In summary $\mathcal{E}_{CF2}(AF_{2.11}) = \{\{a,e\}, \{b,e\}, \{c,e\}\}$. It can be seen that in all other examples considered so far $CF2$ extensions coincide with preferred extensions.

As to general properties, $CF2$ semantics is I-maximal, since its extensions are maximal conflict-free sets of AF, directional [2], and universally defined, since, for any AF, $\mathcal{MCF}(AF) \neq \emptyset$. On the other hand, the "desired" treatment of odd-length cycles entails that $CF2$ semantics gives up the traditional properties of admissibility and reinstatement as shown, for instance, by the example of Figure 2.7 where no extension is an admissible set and all violate the reinstatement property. It is proven however in [2] that the departure from the notion of reinstatement is not radical, since $CF2$ semantics satisfies two weaker versions of this property called $\mathcal{CF}$-reinstatement and weak reinstatement. As another confirmation that $CF2$ semantics has significant relationships with traditional semantics it can be recalled that any preferred extension is included in a $CF2$ extension, any stable extension is a $CF2$ extension and the grounded extension is included in any $CF2$ extension.

5.8 Prudent semantics

The family of prudent semantics [10] is introduced by considering a more extensive notion of attack in the context of traditional semantics. In particular, an argument a *indirectly attacks* an argument b if there is an odd-length attack path from a to b. For instance, in Figure 2.5 a indirectly attacks d, while in Figure 2.6 a indirectly attacks d and f, b indirectly attacks e, and c indirectly attacks f. The odd-length path need not be the shortest path and may include cycles: in Figure 2.10 both a and b indirectly attack d, while in Figure 2.11 a indirectly attacks e. A set S of arguments is free of indirect conflicts, denoted as $icf(S)$, if $\nexists a, b \in S$ such that a indirectly attacks b. The prudent version of the admissibility property and of several traditional notions of extension can then be defined.

Definition 2.22. Given an argumentation framework $AF = \langle \mathcal{A}, \mathcal{R} \rangle$, a set of arguments $S \subseteq \mathcal{A}$ is *p(rudent)-admissible* if and only if $\forall a \in S$ a is acceptable wrt. S

and $icf(S)$. A set of arguments $E \subseteq \mathcal{A}$ is: a *preferred p-extension* if and only if E is a maximal (wrt. set inclusion) p-admissible set; a *stable p-extension* if and only if $icf(E)$ and $\forall a \in (\mathcal{A} \setminus E)$ $E\mathcal{R}a$; a *complete p-extension* if and only if E is p-admissible and there is no $a \notin E$ such that a is acceptable wrt. E and $icf(E \cup \{a\})$.

Definition 2.23. Given an argumentation framework $AF = \langle \mathcal{A}, \mathcal{R} \rangle$, the function $\mathcal{F}^p_{AF} : 2^{\mathcal{A}} \to 2^{\mathcal{A}}$ such that for a given a set $S \subseteq \mathcal{A}$, $\mathcal{F}^p_{AF}(S) = \{a \mid a$ is acceptable with respect to $S \wedge icf(S \cup \{a\})\}$ is called the *p-characteristic function* of AF. Let j be the lowest integer such that the sequence $(\mathcal{F}^p_{AF})^i(\emptyset)$ is stationary for $i \geq j$: $(\mathcal{F}^p_{AF})^j(\emptyset)$ is the *grounded p-extension* of AF, denoted as $\mathrm{GPE}(AF)$.

The prudent versions of grounded, complete, preferred and stable semantics are denoted as $\mathcal{GRP}$, $\mathcal{COP}$, $\mathcal{PRP}$ and $\mathcal{STP}$, respectively.

It is possible to note that the adoption of indirect conflict has a different impact on the various notions of traditional semantics. The definition of stable prudent extension corresponds to the one of stable extension with an additional requirement. This means that, when $\mathcal{STP}$ is defined, its extensions are also stable (and thus have the same properties) but $\mathcal{D}_{\mathcal{STP}} \subsetneq \mathcal{D}_{\mathcal{ST}}$. For instance in the example of Figure 2.12 $\mathcal{STP}$ is not defined since the only stable extension, namely $\{a,d,e\}$ is not prudent due to the indirect attack from a to d. Analogously to the traditional version, the grounded prudent extension, denoted as $\mathrm{GPE}(AF)$, can be conceived as the result of the incremental application of a (p-)characteristic function starting from initial arguments. As $\mathcal{F}^p_{AF}$ is more restrictive than $\mathcal{F}_{AF}$ it follows that the grounded prudent extension is a possibly strict subset of the traditional grounded extension. This entails in particular that reinstatement is given up by $\mathcal{GRP}$, as it can be seen in the example of Figure 2.12 where $\mathrm{GPE}(AF_{2.12}) = \{a,e\} \subsetneq \mathrm{GE}(AF_{2.12}) = \{a,d,e\}$ and d is not reinstated. In the context of complete and preferred prudent semantics a notable effect is that an initial argument may not be included in an extension. This is the case of a in the example of Figure 2.12 where $\mathcal{E}_{\mathcal{COP}}(AF_{2.12}) = \mathcal{E}_{\mathcal{PRP}}(AF_{2.12}) = \{\{a,e\},\{d,e\}\}$. Besides reinstatement this gives up also the directionality property, showing the neat departure of $\mathcal{COP}$ and $\mathcal{PRP}$ from the track of traditional semantics.

6 Advanced topics

This final section provides a quick overview and literature references for some advanced topics in the field of abstract argumentation, namely semantics agreement, skepticism relations, and semantics principles.

As to the first point, while different semantics proposals correspond to alternative intuitions which manifest themselves in distinct behaviors in some argumentation

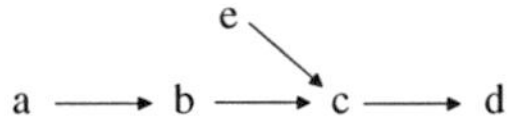

Fig. 2.12 $AF_{2.12}$: an example to illustrate prudent semantics

frameworks, there are also argumentation frameworks where the sets of extensions prescribed by different semantics coincide, as evident from several of the examples seen above. Topological properties of argumentation frameworks providing sufficient conditions for semantics agreement have been investigated in Dung's original paper: for instance the absence of attack cycles is sufficient to ensure agreement among grounded, stable and preferred semantics, while the absence of odd-length attack cycles is sufficient to ensure agreement between stable and preferred semantics. Subsequent results concerning topological families of argumentation frameworks relevant to agreement properties are reported in [11, 1], while a systematic set-theoretical analysis of agreement classes is provided in [5].

As to the notion of skepticism, it has often been used in informal ways to discuss semantics behavior, e.g. by observing that a semantics is "more skeptical" than another one. Intuitively, a semantics is more skeptical than another if it makes less committed choices about the justification of the arguments: a skeptical behavior tends to leave arguments in an "undecided" justification state, while a non-skeptical behavior corresponds to more "resolute" choices about acceptance or rejection of arguments. The issue of formalizing skepticism relations between sets of extension in terms of set theoretical properties and then comparing semantics according to skepticism has been first addressed in [6] and subsequently developed in [4].

Turning finally back to general properties of argumentation semantics, some of them, like admissibility and reinstatement, have regularly been considered in the literature [18], while the task of systematically defining a set of criteria for semantics evaluation and comparison has been undertaken only recently. Besides the principles we have explicitly discussed in Section 3, two families of *adequacy* properties (based on skepticism relations) are introduced in [2], where it is shown that, considering also these properties, none of the literature semantics discussed in this chapter is able to comply with all the desirable criteria. A novel semantics able to satisfy all of them has been proposed in [3]. At a different abstraction level, where argument structure and construction are explicitly dealt with, general *rationality postulates* for argumentation systems have been introduced in [9]. Exploring the definition of general principles for argumentation at different abstraction levels, investigating their relationships and analyzing their suitability for different application domains appear to be open and fruitful research directions. A related research issue concerns the identification of a generic definition scheme able to encompass into a unifying view a large variety of semantics. In this perspective, it is shown in [7] that all traditional semantics adhere to the parametric SCC-recursive scheme, where they differ simply by a *base function* which only specifies the sets of extensions of argumentation frameworks consisting of a single SCC.

The above mentioned results suggest that though there is a wide corpus of literature on abstract argumentation semantics, providing a rich variety of alternative approaches, the field is far from being "mature" and there is still large room for investigating both fundamental theoretical issues and their potential impact on practical applications.

References

1. Baroni, P., Giacomin, M.: Characterizing defeat graphs where argumentation semantics agree. In: G. Simari, P. Torroni (eds.) Proc. 1st Int. Workshop on Argumentation and Non-Monotonic Reasoning (ARGNMR07), pp. 33–48. Tempe, AZ (2007)
2. Baroni, P., Giacomin, M.: On principle-based evaluation of extension-based argumentation semantics. Artif. Intell. (Special issue on Argumentation in A.I.) **171**(10/15), 675–700 (2007)
3. Baroni, P., Giacomin, M.: Resolution-based argumentation semantics. In: P. Besnard, S. Doutre, A. Hunter (eds.) Proc. 2nd Int. Conf. on Computational Models of Argument (COMMA 2008), pp. 25–36. IOS Press, Toulouse, F (2008)
4. Baroni, P., Giacomin, M.: Skepticism relations for comparing argumentation semantics. Int. J. Approx. Reason. **50**(6), 854–866 (2009)
5. Baroni, P., Giacomin, M.: A systematic classification of argumentation frameworks where semantics agree. In: P. Besnard, S. Doutre, A. Hunter (eds.) Proc. 2nd Int. Conf. on Computational Models of Argument (COMMA 2008), pp. 37–48. IOS Press, Toulouse, F (2008)
6. Baroni, P., Giacomin, M., Guida, G.: Towards a formalization of skepticism in extension-based argumentation semantics. In: Proc. 4th Workshop on Computational Models of Natural Argument (CMNA 2004), pp. 47–52. Valencia, Spain (2004)
7. Baroni, P., Giacomin, M., Guida, G.: SCC-recursiveness: a general schema for argumentation semantics. Artif. Intell. **168**(1-2), 165–210 (2005)
8. Caminada, M.: Semi-stable semantics. In: P.E. Dunne, T. Bench-Capon (eds.) Proc. 1st Int. Conf. on Computational Models of Argument (COMMA 2006), pp. 121–130. IOS Press, Liverpool, UK (2006)
9. Caminada, M., Amgoud, L.: An axiomatic account of formal argumentation. In: Proc. 20th National Conf. on Artificial Intelligence (AAAI-05), pp. 608–613. AAAI Press, Menlo Park, CA (2005)
10. Coste-Marquis, S., Devred, C., Marquis, P.: Prudent semantics for argumentation frameworks. In: Proc. 17th IEEE Int. Conf. on Tools with Artificial Intelligence (ICTAI 2005), pp. 568–572. IEEE Computer Society, Hong Kong, China (2005)
11. Coste-Marquis, S., Devred, C., Marquis, P.: Symmetric argumentation frameworks. In: Proc. 8th European Conf. on Symbolic and Quantitative Approaches to Reasoning with Uncertainty (ECSQARU 2005), pp. 317–328. Barcelona, E (2005)
12. Dung, P.M.: Negations as hypotheses: An abductive foundation for logic programming. In: K. Furukawa (ed.) Proc. 8th Int. Conf. on Logic Programming (ICLP 91), pp. 3–17. MIT Press, Paris, F (1991)
13. Dung, P.M.: On the acceptability of arguments and its fundamental role in nonmonotonic reasoning, logic programming, and n-person games. Artif. Intell. **77**(2), 321–357 (1995)
14. Dung, P.M., Mancarella, P., Toni, F.: A dialectic procedure for sceptical, assumption-based argumentation. In: P.E. Dunne, T. Bench-Capon (eds.) Proc. 1st Int. Conf. on Computational Models of Argument (COMMA 2006), pp. 145–156. IOS Press, Liverpool, UK (2006)
15. Gelfond, M., Lifschitz, V.: The stable model semantics for logic programming. In: R.A. Kowalski, K. Bowen (eds.) Proc. 5th Int. Conf. on Logic Programming (ICLP 88), pp. 1070–1080. MIT Press, Cambridge, Massachusetts (1988)
16. Pollock, J.L.: How to reason defeasibly. Artif. Intell. **57**(1), 1–42 (1992)
17. Pollock, J.L.: Justification and defeat. Artif. Intell. **67**(2), 377–407 (1994)
18. Prakken, H., Vreeswijk, G.A.W.: Logics for defeasible argumentation. In: D.M. Gabbay, F. Guenthner (eds.) Handbook of Philosophical Logic, Second Edition. Kluwer Academic Publishers, Dordrecht (2001)
19. Reiter, R.: A logic for default reasoning. Artif. Intell. **13**(1–2), 81–132 (1980)
20. van Gelder, A., Ross, K., Schlipf, J.S.: The well-founded semantics for general logic programs. J. ACM **38**(3), 620–650 (1991)
21. Verheij, B.: Two approaches to dialectical argumentation: admissible sets and argumentation stages. In: Proc. 8th Dutch Conf. on Artificial Intelligence (NAIC'96), pp. 357–368. Utrecht, NL (1996)

Chapter 3
Abstract Argumentation and Values

Trevor Bench-Capon and Katie Atkinson

1 Introduction

Abstract argumentation frameworks, as described in Chapter 2, are directed towards determining whether a claim that some statement is true can be coherently maintained in the context of a set of conflicting arguments. For example, if we use preferred semantics, that an argument is a member of all preferred extensions establishes that its claim must be accepted as true, and membership of at least one preferred extension shows that the claim is at least tenable. In consequence, that admissible sets of arguments are conflict free is an important requirement under all the various semantics.

For many common cases of argument, however, this is not appropriate: two arguments can conflict, and yet both be accepted. For an example suppose that Trevor and Katie need to travel to Paris for a conference. Trevor offers the argument "we should travel by plane because it is quickest". Katie replies with the argument "we should travel by train because it is much pleasanter". Trevor and Katie may continue to disagree as to how to travel, but they cannot deny each other's arguments. The conclusion will be something like "we should travel by train because it is much pleasanter, even though travelling by plane is quicker". The point concerns what Searle [24] calls *direction of fit*. For matters of truth and falsity, we are trying to fit what we believe to the way the world actually is. In contrast, when we consider what we should do we are trying to fit the world to the way we would like it to be. Moreover, because people may have different preferences, values, interests and aspirations, people may rationally choose different options: if Katie prefers comfort

Trevor Bench-Capon
Department of Computer Science, University of Liverpool, UK, e-mail: tbc@liverpool.ac.uk

Katie Atkinson
Department of Computer Science, University of Liverpool, UK, e-mail: katie@liverpool.ac.uk

I. Rahwan, G. R. Simari (eds.), *Argumentation in Artificial Intelligence*,
DOI 10.1007/978-0-387-98197-0_3, © Springer Science+Business Media, LLC 2009

to speed she will rationally choose the train, but this does not mean that Trevor cannot rationally choose the plane if he prefers speed to comfort. We will return to this example throughout this chapter.

Within standard abstract argumentation frameworks one approach to recognising the importance of direction of fit [22] is to require sceptical acceptance for epistemic arguments but only credulous acceptance for practical arguments. This does successfully model the existence of a choice with respect to practical arguments, but it does not motivate the choice, nor does it allow us to predict choices on the basis of choices made in the past. Value based argumentation frameworks (VAFs) [6], described in this chapter, are an attempt to address issues about the rational justification of choices systematically.

Value based justification of choices is common in many important areas: in politics where specific policies are typically justified in terms of the values they promote, and where politicians' values are advanced as reasons to vote for them; in law, where differences in legal jurisdictions and decisions over time can be explained in terms of the values of the societies in which the judgements are made [11]; in matters of morality where individual and group ethical perspectives play a crucial role in reasoning and action [2]; as well as more everyday examples, such as given above.

In this chapter we will first give some philosophical background, in particular introducing the notion of *audience*, and some of the features that we require from practical reasoning. Section 3 will discuss the nature of values in more detail, in particular the distinction between values and goals. Section 4 will introduce the formal machinery of Value Based Argumentation Frameworks, and discuss some of their more important properties. Section 5 describes some applications of value based argumentation. Section 6 discusses some recent developments, and section 7 concludes the chapter with a summary.

2 Audiences

One of the first people to stress the importance of the audience in determining whether an argument is persuasive or not was Chaim Perelman [20], [19]:

> "If men oppose each other *concerning a decision to be taken*, it is not because they commit some error of logic or calculation. They discuss apropos the applicable rule, the ends to be considered, the meaning to be given to *values*, the interpretation and characterisation of facts." [[19] p.150, italics ours].

A similar point was made by John Searle [24]:

> "Assume universally valid and accepted standards of rationality, assume perfectly rational agents operating with perfect information, and you will find that rational disagreement will still occur; because, for example, the rational agents are likely to have different and inconsistent values and interests, each of which may be rationally acceptable." [[24], xv]

Both Perelman and Searle recognise that there may be complete agreement on facts, logic, which arguments are valid, which arguments attack one another and the rules of fair debate, and yet still disagreement as to the correct decision. This was true when Trevor and Katie were thinking about how to travel to Paris, and there are many other examples. Consider an example from politics.

One choice that any government must make is to decide on an appropriate rate of income tax. Typically there will be an argument in favour of increasing the rate of taxation, since this progressive form of taxation will reduce income inequalities. Against this, it can be argued that a decrease in taxation will promote more enterprise, increasing Gross National Product, and so raising the absolute incomes of everyone. It is possible to see both these arguments as valid, since both supply a reason to act: and yet a choice must be made, since the actions are incompatible. Which choice is made will depend on whether the chooser prefers equality or enterprise in the particular circumstances with which he is confronted. Two parties may be in agreement as to the consequences of a movement in the tax rate, and yet disagree as to the choice to be made because they differ in their fundamental aspirations. Different people will prize social values differently, and one may prefer equality to enterprise, while another prefers enterprise to equality. Thus while both arguments are agreed to be valid, one *audience* will ascribe more force to one of the arguments, while a different *audience* will make a different choice. In such cases these different audiences will rationally disagree, and agreement can only be reached by coming up with additional arguments which convince all audiences *in terms of their own preferences*, or by converting those who disagree to a different appraisal of social values. This will often require that different arguments be presented to different audiences. Thus when in the 1980s the UK Conservative Party under Margaret Thatcher were attempting to justify dramatic cuts in income tax for the highly paid, one argument was simply that fairness meant that people deserved to keep a larger proportion of their "earnings". This argument was quite acceptable at Party Conferences where the audience comprised predominately high earners, but was not persuasive to the country at large, since most people were not subject to higher rate taxation. To convince the nation at large a different argument was needed: namely that there would be a "trickle down" effect, benefitting everyone, whatever their level of income. This was clearly persuasive as Thatcher was twice re-elected.

Thus whether an argument is persuasive depends not only on the intrinsic merits of the argument – of course, it needs to be based on plausible premises and must be sound – but also on the audience to which it is addressed. Moreover, for practical reasoning, what is important about the audience is what they want to see happen, and this seems to turn on how they rank the various values that accepting the arguments promote. In the next section we will consider values, and their relation to practical reasoning, in more detail.

3 Values

This far we have seen that whether a particular audience is persuaded by an argument depends on the attitude of that audience to the values on which the argument is founded. Values are used in the sense of fundamental social or personal goods that are desirable in themselves, and should never be confused with any numeric measure of the strength, certainty or probability of an argument. Liberty, Equality and Fraternity, the values of the French Revolution, are paradigmatic examples of values. Values are widely recognised as the basis for persuasive argument. For example, the National Forensic League, which conducts debating competitions throughout the USA uses the "Lincoln-Douglas" (LD) debate format which is based on the notion of a clash of values. In an LD debate the resolution forces each side to take on competing values and argue about which one is supreme. For example, if the resolution is, "*Resolved*: An oppressive government is better than no government at all," the affirmative side might value "order" and the negative side might value "freedom". Such a debate would revolve around whether order is more valuable than freedom. In the original debate between Abraham Lincoln and Stephen Douglas on which LD debates are based, Douglas championed the rights of states to legislate for their particular circumstances, whereas Lincoln argued on the basis that there were certain inviolable human rights that all states had to respect, even though this constrained state autonomy.

But what is the role of values in practical reasoning? Historically the basis for treatments of practical reasoning has been the practical syllogism, first discussed by Aristotle. A standard modern statement is given in [16]:

K1   I'm to be in London at 4.15
     If I catch the 2.30, I'll be in London at 4.15
     So, I'll catch the 2.30.

The first premise is a statement of some desired state of affairs, the second an action which would bring about that state of affairs, and the conclusion is that the action should be performed. There are, however, problems with the formulation: it is abductive rather than deductive, does not consider alternative, possibly better, ways of achieving the desired state of affairs, or possibly undesirable side effects of the action. Walton [26] addresses these issues by regarding the practical syllogism as an argumentation scheme, which he calls the *sufficient condition scheme for practical reasoning*, which provides a presumptive reason to perform the action, but which can be critiqued on the basis of alternatives and undesirable consequences. He states the sufficient condition practical reasoning scheme as:

W2   G is a goal for agent a
     Doing action A is sufficient for agent a to carry out goal G
     Therefore agent a ought to do action A.

This, however, still does not explain why G is a goal for the agent, nor indicate how important bringing about G is to the agent. Neither K1 nor W1 make any mention of values: rather that the agent has certain values is implicit in calling the desired state of affairs a "goal" for that agent. Accordingly, to make this role of values explicit, Walton's scheme was developed by Atkinson and her colleagues [4] into the more elaborated scheme:

A1   In the circumstances R, we should perform action A
     to achieve new circumstances S, which will realise some goal G
     which will promote some value V.

What this scheme does in particular is to distinguish three aspects which are conflated into the notion of goal in K1 and W1. These aspects are: the state of affairs which will result from the action; the goal, which is those aspects of the new state of affairs for the sake of which the action is performed; and the *value*, which is the reason why the agent desires the goal. Making these distinctions opens up several distinct types of alternative to the recommended action. We may perform a different action to realise the same state of affairs; we may act so as to bring about a different state of affairs which realises the same goal; or we may realise a different goal which promotes the same value. Alternatively, since the state of affairs potentially realises several goals, we can justify the action in terms of promoting a different value. In coming to agreement this last possibility may be of particular importance: we may want to promote different values, and so agree to perform the action on the basis of different arguments. Our contention is that, in the spirit of the notion of audience developed in section 2, what is important, what is the appropriate comparison for choosing between alternatives, is the value.

In order to see the distinction between a goal and a value, consider again Trevor and Katie's journey to Paris. The *goal* is to be in Paris for the conference, and this is not in dispute: the dispute is how that goal should be realised and turns on the values promoted by the different methods of travel. What is important is not the state reached, but the way in which the transition is made.

The style of argumentation represented by A1 has been formalised in [1] in terms of a particular style of transition system, Alternating Action Based Transition systems (AATS) [27]. An AATS consists of a set of states and a set of agents and the transitions between the states are in terms of the *joint actions* of the agents, that is, actions composed from the actions available to the agents individually. In terms of A1 the circumstances R and S are represented by the states of the system, the goal G is realised if G holds in S (of course, G may hold in several of the states), and the action is the particular agent's component of a joint action which is a transition from R to S. The value labels the transition, indicating that it is the movement from R to S *using that particular transition* that promotes the value. A fragment of the AATS for Trevor and Katie's travel dilemma is shown in Figure 3.1, t/kt/p is the action of Trevor/Katie travelling by train/plane, C/St/k means that Comfort/Speed is promoted in respect of Trevor/Katie, 00 that both are in Liverpool and 11 that both are in Paris.

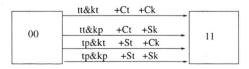

Fig. 3.1 AATS for travel to Paris example

Although there is only one destination state, each of the four potential ways of reaching it promotes different values, and hence give rise to different arguments in their favour. Which arguments will succeed will depend on the preferences between the values of Comfort and Speed of the two agents concerned.

Essentially then, in this problem there will be a number of possible audiences, depending on how the values are ordered. Suppose that Trevor values his own speed over his own comfort and Katie her comfort over her speed, and that neither consider values promoted in respect of the other. Then Trevor will choose to go by plane and Katie by train. Here the agents can choose independently, as their values are affected only by their own actions: in later sections we will introduce a third value which requires them to consider what the other intends to do also.

The basic idea underlying Value Based Argumentation Frameworks is that it is possible to associate practical arguments with values, and that in order to determine which arguments are acceptable we need to consider the audience to which they are addressed, characterised in terms of an ordering on the values involved. We need, however, to recognise that not all the arguments relevant to a practical decision will be practical arguments. For example, if there is a train strike (or it is a UK Bank Holiday when there are often no trains from Liverpool), the argument that the train should be used cannot be accepted no matter how great the audience preference is for Comfort over Speed. In order to recognise that such epistemic arguments constrain choice, such arguments are associated with the value *Truth*, and all audiences are obliged to rank Truth above all other values. In the next section we will give a formal presentation of Value Based Argumentation Frameworks.

4 Value Based Argumentation Frameworks

We present the Value Based Framework as an extension of Dung's original Argumentation Framework [14], defined in Chapter 2 of this book. We do this by extending the standard pair to a 5 tuple.

Definition 3.1. A *value-based argumentation framework* (*VAF*) is a 5-tuple:
VAF = $<\mathcal{A}, \mathcal{R}, V, val, P>$

where $\mathcal{A}$ is a finite set of arguments, $\mathcal{R}$ is an irreflexive binary relation on $\mathcal{A}$ (i.e. $<\mathcal{A}, \mathcal{R}>$ is a standard AF), V is a non-empty set of values, *val* is a function which maps from elements of $\mathcal{A}$ to elements of V and P is the set of possible audiences (i.e. total orders on V). We say that an argument a relates to value v if accepting A promotes or defends v: the value in question is given by $val(a)$. For every $a \in \mathcal{A}$, $val(a) \in V$.

When the VAF is considered by a particular audience, the ordering of values is fixed. We may therefore define an Audience Specific VAF (AVAF) as:

Definition 3.2. An *audience specific value-based argumentation framework* (*AVAF*) is a 5-tuple: VAF$_a$ = $<\mathcal{A}, \mathcal{R}, V, val, Valpref_a>$

where $\mathcal{A}$, $\mathcal{R}$, V and val are as for a VAF, a is an audience, $a \in P$, and $Valpref_a$ is a preference relation (transitive, irreflexive and asymmetric) $Valpref_a \subseteq V \times V$, reflecting the value preferences of audience a. The $AVAF$ relates to the VAF in that $\mathcal{A}$, $\mathcal{R}$, V and val are identical, and $Valpref$ is the set of preferences derivable from the ordering $a \in P$ in the VAF.

Our purpose in introducing VAFs is to allow us to distinguish between one argument *attacking* another, and that attack *succeeding*, so that the *attacked* argument may or may not be defeated. Whether the attack succeeds depends on the value order of the audience considering the VAF. We therefore define the notion of *defeat for an audience*:

Definition 3.3. *An argument $A \in AF$ defeats$_a$ an argument $B \in AF$ for audience a if and only if both $\mathcal{R}(A,B)$ and not $(val(B),val(A)) \in Valpref_a$.*

We can now define the various notions relating to the status of arguments:

Definition 3.4. An argument $a \in \mathcal{A}$ is *acceptable-to-audience-a* (*acceptable$_a$*) with respect to set of arguments S, (*acceptable$_a$(A,S)*) if:
$(\forall x)((x \in \mathcal{A}\ \&\ defeats_a(x,A)) \rightarrow (\exists y)((y \in S)\ \&\ defeats_a(y,x)))$.

Definition 3.5. A set S of arguments is *conflict-free-for-audience-a* if:
$(\forall x)\ (\forall y)((x \in S\ \&\ y \in S) \rightarrow (\neg\ \mathcal{R}(x,y) \vee valpref(val(y),val(x)) \in Valpref_a)))$.

Definition 3.6. A *conflict-free-for-audience-a* set of arguments S is *admissible-for-an-audience-a* if: $(\forall x)(x \in S \rightarrow acceptable_a(x,S))$.

Definition 3.7. A set of arguments S in a value-based argumentation framework VAF is a *preferred extension for-audience-a* (*preferred$_a$*) if it is a maximal (with respect to set inclusion) *admissible-for-audience-a* subset of $\mathcal{A}$.

Now for a given choice of value preferences $valpref_a$ we are able to construct an AF equivalent to the $AVAF$, by removing from $\mathcal{R}$ those attacks which fail because they are faced with a superior value.

Thus for any $AVAF$, $vaf_a = <\mathcal{A}, \mathcal{R}, V, val, Valpref_a>$ there is a corresponding AF, $af_a = <\mathcal{A}, defeats>$, such that an element of $\mathcal{R}$, $\mathcal{R}(x,y)$ is an element of defeats if and only if $defeats_a(x,y)$. The preferred extension of af_a will contain the same arguments as vaf_a, the preferred extension for audience a of the VAF. Note that if vaf_a does not contain any cycles in which all arguments pertain to the same value, af_a will contain no cycles, since the cycle will be broken at the point at which the attack is from an inferior value to a superior one. Hence both af_a and vaf_a will have a unique, non-empty, preferred extension for such cases. A proof is given in [6]. Moreover, since the AF derived from an AVAF contains no cycles, the grounded extension coincides with the preferred extension for this audience, and so there is a straightforward polynomial time algorithm to compute it, also given in [6]. For the moment we will restrict consideration to VAFs which do not contain any cycles in a single value.

For such VAFs, the notions of sceptical and credulous acceptance do not apply, since any given audience will accept only a single preferred extension. These preferred extensions may, and typically will, however, differ from audience to audience. We may therefore introduce two useful notions, objective acceptance, arguments which are acceptable to all audiences irrespective of their particular value order, and subjective acceptance, arguments which can be accepted by audiences with the appropriate value order.

Definition 3.8. *Objective Acceptance.* Given a *VAF*, $<\mathcal{A}, \mathcal{R}, V, val, P>$ an argument $a \in \mathcal{A}$ is objectively acceptable if and only if for all $p \in P$, a is in every *preferred$_p$*.

Definition 3.9. *Subjective Acceptance.* Given a *VAF*, $<\mathcal{A}, \mathcal{R}, V, val, P>$ an argument $a \in \mathcal{A}$ is subjectively acceptable if and only if for some $p \in P$, a is in some *preferred$_p$*.

An argument which is neither objectively nor subjectively acceptable (such as one attacked by an objectively acceptable argument with the same value) is said to be *indefensible*.

All arguments which are not attacked will, of course, be objectively acceptable. Otherwise objective acceptance typically arises from cycles in two or more values. For example, consider a three cycle in two values, say two arguments with V1 and one with V2. The argument with V2 will either resist the attack on it when it is preferred to V1, or, when V1 is preferred, fail to defeat the argument it attacks which will, in consequence, be available to defeat its attacker. Thus the argument in V2 will be objectively acceptable, and both the arguments with V1 will be subjectively acceptable. For a more elaborate example consider Figure 3.2.

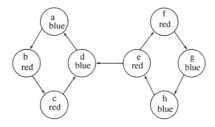

Fig. 3.2 VAF with values red and blue

There will be two preferred extensions, according to whether red > blue, or blue > red. If red > blue, the preferred extension will be {e,g,a,b}, and if blue > red, {e,g,d,b}. Now *e* and *g* and *b* are objectively acceptable, but *d*, which would have been objectively acceptable if *e* had not attacked *d*, is only subjectively acceptable (when blue > red), and *a*, which is indefensible if *d* is not attacked, is also subjectively acceptable (when red > blue). Arguments *c*, *f* and *h* are indefensible. Results characterising the structures which give rise to objective acceptance are given in [6].

4.1 VAF Example

We will illustrate VAFs using our running example of Trevor and Katie's conference travel arrangements. Recall that $VAF_a = <\mathcal{A}, \mathcal{R}, V, val, Valpref_a>$. We therefore need to instantiate the five elements of this tuple.

From Figure 3.1 above we get four arguments:

A1: Katie should travel by train (Kt) to promote her comfort (Ck).

A2: Katie should travel by plane (Kp) to promote her speed (Sk).

A3: Trevor should travel by train (Tt) to promote his comfort (Ct).

A4: Trevor should travel by plane to (Tp) to promote his speed (St).

But there are other considerations: it is far more boring to travel alone than in company. This gives two other arguments:

A5: Both Katie and Trevor should travel by train (Kt&Tt) to avoid boredom (B).

A6: Both Katie and Trevor should travel by plane (Kp&Tp) to avoid boredom (B).

Thus $\mathcal{A}_e = \{A1,A2,A3,A4,A5,A6\}$ and val = $\{A1{\to}Ck, A2{\to}Sk, A3{\to}Ct, A4{\to}St, A5{\to}B, A6{\to}B\}$.

We can now identify attacks between these arguments. Since neither Katie nor Trevor can travel by both train and plane, A1 attacks A2, and vice versa, and A3 attacks and is attacked by A4. Moreover A1 and A3 attack and are attacked by A6, and A2 and A4 attack and are attacked by A5.

Thus $\mathcal{R}_e = \{<A1,A2>, <A2,A1>, <A3,A4>, <A4,A3>, <A1,A6>, <A3,A6>, <A6,A1>, <A6,A3>, <A2,A5>, <A4,A5>,<A5,A2>,<A5,A4>, <A5,A6>, <A6,A5>\}$.

The values are given by the values used in the arguments, but for the present we will make no distinction at first between values promoted in respect of Trevor and values promoted in respect of Katie. Thus $V_e = \{B, C, S\}$. Finally the audiences P will be every possible ordering of the elements in V_e, so P = $\{B>C>S, B>S>C, S>B>C, S>C>B, C>B>S, C>S>B\}$

We can represent the VAF diagrammatically as a directed graph, as shown in Figure 3.3.

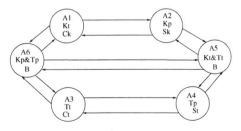

Fig. 3.3 VAF for travel example

Note that here we do have a cycle of two arguments with the same value, namely B. This means that some audiences will not have a unique preferred extension. This does not pose any serious problem in this small example.

Now consider specific audiences. Suppose that Katie, who very much dislikes flying, ranks C as her highest value, and S as her least important.

Now $\text{AVAF}_{katie} = <\mathcal{A}_e, \mathcal{R}_e, V_e, \text{val}, \{<C,B>,<C,S>,<B,S>\}>$.

When we use Katie's preferences to eliminate unsuccessful attacks, this produces the corresponding $\text{AF}_{katie} = < \mathcal{A}_e, \{<A1,A2>,<A3,A4>, <A1,A6>, <A3,A6>, <A5,A2>,<A5,A4>, <A5,A6>\}>$. This AF has a unique preferred extension, $\text{PE}_{katie} = \{A1,A3,A5\}$, which means that she will be in favour of both Trevor and herself travelling by train.

Suppose, however, Trevor, who has no objection to flying, prefers speed to comfort, but dislikes travelling alone, so that he is a member of the audience $\{B>S>C\}$.

Now $\text{AVAF}_{trevor} = <\mathcal{A}_e, \mathcal{R}_e, V_e, \text{val}, \{<B,S>,<B,C>,<S,C>\}>$.

And $\text{AF}_{trevor} = <\mathcal{A}_e, \{<A2,A1>, <A4,A3>, <A6,A1>, <A6,A3>, <A5,A4>, <A5,A6>, <A6,A5>\}>$.

This contains a cycle for the two arguments in B, and so Trevor will have two preferred extensions: $\{A1,A3,A5\}$, and $\{A2,A4,A6\}$. Trevor could solve this dilemma by considering that A3 also promotes C and A4 also promotes S, and so choose $\{A2,A4,A6\}$. But what is required is a joint decision: neither Trevor nor Katie can act independently so as to ensure that A5 or A6 is followed. We therefore need to consider the joint audience, and to distinguish between values promoted in respect of Trevor and values promoted in respect of Katie.

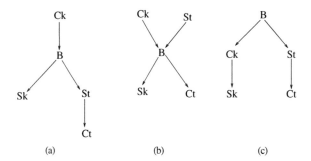

Fig. 3.4 Partial Orders representing combined audiences: (a) Katie C>B>S and Trevor B>S>C; (b) Katie C>B>S and Trevor S>B>C; (c) Katie B>C>S and Trevor B>S>C

Katie's order is Ck > B > Sk, while Trevor's is B > St > Ct. Since they have B in common – either both are bored or neither are bored – we can merge their orderings on B to get the partial order shown in Figure 3.4(a).

The AVAF for the combined audience is thus $<\mathcal{A}_e, \mathcal{R}_e, V_e, \text{val}, \{<B,St>, <B,Ct>, <B,Sk>, <St,Ct>, <Ck,B>, <Ck,Sk>, <Ck,St>, <Ck,Ct>\}>$. This gives rise to the AF shown in Figure 3.5.

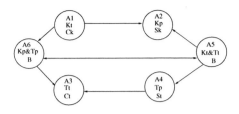

Fig. 3.5 AF for Combined Audience

We can use this VAF to illustrate the algorithm for finding the Preferred Extension given in [6]. First we include the arguments with no attacker: in this case A1. A1 attacks A2 and A6 and so they are excluded. Now A5 has no attacker and so it is included. A5 excludes A4, leaving A3 without an attacker, and so A3 is included to give the preferred extension of the combined audience as {A1,A3,A5}.

This case is straightforward, because the combined audience yields a single preferred extension. The same is true if Trevor preferred S to B, the combined order being shown in Figure 3.4(b). This would cause <A5,A4> to be replaced in $\mathcal{R}$ by <A4,A5>. Now both A1 and A4 are not attacked, and so they defeat the remaining arguments yielding the preferred extension {A1,A4}. This is possible: they simply agree to travel separately by their preferred means.

More complicated is the situation where Katie prefers B to C, so that the merged order is as shown in Figure 3.4(c), and <A6,A1> replaces <A1,A6> in $\mathcal{R}$. Now there is no longer any argument which has no attackers, and the algorithm must be applied twice; first including A5 and then including A6, so that are two preferred extensions, {A1,A3,A5}, and {A2,A4,A6}, both of which are acceptable to them both. Now, since Katie will lean towards the former and Trevor the latter they must find a way to decide between Ck and St. This might depend on who had the strongest opinions, or who is the more altruistic or conciliatory. Alternatively one person might change their preferences: if Katie moved back to her original ordering of C>B>S, Trevor would either have to decide to prefer S to B or to agree to travel by train. This possibility shows how preferences can emerge from the reasoning process: although initially Katie might express a preference for B to C, and Trevor for B to S, when the consequences are realised she may decide that C is actually more important than B, and he may decide S is more important than B.

5 Example Applications

As noted in Section 1, reasoning with values is common to many application domains. In previous work [2, 3, 5, 9] we have shown how the application of abstract argumentation with values can be applied to problems in law, medicine, ethics and e-democracy, and we will briefly discuss these applications here. We begin by considering legal reasoning with values.

5.1 Law

Reasoning with legal cases has often been viewed as a decision being deduced about a particular case through the application of a set of rules, given the facts of the case, e.g. [25]. However, the facts of cases are not set in stone as they can be open to interpretation from different lawyers. Additionally, the rules used to reach decisions are defeasible by their nature and many are derived from precedent cases, so they too may be open to interpretation. Thus, within the AI and Law literature it has been recognised that when considering arguments in legal cases, the purposes of the law – the values intended to be promoted or upheld through the application of the law – must be represented and accounted for, e.g. [8] [21]. In the literature on legal case-based reasoning the issue was first brought to attention in Berman and Hafner's seminal paper on the topic [8] arguing that legal case-based reasoning needs to recognise teleological as well as factual aspects. This is so since the law is not composed arbitrarily, rather it is constructed to serve social ends, so when conflicts in the application of rules occur in legal cases they can be resolved more effectively by considering the purposes of these rules and their relative applicability to the particular case in question. This enables preferences amongst purposes to be revealed, and then the argument can be presented appropriately to the audience through an appeal to the social values that the argument promotes or defends.

In order to demonstrate how the values of the law can be represented and reasoned about within a case, we have previously presented a reconstruction [3] of a famous case in property law by simulating the opinion and dissent in that case. The case is that of *Pierson vs Post*[1] which concerned a dispute about ownership of a hunted fox. The said fox was being pursued by Post who was hunting with hounds on unoccupied waste-land. Whilst Post was in pursuit of the fox another man, Pierson, came along and intercepted the chase, killing and carrying off the fox. Central to the arguments considered in the case was whether ownership of a wild animal can be attributed through mere pursuit. However, there are numerous other arguments that need to be considered which draw out the emphasis placed on the values considered within the case.

Firstly, the value 'public benefit' was considered as it was argued that fox hunting is of benefit to the public because it assists farmers, so it should be encouraged by giving the sportsman such as Post protection of the law. There are of course counter arguments to this based on the humane treatment of animals. Furthermore, there are arguments concerning consideration of public benefit based on the desire to punish malicious behaviour as allegedly shown by Pierson in intercepting the fox that he could see Post was chasing.

---

[1] 3 Cai R 1752 Am Dec 264 (Supreme Court of New York, 1805)

Secondly, there were arguments set forth about the need for the law to be clear: in attributing ownership without bodily possession this would encourage a climate of litigation based on similar claims related to pursuit alone.

Thirdly, the value of 'economic benefit' was considered in relation to the protection of property rights where the claimant is engaged in a profitable enterprise.

Given the facts of the case and the values stated above that have been recognised as pertinent to the reasoning in the case, the argument scheme for practical reasoning can be applied to generate the competing arguments about who to decide for in the case. Once generated these arguments can be organised into a VAF and evaluated in the usual manner. In the actual case the court found for Pierson, thus holding that clarity was more important than the values promoted by finding for Post. Preference orderings of values that led to this decision are reflected in our full representation of the case, which can be found in [3]. Explicitly representing the values promoted by the arguments put forward in the case helps to clarify the justifications for the arguments advanced and ground those justifications within the purposes that law is intended to capture and uphold.

5.2 Medicine

A second example scenario that has been considered in terms of value-based argumentation is one concerning a system for reasoning about the medical treatment of a patient [5]. Decision making in this domain often requires consideration of a wide range of options, some of which may conflict, and may also be uncertain. Thus, value-based argumentation can play a role in supporting the decision making process in this domain.

The scenario modelled in [5] illustrates a running example of a patient whose health is threatened by blood clotting. In deciding which particular treatment to administer to the patient there are a number of policies and concerns that affect the decision, and each must be given its due weight. In the computational model of the scenario a number of different perspectives are represented that are given as values of individual agents. The arguments and subsequent conclusions drawn by the individual agents are then adjudicated by a central agent which comes to a decision based on an evaluation of the competing arguments. Concerning the individual agents' values, these represent perspectives such as: the *treatment* of the patient based on general medical policy; the *safety* of the patient concerning knowledge of contraindications of the various drugs; the *efficacy* of the treatments in reference to specific medical knowledge; and, the *cost* of the different treatments available.

Given the above agent perspectives (and others that we do not detail here), the practical reasoning argument scheme can be used to generate arguments about which drug should be used to treat a particular patient. These arguments can be critiqued by agents other than those that generated the recommendation, based on their individual knowledge, through the posing of the appropriate critical questions. This may lead to different agents recommending different treatments, one of which must be chosen. In order to decide between the competing choices, the arguments justifying each are organised into a VAF and evaluated according to the preference given over the values represented by the individual agents. For example, it may be the case that the treatment agent recommends a particular drug that is known to be highly effective (since no critique from the efficacy agent indicates otherwise) and has no contraindications (according to the safety agent), yet the cost agent has an argument that the drug cannot be used on monetary grounds. The question then is whether treatment is to be preferred to cost (which may be the case if there are no suitable alternatives are identified). Resolution of this issue will be determined by the central adjudicating agent who provides the value ordering to decide upon the winning argument and subsequent treatment recommended, in accordance with the policy of the relevant health authority at the time.

Whilst a key motivation for the example application described above was the representation of the different perspectives within the situation, there are other advantages worthy of note. Firstly, the reasoning involved in medical scenarios is often highly context dependant and relative to specific individuals so there is a high degree of uncertainty. Thus any ordering of preferences must take the specific context into account and the argumentation based approach enables this. Secondly, the argumentation element is effected inside a single agent and the information that it uses is distributed across different information sources, which need not themselves consider every eventuality, and play no part in the evaluation. This simplifies their construction and facilitates their reuse in other applications. Finally, the critiques that are posed against putative solutions are made only as and when they can affect the evaluation status of arguments already advanced. This means that all reasoning undertaken is potentially relevant to the solution.

5.3 Moral Reasoning

The running example that we have presented in this paper concerning travel to a conference is represented in terms of an AATS. We now turn to briefly discussing another example scenario, concerning moral reasoning, that has been modelled in these terms.

The scenario is a particular ethical dilemma discussed by Coleman [12] and Christie [11], amongst others, and it involves two agents, called Hal and Carla, both of whom are diabetic. The situation is that Hal, through no fault of his own, has lost his supply of insulin and urgently needs to take some to stay alive. Hal is aware that Carla has some insulin kept in her house, but Hal does not have permission to enter Carla's house. The question is whether Hal is justified in breaking into Carla's house and taking her insulin in order to save his life. By taking Carla's insulin, Hal may be putting her life in jeopardy, since she will come to need that insulin herself. One possible response is that if Hal has money, he can compensate Carla so that her insulin can be replaced before she needs it. Alternatively if Hal has no money but Carla does, she can replace her insulin herself, since her need is not immediately life threatening. There is, however, a serious problem if neither have money, since in that case Carla's life is really under threat. Coleman argued that Hal may take the insulin to save his life, but should compensate Carla. Christie's argument against this was that even if Hal had no money and was unable to compensate Carla he would still be justified in taking the insulin by his immediate necessity, since no one should die because of poverty.

In [2] we have represented this scenario in terms of an AATS and considered the arguments that can be generated concerning how the agents could justifiably act. Following our methodology, we take the arguments generated and organise them into a VAF to see the attack relations between them and evaluate them in accordance with the particular value preference orderings. An interesting point that can be taken from this particular example concerns the nuances between different 'levels' of morality that can be drawn out by distinguishing the individual agents *within* the value orderings. For example, *prudential reasoning* takes account of the different agents, with the reasoning agent preferring values relating to itself, whereas *strict moral reasoning* ignores the individual agents and treats the values equally. For example, in the insulin scenario two values are recognised: *life*, which is demoted when Hal or Carla ceases to be alive, and *freedom*, which is demoted when Hal or Carla ceases to have money. Thus, an agent may rank life over freedom, but within this value ordering it may discriminate between agents; for example, the agent may place equal value on its own and another's life, or it may be that it prefers its own life to another's (or vice versa). This leads to distinctions such as *selfish* agents who prefer their own interests above all those of other agents, and *noble* agents whose values are ordered, but within a value the agent prefers another's interests.

In addition to the AATS representation set out in [2], simulations have also been run, which are reported in [10], that confirm the reasoning as set out.

5.4 e-Democracy

The final application area that we discuss is an e-Democracy setting whose focus is more on the support given by value based argumentation within a system to facilitate the collection and analysis of human arguments within political debates.

The application is presented as a discussion forum named Parmenides whose underlying structure is based upon the practical reasoning argument scheme and the latest version of the system is described in [9]. The system is intended as a forum by which the government is able to present policy proposals to the public so users can submit their opinions on the justification presented for the particular policy. The justification for action is structured in the form of the practical reasoning argument scheme, though this imposed structure is hidden from the user. Within a particular topic of debate, a justification upholding a proposed government action is presented to users of the system in the form of the argument scheme. Users are then led in a structured fashion through a series of web pages that pose the appropriate critical questions to determine which parts of the justification the users agree or disagree with (the circumstances, the action, the consequences or the value). Users are not aware (and have no need to be aware) of the underlying structure for argument representation but it is, nevertheless, imposed on the information they submit. This enables the collection of information which is structured in a clear and unambiguous fashion from a system which does not require users to gain specialist knowledge before being able to use it.

In addition to collecting arguments, Parmenides also has analysis facilities that make use of AFs. All the information that the users submit through the system is stored in a back-end database. This information is then organised into an argumentation framework to show the attacking arguments between the positions expressed. Associated with the arguments in the AF is statistical information concerning a breakdown of support for the arguments, i.e. the number of users agreeing/disagreeing with a particular element of the justification. Thus, arguments can be assessed by considering which ones are the most controversial to the users.

The Parmenides system is intended to overcome some of the problems faced by existing discussion forum formats, such as unstructured blogs and e-petitions. In such systems where there is no structuring of the information, it is undoubtedly very difficult for the policy maker to adequately address each person's concerns since he or she is not aware of users' specific reasons for disagreeing. Furthermore, it may be difficult to recognise agreement and disagreement *between* multiple user replies. In contrast, the structure imposed by Parmenides allows the administrator of the system to see exactly which particular part of the argument is disagreed with by the majority of users, e.g. arguments based on a description of the circumstances, or arguments based on a disagreement about the importance of promoting a particular value. Identifying these different sources of disagreement allows the policy maker to see why his policy is disliked, so he may be able to better respond to the criticisms made, or indeed change the policy. In particular, it can indicate whether the values motivating the policy are shared by the respondents.

Parmenides has been tested on a number of different political debates, including: the UK debate about banning fox hunting[2]; the justification for the 2003 war in Iraq; and, a debate about the proposal to increase the number of speed cameras on UK roads. Work on the Parmenides system is ongoing to further extend its representation facilities, through the use of schemes additional to the practical reasoning scheme, and to further extend the facilities for analysing the arguments through the use of argumentation frameworks.

6 Developments of Value Based Argumentation

In this section we will mention some developments of Value Based Argumentation.

In [13] there is an interesting exploration of the relation between neural networks, in particular neural-symbolic learning systems, and value based argumentation sys-

---

[2] For this particular debate on the system see:
http://cgi.csc.liv.ac.uk/~parmenides/foxhunting/

tems, including an extensive discussion of the insulin example described in the last section. In [15] there is a formal generalisation of VAFs to allow for arguments that promote multiple values, and in which preferences among values can be specified in various ways. In [7] a method is given to determine which audiences can accept a particular set of arguments. Here, however, we will look in detail only at the application of Modgil's extended argumentation frameworks (EAF) [17] to VAFs. For a preliminary exploration of the relation between EAFs and VAFs see [18].

The core idea of EAFs is, like VAFs, to enable a distinction between an argument attacking an argument, and an argument defeating another argument. Whereas VAFs, however, rely on a comparison of properties of the arguments concerned, EAFs achieve this in an entirely abstract manner by allowing arguments to attack not only other arguments, but also attacks. EAFs thus enable arguments to resist an attack for a number of reasons. In VAFs arguments resist attacks solely in virtue of a preference between the values concerned. This enables VAFs to be rewritten as standards AFs, by introducing some auxiliary arguments to articulate the notion of an attack on an attack. These auxiliary arguments represent the status of arguments, value preferences, and arguments representing particular audiences. Suppose we have a VAF with two arguments, A and B which attack one another. A is associated with value V1 and B with Value V2. A will be defeated if B defeats it, and B will be defeated if A defeats it. Defeat is only possible if the attacking argument is not defeated, and if the value of A is not preferred to that of B. Thus the attack on the attack of A on B in an EAF becomes an attack on the argument that A defeats B.

This enables us to represent a VAF as a standard AF, with preferred extensions depending on the choices made regarding value preferences. We can extend the AF to include audiences as well. Suppose Audience X prefers V1 to V2 and Audience Y prefers V2 to V1. This can be shown as in Figure 3.6.

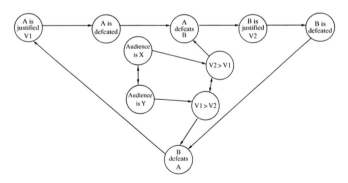

Fig. 3.6 AF representing VAF with audiences

The rewriting of VAFs in this way is shown to be sound and complete with respect to EAFs in [18]. When we rewrite VAFs in this way, subjective acceptance in the VAF is equivalent to credulous acceptance in the rewritten AF, and objective acceptance in the VAF is equivalent to sceptical acceptance in the rewritten AF. This

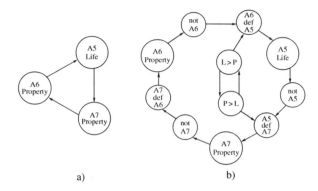

Fig. 3.7 3 cycle and re-write

can be seen by considering the three cycle in the two value case shown in Figure 3.7.

There will be two preferred extensions depending on which preference is chosen: {L> P, A5defA7,not A7,A6,A5} and {P>L,A7,A7defA6,notA6,A5}. Thus A5 is correctly sceptically acceptable in 7b, and objectively acceptable in 7a, and the remaining arguments, other than notA5, are credulously acceptable in 7b, and A6 and A7 are subjectively acceptable in 7a.

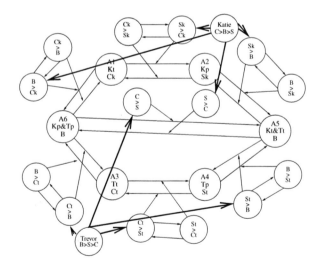

Fig. 3.8 Value based EAF for travel example.

Finally, we apply this to our running example of Trevor and Katie travelling to Paris. The rewritten framework is given in Figure 3.8: note that we have used the EAF style of attacks on attacks rather than the rewrite, for clarity in the diagram.

We have added the audiences Trevor and Katie. Note that, although their preferences differ, these arguments do not conflict, as Trevor and Katie must be allowed to have different preferences: although they are trying to come to a consensus of which arguments to accept, they are free to maintain their own value orders. Trevor's audience attacks the preferences between values in respect of Trevor, and Katie's audience attacks preferences in respect of Katie. Both audiences attack preferences in common.

We evaluate the framework in Figure 3.8 by first removing the arguments attacked by the audiences, and then the attacks attacked by surviving arguments. Reflecting the impact of audiences in this way gives a standard AF, the connected component of which is the same as that shown in Figure 3.5. Now A1 is not attacked, and so the preferred extension will contain the two audiences, the consequent preferences (note that *both* S>C and C>S have been defeated as Trevor and Katie disagree), together with A1, (which is not attacked), A3 and A5 (whose attackers are defeated). Thus, as before, given these preferences both Trevor and Katie choose to travel by train.

7 Summary

Just as deduction is a natural paradigm for justifying beliefs, argumentation is the natural paradigm for explaining and justifying why one course of action is preferred to another, since the notions of defeasibility and individual preference are central to argumentation. We can be coercive about what is the case, but need to be persuasive about what should be the case. But in order to exploit this aspect of argumentation, it is necessary to extend the purely abstract notion of argumentation proposed by Dung to enable individual preferences to explain the choices made in determining which arguments will be accepted by an agent in a particular context. We have discussed such an extension, representing the individual interests and aspirations as values, and individual preferences as orderings on these values.

Using this extension we have shown how different agents can rationally make different choices in accordance with their value orderings, and how in turn these value orderings can emerge from particular situations. In particular we have discussed examples where two agents with different value orderings must agree collectively on what they should do. The range of applications in which reasoning of this sort is required is wide, and we have discussed a number of application areas: law, medicine, politics and moral dilemmas, and an everyday situation. In this chapter we have shown how this important style of reasoning, central to the notion of an autonomous agent, can be captured in a particular form of argumentation framework which, while permitting the expression of individual preferences, retains all the benefits of the clean semantics associated with abstract argumentation frameworks.

References

1. K. Atkinson and T. Bench-Capon. Practical reasoning as presumptive argumentation using action based alternating transition systems. *Artificial Intelligence*, 171(10–15):855–874, 2007.
2. K. Atkinson and T. Bench-Capon. Addressing moral problems through practical reasoning. *Journal of Applied Logic*, 6(2):135–151, 2008.
3. K. Atkinson, T. Bench-Capon, and P. McBurney. Arguing about cases as practical reasoning. In *Proc. of the Tenth International Conference on Artificial Intelligence and Law (ICAIL '05)*, pages 35–44, 2005. ACM Press.
4. K. Atkinson, T. Bench-Capon, and P. McBurney. Computational representation of practical argument. *Synthese*, 152(2):157–206, 2006.
5. K. Atkinson, T. Bench-Capon, and S. Modgil. Argumentation for decision support. In *Proc. of the Seventeenth DEXA Conference*, LNCS 4080, pages 822–831. Springer, 2006.
6. T. Bench-Capon. Persuasion in practical argument using value based argumentation frameworks. *Journal of Logic and Computation*, 13(3):429–448, 2003.
7. T. Bench-Capon, S. Doutre, and P.E. Dunne. Audiences in argumentation frameworks. *Artificial Intelligence*, 171(1):42–71, 2006.
8. D. H. Berman and C. D. Hafner. Representing teleological structure in case-based legal reasoning: the missing link. In *Proc. of the Fourth International Conference on Artificial Intelligence and Law (ICAIL '93)*, pages 50–59, 1993. ACM Press.
9. D. Cartwright and K. Atkinson. Political engagement through tools for argumentation. In P. Besnard, S. Doutre, and A. Hunter, editors, *Proc. of COMMA '08*, pages 116–127, 2008.
10. A. Chorley, T. Bench-Capon, and P. McBurney. Automating argumentation for deliberation in cases of conflict of interest. In P. E. Dunne and T. Bench-Capon, editors, *Proc. of COMMA '06*, pages 279–290. IOS Press, 2006.
11. C. G. Christie. *The Notion of an Ideal Audience in Legal Argument*. Kluwer Academic Publishers, 2000.
12. J. Coleman. *Risks and Wrongs*. Cambridge University Press, 1992.
13. A. S. d'Avila Garcez, D. M. Gabbay, and L. C. Lamb. Value-based argumentation frameworks as neural-symbolic learning systems. *J. of Logic and Computation*, 15(6):1041–1058, 2005.
14. P. M. Dung. On the acceptability of arguments and its fundamental role in nonmonotonic reasoning, logic programming and n-person games. *Artificial Intelligence*, 77:321–357, 1995.
15. S. Kaci, L. van der Torre, and E. Weydert. On the acceptability of incompatible arguments. In *Proc. of the Ninth ECSQARU Conference*, pages 247–258, 2007.
16. A. J. P. Kenny. *Practical Reasoning and Rational Appetite*. 1975. Reprinted in [23].
17. S. Modgil. An abstract theory of argumentation that accommodates defeasible reasoning about preferences. In *Proc. of the Ninth ECSQARU Conference*, pages 648–659, 2007.
18. S. Modgil and T. Bench-Capon. Integrating object and meta-level value based argumentation. In P. Besnard, S. Doutre, and A. Hunter, editors, *Proc. of COMMA '08*, pages 240–251, 2008.
19. C. Perelman. *Justice, Law, and Argument*. D. Reidel Publishing Company, Dordrecht, 1980.
20. C. Perelman and L. Olbrechts-Tyteca. *The New Rhetoric: A Treatise on Argumentation*. University of Notre Dame Press, Notre Dame, IN, USA, 1969.
21. H. Prakken. An exercise in formalising teleological reasoning. In *Proc. of the Thirteenth Annual JURIX Conference*, pages 49–58, 2000. IOS Press.
22. H. Prakken. Combining sceptical epistemic reasoning with credulous practical reasoning. In P. E. Dunne and T. Bench-Capon, editors, *Proc. of COMMA '06*, pages 311–322. IOS Press, 2006.
23. J. Raz, editor. *Practical Reasoning*. Oxford University Press, Oxford, UK, 1978.
24. J. R. Searle. *Rationality in Action*. MIT Press, Cambridge, MA, USA, 2001.
25. M. J. Sergot, F. Sadri, R. A. Kowalski, F. Kriwaczek, P. Hammond, and H. T. Cory. The British Nationality Act as a logic program. *Communications of the ACM*, 29(5):370–386, 1986.
26. D. N. Walton. *Argumentation Schemes for Presumptive Reasoning*. Lawrence Erlbaum Associates, Mahwah, NJ, USA, 1996.
27. M. Wooldridge and W. van der Hoek. On obligations and normative ability: Towards a logical analysis of the social contract. *Journal of Applied Logic*, 3:396–420, 2005.

Chapter 4
Bipolar abstract argumentation systems

Claudette Cayrol and Marie-Christine Lagasquie-Schiex

1 Introduction

In most existing argumentation systems, only one kind of interaction is considered between arguments. It is the so-called attack relation. However, recent studies on argumentation [23, 34, 35, 4] have shown that another kind of interaction may exist between the arguments. Indeed, an argument can attack another argument, but it can also support another one. This suggests a notion of bipolarity, *i.e.* the existence of two independent kinds of information which have a diametrically opposed nature and which represent repellent forces.

Bipolarity has been widely studied in different domains such as knowledge and preference representation [10, 31, 25, 6]. Indeed, in [6] two kinds of preferences are distinguished: the *positive* preferences representing what the agent really wants, and the *negative* ones referring to what the agent rejects. This distinction has been supported by studies in cognitive psychology which have shown that the two kinds of preferences are completely independent and are processed separately in the mind. Another application where bipolarity is largely used is that of decision making. In [3, 19], it has been argued that when making decision, one generally takes into account some information in favour of the decisions and other pieces of information against those decisions.

In [20], a nomenclature of three types of bipolarity has been proposed using particular characteristics like *exclusivity* (can a piece of information be at the same time positive and negative), *duality* (can negative information be computed using positive information), *exhaustivity* (can information be neither positive, nor negative), computation of positive and negative information *on the same data*, computation of positive and negative information *with the same process*, *existence of a consistency constraint* between positive and negative information.

IRIT-UPS, 118 route de Narbonne, 31062 Toulouse, France, e-mail: {ccayrol,lagasq}@irit.fr

I. Rahwan, G. R. Simari (eds.), *Argumentation in Artificial Intelligence*,
DOI 10.1007/978-0-387-98197-0_4, © Springer Science+Business Media, LLC 2009

The first type of bipolarity proposed by [20] (*symmetric univariate bipolarity*) expresses the fact that the negative feature is a reflection of the positive feature (so, they are mutually exclusive and a single bipolar univariate scale is enough for representing them).

The second one (*dual bivariate bipolarity*) expresses the fact that we need two separate scales in order to represent both features, although they stem from the same data (so, an information can be positive and negative at the same time and there is no exclusivity). However a duality must exist between both features.

And the third one (*heterogeneous bipolarity*) expresses the fact that both features do not stem from the same data though there is some minimal consistency requirement between both features.

In this chapter, we focus on the use of bipolarity in the particular domain of argumentation. In all the disparate cases, an argumentation process follows different steps: i) building the arguments and the interactions between them, ii) valuating the arguments and accounting for their interactions or not, iii) finally selecting the most acceptable arguments (or sets of arguments) and using them in order to draw a conclusion or choose a decision. Bipolarity can appear under different forms in each step of this process. In this chapter we are only concerned by the use of bipolarity at the interaction level (a more complete study of bipolarity in each step of the argumentation process is proposed in [4, 5]).

At this level, the main point is the definition of the interactions between arguments. As already said, due for instance to the presence of inconsistency in knowledge bases, arguments may be conflicting. Indeed, in all argumentation systems, an attack relation is considered in order to capture the conflicts.

However, most logical theories of argumentation assume that: if an argument a_1 attacks an argument a_3 and a_3 attacks an argument a_2, then a_1 supports a_2. In this case, the notion of support does not have to be formalized in a way really different from the notion of attack. It is the case of the basic argumentation framework defined by Dung, in which only one kind of interaction is explicitly represented by the *attack* relation. In this context, the support of an argument a by another argument b can be represented only if b defends a in the sense of [21]. So, support and attack are *dependent* notions. It is a parsimonious strategy, but it is not a correct description of the process of argumentation. Let us take several examples for illustrating the difference between "defence" and "support":

Ex. 1 *We want to begin a hike. We prefer a sunny weather, then a sunny and cloudy one, then a cloudy but not rainy weather, in this order. We will cancel the hike only if the weather is rainy. But clouds could be a sign of rain. We look at the sky early in the morning. It is cloudy. The following exchange of informal arguments occurs between Tom, Ben and Dan:*

t_1 *Today we have time, we begin a hike.*

b *The weather is cloudy, clouds are sign of rain, we had better cancel the hike.*

t_2 *These clouds are early patches of mist, the day will be sunny, without clouds, so the weather will be not cloudy (and we can begin the hike).*

d   These clouds are not early patches of mist, so the weather will be not sunny but cloudy; however these clouds will not grow, so it will not rain (and we can begin the hike).

In this exchange, we can identify the following path of conflicts between arguments: argument d attacks argument t_2 which attacks argument b which in turn attacks argument t_1. So, with Dung's framework, argument t_2 is a defender of argument t_1, and argument d is a defeater of argument t_1. Nevertheless, arguments t_2 and d support the hike project. So, the idea of a chain of arguments and counterarguments in which we just have to count the links and take the even one as defeaters and the odd ones as supporters is an oversimplification. So, the notion of defence proposed by [21] is not sufficient to represent support.

The following example also illustrates the need for a new kind of interaction between arguments; the following arguments are exchanged during the meeting of the editorial board of a newspaper:

Ex. 2

a: Assuming agreement and no right of censor, information I concerning X will be published.
b_1:   X is the prime minister who may use the right of censor.
c_0:   We are in democracy and even a prime minister cannot use the right of censor.
c_1:   I believe that X has resigned. So, X is no longer the prime minister.
d: The resignation has been announced officially yesterday on TV Channel 1.
b_2:   I is private information so X denies publication.
e: I is an important information concerning X's son.
c_2:   Any information concerning a prime minister is public information.
repetition of c_1 and d: ...
c_3:   But I is of national interest, so I cannot be considered as private information.

In this example, some conflits appear: for instance, b_1 (resp. b_2) is in conflict with a. But we may also consider that the argument d given by an agent Ag_1 supports the argument c_1 given by another agent Ag_2. It is not only a "dialogue-like speech act": a new piece of information is really given and it is given *after* the production of the argument c_1. So taking d into account leads either to modify c_1, or to find a more intuitive solution for representing the interaction between d and c_1. In this case, we adopt an incremental point of view, considering that pieces of information given by different agents enable them to provide more and more arguments. We do not want to revise already advanced arguments. In contrast, we intend to represent as much as possible all the kinds of interaction between these arguments.

The last example shows how a notion of support between two arguments can be formalized with a logical representation of the structure of the arguments.

Ex. 3 *A murder has been performed and the suspects are Liz, Mary and Peter. The following pieces of information have been gathered:*
The type of murder suggests us that the killer is a female. The killer is certainly small. Liz is tall and Mary and Peter are small. The killer has long hair and uses a

lipstick. A witness claims that he saw the killer who was tall. Moreover, we are told that the witness is short-sighted, so he is no more reliable.

We use the following propositional symbols: sm (the killer is small), fem (the killer is a female), mary (the killer is Mary), lglip (the killer has long hair and uses a lipstick), wit (the witness is reliable), bl (the witness is short-sighted).

Here, an argument takes the form of a set of premises which entails a conclusion. So the following arguments can be formed: a_1 in favour of mary (with premises $\{sm, fem, (sm \wedge fem) \rightarrow mary\}$), a_2 in favour of $\neg sm$ (with premises $\{wit, wit \rightarrow \neg sm\}$), a_3 in favour of $\neg wit$ (with premises $\{bl, bl \rightarrow \neg wit\}$), a_4 in favour of fem (with premises $\{lglip, lglip \rightarrow fem\}$).

a_3 attacks a_2 which attacks a_1. So a_3 defends a_1 against a_2.

Moreover, a_4 confirms the premise fem of a_1. So, a_4 supports a_1 (in the sense that a_4 strengthens a_1). Contrastedly, a_3 defends a_1 against a_2 means that a_3 weakens the attack on a_1 brought by a_2. So, on one side, a_1 gets a support and on the other side a_1 suffers a weakened attack.

The above examples show that the argumentation process uses arguments and counter-arguments, support and attack relations, but not always in the same way. The arguments which are available in a dynamic argumentation process rely upon premises which are not always pieces of evidence. If we accept that a new fact can undermine one of the premises (thus forming an attack), we must also accept that a new fact can enforce, or confirm a premise (thus forming a support interaction).

Following all these remarks, and in order to formalise realistic examples, a more powerful tool than the abstract argumentation framework proposed by Dung is needed. In particular, we are interested in modelling situations where two *independent* kinds of interactions are available: a positive and a negative one (see for example in the medical domain the work [23]). So, following [23, 35], we present a new argumentation framework: an abstract bipolar argumentation framework.

The chapter is organized as follows: Section 2 introduces the formal definitions of an abstract Bipolar Argumentation Framework (BAF). Then, we consider the fundamental problem of determining which arguments (or sets of arguments) can be considered as acceptable. The formal way to handle this problem is to define argumentation semantics. Section 3 introduces extension-based acceptability semantics for a BAF. These new semantics rely upon criteria which make explicitly use of both support and attack relations. In Section 4, another way to define extension-based semantics for a BAF is followed. First, a transformation of a BAF into a Dung's meta-argumentation framework is given. The support relation is used to form meta-arguments (called coalitions) in such a way that at the meta-level only conflict interactions may appear. Extensions of a BAF can then be defined from Dung's extensions of the meta framework. Section 5 addresses the question of labelling-based semantics in a BAF. Some labelling functions are proposed for a BAF. Section 6 is devoted to the related issues and to some concluding remarks. Note that the proofs of the properties given in this chapter can be found in the associated original papers.

2 Abstract bipolar frameworks

An abstract bipolar argumentation framework is an extension of the basic abstract argumentation framework introduced by [21] in which a new kind of interaction between arguments is represented by the *support*[1] relation[2]. This new relation is assumed to be totally independent of the attack relation (*i.e.* it is not defined using the attack relation). So, we have a bipolar representation of the interactions between arguments.

Def. 1 *An abstract bipolar argumentation framework (BAF)* $\langle A, \mathcal{R}_{att}, \mathcal{R}_{sup} \rangle$ *consists of: a set* A *of arguments, a binary relation* $\mathcal{R}_{att}$ *on* A *called the* attack *relation and another binary relation* $\mathcal{R}_{sup}$ *on* A *called the* support *relation. These binary relations must verify the following consistency constraint:* $\mathcal{R}_{att} \cap \mathcal{R}_{sup} = \varnothing$[3].
Consider a_i *and* $a_j \in A$, $a_i \mathcal{R}_{att} a_j$ *(resp.* $a_i \mathcal{R}_{sup} a_j$*) means that* a_i *attacks (resp. supports)* a_j. *Let* $a \in A$, $\mathcal{R}_{att}^{-}(a)$ *(resp.* $\mathcal{R}_{sup}^{-}(a)$*) denotes the set of attackers (resp. supporters) of* a.

In the following, we assume that A represents the set of arguments proposed by rational agents at a given time, so we will assume that A is finite.

A BAF can be represented by a directed graph $\mathcal{G}^b$ called the *bipolar interaction graph*, with two kinds of edges, one for the attack relation ($\rightarrow$) and another one for the support relation ($\rightsquigarrow$). See for instance the following representations:

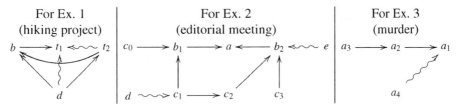

| For Ex. 1 | For Ex. 2 | For Ex. 3 |
| (hiking project) | (editorial meeting) | (murder) |

In the following, we abstract from the structure of the arguments and we consider arbitrary independent relations $\mathcal{R}_{att}$ and $\mathcal{R}_{sup}$.

Def. 2 *Let* $\text{BAF} = \langle A, \mathcal{R}_{att}, \mathcal{R}_{sup} \rangle$ *be a bipolar argumentation framework and* $\mathcal{G}^b$ *be the associated interaction graph. Let* $a, b \in A$. *A path from* a *to* b *in* $\mathcal{G}^b$ *is a sequence* $(a_1, \ldots, a_n)$ *of elements of* A *s.t.* $n \geq 2$, $a = a_1$, $b = a_n$, $a_1 \mathcal{R} a_2, \ldots, a_{n-1} \mathcal{R} a_n$, *with* $\mathcal{R} = \mathcal{R}_{att}$ *or* $\mathcal{R}_{sup}$. *Such a path has length* $n - 1$.
Note that if $n = 2$ *and* $a = b$ *then the path is a* loop *and if the relation* $\mathcal{R}$ *used in the loop is* $\mathcal{R}_{att}$ *then* a *is said* self-attacking.

The use of bipolarity suggests new kinds of interaction between arguments: in Ex. 2, the fact that d supports an attacker of b_1 may be considered as a kind of

---

[1] Note that the term "support" refers to a relation between two arguments and not a relation between premises and conclusion, as in Toulmin [32].

[2] If the support relation is removed, we retrieve Dung's framework.

[3] In the context of the argumentation, this consistency constraint is essential: it does not seem rational to advance an argument which simultaneously attacks and supports the same other argument.

negative interaction between d and b_1, which is however weaker than a direct attack. From a cautious point of view, such arguments cannot appear together in a same extension. In order to address this problem, a new kind of attack has been introduced [13, 14] which combines a sequence of supports with a direct attack.

Def. 3 *Let a, $b \in \mathcal{A}$. There is a* sequence of supports for b by a *(or for short a supports b) iff there exists a sequence $(a_1,\dots,a_n)$ of elements of $\mathcal{A}$ s.t. $n \geq 2$, $a = a_1$, $b = a_n$, $a_1 \mathcal{R}_{sup} a_2$, $\dots$, $a_{n-1} \mathcal{R}_{sup} a_n$.*

Def. 4 *A* supported attack *for an argument b by an argument a is a sequence (a,x,b) of arguments of $\mathcal{A}$ s.t. a supports x[4] and $x \mathcal{R}_{att} b$.*

In Ex. 2, there is a supported attack for b_1 by d.
Then, taking into account attacks and sequences of supports leads to the following definitions applying to sets of arguments:

Def. 5 *Let $S \subseteq \mathcal{A}$, let $a \in \mathcal{A}$. S set-attacks a iff there exists a supported attack or a direct attack for a from an element of S. S set-supports a iff there exists a sequence of supports for a from an element of S.*

The above definitions are illustrated on the following example:

Ex. 4 *Consider the following graph:*

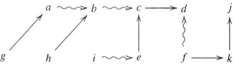

In this graph, the paths $a - b - c - d$ and $i - c$ correspond to supported attacks. The set $\{a, h\}$ set-attacks d and b and set-supports b and c.

3 Extension-based semantics for acceptability

In Dung's framework, the *acceptability* of an argument depends on its membership to some sets, called acceptable sets or extensions. These extensions are characterised by particular properties. It is a collective acceptability. Following Dung's methodology, we propose characteristic properties that a set of arguments must satisfy in order to be an output of the argumentation process, in a bipolar framework. We recall that such a set of arguments must be in some sense coherent and must enable to win a dispute. Maximality for set-inclusion is also often required.

Considering a BAF $\langle \mathcal{A}, \mathcal{R}_{att}, \mathcal{R}_{sup} \rangle$ and using the notion of "set-attack" and "set-support" given by Def. 5, we first investigate the notion of coherence, then we propose new semantics for acceptability in bipolar argumentation frameworks.

---

[4] In the sense of Def. 3.

3.1 Managing the conflicts

In the basic argumentation framework, whatever the considered semantics, selected acceptable sets of arguments are constrained to be coherent in the sense that they must be conflict-free. In a bipolar argumentation framework, the concept of coherence can be extended along two different lines:

- forbidding not only direct attacks but also supported attacks enforces a kind of *internal* coherence: we do not accept a set S of arguments which set-attacks one of its elements (this a generalization of Dung's notion of conflict-free).
- extending the consistency constraint between support and attack relations leads to define a kind of *external* coherence: we do not accept a set S of arguments which set-attacks *and* set-supports the same argument.

Def. 6 *Let* $S \subseteq A$. *S is* +conflict-free[5] *iff* $\nexists a, b \in S$ *s.t.* $\{a\}$ *set-attacks b.*
S is safe[6] *iff* $\nexists b \in A$ *s.t. S set-attacks b and either S set-supports b, or* $b \in S$.

Ex. 4 (cont'd) *The set* $\{h, b\}$ *is not* +conflict-free *(there is a direct attack). The set* $\{b, d\}$ *is not* +conflict-free *since d suffers a supported attack from b. Contrastedly,* $\{a, h\}$ *and* $\{b, f\}$ *are* +conflict-free.
The set $\{a, h\}$ *is not safe since a supports b and h attacks b. The set* $\{b, f\}$ *is not safe since d suffers a supported attack from b and f supports d. Contrastedly,* $\{g, i, h\}$ *is safe.*

Note that the notion of safe set encompasses the notion of +conflict-free set:

Prop. 1 ([14]) *Let* $S \subseteq A$. *If S is safe, then S is* +conflict-free. *If S is* +conflict-free *and closed for* $\mathcal{R}_{sup}$ *then S is safe.*

Ex. 4 (cont'd) *The set* $\{g, h, i, e\}$ *is* +conflict-free *and closed for* $\mathcal{R}_{sup}$. *So it is safe.*

3.2 New acceptability semantics

According to the methodology proposed by [21], two notions play an important role in the definition of extension-based semantics: the notion of coherence, and the notion of defence (that is for short attack against attack). In a BAF, several notions of coherence, and two kinds of attack (direct and supported) are available. So several extensions of the notion of defence could be proposed. However, we have chosen to restrict to the classical defence, for the following reasons. First, the purpose of this chapter is to present some principles governing bipolar frameworks, rather than an exhaustive survey. Secondly, most of the works talking about bipolarity consider that

---

[5] This notation means that checking if a set is +conflict-free needs to consider more conflicts than with the basic notion of conflict-free suggested by Dung.

[6] This definition is inspired by [35] and by the notion of a controversial argument given in [21].

a support does not have the same strength as an attack. In that sense, an argument can be considered as defended if and only if its direct attackers are directly attacked.

The above remark is illustrated by the following example: $a_1 \longrightarrow a_2 \leftsquigarrow a_3$

There is a supported attack for a_1 by a_3 and no attack for a_3. However, a_1 directly attacks a_2 and it seems sufficient to resinstate a_1.

Let us recall the definition of defence given in [21].

Def. 7 *Let $S \subseteq \mathcal{A}$. Let $a \in \mathcal{A}$. S defends a iff $\forall b \in \mathcal{A}$, if $b\mathcal{R}_{att}a$ then $\exists c \in S$ s.t. $c\mathcal{R}_{att}b$.*

In the following, the concept of admissibility is first extended. The idea is to reinforce the coherence of the admissible sets. Then, extensions under the preferred semantics will be defined as maximal (for $\subseteq$) admissible sets of arguments.

Three different definitions for admissibility can be given, from the most general one to the most specific one. First, a direct translation of Dung's definition gives the definition of d-admissibility ("d" means "in the sense of Dung"). Taking into account external coherence leads to s(afe)-admissibility. Finally, external coherence can be strengthened by requiring that an admissible set is closed for $\mathcal{R}_{sup}$. So, we obtain the definition of c(losed)-admissibility.

Def. 8 *Let $S \subseteq \mathcal{A}$.*
S is d-admissible iff S is +conflict-free and defends all its elements.
S is s-admissible iff S is safe and defends all its elements.
S is c-admissible iff S is +conflict-free, closed for $\mathcal{R}_{sup}$ and defends all its elements.

From the above definitions, it follows that each c-admissible set is s-admissible, and each s-admissible set is d-admissible.

Def. 9 *A set $S \subseteq \mathcal{A}$ is a d-preferred (resp. s-preferred, c-preferred) extension iff S is maximal for $\subseteq$ (or for short $\subseteq$-maximal) among the d-admissible (resp. s-admissible, c-admissible) subsets of $\mathcal{A}$.*

Ex. 1 (cont'd) *In this case, the three semantics give the same result: $\{d, t_1\}$ is the unique d-preferred, s-preferred and c-preferred extension.*

Ex. 4 (cont'd) *The set $\{g, h, i, e, f, d, j\}$ is the unique c-preferred extension.*

Ex. 5 *Consider the BAF represented by $a \rightsquigarrow b \leftarrow h$. The set $\{a, h\}$ is the unique d-preferred extension. There are two s-preferred extensions $\{a\}$ and $\{h\}$. And there is only one c-preferred extension $\{h\}$.*

One of the most important issues with regard to extensions concerns their existence. The existence of d-preferred (resp. s-preferred, c-preferred) extensions is guaranteed since the empty set is d-admissible (resp. s-admissible, c-admissible), and each d-admissible (resp. s-admissible, c-admissible) is included in a d-preferred (resp. s-preferred, c-preferred) extension. Note that analogous definitions for admissibility could be proposed using a stronger notion of defence (a stronger defence would be defined for instance by replacing *attack* with *set-attack* in Def. 7).

Considering another well-known semantics, the stable semantics, nice results can be obtained if we keep the basic definition of a stable extension, but replace *attack* with *set-attack*. It is a straightforward way to extend the stable semantics in a BAF.

Def. 10 *S is a* stable extension *iff S is +conflict-free and* $\forall a \notin S$, *S set-attacks a.*

In the following, we restrict to acyclic BAF, in the sense that the associated interaction graph is acyclic. In Dung's basic framework, it has been proved that, in the case of an acyclic attack graph, there is always a unique stable (which is also preferred) extension. So, Def. 10 ensures the existence of a unique stable extension in an acyclic BAF[7]. However, the unique stable extension is not always safe.

Ex. 5 (cont'd) *The set* $\{a, h\}$ *is the unique stable extension, and it is not safe.*

Indeed, the following result can be proved:

Prop. 2 ([14]) *Let S be a stable extension. S is safe iff S is closed for* $\mathcal{R}_{sup}$.

The following results enable to characterize d-preferred, s-preferred and c-preferred extensions when the BAF is acyclic:

Prop. 3 ([14]) *Let S be the unique stable extension of an acyclic BAF.*

1. *S is also the unique d-preferred extension.*
2. *The s-preferred extensions and the c-preferred extensions are subsets of S.*
3. *Each s-preferred extension which is closed for* $\mathcal{R}_{sup}$ *is c-preferred.*
4. *If S is safe, then S is the unique c-preferred and the unique s-preferred extension.*
5. *If* $\mathcal{A}$ *is finite, each c-preferred extension is included in a s-preferred extension.*
6. *If S is not safe, the s-preferred extensions are the subsets of S which are* $\subseteq$-*maximal among the s-admissible sets.*
7. *If S is not safe, and* $\mathcal{A}$ *is finite, there is only one c-preferred extension.*

Ex. 5 (cont'd) $\{h\}$ *is the only s-preferred extension which is also closed for* $\mathcal{R}_{sup}$. *So,* $\{h\}$ *is the unique c-preferred extension.*

Ex. 6 *Consider the BAF represented by:*

$\{a_1, a_2, h\}$ *is the only d-preferred extension.* $\{a_1, a_2\}$ *and* $\{h\}$ *are the only two s-preferred extensions. None of them is closed for* $\mathcal{R}_{sup}$. $\varnothing$ *is the unique c-preferred extension. If we add an isolated argument* a_3 *(for which no interaction exists with the other available arguments), then we obtain:* $\{a_1, a_2, a_3, h\}$ *is the only d-preferred extension.* $\{a_1, a_2, a_3\}$ *and* $\{h, a_3\}$ *are the only two s-preferred extensions. None of them is closed, and* $\{a_3\}$ *is the unique c-preferred extension.*

---

[7] We instantiate Dung's AF with the relation set-attacks and the resulting graph is still acyclic.

The above discussion enables to draw the following conclusions. In the particular case of an acyclic BAF, two semantics present nice features: the stable semantics and the c-preferred semantics. If we are interested in internal coherence only, we will have to determine the unique stable extension, which is also the unique d-preferred extension. If we are interested in a more constrained concept of coherence, we will compute the unique c-preferred extension.

4 Turning a bipolar framework into a Dung meta-framework

The extension-based acceptability semantics introduced in Section 3 rely upon criteria which make explicitly use of support and attack relations, through the concept of supported attack. Here, we follow another way to define extension-based semantics for a BAF. First, a transformation of a BAF into a Dung's meta-argumentation framework is given. This meta-argumentation framework consists only of a set of meta-arguments (called coalitions), and a conflict relation between these meta-arguments. The attack relation of the initial BAF will appear only at the meta-level. As a consequence, a meta-argument will gather arguments which are not in conflict. The support relation of the initial BAF will not appear at the meta-level, but will be used to gather arguments in a coalition. The idea is that a meta-argument makes sense only if its members are somehow related by the support relation. So, the two fundamental principles governing the definition of a coalition are: the *Coherence principle* (there is no direct attack between two arguments of a same coalition) and the *Support principle* (if two arguments belong to a same coalition, they must be somehow, directly or indirectly, related by the support relation).

4.1 The concept of coalition

Consider $\mathrm{BAF} = \langle \mathcal{A}, \mathcal{R}_{\mathrm{att}}, \mathcal{R}_{\mathrm{sup}} \rangle$ represented by the graph $\mathcal{G}^b$. $\mathcal{G}^b_{\mathrm{sup}}$ will denote the partial graph representing the partial system $\langle \mathcal{A}, \mathcal{R}_{\mathrm{sup}} \rangle$[8]. AF will denote the partial argumentation system $\langle \mathcal{A}, \mathcal{R}_{\mathrm{att}} \rangle$ associated with BAF and represented by the partial graph denoted by $\mathcal{G}^b_{\mathrm{att}}$.

Def. 11 $C \subseteq \mathcal{A}$ *is a* coalition *of* BAF *iff:* (i) *The subgraph of* $\mathcal{G}^b_{\mathrm{sup}}$ *induced by* C *is connected;* (ii) C *is conflict-free*[9] *for* AF; (iii) C *is* $\subseteq$-*maximal among the sets satisfying* (i) *and* (ii).

---

[8] We consider that the reader knows the basic concepts of graph theory (chain, connexity,...). See for instance [7] for a background on graph theory.

[9] In the basic sense proposed by Dung.

Note that when $\mathcal{R}_{att}$ is empty, the coalitions are exactly the connected compo-nents[10] of the partial graph $\mathcal{G}^b_{sup}$.

Prop. 4 ([17]) *An argument which is not self-attacking is in at least one coalition.*

Ex. 7 *Consider the BAF:*

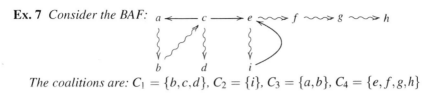

The coalitions are: $C_1 = \{b,c,d\}$, $C_2 = \{i\}$, $C_3 = \{a,b\}$, $C_4 = \{e,f,g,h\}$

The following result shows that coalitions can be restated in terms of connected components of an appropriate subgraph. By the way, it gives a constructive way for computing coalitions.

Prop. 5 ([17]) $C \subseteq \mathcal{A}$ *is a coalition of* BAF *iff: (i) There exists* $S \subseteq \mathcal{A}$ $\subseteq$-*maximal conflict-free for* AF *s.t.* C *is a connected component of the subgraph of* $\mathcal{G}^b_{sup}$ *induced by* S *and (ii)* C *is* $\subseteq$-*maximal among the subsets of* $\mathcal{A}$ *satisfying* **(i)**.

Prop. 5 suggests a procedure for computing the coalitions of BAF:

Step 1:   Consider AF and determine the maximal conflict-free sets for AF.
Step 2:   For each set of arguments S_i obtained at Step 1, determine the connected components of the subgraph of $\mathcal{G}^b_{sup}$ induced by S_i.
Step 3:   Keep the $\subseteq$-maximal sets obtained at Step 2.

The notion of conflict-free set is related to the notion of independent set:

Prop. 6 ([17]) *Let* $S \subseteq \mathcal{A}$. S *is conflict-free for* AF *iff* S *is an independent subset of* $\mathcal{A}$ *in the graph* $\mathcal{G}^b_{att}$.

So, S is $\subseteq$-maximal conflict-free for AF iff S is a $\subseteq$-maximal independent set of vertices in the graph $\mathcal{G}^b_{att}$ and Step 1 of the computational procedure consists in determining all the $\subseteq$-maximal independent subsets of $\mathcal{G}^b_{att}$. Remark that the time complexity of the best algorithms providing all the $\subseteq$-maximal independent sets is exponential. Note also that there exist several algorithms in the literature for finding all the $\subseteq$-maximal independent sets (see for instance the work of J.M. Nielsen [26]). We also know that:

- For Step 2, a depth-first exploration of a graph provides the connected compo-nents in linear time $\mathcal{O}$(number of vertices + number of edges).
- And for Step 3, maximization with respect to $\subseteq$ is also an exponential process.

---

[10] Let $G = (V,E)$ be a graph. Let $S \subseteq V$. S is a *connected component of* G iff the subgraph of G induced by S is connected and there exists no $S' \subseteq V$ s.t. $S \subset S'$ and the subgraph of G induced by S' is connected.

4.2 A meta-argumentation framework

Let $C(\mathcal{A})$ denote the set of coalitions of BAF. We define a conflict relation on $C(\mathcal{A})$ as follows.

Def. 12 *Let C_1 and C_2 be two coalitions of BAF. C_1 C-attacks C_2 iff there exists an argument a_1 in C_1 and an argument a_2 in C_2 s.t. $a_1 \mathcal{R}_{att} a_2$.*

It can be proved that:

Prop. 7 ([17]) *Let C_1 and C_2 be two distinct coalitions of BAF. If $C_1 \cap C_2 \neq \varnothing$ then C_1 C-attacks C_2 or C_2 C-attacks C_1.*

So a new argumentation framework $\text{CAF} = \langle C(\mathcal{A}), \text{C-attacks} \rangle$ can be defined, referred to as the coalition framework associated with BAF.

Ex. 7 (cont'd) *In this example, CAF can be represented by (by abusing notations, $\rightarrow$ represents the attack relation in BAF and also the C-attack relation in CAF):*

$$C_3 \longleftarrow C_1 \longrightarrow C_4 \longleftarrow C_2$$

Dung's definitions apply to CAF, and it can be proved that:

Prop. 8 ([17]) *Let $\{C_1, \ldots, C_p\}$ be a finite set of distinct coalitions. $\{C_1, \ldots, C_p\}$ is conflict-free for CAF iff $C_1 \cup \ldots \cup C_p$ is conflict-free for AF.*

So, CAF is a "meta-argumentation" framework with a set of "meta-arguments" (the set of coalitions $C(\mathcal{A})$) and a "meta-attack" relation on these coalitions (the C-attacks relation). A coalition gathers arguments which are close in some sense and can be produced together. However, as coalitions may conflict, following Dung's methodology, preferred and stable extensions of CAF can be computed. Such extensions will contain coalitions which are collectively acceptable. The last step consists in gathering the elements of the coalitions of an extension of CAF. By this way, the best groups of arguments (w.r.t. the given interaction relations) will be selected.

Def. 13 *Let $S \subseteq \mathcal{A}$. S is a Cp-extension (Cp means "Coalition-preferred") of BAF iff there exists $\{C_1, \ldots, C_p\}$ a preferred extension of CAF s.t. $S = C_1 \cup \ldots \cup C_p$. S is a Cs-extension (Cs means "Coalition-stable") of BAF iff there exists $\{C_1, \ldots, C_p\}$ a stable extension of CAF s.t. $S = C_1 \cup \ldots \cup C_p$.*

When the only preferred extension of CAF is the empty set, we define the empty set as the unique Cp-extension of BAF.

Ex. 7 (cont'd) *There is only one preferred extension of CAF, which is also stable: $\{C_1, C_2\}$. So, $S = \{b, c, d, i\}$ is the Cp-extension (and also the Cs-extension) of BAF.*

Some nice properties of Dung's basic framework are preserved:

- A BAF has always a (at least one) Cp-extension. It is a consequence of Def. 13.
- In contrast, there does not always exist a Cs-extension of BAF. The reason is that there may be no stable extension of CAF.
- Each Cs-extension is also a Cp-extension. The converse is false.

- There cannot exist two Cp-extensions s.t. one strictly contains the other one. It follows from Def. 11 and 13.

However, other properties are lost. A Cp-extension is not always admissible for AF, and a Cs-extension is not always a stable extension of AF:

Ex. 8 *Consider the BAF represented by:* $a \longrightarrow b \leftsquigarrow c \rightsquigarrow d \longrightarrow e$

The coalitions are: $C_1 = \{a\}$, $C_2 = \{b,c,d\}$, $C_3 = \{e\}$. *And the associated CAF can be represented by:* $C_1 \longrightarrow C_2 \longrightarrow C_3$

There is only one preferred extension of CAF, which is also stable: $\{C_1, C_3\}$. *So, $S = \{a,e\}$ is the Cp-extension (and also the Cs-extension) of BAF. We have $d \mathcal{R}_{att} e$, but a does not defend e against d (neither by a direct attack, nor by a supported attack, though a attacks an element of the coalition which attacks e). So, S is not admissible for AF. S does not contain c, but there is no attack (no supported attack) of an element of S against c. So, S is not a stable extension of AF.*

Note that a coalition is considered as a whole and its members cannot be used separately in an attack process. Ex. 8 suggests that admissibility is lost due to the size of the coalition $\{b,c,d\}$, and that it would be more fruitful to consider two independent coalitions $\{c,b\}$ and $\{c,d\}$. A new formalization of coalitions in terms of conflict-free maximal support paths has been proposed in [17]. However, it does not enable to recover Dung's properties.

Note that the lost of admissibility in Dung's sense is not surprising: admissibility is lost because it takes into account "individual" attack and defence, whereas, with meta-argumentation and coalitions, "collective" attack and defence are considered.

5 Labellings in bipolar frameworks

This section addresses the question of labelling-based semantics in a BAF. A labelling-based semantics relies upon a set of labels and is defined by specifying the criteria for assigning labels to arguments. An example of labelling-based semantics in a basic argumentation framework is given by [22] with the robust semantics. More generally, several approaches have been proposed for valuing the arguments in a classical argumentation framework (for example [24, 29, 30, 8, 15, 1, 33]). In some of them, the value of an argument depends on its interactions with the other arguments; in other ones, it depends on an intrinsic strength of the argument. Besides, Karacapilidis & Papadias [23] have proposed an argumentation web-tool, named HERMES, for decision making in the medical field. Taking into account notions of attacks and supports between arguments, this system permits the expression and the weighting of arguments. The basic elements of this system are: a *solution* (an answer to the question which is discussed) and a *position* (expressing the support for, or the opposition to a solution or to another position). HERMES can label the solutions and the positions by the status "active" or "inactive". At the end of the discussion, the "active" (resp. "inactive") solutions are accepted (resp. rejected). An "active" solution is a recommended choice among the other solutions concerning a same question. Different recursive labellings are proposed in HERMES. But, the value of a position p depends only on the *active* positions which are linked to p in the acyclic discussion graph, and the value of a position is always binary.

In this section, we propose a limited use of the notion of labelling-based semantics for a BAF: we show how bipolar interactions can be used for defining valuations over the set of arguments, *i.e.* functions which assign a value to each argument of the BAF (a further step would be to use such a valuation in order to select arguments, that is to completely define labelling-based semantics in a BAF, in an analogous way as what has been done in [16] for basic argumentation frameworks).

The approach presented here (see [13]) has the following features: the valuation process takes place before the selection process; the valuation process makes use of a rich set of values and not only two as in HERMES (so, it is called a gradual valuation); the value assigned to an argument takes into account all the direct attackers and supporters of this argument (it is not the case in HERMES in which the value of an argument only depends on the *active* positions); so it is called a local valuation.

This proposition extends the works [22, 8, 16] to bipolar argumentation frameworks as defined in Section 2. It follows the same principles as those already described in [15] augmented with new principles corresponding to the "support" information. So, the three underlying principles for a gradual interaction-based local valuation are:

- **P1**: The value of an argument depends on the values of its direct attackers and of its direct supporters.
- **P2**: If the quality of the support (resp. attack) increases then the value of the argument increases (resp. decreases).
- **P3**: If the quantity of the supports (resp. attacks) increases then the quality of the support (resp. attack) increases.

The value of an argument is obtained with the composition of several functions:

- one for aggregating the values of all the direct attackers; this function computes the value of the "attack"
- one for aggregating the values of all the direct supporters; this function computes the value of the "support"
- one for computing the effect of the attack and of the support on the value of the argument.

In the respect of the previous principles, we assume that there exists a completely ordered set $\mathcal{V}$ with a minimum element $\mathcal{V}_{min}$ and a maximum element $\mathcal{V}_{max}$. The following formal definition for a gradual local valuation can be given.

Def. 14 *Let* $\langle \mathcal{A}, \mathcal{R}_{att}, \mathcal{R}_{sup} \rangle$ *be a bipolar argumentation framework. Let* $a \in \mathcal{A}$ *with* $\mathcal{R}_{att}^-(a) = \{b_1, \ldots, b_n\}$ *and* $\mathcal{R}_{sup}^-(a) = \{c_1, \ldots, c_p\}$.
A local gradual valuation on $\langle \mathcal{A}, \mathcal{R}_{att}, \mathcal{R}_{sup} \rangle$ *is a function* $v : \mathcal{A} \to \mathcal{V}$ *s.t.:*
$$v(a) = g(h_{sup}(v(c_1), \ldots, v(c_p)), h_{att}(v(b_1), \ldots, v(b_n))) \text{ with}$$

the function h_{att} (resp. h_{sup}): $\mathcal{V}^* \to \mathcal{H}_{att}$ (resp. $\mathcal{V}^* \to \mathcal{H}_{sup}$)[11] valuing the quality of the attack (resp. support) on a, and the function g: $\mathcal{H}_{sup} \times \mathcal{H}_{att} \to \mathcal{V}$ with $g(x,y)$ increasing on x and decreasing on y. The function h, $h = h_{att}$ or h_{sup}, must satisfy:

1. if $x_i \geq x_i'$ then $h(x_1,\ldots,x_i\ldots,x_n) \geq h(x_1,\ldots,x_i'\ldots,x_n)$,
2. $h(x_1,\ldots,x_n,x_{n+1}) \geq h(x_1,\ldots,x_n)$,
3. $h() = \alpha \leq h(x_1,\ldots,x_n) \leq \beta$, for all $x_1,\ldots,x_n$[12].

Def. 14 produces a generic local gradual valuation. Let us give two instances of the generic definition, to illustrate the different principles.

- A first instance is defined by $\mathcal{H}_{att} = \mathcal{H}_{sup} = \mathcal{V} = [-1,1]$ interval of the real line, $h_{att}(x_1,\ldots,x_n) = h_{sup}(x_1,\ldots,x_n) = \max(x_1,\ldots,x_n)$, and $g(x,y) = \frac{x-y}{2}$ (so, we have $\alpha = -1$, $\beta = 1$ and $g(\alpha,\alpha) = 0$).
- Another one is defined by $\mathcal{V} = [-1,1]$ interval of the real line, $\mathcal{H}_{att} = \mathcal{H}_{sup} = [0,\infty[$ interval of the real line, $h_{att}(x_1,\ldots,x_n) = h_{sup}(x_1,\ldots,x_n) = \Sigma_{i=1}^n \frac{x_i+1}{2}$, and $g(x,y) = \frac{1}{1+y} - \frac{1}{1+x}$ (so, we have $\alpha = 0$, $\beta = \infty$ and $g(\alpha,\alpha) = 0$).

The following table shows the values computed with both instances on some simple examples:

Example	with 1st instance	with 2nd instance
No attack, no support: a	$v(a) = 0$	$v(a) = 0$
Direct attack: $a \longrightarrow b$	$v(b) = -0.5$	$v(b) = -0.33$
Direct support: $a \rightsquigarrow b$	$v(b) = 0.5$	$v(b) = 0.33$
Defence: $a \longrightarrow b \longrightarrow c$	$v(c) = -0.25$	$v(c) = -0.25$
Sequence of supports: $a \rightsquigarrow b \rightsquigarrow c$	$v(c) = 0.75$	$v(c) = 0.4$
Supported attack: $a \rightsquigarrow b \longrightarrow c$	$v(c) = -0.75$	$v(c) = -0.4$

Ex. 1 (cont'd) *With the first (resp. second) instance, $v(t_1) = \frac{1}{4}$ (resp. $\frac{37}{154}$).*

Ex. 5 (cont'd) *With the first and the second instances, $v(b) = 0$. In this case, there is a perfect equilibrium[13] between support and attack.*

A local gradual valuation defined as above satisfies the following properties [13]:

- If $\mathcal{R}_{att}^-(a) = \mathcal{R}_{sup}^-(a) = \varnothing$ then $v(a) = g(\alpha,\alpha)$.
- If $\mathcal{R}_{att}^-(a) \neq \varnothing$ and $\mathcal{R}_{sup}^-(a) = \varnothing$ then $v(a) = g(\alpha,y) \leq g(\alpha,\alpha)$ for $y \geq \alpha$.
- If $\mathcal{R}_{att}^-(a) = \varnothing$ and $\mathcal{R}_{sup}^-(a) \neq \varnothing$ then $v(a) = g(x,\alpha) \geq g(\alpha,\alpha)$ for $x \geq \alpha$.

---

[11] $\mathcal{V}^*$ denotes the set of the finite sequences of elements of $\mathcal{V}$, including the empty sequence. $\mathcal{H}_{att}$ and $\mathcal{H}_{sup}$ are ordered sets.

[12] So, α is the minimal value for an attack (resp. a support) – i.e. there is no attack (resp. no support) –, and β is the maximal value for an attack (resp. a support).

[13] Note that it is not necessarily the case, and an appropriate choice of the function g enables to give more importance to the attack than to the support.

And we have the following comparative scale[14]:

$$\mathcal{V}_{\min} \leq \quad g(\alpha,y) \quad \leq g(\alpha,\alpha) \leq \quad g(x,\alpha) \quad \leq \mathcal{V}_{\max}$$
$$\text{(for } y \geq \alpha) \qquad\qquad\qquad \text{(for } x \geq \alpha)$$

Moreover the valuation proposed in Def. 14 satisfies the principles **P1** to **P3** (see [13] for a more detailed discussion).

6 Related issues and conclusion

In this chapter, an extension of [21]'s abstract argumentation framework has been proposed in order to take into account two kinds of interaction between arguments modelled with a support relation and an attack relation. In this abstract BAF, two issues have been considered:

- taking into account bipolarity for defining acceptability semantics: either by enforcing the coherence of the admissible sets, or by turning a BAF into a meta-argumentation framework using the concept of coalition;
- taking into account bipolar interactions for proposing gradual labellings for the arguments.

6.1 Related issues about acceptability and bipolarity

Deflog [35]: DEFLOG argumentation system enables to express a support or an attack between sentences in the language, with a new sentence using specific connectors (one for each kind of interaction). Examples of sentences (with $\rightarrow$ for the attack relation and $\rightsquigarrow$ for the support relation) are: a, b, $(a \rightsquigarrow b)$, $(a \rightarrow b)$, $(c \rightsquigarrow (a \rightsquigarrow b))$, $(d \rightarrow (a \rightsquigarrow b))$. In DEFLOG, the notions of sequence of supports and of supported attacks can be retrieved but at the language level (between sentences). Moreover, the notion of conflict-free set proposed in DEFLOG corresponds to the notion of safe set (no sentence which is, at the same time, supported and attacked by the set).

DEFLOG enables to define the dialectical interpretations (or extensions) of a given set of sentences S: an extension is built from a partition (J,D) of S such that J is conflict-free and attacks the sentences of D.

Note that the attack relation and the support relation are explicitly expressed in the sentences. So, one can have an extension of a set S s.t. some supported sentences by J do not belong to S. DEFLOG extensions correspond to [21]'s stable extensions for DEFLOG theories that do not go beyond the expressiveness of Dung's argumentation frameworks, and note that a Dung's AF can always be expressed in DEFLOG. So in this precise sense, DEFLOG's extensions are a faithful generalization of Dung's stable extensions, allowing more expressiveness. Moreover, [35] gives also a faithful generalization of Dung's preferred extensions.

---

[14] Using this scale, the values $\leq$ (resp. $\geq$) to $g(\alpha,\alpha)$ are considered as negative (resp. positive) ones even if $g(\alpha,\alpha) \neq 0$.

Evidence-based argumentation [28]: In this work, the fundamental claim is that an argument cannot be accepted unless it is supported by evidence. So, special arguments are distinguished: the *prima-facie* arguments (which do not require any support to stand).

Arguments may be acceptable only if they are supported (indirectly) by *prima-facie* arguments. This is evidential support. Moreover, only supported arguments may attack other arguments.

Then, the notion of defence is rather complex: A set of arguments S defends an argument a if S provides evidential support for a and S invalidates each attack on a (either by a direct attack on the attacker of a or by rendering this attack unsupported).

Following our definitions, a BAF is an abstract framework, where arguments may stand and attack with or without support. However, evidential reasoning as proposed by [28] could also be handled in a BAF in the following way: Given X a set of arguments (which are considered as *prima-facie* arguments in a given application), a notion of evidential support can be defined via a sequence of supports from an argument of X. Then, the notion of attack can be restricted so that attackers be elements of X, or receive evidential support from X. Finally, instead of choosing the classical definition for "S defends a" (as presented in Def. 7), it can be required first that S provides support for a and secondly that for each supported attack on a, one argument of the sequence of supports is directly attacked by S.

6.2 Related issues about coalitions of arguments

Another way for defining acceptability semantics in a bipolar framework is to turn a *bipolar* argumentation framework into a *meta-argumentation framework* . This transformation has the following characteristics: the support relation is used in order to identify "coalitions" (sets of arguments which can be used together without conflict and which are related by the support relation) and the attack relation is used in order to identify conflicts between coalitions and then to define new acceptability semantics as in Dung's framework.

The concept of coalition has already been related to argumentation.

Collective argumentation framework [9, 27]: A collective argumentation framework is an abstract framework where the initial data are a set of arguments and a binary "attack" relation between *sets* of arguments. The key idea is the following: a set of arguments can produce an attack against other arguments, which is not reducible to attacks between particular arguments. That is in agreement with our notion of coalition, since in our work, a coalition is considered as a whole and its members cannot be used separately in an attack process. The proposal by Nielsen and Parsons is similar to Bochman's proposal. Both proposals take the attacks between sets of arguments as initial data, and define semantics by properties on subsets of arguments. However, Nielsen and Parsons propose an abstract framework which allows sets of arguments to attack single arguments only, and they stick as close as possible to the semantics provided by Dung. In contrast, Bochman departs from Dung's methodology and give new specific definitions for stable and admissible sets of arguments. Our proposal essentially differs from collective argumentation in two points. First, we keep exactly Dung's construction for defining semantics, but we apply this construction in a meta-argumentation framework (the coalition framework). The second main difference lies in the meaning of a coalition: we intend to gather as many arguments as possible in a coalition, and a coalition cannot be broken in the defence process.

Generation of coalition structures in MAS [18, 2]: In multi-agent systems (MAS), the coalition formation is a process in which independent and autonomous agents come together to act as a collective. A coalition structure (CS) is a partition of the set of agents into coalitions. Each coalition has a value (the utility that the agents in the coalition can jointly get minus the cost which this coalition induces for each agent). So the value of a CS is obtained by aggregating the values of the different coalitions in the structure. One of the main problems is to generate a preferred CS, that is a structure which maximizes the global value. Recently, [2] has proposed an abstract system where the initial data are a set of coalitions equipped with a conflict relation. A preferred CS is a subset of coalitions which is conflict-free and defends itself against attacks. Coalitions may conflict for instance if they are non-disjoint or if they achieve a same task.

However, the generation of the coalitions is not studied in [2]. So, one perspective is to apply our work to the formation of coalitions taking into account interactions between the agents. Arguments represent agents in that case. Indeed, it is very important to put together agents which want to cooperate ("supports" relation) and to avoid gathering agents who do not want to cooperate ("attacks" relation). Then, the concept of Cp-extension provides a tool for selecting the best groups of agents (w.r.t. the given interaction relations).

More generally, the work reported here is generic and takes place in abstract frameworks, since no assumption is made on the nature of the arguments. Arguments may have a logical structure such as a pair ⟨explanation, conclusion⟩, may just be positions advanced in a discussion, or may be agents interacting in a multi-agent system. All that we need is the bipolar interaction graph describing how the arguments under consideration are interrelated. We think that this generic work should stimulate discussion across boundaries.

6.3 Related issues about valuation and bipolarity

Most works about valuations of arguments take place in the basic framework. Some of them consider intrinsic valuations, which express to what extent an argument increases the confidence in the statement it promotes. Other approaches consider interaction-based valuations. These approaches usually differ in the set of values which are available.

However, very few works have been interested in valuations which handle both support and attack interactions. Most of these works have been developed for specific applications.

Medical applications: The most influential work has been proposed in HERMES system [23]. But there is no graduality (only two possible values with HERMES), and some parts of the interacting arguments are not taken into account for the computation of the value. See in Section 5.

Valued maps of argumentations: The bipolar valuation in argumentation has been used for a collective annotation of documents.

Collective annotation models supporting exchange through discussion threads. A discussion thread is initiated by an annotation about a given document. Then, users can reply with annotations which confirm or refute the previous ones. Annotations are associated with a social validation which provides a synthetic view of the discussions. The purpose of this validation is to identify annotations which are globally confirmed by the discussion thread. It can also take into account an intrinsic value of the annotations.

In [11, 12] a discussion thread is modelled by a BAF. The set of arguments contains the nodes of the thread. Pairs of the support (resp. attack) relation correspond to replies in the thread of the confirm (resp. refute) type. The social validation of a given annotation is computed with the local bipolar valuation. Moreover, the bipolar valuation procedure has been slightly modified in order to take into account an intrinsic value of each annotation.

References

1. L. Amgoud. *Contribution à l'intégration des préférences dans le raisonnement argumentatif.* PhD thesis, Université Paul Sabatier, Toulouse, July 1999.
2. L. Amgoud. Towards a formal model for task allocation via coalition formation. In *Proc. of AAMAS*, pages 1185–1186, 2005.
3. L. Amgoud, J.-F. Bonnefon, and H. Prade. An argumentation-based approach to multiple criteria decision. In *Proc. of ECSQARU*, pages 269–280, 2005.
4. L. Amgoud, C. Cayrol, and M. Lagasquie-Schiex. On the bipolarity in argumentation frameworks. In *Proc. of the 10th NMR-UF workshop*, pages 1–9, 2004.
5. L. Amgoud, C. Cayrol, M.-C. Lagasquie-Schiex, and P. Livet. On bipolarity in argumentation frameworks. *International Journal of Intelligent Systems*, 23:1062–1093, 2008.
6. S. Benferhat, D. Dubois, S. Kaci, and H. Prade. Bipolar representation and fusion of preferences in the possibilistic logic framework. In *Proc. of KR*, pages 158–169, 2002.
7. C. Berge. *Graphs and Hypergraphs*. North-Holland Mathematical Library, 1973.
8. P. Besnard and A. Hunter. A logic-based theory of deductive arguments. *Artificial Intelligence*, 128 (1-2):203–235, 2001.
9. A. Bochman. Collective argumentation and disjunctive programming. *Journal of Logic and Computation*, 13 (3):405–428, 2003.
10. C. Boutilier. Towards a logic for qualitative decision theory. In *Proc. of KR*, pages 75–86, 1994.
11. G. Cabanac, M. Chevalier, C. Chrisment, and C. Julien. A social validation of collaborative annotations on digital documents. In *Proc. of IWAC*, pages 31–40, 2005.

12. G. Cabanac, M. Chevalier, C. Chrisment, and C. Julien. Collective annotation: Perspectives for information retrieval improvement. In *Proc. of RIAO*, 2007.

13. C. Cayrol and M. Lagasquie-Schiex. Gradual valuation for bipolar argumentation frameworks. In *Proc of the 8th ECSQARU*, pages 366–377, 2005.

14. C. Cayrol and M. Lagasquie-Schiex. On the acceptability of arguments in bipolar argumentation frameworks. In *Proc of the 8th ECSQARU*, pages 378–389, 2005.

15. C. Cayrol and M.-C. Lagasquie-Schiex. Gradual handling of contradiction in argumentation frameworks. In *Intelligent Systems for Information Processing: From representation to Applications*, chapter Reasoning, pages 179–190. Elsevier, 2003.

16. C. Cayrol and M.-C. Lagasquie-Schiex. Graduality in argumentation. *Journal of Artificial Intelligence Research*, 23:245–297, 2005.

17. C. Cayrol and M.-C. Lagasquie-Schiex. Coalitions of arguments in bipolar argumentation frameworks. In *Proc. of CMNA*, pages 14–20, 2007.

18. V. Dang and N. Jennings. Generating coalition structures with finite bound from the optimal guarantees. In *Proc. of AAMAS*, pages 564–571, 2004.

19. D. Dubois and H. Fargier. On the qualitative comparison of sets of positive and negative affects. In *Proc. of ECSQARU*, pages 305–316, 2005.

20. D. Dubois and H. Prade. A bipolar possibilitic representation of knowledge and preferences and its applications. In *Proc. of WILF (LNCS 3849)*, pages 1–10, 2006.

21. P. M. Dung. On the acceptability of arguments and its fundamental role in nonmonotonic reasoning, logic programming and n-person games. *Artificial Intelligence*, 77:321–357, 1995.

22. H. Jakobovits and D. Vermeir. Robust semantics for argumentation frameworks. *Journal of logic and computation*, 9(2):215–261, 1999.

23. N. Karacapilidis and D. Papadias. Computer supported argumentation and collaborative decision making: the HERMES system. *Information systems*, 26(4):259–277, 2001.

24. P. Krause, S. Ambler, M. Elvang, and J. Fox. A logic of argumentation for reasoning under uncertainty. *Computational Intelligence*, 11 (1):113–131, 1995.

25. J. Lang, L. Van der Torre, and E. Weydert. Utilitarian desires. *Journal of Autonomous Agents and Multi-Agents Systems*, 5(3):329–363, 2002.

26. J. Nielsen. On the number of maximal independent sets in a graph. Technical Report RS 02-15, Center for Basic Research in Computer Science (BRICS), April 2002.

27. S. Nielsen and S. Parsons. A generalization of Dung's abstract framework for argumentation. In *Proc. of the 3rd WS on Argumentation in multi-agent systems*, 2006.

28. N. Oren and T. J. Norman. Semantics for evidence-based argumentation. In *Proc. of COMMA*, pages 276–284, 2008.

29. S. Parsons. Normative argumentation and qualitative probability. In *Proc. of ECSQARU*, pages 466–480, 1997.

30. H. Prakken and G. Sartor. Argument-based extended logic programming with defeasible priorities. *Journal of Applied Non-Classical Logics*, 7:25–75, 1997.

31. S. W. Tan and J. Pearl. Specification and evaluation of preferences under uncertainty. In *Proc. of KR*, pages 530–539, 1994.

32. S. Toulmin. *The Uses of Arguments*. Cambridge University Press, Mass., 1958.

33. B. Verheij. Two Approaches to Dialectical Argumentation: Admissible Sets and Argumentation Stages. In *Proc. of Dutch Conference on Artificial Intelligence*, 357–368, 1996.

34. B. Verheij. Automated argument assistance for lawyers. In *Proc. of International Conference on Artificial Intelligence and Law*, 43–52, 1999.

35. B. Verheij. Deflog: on the logical interpretation of prima facie justified assumptions. *Journal of Logic in Computation*, 13:319–346, 2003.

Chapter 5
Complexity of Abstract Argumentation

Paul E. Dunne and Michael Wooldridge

1 Introduction

The semantic models discussed in Chapter 2 provide an important element of the
formal computational theory of abstract argumentation. Such models offer a variety
of interpretations for "collection of acceptable arguments" but are unconcerned with
issues relating to their implementation. In other words, the extension-based semantics described earlier distinguish different views of what it *means* for a set, S, of
arguments to be acceptable, but do not consider the procedures by which such a set
might be *identified*.

This observation motivates the study of natural questions relating to the actual
implementation of different semantics, e.g., using semantics s what can be stated
regarding methods that: decide if $S \in \mathcal{E}_s(\langle \mathcal{A}, \mathcal{R} \rangle)$ for $S \subseteq \mathcal{A}$; or determine if $x \in S$
for at least one (alternatively every) $S \in \mathcal{E}_s(\langle \mathcal{A}, \mathcal{R} \rangle)$, etc? Such questions raise two
separate issues: that of *algorithms* by which upper bounds can be obtained; and that
of mechanisms by which lower bounds can be established. Some discussion of the
former will be given in Chapter 6; the field of *Computational Complexity Theory*
provides a number of approaches by which the latter issue can be addressed: these
methods and their application within abstract argument systems are the subject of
the current chapter. In the next section we give an overview of some basic notions
in complexity theory and continue with a review of some fundamental results on
complexity in abstract argument systems in Section 3. In Section 4 we consider
analogous results within deductive frameworks, *assumption-based frameworks* and
a number of complexity-theoretic properties of value-based frameworks. Section 5

Paul E. Dunne
Dept. of Computer Science, University of Liverpool Liverpool UK, e-mail: ped@csc.liv.ac.
uk

Michael Wooldridge
Dept. of Computer Science, University of Liverpool Liverpool UK, e-mail: mjw@csc.liv.ac.
uk

I. Rahwan, G. R. Simari (eds.), *Argumentation in Artificial Intelligence*,
DOI 10.1007/978-0-387-98197-0_5, © Springer Science+Business Media, LLC 2009

summarises some recent developments concerning novel semantics. Conclusions and selected open questions are discussed in the final section.

2 Elements of Computational Complexity Theory

In crude terms, computational complexity theory deals with classifying computational problems with respect to the resources needed for their solution, e.g., the time required by the fastest program that will solve the problem. In this section we introduce some of the basic concepts in the field of computational complexity.

2.1 Languages and Decision Problems

We think of "computational problems" in terms of *recognising* objects, (e.g., propositional formulae, argumentation frameworks, etc.), which have some *property* of interest, (e.g., instantiations that make the formula true ($\top$), non-empty subsets of arguments that define preferred extensions). For such problems one has a set of *problem instances*, and the goal is to decide whether or not a given instance should be accepted, i.e., has the property of interest. With this approach, *decision problems* are defined by describing the *form* taken by instances *and* the *question* asked of these instances, i.e., the property we want to check. The subset of instances for which positive answers are given is often referred to as a *language*. For example, the decision problem (language) 3-CNF *Satisfiability* (3-SAT) has,

Instance: Propositional formula, $\varphi(x_1, x_2, \ldots, x_n)$ over the variables $\{x_1, \ldots, x_n\}$ in conjunctive normal form with at most three literals in each clause, i.e., φ is specified by a set of m *clauses*, $\{C_1, C_2, \ldots, C_m\}$, with $C_j = y_{j,1} \vee y_{j,2} \vee y_{j,3}$ where $y_{j,k}$ is a literal from $\{x_1, \ldots, x_n, \neg x_1, \ldots, \neg x_n\}$, so that $\varphi = \wedge_{j=1}^{m} C_j$.
Question: Is there an instantiation, $\alpha = \langle a_1, a_2, \ldots, a_n \rangle \in \langle \bot, \top \rangle^n$ for which setting $x_i := a_i$ results in every clause, C_j having at least one literal given the value $\top$?

Notice that this approach allows us to distinguish ideas of problem *size*. Although this could be captured in terms of the number of bits used to encode an instance, there is often some natural parameter that can be used as an alternative, e.g., the size of a 3-CNF formula is usually measured as the number of propositional variables in its definition (n). In general we use $|x|$ to denote the size of a problem instance x.

2.2 Complexity Classes – P, NP, coNP and PH

The concept of *complexity class* is used to describe problems whose resource requirements are similar. Given a language, L, the problem of deciding whether $x \in L$

is viewed as having an efficient algorithm if there is a *constant value*, k, and program M, for which

- **if** $x \in L$, then M returns *"accept"* **else** M returns *"reject"*.
- M returns its answer after at most $|x|^k$ steps.

The program M is said to provide an algorithm for L with run-time n^k, so leading to the complexity class, P, (of *polynomial time decidable* languages) as

$$
\text{P} \;=\; \bigcup_{k=0}^{\infty} \; \{\, L \,:\, \text{There is an algorithm with run-time } n^k \text{ deciding } x \in L.\}
$$

Note that we generally regard problems as being *computationally easy* or *tractable* if they are polynomial time decidable, although of course, if k is very large, polynomial time decidability may not in fact imply the existence of a *practicable* algorithm to solve the problem.

It is often the case that the question $x \in ?L$ can be phrased in terms of identifying some auxiliary structure (or *witness*) that x is indeed a member of L, e.g., $\varphi \in 3 - \text{SAT}$, is witnessed by any instantiation, α, for which $\varphi(\alpha) = \top$. In general, associated with x one may have a set of *possible witnesses*, $W(x)$ to $x \in L$, any such witness having size at most $|x|^r$, for some constant r. Suppose that L_W is the language of pairs $\langle x, y \rangle$ defined by instances, x of L and witnesses $y \in W(x)$ to $x \in L$. Concentrating on languages, L_W in P, we get the complexity classes NP and coNP –

$$
L \in \text{NP} \quad \text{if } (x \in L) \;\Leftrightarrow\; \exists\, y \in W(x) \,:\, \langle x, y \rangle \in L_W
$$
$$
L \in \text{coNP} \;\; \text{if } (x \in L) \;\Leftrightarrow\; \forall\, y \in W(x) \,:\, \langle x, y \rangle \notin L_W
$$

So, for the *complementary* problem to 3-SAT, called 3-UNSAT, $\varphi \in 3 - \text{UNSAT}$ if and only if φ has no satisfying instantiation: $3 - \text{SAT} \in \text{NP}$ while $3 - \text{UNSAT} \in \text{coNP}$.

Looking at the requirements for $L \in \text{P}$, $L \in \text{NP}$, $L \in \text{coNP}$, we note the following pattern: polynomial time decidable languages are characterised by *unary* predicates – P_L – over instances of L, i.e., tests $x \in L$ equate to evaluating the predicate $P_L(x) \equiv (x \in L)$; languages in NP and coNP are characterised by polynomial time decidable *binary* predicates – $P_L(x, y)$ over instances and possible witnesses so that NP languages are those expressible as $\exists\, y\, P_L(x, y)$ and coNP expressible as $\forall\, y\, P_L(x, y)$. This view naturally suggests extending to $(k+1)$-ary polynomial time decidable predicates $P_L(x, y_1, y_2, \ldots, y_k)$ and the languages characterised as

$$
(x \in L) \;\Leftrightarrow\; Q_k\, y_k\, Q_{k-1}\, y_{k-1} \;\cdots\; Q_2\, y_2\, Q_1\, y_1\, P_L(x, y_1, y_2, \ldots, y_k)
$$

where $Q_i \in \{\exists, \forall\}$, $Q_i \neq Q_{i+1}$. When $Q_k = \exists$ (respectively $\forall$) the corresponding class is denoted by Σ_k^p (respectively, Π_k^p). The collection $\cup_{k=0}^{\infty} \Sigma_k^p$ ($= \cup_{k=0}^{\infty} \Pi_k^p$) is called the *Polynomial Hierarchy* (PH) .

As examples of languages in Σ_k^p and Π_k^p we have the so-called *quantified satisfiability* problems – QSAT_k^{Σ} and QSAT_k^{Π} – whose instances are 3-CNF formulae defined on k disjoint sets of n propositional variables – $X_1, X_2, \ldots, X_k$ – so that

$$\varphi \in \text{QSAT}_k^\Sigma \quad \Leftrightarrow \quad \begin{cases} \exists \alpha_1 \forall \alpha_2 \cdots \exists \alpha_{k-1} \forall \alpha_k \ \varphi(\alpha_1, \alpha_2, \ldots, \alpha_k) = \bot \ (k \text{ even}) \\ \exists \alpha_1 \forall \alpha_2 \cdots \forall \alpha_{k-1} \exists \alpha_k \ \varphi(\alpha_1, \alpha_2, \ldots, \alpha_k) = \top \ (k \text{ odd}) \end{cases}$$

$$\varphi \in \text{QSAT}_k^\Pi \quad \Leftrightarrow \quad \begin{cases} \forall \alpha_1 \exists \alpha_2 \cdots \forall \alpha_{k-1} \exists \alpha_k \ \varphi(\alpha_1, \alpha_2, \ldots, \alpha_k) = \top \ (k \text{ even}) \\ \forall \alpha_1 \exists \alpha_2 \cdots \exists \alpha_{k-1} \forall \alpha_k \ \varphi(\alpha_1, \alpha_2, \ldots, \alpha_k) = \bot \ (k \text{ odd}) \end{cases}$$

It is immediate from the formal definitions of P, NP, CONP and PH that the corresponding sets (of languages) satisfy

$$\text{P} \subseteq \begin{Bmatrix} \text{NP} = \Sigma_1^p \\ \text{CONP} = \Pi_1^p \end{Bmatrix} \subseteq \cdots \subseteq \begin{Bmatrix} \Sigma_k^p \\ \Pi_k^p \end{Bmatrix} \subseteq \begin{Bmatrix} \Sigma_{k+1}^p \\ \Pi_{k+1}^p \end{Bmatrix} \subseteq \cdots$$

It is conjectured that all of these containments are *strict* and that $\Sigma_k^p \neq \Pi_k^p$ for any $k \geq 1$: these generalize the well-known P $\neq$ NP conjecture and, to date, are unproven.

2.3 Hardness, Completeness, and Reducibility

The forms presented in Section 2.2 allow problems to be grouped together via *upper bounds*: expressing membership in L in terms of some polynomial time decidable finite arity predicate P_{k+1} places L (at worst) in one of Σ_k^p or Π_k^p. The relationship of *polynomial time many one reducibility* between languages is one key technique underlying arguments that such upper bounds are "optimal". Suppose, given some complexity class, $\mathcal{C}$, we can show that L has the following property:
For *every* $L' \in \mathcal{C}$ there is a *polynomial time* procedure, τ, that transforms instances x of L' to instances $\tau(x)$ of L in such a way that $x \in L'$ *if and only if* $\tau(x) \in L$. We write $L' \leq_m^p L$ to describe this relationship.
   What may be said of L in such cases? Certainly, were $L \in$ P then we could deduce $\mathcal{C} \subseteq$ P: given an instance x of $L' \in \mathcal{C}$, construct the instance $\tau(x)$ of L (polynomial time) and then use the polynomial time method to decide $\tau(x) \in L$. We can thereby deduce that the complexity of L is *at least as high* as the complexity of *any* language in $\mathcal{C}$. A language L for which every $L' \in \mathcal{C}$ has $L' \leq_m^p L$ is said to be $\mathcal{C}$–*hard* . If, in addition, $L \in \mathcal{C}$ then L is called $\mathcal{C}$–*complete* . Just as P is considered as encapsulating all efficiently decidable languages, so the classes of NP–hard, CONP–hard, Σ_k^p–hard and Π_k^p–hard languages are viewed as progressively more and more demanding in terms of their time requirements. Noting the long-standing conjecture about the relationship between these classes a proof that $L \in$ P is a *positive* statement that L is *tractable*; a proof that L is $\mathcal{C}$-hard for some $\mathcal{C} \in$ PH (other than P) provides a strong indication that $L \notin$ P, i.e., that L is *intractable*.[1]
   While the condition $L' \leq_m^p L$ for *every* $L' \in \mathcal{C}$ may seem somewhat demanding, noting that the relation $\leq_m^p$ is transitive we can replace "$\forall L' \in \mathcal{C} \ L' \leq_m^p L$" by "For

---

[1] It should be noted that $\mathcal{C} \in$ PH is, almost without exception a class such as Σ_k^p or Π_k^p for some fixed $k > 0$. There are a number of technical consequences which suggest it is extremely unlikely the class PH itself has complete languages, i.e., L such that $\forall L' \in$ PH $L' \leq_m^p L$.

some $\mathcal{C}$-hard, L' : $L' \leq_m^p L$". For the classes introduced in Section 2.2 we have the following results of Cook [10] and Wrathall [45].

Theorem 5.1.

a. *3*-SAT *is* NP–*complete; 3*-UNSAT *is* coNP–*complete.*
b. QSAT$_k^\Sigma$ *is* Σ_k^p–*complete;* QSAT$_k^\Pi$ *is* Π_k^p–*complete.*

For the results discussed later in this Chapter with very few exceptions the complexity classifications use reductions from 3-SAT or 3-UNSAT.

2.4 More Advanced Ideas

The topics outlined above provide sufficient background for the majority of complexity analyses on decision problems for AFs. There are, however, a number of developments – in particular in the related frameworks discussed in Section 4.1 – which occur in more recent work on complexity of abstract argumentation: here we briefly introduce the basic notions of *oracle-based* complexity classes and the models proposed in work of Cook and Reckhow [11] in order to capture relative complexity of *proof systems*.

Oracle computations, are defined in terms of the availability of a device (or *oracle*) that at the cost of a single step in the algorithm provides the answer to a given language membership query, e.g., oracle computations using 3-SAT may construct a 3-CNF φ, query the 3-SAT oracle as to whether $\varphi \in 3 - \text{SAT}$ with the answer determining subsequent steps taken. This notion, when coupled with oracles for NP-complete languages, gives rise to a range of complexity classes differentiated by the particular restrictions placed on the manner in which such calls are made. One important representative of such classes is the so-called *difference* class, D^p formally defined as those languages, L whose members are the intersection of a language $L_1 \in$ NP with a language $L_2 \in$ coNP: a language $L \in$ D^p can thus be decided by a polynomial time algorithm that is allowed to make at most two calls on an NP oracle (which, by virtue of Thm 5.1(a) can be assumed to be 3-SAT): given an instance x of L, test $x \in L_1$ by forming the appropriate 3-SAT instance, $\tau_1(x)$, and calling the oracle; if the response is positive, then $x \in L_2$ is tested in the same way, forming the instance $\tau_2(x)$ using a second oracle call to verify $\tau_2(x) \notin 3 - \text{SAT}$, i.e. $\tau_2(x) \in 3 - \text{UNSAT}$. More generally, the class of languages for which polynomial time algorithms using at most $f(|x|)$ calls on some oracle for a language complete in a class $\mathcal{C}$ is denoted by P$^{\mathcal{C}[f(|x|)]}$ (so that D$^p \subseteq$ P$^{\text{NP}[2]}$). Where no restriction is placed on the oracle invocation the notation P$^{\mathcal{C}}$ is used. As will be seen from the results reviewed in Sect. 4.1, the algorithmic "base class" can be defined within arbitrary complexity classes, not simply P: this leads to classes such as NP$^{\mathcal{C}}$, etc.

The formalism from [11] has been adopted in order to relate the efficiency of proof procedures for credulous reasoning in AFs to more widely known proof procedures in propositional logic, e.g., resolution, tableau-based, sequents, etc. The model starts from an abstraction of "proof system" Π for a (coNP) language, L as a procedure which given $x \in L$ admits a formal derivation of this fact: the relative efficiency of two processes Π_1 and Π_2 being viewed as the number of derivation steps each requires.[2] This approach precisely formalises two systems as equivalent whenever derivations in one can be simulated by polynomially longer derivations in the other.

3 Fundamental Complexity Results in Argument Frameworks

Faced with a particular semantics and framework there are a number of questions which one may wish to decide: whether a given collection of arguments satisfies the conditions specified by the semantics; whether a particular argument belongs to at least one or every such set; whether there is *any* (non-empty) collectively acceptable subset, etc.. We shall refer to these subsequently as *Verification* (VER$_s$) ; *Credulous Acceptance* (CA$_s$) ; *Sceptical Acceptance* (SA$_s$) ; *Existence* (EX$_s$); and *Non-emptiness* (NE$_s$). Table 5.1 presents the formal definitions.

Table 5.1 Decision Problems in AFs

Problem	Instance	Question
VER$_s$	$\mathcal{G}(\mathcal{A},\mathcal{R}); S \subseteq \mathcal{A}$	Is $S \in \mathcal{E}_s(\mathcal{G})$?
CA$_s$	$\mathcal{G}(\mathcal{A},\mathcal{R}); x \in \mathcal{A}$	Is there *any* $S \in \mathcal{E}_s(\mathcal{G})$ for which $x \in S$?
SA$_s$	$\mathcal{G}(\mathcal{A},\mathcal{R}); x \in \mathcal{A}$	Is x a member of *every* $T \in \mathcal{E}_s(\mathcal{G})$?
EX$_s$	$\mathcal{G}(\mathcal{A},\mathcal{R})$	Is $\mathcal{E}_s(\mathcal{G})$ *non-empty*?
NE$_s$	$\mathcal{G}(\mathcal{A},\mathcal{R})$	Is there any $S \in \mathcal{E}_s(\mathcal{G})$ for which $S \neq \emptyset$?

Before discussing the intractability results that form the main concern of this chapter, we briefly review the cases for which efficient methods are known.

Theorem 5.2.

a. *For $s = GR$ (the grounded semantics), all of the decision problems in Table 5.1 are in* P. *Furthermore the unique subset S for which $S \in \mathcal{E}_{GR}(\langle \mathcal{A},\mathcal{R} \rangle)$ can be constructed in polynomial time.*

b. *Given $\langle \mathcal{A},\mathcal{R} \rangle$ and $S \subseteq \mathcal{A}$ deciding if S is conflict-free, admissible, or stable, i.e., the decision problem* VER$_{ST}(\langle \mathcal{A},\mathcal{R} \rangle, S)$, *are all in* P.

---

[2] In carrying out such comparisons it is presumed that basic derivations in each system are comparable, e.g., can be implemented in polynomial time.

3.1 Intractability Results in Preferred and Stable Semantics

We now turn to the problems defined in Table 5.1 with respect to the other extension based semantics - Preferred and Stable - introduced in Dung [22]. Our main aim is to outline the constructions of Dimopoulos and Torres [21] and Dunne and Bench-Capon [28] from which the classifications shown in Table 5.2 result.

Table 5.2 Complexity of Decision Problems in Preferred (PR) and Stable Semantics (ST)

A	VER$_{PR}$	coNP–complete	[21]
B	CA$_{PR}$	NP–complete	[21]
C	SA$_{PR}$	Π_2^p–complete	[28]
D	NE$_{PR}$	NP–complete	[21]
E	CA$_{ST}$	NP–complete	[21]
F	SA$_{ST}$	coNP–complete/D^p–complete	See discussion below.
G	EX$_{ST}$	NP–complete	attributed to Chvatal in [33]; also [16, 21, 32].

All of the lower bound results in Table 5.2 are obtained as variations on what we shall refer to as the *standard translation* from 3-CNF formulae to AFs.

Definition 5.1. Given $\varphi(z_1,\ldots,z_n)$ a 3-CNF with clauses $\{C_1,\ldots,C_m\}$ the AF, $\mathcal{G}_\varphi(\mathcal{A}_\varphi,\mathcal{R}_\varphi)$ constituting the *standard translation* from φ has

$$\mathcal{A}_\varphi = \{\varphi\}\cup\{C_1,\ldots,C_m\}\cup\{z_1,\ldots,z_n\}\cup\{\neg z_1,\ldots,\neg z_n\}$$
$$\mathcal{R}_\varphi = \{\langle C_j,\varphi\rangle : 1\leq j\leq m\} \cup \{\langle z_i,\neg z_i\rangle,\langle\neg z_i,z_i\rangle : 1\leq i\leq n\}$$
$$\cup \{\langle y_i,C_j\rangle : y_i \text{ is a literal (i.e., } z_i \text{ or } \neg z_i) \text{ of the clause } C_j\}$$

The AF described in Defn 5.1 is, modulo some minor simplifications, identical to that originally used in [21]. This framework provides an extremely versatile mechanism that underpins almost all the complexity analyses of extension based semantics in abstract argumentation frameworks.[3] The basic form of the standard translation suffices to establish (B) and (E) of Table 5.2, whereas (A) and (D) follow from quite simple modifications to it.

For example consider the claim in Table 5.2(B) that CA$_{PR}$ is NP–complete. First note that CA$_{PR} \in$ NP since we may use the set of all admissible subsets of $\mathcal{A}$ containing x as witnesses to $\langle\mathcal{G},x\rangle \in$ CA$_{PR}$. We may then use the standard translation to prove 3-SAT $\leq_m^p$ CA$_{PR}$: given φ form the instance $\langle\mathcal{G}_\varphi,\varphi\rangle$ of CA$_{PR}$. If $\varphi \in$ 3-SAT then the literals instantiated to $\top$ by a satisfying assignment indicate a subset S of the arguments $\{z_1,\ldots,z_n,\neg z_1,\ldots,\neg z_n\}$ for which $S\cup\{\varphi\}$ is admissible. On the other hand if $\langle\mathcal{G}_\varphi,\varphi\rangle \in$ CA$_{PR}$ then an admissible set containing φ must include a conflict-free subset of literals arguments that collectively attack all of the clause arguments: instantiating the corresponding literals to $\top$ produces a satisfying assignment of φ.

---

[3] Exceptions are a specialized case of CA$_{PR}$ and a select number of reductions dealing with value-based argumentation frameworks, cf. [25, Thm. 8(a), Thms. 23–25], and later in this chapter.

Adapting the standard translation by adding a new argument, ψ that is attacked by φ and attacks all of the literal arguments yields an AF, $\mathcal{H}_\varphi$ for which (both) $\mathcal{H}_\varphi \in$ NE$_{PR}$ and $\mathcal{H}_\varphi \in$ EX$_{ST}$ hold if and only if $\varphi \in$ 3-SAT. Table 5.2(A) is an immediate consequence of the former property using the special case of verifying if the empty set is a preferred extension.

The discussion above accounts for all the cases given in Table 5.2 with the exceptions of SA$_{PR}$ and SA$_{ST}$. We first address the apparent ambiguity in the classification of SA$_{ST}$ – Table 5.2(F). A further modification to the framework $\mathcal{H}_\varphi$ by which the new argument ψ now attacks *every* argument in $\mathcal{G}_\varphi$, gives an AF in which ψ belongs to every stable extension if and only if $\varphi \in$ 3-UNSAT so giving a coNP-hardness lower bound.[4] In principle, one appears to have a coNP method via "$\langle\langle\mathcal{A},\mathcal{R}\rangle,x\rangle \in$ SA$_{ST}$ $\Leftrightarrow$ $\forall S \subseteq \mathcal{A}$ (VER$_{ST}(\langle\mathcal{A},\mathcal{R}\rangle,S) \Rightarrow (x \in S)$)". There is, however, a possible objection: $\langle\mathcal{G},x\rangle \in$ SA$_{ST}$ even when $\mathcal{G}$ has *no* stable extension whatsoever, i.e., $\mathcal{G} \notin$ EX$_{ST}$.[5] In order to deal with this objection one might require as a precondition of $\langle\mathcal{G},x\rangle \in$ SA$_{ST}$ that $\mathcal{G} \in$ EX$_{ST}$ leading to an easy D^p upper bound: positive instances are characterised as those in CA$_{ST} \cap \{\langle\langle\mathcal{A},\mathcal{R}\rangle,x\rangle : \forall S \subseteq \mathcal{A}$ (VER$_{ST}(\langle\mathcal{A},\mathcal{R}\rangle,S) \Rightarrow (x \in S)\}$

The matching D^p–hardness lower bound provides another illustration of the flexibility of the standard translation: instances $\langle\varphi_1,\varphi_2\rangle$ of the canonical D^p–hard problem $\langle$3-SAT,3-UNSAT$\rangle$ being transformed to an instance $\langle\mathcal{K},\psi_2\rangle$ of SA$_{ST}$. The construction is illustrated in Fig. 5.1. We leave the reader to verify that this framework satisfies both EX$_{ST}$ *and* has ψ_2 a member of every stable extension if and only if $\varphi_1 \in$ 3-SAT *and* $\varphi_2 \in$ 3-UNSAT.[6]

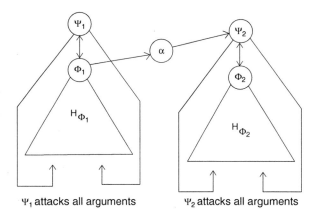

Ψ_1 attacks all arguments Ψ_2 attacks all arguments

Fig. 5.1 The reduction from $\langle\varphi_1,\varphi_2\rangle \in \langle$3-SAT,3-UNSAT$\rangle$ to $\langle\mathcal{K},\psi_2\rangle \in$ SA$_{ST}$

[4] In [28] the coNP-hardness result is attributed to Dimopolous and Torres who do not explicitly consider this problem: the commentary of [28, p. 189] observes the lower bound follows from an easy modification to a construction in [21].

[5] Resulting in AFs for which $\langle\langle\mathcal{A},\mathcal{R}\rangle,x\rangle \in$ SA$_{ST}$ and $\langle\langle\mathcal{A},\mathcal{R}\rangle,x\rangle \notin$ CA$_{ST}$ for *every* $x \in \mathcal{A}$, i.e. *every* argument is sceptically accepted but *none* credulously so.

[6] The construction in Fig. 5.1 has not previously appeared in the literature. The issues concerning precise formulations of SA$_{ST}$ appear first to have been raised in [31].

Although the remaining case in Table 5.2 – Π_2^p-completeness of SA$_{PR}$ deals with a, notionally, harder class of languages, again the lower bound follows by adapting the standard translation: in this case to instances $\varphi(y_1, \ldots, y_n, z_1, \ldots, z_n)$ of QSAT$_2^{\Pi}$.[7] It is worth noting that the decision problem actually considered via this reduction, in [28], is the so-called *coherence property* of AFs, i.e., whether $\mathcal{G}$ is such that $\mathcal{E}_{PR}(\mathcal{G}) = \mathcal{E}_{ST}(\mathcal{G})$: this problem is shown to be Π_2^p-complete with the classification of SA$_{PR}$ an immediate consequence of the reduction used.

3.2 Dialogue and Relationships to Proof Complexity

The standard translation from 3-CNF (which easily generalises to arbitrary CNF) gives rise to one concrete interpretation of argumentation process in terms of logical proof: in particular, the concept of dialogue based procedures by which two parties attempt to reach agreement on the (credulous) acceptability status of some argument, will be discussed in Chapter 6. If one considers applying such procedures to determining the status of φ (in the standard translation) then a demonstration that φ is *not* admissible corresponds to a formal logical proof that the propositional formula $\neg\varphi$ is a tautology. There are, of course, a number of widely used and well-studied proof mechanisms for propositional logic, the question of interest in terms of complexity in argumentation, is what one can state about the efficiency of dialogue based argumentation processes: that is to say, using the comparative schema proposed in [11], how does the use of dialogue approaches compare to other techniques? This question has been examined with respect to one particular credulous reasoning process: the *two-party immediate response* protocol (TPI) introduced in [44]. Informally, TPI-dialogues involve two protagonists (PRO and CON) debating the acceptability of a given argument x: PRO claiming x to be acceptable and CON adopting the opposite stance. The dialogue is set in the context of an AF where each player takes turns advancing arguments in $\mathcal{A}$: PRO starts by putting forward x. A requirement of the game is that, *whenever possible to do so*, a player must put forward an argument that attacks the most recent argument put forward by their opponent: where this is not possible the player must backtrack to a (specified) earlier point in the discussion or concede. In [29] the number of moves required in this game when played on the standard translation of an *unsatisfiable* CNF is considered. The TPI procedure turns out to be equivalent to a standard propositional proof theory – the so-called CUT-free Gentzen calculus [34] and, as a consequence of [42], there are TPI-disputes requiring exponentially many moves in order to resolve the status of particular arguments.

---

[7] The reduction originally presented in [28] is not restricted to 3-CNF formulae but describes a general translation from arbitrary propositional formulae over the logical basis $\{\wedge, \vee, \neg\}$.

4 Complexity in Related Abstract Frameworks

As described in several chapters there are a number of abstract treatments of argumentation that build on the basic structures and semantics proposed in Dung [22]. Among such are *assumption-based frameworks* (ABFs) discussed in Chapter 10; the closely related deductive systems considered in Chapter 7; and the value-based argumentation frameworks (VAFs) whose elements have been presented in Chapter 3. Our aim in this section is to review the range of complexity-theoretic results that have been proved within these models. In general we will not give detailed definitions of relevant ideas and refer the reader to the appropriate chapter for these.

4.1 Complexity in Assumption-based Argumentation

Assumption-based frameworks [5], can be interpreted as specific concrete interpretations of abstract argumentation frameworks, i.e. as mechanisms for constructing the structure $\langle \mathcal{A}, \mathcal{R} \rangle$ by generating arguments in $\mathcal{A}$ *and* attacks between these. This approach starts from some *deductive system* – (L, R) in which L is a formal language, e.g., well-formed propositional sentences, and R a set of *inference rules* of the form $\alpha \leftarrow \{\alpha_1, \ldots, \alpha_n\}$ describing the *conclusions* ($\alpha \in L$) that are supported by the *premises* $\{\alpha_1, \ldots, \alpha_n\} \subseteq L$. Such systems have an associated *derivability relation*, $\vdash \; : \; 2^L \to L$; $\Delta \vdash \alpha$ holds whenever α may be obtained (via R) from Δ. It should be noted that attention is restricted to theories in which the underlying derivability relation is *monotonic*, i.e., $(\Delta \vdash \alpha) \Rightarrow (\Delta' \vdash \alpha)$ for any $\Delta' \supseteq \Delta$.

The key elements added are *assumption sets*, $A \subseteq L$ and the *contrary* function, $^-$ which is a (total) mapping from $\alpha \in A$ to its *contrary* $\overline{\alpha} \in L$. In very simplified terms, (sets of) assumptions define the basis for atomic arguments (in AFs), and the contrary mapping provides the reasons underpinning attacks between arguments. Just as the semantics of "collection of acceptable arguments" in AFs is given by different notions of extension, so too in ABFs the objects of interest are subsets of assumptions defining extensions. In total, viewing an argument as "a statement derivable from some set of assumptions", leads to the notion of attack between arguments as (the argument) $\Delta \vdash \alpha$ attacks (the argument) $\Delta' \vdash \beta$ if $\Delta \vdash \overline{\gamma}$ for an assumption $\gamma \in \Delta'$. In this way we can take any basic semantics w.r.t. AFs, and define analogues w.r.t. ABFs, e.g., a set of assumptions, Δ, is conflict-free if for every $\alpha \in \Delta$ it is *not* the case that $\Delta \vdash \overline{\alpha}$.

Similarly, one may formulate each of the decision problems of Table 5.1 in ABF settings. There are, however, a number of important distinctions: as a result complexity-theoretic treatments of ABFs use significantly different techniques to those discussed in Section 3. In particular,

a. In AFs both arguments, $\mathcal{A}$, and the attack relation, $\mathcal{R}$, are specified *explicitly*. In ABFs these are *implicit* and dependent on the underlying set of assumptions A *and* the precise deductive theory embodied within (L, R).

b. The deductive system (L,R) is *not* limited to classical propositional logic with the contrary being simply logical negation, e.g., (L,R) and $^-$ could be instantiated in terms of a number of non-monotonic logics such as the default logic of [39].

Since the attack relation is defined between assumption sets, in principal one may express any ABF $\langle(L,R),A,^-\rangle$ as an AF, $\langle\mathcal{A},\mathcal{R}\rangle$: $\mathcal{A} = 2^A$, $\mathcal{R} = \{\langle\Delta,\Delta'\rangle : \Delta \vdash \overline{\gamma}$ for some $\gamma \in \Delta'\}$. There is, however, one complication: in practice not *every* subset of A is of interest, only those that satisfy the technical requirement of being *closed*, i.e., $\Delta \subseteq A$ is closed if and only if $\alpha \in A \setminus \Delta \Rightarrow \neg(\Delta \vdash \alpha)$. While this provides a starting point for algorithms and upper bound constructions, for *lower bounds* such approaches yield little of benefit: $|\langle(L,R),A,^-\rangle|$ is exponentially smaller than the corresponding AF.

A detailed investigation of complexity-theoretic issues within ABFs has been presented in a series of papers by Dimopolous, Nebel and Toni [18, 19, 20]. Using the notation L^{ABF} to distinguish ABF instantiations of decision problems L as presented in Table 5.1 and $L^{ABF,LT}$ with reference to different formal theories $LT = (L,R)$, a key element in exact complexity characterisations is the computational complexity of the derivability relation for the underlying logic, i.e., the *derivability problem* (DER) for the formal theory (L,R), has instances $\langle\Delta,\alpha\rangle - \Delta \subseteq L$, $\alpha \in L$ – accepted if and only if $\Delta \vdash \alpha$. For example, in standard propositional logic the derivability problem is coNP–complete: $\Delta \vdash \alpha$ if and only if the formula $\alpha \vee \bigvee_{\varphi \in \Delta} \neg\varphi$ is a tautology.

Combining the notion of "oracle complexity classes" as described in Section 2.4 using oracles for $\text{DER}(\Delta,\alpha)$ provides a generic approach to obtaining *upper bounds* on the complexity of decision problems within ABFs. For example, consider the decision problem $\text{VER}_{ST}^{ABF,LT}$ of verifying that a given set of assumptions defines a stable extension within $\langle(L,R),A,^-\rangle$, where the derivability problem for LT is in some class $\mathcal{C}$. In order to decide if Δ is accepted:

1. Check that Δ is *closed*.
2. Check that Δ is conflict-free, i.e., $\forall \alpha \in \Delta \; \neg(\Delta \vdash \overline{\alpha})$.
3. Check that Δ attacks every assumption $\alpha \notin \Delta$, i.e., $\Delta \vdash \overline{\alpha}$ for each $\alpha \in A \setminus \Delta$.

All of these stages can be carried out using $|A|$ calls to an oracle for DER: (1) tests $(\Delta,\alpha) \notin \text{DER}$ for $\alpha \in A \setminus \Delta$; (2) involves a further $|\Delta|$ calls; and (3) a final set of $|A \setminus \Delta|$ calls. In consequence, $\text{VER}_{ST}^{ABF,LT} \in \text{P}^{\mathcal{C}}$.

Concentrating on upper bounds for Table 5.1 within the most general settings[8] the upper bounds obtained in [20] are stated in Table 5.3.

It may be noted that with the exception of upper bounds on stability related problems, those relating to preferred and admissible sets of assumptions are rather higher than might be expected having allowed for the additional overhead associated with calls to the DER oracle, e.g., $\text{CA}_{ADM} \in \text{NP}$ whereas $\text{CA}_{ADM}^{ABF} \in \text{coNP}^{\text{NP}^{\mathcal{C}}}$ rather than

---

[8] That is to say, no specific properties of the underlying frameworks are assumed, e.g., the property "flatness" described in [5].

Table 5.3 Upper bounds for main decision problems in ABFs

Problem	Semantics	Instance (ABF)	ABF bound (DER $\in C$)	Instance (AF)	AF bound
VER_s	Admissible	$\langle (L,R),A,^- \rangle, \Delta \subseteq A$	coNP^C	$\langle A,R \rangle, S \subseteq A$	P
VER_s	Preferred	$\langle (L,R),A,^- \rangle, \Delta \subseteq A$	$\mathrm{coNP}^{\mathrm{NP}^C}$	$\langle A,R \rangle, S \subseteq A$	coNP
VER_s	Stable	$\langle (L,R),A,^- \rangle, \Delta \subseteq A$	P^C	$\langle A,R \rangle, S \subseteq A$	P
CA_s	Admissible	$\langle (L,R),A,^- \rangle, \varphi \in L$	$\mathrm{NP}^{\mathrm{NP}^C}$	$\langle A,R \rangle, x \in A$	NP
CA_s	Preferred	$\langle (L,R),A,^- \rangle, \varphi \in L$	$\mathrm{NP}^{\mathrm{NP}^C}$	$\langle A,R \rangle, x \in A$	NP
CA_s	Stable	$\langle (L,R),A,^- \rangle, \varphi \in L$	NP^C	$\langle A,R \rangle, x \in A$	NP
SA_s	Preferred	$\langle (L,R),A,^- \rangle, \varphi \in L$	$\mathrm{coNP}^{\mathrm{NP}^{\mathrm{NP}^C}}$	$\langle A,R \rangle, x \in A$	Π_2^p
SA_s	Stable	$\langle (L,R),A,^- \rangle, \varphi \in L$	NP^C	$\langle A,R \rangle, x \in A$	$\mathrm{coNP}/\mathrm{D}^p$

NP^C. That the reasoning problems exhibit "higher than expected" complexity in ABFs is not on account of the (additional) closure checking stage, despite the fact this does not feature in corresponding AF algorithms.[9] The increased complexity arises from the nature of the attack relation, e.g. deciding $\langle 9,x \rangle \in \mathrm{CA}_{PR}$ involves: guess $S \subseteq A$, confirm that $x \in S$ and S is conflict-free; check S attacks each y that attacks S. Suppose, however, we consider the analogous version for $\mathrm{CA}_{PR}^{\mathrm{ABF,LT}}$: guess $\Delta \subseteq A$; confirm that Δ is closed, $\Delta \vdash \varphi$, and Δ does not attack itself; finally check that any *closed assumption set* attacking Δ is itself attacked by Δ. This final stage requires tests involving Δ and *all* other *sets* of assumptions, rather than (as is effectively the case in AFs and suffices for stability) checking a property of Δ in relation to *single* assumptions.

We conclude this overview of complexity in ABFs by noting that for the credulous and sceptical reasoning variants, the classifications of Table 5.3 turn out to be optimal for a wide range of instantiations of $\langle (L,R),A,^- \rangle$ modelling non-classical logics such as DL [39], AEL [38], etc. The typical approach to lower bound proofs, e.g., as illustrated in the specific examples of DL and AEL, uses bounds on the complexity of DER: the cases DL and AEL being coNP–complete. While for DL, one can show $\mathrm{CA}_{PR}^{\mathrm{ABF,DL}} \in \mathrm{NP}^{\mathrm{NP}} = \Sigma_2^p$, no reduction in the generic upper bound is possible for AEL: $\mathrm{CA}_{PR}^{\mathrm{ABF,AEL}} \in \mathrm{NP}^{\mathrm{NP}^{\mathrm{NP}}}$, i.e Σ_3^p. The Σ_2^p (resp. Σ_3^p) hardness reductions use instances of QSAT_2^Σ (resp. QSAT_3^Σ) to define ABFs instantiated as DL (resp. AEL) systems: detailed constructions may be found in [20].

4.2 Complexity in Value-based Argumentation Frameworks

We recall, from Chapter 3, that *value-based argumentation frameworks* (VAFs) augment the basic $\langle A,R \rangle$ abstraction of Dung's AFs by introducing a finite set of *values*, V, and a mapping $\eta : A \to V$ describing the abstract value, $\eta(x)$ endorsed by $x \in A$, so a VAF is described via a four tuple, $9^{(V)} = \langle A,R,V,\eta \rangle$. In VAFs the underlying structures are the completely abstract frameworks of [22]: whereas ABFs provide

---

[9] In fact this stage is redundant in a number of ABF models, e.g DL.

a basis for argument *construction* and attacks between arguments, the motivation behind VAFs is to offer an *explanatory* mechanism accounting for choices between distinct justifiable collections, S and T, which are not collectively acceptable, i.e., S and T may be admissible under Dung's semantics, however, $S \cup T$ fails to be. Such occurrences raise the question of the supporting reasons as to which of S or T is adopted: as developed in Chapter 3, VAFs rationalize these choices in terms of *value orderings* on $\mathcal{V}$. Any commitment to a preference of $v_i \in \mathcal{V}$ over $v_j \in \mathcal{V}$ (written $v_i \succ v_j$) induces a simplification of $\langle \mathcal{A}, \mathcal{R}, \mathcal{V}, \eta \rangle$ whereby every attack $\langle x, y \rangle \in \mathcal{R}$ for which $\eta(x) = v_j$ and $\eta(y) = v_i$ can be removed. Under the restrictions discussed in Chapter 3, applying this refinement of $\mathcal{R}$, any total ordering, α of $\mathcal{V}$, will result in an *acyclic* framework, $\mathcal{G}_\alpha^{(\mathcal{V})}$: as has been noted elsewhere such a framework will have $\mathcal{E}_{GR}(\mathcal{G}_\alpha^{(\mathcal{V})}) = \mathcal{E}_{PR}(\mathcal{G}_\alpha^{(\mathcal{V})}) = \mathcal{E}_{ST}(\mathcal{G}_\alpha^{(\mathcal{V})})$. Value orderings thus motivate the two principal decision problems that have been reviewed in algorithmic and complexity studies of VAFs: *Subjective Acceptance* (SBA) and *Objective Acceptance* (OBA) . Both take as an instance a VAF $\mathcal{G}^{(\mathcal{V})}$ and argument $x \in \mathcal{A}$.

$$\langle \mathcal{G}^{(\mathcal{V})}, x \rangle \in \text{SBA} \ \Leftrightarrow \ \exists \, \alpha \text{ a total ordering of } \mathcal{V} : \text{CA}_{PR}(\mathcal{G}_\alpha^{(\mathcal{V})}, x)$$
$$\langle \mathcal{G}^{(\mathcal{V})}, x \rangle \in \text{OBA} \ \Leftrightarrow \ \forall \, \alpha \text{ total orderings of } \mathcal{V} : \text{CA}_{PR}(\mathcal{G}_\alpha^{(\mathcal{V})}, x)$$

The acyclic form of $\mathcal{G}_\alpha^{(\mathcal{V})}$ gives $\text{CA}_{PR}(\mathcal{G}_\alpha^{(\mathcal{V})}, x) \in \text{P}$ hence SBA$\in$NP and OBA$\in$coNP.

Both bounds turn out to be exact, as shown in [30, 3]: these again use variants of the standard translation from Defn 5.1. This may appear surprising given that although the standard translation is well-suited to relating *subsets* (of arguments) to instantiations of propositional variables, it is less clear how it could be applied to deal with relating *orderings* of values to such instantiations. The device used in [30] associates a "neutral" value with the formula and clause arguments in the VAF defined from $\varphi(Z_n)$ and replaces the mutually attacking pairs $\{z_i, \neg z_i\}$ with a cycle of four arguments $p_i \rightarrow q_i \rightarrow r_i \rightarrow s_i \rightarrow p_i$. Two arguments ($p_i$ and r_i) are assigned the value pos_i to promote "$z_i = \top$ in a satisfying assignment of φ" while the others (q_i and s_i) are given the value neg_i in order to promote "$z_i = \bot$ in a satisfying assignment of φ". Although their definition and these classifications suggest that SBA (resp. OBA) are closely related to CA_{PR} (resp. SA_{PR} for *coherent* AFs) , recent work, discussed in Section 5 highlights several differences between the nature of decision problems in VAFs and, what appear to be analogous problems in AFs.

5 Recent Developments

The computational complexity of the standard semantics (preferred, stable, grounded) in AFs settings is, in the most general case, now well understood: exact complexity bounds having been established for each of the canonical decision problems given in Table 5.1 with respect to these semantics. There has, however, continued to be extensive development of this aspect of the formal theory of ar-

gumentation, driven by a number of reasons. Among these – and forming the topics reviewed in this section – one has: the various proposals for novel extension-
based semantics, some of which have been discussed in Chapter 2, e.g., Ideal semantics [23, 24], Semi-stable semantics [6, 7], Prudent semantics [12]. A second
consideration concerns the extent to which intractability issues may be alleviated by
constructing efficient algorithmic approaches applicable to AFs which are restricted
in some way, e.g., by analogy with the known tractable case of *acyclic* topologies.

5.1 Novel extension-based semantics and their complexity

In this section we outline recent treatments of complexity in three of the developments of Dung's standard AF semantics: prudent, ideal, and semi-stable semantics.

We recall that the rationale underlying *prudent semantics* stems from the potential problematic side effects that might eventuate by regarding as collectively
acceptable, arguments $\{x, y\}$ for which x "indirectly attacks" y. An indirect attack
by x on y is present in $\langle \mathcal{A}, \mathcal{R} \rangle$ if "there exists a finite sequence $x_0, \ldots, x_{2n+1}$ such that
(1) $x = x_0$ and $y = x_{2n+1}$ and (2) for each $0 \le i < 2n$, $\langle x_i, x_{i+1} \rangle \in \mathcal{R}$" [22, p. 332].
It should be noted that this formulation, which we have quoted *verbatim*, presents
some ambiguity, which is significant from complexity-theoretic and semantic perspectives: it fails to distinguish "indirect attacks" in which no argument is repeated,
i.e., "simple paths"; from those in which *arguments* but not attacks may be repeated;
from those in which attacks may be repeated, e.g. the cases in Fig. 5.2.

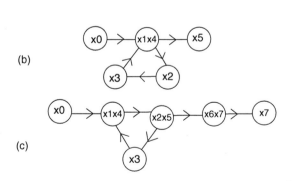

Fig. 5.2 Three possible forms of "indirect" attack – (a) Simple; (b) $x1 = x4$; (c) $\langle x1, x2 \rangle = \langle x4, x5 \rangle$

The concept of conflict-free set from [22], is replaced under the prudent semantics by that of *prudently conflict-free set*, i.e., one in which there is no indirect attack
between any two members. There are evident interpretative issues with cases (b) and

(c) in Fig. 5.2, however, the most natural interpretation (where an indirect attack is a simple path) has one significant computational drawback.

Fact 1 *Given $\langle A, \mathcal{R} \rangle$ and $S \subseteq A$ deciding if S is prudently conflict-free is coNP–complete even if S contains only two arguments.*

Proof. Immediate from the result of Lapaugh and Papadimitriou [35] which shows deciding the existence of a simple *even* length path between two specified arguments in a directed graph to be NP–complete. The extension to *odd* length simple path is trivial, so the lemma follows by observing that a prudently conflict-free set is one in which no simple odd length path is present between two arguments.

Noting the definitions of admissible set, preferred and stable extensions from [22] and the fact that conflict-freeness is an integral part of these, the result of Fact 1 immediately allows us to deduce that under the prudent semantics (so that "conflict-free set" becomes "prudently conflict-free") the respective verification problems are all coNP–complete. Complexity of credulous and sceptical acceptance under the prudent semantics has yet to be studied in depth. The intractability status of key decision problems in this semantics is predicated on the interpretation of "indirect attack" given by (a), i.e., as a simple path. These do not hold if repeated *attacks* – Fig 5.2(c) – are used: here polynomial time methods are available. The status of allowing repeated *arguments* – Fig 5.2(b) – is, to the authors' knowledge still open.

The *ideal semantics* were originally proposed with respect to ABFs, but have a natural formulation in AFs: $S \subseteq A$ is an ideal *set* within $\langle A, \mathcal{R} \rangle$ if S is both admissible and a subset of *every* set in $\mathcal{E}_{PR}(A, \mathcal{R})$; S is an ideal *extension* if it a maximal ideal set. Detailed studies of the complexity of ideal semantics in AFs are presented in [26, 27]. The treatment of complexity issues presented in these papers exploit a number of more advanced techniques, however, the hardness proofs continue to be built on the standard translation of CNF formulae to AFs. In terms of the canonical problems in Table 5.1, the verification problem (for ideal sets) is shown to be coNP-complete, placing this decision problem at the same level of complexity as the verification problem for preferred extensions. Arguably the most radical technique exploited – although widely applied in a number of earlier complexity-theoretic analyses – is the use of *randomized* reductions coupled with structural complexity results from [8, 9], as opposed to standard many-one reducibility ($\leq_m^p$) which features in all of the results discussed earlier.[10] Combining these elements, the verification problem (for ideal extensions) and credulous acceptance problems are shown to be complete for the (conjectured to be) subclass of P^{NP} in which oracle queries are *non-adaptive* (denoted $P_{||}^{NP}$). We note that the upper bounds from [26, 27] do not use randomized elements. This complexity class also arises in the known *lower bounds* for both credulous and sceptical acceptance in semi-stable semantics presented in [31]. These lower bounds again apply the structural characterizations of [8] (using $\leq_m^p$ reducibility, i.e., not randomized). Upper bounds, however, are Σ_2^p and Π_2^p, i.e., exact classifications of reasoning problems in semi-stable semantics is open.

---

[10] Relevant background is outlined in [27] and described in full in [26]. The actual "randomized" element is not explicit but arises from results of [43] for the satisfiability variant used.

5.2 Properties of restricted frameworks

The complexity lower bounds discussed above describe *worst-case* scenarios, i.e., the fact that, for example CA$_{PR}$ is NP–hard, does not imply that every algorithm on every instance will entail unrealistic computational overheads. As will be seen in Chapter 6, if the AF is acyclic, then all of the canonical decision problems of Table 5.1 have polynomial time solutions. In consequence a natural question to consider is whether other graph-theoretic restrictions also result in frameworks with efficient decision processes. Examining this question leads to two classes of results: positive outcomes of the form "decision problem L has a polynomial time algorithm in AFs satisfying some property P"; and negative classifications of the form "decision problem L in frameworks satisfying property P are no easier than the general case". Results of the first type extend (beyond acyclic frameworks) the range of AFs for which tractable solutions exist. Recent work has added to the class of such frameworks: *symmetric* AFs – those for which $\langle x,y \rangle \in \mathcal{R} \Leftrightarrow \langle y,x \rangle \in \mathcal{R}$ – in work of Coste-Marquis *et al.* [13]; *bipartite* AFs (those for which $\mathcal{A}$ may be partitioned into two conflict-free sets) [25]. Using the notion of "treewidth decomposition", see e.g., [4] a select number of problems whose instances are single AFs such as EX$_{ST}$, NE$_{PR}$ admit linear time algorithms given a treewidth decomposition of width k as part of the instance: the construction of these algorithms rely on a deep result (Courcelle's Theorem [14, 15]) demonstrating how efficient algorithms for testing graph-theoretic properties may be obtained given an appropriate logical description of the property (the so-called Monadic Second Order Logic) and a bounded treewidth decomposition of the graph. For more details on this approach and its application in AF settings we refer the reader to [2] and [25].

There are, however, a number of natural properties that fail to yield any reduction in complexity. Typically the approach adopted in proving such results is to demonstrate that frameworks with the property of interest are general enough to effectively "simulate" any framework, e.g., if S is admissible in $\langle \mathcal{A}, \mathcal{R} \rangle$ then $S \cup T$ is admissible in $\langle \mathcal{A} \cup \mathcal{B}, \mathcal{R}' \rangle$ where the latter AF has a particular property. Using such methods, [25] shows that no reduction in complexity arises in: k-partite AFs ($k \geq 3$); *planar* systems; and those in which no argument attacks or is attacked by more than two other arguments. This remains the case when all restrictions hold simultaneously.

We conclude this overview of recent work by returning to the issue of complexity in VAFs. In contrast to the class of positive cases that have been identified with AFs, the situation with VAFs turns outs out to be far more negative. The most extreme indication of this status is the following result of [25].

Fact 2

a. SBA *is* NP–*complete and* OBA *is* coNP–*complete even if the underlying graph is a* binary tree *and every* $v \in \mathcal{V}$ *is associated with* at most *three arguments*.

b. *For every* $\varepsilon > 0$ SBA *is* NP–*complete and* OBA *is* coNP–*complete even if the underlying graph is a* binary tree *and* $|\mathcal{V}| \leq |\mathcal{A}|^{\varepsilon}$.

Both constructions use reductions from variants of 3-SAT/3-UNSAT, however, these differ in a number of ways from the standard translation (which is clearly is not a binary tree). The situation highlighted by results such as Fact 2 provides further indications that the nature of SBA/OBA in VAFs, while superficially similar to, is in fact radically different from that of CA/SA in AFs.

6 Conclusions and Further Research

In this final section we outline some areas of research which offer a variety of challenging directions through which the algorithmic and complexity foundations of abstract argumentation may be further advanced. We stress that our aim is to focus on general areas rather than particular open questions as such: the reader who has followed the earlier exposition will have noted that a number of specific open issues have already been raised in the text.

6.1 Average case properties

As discussed in Section 5.2, the lower bounds on problem complexity are worst-case, so leaving open the possibility that feasible algorithms may be available in suitable contexts. In addition to the use of restrictions on the form of instances one other approach that has been widely considered in the theory of algorithms is the study of *average-case complexity*. Underpinning this approach one considers a probability distribution, μ, on instances of a decision problem – often, but not invariably so, μ is the uniform distribution whereby each instance is equally likely, proceeding to define the average-case run time of an algorithm P on instances of size n of L as $\sum_{x \in I(n)} \mu(x)\rho(P,x)$ where $\rho(P,x)$ is the run-time of P on instance x. Formal definitions of average-case complexity classes may be found in [36]. To date surprisingly little work has been carried out concerning the application of average-case methods to decision problems in AFs either in terms of algorithmic development or in considering the limitations of such approaches. It remains open to what extent techniques such as those applied to other intractable problems, e.g., [1] for the NP–complete Hamiltonian cycle problem, or [46] for CNF satisfiability could be replicated in AF settings. Of some relevance to such approaches are so-called "phase-transition" effects, which received much attention in the mid-late 1990s as potential indicators of factors separating tractable and intractable classes of problem instances, e.g., the studies of random CNF-SAT from [37, 40]. Analytic studies of such effects appears to indicate connections between suitable witnessing structures, e.g., satisfying assignment, being present "almost certainly" and the performance of algorithms to identify such structures. Of some interest in the context of AF semantics are the results of [41, 17] which give conditions ensuring that a random AF "almost certainly" has a stable extension. There has as yet, however, been no detailed study of the implications of these results for fast on average methods for identifying or enumerating stable extensions. In the same way that the analyses of [41, 17] relate to the existence of stable extensions in AFs, it would be of some interest to examine to consider existence properties of other solution structures in random AFs and algorithmic consequences.

6.2 Approaches to dynamic updates

An important feature of the argumentation forms discussed so far is that, in practice, these are not *static* systems: typically an AF, $\langle \mathcal{A}, \mathcal{R} \rangle$, represents only a "snapshot" of the environment, and, as further facts, information and opinions emerge the form of the initial view may change significantly in order to accommodate these. For example, additional arguments may have to be considered so changing $\mathcal{A}$; existing attacks may cease to apply and new attacks (arising from changes to $\mathcal{A}$) come into force. It is clear that accounting for such dynamic aspects raises a number of issues in terms of assessing the acceptability status of individual arguments. As with the study of average-case properties, the treatment of algorithms and complexity issues relating to determining argument status in dynamically changing environments has been somewhat neglected. Thus, given $\langle \mathcal{A}, \mathcal{R} \rangle$ and $S \subseteq \mathcal{A}$ for which $S \in \mathcal{E}_s(\langle \mathcal{A}, \mathcal{R} \rangle)$ according to some semantics s, natural decision questions are: does $x \in S$ continue to be credulously accepted (w.r.t. to semantics s) in the AF $\langle \mathcal{B}, \mathcal{S} \rangle$ where $\mathcal{B}$ results by removing some arguments from $\mathcal{A}$ and replacing these; similarly $\mathcal{T}$ modifies the attack relation $\mathcal{R}$.

Summary

Complexity issues provide an important foundational element of the formal computational theory of abstract argumentation. Our review of the preceding pages is intended to give a flavour of the class of questions of interest and an appreciation of the techniques that have been brought to bear in addressing these. While some notable progress has been achieved since the appearance of [22] – particularly in understanding of decision properties of the standard semantics and the canonical problems of Table 5.1, nevertheless a significant number of areas and potential analytic tools originating from complexity-theoretic studies, remain unexplored.

References

1. D. Angluin and L. Valiant. Fast probabilistic algorithms for hamiltonian circuits and matchings. *Jnl. of Comp. and System Sci.*, 18:82–93, 1979.
2. S. Arnborg, J. Lagergren, and D. Seese. Easy problems for tree-decomposable graphs. *Jnl. of Algorithms*, 12:308–340, 1991.

3. T. J. M. Bench-Capon, S. Doutre, and P. E. Dunne. Audiences in argumentation frameworks. *Artificial Intelligence*, 171:42–71, 2007.

4. H. L. Bodlaender. A partial k-arboretum of graphs with bounded treewidth. *Theoretical Computer Science*, 209:1–45, 1998.

5. A. Bondarenko, P. Dung, R. Kowalski, and F. Toni. An abstract, argumentation-theoretic approach to default reasoning. *Artificial Intelligence*, 93:63–101, 1997.

6. M. Caminada. Semi-stable semantics. In P. E. Dunne and T. J. M. Bench-Capon, editors, *Proc. 1st Int. Conf. on Computational Models of Argument*, volume 144 of *FAIA*, pages 121–130. IOS Press, 2006.

7. M. Caminada. An algorithm for computing semi-stable semantics. In *Proc. of ECSQARU 2007, 9th European Conference on Symbolic and Quantitative Approaches to Reasoning with Uncertainty*, pages 222–234, Hammamet, Tunisia, 2007.

8. R. Chang and J. Kadin. On computing Boolean connectives of characteristic functions. *Math. Syst. Theory*, 28:173–198, 1995.

9. R. Chang, J. Kadin, and P. Rohatgi. On unique satisfiability and the threshold behavior of randomised reductions. *Jnl. of Comp. and Syst. Sci.*, pages 359–373, 1995.

10. S. A. Cook. The complexity of theorem-proving procedures. In *STOC '71: Proc. of the 3rd Annual ACM Symposium on Theory of Computing*, pages 151–158, New York, NY, USA, 1971. ACM.

11. S. A. Cook and R. A. Reckhow. The relative complexity of propositional proof systems. *Journal of Symbolic Logic*, 44(1):36–50, 1979.

12. S. Coste-Marquis, C. Devred, and P. Marquis. Prudent semantics for argumentation frameworks. In *Proc. 17th IEEE Intnl.Conf. on Tools with AI (ICTAI 2005)*, pages 568–572. IEEE Computer Society, 2005.

13. S. Coste-Marquis, C. Devred, and P. Marquis. Symmetric argumentation frameworks. In L. Godo, editor, *Proc. 8th European Conf. on Symbolic and Quantitative Approaches to Reasoning With Uncertainty (ECSQARU)*, volume 3571 of *LNAI*, pages 317–328. Springer-Verlag, 2005.

14. B. Courcelle. The monadic second-order logic of graphs. I. recognizable sets of finite graphs. *Information and Computation*, 85(1):12–75, 1990.

15. B. Courcelle. The monadic second-order logic of graphs III: tree-decompositions, minor and complexity issues. *Informatique Théorique et Applications*, 26:257–286, 1992.

16. N. Creignou. The class of problems that are linearly equivalent to satisfiability or a uniform method for proving np-completeness. *Theoretical Computer Science*, 145(1-2):111–145, 1995.

17. W. F. de la Vega. Kernels in random graphs. *Discrete Math.*, 82(2):213–217, 1990.

18. Y. Dimopoulos, B. Nebel, and F. Toni. Preferred arguments are harder to compute than stable extensions. In D. Thomas, editor, *Proc. of the 16th International Joint Conference on Artificial Intelligence (IJCAI-99-Vol1)*, pages 36–43, San Francisco, 1999. Morgan Kaufmann Publishers.

19. Y. Dimopoulos, B. Nebel, and F. Toni. Finding admissible and preferred arguments can be very hard. In A. G. Cohn, F. Giunchiglia, and B. Selman, editors, *KR2000: Principles of Knowledge Representation and Reasoning*, pages 53–61, San Francisco, 2000. Morgan Kaufmann.

20. Y. Dimopoulos, B. Nebel, and F. Toni. On the computational complexity of assumption-based argumentation for default reasoning. *Artificial Intelligence*, 141:55–78, 2002.

21. Y. Dimopoulos and A. Torres. Graph theoretical structures in logic programs and default theories. *Theoretical Computer Science*, 170:209–244, 1996.

22. P. M. Dung. On the acceptability of arguments and its fundamental role in nonmonotonic reasoning, logic programming, and N-person games. *Artificial Intelligence*, 77:321–357, 1995.

23. P. M. Dung, P. Mancarella, and F. Toni. A dialectical procedure for sceptical assumption-based argumentation. In P. E. Dunne and T. J. M. Bench-Capon, editors, *Proc. 1st Int. Conf. on Computational Models of Argument*, volume 144 of *FAIA*, pages 145–156. IOS Press, 2006.

24. P. M. Dung, P. Mancarella, and F. Toni. Computing ideal sceptical argumentation. *Artificial Intelligence*, 171:642–674, 2007.

25. P. E. Dunne. Computational properties of argument systems satisfying graph-theoretic constraints. *Artificial Intelligence*, 171:701–729, 2007.
26. P. E. Dunne. The computational complexity of ideal semantics. Technical Report ULCS-08-015, Dept. of Comp. Sci., Univ. of Liverpool, August 2008.
27. P. E. Dunne. The computational complexity of ideal semantics I: abstract argumentation frameworks. In *Proc. 2nd Int. Conf. on Computational Models of Argument*, volume 172 of *FAIA*, pages 147–158. IOS Press, 2008.
28. P. E. Dunne and T. J. M. Bench-Capon. Coherence in finite argument systems. *Artificial Intelligence*, 141:187–203, 2002.
29. P. E. Dunne and T. J. M. Bench-Capon. Two party immediate response disputes: properties and efficiency. *Artificial Intelligence*, 149:221–250, 2003.
30. P. E. Dunne and T. J. M. Bench-Capon. Complexity in value-based argument systems. In *Proc. 9th JELIA*, volume 3229 of *LNAI*, pages 360–371. Springer-Verlag, 2004.
31. P. E. Dunne and M. Caminada. Computational complexity of semi-stable semantics in abstract argumentation frameworks. In *Proc. 11th JELIA*, volume 5293 of *LNAI*, pages 153–165. Springer-Verlag, 2008.
32. A. Fraenkel. Planar kernel and grundy with $d \leq 3$, $d_{out} \leq 2$, $d_{in} \leq 2$ are NP–complete. *Discrete Appl. Math.*, 3(4):257–262, 1981.
33. M. R. Garey and D. S. Johnson. *Computers and Intractability: A Guide to the Theory of NP-Completeness*. W. H. Freeman: New York, 1979.
34. G. Gentzen. Investigations into logical deductions, 1935. In M. E. Szabo, editor, *The Collected Papers of Gerhard Gentzen*, pages 68–131. North-Holland Publishing Co., Amsterdam, 1969.
35. A. S. Lapaugh and C. H. Papadimitriou. The even path problem for graphs and digraphs. *Networks*, 14(4):597–614, 1984.
36. L. Levin. Average case complete problems. *SIAM J. Comput.*, 15:285–286, 1986.
37. D. Mitchell, B. Selman, and H. Levesque. Hard and easy distributions of sat problems. In *Proc. AAAI-92*, pages 459–465. AAAI/MIT Press, 1992.
38. R. C. Moore. Semantical considerations on nonmonotonic logic. *Artificial Intelligence*, 25:75–94, 1985.
39. R. Reiter. A logic for default reasoning. *Artificial Intelligence*, 13:81–132, 1980.
40. B. Selman, H. Levesque, and D. Mitchell. A new method for solving hard satisfiability problems. In *Proc. 10th National Conf. on Art. Intellig.*, pages 440–446, 1992.
41. I. Tomescu. Almost all digraphs have a kernel. *Discrete Math.*, 84(2):181–192, 1990.
42. A. Urquhart. The complexity of Gentzen systems for propositional logic. *Theoretical Computer Science*, 66(1):87–97, 1989.
43. L. G. Valiant and V. V. Vazirani. NP is as easy as detecting unique solutions. *Theoretical Computer Science*, 47:85–93, 1986.
44. G. Vreeswijk and H. Prakken. Credulous and sceptical argument games for preferred semantics. In *Proc. of JELIA'2000, The 7th European Workshop on Logic for Artificial Intelligence.*, pages 224–238, Berlin, 2000. Springer LNAI 1919, Springer Verlag.
45. C. Wrathall. Complete sets and the polynomial-time hierarchy. *Theoretical Computer Science*, 3:23–33, 1976.
46. L. Wu and C. Tang. Solving the satisfiability problem by using randomized approach. *Inf. Proc. Letters*, 41:187–190, 1992.

Chapter 6
Proof Theories and Algorithms for Abstract Argumentation Frameworks

Sanjay Modgil and Martin Caminada

1 Introduction

Previous chapters have focussed on abstract argumentation frameworks and properties of sets of arguments defined under various extension-based semantics. The main focus of this chapter is on more procedural, proof-theoretic and algorithmic aspects of argumentation. In particular, Chapter 2 describes properties of extensions of a Dung argumentation framework $\langle \mathcal{A}, \mathcal{R} \rangle$ under various semantics. In this context a number of questions naturally arise:

1. For a given semantics s, "global" questions concerning the existence and construction of extensions can be addressed:

   a. Does an extension exist?
   b. Give an extension (it does not matter which, just give one)
   c. Give all extensions.

2. For a given semantics s, "local" questions concerning the existence and construction of extensions, relative to a set $A \subseteq \mathcal{A}$ can be addressed. Note that it is often the case that $|A| = 1$, in which case the member of A is called the query argument.

   a. Is A contained in an extension ? (Credulous membership question.)
   b. Is A contained in all extensions ? (Sceptical membership question.)
   c. Is A attacked by an extension?
   d. Is A attacked by all extensions?
   e. Give an extension containing A.

Sanjay Modgil
Department of Computer Science, King's College London, e-mail: `sanjay.modgil@kcl.ac.uk`

Martin Caminada
Interdisciplinary Lab for Intelligent and Adaptive Systems, University of Luxembourg e-mail: `martin.caminada@uni.lu`

I. Rahwan, G. R. Simari (eds.), *Argumentation in Artificial Intelligence*,   105
DOI 10.1007/978-0-387-98197-0_6, © Springer Science+Business Media, LLC 2009

   f. Give all extensions containing A.

   g. Give an extension that attacks A.

   h. Give all extensions that attack A.

In this chapter, procedures will be described for answering a selection of the above questions with respect to finite argumentation frameworks $\langle A, \mathcal{R} \rangle$ (in which A is finite). Notice that for some semantics, such as the grounded and preferred semantics, extensions always exist, so that 1a will be answered in the positive for any framework. Also, for the grounded semantics, at most one extension exists, so that questions distinguished by reference to 'an' or 'all' extensions are equivalent (e.g., questions 2a and 2b).

Sections 2 and 3 will introduce some key concepts underpinning the approaches that we will use in the description of proof theories and algorithms. Sections 4 - 6 will then focus on application of these approaches to the core semantics defined by Dung [13]; namely grounded, preferred and stable.

Broadly speaking, two approaches will be presented. Firstly, Section 2 formally describes the argument graph *labelling* approach that was originally proposed by Pollock [23], and has more recently been the subject of renewed analysis and investigation [5, 6, 25, 27]. The basic idea is that the status assignment to arguments defined by the extension-based approach (see Chapter 2), can be directly defined through assignment of labels to the arguments (nodes) in the framework's corresponding argument graph. Section 2 provides formal underpinnings for the definition of argument graph labelling algorithms that are used to address a selection of the above questions in Sections 4 - 6.

Section 3 then describes a framework for *argument game* based proof theories [9, 16, 17, 28]. The inherently dialectical nature of argumentation lends itself to formulation of argument games in which a proponent starts with an initial argument to be tested, and then an opponent and the proponent successively attack each other's arguments. The initial argument provably has a certain status if the proponent has a winning strategy whereby he can win irrespective of the moves made by the opponent. In Sections 4 - 6 we describe specific games, emphasising the way in which the rules of each specific game correspond to the semantics they are meant to capture.

2 Labellings

In this section the labelling approach (based on its formulation in [5, 6]) is briefly reviewed. Given an argumentation framework $AF = \langle A, \mathcal{R} \rangle$, a labelling assigns to each argument exactly one label, which can be either IN, OUT or UNDEC. The label IN indicates that the argument is justified, OUT indicates that the argument is overruled, and UNDEC indicates that the status of the argument is undecided.

Definition 6.1. Let $\langle A, \mathcal{R} \rangle$ be an argumentation framework.

- A labelling is a total function $\mathcal{L} : A \mapsto \{\text{IN}, \text{OUT}, \text{UNDEC}\}$

- We define: $\text{in}(\mathcal{L}) = \{x | \mathcal{L}(x) = \text{IN}\}$; $\text{out}(\mathcal{L}) = \{x | \mathcal{L}(x) = \text{OUT}\}$; $\text{undec}(\mathcal{L}) = \{x | \mathcal{L}(x) = \text{UNDEC}\}$

Notice that from hereon, we may represent a labelling $\mathcal{L}$ as a triple of the form $(\text{in}(\mathcal{L}), \text{out}(\mathcal{L}), \text{undec}(\mathcal{L}))$.

We now define what it is for an argument to be assigned a legal labelling:

Definition 6.2. Let $\mathcal{L}$ be a labelling for $\langle \mathcal{A}, \mathcal{R} \rangle$ and $x \in \mathcal{A}$

- x is legally IN iff x is labelled IN and every y that attacks x $(y\mathcal{R}x)$ is labelled OUT
- x is legally OUT iff x is labelled OUT and there is at least one y that attacks x and y is labelled IN
- x is legally UNDEC iff x is labelled UNDEC, there is no y that attacks x such that y is labelled IN, and it is not the case that: for all y, y attacks x implies y is labelled OUT.

The rules defining legal labelling assignments encode one's intuitive understanding of the status assignments defined by the extension-based semantics and their use of the reinstatement principle, as described in Chapter 2. An argument x is IN only if all its attackers are OUT, and each attacker is OUT only if it is itself attacked by an argument that is IN. Thus, the arguments that are IN in a legal labelling correspond to a single extension. It is sometimes not possible to obtain a labelling where each argument is either legally IN or legally OUT; consider for example an argumentation framework with just a single argument that attacks itself. This is why we need a third label UNDEC, which basically means that there is insufficient ground to explicitly justify the argument and insufficient ground to explicitly overrule the argument. Notice that from Definition 6.2 it follows that x is legally UNDEC iff it is labelled UNDEC, and at least one y that attacks x is labelled UNDEC, and no y attacking x is labelled IN.

Definition 6.3. For $l \in \{\text{IN}, \text{OUT}, \text{UNDEC}\}$ an argument x is said to be illegally l iff x is labelled l, and it is not legally l.

- An admissible labelling $\mathcal{L}$ is a labelling without arguments that are illegally IN and without arguments that are illegally OUT.
- A complete labelling $\mathcal{L}$ is an admissible labelling without arguments that are illegally UNDEC

Notice that the additional requirement on complete labellings corresponds intuitively to Chapter 2's characterisation of a complete extension as a fixed point of a framework AF's characteristic function $\mathcal{F}_{AF}$. Since the grounded and preferred extensions of a framework are the minimal, respectively maximal, fixed points (complete extensions) of a framework, then as one would expect, grounded and preferred labellings are given by complete labellings that minimise, respectively maximise, the arguments that are made legally IN. A stable labelling is a complete labelling in which all arguments are either legally IN or legally OUT, and hence no argument is UNDEC.

Definition 6.4. Let $\mathcal{L}$ be a complete labelling. Then:

- $\mathcal{L}$ is a grounded labelling iff there there does not exist a complete labelling $\mathcal{L}'$ such that $\mathrm{in}(\mathcal{L}') \subset \mathrm{in}(\mathcal{L})$ [1]
- $\mathcal{L}$ is a preferred labelling iff there there does not exist a complete labelling $\mathcal{L}'$ such that $\mathrm{in}(\mathcal{L}') \supset \mathrm{in}(\mathcal{L})$
- $\mathcal{L}$ is a stable labelling iff $\mathrm{undec}(\mathcal{L}) = \emptyset$

In [6], the following theorem is shown to hold:

Theorem 6.1. *Let* $AF = \langle \mathcal{A}, \mathcal{R} \rangle$ *be an argumentation framework, and* $E \subseteq \mathcal{A}$*. For* $s \in \{admissible, complete, grounded, preferred, stable\}$:

E *is an s extension of AF iff there exists an s labelling* $\mathcal{L}$ *with* $\mathrm{in}(\mathcal{L}) = E$ [2]

In Sections 4 - 6 we will describe algorithms that compute labellings and so address a subset of the questions enumerated in Section 1. We conclude this section with an example:

Example 6.1. Consider the framework in Figure 6.1. There exists three complete labellings: 1. $(\emptyset, \emptyset, \{a,b,c,d,e\})$; 2. $(\{a\}, \{b\}, \{c,d,e\})$; and 3. $(\{b,d\}, \{a,c,e\}, \emptyset)$. 1 is the grounded labelling, 2 and 3 are preferred, and 3 is also stable.

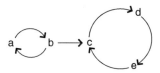

Fig. 6.1 An argumentation framework

3 Argument Games

In general, proof theories license the way in which pieces of information can be articulated in order to prove a fact. They therefore provide a basis for algorithm development, and proofs constructed according to these theories provide explanations as to why a given fact is believed to be true. For example, a proof that argument x is in an admissible extension, would consist of showing *how* one can establish the existence of such an extension, rather than simply identifying the extension. Intuitively,

---

[1] Since every framework has a unique minimal fixed point, one could alternatively define $\mathcal{L}$ to be a grounded labelling iff for each complete labelling $\mathcal{L}'$ it holds that $\mathrm{in}(\mathcal{L}) \subset \mathrm{in}(\mathcal{L}')$

[2] Note that for $s \neq$ admissible there is a 1-1 mapping between s extensions and s labellings. An admissible extension may have more than one admissible labelling. For example, the admissible extension $\{c\}$, of $c \rightarrow \underline{b}$, $\underline{c} \rightarrow a$, has two admissible labellings: $(\{c\},\{b\},\{a\})$ and $(\{c\},\{b,a\},\emptyset)$.

one would need to show how to *defend* x by showing that for every argument y that is put forward (moved) as an attacker of x, one must move an argument z that attacks y, and then subsequently show how any such z can be reinstated against attacks (in the same way that z reinstates x). The arguments moved can thus be organised into a graph of attacking arguments that constitutes an explanation as to why x is in an admissible extension.

The *process* of moving arguments and counter-arguments can be implemented as an algorithm [27]. In this chapter we follow the approach of [9, 14, 16, 17, 26, 28] and present the moving of arguments as 2-person dialogue games that provide a natural way in which to lay out and understand the algorithms that implement them. To be sure, the actual algorithms themselves, should, except for didactic purposes, not be implemented as dialogue games, but rather as monological procedures (or *methods* in OO-languages) that are called recursively.

A dialogue game is played by two players, PRO (for "proponent") and OPP (for "opponent"), each of which are referred to as the other's 'counterpart'. A game begins with PRO moving an initial argument x that it wants to put to the test. OPP and PRO then take turns in moving arguments that attack their counterpart's last move. From hereon:

> a sequence of moves in which each player moves against its counterpart's last move is referred to as a *dispute*.

If the last move in a dispute is by player Pl, and Pl's counterpart cannot respond to this last move, then Pl is said to win the dispute. If a dispute with initial argument x is won by PRO, we call the dispute a *line of defense* for x.

The rules of the game encode restrictions on the legality of moves in a dispute, and different sets of rules capture the different semantics under which justification of the initial argument x is to be shown, by effectively establishing when OPP or PRO run out of legal moves. In general, however, a player can backtrack to a counterpart's previous move and initiate a new dispute. Consider the dispute $a_{PRO} - b_{OPP} - c_{PRO} - d_{OPP} - e_{PRO} - f_{OPP}$ won by OPP ($x_{Pl} - y_{Pl'}$ denotes player Pl' moving argument y against counterpart Pl's argument x). PRO must then try and backtrack to move an argument against either b_{OPP} or d_{OPP} and establish an alternative line of defense for a. Suppose such a line of defense $a_{PRO} - b_{OPP} - g_{PRO}$. Then OPP can backtrack and try an alternative line of attack moving h against a, so that PRO must now try and win the newly initiated dispute $a_{PRO} - h_{OPP}$. Thus, the 'playing field' of a game — the data structure on the basis of which argument games are played — can be represented by an argumentation framework's induced *dispute tree*, in which every branch from root to leaf is a dispute:

Definition 6.5. Let $AF = \langle \mathcal{A}, \mathcal{R} \rangle$ be an argumentation framework, and let $a \in \mathcal{A}$. The dispute tree induced by a in AF is a tree T of arguments, such that T's root node is a, and $\forall x, y \in \mathcal{A}$: x is a child of y in T iff $x\mathcal{R}y$.

Figure 6.2i) shows an argumentation framework, and part of the tree induced by a is shown in Figure 6.2ii). Notice that multiple instances of arguments are individuated by numerical indicies. Any game played by PRO and OPP in which PRO

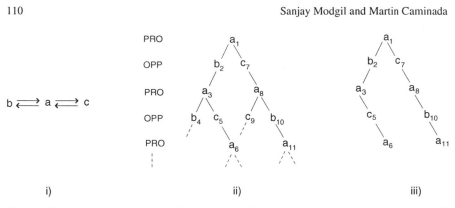

Fig. 6.2 i) shows an argumentation framework, and ii) shows the dispute tree induced in a. iii) shows the dispute tree induced under the assumption that OPP cannot repeat moves in the same dispute (branch of the tree)

attempts to show that a is justified, must necessarily involve the submission of attacking arguments conforming to some sub-tree of the induced tree in Figure 6.2ii). In particular, PRO must show that it fully fulfills its burden of proof, in response to OPP who fully fulfills its burden of attack. In other words, OPP moves *all* ys that attack an x moved by PRO, and each such y must in turn be responded to by PRO moving *at least one* x' that attacks y. This does of course capture the reinstatement principle used to define the extensions of an argumentation framework, and correlates with Section 2's definition of legal labellings and the extensions they define[3]. In the context of a game, this is captured by the notion of a *winning strategy* for an argument. Notice that in the following definition we refer to the notion of a *sub-dispute d'* of a dispute d, which, intuitively is any sub-sequence of d that starts with the same initial argument as d.

Definition 6.6. Let $AF = \langle \mathcal{A}, \mathcal{R} \rangle$, T the dispute tree induced by a in AF, and T' a sub-tree of T. Then T' is a winning strategy for a iff:

1. The set $D_{T'}$ of disputes in T' is a non-empty finite set such that each dispute $d \in D_{T'}$ is finite and is won by PRO (terminates in an argument moved by PRO)
2. $\forall d \in D_{T'}$, $\forall d'$ such that d' is some sub-dispute of d and the last move in d' is an argument x played by PRO, then for any y such that $y\mathcal{R}x$, there is a $d'' \in D_{T'}$ such that $d' - y_{OPP}$ is a sub-dispute of d''.

If PRO plays moves as described in a winning strategy sub-tree, then PRO is guaranteed to win.

As stated earlier, the rules of a game encode restrictions on the arguments a player can legally move in a dispute in order to attack its counterpart's argument. These restrictions vary according to the semantics of interest, and are encoded in a legal move function:

---

[3] Recall that x is legally IN iff *all* ys that attack an x are legally OUT, and each such y is legally OUT iff there is *at least one* x' attacking y that is legally IN

Definition 6.7. Let $AF = \langle \mathcal{A}, \mathcal{R} \rangle$, T the dispute tree induced by a in AF. Let D_T be the set of all disputes in T. Then ϕ is a legal move function such that $\phi : D_T \mapsto 2^{\mathcal{A}}$.

Given a dispute tree T induced by a, the legal move function ϕ for a semantics s, prunes T to obtain the sub-tree T' of T that we call the ϕ tree induced by a. T' is the playing field of the game for semantics s. Thus, we define a ϕ-*winning strategy for a* [9, 17] as a sub-tree of the ϕ dispute tree induced by a, in the same way as Definition 6.6, except that we replace 'for any x such that $x\mathcal{R}y$' in condition 2, with 'for any x that OPP can ϕ legally move against y'. Intuitively, ϕ is defined such that a is in an admissible extension that conforms to the semantics s iff there is a ϕ-winning strategy for a in the ϕ tree induced by a, where the arguments moved by PRO in the ϕ-winning strategy are conflict free (recall that an admissible extension must contain no arguments that attack each other).

For example, consider games whose legal move function ϕ prohibits OPP from repeating arguments in the same dispute. Figure 6.2iii) shows the ϕ-*dispute tree* that is a sub-tree of the *dispute tree* induced by a (Figure 6.2ii)). After PRO plays a_6, OPP cannot backtrack and extend the dispute $d = a_1 - b_2 - a_3$ by moving b against a_3, since b has already been moved by OPP in d. Similarly, OPP cannot backtrack to move c against a_8 in order to extend $d' = a_1 - c_7 - a_8$. Note also that both $D_{T_1} = \{d_1 = a_1 - b_2 - a_3 - c_5 - a_6\}$ and $D_{T_2} = \{d_2 = a_1 - c_7 - a_8 - b_{10} - a_{11}\}$ are winning strategies. In the former case, consider the sub-dispute $d'_1 = a_1 - b_2 - a_3$ of d_1. OPP can legally move c against a_3, but there is a dispute in D_{T_1} that extends d'_1 (d_1 itself) in which PRO moves against OPP's move of c.

To summarise, suppose PRO wishes to show that x is a member of an extension E under the semantics s. The associated legal move function ϕ for s defines some ϕ-dispute tree T that is a sub-tree of the dispute tree induced by x, and defines all possible disputes the players can play in a game. The ϕ-dispute tree T should be such that: $x \in E$ iff there is a ϕ-winning strategy T' in T, such that the arguments moved by PRO in T' do not attack each other (are conflict free). A ϕ-winning strategy is a set of disputes won by PRO in which PRO has fulfilled its burden of proof by countering all possible ϕ-legal moves of OPP.

4 Grounded Semantics

For any argumentation framework, there is guaranteed to be exactly one grounded extension. Hence, questions 1b, 1c and 2a - 2h can all be addressed by construction of a framework's grounded extension. In Section 4.1 we present an algorithm that generates the grounded labelling of an argumentation framework. Section 4.2 then describes an argument game for deciding whether a given argument is in the grounded extension, thus providing an alternative way for addressing the questions 2a and 2b.

The grounded semantics places the highest burden of proof on membership of the extension that it defines. This equates with Chapter 2's definition of the extension as the *least* fixed point of a framework AF's characteristic function $\mathcal{F}_{AF}$ (i.e., the smallest admissible E that contains exactly those arguments that are acceptable w.r.t. E). The extra burden of proof is intuitively captured by the fact that in defending x's membership of the grounded extension E, one must 'appeal to' some argument other than x itself. That is to say, for any y such that y attacks x, y is attacked by at least one $z_1 \in E$ such that $z_1 \neq x$, and in turn, z_1 must be reinstated against any attack, by some $z_2 \in E$ such that $z_2 \neq x$, $z_2 \neq z_1$, and so on. This property is exploited by both the algorithm for generating the grounded labelling, and argument games for the grounded semantics. The property is relatively straightforward to show given Chapter 2's description of how, starting with the empty set, iteration of the characteristic function yields the grounded extension. We have that $x \in \mathcal{F}_{AF}^i$ iff for every attack on x, x is reinstated by some $z \in \mathcal{F}_{AF}^j$, where $z \neq x$ and $j < i$.

4.1 A labelling algorithm for the Grounded Semantics

An algorithm for generating the grounded labelling starts by assigning IN to all arguments that are not attacked, and then iteratively: OUT is assigned to any argument that is attacked by an argument that has just been made IN, and then IN to those arguments *all* of whose attackers are OUT. Thus, the arguments assigned IN on each iteration, are those that are reinstated by the arguments assigned IN on the previous iteration. The iteration continues until no more new arguments are made IN or OUT. Any arguments that remain unlabelled are then assigned UNDEC. One can straightforwardly show that the algorithm is sound and complete since it effectively mimics construction of the grounded extension through iteration of a framework's characteristic function. The algorithm for generating the grounded labelling $\mathcal{L}_G$ of a framework $\langle \mathcal{A}, \mathcal{R} \rangle$ is presented more formally below, in which we use Section 2's representation of a labelling $\mathcal{L}$ as a triple $(\text{in}(\mathcal{L}), \text{out}(\mathcal{L}), \text{undec}(\mathcal{L}))$.

Algorithm 6.1 Algorithm for Grounded Labelling

1: $\mathcal{L}_0 = (\emptyset, \emptyset, \emptyset)$
2: **repeat**
3:      $\text{in}(\mathcal{L}_{i+1}) = \text{in}(\mathcal{L}_i) \cup \{x \mid x \text{ is not labelled in } \mathcal{L}_i, \text{ and } \forall y : \text{if } y\mathcal{R}x \text{ then } y \in \text{out}(\mathcal{L}_i) \}$
4:      $\text{out}(\mathcal{L}_{i+1}) = \text{out}(\mathcal{L}_i) \cup \{x \mid x \text{ is not labelled in } \mathcal{L}_i, \text{ and } \exists y : y\mathcal{R}x \text{ and } y \in \text{in}(\mathcal{L}_{i+1}) \}$
5: **until** $\mathcal{L}_{i+1} = \mathcal{L}_i$
6: $\mathcal{L}_G = (\text{in}(\mathcal{L}_i), \text{out}(\mathcal{L}_i), \mathcal{A} - (\text{in}(\mathcal{L}_i) \cup \text{out}(\mathcal{L}_i)))$

Consider the following example framework:

$$a \rightarrow b \rightarrow c \, , d \rightleftarrows e$$

$\mathcal{L}_1 = (\{a\}, \{b\}, \emptyset), \mathcal{L}_2 = (\{a,c\}, \{b\}, \emptyset), \mathcal{L}_3 = \mathcal{L}_2$ and so $\mathcal{L}_G = (\{a,c\}, \{b\}, \{d,e\})$.

Finally, notice that the algorithm presented here can be made more efficient in a number of ways. For example, when assigning IN to arguments in line 3, checking whether all attackers are OUT can be made more efficient by giving each argument a counter `attackers-out` that represents the number of attackers that are labelled OUT. Since all arguments are initially unlabelled, this counter is set to zero before the actual labelling begins. Every time that an argument is labelled OUT, it sends a message to each of the arguments that it attacks to increase its variable `attackers-out`. Evidently, if this variable equals the number of attackers, the attacked argument can be labelled IN.

4.2 Argument games for the Grounded Semantics

We have discussed how, in defending an argument x's membership of the grounded extension, one must not loop back to x itself, and how the same restriction applies to any argument moved in x's line of defence. Intuitively, this is captured by a legal move function ϕ_{G_1} that prohibits PRO from repeating arguments it has already moved in a dispute.

Definition 6.8. Given $\langle A, \mathcal{R} \rangle$, a dispute d such that x is the last argument in d, and PRO(d) the arguments moved by PRO in d, then ϕ_{G_1} is a legal move function such that:

- If d is of odd length (next move is by OPP) then $\phi_{G_1}(d) = \{ y \mid y\mathcal{R}x \}$
- If d is of even length (next move is by PRO) then:

$$\phi_{G_1}(d) = \{ y \mid$$
$$\qquad 1.\ y\mathcal{R}x$$
$$\qquad 2.\ y \notin \mathrm{PRO}(d)$$
$$\}$$

Theorem 6.2. *Let $AF = \langle A, \mathcal{R} \rangle$ be a finite argumentation framework. Then, there exists a ϕ_{G_1}-winning strategy T for x such that the set PRO(T) of arguments moved by PRO in T is conflict free, iff x is in the grounded extension of AF.*

One can give an intuitive proof of Theorem 6.2 by appealing to the correspondence between the grounded extension and grounded labelling of an argumentation framework (see Theorem 6.1). That is to say, by showing that:

1. Let T be a ϕ_{G_1}-winning strategy for x such that $PRO(T)$ is conflict free. Then there is a grounded labelling $\mathcal{L}$ with $\mathcal{L}(x) = \mathrm{IN}$.
2. Let $\mathcal{L}$ be a labelling with $\mathcal{L}(x) = \mathrm{IN}$. Then there exists a ϕ_{G_1}-winning strategy for x such that $PRO(T)$ is conflict free.

Proof of the above correspondences can be found in [21].

Consider the example framework in Figure 6.3i). Part of the dispute tree induced by a is shown in Figure 6.3ii), and the ϕ_{G_1} dispute tree induced by a is shown in Figure 6.3iii). Observe that $\{(a_1 - b_2 - c_3 - d_4 - e_6)\}$ is a ϕ_{G_1}-winning strategy for a (a is in the grounded extension $\{a, c, e\}$). Finally, consider the example framework in Figure 6.3iv). In this case the ϕ_{G_1}-winning strategy for a consists of two disputes:

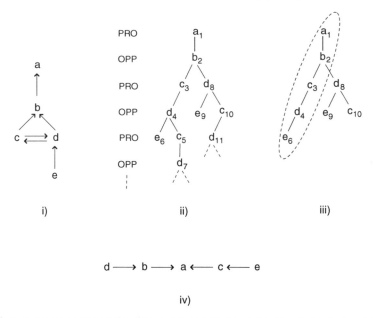

Fig. 6.3 i) shows an argumentation framework and ii) shows the dispute tree induced in a. iii) shows the ϕ_{G_1}-dispute tree induced by a and the ϕ_{G_1} winning strategy encircled. The ϕ_{G_1} winning strategy for a, in the framework in iv), consists of two disputes.

$$\{(a_{PRO} - b_{OPP} - d_{PRO}), (a_{PRO} - c_{OPP} - e_{PRO})\}.$$

Some gain in efficiency can be obtained by a legal move function ϕ_{G_2} that additionally prohibits PRO from moving a y that is itself attacked by the x that PRO moves against (i.e., augmenting 1 and 2 in Definition 6.8 with $\neg(x\mathcal{R}y)$). This is because if PRO moves such a y against x, then OPP can simply repeat x and move against y, and then PRO will be prevented from repeating y. The ϕ_{G_2} game is instantiated by Prakken and Sartor for their argument-based system of prioritized extended logic programming [24]. Amgoud and Cayrol [1] do the same for their argument based system for inconsistency handling in propositional logic. The following soundness and completeness result can be proved as a straightforward generalisation of proofs for the specific systems in [24, 1]. Such a generalised proof can be found in [4].

Theorem 6.3. *Let $AF = \langle \mathcal{A}, \mathcal{R} \rangle$ be a finite argumentation framework. Then, there exists a ϕ_{G_2}-winning strategy T for x such that the set $PRO(T)$ of arguments moved by PRO in T is conflict free, iff x is in the grounded extension of AF*

Since the arguments moved by PRO in a winning strategy are required to be conflict free, it is obvious to see that shorter proofs may also be obtained by preventing PRO from moving arguments in a dispute d that attack themselves or attack or are attacked by arguments that PRO has already moved in d.

Definition 6.9. Let $POSS(d) = \{y \mid \neg(y\mathcal{R}y) \text{ and } \forall z \in PRO(d), \neg(z\mathcal{R}y) \text{ and } \neg(y\mathcal{R}z)\}$.

One can then further restrict PRO's moves in Definition 6.8, by adding the condition that $y \in POSS(d)$, thus obtaining the legal move function ϕ_{G_3}.

Finally, further gains in efficiency can be obtained by noticing that if T is a ϕ_{G_1}, ϕ_{G_2} or ϕ_{G_3} winning strategy, then $PRO(T)$ is conflict free. Thus, one need not instigate the conflict free check on winning strategies suggested by the above soundness and completeness results. To see why, notice that ϕ_{G_1}, ϕ_{G_2} and ϕ_{G_3} make no restrictions on moves by OPP, and one can show that the following theorem holds:

Theorem 6.4. *Let T be a ϕ winning strategy such that ϕ makes no restrictions on moves by OPP. Then $PRO(T)$ is conflict free.*

We refer the reader to [21] for a proof of the above theorem.

5 Preferred Semantics

For any argumentation framework, existence of a preferred extension is guaranteed, and there can be more than one preferred extension. Hence, the decision questions 2a (credulous membership) and 2b (sceptical membership) are distinct. In Section 5.2 we describe argument games for addressing the credulous membership question. Section 5.3 then describes argument games for addressing the more difficult sceptical membership question. Solution-oriented questions 2c - 2h require procedures for identifying one or all preferred extensions. Such questions become relevant when end-users would like to be informed about the reasons as to how and why an argument is justified or overruled, and can be addressed by labelling algorithms that compute one or all preferred labellings. We describe labelling algorithms in the following section.

5.1 A Labelling Algorithm for the Preferred Semantics

In this Section we review Caminada's work on labelling algorithms [6]. Theorem 6.1 in Section 2 establishes an equivalence between an argumentation framework's preferred extensions and the framework's preferred labellings. In [5] it is shown that:

$\mathcal{L}$ is a preferred labelling iff $\mathcal{L}$ is an admissible labelling such that for no admissible labelling $\mathcal{L}'$ is it the case that $\text{in}(\mathcal{L}') \supset \text{in}(\mathcal{L})$. **(R1)**

Hence, a framework's preferred extensions can be identified by algorithms that compute admissible labellings that maximise the number of arguments that are legally IN. In [6], admissible labellings are generated by starting with a labelling that labels all arguments IN and then iteratively, selects arguments that are illegally IN and applies a *transition step* to obtain a new labelling, until a labelling is reached in which no argument is illegally IN.

Definition 6.10. Let $\mathcal{L}$ be a labelling for $\langle \mathcal{A}, \mathcal{R} \rangle$ and x an argument that is illegally IN in $\mathcal{L}$. A *transition step* on x in $\mathcal{L}$ consists of the following:

1. the label of x is changed from IN to OUT
2. for every $y \in \{x\} \cup \{z | x\mathcal{R}z\}$, if y is illegally OUT, then the label of y is changed from OUT to UNDEC (i.e., any argument made illegally OUT by 1 is changed to UNDEC)

In what follows, we assume a function *transition step* that takes as input x and $\mathcal{L}$, and applies the above operations to yield a labelling $\mathcal{L}'$. We then define a *transition sequence* as follows:

A *transition sequence* is a list $[\mathcal{L}_0, x_1, \mathcal{L}_1, x_2, \ldots, x_n, \mathcal{L}_n]$ $(n \geq 0)$, where for $i = 1 \ldots n$, x_i is illegally IN in $\mathcal{L}_{i-1}$, and $\mathcal{L}_i = transition\ step(\mathcal{L}_{i-1}, x_i)$.

A *transition sequence* is said to be terminated iff $\mathcal{L}_n$ does not contain any argument that is illegally IN.

Let us examine a transition sequence that starts with the initial labelling $\mathcal{L}_0$ in which all arguments are labelled IN (from hereon any such labelling is referred to as an 'all-in' labelling and we assume that any initial labelling $\mathcal{L}_0$ is an all-in labelling). Any labelling containing an argument x that is illegally IN cannot be a candidate admissible labelling (since not all of x's attackers are OUT and so x is not reinstated against all attackers), and so must be relabelled OUT. One might expect that the second part of the transition step relabels to IN, those arguments that are made illegally OUT by the first step. However this may not only result in a loop, but would also 'overcommit' arguments to membership of an admissible labelling (and so extension); just because an argument may be acceptable w.r.t. an admissible extension E does not mean that it must be in E.

For finite frameworks it can be shown that:

For any terminated transition sequence $[\mathcal{L}_0, x_1, \mathcal{L}_1, x_2, \ldots, x_n, \mathcal{L}_n]$, it holds that $\mathcal{L}_n$ is an admissible labelling. **(R2)**

To see why, observe that $\mathcal{L}_0$ contains no arguments that are illegally OUT, and it is straightforward to show that a transition step preserves the absence of arguments that are illegally OUT. Hence, since the terminated sequence contains no arguments that are illegally IN, then by Definition 6.3, $\mathcal{L}_n$ is admissible.

In [6], it is also shown that:

For any preferred labelling $\mathcal{L}$, it holds that there exists a terminated transition sequence $[\mathcal{L}_0, x_1, \mathcal{L}_1, x_2, \ldots, x_n, \mathcal{L}_n]$, where $\mathcal{L}_n = \mathcal{L}$.

(R3)

The above results R1, R2 and R3, imply that terminated transition sequences whose final labellings maximise the arguments labelled *IN* are exactly the preferred labellings. Before presenting the algorithm for generating such sequences, let us consider how admissible labellings are generated for the argumentation framework in Figure 6.4i). Starting with the initial all-in labelling $\mathcal{L}_0 = (\{a,b,c\}, \emptyset, \emptyset)$, then selecting a on which to perform a transition step obtains $\mathcal{L}_1 = (\{b,c\}, \{a\}, \emptyset)$. Now only c is illegally IN, and relabelling it to OUT results in a being illegally *OUT*, and so $\mathcal{L}_2 = (\{b\}, \{c\}, \{a\})$. Now b is illegally IN, and relabelling b to OUT results in both b and c being illegally OUT, so that they are both labelled UNDEC. Thus, the transition sequence terminates with the labelling $\mathcal{L}_3 = (\emptyset, \emptyset, \{a,b,c\})$ in which all arguments are UNDEC. It is easy to verify that irrespective of whether a, b or c is selected on the first transition step, every terminated transition sequence will result in $\mathcal{L}_3$.

Consider now the framework in Figure 6.4ii). Starting with the initial all-in labelling $\mathcal{L}_0 = (\{a,b,c\}, \emptyset, \emptyset)$, we observe that B and C are illegally IN:

1. Selecting b for the first transition step obtains the terminated sequence $[\mathcal{L}_0, b, \mathcal{L}_1 = (\{a,c\}, \{b\}, \emptyset)]$. $\mathcal{L}_1$ is an admissible and complete labelling, yielding the admissible and complete extension $\{a,c\}$.
2. Selecting c for the first transition step obtains the terminated sequence $[\mathcal{L}_0, c, \mathcal{L}_1 = (\{a,b\}, \{c\}, \emptyset), b, \mathcal{L}_2 = (\{a\}, \{b\}, \{c\})]$, yielding the admissible extension $\{a\}$

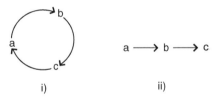

i)   ii)

Fig. 6.4 Two argumentation frameworks

Notice that in the second sequence, the label of c is changed from OUT to UNDEC since c is made illegally OUT by the second transition step's assignment of OUT to the illegally IN b. $\mathcal{L}_2$ is an admissible but not complete labelling, since c is illegally UNDEC. To help avoid non-complete labellings, one can guide the choice of arguments on which to perform transition steps: *choose an argument that is super-illegally IN, if such an argument is available.*

Definition 6.11. An argument x in $\mathcal{L}$ that is illegally IN, is also *super-illegally* IN iff it is attacked by a y that is legally IN in $\mathcal{L}$, or UNDEC in $\mathcal{L}$.

Thus, b would preferentially be selected according to the above strategy, since b and not c is super-illegally IN in $(\{a,b,c\},\emptyset,\emptyset)$. As shown in [6], both the results R2 and R3 are preserved under such a strategy.

Algorithm 6.2 Algorithm for Preferred Labellings

```
 1: candidate-labellings := ∅;
 2: find_labellings(all-in);
 3: print candidate-labellings;
 4: end.
 5: .
 6: .
 7: procedure find_labellings(𝓛)
 8: .
```
 9: # if $\mathcal{L}$ is worse than an existing candidate labelling then prune the search tree
10: # and backtrack to select another argument for performing a transition step
11: **if** $\exists\mathcal{L}' \in$ candidate-labellings: in($\mathcal{L}$) $\subset$ in($\mathcal{L}'$) **then return**;
12: .
13: # if the transition sequence has terminated
14: **if** $\mathcal{L}$ does not have an argument that is illegally IN **then**
15:     **for** each $\mathcal{L}' \in$ candidate-labellings **do**
16:        # if $\mathcal{L}'$'s IN arguments are a strict subset of $\mathcal{L}$'s IN arguments
17:        # then remove $\mathcal{L}'$
18:        **if** in($\mathcal{L}'$) $\subset$ in($\mathcal{L}$) **then**
19:           candidate-labellings :=
20:           candidate-labellings $- \{\mathcal{L}'\}$;
21:        **end if**
22:     **end for**
23:     # add $\mathcal{L}$ as a new candidate
24:     candidate-labellings := candidate-labellings $\cup \{\mathcal{L}\}$;
25:     **return**; # we are done, so try the next possibility
26: **else**
27:     **if** $\mathcal{L}$ has an argument that is super-illegally IN **then**
28:        $x :=$ some argument that is super-illegally IN in $\mathcal{L}$;
29:        find_labellings(*transition_step*($\mathcal{L}, x$));
30:     **else**
31:        **for** each x that is illegally IN in $\mathcal{L}$ **do**
32:           find_labellings(*transition_step*($\mathcal{L}, x$))
33:        **end for**
34:     **end if**
35: **end if**
36: **endproc**

We now describe the above listed algorithm for generating preferred labellings. The main procedure find_labellings starts with the all-in labelling, and then iteratively applies transitions steps in an attempt to generate terminated transition sequences that update the global variable candidate-labellings. The algorithm preferentially selects from amongst super-illegal arguments for performing transition steps, if such arguments are available. If at any stage in the generation of a transition sequence, the arguments that are IN in the labelling $\mathcal{L}_i$ thus far obtained are a strict subset of $\text{in}(\mathcal{L}')$ for some $\mathcal{L}' \in$ candidate-labellings, then no further transition steps on $\mathcal{L}_i$ can result in a preferred labelling (that maximises the arguments that are IN). This follows from the result that during the course of a transition sequence, the set of IN labelled arguments monotonically decreases (as shown in [6]). Thus, any further transition steps on $\mathcal{L}_i$ will only reduce the arguments that are IN. In such cases, the algorithm backtracks to $\mathcal{L}_{i-1}$ and, if possible, selects another argument on which to perform a transition step. In the case that a transition sequence terminates, the obtained labelling $\mathcal{L}$ is compared with all labellings $\mathcal{L}'$ in candidate-labellings. If for any $\mathcal{L}'$, $\text{in}(\mathcal{L}')$ is a strict subset of $\text{in}(\mathcal{L})$, then $\mathcal{L}'$ is removed from candidate-labellings. Thus, given a finite argumentation framework $\langle \mathcal{A}, \mathcal{R} \rangle$, the algorithm calculates the preferred labellings and so preferred extensions.

5.2 Argument Games for the Credulous Preferred Semantics

Since the admissible extensions of a framework form a complete partial order with respect to set inclusion (and so every admissible extension is a subset of a preferred extension), then for argument games addressing the credulous membership question, it suffices to show an admissible extension containing the argument in question. In contrast with the grounded semantics, x's membership of an admissible extension E can now 'appeal to' x itself, in the sense that in defending x's membership of E, and membership of all subsequent defenders, one can loop back to x itself. This then means, that to prevent infinite disputes, it is now OPP, rather than PRO, that should not be allowed to repeat an argument y it has already moved in a dispute, since y can then be attacked by PRO repeating the argument it moved against OPP's first move of y.

Consider the framework in Figure 6.5i), and the dispute tree induced in a in Figure 6.5ii). In both disputes (branches) PRO is allowed to repeat its arguments (c_5 and d_9). OPP repeats its arguments, and the disputes continue with PRO repeatedly fulfilling its burden of proof w.r.t. c (d). It is of course sufficient that PRO fulfill its burden of proof only once. Hence, as well as preventing PRO from introducing a conflict into a dispute, the following legal move function prohibits OPP from repeating arguments.

Definition 6.12. Given $\langle \mathcal{A}, \mathcal{R} \rangle$, a dispute d such that x is the last argument in d, and OPP(d) the arguments moved by OPP in d, then ϕ_{PC_1} is a legal move function such that:

- If d is of odd length (next move is by OPP) then:

$$\phi_{PC_1}(d) = \{ y \mid$$
$$1.\ y\mathcal{R}x$$
$$2.\ y \notin \text{OPP}(d)$$
$$\}$$

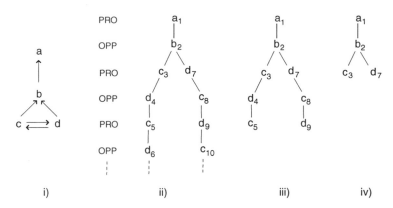

Fig. 6.5 i) shows an argumentation framework and ii) shows the dispute tree induced in a. iii) and iv) respectively shows the ϕ_{PC_1} and ϕ_{PC_2} dispute trees induced by a.

- If d is of even length (next move is by PRO) then:

$\phi_{PC_1}(d) = \{y \mid$

      1. $y \mathcal{R} x$

      2. $y \in POSS(d)$

$\}$

Notice that ϕ_{PC_1} mirrors Section 4.2's grounded game function ϕ_{G_3} (that augments ϕ_{G_1} to restrict PRO to moving arguments in $POSS(d)$). They differ only in that ϕ_{PC_1} prevents repetition by OPP, and ϕ_{G_3} prevents repetition by PRO.

Consider again the framework in Figure 6.5i). The ϕ_{PC_1} dispute tree induced by a is shown in Figure 6.5iii), and both disputes in the tree individually constitute ϕ_{PC_1} winning strategies. Notice that for the example framework in Figure 6.3iv), the ϕ_{PC_1}-winning strategy for a consists of two disputes: $\{(a_{PRO} - b_{OPP} - d_{PRO}), (a_{PRO} - c_{OPP} - e_{PRO})\}$.

The following theorem states the soundness and completeness result for ϕ_{PC_1} games:

Theorem 6.5. *Let $AF = \langle \mathcal{A}, \mathcal{R} \rangle$ be a finite argumentation framework. Then, there exists a ϕ_{PC_1}-winning strategy T for x such that the set $PRO(T)$ of arguments moved by PRO in T is conflict free, iff x is in an admissible (and hence preferred) extension of AF.*

One can give an intuitive proof of the above by using the correspondence between admissible extensions and admissible labellings of an argumentation framework (see Theorem 6.1). That is, it suffices to prove that:

1. Let T be a ϕ_{PC_1}-winning strategy for x such that $PRO(T)$ is conflict free. Then there exists an admissible labelling $\mathcal{L}$ with $\mathcal{L}(x) = \text{IN}$.

2. Let $\mathcal{L}$ be an admissible labelling with $\mathcal{L}(x) = \text{IN}$. Then there exists a ϕ_{PC_1}-winning strategy for x such that $PRO(T)$ is conflict free.

Proof of the above correspondences can be found in [21].

Observe that the spectrum of outcomes would not be changed by a function ϕ_{PC_2} that augments ϕ_{PC_1} by prohibiting OPP from moving *any* argument y (and not just a y already moved by OPP) that is attacked by an argument x in PRO(d). This is because PRO can then simply move x against y, and if $y\mathcal{R}x$, prohibiting repetition by OPP will mean that y cannot be moved against this second move of x by PRO. Notice that if this prohibition on OPP is in place, then one cannot have a dispute of the form $(\ldots y_{PRO} \ldots x_{OPP} - y_{PRO} \ldots)$ in which PRO repeats an argument, since the prohibition on OPP would prevent the move x_{OPP}. Hence, shorter proofs can be obtained by a function ϕ_{PC_2} that augments ϕ_{PC_1} by prohibiting OPP from moving any argument attacked by an argument in PRO(d), and prohibiting repetition by PRO. Indeed, [9] prove that the following theorem holds:

Theorem 6.6. *Let $AF = \langle \mathcal{A}, \mathcal{R} \rangle$ be a finite argumentation framework. Then, there exists a ϕ_{PC_2}-winning strategy for x such that the set $PRO(T)$ of arguments moved by PRO in T is conflict free, iff a is in a preferred extension of AF.*

Figure 6.5iv) shows the ϕ_{PC_2} dispute tree induced by a for the framework in Figure 6.5i), where both disputes in the tree are ϕ_{PC_2} winning strategies. However, notice that neither dispute fully fulfills the remit of a proof to *explain* the credulous membership of a, since neither demonstrates the reinstatement of c, respectively d, against its attacker d, respectively c, and so provides an explanation for the admissibility of $\{a,c\}$, respectively $\{a,d\}$. This illustrates a more general point that efficiency gains often come at the expense of explanatory power.

Finally, note that unlike games for the grounded semantics, checking that the arguments moved by PRO in a ϕ_{PC_1} (or ϕ_{PC_2}) winning strategy are conflict free, is required. This is because ϕ_{PC_1} and ϕ_{PC_2} games place restrictions on moves by OPP (and hence the result concluding Section 4.2 does not hold). For example, consider that a is not in an admissible, and hence preferred, extension of the framework in Figure 6.6. Now, $\{(a_{PRO} - b_{OPP} - c_{PRO} - d_{OPP} - g_{PRO}), (a_{PRO} - e_{OPP} - f_{PRO} - g_{OPP} - d_{PRO})\}$ is a ϕ_{PC_1} winning strategy since OPP cannot legally extend either dispute. However, the arguments moved by PRO are not conflict free (PRO has moved g and d).

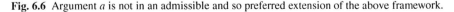

Fig. 6.6 Argument a is not in an admissible and so preferred extension of the above framework.

5.3 Argument Games for the Sceptically Preferred Semantics

The question of whether an argument is sceptically preferred is much harder to answer than the credulously preferred membership problem. To understand why, it may first help to realise that the credulous membership problem only requires us to point at one extension, while the sceptical membership problem requires us to prove something about all possible extensions. Thus, the credulously preferred membership problem is an existence problem while the sceptically preferred membership problem is a verification problem. To understand better why verification is hard in this case, we recall the definition of sceptically preferred membership: an argument a is *sceptically preferred* iff it is a member of all preferred extensions. The crux of the problem is that we have to verify whether there exists preferred extensions that do not contain a. In so doing, it is not immediately clear where to begin to search for such extensions.

The following result establishes a connection between a and preferred extensions that might possibly exclude a (we refer the reader to [21] for a proof of this result). It basically ensures that the search space for the sceptical decision problem is confined to elements that are indirectly connected to defense sets of a.

Theorem 6.7 (Complement lemma). *An argument a is sceptically preferred if and only if for every admissible extension B, there is an admissible extension A, containing a, that is consistent with B.*

Thus, conversely, a is not sceptically preferred if there exists an admissible extension B that conflicts with all admissible extensions around a. Because such an extension B blocks sceptically preferred membership, such an extension is called a *block*. With the help of Theorem 6.7 we may now formulate an abstract and inefficient, but conceptually correct proof procedure to determine sceptical membership. This procedure works by falsification, as follows. Try to construct a block B. If this attempt fails, we may, with the help of Theorem 6.7 conclude that a is sceptically preferred.

The procedure to block a can be described as an argument game that we informally describe here. The difference with the games described earlier, is that the players exchange entire admissible extensions rather than single arguments. The game works as follows. Suppose PRO's goal is to show that a is sceptically preferred. To this end, PRO starts by constructing an admissible extension, $A\{1\}$ around a. Since $A\{1\}$ is the only admissible extension known at this stage, it follows that at this stage a is sceptically preferred. To invalidate this temporary conclusion, the burden of proof shifts to OPP who must show that a is not sceptically preferred. By virtue of Theorem 6.7 it suffices for OPP to show that there exists an admissible extension that conflicts with $A\{1\}$. If OPP does not manage to construct such an extension, the procedure ends and OPP has lost. Suppose OPP manages to produce $A\{1,1\}$ as a response to $A\{1\}$. Thus, $A\{1,1\}$ is an admissible extension that conflicts with $A\{1\}$. Once $A\{1,1\}$ is advanced, a is no longer sceptically preferred, because $A\{1,1\}$ conflicts with every admissible extension around a constructed thus far, viz. $A\{1\}$. To invalidate this temporary conclusion, the burden of proof shifts back to PRO who must now show that there exists another admissible extension around a that does not conflict with $A\{1,1\}$. If PRO fails to do so (and PRO's search was adequate and exhaustive), it follows that $A\{1,1\}$ conflicts with all admissible extensions around A, so that a is not sceptically preferred. Suppose otherwise, i.e, suppose that PRO is able to construct an admissible extension, $A\{1,1,1\}$, that does not conflict with $A\{1,1\}$. OPP must now either extend $A\{1,1\}$ such that it also conflicts with $A\{1,1,1\}$ or else drop $A\{1,1\}$ to start all over to attack another member of $A\{1\}$. Continuing this way (including backtracking), OPP is busy with extending an admissible extension until either PRO is unable to produce another admissible extension around a, or else until OPP's admissible extension cannot be further extended (on pain of becoming inconsistent).

More generally, we may suppose that $A\{1\},\ldots,A\{n\}$ are possible begin moves of PRO, and $A\{i_1,\ldots,i_k,m\}$, $k \geq 1$ is the mth possible response of either PRO or OPP to $A\{i_1,\ldots,i_k\}$. Naturally, all the $A\{\bar{i}\}$ are admissible extensions. The following constraints hold:

1. Every extension advanced by PRO must contain the main argument, a.
2. Every response of PRO must be consistent with the extension that is previously advanced by OPP.
3. Every response of OPP must attack PRO's immediately preceding extension.
4. Within one branch, every extension advanced by OPP must be an extension of OPP's previous extension in the same branch.
5. Both parties may backtrack and construct alternative replies.
6. OPP has won if it is able to move last; else PRO has won.

If OPP has won this means that OPP was able to create a block $B = A\{i_1,\ldots,i_{2k}\}$, where $k \geq 1$ (note that we have '$2k$' since all moves by OPP have an even number of indices). With B, OPP is able to move last in the particular branch where that block was created and all sub-branches emanating from the main branch. It must be noted that all this only works in finitary argument systems, i.e., argument systems where all arguments have a finite number of attackers. Algorithms for non-finitary argument systems require additional constraints such as *fairness* which must guarantee that every possibility is enumerated eventually.

The above ideas are taken from earlier work on the sceptically preferred membership problem, notably that of Doutre *et al.* [12] and Dung *et al.* [15]. In [12], the procedure to find a possible block is presented as a so-called meta-acceptance dialogue. As above, moves in this dialogue are extensions (hence the *meta*), and a dialogue is won by OPP if it is able to move last in at least one branch. In Dung *et al.* [15] the procedure to construct a "fan" of admissible extensions around A that together represent all preferred extensions is called *generating a complete base* for a. A *base* for a is a set of admissible extensions, $\mathcal{B}$, such that every preferred extension around a includes at least one element of $\mathcal{B}$. A *complete base* for a, then, is a set of admissible extensions, $\mathcal{B}$, such that *every* preferred extension includes at least one element of $\mathcal{B}$. In line with Theorem 6.7, Dung *et al.* proceed to show that a base $\mathcal{B}$ is incomplete if and only if there exists a preferred extension that attacks every element of $\mathcal{B}$. Their proof procedure is a combination of a so-called BG-derivation (base generation derivation) followed by a CB-verification (complete base verification). With BG a base for a is generated, such that every preferred extension around a contains an element of $\mathcal{B}$. Such a base always exists, but not every base may serve as a representant of sceptical membership. To check whether $\mathcal{B}$ indeed represents sceptical membership, it is checked for completeness, which effectively means that it must hold out against every candidate block that might undermine $\mathcal{B}$. Again, all decision procedures only work in finitary argument systems.

6 Stable and Semi-Stable Semantics

Stable semantics are, what one might call 'xenophobic', since every argument outside of a stable extension is attacked by an argument in the stable extension. Unlike the preferred semantics, existence of a stable extension is not guaranteed; consider that a framework consisting of a single argument that attacks itself has no stable extension. However, as in the case of the preferred semantics, there may be more than one extension, and so decision questions 2a (credulous membership) and 2b (sceptical membership) are distinct. These questions, questions 1b, 1c, and the solution-orientated questions 2a - 2h can be addressed by an algorithm (taken from [6]) that generates all stable extensions of a framework. Since a stable labelling makes all arguments either OUT or IN, one can straightforwardly adapt the algorithm for preferred labellings in Section 5.1, so as to only yield labellings without UNDEC labelled arguments. Thus, line 11 in the algorithm is replaced by:

if undec($\mathcal{L}$) $\neq \emptyset$ **then return**;

Furthermore, we do not have to compare the arguments made IN by other candidate labellings, and so we can remove lines 15 to 22. The result is an algorithm that calculates all stable extensions of a finite framework.

Argument games for stable semantics have only recently been studied. In [28], the authors study *coherent* argumentation frameworks, in which every preferred extension is also stable (meaning that the preferred and stable extensions coincide, since each stable extension is by definition also a preferred extension). Thus, for coherent argumentation frameworks, one can simply apply existing games for the preferred semantics to decide membership under stable semantics.

For the general case, where one is not restricted to coherent argumentation frameworks, the situation is more complex, but can still be expressed in terms of the credulous games defined in Section 5.2. Given a framework $\langle \mathcal{A}, \mathcal{R} \rangle$, and letting $PRO(T)$, respectively $OPP(T)$, denote the arguments moved by PRO, respectively OPP, in a dispute tree T, then an argument x is in a stable extension iff there exists a set S of ϕ_{PC_1} winning strategies such that:

1. at least one winning strategy in S is for x.
2. $\bigcup \{PRO(T) | T \in S\}$ is conflict free.
3. $\bigcup \{PRO(T) \cup OPP(T) | T \in S\} = \mathcal{A}$

This can be seen as follows. First of all, each ϕ_{PC_1} winning strategy corresponds to an admissible labelling. A set of winning strategies that do not attack each other (point 2) again corresponds to an admissible labelling. If this resulting admissible labelling spans the entire argumentation framework (each argument is either IN or OUT) then this labelling is also stable (point 3). Then, if x is IN in this labelling, then x is labelled IN in at least one stable labelling (point 1).

It is also possible to define a single dispute game that determines credulous acceptance w.r.t. stable semantics. Such a game has recently been stated by Caminada and Wu [7]. One particular feature of their approach, which builds on the work of Vreeswijk and Prakken [28], is that they do not use the concept of a winning strategy. Instead, for an argument x to be in a stable extension, it suffices to have at least one game for x that is won by PRO. Caminada and Wu are able to do this by first defining a game for credulous preferred in which PRO may repeat its own moves, but not the moves of OPP, and in which OPP may repeat PRO's moves but not its own moves. Moreover, PRO has to react to the directly preceding move of OPP, whereas OPP is free to react either to the directly preceding move of PRO, *or* to a previous PRO move. A dispute is won by PRO iff OPP cannot move. A dispute is won by OPP iff PRO cannot move, or if OPP managed to repeat one of PRO's moves.

Basically, the game can be understood in terms of PRO and OPP building an admissible labelling in which PRO makes IN moves, and OPP makes OUT moves. This game can be altered to implement stable semantics by introducing a third kind of move, which is called *QUESTION*. By uttering *QUESTION x*, OPP asks PRO for an explicit opinion on argument x. PRO is then obliged to reply with either IN x or with IN y, where y is an attacker of x. Caminada and Wu show that this game indeed models credulous acceptance under the stable semantics.

Once a procedure for credulous acceptance w.r.t. stable semantics has been defined, the issue of sceptical acceptance w.r.t. stable semantics becomes relatively straightforward: an argument x is in all stable extensions iff one fails to establish credulous membership of any attacker of x. For the left to right half, observe that if x is in all stable extensions, then all attackers of x are attacked by all such extensions (an argument y is *attacked by an extension* if it is attacked by an argument in that extension), and so no attacker of x can be in any such extension, since each such extension is conflict free. For the right to left half, observe that if any attacker of x does not belong to any stable extension, then it is attacked by all such extensions. Thus every extension contains an argument that reinstates x, and so contains x.

Caminada has recently proposed *semi-stable* semantics [5, 6], that unlike the stable semantics, guarantees that every (finite) framework has at least one semi-stable extension. In the case that there exists at least one stable extension for a framework, semi-stable semantics yield the same extensions as stable semantics. From the perspective of argument labellings, semi-stable semantics select those labellings in which the set of UNDEC arguments is minimal. Referring to Definition 6.4, this can be expressed as follows:

Let $\mathcal{L}$ be a complete labelling. Then $\mathcal{L}$ is a semi-stable labelling iff there does not exist a complete labelling $\mathcal{L}'$ such that $\mathrm{undec}(\mathcal{L}') \subset \mathrm{undec}(\mathcal{L})$

For example, consider the framework in Figure 6.4ii) augmented by an additional argument d that attacks itself. The augmented framework has no stable extension, but $\{a,c\}$ is the single semi-stable extension equating with the semi-stable labelling $(\{a,c\},\{b\},\{d\})$. Notice that although $\{a,c\}$ is also the single preferred extension, in general not every preferred extension is a semi-stable extension since not every preferred extension minimises UNDEC. However, every semi-stable extension is a preferred extension, which suggests that we can adapt Section 5.1's algorithm for preferred labellings in order to compute semi-stable labellings.

In [6] it is also shown that:

$\mathcal{L}$ is a semi-stable labelling iff $\mathcal{L}$ is an admissible labelling such that for no admissible labelling $\mathcal{L}'$ is it the case that $\mathrm{undec}(\mathcal{L}') \subset \mathrm{undec}(\mathcal{L})$.

                                                                                        (R1')

Since every semi-stable extension is a preferred extension then R3 in Section 5.1 also holds for semi-stable labellings $\mathcal{L}$. This result, together with R1' and R2 in Section 5.1, implies that terminated transition sequences whose final labellings minimise the arguments labelled *UNDEC* are exactly the semi-stable labellings. Hence, one can adapt Section 5.1's algorithm by replacing line 11 by:

if $\exists \mathcal{L}' \in$ candidate-labellings: $\mathrm{undec}(\mathcal{L}') \subset \mathrm{undec}(\mathcal{L})$ **then return**;

In other words, if at any stage in the generation of a transition sequence, the UNDEC arguments of the labelling $\mathcal{L}_i$ thus far obtained, are a strict superset of $\mathrm{undec}(\mathcal{L}')$ for some $\mathcal{L}' \in$ candidate-labellings, then no further transition steps on $\mathcal{L}_i$ can result in a semi-stable labelling, and so one can backtrack to perform a transition step on another choice of argument. This follows from the result that during the course of a transition sequence, the set of UNDEC labelled arguments monotonically increases (as shown in [6]). Finally, we replace line 18 with:

if $\mathrm{undec}(\mathcal{L}) \subset \mathrm{undec}(\mathcal{L}')$;

and we are done. We have an algorithm that calculates the semi-stable labellings of a finite argumentation framework.

7 Conclusions

In this chapter we have described labelling algorithms and argument game proof theories for various argumentation semantics. Labellings and argument games can be seen as alternatives to the *extension-based* approach to specifying argumentation semantics described in Chapter 2. We conclude with some further reflections on these different ways of specifying argumentation semantics.

One of the original motivations for developing the labelling approach was to provide an easy and intuitive account of formal argumentation. After all, principles like "In order to accept an argument, one has to be able to reject all its counterarguments" and "In order to reject an argument, one has to be able to accept at least one counterargument" are easy to explain and have therefore been used as the basis of the labelling approach. Also, our teaching experiences indicate that students who are new to argumentation tend to find it easier to understand the labelling approach rather than the extension-based approach to argumentation. In fact, it is often easier for them to understand the extension-based approach after having been introduced to the labelling approach.

Another advantage of the labelling approach is that it allows one to specify a number of relatively small and simple properties, each of which can be individually satisfied or not, and that collectively define the argumentation semantics. This modular approach can be of assistance when constructing formal proofs. Also, by explicitly distinguishing between IN, OUT and UNDEC (instead of merely specifying the set of IN-labelled arguments as in the extension-based approach) one is provided with more detailed information. For instance, Section 5.1's algorithm for generating all preferred extensions, would be much more difficult to specify using the extension-based approach.

Finally, we note that the labelling approach essentially identifies a graph or 'network' labelling problem, suggesting that the approach more readily lends itself to extensions of argument frameworks that accommodate: different types of relation between arguments (e.g. support [10] and collective attack [22]); attacks on attacks [20]; multi-valued and quantitative valuations of arguments [2, 11], and so on. In essence, these extensions of Dung's abstract argumentation framework can be understood as instantiating a more general network reasoning model in which the valuations of nodes (arguments) is determined by propagating the valuations of the connected nodes, as mediated by the semantics of the connecting arcs. Algorithms for determining these valuations will thus generalise the three value labelling algorithms described in this chapter.

With regard to the argument game approach, we recall that Dung's abstract argumentation semantics can be understood as a semantics for a number of non-monotonic and defeasible logics [3, 13], in the sense that:

α is an inference from a theory Δ in a logic $\mathcal{L}$, iff α is the conclusion of a justified argument of the argumentation framework $\langle \mathcal{A}, \mathcal{R} \rangle$ defined by Δ and $\mathcal{L}$.

The argument game approach places an emphasis on the dialectical nature of argumentation, in the sense that the approach appeals more directly to an intersubjective notion of truth: truth becomes that which can be defended in a rational exchange and evaluation of interacting arguments. Thus, what accounts for the correctness of an inference is that it can be *shown* to rationally prevail in the face of arguments for opposing inferences, where it is application of the reinstatement principle that encodes logic neutral, rational means for establishing such standards of correctness. This account of argumentation as a semantics, contrasts with model-based semantics for formal entailment that appeal to an objective notion of truth: true is that which holds in every possible model. Notice that dialectical semantics are not unique to formal argumentation. For instance, Lorenzen and Lorenz [18, 19] have proposed dialectical devices as a method of demonstration in formal logic.

An advantage of dialectical semantics is that they are able to relate formal entailment to something most people are familiar with in everyday life: debates and discussions. Argument games of the type described in this chapter are therefore useful not only for providing guidelines and principles for the design of algorithms, but also for bridging the gap between formal and informal reasoning.

Finally, we note that the dialectical view also accords with our understanding of reasoning as an incremental process. Rather than have all the arguments and their attacks defined from the outset, we incrementally acquire knowledge in order to construct arguments required to counter-argue existing arguments. At any stage in this incremental process we can evaluate the status of arguments, which in turn motivates acquisition of further knowledge for construction and submission of arguments. Argument games allow one to model such processes. Provided that there is a well understood notion of what constitutes an attack between any two arguments, one can then formalise the games described in this chapter, without reference to a pre-existing framework. This also allows one to acknowledge that reasoning agents are resource bounded, and suggests that bounds on reasoning resources may be characterised by bounds on the breadth and depth of the dispute trees constructed in order to prove the claim of the argument under test.

Acknowledgements The authors would like to thank Gerard Vreeswijk for his contributions to the contents of this chapter. Thanks also to Nir Oren for commenting on a draft of the chapter.

References

1. L. Amgoud and C. Cayrol. A Reasoning Model Based on the Production of Acceptable Arguments. *Annals of Mathematics and Artificial Intelligence*, 34(1–3),197–215, 2002.
2. H. Barringer, D. M. Gabbay and J. Woods. Temporal Dynamics of Support and Attack Networks: From Argumentation to Zoology. *Mechanizing Mathematical Reasoning*, 59–98, 2005.
3. A. Bondarenko and P.M. Dung and R.A. Kowalski and F. Toni. An abstract, argumentation-theoretic approach to default reasoning. *Artificial Intelligence*, 93:63–101, 1997.
4. M. Caminada. *For the sake of the Argument. Explorations into argument-based reasoning.* Doctoral dissertation Free University Amsterdam, 2004.
5. M. Caminada. On the Issue of Reinstatement in Argumentation. In *European Conference on Logic in Artificial Intelligence (JELIA)*, 111–123, 2006.
6. M. Caminada. An Algorithm for Computing Semi-stable Semantics. In *European Conference on Symbolic and Quantitative Approaches to Reasoning with Uncertainty (ECSQARU)*, 222–234, 2007.

7. M. Caminada and Y. Wu. Towards an Argument Game for Stable Semantics. In *Computational Models of Natural Argument*, to appear, 2008.
8. C. Cayrol, S. Doutre and J. Mengin. Dialectical Proof Theories for the Credulous Preferred Semantics of Argumentation Frameworks. In *European Conference on Symbolic and Quantitative Approaches to Reasoning with Uncertainty (ECSQARU)*, 668–679, 2001.
9. C. Cayrol, S. Doutre and J. Mengin. On Decision Problems related to the preferred semantics for argumentation frameworks. *Journal of Logic and Computation*, 13(3), 377–403, 2003.
10. C. Cayrol and M. Lagasquie-Schiex. On the Acceptability of Arguments in Bipolar Argumentation Frameworks. In *European Conference on Symbolic and Quantitative Approaches to Reasoning with Uncertainty (ECSQARU)*, 378–389, 2005.
11. C. Cayrol and M.-Ch. Lagasquie-Schiex. Graduality in argumentation. *Journal of Artificial Intelligence Research*, 23:245–297, 2005.
12. S. Doutre and J. Mengin. On sceptical vs credulous acceptance for abstract argument systems. In *Ninth European Conference on Logics in Artificial Intelligence (JELIA 2004)*, 462–473, 2004.
13. P. M. Dung. On the acceptability of arguments and its fundamental role in nonmonotonic reasoning, logic programming and *n*-person games. *Artificial Intelligence*, 77:321–357, 1995.
14. P.M. Dung, P. Mancarella and F. Toni. Computing ideal sceptical argumentation. *Artificial Intelligence Journal*, 171(10–15):642–674, 2007.
15. P.M. Dung and P.M. Thang. A Sound and Complete Dialectical Proof Procedure for Sceptical Preferred Argumentation. In *Proc. of the LPNMR-Workshop on Argumentation and Nonmonotonic Reasoning (ArgNMR07)*, 49–63, 2007.
16. P.E. Dunne and T.J.M. Bench-Capon. Two Party Immediate Response Disputes: Properties and Efficiency. *Artificial Intelligence Journal*, 149(2),221–250, 2003.
17. H. Jakobovits and D. Vermeir. Dialectic Semantics for Argumentation Frameworks. *Journal of Logic and Computation*, 53–62, 1999.
18. P. Lorenzen. Dialectical foundations of logical calculi. *Constructive Philosophy*, Univ. of Massachusetts Press, 1987.
19. P. Lorenzen and K.Lorenz". Dialogische Logik. Wissenschaftliche Buchgesellschaft, Darmstadt, 1978.
20. S. Modgil. Reasoning About Preferences in Argumentation Frameworks. *Artificial Intelligence Journal*, 173(9–10), 901–934, 2009.
21. S. Modgil and M. Caminada. Proof Theories and Algorithms for Abstract Argumentation Frameworks. *Technical Report*, Department of Computer Science, King's College London, *www.dcs.kcl.ac.uk/staff/modgilsa/ProofTheoriesAlgorithms.pdf*, 2008.
22. S. Nielsen and S. Parsons. A generalization of Dung's abstract framework for argumentation: Arguing with sets of attacking arguments. In *Proc. Third International Workshop on Argumentation in Multiagent Systems (ArgMAS 2006)*, 54–73, 2006.
23. J. L. Pollock. *Cognitive Carpentry. A Blueprint for How to Build a Person*. MIT Press, Cambridge, MA, 1995.
24. H. Prakken and G. Sartor. Argument-based extended logic programming with defeasible priorities. *Journal of Applied Non-Classical Logics*, 7:25–75, 1997.
25. B. Verheij. A Labeling Approach to the Computation of Credulous Acceptance in Argumentation. In *International Joint Conference on Aritificial Intelligence (IJCAI)*, 623–628, 2007.
26. G. A. W. Vreeswijk. Defeasible dialectics: A controversy-oriented approach towards defeasible argumentation. *Journal of Logic and Computation*, 3:3–27, 1993.
27. G. A. W. Vreeswijk. An algorithm to compute minimally grounded and admissible defence sets in argument systems. In *Proc. 1st International Conference on Computational Models of Argument*, 109–120, 2006.
28. G. A. W. Vreeswijk and H. Prakken. Credulous and sceptical argument games for preferred semantics. In *Proc. 7th European Workshop on Logic for Artificial Intelligence*, 239–253, 2000.

Part II
Arguments with Structure

Chapter 7
Argumentation Based on Classical Logic

Philippe Besnard and Anthony Hunter

1 Introduction

Argumentation is an important cognitive process for dealing with conflicting information by generating and/or comparing arguments. Often it is based on constructing and comparing deductive arguments. These are arguments that involve some premises (which we refer to as the support of the argument) and a conclusion (which we refer to as the claim of the argument) such that the support deductively entails the claim.

In order to formalize argumentation, we could potentially use any logic to define the logical entailment of the claim from the support. Possible logics include defeasible logics, description logics, paraconsistent logics, modal logics, and classical logic. In this chapter, we focus on deductive arguments in the setting of classical logic. Hence, our starting position is that a deductive argument consists of a claim entailed by a collection of statements such that the claim as well as the statements are denoted by formulae of classical logic and entailment is deduction in classical logic. Classical logic is a well-known formalism. It is widely used in philosophy, mathematics, and computer science for capturing deductive reasoning. It has a simple and intuitive syntax and semantics, and it is supported by a proof theory and extensive foundational results. By using classical logic, we can provide a simple and efficient formalization of argument and counterargument.

So in our framework, an argument is simply a pair $\langle \Phi, \alpha \rangle$ where the first item in the pair is a minimal consistent set of formulae that proves the second item. That is, we account for the support and the claim of an argument though we do not indicate the method of inference since it does not differ from one argument to another: We

Philippe Besnard
IRIT, Universite Paul Sabatier, Toulouse, France

Anthony Hunter
Department of Computer Science, University College London, London, UK

I. Rahwan, G. R. Simari (eds.), *Argumentation in Artificial Intelligence,*
DOI 10.1007/978 0 387 98197 0_7, © Springer Science+Business Media, LLC 2009

only consider deductive arguments, hence the method of inference for each and every argument is always entailment according to classical logic.

A counterargument for an argument $\langle \Phi, \alpha \rangle$ is an argument $\langle \Psi, \beta \rangle$ where the claim β contradicts the support Φ. Furthermore, we identify a particular kind of counterargument called a canonical undercut $\langle \Psi, \beta \rangle$ where β is equivalent to $\neg(\phi_1 \wedge .. \wedge \phi_n)$ and $\{\phi_1, ..., \phi_n\}$ is the support of the argument being undercut. This is a valuable form of undercut since it subsumes many other kinds of undercut, and hence focusing on only canonical undercuts renders the presentation and evaluation of counterarguments as a more manageable process.

Each undercut to an argument is itself an argument, and so may be undercut, and hence by recursion each undercut needs to be considered for its undercuts. Exploring systematically the universe of arguments in order to present an exhaustive synthesis of the relevant chains of undercuts for a given argument is the basic principle of our approach.

Following on from the idea that we can capture undercuts, and by recursion undercuts to undercuts, our notion of an argument tree is that it is a synthesis of all the arguments that challenge the argument at the root of the tree, and it also contains all counterarguments that challenge these arguments and so on recursively. In each instance, the only counterarguments we consider are the canonical undercuts.

In the rest of this chapter, we formalize and illustrate arguments and counterarguments (including canonical undercuts), and show how these can be collected into argument trees. We conclude the chapter with a comparison with other approaches to formalising argumentation. Since the aim of this chapter is to just introduce some of the basic ideas to argumentation based on classical logic, the interested reader is requested to refer to [3, 6] for more details including formal results.

2 Preliminaries

We assume the reader has some knowledge of classical logic. We will represent atoms by lower case roman letters ($a,b,c,d,...$), formulae by greek letters ($\alpha, \beta, \gamma, ...$), and use $\wedge, \vee, \rightarrow$, and $\neg$ to denote the logical connectives conjunction, disjunction, negation, and implication (respectively). We use $\vdash$ to denote the classical consequence relation, and so if Δ is a knowledgebase, and α is a formula, then $\Delta \vdash \alpha$ denotes that Δ entails α (or equivalently α is a consequence of Δ). We also use $\bot$ to denote a contradiction, and so $\Delta \vdash \bot$ denotes that Δ is contradictory (or equivalently inconsistent).

For the knowledgebase, we first assume a fixed Δ (a finite set of formulae) and use this Δ throughout. So when we consider arguments and counterarguments, they will be formed from this Δ. For examples, we will explicitly give the elements of the knowledgebase.

We further assume that every subset of Δ is given an enumeration $\langle \alpha_1, ..., \alpha_n \rangle$ of its elements, which we call its canonical enumeration. This really is not a demanding constraint: In particular, the constraint is satisfied whenever we impose an arbitrary total ordering over Δ. Importantly, the order has no meaning and is not meant to represent any respective importance of formulae in Δ. It is only a convenient way to indicate the order in which we assume the formulae in any subset of Δ are conjoined to make a formula logically equivalent to that subset.

The paradigm for our approach is a large repository of information, represented by Δ, from which arguments can be constructed for and against arbitrary claims. Apart from information being understood as declarative statements, there is no *a priori* restriction on the contents and the pieces of information in the repository can be arbitrarily complex. Therefore, Δ is not expected to be consistent. It need not even be the case that individual formulae in Δ are consistent.

The formulae in Δ can represent certain or uncertain information, and they can represent objective, subjective, or hypothetical statements. So Δ can represent facts, beliefs, views, ... Furthermore, the items in Δ can be beliefs from different agents who need not even have the same opinions. It can indeed be the case that an argument formed from such a Δ takes advantage of partial views from different agents. In any case, it is quite possible for Δ to have two or more formulae which are logically equivalent (Δ can be such that it contains both $\alpha \vee \beta$ and $\beta \vee \alpha$ for example). But wherever they come from, all formulae in Δ are on *a par* and treated equitably.

Note, we do not assume any meta-level information about formulae. In particular, we do not assume some preference ordering or "certainty ordering" over formulae. This is in contrast to numerous proposals for argumentation which do assume some form of ordering over formulae. Such orderings can be useful to resolve conflicts by, for example, selecting formulae from a more reliable source. However, this, in a sense, pushes the problem of dealing with conflicting information to one of finding and using orderings over formulae, and as such raises further questions such as: Where does the knowledge about reliability of the sources come from? How can it be assessed? How can it be validated? Besides, reliability is not universal, it usually comes in specialized domains.

This is not to say priorities (or indeed other forms of meta-level information) are not useful. Indeed it is important to use them in some situations when they are available, but we believe that to understand the elements of argumentation, we need to avoid drawing on them — we need to have a comprehensive framework for argumentation that works without recourse to priorities over formulae.

3 Arguments

We adopt a very common intuitive notion of an argument and consider some of the ramifications of the definition. Essentially, an argument is a set of appropriate formulae that can be used to classically prove some claim, together with that claim (formulae represent statements, including claims).

Definition 7.1. An **argument** is a pair $\langle \Phi, \alpha \rangle$ such that

1. $\Phi \not\vdash \bot$.

2. $\Phi \vdash \alpha$.

3. Φ is a minimal subset of Δ satisfying 2.

If $A = \langle \Phi, \alpha \rangle$ is an argument, we say that A is an argument for α (which in general is not an element of Δ) and we also say that Φ is a support for α. We call α the **claim** of the argument and we call Φ the **support** of the argument.

Example 7.1. Let $\Delta = \{a, a \to b, c \to \neg b, c, d, d \to b, \neg a, \neg c\}$. Some arguments are:

$$\langle \{a, a \to b\}, b \rangle$$
$$\langle \{c \to \neg b, c\}, \neg b \rangle$$
$$\langle \{d, d \to b\}, b \rangle$$
$$\langle \{\neg a\}, \neg a \rangle$$
$$\langle \{\neg c\}, \neg c \rangle$$
$$\langle \{a \to b\}, \neg a \lor b \rangle$$
$$\langle \{\neg c\}, d \to \neg c \rangle$$

The need for the first condition of Definition 7.1 can be illustrated by means of the next example.

Example 7.2. Consider the following atoms.

   a The office phone number is 020 4545 8721
   b I am a billionaire

Now let $\{a, \neg a\} \subseteq \Delta$, and so by classical logic, we have

$$\{a, \neg a\} \vdash b$$

However, we do not want to have $\{a, \neg a\}$ as the support for an argument with claim *b*. If we were to allow that as an argument, then we would have an argument with this support and with any claim in the language. Hence, if we were to allow inconsistent supports, then we would have an overwhelming number of useless arguments.

The second condition of Definition 7.1 aims at ensuring that the support is sufficient for the consequent to hold, as is illustrated in the next example.

Example 7.3. Consider the informal argument which is acceptable.

   It is an even number, and therefore we can infer it is not an odd number.

Now consider the following atoms.

   e It is an even number
   o It is an odd number

So we can represent the premise of informal argument by the set $\{e\}$. However, by classical logic we have that $\{e\} \nvdash \neg o$, and hence the following is not an argument.

$$\langle \{e\}, \neg o \rangle$$

If we want to turn the informal argument (which is an enthymeme) into an argument, we need to make explicit all the premises. So we can represent the above informal argument by the following formal argument.

$$\langle \{e, \neg e \lor \neg o\}, \neg o \rangle$$

An enthymeme is a form of reasoning in which some premises are implicit, most often because they are obvious. As another example, "The baby no longer has her parents, therefore she is an orphan" (in symbols, $\neg p$ hence o) is an enthymeme: The reasoning is correct despite omitting the trivial premise stating that "if a baby no longer has her parents, then she is an orphan" (in symbols, $\{\neg p, \neg p \rightarrow o\} \vdash o$).

Minimality (i.e., condition 3 Definition 7.1) is not an absolute requirement, although some properties depend on it. Importantly, the condition is not of a mere technical nature.

Example 7.4. Consider the following formulae.

p I like paprika
r It is raining
$r \rightarrow q$ If it is raining, then I should use my umbrella

It is possible to argue that "I should use my umbrella, because I should use my umbrella, if it is raining, and indeed it is", to be captured formally by the argument

$$\langle \{r, r \rightarrow q\}, q \rangle$$

In contrast, it is counter-intuitive to argue that "I should use my umbrella, because I like paprika and I should use my umbrella, if it is raining, and indeed it is", to be captured formally by

$$\langle \{p, r, r \rightarrow q\}, q \rangle$$

which fails to be an argument because condition 3 is not satisfied.

The underlying idea for condition 3 is that an argument makes explicit the connection between reasons for a claim and the claim itself. But that would not be the case if the reasons were not exactly identified. In other words, if reasons incorporated irrelevant information and so included formulae not used in the proof of the claim.

Arguments are not necessarily independent. In a sense, some encompass others (possibly up to some form of equivalence), which is the topic we now turn to.

Definition 7.2. An argument $\langle \Phi, \alpha \rangle$ is **more conservative** than an argument $\langle \Psi, \beta \rangle$ iff $\Phi \subseteq \Psi$ and $\beta \vdash \alpha$.

Example 7.5. $\langle \{a\}, a \lor b \rangle$ is more conservative than $\langle \{a, a \rightarrow b\}, b \rangle$.

Roughly speaking, a more conservative argument is more general: It is, so to speak, less demanding on the support and less specific about the consequent.

Example 7.6. Consider the following atoms.

p The number is divisible by 10
q The number is divisible by 2
r The number is an even number

We use these for the following set of formulae.

$$\Delta = \{p, p \to q, q \to r\}$$

Hence, the following is an argument with the claim "The number is divisible by 2".

$$\langle \{p, p \to q\}, q \rangle$$

Similarly, the following is argument with claim "The number is divisible by 2 and the number is an even number".

$$\langle \{p, p \to q, q \to r\}, r \wedge q \rangle$$

However, the first argument $\langle \{p, p \to q\}, q \rangle$ is more conservative than the second argument $\langle \{p, p \to q, q \to r\}, r \wedge q \rangle$ which can be retrieved from it:

$$\left. \begin{array}{l} \langle \{p, p \to q\}, q \rangle \\ \{q, q \to r\} \models r \wedge q \end{array} \right\} \quad \Rightarrow \quad \langle \{p, p \to q, q \to r\}, r \wedge q \rangle$$

We will use the notion of "more conservative" to help us identify the most useful counterarguments amongst the potentially large number of counterarguments.

4 Counterarguments

Informally, an argument that disagrees with another argument is described as a counterargument. So counterarguments are an important part of the argumentation process. They highlight points of contention.

In logic-based approaches to argumentation, an intuitive notion of counterargument is captured with the idea of defeaters, which are arguments whose claim refutes the support of another argument [23, 14, 19, 25, 24, 22]. This gives us a general way for an argument to challenge another.

Definition 7.3. A **defeater** for an argument $\langle \Phi, \alpha \rangle$ is an argument $\langle \Psi, \beta \rangle$ such that $\beta \vdash \neg(\phi_1 \wedge \ldots \wedge \phi_n)$ for some $\{\phi_1, \ldots, \phi_n\} \subseteq \Phi$.

Example 7.7. Let $\Delta = \{\neg a, a \vee b, a \leftrightarrow b, c \to a\}$. Then, $\langle \{a \vee b, a \leftrightarrow b\}, a \wedge b \rangle$ is a defeater for $\langle \{\neg a, c \to a\}, \neg c \rangle$. A more conservative defeater for $\langle \{\neg a, c \to a\}, \neg c \rangle$ is $\langle \{a \vee b, a \leftrightarrow b\}, a \vee c \rangle$.

The notion of assumption attack to be found in the literature is less general than the above notion of defeater, of which special cases are undercut and rebuttal as discussed next.

Some arguments directly oppose the support of others, which amounts to the notion of an undercut.

Definition 7.4. An **undercut** for an argument $\langle \Phi, \alpha \rangle$ is an argument $\langle \Psi, \neg(\phi_1 \wedge \ldots \wedge \phi_n) \rangle$ where $\{\phi_1, \ldots, \phi_n\} \subseteq \Phi$.

Example 7.8. Let $\Delta = \{a, a \rightarrow b, c, c \rightarrow \neg a\}$. Then, $\langle \{c, c \rightarrow \neg a\}, \neg(a \wedge (a \rightarrow b)) \rangle$ is an undercut for $\langle \{a, a \rightarrow b\}, b \rangle$. A less conservative undercut for $\langle \{a, a \rightarrow b\}, b \rangle$ is $\langle \{c, c \rightarrow \neg a\}, \neg a \rangle$.

The most direct form of a conflict between arguments is when two arguments have opposite claims. This case is captured in the literature through the notion of a rebuttal.

Definition 7.5. An argument $\langle \Psi, \beta \rangle$ is a **rebuttal** for an argument $\langle \Phi, \alpha \rangle$ iff $\beta \leftrightarrow \neg \alpha$ is a tautology.

Example 7.9. Consider a discussion in a newspaper editorial office about whether or not to proceed with the publication of some indiscretion about a prominent politician. Suppose the key bits of information are captured by the following five statements.

p Simon Jones is a Member of Parliament

$p \rightarrow \neg q$ If Simon Jones is a Member of Parliament then we need not keep quiet about details of his private life

r Simon Jones just resigned from the House of Commons

$r \rightarrow \neg p$ If Simon Jones just resigned from the House of Commons then he is not a Member of Parliament

$\neg p \rightarrow q$ If Simon Jones is not a Member of Parliament then we need to keep quiet about details of his private life

The first two statements form an argument A whose claim is that we can publicize details about his private life. The next two statements form an argument whose claim is that he is not a Member of Parliament (contradicting an item in the support of A) and that is a counterargument against A. The last three statements combine to give an argument whose claim is that we cannot publicize details about his private life (contradicting the claim of A) and that, too, is a counterargument against A. In symbols, we obtain the following argument (below left), and counterarguments (below right).

$$\langle \{p, p \rightarrow \neg q\}, \neg q \rangle \quad \left\{ \begin{array}{l} \text{An undercut is } \langle \{r, r \rightarrow \neg p\}, \neg p \rangle \\ \text{A rebuttal is } \langle \{r, r \rightarrow \neg p, \neg p \rightarrow q\}, q \rangle \end{array} \right.$$

Trivially, undercuts are defeaters but it is also quite simple to establish that rebuttals are defeaters. Furthermore, if an argument has defeaters then it has undercuts, naturally. It may happen that an argument has defeaters but no rebuttals as illustrated next.

Example 7.10. Let $\Delta = \{a \wedge b, \neg b\}$. Then, $\langle \{a \wedge b\}, a \rangle$ has at least one defeater but no rebuttal.

There are some important differences between rebuttals and undercuts that can be seen in the following examples. In the first, we see how an undercut for an argument need not be a rebuttal for that argument, and in the second, we see how rebuttal for an argument need not be an undercut for that argument.

Example 7.11. $\langle \{\neg a\}, \neg a \rangle$ is an undercut for $\langle \{a, a \rightarrow b\}, b \rangle$ but is not a rebuttal for it. Clearly, $\langle \{\neg a\}, \neg a \rangle$ does not rule out b. Actually, an undercut may even agree with the claim of the objected argument: $\langle \{b \wedge \neg a\}, \neg a \rangle$ is an undercut for $\langle \{a, a \rightarrow b\}, b \rangle$. In this case, we have an argument with an undercut that conflicts with the support of the argument but implicitly provides an alternative way to deduce the claim of the argument. This should make it clear that an undercut need not question the claim of an argument but only the reason(s) given by that argument to support its claim. Of course, there are also undercuts that challenge an argument on both counts: Just consider $\langle \{\neg a \wedge \neg b\}, \neg a \rangle$ which is such an undercut for the argument $\langle \{a, a \rightarrow b\}, b \rangle$.

Example 7.12. $\langle \{\neg b\}, \neg b \rangle$ is a rebuttal for $\langle \{a, a \rightarrow b\}, b \rangle$ but is not an undercut for it because b is not in $\{a, a \rightarrow b\}$. Observe that there is not even an argument equivalent to $\langle \{\neg b\}, \neg b \rangle$ which would be an undercut for $\langle \{a, a \rightarrow b\}, b \rangle$: In order to be an undercut for $\langle \{a, a \rightarrow b\}, b \rangle$, an argument should be of the form $\langle \Phi, \neg a \rangle$, $\langle \Phi, \neg(a \rightarrow b) \rangle$ or $\langle \Phi, \neg(a \wedge (a \rightarrow b)) \rangle$ but $\neg b$ is not logically equivalent to $\neg a$, $\neg(a \rightarrow b)$ or $\neg(a \wedge (a \rightarrow b))$.

Both undercuts and rebuttals are useful kinds of counterargument. However, we will see in the next section that we can effectively capture all we need to know about the counterarguments to an argument by just using a special kind of undercut called a canonical undercut.

5 Canonical undercuts

A particularly useful kind of undercut is the maximally conservative undercut which we define next.

Definition 7.6. $\langle \Psi, \beta \rangle$ is a **maximally conservative undercut** of $\langle \Phi, \alpha \rangle$ iff for all undercuts $\langle \Psi', \beta' \rangle$ of $\langle \Phi, \alpha \rangle$, if $\Psi' \subseteq \Psi$ and $\beta \vdash \beta'$ then $\Psi \subseteq \Psi'$ and $\beta' \vdash \beta$.

Evidently, $\langle \Psi, \beta \rangle$ is a maximally conservative undercut of $\langle \Phi, \alpha \rangle$ iff $\langle \Psi, \beta \rangle$ is an undercut of $\langle \Phi, \alpha \rangle$ such that no undercuts of $\langle \Phi, \alpha \rangle$ are strictly more conservative than $\langle \Psi, \beta \rangle$.

The next example shows that a collection of counterarguments to the same argument can sometimes be summarized in the form of a single maximally conservative undercut of the argument, thereby avoiding some amount of redundancy among counterarguments.

Example 7.13. Consider the following formulae concerning who is going to a party.

$r \rightarrow \neg p \wedge \neg q$ If Rachel goes, neither Paul nor Quincy go
p Paul goes
q Quincy goes

Hence both Paul and Quincy go (initial argument)

$$\langle \{p,q\}, p \wedge q \rangle$$

Now assume the following additional piece of information

r Rachel goes

Hence Paul does not go (a first counterargument)

$$\langle \{r, r \rightarrow \neg p \wedge \neg q\}, \neg p \rangle$$

Hence Quincy does not go (a second counterargument)

$$\langle r, r \rightarrow \neg p \wedge \neg q\}, \neg q \rangle$$

A maximally conservative undercut (for the initial argument) that subsumes both counterarguments above is

$$\langle \{r, r \rightarrow \neg p \wedge \neg q\}, \neg(p \wedge q) \rangle$$

The fact that the maximally conservative undercut in Example 7.13 happens to be a rebuttal of the argument is only accidental. Actually, the claim of a maximally conservative undercut for an argument is exactly the negation of the full support of the argument. In other words, if $\langle \Psi, \neg(\phi_1 \wedge \ldots \wedge \phi_n) \rangle$ is a maximally conservative undercut for an argument $\langle \Phi, \alpha \rangle$, then $\Phi = \{\phi_1, \ldots, \phi_n\}$.

Note that if $\langle \Psi, \neg(\phi_1 \wedge \ldots \wedge \phi_n) \rangle$ is a maximally conservative undercut for an argument $\langle \Phi, \alpha \rangle$, then so are $\langle \Psi, \neg(\phi_2 \wedge \ldots \wedge \phi_n \wedge \phi_1) \rangle$ and $\langle \Psi, \neg(\phi_3 \wedge \ldots \wedge \phi_n \wedge \phi_1 \wedge \phi_2) \rangle$ and so on. However, they are all identical (in the sense that each is more conservative than the others). We can ignore the unnecessary variants by just considering the canonical undercuts defined as follows.

Definition 7.7. An argument $\langle \Psi, \neg(\phi_1 \wedge \ldots \wedge \phi_n) \rangle$ is a **canonical undercut** for $\langle \Phi, \alpha \rangle$ iff it is an undercut for $\langle \Phi, \alpha \rangle$ and $\langle \phi_1, \ldots, \phi_n \rangle$ is the canonical enumeration of Φ.

Recall (from the Preliminaries section) that the ordering given by the canonical enumeration has no meaning and is not meant to represent any respective importance of formulae in Δ. It is only a convenient way to indicate the order in which we assume the formulae in any subset of Δ are conjoined to make a formula logically equivalent to that subset.

Example 7.14. Returning to Example 7.13, suppose the canonical enumeration is as follows.

$$\langle r, p, r \rightarrow \neg p \wedge \neg q, q \rangle$$

Then both the following are maximally conservative undercuts, but only the first is a canonical undercut.

$$\langle \{r, r \rightarrow \neg p \wedge \neg q\}, \neg(p \wedge q) \rangle$$
$$\langle \{r, r \rightarrow \neg p \wedge \neg q\}, \neg(q \wedge p) \rangle$$

The nice feature of canonical undercuts is that they are all maximally conservative undercuts. In other words, an argument $\langle \Psi, \neg(\phi_1 \wedge \ldots \wedge \phi_n) \rangle$ is a canonical undercut for $\langle \Phi, \alpha \rangle$ iff it is a maximally conservative undercut for $\langle \Phi, \alpha \rangle$ and $\langle \phi_1, \ldots, \phi_n \rangle$ is the canonical enumeration of Φ.

Clearly, an argument may have more than one canonical undercut. This raises the question of how do the canonical undercuts for the same argument look like, and how do they differ from one another? In response to the first question, any two different canonical undercuts for the same argument have the same claim, but distinct supports, and in response to the second question, given two different canonical undercuts for the same argument, none is more conservative than the other.

Example 7.15. Let $\Delta = \{a, b, \neg a, \neg b\}$. Both the following are canonical undercuts for $\langle \{a, b\}, a \leftrightarrow b \rangle$, but neither is more conservative than the other.

$$\langle \{\neg a\}, \neg(a \wedge b) \rangle$$
$$\langle \{\neg b\}, \neg(a \wedge b) \rangle$$

A further important property of canonical undercuts is the following which shows how they give us the useful information concerning counterarguments for an argument: For each defeater $\langle \Psi, \beta \rangle$ of an argument $\langle \Phi, \alpha \rangle$, there exists a canonical undercut for $\langle \Phi, \alpha \rangle$ that is more conservative than $\langle \Psi, \beta \rangle$. Therefore, the set of all canonical undercuts of an argument represent all the defeaters of that argument (informally, all its counterarguments). This is to be taken advantage of in the next section.

6 Argument trees

How does argumentation usually take place? Argumentation starts when an initial argument is put forward, making some claim. An objection is raised, in the form of a counterargument. The latter is addressed in turn, eventually giving rise to a counter-counterargument, if any. And so on. However, there often is more than one counterargument to the initial argument, and if the counterargument actually raised in the first place had been different, the counter-counterargument would have been different, too, and similarly the counter-counter-counterargument, if any, and so on, and hence the argumentation would have taken a possibly quite different course.

So do we find all the alternative courses which could take place from a given initial argument? And is it possible to represent them in a rational way? Let alone the most basic question: How do we make sure that no further counterargument can be expressed from the information available?

Example 7.16. Let the following be our knowledgebase.

$$\{a, b, c, \neg a \vee \neg b \vee \neg c\}$$

Suppose we start with the following argument.

$$\langle \{a, b, c\}, a \wedge b \wedge c \rangle$$

Now we have numerous undercuts to this argument including the following.

$$\langle \{b, c, \neg a \vee \neg b \vee \neg c\}, \neg a \rangle$$
$$\langle \{a, c, \neg a \vee \neg b \vee \neg c\}, \neg b \rangle$$
$$\langle \{a, b, \neg a \vee \neg b \vee \neg c\}, \neg c \rangle$$
$$\langle \{a, \neg a \vee \neg b \vee \neg c\}, \neg b \vee \neg c \rangle$$
$$\langle \{b, \neg a \vee \neg b \vee \neg c\}, \neg a \vee \neg c \rangle$$
$$\langle \{c, \neg a \vee \neg b \vee \neg c\}, \neg a \vee \neg b \rangle$$
$$\langle \{\neg a \vee \neg b \vee \neg c\}, \neg a \vee \neg b \vee \neg c \rangle$$

All these undercuts say the same thing which is that the set $\{a, b, c\}$ is inconsistent together with the formula $\neg a \vee \neg b \vee \neg c$. As a result, this can be captured by the last undercut listed above. Note this is the maximally conservative undercut amongst the undercuts listed, and moreover it is a canonical undercut. This example therefore illustrates how the canonical undercuts are the undercuts that represent all the other undercuts.

Often each undercut may itself be undercut, as illustrated by the next example.

Example 7.17. Consider the following atoms that concern the debate on addressing the shortage of oil with biofuel and thereby addressing the effect of the shortage on inflation. However, when grain is used to produce biofuel, then this can cause inflation because it causes shortages of grain for food. But, biofuel can be produced from the large unexploited sources of biowaste (such as the remainder of the wheat plant after the grain has been removed).

o there is decreased availability of oil
b there is increased production of biofuel
g there is decreased availability of food grain
i there is increased inflation of prices
w there is unexploited availability of biowaste

We can use these for the following formulae.

$$\{o, o \to b, b \to g, b \to \neg i, g \to i, w, w \to b \land \neg g\}$$

Now we can form the the following argument to capture the first part of the above discussion.

$$\langle \{o, o \to b, b \to \neg i\}, \neg i \rangle$$

The following canonical undercut captures the counterargument to the above.

$$\langle \{o, o \to b, b \to g, g \to i\}, \neg(o \land (o \to b) \land (b \to \neg i)) \rangle$$

We can capture the counterargument to the above undercut by the following canonical undercut.

$$\langle \{w, w \to b \land \neg g\}, \neg(o \land (o \to b) \land (b \to g) \land (g \to i)) \rangle$$

So we can represent the above discussion by three arguments, where we start with an argument, we have an undercut to that argument, and an undercut to the undercut.

It is also common to have more than one canonical undercut for an argument. Multiple undercuts are illustrated by the following example.

Example 7.18. Suppose we have the following knowledgebase.

$$\{(\neg r \to \neg p) \to \neg q, (p \to s) \to \neg\neg q, r, s, \neg p\}$$

Also suppose we construct the following argument.

$$\langle \{r, (\neg r \to \neg p) \to \neg q\}, \neg q \rangle$$

Then the following two arguments are each a canonical undercut to the above argument.

$$\langle \{s, (p \to s) \to \neg\neg q\}, \neg(r \land (\neg r \to \neg p) \to \neg q) \rangle$$
$$\langle \{\neg p, (p \to s) \to \neg\neg q\}, \neg(r \land (\neg r \to \neg p) \to \neg q) \rangle$$

Finally, the following argument is a canonical undercut to the first of the above canonical undercuts.

$$\langle \{\neg p, (\neg r \to \neg p) \to \neg q\}, \neg(s \land (p \to s) \to \neg\neg q) \rangle$$

We now turn to one final issue before we formalize the notion of argument trees.

Example 7.19. Argumentation sometimes falls into a repetitive and uninformative cycle as illustrated below with a case of the "Chicken and Egg dilemma".

> Dairyman: – Egg was first
> Farmer: – Chicken was first
> Dairyman: – Egg was first
> Farmer: – Chicken was first
>   . . .   – . . .

The following propositional atoms are introduced:

p Egg was first
q Chicken was first
r The chicken comes from the egg
s The egg comes from the chicken

It can be assumed that the chicken was first and that the egg was first are not equivalent. (i.e. $\neg(p \leftrightarrow q)$). Also, it can be assumed that the egg comes from the chicken (i.e. s) and the chicken comes from the egg (i.e. r). Moreover, if the egg comes from the chicken then the egg was not first. (i.e. $s \rightarrow \neg p$). Similarly, if the chicken comes from the egg then the chicken was not first (i.e. $r \rightarrow \neg q$). Then, the above dispute can be represented as follows:

$$\langle \{s \rightarrow \neg p, s, \neg(p \leftrightarrow q)\}, q \rangle$$
$$\uparrow$$
$$\langle \{r \rightarrow \neg q, r, \neg(p \leftrightarrow q)\}, p \rangle$$
$$\uparrow$$
$$\langle \{s \rightarrow \neg p, s, \neg(p \leftrightarrow q)\}, q \rangle$$
$$\uparrow$$
$$\langle \{r \rightarrow \neg q, r, \neg(p \leftrightarrow q)\}, p \rangle$$
$$\uparrow$$
$$\vdots$$

We are now ready for our definition (below) of an argument tree in which the root of the tree is an argument of interest, and the children for any node are the canonical undercuts for that node. In the definition, we avoid the circularity seen in the above example by incorporating an intuitive constraint.

Definition 7.8. An **argument tree** for α is a tree where the nodes are arguments such that

1. The root is an argument for α.
2. For no node $\langle \Phi, \beta \rangle$ with ancestor nodes $\langle \Phi_1, \beta_1 \rangle, \ldots, \langle \Phi_n, \beta_n \rangle$ is Φ a subset of $\Phi_1 \cup \cdots \cup \Phi_n$.
3. The children nodes of a node N consist of all canonical undercuts for N that obey 2.

We illustrate the definition of an argument tree in the following examples.

Example 7.20. Returning to Example 7.9, we have the following five formulae.

p Simon Jones is a Member of Parliament
$p \rightarrow \neg q$ If Simon Jones is a Member of Parliament then we need not keep quiet about details of his private life
r Simon Jones just resigned from the House of Commons
$r \rightarrow \neg p$ If Simon Jones just resigned from the House of Commons then he is not a Member of Parliament
$\neg p \rightarrow q$ If Simon Jones is not a Member of Parliament then we need to keep quiet about details of his private life

These can be used to construct the argument tree below.

$$\langle \{p, p \rightarrow \neg q\}, \neg q \rangle$$
$$\uparrow$$
$$\langle \{r, r \rightarrow \neg p\}, \neg(p \wedge (p \rightarrow \neg q))) \rangle$$

Example 7.21. Given $\Delta = \{a, a \rightarrow b, c, c \rightarrow \neg a, \neg c \vee \neg a\}$, we have the following argument tree.

$$\langle \{a, a \rightarrow b\}, b \rangle$$

$$\langle \{c, c \rightarrow \neg a\}, \neg(a \wedge (a \rightarrow b))) \rangle \qquad \langle \{c, \neg c \vee \neg a\}, \neg(a \wedge (a \rightarrow b))) \rangle$$

Note the two undercuts are equivalent. They do count as two arguments because they are based on two different items of the knowledgebase (even though these items turn out to be logically equivalent).

For the rest of this chapter, we adopt a lighter notation, writing $\langle \Psi, \diamond \rangle$ for a canonical undercut of $\langle \Phi, \beta \rangle$. Clearly, $\diamond$ is $\neg(\phi_1 \wedge \ldots \wedge \phi_n)$ where $\langle \phi_1, \ldots, \phi_n \rangle$ is the canonical enumeration for Φ.

Example 7.22. Consider the following atoms concerning the safety of mobiles phones for children.

q_1 Mobile phones are safe for children
q_2 Mobile phones have a health risk
q_3 Mobile phones heat the brain
q_4 Mobile phones emit strong electromagnetic radiation
q_5 There is a high density of phone masts
q_6 Mobile phones can be used hands-free
q_7 Hot baths heat the brain

Now suppose we have the following knowledgebase

$$\{\neg q_2, \neg q_2 \rightarrow q_1, q_4, q_4 \rightarrow q_3, q_3 \rightarrow q_2, q_5, q_5 \rightarrow \neg q_4, q_6, q_6 \rightarrow \neg q_3, q_7, q_7 \rightarrow \neg q_2\}$$

From this knowledgebase, we can obtain the following argument tree.

$$\langle \{\neg q_2, \neg q_2 \rightarrow q_1\}, q_1 \rangle$$
$$\uparrow$$
$$\langle \{q_4, q_4 \rightarrow q_3, q_3 \rightarrow q_2\}, \diamond \rangle$$
$$\langle \{q_5, q_5 \rightarrow \neg q_4\}, \diamond \rangle \quad \langle \{q_6, q_6 \rightarrow \neg q_3\}, \diamond \rangle \quad \langle \{q_7, q_7 \rightarrow \neg q_2\}, \diamond \rangle$$

We motivate the conditions of Definition 7.8 as follows: Condition 2 is meant to avoid the situation illustrated by Example 7.23; and Condition 3 is meant to avoid the situation illustrated by Example 7.24.

Example 7.23. Let $\Delta = \{a, a \to b, c \to \neg a, c\}$.

$$\langle \{a, a \to b\}, b \rangle$$
$$\uparrow$$
$$\langle \{c, c \to \neg a\}, \diamondsuit \rangle$$
$$\uparrow$$
$$\langle \{a, c \to \neg a\}, \diamondsuit \rangle$$

This is not an argument tree because Condition 2 is not met. The undercut to the undercut is actually making exactly the same point (that a and c are incompatible) as the undercut itself does, just by using modus tollens instead of modus ponens.

Example 7.24. Given $\Delta = \{a, b, a \to c, b \to d, \neg a \vee \neg b\}$, consider the following tree.

$$\langle \{a, b, a \to c, b \to d\}, c \wedge d \rangle$$

$$\langle \{a, \neg a \vee \neg b\}, \neg b \rangle \qquad\qquad \langle \{b, \neg a \vee \neg b\}, \neg a \rangle$$

This is not an argument tree because the two children nodes are not maximally conservative undercuts. The first undercut is essentially the same argument as the second undercut in a rearranged form (relying on a and b being incompatible, assume one and then conclude that the other doesn't hold). If we replace these by the maximally conservative undercut $\langle \{\neg a \vee \neg b\}, \diamondsuit \rangle$, we obtain an argument tree.

The form of an argument tree is not arbitrary. It summarizes all possible courses of argumentation about the argument in the root node. Each node except the root node is the starting point of an implicit series of related arguments. What happens is that for each possible course of argumentation (from the root), an initial sequence is provided as a branch of the tree up to the point that no subsequent counter[n]-argument needs a new item in its support (where new means not occurring somewhere in that initial sequence). Also, the counterarguments in a course of argumentation may somewhat differ from the ones in the corresponding branch of the argument tree:

Example 7.25. We return to Example 7.18 which has the following knowledgebase.

$$\{(\neg r \to \neg p) \to \neg q, (p \to s) \to \neg\neg q, r, s, \neg p\}$$

The argument tree with $\langle \{r, (\neg r \to \neg p) \to \neg q\}, \neg q \rangle$ as its root is

$$\langle \{r, (\neg r \to \neg p) \to \neg q\}, \neg q \rangle$$

$$\langle \{s, (p \to s) \to \neg\neg q\}, \diamondsuit \rangle \qquad \langle \{\neg p, (p \to s) \to \neg\neg q\}, \diamondsuit \rangle$$
$$\uparrow$$
$$\langle \{\neg p, (\neg r \to \neg p) \to \neg q\}, \diamondsuit \rangle$$

Example 7.26. We return to the "Chicken and Egg dilemma" presented in Example 7.19

> Dairyman: – Egg was first
> Farmer: – Chicken was first
> Dairyman: – Egg was first
> Farmer: – Chicken was first
>   ...   – ...

Here are the formulae again:

> p Egg was first
> q Chicken was first
> r The chicken comes from the egg
> s The egg comes from the chicken
> $\neg(p \leftrightarrow q)$ That the egg was first and that the chicken was first are not equivalent
> $r \rightarrow \neg q$ The chicken comes from the egg implies that the chicken was not first
> $s \rightarrow \neg p$ The egg comes from the chicken implies that the egg was not first

So, $\Delta = \{\neg(p \leftrightarrow q), r \rightarrow \neg q, s \rightarrow \neg p, r, s\}$. The argument tree with the dairyman's argument as its root is

$$\langle\{r \rightarrow \neg q, r, \neg(q \leftrightarrow p)\}, p\rangle$$
$$\uparrow$$
$$\langle\{s \rightarrow \neg p, s, \neg(q \leftrightarrow p)\}, \Diamond\rangle$$

but it does not mean that the farmer has the last word nor that the farmer wins the dispute! The argument tree is merely a representation of the argumentation (in which the dairyman provides the initial argument). Although the argument tree is finite, the argumentation here is infinite and unresolved.

We now consider a widely used criterion in argumentation theory for determining whether the argument at the root of the argument tree is warranted (e.g. [21, 15]). For this, each node is marked as either U for **undefeated** or D for **defeated**.

Definition 7.9. The **judge function**, denoted Judge, assigns either Warranted or Unwarranted to each argument tree T such that $\text{Judge}(T) = \text{Warranted}$ iff $\text{Mark}(A_r) = U$ where A_r is the root node of T. For all nodes A_i in T, if there is child A_j of A_i such that $\text{Mark}(A_j) = U$, then $\text{Mark}(A_i) = D$, otherwise $\text{Mark}(A_i) = U$.

As a direct consequence of the above definition, the root is undefeated iff all its children are defeated.

Example 7.27. Returning to Example 7.22, we see that the root of the tree T is undefeated, and hence $\text{Judge}(T) = \text{Warranted}$.

Example 7.28. Returning to Example 7.26, we see that the root of the tree T is defeated, and hence $\text{Judge}(T) = \text{Unwarranted}$.

In general, a complete argument tree (i.e. an argument tree with all the canonical undercuts for each node as children of that node) provides an efficient representation of the arguments and counterarguments. Furthermore, if Δ is finite, there is a finite number of argument trees with the root being an argument with claim α that can be formed from Δ, and each of these trees has finite branching and a finite depth.

7 Discussion

In this chapter, we have reviewed a framework for argumentation based on classical logic. The key features of this framework are the clarification of the nature of arguments and counterarguments, the identification of canonical undercuts which we argue are the only undercuts that we need to take into account, and the representation of argument trees which provide a way of exhaustively collating arguments and counterarguments. This chapter is based on a particular proposal for logic-based argumentation for the propositional case [3, 6]. In comparison with the previous proposals based on classical logic (e.g. [1, 20]), our proposal provides a much more detailed analysis of counterarguments, and ours is the first proposal to consider canonical undercuts. We believe that without the notion of canonical undercuts, the number of undercuts available is unmanageable, and so restricting to canonical undercuts reduces the number of undercuts to consider, and renders it manageable.

It is interesting to compare our approach with other logic-based approaches to argumentation that use logics other than classical logic for the definition of deduction. The most common alternative is a form of defeasible logic such as defeasible logic programming [15], defeasible argumentation with specificity-based preferences [23], and argument-based extended logic programming [21]. For a general coverage of defeasible logics in argumentation see [10, 22, 6].

Whilst there are various positive features of these proposals based on defeasible logic, including computational viability, and modeling of intuitive features of defeasible reasoning, there are complications with these proposals with respect to the interplay between strict rules and defeasible rules, and the interplay between these rules and the use of priorities over rules. This can render the deductive process to be less than transparent. In comparison, we believe that using classical logic provides a simpler and clear notion of deduction, of argument, and of counterargument.

Furthermore, various questions of rationality have been raised concerning the use of defeasible logic for deduction in argumentation [8]. One of the proposals made for rationality is that contrapositive reasoning needs to be supported. Introducing contrapositive reasoning is controversial in defeasible logic [9], but it is an intrinsic feature of classical logic. In other words, classical logic offers a nice solution to the problems raised in [8].

A more general approach to logic-based argumentation is to leave the logic for deduction as a parameter. This was proposed in abstract argumentation systems [25], and developed in assumption-based argumentation (ABA) [11]. A substantial part of the development of the theory and implement of ABA is focused on defeasible logic. However, ABA is a general framework allowing for the use classical logic for deduction, and thereby we could instantiate ABA with our proposal.

It is also interesting to compare our approach with abstract argument systems. Superficially, an argument tree could be viewed as an argument framework in Dung's system. An argument in an argument tree could be viewed as an argument in a Dung argument framework, and each arc in an argument tree could be viewed as an attack relation. However, the way sets of arguments are compared is different.

Some differences between Dung's approach and our approach can be seen in the following examples.

Example 7.29. Consider a set of arguments $\{A_1, A_2, A_3, A_4\}$ with the attack relation $\mathcal{R}$ s.t. $A_2 \mathcal{R} A_1$, $A_3 \mathcal{R} A_2$, $A_4 \mathcal{R} A_3$, and $A_1 \mathcal{R} A_4$. Here there is an admissible set $\{A_1, A_3\}$. We can try to construct an argument tree with A_1 at the root. As a counterpart to the attack relation, we regard that A_1 is undercut by A_2, A_2 is undercut by A_3, and so on. However, the corresponding sequence of nodes A_1, A_2, A_3, A_4, A_1 is not an argument tree because A_1 occurs twice in the branch (violating Condition 2 of Definition 7.8). So, the form of the argument tree for A_1 fails to represent the fact that A_1 attacks A_4.

Example 7.30. Let $\Delta = \{b, b \to a, d \wedge \neg b, \neg d \wedge \neg b\}$, giving the following argument tree for a.

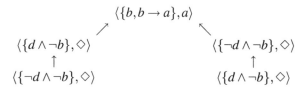

$$\langle \{b, b \to a\}, a \rangle$$

$$\langle \{d \wedge \neg b\}, \Diamond \rangle \qquad\qquad \langle \{\neg d \wedge \neg b\}, \Diamond \rangle$$
$$\uparrow \qquad\qquad\qquad\qquad\qquad \uparrow$$
$$\langle \{\neg d \wedge \neg b\}, \Diamond \rangle \qquad\qquad \langle \{d \wedge \neg b\}, \Diamond \rangle$$

For this let A_1 be $\langle \{b, b \to a\}, a \rangle$, A_2 be $\langle \{d \wedge \neg b\}, \Diamond \rangle$ and A_3 be $\langle \{\neg d \wedge \neg b\}, \Diamond \rangle$. Disregarding the difference between the occurrences of $\Diamond$, this argument tree rewrites as $A_2 \mathcal{R} A_1$, $A_3 \mathcal{R} A_1$, $A_3 \mathcal{R} A_2$, and $A_2 \mathcal{R} A_3$ where A_1 denotes the root node $\langle \{b, b \to a\}, a \rangle$. In this argument tree, each defeater of the root node is defeated. Yet no admissible set of arguments contains A_1.

Our proposal has been extended in a number of ways. As covered in [6], we have proposed techniques that take into account intrinsic aspects of the arguments and counterargument such as the degree of conflict between them, and the degree of similarity between them, and extrinsic aspects such as the impact on the audience and the empathy or antipathy the audience may have for individual arguments.

Further developments include formalization of enthymemes in our logic-based framework [16, 7], a generalization of the framework to also consider the proponent of each argument, and thereby argue about whether a proponent is an appropriate proponent for that argument [17], and a refinement of the proposal to reason with temporal knowledge [18].

We have also generalised the proposal reviewed in this chapter to handle first-order logic [4]. Indeed, this is straightforward since all we need to do is to use a first-order language and to use the classical first-order consequence relation instead of the classical propositional logic. The key finiteness results still hold: So for a finite number of formulae in the knowledgebase, there is a finite number of argument trees for a claim, and each of these trees contains a finite number of nodes.

We have developed algorithms for generating arguments [12, 13], formalizations of decision problems concerning arguments and counterarguments in quantified Boolean formulas [2], and compilation techniques with the aim of improving the viability of argumentation based on classical logic [5].

Acknowledgements

We wish to thank Maria Vanina Martinez for feedback on an earlier draft of this chapter.

References

1. L. Amgoud and C. Cayrol. On the acceptability of arguments in preference-based argumentation. In G. Cooper and S. Moral, editors, *Proceedings of the 14th Conference on Uncertainty in Artificial Intelligence (UAI 1998)*, pages 1–7. Morgan Kaufmann, 1998.
2. Ph. Besnard, A. Hunter, and S. Woltran. Encoding deductive argumentation in quantified boolean formulae. Technical Report DBAI-TR-2008-60, Database and Artificial Intelligence Group, Institute of Information Systems, Technischen Universität Wien, 2008.
3. Ph. Besnard and A. Hunter. A logic-based theory of deductive arguments. *Artificial Intelligence*, 128:203–235, 2001.
4. Ph. Besnard and A. Hunter. Practical first-order argumentation. In *Proceedings of the 20th National Conference on Artificial Intelligence (AAAI 2005)*, pages 590–595. MIT Press, 2005.
5. Ph. Besnard and A. Hunter. Knowledgebase compilation for efficient logical argumentation. In *Proceedings of the 10th International Conference on Knowledge Representation (KR 2006)*, pages 123–133. AAAI Press, 2006.
6. Ph. Besnard and A. Hunter. *Elements of Argumentation*. MIT Press, 2008.
7. E. Black and A. Hunter. Using enthymemes in an inquiry dialogue system. In *Proceedings of the Seventh International Joint Conference on Autonomous Agents and Multi-Agent Systems (AAMAS'08)*, pages 437–444. ACM Press, 2008.
8. M. Caminada and L. Amgoud. An axiomatic account of formal argumentation. In *Proceedings of the 20th National Conference on Artificial Intelligence (AAAI 2005)*, pages 608–613, 2005.
9. M. Caminada. On the issue of contraposition of defeasible rules. In *Computational Models of Argument: Proceedings of COMMA 2008*, pages 109–115. IOS Press, 2008.
10. C. Chesñevar, A. Maguitman, and R. Loui. Logical models of argument. *ACM Computing Surveys*, 32:337–383, 2000.
11. P. Dung, R. Kowalski, and F. Toni. Dialectical proof procedures for assumption-based admissible argumentation. *Artificial Intelligence*, 170:114–159, 2006.
12. V. Efstathiou and A. Hunter. Algorithms for effective argumentation in classical propositional logic. In *Proceedings of the International Symposium on Foundations of Information and Knowledge Systems (FOIKS'08)*, volume 4932 of *LNCS*, pages 272–290. Springer, 2008.
13. V. Efstathiou and A. Hunter. Focused search for arguments from propositional knowledge. In *Computation Models of Argument: Proceedings of COMMA 2008*, pages 159–170. IOS Press, 2008.
14. J. Fox, P. Krause, and M. Elvang-Gøransson. Argumentation as a general framework for uncertain reasoning. In *Proceedings of the 9th Conference on Uncertainty in Artificial Intelligence (UAI 1993)*, pages 428–434. Morgan Kaufmann, 1993.
15. A. García and G. Simari. Defeasible logic programming: An argumentative approach. *Theory and Practice of Logic Programming*, 4:95–138, 2004.
16. A. Hunter. Real arguments are approximate arguments. In *Proceedings of the 22nd AAAI Conference on Artificial Intelligence (AAAI'07)*, pages 66–71. MIT Press, 2007.
17. A. Hunter. Reasoning about the appropriateness of proponents for arguments. In *Proceedings of the 23rd AAAI Conference on Artificial Intelligence (AAAI'08)*. MIT Press, 2008.
18. N. Mann and A. Hunter. Argumentation using temporal knowledge. In *Computational Models of Argument: Proceedings of COMMA'08*, pages 204–215. IOS Press, 2008.

19. D. Nute. Defeasible logics. In *Handbook of Logic in Artificial Intelligence and Logic Programming, Volume 3: Nonmonotonic Reasoning and Uncertainty Reasoning*, pages 355–395. Oxford University Press, 1994.
20. J. Pollock. How to reason defeasibly. *Artificial Intelligence*, 57:1–42, 1992.
21. H. Prakken and G. Sartor. Argument-based extended logic programming with defeasible priorities. *Journal of Applied Non-classical Logic*, 7:25–75, 1997.
22. H. Prakken and G. Vreeswijk. Logical systems for defeasible argumentation. In D. Gabbay, editor, *Handbook of Philosophical Logic*, pages 219–318. Kluwer, 2002.
23. G. Simari and R. Loui. A mathematical treatment of defeasible reasoning and its implementation. *Artificial Intelligence*, 53:125–157, 1992.
24. B. Verheij. Automated argument assistance for lawyers. In *Proceedings of the 7th International Conference on Artificial Intelligence and Law (ICAIL 1999)*, pages 43–52. ACM Press, 1999.
25. G. Vreeswijk. Abstract argumentation systems. *Artificial Intelligence*, 90:225–279, 1997.

Chapter 8
Argument-based Logic Programming

Alejandro J. García, Jürgen Dix and Guillermo R. Simari

1 Introduction

In this chapter we describe several formalisms for integrating *Logic Programming* and *Argumentation*. Research on the relation between logic programming and argumentation has been and still is fruitful in both directions: Some argumentation formalisms were used to define semantics for logic programming and also logic programming was used for providing an underlying representational language for non-abstract argumentation formalisms.

One of the first attempts dates back to 1987, when Donald Nute [19] introduced a formalism called LDR (*Logic for Defeasible Reasoning*) with a simple representational language consisting of three types of rules: *Strict, defeasible* and *defeaters*. Although LDR is not a defeasible argumentation formalism in itself, its implementation, d-Prolog, defined as an extension of PROLOG, was the first language that introduced defeasible reasoning programming *with specificity* as a comparison criterion between rules.

Another important step was taken in the nineties, when Phan M. Dung [10] emphasized that *"there are extremely interesting relations between argumentation and logic programming"*. Dung showed that argumentation can be viewed as a special form of logic programming with negation as failure. He introduced a general logic

Alejandro J. García
Consejo Nacional de Investigaciones Científicas y Técnicas (CONICET)
Department of Computer Science and Engineering, Universidad Nacional del Sur
e-mail: ajg@cs.uns.edu.ar

Guillermo R. Simari
Department of Computer Science and Engineering, Universidad Nacional del Sur
e-mail: grs@cs.uns.edu.ar

Jürgen Dix
Department of Informatics Clausthal University of Technology
e-mail: dix@tu-clausthal.de

I. Rahwan, G. R. Simari (eds.), *Argumentation in Artificial Intelligence*,
DOI 10.1007/978-0-387-98197-0 8, © Springer Science+Business Media, LLC 2009
153

programming based method for generating meta-interpreters for argumentation systems.

A few years later, in 1997, inspired by legal reasoning, Prakken and Sartor [24] introduced an argument-based formalism for extended logic programming with defeasible priorities. In their formalism, arguments are expressed in a logic programming language with both strong and default negation. Conflicts between arguments are decided with the help of priorities on the rules. These priorities can be defeasibly derived as conclusions within the system. The semantics of the system is given by a fixed point definition, while its proof theory is stated in dialectical style. A proof takes the form of a *dialogue between a proponent and an opponent*: An argument is shown to be justified if the proponent can make the opponent run out of moves in whatever way the opponent attacks.

Another formalism for combining logic programming and argumentation, *Defeasible Logic Programming* (DeLP) has been introduced by García and Simari in [15]. The representational language of DeLP is defined as an extension of a logic programming language that considers two types of rules: Strict and defeasible, and allows for both strong and default negation. A DeLP-query succeeds, *i.e.*, it is warranted from a DeLP-program, if it is possible to build an argument that supports the query and this argument is found to be undefeated by a warrant procedure. This process implements an exhaustive dialectical analysis that involves the construction and evaluation of arguments that either support or interfere with the given query. The DeLP dialectical analysis is based on previous works on defeasible argumentation conducted by Simari and Loui [28], and Simari, Chesñevar, and García [27].

In [26], Schweimeier and Schroeder formulate a variety of notions of attack for extended logic programs from combinations of undercut and rebuttal. As shown in Section 4, their language corresponds to that used by Prakken and Sartor [24] *without strict rules and any priorities*. They also define a general hierarchy of argumentation semantics parameterized by the notions of attack chosen by the proponent and the opponent. They prove the equivalence and subset relationships between the semantics and examine some essential properties concerning consistency and the coherence principle, which relates default negation and explicit negation.

The rest of the chapter is organized as follows. Section 2 describes Defeasible Logic Programming. Section 3 introduces Prakken's approach of argument-based extended logic programming with defeasible priorities. Section 4 gives an overview of argumentation semantics for extended logic programming by Schweimeier and Schroeder. Section 5 introduces Dung's approach and Section 6 illustrates Nute's framework. Finally, in Section 7 we discuss more recent developments before concluding with Section 8.

2 Defeasible Logic Programming

Defeasible Logic Programming (DeLP), as introduced in [15], is a formalism that combines techniques of both logic programming and defeasible argumentation. As in logic programming, in DeLP knowledge is represented using facts and rules; however, DeLP also provides the possibility of representing information in the form of *weak rules* in a declarative manner. These weak rules are the key element for introducing *defeasibility* [21] and they are used to represent a relation between pieces of knowledge that could be *defeated* when all things have been considered. DeLP uses a defeasible argumentation inference mechanism for warranting the entailed conclusions.

A *defeasible logic program* (*DeLP-program* for short), is a set of facts, strict rules and defeasible rules, defined as follows.

- *Facts* are ground literals representing atomic information or the negation of atomic information using strong negation "$\sim$", (*e.g.,* *chicken*(*little*) and $\sim$*scared*(*little*)).
- *Strict rules*, denoted by $L_0 \leftarrow L_1, \ldots, L_n$, represent non-defeasible information. The *head* of the rule, L_0, is a ground literal and the *body* $\{L_i\}_{i>0}$ is a non-empty set of ground literals, (*e.g., bird $\leftarrow$ chicken* and $\sim$*innocent $\leftarrow$ guilty*).
- *Defeasible rules*, denoted by $L_0 \prec L_1, \ldots, L_n$, represent tentative information. The head L_0 is a ground literal and the body $\{L_i\}_{i>0}$ is a non-empty set of ground literals (*e.g., $\sim$flies $\prec$ chicken* or *flies $\prec$ chicken, scared*).

Syntactically, the symbol "$\prec$" is all that distinguishes a defeasible rule from a strict one. Pragmatically, a defeasible rule is used to represent tentative information that may be used if nothing could be posed against it. A defeasible rule "*H $\prec$ B*" is understood as expressing that "*reasons to believe in the antecedent B provide reasons to believe in the consequent H*" [28]. For instance, "*lights_on $\prec$ switch_on*" expresses that reasons to believe that the switch of a room is on, provide reasons to believe that lights will be on. Note that this rule represents *tentative information* because it may happen that the switch is on and the lights are not on, for example, if light bulbs are broken, or there is no electricity (as represented by the following rule: "$\sim$*lights_on $\prec$ $\sim$electricity*").

The information that represents a strict rule is not tentative. For instance, given "$\sim$*innocent $\leftarrow$ guilty*" and the fact *guilty*, then it will not be possible to infer *innocent*. That is, if *guilty* has a strict derivation then $\sim$*innocent* will also have a strict derivation and *innocent* cannot be concluded. However, as it will be shown below, if *guilty* is a tentative conclusion, then $\sim$*innocent* will also be a tentative conclusion, and *innocent* may be concluded if there is information that supports it.

When required, a DeLP-program is denoted by the pair (Π, Δ) distinguishing the subset Π of facts and strict rules (that represents non-defeasible knowledge), and the subset Δ of defeasible rules. Observe that strict and defeasible rules are ground. However, following the usual convention [17], some examples will use "schematic rules" with variables. To distinguish variables, they are written with an uppercase letter. In examples, a period may be used as a delimiter between rules or facts. As in logic programming, queries can be posed to a program. A DeLP-*query* is a ground literal that DeLP will try to warrant. For example, *dark*(*a*) or *illuminated*(*b*) are DeLP-queries.

Example 8.1. Consider the DeLP-program $(\Pi_{8.1}, \Delta_{8.1})$ where:

$$\Pi_{8.1} = \begin{cases} night. & switch\_on(a). \\ \sim day \leftarrow night. & switch\_on(b). \\ \sim dark(X) \leftarrow illuminated(X). & switch\_on(c). \\ sunday. & \sim electricity(b). \\ deadline. & \sim electricity(c). \\ & emergency\_lights(c). \end{cases}$$

$$\Delta_{8.1} = \begin{cases} lights\_on(X) \prec switch\_on(X). \\ \sim lights\_on(X) \prec \sim electricity(X). \\ lights\_on(X) \prec \sim electricity(X), emergency\_lights(X). \\ dark(X) \prec \sim day. \\ illuminated(X) \prec lights\_on(X), \sim day. \\ working\_at(X) \prec illuminated(X). \\ \sim working\_at(X) \prec sunday. \\ working\_at(X) \prec sunday, deadline. \end{cases}$$

The set $\Pi_{8.1}$ has information about three rooms: a, b and c. For instance, there are facts expressing that in room a the light switch is on, in room b there is no electricity and in room c there are emergency lights. There are also facts expressing that it is Sunday night and that people working there have a deadline. Observe that $\Pi_{8.1}$ has also two strict rules. For instance, the second one express that an illuminated room is not dark.

The set $\Delta_{8.1}$ provides defeasible rules representing tentative information, that can be used to infer, for instance, which room is illuminated, or if someone is working in a particular room. For example, the first defeasible rule states that "reasons to believe that the switch of a room is on, provides reasons to believe that the lights of that room are on". The second rule express that "usually if there is no electricity then lights of a room are not on". The third defeasible rule states that " normally, if there is no electricity but there are emergency lights, then lights will be on". The last two rules state that "normally there is nobody working in a room on a Sunday", however, "if they have a deadline, people may be working on a Sunday".

As it will be explained below, there are several queries that succeed with respect to this program because they are warranted (*e.g.*, $illuminated(a)$, $illuminated(c)$, $\sim dark(c)$, $dark(b)$ and working_at(a)), whereas other queries are not warranted (*e.g.*, $illuminated(b)$, $\sim illuminated(c)$).

Defeasible rules allow to infer tentative conclusions. A *defeasible derivation* of a literal Q from a DeLP-program (Π, Δ), denoted by $(\Pi, \Delta) \mid\sim Q$, is a finite sequence of ground literals $L_1, L_2, \ldots, L_n = Q$, where either:

1. L_i is a fact in Π, or
2. there exists a rule R_i in (Π, Δ) (strict or defeasible) with head L_i and body $B_1, B_2, \ldots, B_k$ and every literal of the body is an element L_j of the sequence appearing before L_i ($j < i$.)

The sequence: $switch\_on(b)$, $lights\_on(b)$, $night$, $\sim day$, $illuminated(b)$, is a defeasible derivation for $illuminated(b)$ from $(\Pi_{8.1}, \Delta_{8.1})$. In particular, a derivation from $(\Pi, \emptyset)$ is called a *strict derivation*, (*e.g., night, ~day* in Example 8.1). That is, a derivation is defeasible if at least one defeasible rule is used, otherwise it is strict. Two literals are considered contradictory if one is the complement of the other with respect to strong negation, (*e.g., day* and *~day*). Since Π represents non-defeasible information, then it is natural to require certain internal coherence. Therefore, in DeLP, two contradictory literals cannot have a strict derivation from a valid program.

Nevertheless, as expected, from a valid DeLP-program, there can result contradictory literals that have defeasible derivations (*e.g., lights_on(b)* and *~lights_on(b)* from $(\Pi_{8.1}, \Delta_{8.1})$). In these situations, in order to decide which literal is accepted as warranted, DeLP incorporates a defeasible argumentation formalism that allows the identification of the pieces of knowledge that are in contradiction. Then, a dialectical process is used for deciding which information prevails as warranted. This process involves the construction and evaluation of arguments and counter-arguments, as described next.

Definition 8.1 (Argument Structure). Let H be a ground literal, (Π, Δ) a DeLP-program, and $\mathcal{A} \subseteq \Delta$. The pair $\langle \mathcal{A}, H \rangle$ is an argument structure if:

1. there exists a defeasible derivation for H from $(\Pi, \mathcal{A})$,
2. there is no defeasible derivation from $(\Pi, \mathcal{A})$ of contradictory literals,
3. and there is no proper subset $\mathcal{A}'$ of $\mathcal{A}$ such that $\mathcal{A}'$ satisfies (1) and (2).

In an argument structure $\langle \mathcal{A}, H \rangle$, H is the claim and $\mathcal{A}$ is the argument supporting that claim. For instance, from the DeLP-program of Example 8.1 the following argument structures can be obtained: $\langle \mathcal{A}_1, dark(b) \rangle$, $\langle \mathcal{A}_2, illuminated(b) \rangle$, and $\langle \mathcal{A}_3, \sim lights\_on(b) \rangle$, where
$\mathcal{A}_1 = \{dark(b) \prec \sim day\}$
$\mathcal{A}_2 = \{(illuminated(b) \prec lights\_on(b), \sim day), (lights\_on(b) \prec switch\_on(b)\}$
$\mathcal{A}_3 = \{\sim lights\_on(b) \prec \sim electricity(b)\}$
Observe that an argument is a set of defeasible rules; however, strict rules may be used for the defeasible derivation of its claim. For instance, $\mathcal{A}_1$ uses the strict rule $\sim day \leftarrow night$ for the derivation of $\sim day$.

A DeLP-query Q succeeds, *i.e.*, it is warranted from a DeLP-program, if it is possible to build an argument $\mathcal{A}$ that supports Q and $\mathcal{A}$ is found to be undefeated by a warrant procedure. This process implements an exhaustive dialectical analysis that involves the construction and evaluation of arguments that either support or interfere with the query under analysis. That is, given an argument $\mathcal{A}$ that supports Q, the warrant procedure will evaluate if there are other arguments that counter-argue or attack $\mathcal{A}$ or a sub-argument of $\mathcal{A}$. An argument $\langle \mathcal{C}, P \rangle$ is a *sub-argument* of $\langle \mathcal{A}, Q \rangle$ if $\mathcal{C} \subseteq \mathcal{A}$.

Definition 8.2 (Counter-Argument).
An argument $\langle \mathcal{B}, S \rangle$ is a *counter-argument* for $\langle \mathcal{A}, H \rangle$ at literal P, if there exists a sub-argument $\langle \mathcal{C}, P \rangle$ of $\langle \mathcal{A}, H \rangle$ such that P and S disagree, that is, there exist two contradictory literals that have a strict derivation from $\Pi \cup \{S, P\}$. The literal P

is referred to as the counter-argument point and $\langle \mathcal{C}, P \rangle$ as the disagreement sub-argument.

Two contradictory literals trivially disagree (*e.g.*, *day* and $\sim day$), however, two literals that are non-contradictory can also disagree. For instance, in Example 8.1, the literals *dark*(*b*) and *illuminated*(*b*) disagree because from $\Pi_{8.1} \cup \{illuminated(b), dark(b)\}$ there exists a strict derivation for $\sim dark(b)$. Hence, following the example above, $\langle \mathcal{A}_2, illuminated(b) \rangle$ is a counter-argument for $\langle \mathcal{A}_1, dark(b) \rangle$ (and vice versa). Observe that the argument $\langle \mathcal{A}_3, \sim lights\_on(b) \rangle$ is a counter-argument for $\langle \mathcal{A}_2, illuminated(b) \rangle$ at (the inner point) *lights_on*(*b*) and the disagreement sub-argument in $\mathcal{A}_2$ is $\langle \{lights\_on(b) \prec switch\_on(b)\}, lights\_on(b) \rangle$.

Given an argument $\langle \mathcal{A}, H \rangle$, there could be several counter-arguments attacking different points in $\mathcal{A}$, or different counter-arguments attacking the same point in $\mathcal{A}$. In DeLP, in order to verify whether an argument is non-defeated, all of its associated counter-arguments $\mathcal{B}_1, \mathcal{B}_2, \ldots, \mathcal{B}_k$ have to be examined, each of them being a potential reason for rejecting $\mathcal{A}$. If any $\mathcal{B}_i$ is (somehow) "better" than, or unrelated to, $\mathcal{A}$, then $\mathcal{B}_i$ is a candidate for defeating $\mathcal{A}$. However, if for some $\mathcal{B}_i$, the argument $\mathcal{A}$ is "better" than $\mathcal{B}_i$, then $\mathcal{B}_i$ will not be a defeater for $\mathcal{A}$. To compare arguments and counter-arguments a preference relation among arguments is needed.

In DeLP the *argument comparison criterion* is modular, and thus the most appropriate criterion for the domain that is being represented can be introduced. In the literature of DeLP different criteria have been defined. For example in [15] a criterion that uses rule priorities was introduced. Recently, in [11] a comparison criterion based on priorities among selected literals of the program was defined. In the following examples we will use a syntactic criterion called *generalized specificity* [15, 29]. This criterion favors two aspects in an argument: It prefers (1) a *more precise* argument or (2) a *more concise* argument. For instance, $\langle \mathcal{A}_2, illuminated(b) \rangle$, is more specific (more precise) than $\langle \mathcal{A}_1, dark(b) \rangle$. For the following definitions we will abstract away from the comparison criterion, assuming there exists one (denoted "$\succ$").

Definition 8.3 (Defeaters: Proper and Blocking). Let $\langle \mathcal{B}, S \rangle$ be a *counter-argument* for $\langle \mathcal{A}, H \rangle$ at point P, and $\langle \mathcal{C}, P \rangle$ the disagreement sub-argument. If $\langle \mathcal{B}, S \rangle \succ \langle \mathcal{C}, P \rangle$ (*i.e.*, $\langle \mathcal{B}, S \rangle$ is "better" than $\langle \mathcal{C}, P \rangle$) then $\langle \mathcal{B}, S \rangle$ is a proper defeater for $\langle \mathcal{A}, H \rangle$. If $\langle \mathcal{B}, S \rangle$ is unrelated by the preference relation to $\langle \mathcal{C}, P \rangle$, (*i.e.*, $\langle \mathcal{B}, S \rangle \nsucc \langle \mathcal{C}, P \rangle$, and $\langle \mathcal{C}, P \rangle \nsucc \langle \mathcal{B}, S \rangle$) then $\langle \mathcal{B}, S \rangle$ is a blocking defeater for $\langle \mathcal{A}, H \rangle$. Finally, $\langle \mathcal{B}, S \rangle$ is a *defeater* for $\langle \mathcal{A}, H \rangle$, if $\langle \mathcal{B}, S \rangle$ is either a proper or blocking defeater for $\langle \mathcal{A}, H \rangle$.

In a previous example, we have shown that $\langle \mathcal{A}_2, illuminated(b) \rangle$ is a counter-argument for $\langle \mathcal{A}_1, dark(b) \rangle$ (and vice versa). Considering generalized specificity as the comparison criterion, then $\mathcal{A}_2 \succ \mathcal{A}_1$. Therefore, $\langle \mathcal{A}_2, illuminated(b) \rangle$ is a proper defeater for $\langle \mathcal{A}_1, dark(b) \rangle$. The argument $\langle \mathcal{A}_3, \sim lights\_on(b) \rangle$ is a blocking defeater for $\langle \mathcal{A}_2, illuminated(b) \rangle$ because $\mathcal{A}_3$ and the disagreement sub-argument $\mathcal{D}_1 = \{lights\_on(b) \prec switch\_on(b)\}$ of $\mathcal{A}_2$ are unrelated by this comparison criterion.

If an argument $\langle \mathcal{A}_1, H_1 \rangle$ is defeated by $\langle \mathcal{A}_2, H_2 \rangle$, then $\langle \mathcal{A}_2, H_2 \rangle$ represents a reason for rejecting $\langle \mathcal{A}_1, H_1 \rangle$. Nevertheless, a defeater $\langle \mathcal{A}_3, H_3 \rangle$ for $\langle \mathcal{A}_2, H_2 \rangle$ may also exist, rejecting $\langle A_2, H_2 \rangle$ and reinstating $\langle A_1, H_1 \rangle$. Note that the argument $\langle A_3, H_3 \rangle$ may be in turn defeated, reinstating $\langle A_2, H_2 \rangle$, and so on. In this manner, a sequence of arguments (called argumentation line) can arise, where each element is a defeater of its predecessor.

Definition 8.4 (Argumentation Line). An *argumentation line* for $\langle A_1, H_1 \rangle$ is a sequence of argument structures, $\Lambda = [\langle A_1, H_1 \rangle, \langle A_2, H_2 \rangle, \langle A_3, H_3 \rangle, \ldots]$, where each element of the sequence $\langle A_i, H_i \rangle$, $i > 1$, is a defeater of its predecessor $\langle A_{i-1}, H_{i-1} \rangle$.

In an argumentation line $\Lambda = [\langle A_1, H_1 \rangle, \langle A_2, H_2 \rangle, \langle A_3, H_3 \rangle, \ldots]$, the first element, $\langle A_1, H_1 \rangle$, becomes a *supporting* argument for H_1, $\langle A_2, H_2 \rangle$ an *interfering* argument, $\langle A_3, H_3 \rangle$ a supporting argument, $\langle A_4, H_4 \rangle$ an interfering one, and so on. Thus, an argumentation line can be split into two disjoint sets: $\Lambda_S = \{\langle A_1, H_1 \rangle, \langle A_3, H_3 \rangle, \langle A_5, H_5 \rangle, \ldots\}$ of supporting arguments, and $\Lambda_I = \{\langle A_2, H_2 \rangle, \langle A_4, H_4 \rangle, \ldots\}$ of interfering arguments. Considering the arguments generated above from $(\Pi_{8.1}, \Delta_{8.1})$ of Example 8.1, $\Lambda_1 = [\langle A_1, dark(b) \rangle, \langle A_2, illuminated(b) \rangle, \langle A_3, \sim lights\_on(b) \rangle]$ is an argumentation line, with two supporting arguments and an interfering one.

Note that an infinite argumentation line may arise if an argument structure is reintroduced in the sequence. For instance, $\Lambda_i = [\langle A_3, \sim lights\_on(b) \rangle, \langle D_1, lights\_on(b) \rangle, \langle A_3, \sim lights\_on(b) \rangle, \langle D_1, lights\_on(b) \rangle, \ldots]$. This is an example of *circular argumentation* where an argument structure is reintroduced again in the argumentation line to defend itself. Clearly, this situation is undesirable as it leads to the construction of an infinite sequence of arguments. Circular argumentation and other forms of *fallacious argumentation* were studied in detail in [27, 15]. In DeLP, argumentation lines have to be *acceptable*, that is, they have to be finite, an argument cannot appear twice, and supporting (resp. interfering) arguments have to be non-contradictory.

Definition 8.5 (Acceptable Argumentation Line).
An argumentation line $\Lambda = [\langle A_1, H_1 \rangle, \ldots \langle A_n, H_n \rangle]$ is *acceptable* iff:

1. Λ is a finite sequence.
2. The set Λ_S of supporting arguments (resp. Λ_I), is concordant (a set $\{\langle A_i, H_i \rangle\}_{i=1}^n$ is concordant iff $\Pi \cup \bigcup_{i=1}^n A_i$ is non-contradictory.).
3. No argument $\langle A_k, H_k \rangle$ in Λ is a disagreement sub-argument of an argument $\langle A_i, H_i \rangle$ appearing earlier in Λ ($i < k$.)
4. For all i, such that $\langle A_i, H_i \rangle$ is a blocking defeater for $\langle A_{i-1}, H_{i-1} \rangle$, if $\langle A_{i+1}, H_{i+1} \rangle$ exists, then $\langle A_{i+1}, H_{i+1} \rangle$ is a proper defeater for $\langle A_i, H_i \rangle$.

A single acceptable argumentation line for $\langle A_1, H_1 \rangle$ may not be enough to establish whether $\langle A_1, H_1 \rangle$ is an undefeated argument. The reason is that there can be several defeaters ($\langle B_1, Q_1 \rangle$, $\langle B_2, Q_2 \rangle$, ..., $\langle B_k, Q_k \rangle$) for $\langle A_1, H_1 \rangle$, and therefore k argumentation lines for $\langle A_1, H_1 \rangle$ need to be considered. Since for each defeater $\langle B_i, Q_i \rangle$ there can be in turn several defeaters, then a tree structure (called dialectical tree) is defined. In this tree, the root is labeled with $\langle A_1, H_1 \rangle$ and every node (except the root) represents a defeater (proper or blocking) of its parent. Each path from the root to a leaf corresponds to a different acceptable argumentation line. The definition follows.

Definition 8.6 (Dialectical Tree). A dialectical tree for $\langle \mathcal{A}_1, H_1 \rangle$, $\mathcal{T}_{\langle \mathcal{A}_1, H_1 \rangle}$, is defined as follows:

1. The root of the tree is labeled with $\langle \mathcal{A}_1, H_1 \rangle$.
2. Let N be a non-root node labeled $\langle \mathcal{A}_n, H_n \rangle$, and $[\langle \mathcal{A}_1, H_1 \rangle, \ldots, \langle \mathcal{A}_n, H_n \rangle]$ be the sequence of labels of the path from the root to N. Let $\{\langle \mathcal{B}_1, Q_1 \rangle, \langle \mathcal{B}_2, Q_2 \rangle, \ldots, \langle \mathcal{B}_k, Q_k \rangle\}$ be the set of all the defeaters for $\langle \mathcal{A}_n, H_n \rangle$. For each defeater $\langle \mathcal{B}_i, Q_i \rangle$ ($1 \leq i \leq k$), such that the argumentation line $\Lambda' = [\langle \mathcal{A}_1, H_1 \rangle, \ldots, \langle \mathcal{A}_n, H_n \rangle, \langle \mathcal{B}_i, Q_i \rangle]$ is acceptable, the node N has a child N_i labeled $\langle \mathcal{B}_i, Q_i \rangle$. If there is no defeater for $\langle \mathcal{A}_n, H_n \rangle$ or there is no $\langle \mathcal{B}_i, Q_i \rangle$ such that Λ' is acceptable, then N is a leaf.

In Example 8.1, $\langle \mathcal{C}_1, working\_at(c) \rangle$ has two defeaters: $\langle \mathcal{C}_2, \sim lights\_on(c) \rangle$, and $\langle \mathcal{C}_3, \sim working\_at(c) \rangle$, where: $\mathcal{C}_1 = \{(working\_at(c) \prec illuminated(c)), (illuminated(c) \prec lights\_on(c), \sim day), (lights\_on(c) \prec switch\_on(c))\}$; $\mathcal{C}_2 = \{\sim lights\_on(c) \prec \sim electricity(c)\}$ and $\mathcal{C}_3 = \{\sim working\_at(c) \prec sunday\}$. Since $\mathcal{C}_2$ and $\mathcal{C}_3$ have defeaters, then the following acceptable argumentation lines arise: $[\mathcal{C}_1, \mathcal{C}_2, \mathcal{C}_4]$ where $\mathcal{C}_4 = \{working\_at(c) \prec sunday, deadline\}$, and $[\mathcal{C}_1, \mathcal{C}_3, \mathcal{C}_5]$ where $\mathcal{C}_5 = \{lights\_on(c) \prec \sim electricity(c), emergency\_lights(c)\}$. These two lines are considered in the dialectical tree $\mathcal{T}_1^*$ of Figure 8.1.

A dialectical tree provides a structure integrating all the possible acceptable argumentation lines that can be generated for deciding whether an argument is undefeated. In order to compute whether the status of the root is defeated or undefeated, a recursive marking process is introduced next. Let $\mathcal{T}$ be a dialectical tree, a *marked dialectical tree*, $\mathcal{T}^*$, can be obtained marking every node in $\mathcal{T}$ as follows: (1) Each leaf in $\mathcal{T}$ is marked as **U** in $\mathcal{T}^*$. (2) An inner node N of $\mathcal{T}$ is marked as **D** in $\mathcal{T}^*$ iff N has at least a child marked as **U**, otherwise N is marked as **U** in $\mathcal{T}^*$. Thus, the root $\langle \mathcal{A}, H \rangle$ of a dialectical tree is marked with **U** if all its children are marked as **D** (*i.e.*, all the defeaters for $\langle \mathcal{A}, H \rangle$ are defeated).

Figure 8.1 shows three different marked dialectical trees. Nodes are depicted as triangles with marks (**D** or **U**) on their right. **D**-nodes are also grey colored. The marked dialectical tree $\mathcal{T}_1^*$ has also the argument names of the example introduced above as labels inside the triangles.

A ground literal H is considered to be *warranted* if an argument $\mathcal{A}$ for H exists, and all the defeaters for $\langle \mathcal{A}, H \rangle$ are defeated. Therefore, this marking procedure provides an effective way of determining if a DeLP-query H is warranted. Note that given a DeLP-query H, there can be several arguments that support H. Therefore, H is warranted if there is at least one argument $\mathcal{A}$ for H such that the root of a dialectical tree for $\langle \mathcal{A}, H \rangle$ is marked as **U**.

Definition 8.7 (Warranted Literals). Let $\mathcal{P}$ be a DeLP-program, H a ground literal, $\langle \mathcal{A}, H \rangle$ an argument from $\mathcal{P}$ and $\mathcal{T}^*$ a marked dialectical tree for $\langle \mathcal{A}, H \rangle$. Literal H is warranted from $\mathcal{P}$ iff the root of $\mathcal{T}^*$ is marked as **U**.

Example 8.2. Consider again the DeLP-program $(\Pi_{8.1}, \Delta_{8.1})$ of Example 8.1. The set ω includes some literals that are warranted from the program $(\Pi_{8.1}, \Delta_{8.1})$ $\omega = \{working\_at(c), illuminated(c), illuminated(a), dark(b), \sim dark(a)\}$, whereas the set ω' includes literals that are not warranted from $(\Pi_{8.1}, \Delta_{8.1})$ $\omega' = \{dark(a),$

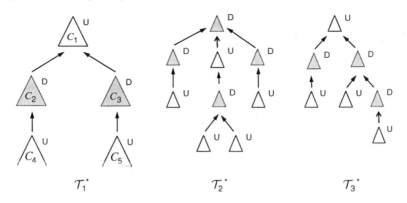

Fig. 8.1 Marked Dialectical Trees

$illuminated(b)$, $\sim lights\_on(b)$, $\sim empty(a), illuminated(r)$}. Observe that the last two literals of ω' have no supporting argument at all.

DeLP Implementation and Extensions

An interpreter for DeLP is available (http://lidia.cs.uns.edu.ar/DeLP). This interpreter takes a DeLP-program $\mathcal{P}$, and a DeLP-query Q as input. It then returns one of the following four possible answers: YES, if Q is warranted from $\mathcal{P}$; NO, if the complement of Q is warranted from $\mathcal{P}$; UNDECIDED, if neither Q nor its complement are warranted from $\mathcal{P}$; or UNKNOWN, if Q is not in the language of the program $\mathcal{P}$. For instance, considering the program $(\Pi_{8.1}, \Delta_{8.1})$ of Example 8.1 the answer for $illuminated(c)$, is YES, the answer for $dark(a)$ is NO, the answer for $\sim lights\_on(b)$ is UNDECIDED, and the answer for $\sim empty(a)$ is UNKNOWN. Observe that for all the literals of the set ω in Example 8.2 the answer is YES. However, as shown above, literals of ω' may have different answers.

The reader may have noticed in Figure 8.1 that in some dialectical trees it is not necessary to explore the whole tree in order to mark the root. Thus, some pruning is possible. For instance, in the tree $\mathcal{T}_2^*$ of Figure 8.1 as one of the children of the root is marked **U**, then the mark of the other two children does not affect the mark of the root. As an optimization, the DeLP interpreter implements a marking procedure with pruning that is similar to the classic α-β pruning algorithm (see [15] for details). It is interesting to note that changes in the definition of acceptable argumentation line may produce a different behavior of the formalism. Therefore, Definition 8.5 could be modified by providing a way of tuning the system in order to have a different behavior.

In [15] an extension of DeLP that allows default negation in the body of defeasible rules was defined (*e.g.*, $a \prec not\ b, c, not \sim d$). In DeLP '*not F*' is assumed when the literal F is not warranted. The definition of argument was adapted for this extension and a new form of defeat (attack to an assumption) was introduced (see [15] for details). Thus, default negated literals become new points of attack, and when the dialectical analysis is carried out, default negated literals can be defeated by arguments.

In [14] dialectical explanations for DeLP-queries (called δ-Explanations) were introduced. δ-Explanations allow to visualize the reasoning carried out by the system, and the support for the answer. It is clear that without this information at hand it is very difficult to understand the returned answer. δ-Explanations were also defined for *schematic queries*, i.e., a DeLP-query with at least one variable that represents the set of DeLP-queries that unify with the schematic one (*e.g., illuminated(X)*.)

Possibilistic Defeasible Logic Programming (P-DeLP) represents an important extension of DeLP in which the elements of the language have the form (φ, α), where φ is of the form $L_0 \leftarrow L_1, \ldots, L_n$ or just L_0, where the $L_i, (0 \leq i \leq n)$ are ground literals as in DeLP, and α is a *certainty weight* associated with φ.

A P-DeLP-program Γ is a set of clauses. To define the possibilistic entailment we only need the triviality axiom of Possibilistic Gödel Logic (PGL) and the generalized modus ponens rule (GMP). The triviality axiom says that we can add $(\varphi, 0)$ for any formula φ in the language and the GMP says that from $(L_0 \leftarrow L_1, \ldots, L_n, \gamma)$ and $(L_1, \beta_n), \ldots, (L_1, \beta_n)$ we can obtain $(L_0, \min(\gamma, \beta_1, \ldots, \beta_n))$. A derivation of a weighted literal (Q, α) from Γ, denoted $\Gamma \vdash (Q, \alpha)$, is a sequence of clauses $C_1, \ldots, C_m$ such that $C_m = (Q, \alpha)$, and for each $1 \leq i \leq m$ it holds that $C_i \in \Gamma$, or C_i is an instance of the triviality axiom, C_i is obtained by using GMP over its preceding clauses in the sequence.

The set of clauses Γ of a P-DeLP program can be split, like in DeLP, as (Π, Δ) distinguishing the subset Π of facts and strict rules with certainty weight $\alpha = 1$ (representing non-defeasible knowledge), and the subset Δ of clauses with certainty weight $\alpha < 1$ (representing defeasible knowledge). An argument for a literal (Q, α) built from a P-DeLP program (Π, Δ) is a subset $\mathcal{A} \subseteq \Delta$ such that: $\Pi \cup \mathcal{A} \vdash (Q, \alpha)$, $\Pi \cup \mathcal{A}$ is non-contradictory, and $\mathcal{A}$ is minimal with respect to set inclusion satisfying the two previous conditions; and it is denoted $\langle \mathcal{A}, Q, \alpha \rangle$.

From these extended notions, a complete argumentation system has been developed which incorporates possibilistic reasoning. Complete details of P-DeLP can be found in [1, 2].

3 Argument-based extended logic programming with defeasible priorities

Inspired by legal reasoning, Prakken and Sartor have introduced in [24] an argument-based formalism for *extended logic programming with defeasible priorities*. In their formalism, arguments are expressed in a logic programming language with both strong and default negation. Conflicts between arguments are decided with the help of priorities on the rules. These priorities can be defeasibly derived as conclusions within the system. Its semantics is given with a fixed point definition, while its proof theory is stated in dialectical style, where a proof takes the form of a dialogue between a proponent and an opponent: an argument is shown to be justified if the proponent can make the opponent run out of moves in whatever way the opponent attacks.

We give a brief description of this formalism and refer the interested reader to [24, 22, 25] for details. Their proposed system assumes input information in the form of an *ordered theory* (S,D) where S and D are sets of, respectively, strict and defeasible rules. In their language, $\sim$ represents default negation and $\neg$ strong negation, and rules are denoted by

$$r: L_0 \wedge \ldots \wedge L_j \wedge \sim L_k \wedge \ldots \wedge \sim L_m \Rightarrow L_n$$

where r, a term, is the name of the rule, each L_i ($0 \leq i \leq n$) is a strong literal, and each $\sim L_k$ is a weak literal. Only defeasible rules can contain weak literals.

An *argument* is a finite sequence $A = [r_0, \ldots, r_n]$ of ground instances of rules such that

1. for every i ($0 \leq i \leq n$), for every strong literal L_j in the antecedent of r_i there is a $k < i$ such that L_j is the consequent of r_k; and
2. no two distinct rules in the sequence have the same consequent.

Each consequent of a rule in A is a conclusion of A, and every literal L is an assumption of A iff $\sim \overline{L}$ occurs in some rule in A. An argument is strict iff it does not contain a defeasible rule; it is defeasible otherwise. Note that arguments are not assumed to be either minimal or consistent.

The presence of assumptions in a rule gives rise to two kinds of conflicts between arguments, *conclusion-to-conclusion attack* and *conclusion-to-assumption attack*. An argument A_1 *attacks* A_2 iff there are sequences of strict rules S_1 and S_2, such that the concatenation $A_1 + S_1$ is an argument with conclusion L and (1) $A_2 + S_2$ is an argument with conclusion $\overline{L}$, or (2) $\overline{L}$ is an assumption of A_2. In order to compare conflicting arguments, priorities among rules (that are relevant to the conflict) are used. For any two sets R and R' of defeasible rules, $R < R'$ iff for some $r \in R$ and all $r' \in R'$ it holds that $r < r'$.

Defeat among arguments is built up from two other notions, *rebutting* and *undercutting* an argument. An argument A defeats an argument B iff (1) $A=[\ ]$ and B attacks itself, or else if (2a) A undercuts B or (2b) A rebuts B and B does not undercut A. As explained in [25], an argument A *rebuts* an argument B iff A conclusion-to-conclusion attacks B and either A is strict and B is defeasible, or A's rules involved in the conflict have no lower priority than B's rules involved in the conflict (see [24, 22] for details). An argument A *undercuts* an argument B precisely in case of the second kind of conflict (attack on an assumption). Note that it is not necessary that the rules responsible for the attack on the assumption have no lower priority than the one containing the assumption. An argument A *strictly defeats* B iff A defeats B and B does not attack A.

As stated above, priorities between rules can be defeasibly derived as conclusions within the system. Hence, the language is extended with a special predicate $\prec$, where $r_1 \prec r_2$ means that rule r_2 has priority over r_1. This new predicate symbol denotes a strict partial order, and therefore the set S must contain the axioms of a strict partial order. Thus, the rebut and defeat relations must be made relative to an ordering relation that might vary during the reasoning process.

Since priorities are not fixed, in order to determine if an argument A is acceptable with respect to a set T of arguments, the relevant defeat relations are verified relative to the priority conclusions drawn by the arguments in T. Therefore, given a set of arguments T, priorities between rules are defined as $<_T = \{r < r' \mid r \prec r'$ is a conclusion of some $A \in T\}$. Hence, an argument A (strictly) T-defeats B iff, assuming the ordering $<_T$, A (strictly) defeats B.

An argument A is *acceptable* with respect to a set T of arguments iff all arguments T-defeating A are strictly T-defeated by some argument in T. Thus, acceptability of an argument with respect to a set T depends on the priority conclusions of the arguments in T. Let Γ be an ordered theory (S,D), and T be any set of arguments from Γ; the characteristic function of Γ is $F_\Gamma(T) = \{A \mid A$ is acceptable with respect to $T\}$. Then, the status of an argument A is defined as follows: A is *justified* iff A is in the least fixed point of F_Γ, A is *overruled* iff A is attacked by a justified argument, and A is *defensible* iff A is neither justified nor overruled.

For example, consider a theory (S,D) where D has the following rules:

$$r_0: \Rightarrow a \qquad r_2: \sim b \Rightarrow c \quad r_4: \Rightarrow r_0 \prec r_3 \quad r_6: \Rightarrow r_5 \prec r_4$$
$$r_1: a \Rightarrow b \quad r_3: \Rightarrow \neg a \qquad r_5: \Rightarrow r_3 \prec r_0$$

The set of justified arguments is constructed as follows. The only $\emptyset$-undefeated argument is $[r_6]$, then, $F_\Gamma(\emptyset) = F^1 = \{[r_6]\}$ and $<_{F^1} = \{r_5 < r_4\}$. Now, the conflict between $[r_4]$ and $[r_5]$ can be solved because $[r_4]$ strictly F^1-defeats $[r_5]$. Then, $F_\Gamma(F^1) = F^2 = \{[r_6], [r_4]\}$ and $<_{F^2} = \{r_5 < r_4, r_0 < r_3\}$. Hence, the conflict between $[r_0]$ and $[r_3]$ can be solved because $[r_3]$ strictly F^2-defeats $[r_0]$. Thus, $F_\Gamma(F^2) = F^3 = \{[r_6], [r_4], [r_3]\}$ and $<_{F^3} = <_{F^2}$. Finally, $F_\Gamma(F^3) = F^4 = \{[r_6], [r_4], [r_3], [r_2]\}$ and $F_\Gamma(F^4) = F^4$.

The proof theory of this formalisms is stated in dialectical style, where a proof takes the form of a dialogue between a proponent (P) and an opponent (O). An argument is shown to be justified if P can make O run out of moves.

A *priority dialogue* is a finite sequence of moves $(Player_i, A_i)$, where:
1. $Player_i = P$ iff i is odd, and $Player_i = O$ iff i is even;
2. If $Player_i = Player_j = P$ and $i \neq j$, then $A_i \neq A_j$;
3. If $Player_i = P(i > 1)$ then A_i is a minimal argument such that A_i strictly $\{A_i\}$-defeats A_{i-1}; or A_{i-1} does not $\{A_i\}$-defeat A_{i-2};
4. If $Player_i = O(i > 1)$ then A_i strictly $\emptyset$-defeats A_{i-1};

A *priority dialogue tree* is a finite tree of moves such that (1) each branch is a dialogue and (2) if $Player_i = P$ then the children of $move_i$ are all $\emptyset$-defeat A_i. A player wins a dialogue if the other player cannot move, and a player wins a dialogue tree iff it wins all branches of the tree. Finally, an argument A is *provably justified* iff there is a dialogue tree with A as its root, and won by the proponent.

The semantics of this formalism was very much inspired by Dung's work. If it is restricted to static priorities (given as input instead of derived within the system) then it instantiates Dung's grounded semantics [10]. However, the semantics slightly differs from Dung's when dynamic priorities are considered. In [23] some detailed legal examples are given, and a third way of attacking arguments, namely by arguing that a rule is not applicable, is introduced.

4 Argumentation Semantics for Extended Logic Programming

In [26], Schweimeier and Schroeder formulate a variety of notions of *attack for extended logic programs* from combinations of undercutting and rebuttal. A general *hierarchy of argumentation semantics* is defined, parameterized by the notions of attack chosen by proponent and opponent, and the equivalence and subset relationships between the semantics is shown. The placement of existing semantics in this hierarchy is determined.

The language corresponds to [24] *without strict rules*, and *either without priorities, or, equivalently, if all rules have the same priority*. An extended logic program (ELP) P is a (possibly infinite) set of rules of the form $L_0 \leftarrow L_1, \ldots, L_m, not\, L_{m+1}, \ldots, not\, L_{m+n}$ $(m, n \geq 0)$ where each L_i $(0 \leq i \leq m+n)$ is an *objective literal*, i.e., an atom M or its explicit negation $\neg M$.

An *argument associated with P* is a finite sequence $A = [r_0, \ldots, r_n]$ of ground instances of rules $r_i \in P$ such that for every $0 \leq i \leq n$, for every objective literal L_j in the body of r_i there is a $k > i$ such that $L_j = head(r_k)$. The head of a rule in A is called a *conclusion of A*, and a default literal $not\, L$ in a rule of A is called an *assumption of A*. An argument A with a conclusion L is a *minimal* argument for L if there is no subargument of A with conclusion L. Given an ELP P, the set of minimal arguments associated with P is denoted by $Args_P$.

From the two basic notions of attack (undercut u, and rebut r), they introduce further notions: Attacks (a), defeats (d), strongly attacks (sa) and strongly undercuts (su). Here are the precise definitions. Let A_1 and A_2 be arguments.

- A_1 *undercuts* A_2 if there is an objective literal L such that L is a conclusion of A_1 and $not\, L$ is an assumption of A_2.
- A_1 *rebuts* A_2 if there is an objective literal L such that L is a conclusion of A_1 and $\neg L$ is a conclusion of A_2.
- A_1 *attacks* A_2 if A_1 undercuts or rebuts A_2.
- A_1 *defeats* A_2 if A_1 undercuts A_2, or A_1 rebuts A_2 and A_2 does not undercut A_1.
- A_1 *strongly attacks* A_2 if A_1 attacks A_2 and A_2 does not undercut A_1.
- A_1 *strongly undercuts* A_2 if A_1 undercuts A_2 and A_2 does not undercut A_1.

A *notion of attack* is defined as a function x that assigns to each ELP P a binary relation $x_P \subseteq Args_P \times Args_P$. Different notions of attack are partially ordered by defining: $x \subseteq y$ iff $\forall P : x_P \subseteq y_P$. The inverse of a notion of attack x, denoted by x^{-1}, is defined as: $x_P^{-1} = \{(B, A) | (A, B) \in x_P\}$. Thus, $\mathsf{a} = \mathsf{u} \cup \mathsf{r}$, $\mathsf{d} = \mathsf{u} \cup (\mathsf{r} - \mathsf{u}^{-1})$, $\mathsf{sa} = (\mathsf{u} \cup \mathsf{r}) - \mathsf{u}^{-1}$, and $\mathsf{su} = \mathsf{u} - \mathsf{u}^{-1}$. Since their framework does not consider priorities, undercuts play the prime role and notions of attack which are based on rebuttals, such as r or $\mathsf{r} - \mathsf{u}^{-1}$, are not considered.

Their definition of *acceptability* is parameterized on the notions of attack allowed for the proponent and the opponent. Basically, an argument is acceptable if it can be defended against any attack.

Let x and y be notions of attack, A an argument, and S a set of arguments. Then A is x/y-*acceptable* with respect to S if for every argument B such that $(B,A) \in x$ there exists an argument $C \in S$ such that $(C,B) \in y$. A particular semantics can be obtained by choosing one notion of attack for the opponent, and another notion of attack as defense for the proponent. The uniformity of the definition makes it a convenient framework for comparing different argumentation semantics.

Based on the notion of acceptability, they define a fixed point semantics for arguments: $F_{P,x/y}(S) = \{A \mid A \text{ is } x/y\text{-acceptable with respect to } S\}$ and its least fixed point is denoted by $J_{P,x/y}$. Thus, an argument A is x/y-justified if $A \in J_{P,x/y}$, A is x/y-overruled if it is attacked by an x/y-justified argument, and A is x/y-defensible if it is neither x/y-justified nor x/y-overruled. For example, Dung's grounded semantics is $J_{a/u}$, and Prakken and Sartor's semantics without priorities or strict rules is $J_{d/su}$ (see [26] for other examples).

Consider, for instance, $P_1 = \{(p \leftarrow not\, q), (q \leftarrow not\, p), (\neg q \leftarrow r), (r \leftarrow not\, s), (\neg s \leftarrow not\, s), (s)\}$. Here, all arguments (except $[s]$) are undercut by another argument, and $[\neg s \leftarrow not\, s]$ rebuts (but does not defeat) $[s]$. Thus, $[s]$ is identified as a justified argument in all semantics, except if a is allowed as an attack. We state several results (for other semantics see [26]).

$$J_{P_1,a/x} = \emptyset \qquad\qquad J_{P_1,u/sa} = \{[s],[\neg q \leftarrow r],[p \leftarrow not\, q]\}$$
$$J_{P_1,d/x} = \{[s]\} \qquad\qquad J_{P_1,sa/su} = \{[s],[p \leftarrow not\, q]\}$$
$$J_{P_1,u/u} = \{[s],[\neg q \leftarrow r]\} \; J_{P_1,su/x} = \{[s],[\neg q \leftarrow r],[q \leftarrow not\, p],[p \leftarrow not\, q]\}$$

Schweimeier and Schroeder proved a series of theorems, showing that some of the argumentation semantics defined above are subsumed by others. In fact some are actually equivalent. Thus, they established a *hierarchy of argumentation semantics*, where **WFS** and **WFSX**$_p$ also occur. One of their results states that **WFS**=u/u and **WFSX**$_p$=u/a. They also showed which semantics satisfy the coherence principle and which ones generate a conflict free set of justified arguments. Finally, based on the dialectical proof theory of [24] they introduce a proof theory for x/y-justified arguments.

5 Dung's approach

In [10], Phan Minh Dung states that *"there are extremely interesting relations between argumentation and logic programming"*. For example, he shows that logic programming can be shown to be a particular form of argumentation. He considers a logic program P as a finite set of clauses of the form $B_0 \leftarrow B_1, \ldots, B_m, \neg B_{m+1}, \ldots, \neg B_{m+n}$ (where the B_i's are atoms). To capture the semantics of *negation as finite failure* (*naff*), he proposes that P can be transformed in an argumentation framework $AF_{naff} = \langle AR, attacks \rangle$ as follows: $AR = \{(K,k) \mid \text{there exists a ground clause of } P \text{ with head } k \text{ and body } K\} \cup \{(\{\neg k\}, k) \mid k \text{ is a ground atom}\}$, and (K', h') attacks (K, h) iff the complement of h belongs to K'. That is, each ground instance of a clause of P constitutes an argument for its head. Then, Dung gives a series of theorems that relate semantics of logic programs and semantics of argumentation frameworks. Similarly, an argumentation framework AF_{napif} that captures the semantics of negation of possibly infinite failure (general loop checking, as in the stable semantics) is introduced.

In [10], Dung also shows that argumentation can be "viewed" as logic programming by introducing a general method for generating an interpreter for argumentation. This method consists of a very simple logic program consisting of the following two clauses:

$$C_1 = acceptable(A) \leftarrow not\,defeated(A)$$
$$C_2 = defeated(A) \leftarrow attacks(B,A), acceptable(B)$$

Consider an argumentation framework $AF = (AR, attacks)$ where AR is a set of arguments and $attack$ a relation over $AR \times AR$. Let P_{AF} be the logic program, $P_{AF} = \{C_1, C_2\} \cup \{attacks(B,A) \,|\, (B,A) \in attacks\}$. For each extension E of AF, let $m(E) = \{attacks(B,A) \,|\, (B,A) \in attacks\} \cup \{acceptable(A) \,|\, A \in E\}$ $\cup \{defeated(B) \,|\, B$ is attacked by some $A \in E\}$. Then, Dung shows that

1. E is a stable extension of AF iff $m(E)$ is stable model of P_{AF}.
2. E is grounded extension of AF iff $m(E) \cup \{not\,defeated(A) \,|\, A \in E\}$ is the well-founded model of P_{AF}.

6 Nute's Defeasible Logic

In [19, 20], Donald Nute introduced *Logic for Defeasible Reasoning* (LDR), a formalism that provides defeasible reasoning with a simple representational language. Although LDR is not a defeasible argumentation formalism in itself, its implementation, d-Prolog, defined as an extension of PROLOG, was the first language that introduced defeasible reasoning programming with specificity as a comparison criterion between rules.

In LDR there are three types of rules: strict rules (*e.g., emus* $\rightarrow$ *birds* that represents "emus are birds"), defeasible rules (*e.g., birds* $\Rightarrow$ *fly* "birds usually fly") and defeater rules (*e.g., heavy* $\rightsquigarrow \neg fly$ "heavy animals may not fly"). The purpose of a defeater rule is to account for the exceptions to defeasible rules. Therefore, in contrast with the other two types of rules, defeater rules cannot be used to derive formulas. They can only be used to block an application of a defeasible rule. As shown below, the derivation of contradictory literals is prevented by the definition of a *defeasible derivation*.

The original definitions of strict and defeasible derivation, introduced in [19], have evolved in successive articles [20, 4, 3]. For strict derivations only facts and strict rules can be used. However, for defeasible derivations a more sophisticated analysis is performed. A literal p has a defeasible derivation if p is the consequent of a rule (strict or defeasible) with antecedent A, such that (1) for every $a \in A$, a has a defeasible derivation, (2) the complement of p ($\overline{p}$) has no strict derivation, and (3) for every rule R_1 (strict, defeasible or defeater) with consequent $\overline{p}$ and antecedent B, it holds that (3a) there is some $b \in B$ that has no defeasible derivation or (3b) there exists a (strict or defeasible) rule R_2 with consequent p and antecedent C such that every $c \in C$ has a defeasible derivation and $R_2 > R_1$. Observe that only rules with complementary consequents can be compared.

Thus, if a literal has a defeasible derivation, then no further analysis is performed. Therefore, a defeasible derivation cannot be considered as a single argument. A defeasible derivation is related to a tree of arguments because it encodes the analysis of all possible attacks and, by condition (3b), also counter-attacks. A comparison of d-Prolog with defeasible argumentation formalisms can be found in [25] and [15].

7 Recent Developments

In this section, we will briefly comment some recent developments that extend the formalisms mentioned above and provide new proposals. We also refer the interested reader to [5], where an extensive review of current defeasible reasoning implementations is given.

In [13], an argumentative reasoning service for multi-agent systems called DeLP-server is proposed. A DeLP-server is a stand-alone program that can interact with multiple client agents. A common (or public) DeLP-program can be stored in a server, and client agents (that can be distributed in remote hosts) may send queries to the server and receive the corresponding answer together with the explanation for that answer [14]. A DeLP-server can be consulted by several agents, and one particular agent can consult several DeLP-servers, each of them providing a different shared knowledge base.

To answer queries, a DeLP-server will use the common knowledge stored in it, together with individual knowledge that clients can send attached to a query, creating a particular *context* for that query (see [13] for details). This context is private knowledge that the server will use for answering the query and will not affect other future queries. That is, a client agent cannot make permanent changes to the public DeLP-program stored in a server. The temporal scope of the context sent in a query $[Context, Q]$ is limited and disappears once the query Q has been answered.

For instance, consider a DeLP-server that has the set $\Delta_{8.1}$ of Example 8.1 stored. An agent may send the contextual query $[\{\sim electricity(d), emergency\_lights(d)\}, lights\_on(d)]$ where the context $\{\sim electricity(d), emergency\_lights(d)\}$ will provide to the server information about a particular room d. The server will use this context and $\Delta_{8.1}$ in order to return the answer for the query $lights\_on(d)$.

Since contextual information can be in contradiction with the information stored in the server, different types of contextual queries were defined [13]: *prioritized*, *non-prioritized* and *restrictive*. For instance, a prioritized contextual assigns more importance to the information sent by the agent and overrides the information stored in the server that produces the contradiction.

Agents are not restricted to consult a unique DeLP-server, they may perform the same contextual query to different servers, and they may share different knowledge with other agents through different servers. Thus, several configurations of agents and servers can be established (statically or dynamically). For example, special-purpose DeLP-servers can be used, each of them representing particular shared knowledge of a specific domain.

Argue tuProlog (AtuP) [6] is a prototype implementation of an argumentation engine based on Vreeswijk's Argumentation System (AS) that can be used to implement a non-monotonic reasoning component in the Internet or agent-based applications. The following description is taken from [5]. AtuP accepts formulae in an extended first-order language and returns answers to queries of acceptability on the basis of the semantics of credulously preferred sets. The language can be considered to be a conservative extension of the basic language of PROLOG, enriched with numbers that quantify rule strength and degree of belief. Strict and defeasible rules can be entered into the system and typically exactly one query is supplied. The core prover of the implementation attempts to find an argument with a conclusion for the query. On the macro level arguments are constructed as nodes in a digraph, and AtuP tries to build an admissible set around an argument for the main claim. AtuP is currently implemented in Java.

Finally, the issue of studying which properties are satisfied by the set of consequences of an argument-based reasoning system has been gaining attention in the community [8, 7]. A similar effort was conducted in the general area of nonmonotonic reasoning formalisms since very early [12, 16, 18]. In [7] three postulates are advanced: *Closure, Direct Consistency*, and *Indirect Consistency*. The properties are studied in the context of the possible extensions that could be obtained from the argumentation system via different semantics such as the ones proposed in [10]. Closure is a form of completeness, *i.e.,* all possible consequences of the knowledge base are obtained. Consistency (direct and indirect) requires that the set of conclusions be non contradictory in a logical sense.

The idea of introducing postulates such as these is to guide the design of the reasoners in a manner that their consequences would satisfy the intuitions of the users of these systems. Even though the importance of this issue cannot be overstated, the discussion of the problems of properly characterizing the behavior of an argument-based consequence operator is out of the scope of this chapter.

8 Conclusions

In this chapter we have described several formalisms that integrate Logic Programming and Argumentation. In particular, we have described Defeasible Logic Programming (DeLP), which provides an extension of a logic programming language with a defeasible argumentation formalism. In DeLP a query succeeds if it is warranted, *i.e.*, if it is possible to build an argument that supports the query and this argument is found to be undefeated by a warrant procedure. We have described an argument-based extended logic programming formalism with defeasible priorities developed by Prakken and Sartor. In their formalism, arguments are expressed in a logic programming language with both strong and default negation. Conflicts between arguments are decided with the help of priorities on the rules. These priorities can be defeasibly derived as conclusions within the system. An overview of the argumentation semantics for extended logic programming developed by Schweimeier and Schroeder was given. Their proposal introduces a variety of notions of attack for extended logic programs from combinations of undercutting and rebuttal.

As Phan Minh Dung emphasized in [10] *"there are extremely interesting relations between argumentation and logic programming"*. In this chapter we have covered some of them.

Acknowledgements This research was funded by CONICET Argentina Project PIP 5050, and SGCyT, Universidad Nacional del Sur, Argentina.

References

1. T. Alsinet, C. Chesñevar, L. Godo, S. Sandri, and G. Simari. Formalizing argumentative reasoning in a possibilistic logic programming setting with fuzzy unification. *International Journal of Approximate Reasoning*, 48(3):711–729, 2008.
2. T. Alsinet, C. Chesñevar, L. Godo, and G. Simari. A logic programming framework for possibilistic argumentation: Formalization and logical properties. *Fuzzy Sets and Systems*, 159(10):208–1228, 2008.
3. G. Antoniou, D. Billington, G. Governatori, M. J. Maher, and A. Rock. A family of defeasible reasoning logics and its implementation. In *Proceedings of European Conference on Artificial Intelligence (ECAI)*, pages 459–463, 2000.
4. G. Antoniou, D. Billington, and M. J. Maher. Normal forms for defeasible logic. In *Proceedings of International Joint Conference and Symposium on Logic Programming*, pages 160–174. MIT Press, 1998.
5. D. Bryant and P. J. Krause. A review of current defeasible reasoning implementations. *The Knowledge Engineering Review*, 23:1–34, 2008.
6. D. Bryant, P. J. Krause, and G. Vreeswijk. Argue tuProlog: A Lightweight Argumentation Engine for Agent Applications. In *Proc. of 1st Int. Conference on Computational Models of Argument (COMMA06)*, pages 27–32. IOS Press, 2006.
7. M. Caminada and L. Amgoud. On the evaluation of argumentation formalisms. *Artificial Intelligence*, 171(5-6):286–310, 2007.
8. C. Chesñevar and G. Simari. Modelling inference in argumentation through labelled deduction: Formalization and logical properties. *Logica Universalis*, 1(1):93–124, 2007.
9. J. Dix, C. Chesñevar, F. Stolzenburg, and G. Simari. Relating Defeasible and Normal Logic Programming through Transformation Properties. *Theoretical Computer Science*, 290(1):499–529, 2002.
10. P. M. Dung. On the acceptability of arguments and its fundamental role in nonmonotonic reasoning and logic programming and *n*-person games. *Artificial Intelligence*, 77:321–357, 1995.
11. E. Ferretti, M. Errecalde, A. García, and G. Simari. Decision rules and arguments in defeasible decision making. In P. Besnard, S. Doutre, and A. Hunter, editors, *Proc. 2nd Int.*

Conference on Computational Models of Arguments (COMMA), volume 172 of Frontiers in Artificial Intelligence and Applications, pages 171–182. IOS Press, 2008.

12. D. Gabbay. Theoretical foundations for non-monotonic reasoning in expert systems. In K. Apt, editor, Logics and Models of Concurrent Systems, pages 439–459. Springer-Verlag, 1985.

13. A. García, N. Rotstein, M. Tucat, and G. Simari. An argumentative reasoning service for deliberative agents. In Z. Zhang and J. Siekmann, editors, LNAI 4798 Proceedings of the 2nd. International Conference on Knowledge Science, Engineering and Management (KSEM 2007), pages 128–139. Springer-Verlag, 2007.

14. A. J. García, N. D. Rotstein, and G. R. Simari. Dialectical explanations in defeasible argumentation. In K. Mellouli, editor, ECSQARU, volume 4724 of Lecture Notes in Computer Science, pages 295–307. Springer, 2007.

15. A. J. García and G. R. Simari. Defeasible logic programming: An argumentative approach. TPLP, 4(1-2):95–138, 2004.

16. S. Kraus, D. Lehmann, and M. Magidor. Nonmonotonic reasoning, preferential models and cumulative logics. Artificial Intelligence, 44:167–207, 1990.

17. V. Lifschitz. Foundations of logic programs. In G. Brewka, editor, Principles of Knowledge Representation, pages 69–128. CSLI Pub., 1996.

18. D. Makinson. General patterns in nonmonotonic reasoning. In D. Gabbay, editor, Handbook of Logic in Artificial Intelligence and Logic Programming (vol 3): Nonmonotonic and Uncertain Reasoning, pages 35–110. Oxford University Press, 1994.

19. D. Nute. Defeasible reasoning. In Proc. of the 20th annual Hawaii Int. Conf. on System Sciences, 1987.

20. D. Nute. Defeasible logic. In D. Gabbay, C. Hogger, and J.A.Robinson, editors, Handbook of Logic in Artificial Intelligence and Logic Programming, Vol 3, pages 355–395. Oxford University Press, 1994.

21. J. Pollock. Cognitive Carpentry: A Blueprint for How to Build a Person. MIT Press, 1995.

22. H. Prakken. Logical Tools for Modelling Legal Argument. A Study of Defeasible Reasoning in Law. Kluwer Law and Philosophy Library, 1997.

23. H. Prakken and G. Sartor. A dialectical model of assessing conflicting arguments in legal reasoning. Artificial Intelligence and Law, 4(331-368), 1996.

24. H. Prakken and G. Sartor. Argument-based logic programming with defeasible priorities. J. of Applied Non-classical Logics, 7(25-75), 1997.

25. H. Prakken and G. Vreeswijk. Logical systems for defeasible argumentation. In D.Gabbay, editor, Handbook of Philosophical Logic, 2nd ed. Kluwer, 2000.

26. R. Schweimeier and M. Schroeder. A parameterised hierarchy of argumentation semantics for extended logic programming and its application to the well-founded semantics. TPLP, 5(1-2):207–242, 2005.

27. G. R. Simari, C. I. Chesñevar, and A. J. García. The role of dialectics in defeasible argumentation. In Proc. of the XIV Int. Conf. of the Chilenean Computer Science Society, pages 335–344, 1994.

28. G. R. Simari and R. P. Loui. A Mathematical Treatment of Defeasible Reasoning and its Implementation. Artificial Intelligence, 53:125–157, 1992.

29. F. Stolzenburg, A. J. García, C. I. Chesñevar, and G. R. Simari. Computing generalized specificity. Journal of Applied Non-Classical Logics, 13(1):87–113, 2003.

Chapter 9
A Recursive Semantics for Defeasible Reasoning

John L. Pollock

1 Reasoning in the Face of Pervasive Ignorance

One of the most striking characteristics of human beings is their ability to function successfully in complex environments about which they know very little. Reflect on how little you really know about all the individual matters of fact that characterize the world. What, other than vague generalizations, do you know about the apples on the trees of China, individual grains of sand, or even the residents of Cincinnati? But that does not prevent you from eating an apple while visiting China, lying on the beach in Hawaii, or giving a lecture in Cincinnati. Our ignorance of individual matters of fact is many orders of magnitude greater than our knowledge. And the situation does not improve when we turn to knowledge of general facts. Modern science apprises us of some generalizations, and our experience teaches us numerous higher-level although less precise general truths, but surely we are ignorant of most general truths.

In light of our pervasive ignorance, we cannot get around in the world just reasoning deductively from our prior beliefs together with new perceptual input. This is obvious when we look at the varieties of reasoning we actually employ. We tend to trust perception, assuming that things are the way they appear to us, even though we know that sometimes they are not. And we tend to assume that facts we have learned perceptually will remain true, at least for awhile, when we are no longer perceiving them, but of course, they might not. And, importantly, we combine our individual observations inductively to form beliefs about both statistical and exceptionless generalizations. None of this reasoning is deductively valid. On the other hand, we cannot be criticized for drawing conclusions on the basis of such non-conclusive evidence, because there is no feasible alternative. Our non-deductive reasoning makes our conclusions reasonable, but does not guarantee their truth. As our conclusions

John L. Pollock
Department of Philosophy, University of Arizona, Tucson, Arizona 85721.
This work was supported by NSF grant no. IIS- 0412791

are not guaranteed to be true, we must countenance the possibility that new information will lead us to change our minds, withdrawing previously adopted beliefs. In this sense, our reasoning is "defeasible". That is, it makes it reasonable for us to form beliefs, but it can be "defeated" by considerations that make it unreasonable to maintain the previously reasonable beliefs.

If we are to understand how rational cognition works, we must know how defeasible reasoning works, or ought to work. This chapter attempts to answer that question.

2 The Structure of Defeasible Reasoning

2.1 Inference Graphs

I assume that much of our reasoning proceeds by stringing together individual inferences into more complex arguments. In philosophy it is customary to think of arguments as linear sequences of propositions, with each member of the sequence being either a premise or the conclusion of an inference (in accordance with some inference scheme) from earlier propositions in the sequence. However, this representation of arguments is an artifact of the way we write them. In many cases the ordering of the elements of the sequence is irrelevant to the structure of the argument. For instance, consider an argument that proceeds by giving a subargument for P and an unrelated subargument for $(P \rightarrow Q)$, and then finishes by inferring Q by modus ponens. We might diagram this argument as in figure 9.1. The ordering of the elements of the two subarguments with respect to each other is irrelevant. If we write the argument for Q as a linear sequence of propositions, we must order the elements of the subarguments with respect to each other, thus introducing artificial structure in the representation. For many purposes it is better to represent the argument graphically, as as in figure 9.1. Such a graph is an *inference graph*. The compound arrows linking elements of the inference graph represent the application of inference schemes.

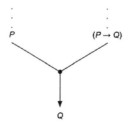

Fig. 9.1 An inference graph

More generally, we can take the elements of arguments to be Fitch-style *sequents* – ordered pairs of propositions and suppositions (sets of propositions), and inference rules like *conditionalization* can take advantage of that. However, for the purposes of this chapter, I will ignore that sophistication. In deductive reasoning, the inference schemes employed are deductive inference rules. What distinguishes deductive reasoning from reasoning more generally is that the reasoning is not defeasible. More precisely, given a deductive argument for a conclusion, you cannot rationally deny the conclusion without denying one or more of the premises. In contrast, consider an inductive argument. Suppose we observe a number of swans and they are all white. This gives us a reason for thinking that all swans are white. If we subsequently journey to Australia and observe a black swan, we must retract that conclusion. But notice that this does not give us a reason for retracting any of the premises. It is still reasonable to believe that each of the initially observed swans is white. What distinguishes defeasible arguments from deductive arguments is that the *addition* of information can mandate the retraction of the conclusion of a defeasible argument without mandating the retraction of any of the premises or conclusions from which the retracted conclusion was inferred.

2.2 Rebutting defeaters

Information that can mandate the retraction of the conclusion of a defeasible argument constitutes a *defeater* for the argument. There are two kinds of defeaters. The simplest are *rebutting defeaters*, which attack an argument by attacking its conclusion. In the inductive example concerning white swans, what defeated the argument was the discovery of a black swan, and the reason that was a defeater is that it entails the negation of the conclusion, i.e., it entails that not all swans are white. More generally, a rebutting defeater could be any reason for denying the conclusion (deductive or defeasible). For instance, I might be informed by Herbert, an ornithologist, that not all swans are white. People do not always speak truly, so the fact that he tells me this does not entail that it is true that not all swans are white. Nevertheless, because Herbert is an ornithologist, his telling me that gives me a defeasible reason for thinking that not all swans are white, so it is a rebutting defeater.

2.3 Undercutting defeaters

Not all defeaters are rebutting defeaters. Suppose Simon, whom I regard as very reliable, tells me, "Don't believe Herbert. He is incompetent." That Herbert told me that not all swans are white gives me a reason for believing that not all swans are white, but Simon's remarks about Herbert give me a reason for withdrawing my belief, and they do so without either (1) making me doubt that Herbert said what I took him to say or (2) giving me a reason for thinking it false that not all swans are white. Even if

Herbert is incompetent, he might have accidentally gotten it right that not all swans
are white. Thus Simon's remarks constitute a defeater, but not a rebutting defeater.
This is an example of an *undercutting defeater*. The difference between rebutting defeaters and undercutting defeaters is that rebutting defeaters attack the conclusion of
a defeasible inference, while undercutting defeaters attack the defeasible inference
itself, without doing so by giving us a reason for thinking it has a false conclusion.
We can think of an undercutting defeater as a reason for thinking that it is false that
the premises of the inference would not be true unless the conclusion were true.
More simply, we can think of it as giving us a reason for believing that (under the
present circumstances) the truth of the premises does not guarantee the truth of the
conclusion. It will be convenient to symbolize this as "premises⊗conclusion". It is
useful to expand our graphical representation of reasoning by including defeat relations. Thus we might represent the preceding example as in figure 9.2. Here I have
drawn the defeat relations using thick grey arrows. Note that the rebutting defeat is
symmetrical, but undercutting defeat is not.

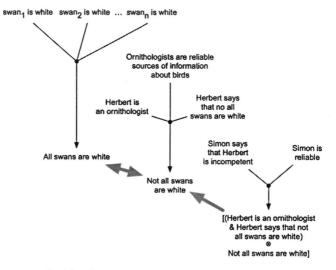

Fig. 9.2 Inference graph with defeat

2.4 Computing Defeat-statuses

We can combine all of a cognizer's reasoning into a single inference graph and regard that as a representation of those aspects of his cognitive state that pertain to
reasoning. The hardest problem in a theory of defeasible reasoning is to give a precise account of how the structure of the cognizer's inference graph determines what
he should believe. Such an account is called a "semantics" for defeasible reasoning,

although it is not a semantics in the same sense as, for example, a semantics for first-order logic. If a cognizer reasoned only deductively, it would be easy to provide an account of what he should believe. In that case, a cognizer should believe all and only the conclusions of his arguments (assuming that the premises are somehow initially justified). However, if an agent reasons defeasibly, then the conclusions of some of his arguments may be defeaters for other arguments, and so he should not believe the conclusions of all of them. For example, in figure 9.2, the cognizer first concludes "All swans are white". Then he constructs an argument for a defeater for the first argument, at which point it would no longer be reasonable to believe its conclusion. But then he constructs a third argument supporting a defeater for the second (defeating) argument, and that should reinstate the first argument. Obviously, the relationships between interacting arguments can be very complex. We want a general account of how it is determined which conclusions should be believed, or to use philosophical parlance, which conclusions are "justified" and which are not. This distinction enforces a further distinction between beliefs and conclusions. When a cognizer constructs an argument, he entertains the conclusion and he entertains the propositions comprising the intervening steps, but he need not believe them. Constructing arguments is one thing. Deciding which conclusions to accept is another. What we want is a criterion which, when applied to the inference graph, determines which conclusions are defeated and which are not, i.e., a criterion that determines the defeat-statuses of the conclusions. The conclusions that ought to be believed are those that are undefeated. The remainder of the chapter will be devoted to proposing such a criterion.

3 The Multiple-Assignment Semantics

Let us collect all of an agent's arguments into an inference-graph, where the nodes are labeled by the conclusions of arguments, *support-links* tie nodes to the nodes from which they are inferred, and *defeat-links* indicate defeat relations between nodes. These links relate their roots to their targets. The root of a defeat-link is a single node, and the root of a support-link is a set of nodes. The analysis is somewhat simpler if we construct the inference-graph in such a way that when the same conclusion is supported by two or more arguments, it is represented by a separate node for each argument. For example, consider the inference-graph diagrammed in figure three, which represents two different arguments for $(P \& Q)$ given the premises, P, Q, A, and $(A \rightarrow (P \& Q))$. The nodes of such an inference-graph represent arguments rather than just representing their conclusions. In such an inference-graph, a node has at most one support-link. When it is unambiguous to do so, I will refer to the nodes in terms of the conclusions they encode.

Because a conclusion can be supported by multiple arguments, it is the arguments themselves to which we must first attach defeat-statuses. Then a conclusion is undefeated iff it is supported by at least one undefeated argument. The only exception to this rule is "initial nodes", which (from the perspective of the inference graph)

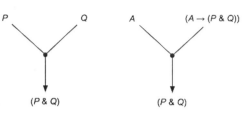

Fig. 9.3 An inference graph

are simply "given" as premises. Initial nodes are unsupported by arguments, but are taken to be undefeated. Ultimately, we want to use this machinery to model rational cognition. In that case, all that can be regarded as "given" is perceptual input (construed broadly to include such modes of perception as proprioception, introspection, etc.), in which case it may be inaccurate to take the initial nodes to encode propositions. It is probably better to regard them as encoding percepts.[1]

The node-basis of a node is the set of roots of its support-link (if it has one), i.e., the set of nodes from which the node is inferred in a single step. If a node has no support-link (i.e., it is initial) then the node-basis is empty. The node-defeaters are the roots of the defeat-links having the node as their target. Given an inference-graph, a semantics must determine which nodes encode (the conclusions of) arguments that ought to be accepted, i.e., that are not defeated. This is the defeat-status computation, and nodes are marked "defeated" or "undefeated". The defeat-status computation is made more complex by the fact that some arguments support their conclusions more strongly than other arguments. For instance, if Jones tells me it is raining, and Smith denies it, and I regard them as equally reliable, then I have equally strong arguments both for believing that it is raining and for believing that it is not raining. In that case, I should withhold belief, not accepting either conclusion. On the other hand, if I regard Jones as much more reliable than Smith, then I have a stronger argument for believing that it is raining, and if the difference is great enough, that is the conclusion I should draw. So argument-strengths make a difference. However, most semantics for defeasible reasoning ignore argument strengths, pretending that all initial nodes are equally well justified and all inference schemes equally strong. I will make this same simplifying assumption in this chapter. What can we say about the semantics in this simplified case?

Let us define:

A node of the inference-graph is *initial* iff its node-basis and list of node-defeaters are empty.

It is initially tempting to try to characterize defeat-statuses recursively using the following two rules:

(D1)   Initial nodes are undefeated.
(D2)   A non-initial node is undefeated iff all the members of its node-basis

---

[1] See [11] and [12] for a fuller discussion of this.

are undefeated and all node-defeaters are defeated.

However, this recursion turns out to be ungrounded because we can have nodes of an inference-graph that defeat each other, as in inference-graph (4), where dashed arrows indicate defeasible inferences and heavy arrows indicate defeat-links. In computing defeat-statuses in inference-graph (4), we cannot proceed recursively using rules (D1) and (D2), because that would require us to know the defeat-status of Q before computing that of ~Q, and also to know the defeat-status of ~Q before computing that of Q. The general problem is that a node Q can have an inference/defeat-descendant that is a defeater of Q, where an inference/defeat-descendant of a node is any node that can be reached from the first node by following support-links and defeat-links. I will say that a node is *Q-dependent* iff it is an inference/defeat-descendant of a node Q. So the recursion is blocked in inference-graph (4) by there being Q-dependent defeaters of Q and ~Q-dependent defeaters of ~Q.

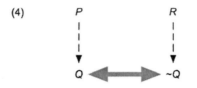

Inference-graph (4) is a case of "collective defeat". For example, let P be "Jones says that it is raining", R be "Smith says that it is not raining", and Q be "It is raining". Given P and Q, and supposing you regard Smith and Jones as equally reliable, what should you believe about the weather? It seems clear that you should withhold belief, accepting neither Q nor ~Q. In other words, both Q and ~Q should be defeated. This constitutes a counter-example to rule (D2). So not only do rules (D1) and (D2) not provide a recursive characterization of defeat-statuses – they are not even true. The failure of these rules to provide a recursive characterization of defeat-statuses suggests that no such characterization is possible, and that in turn suggested to me (see [9, 10]) that rules (D1) and (D2) might be used to characterize defeat-statuses in another way. Reiter's default logic [13] proceeded in terms of multiple "extensions", and "skeptical default logic" characterizes a conclusion as following nonmonotonically from a set of premises and defeasible inference-schemes iff it is true in every extension. There are simple examples showing that this semantics is inadequate for the general defeasible reasoning of epistemic agents (see below), but the idea of having multiple extensions suggested to me that rules (D1) and (D2) might be used to characterize multiple "status assignments". On this approach, a partial status assignment is an assignment of defeat-statuses to a subset of the nodes of the inference-graph in accordance with (D1) and (D2):

An assignment σ of "defeated" and "undefeated" to a subset of the nodes of an inference-graph is a *partial status assignment* iff:

1. σ assigns "undefeated" to any initial node;
2. σ assigns "undefeated" to a non-initial node α iff σ assigns "undefeated" to all the members of the node-basis of α and all node-defeaters of α are assigned "defeated".

My (1995) semantics defined:

σ is a *status assignment* iff σ is a partial status assignment and σ is not properly contained in any other partial status assignment.

My proposal was then:

A node is *undefeated* iff every status assignment assigns "undefeated" to it; otherwise it is defeated.

Belief in P is *justified* for an agent iff P is encoded by an undefeated node of the inference-graph representing the agent's current epistemological state.

I will refer to this semantics as the *multiple-assignment semantics*. To illustrate, consider inference-graph (4) again. There are two status assignments for this inference graph:

assignment 1:

P "undefeated"
R "undefeated"
Q "undefeated"
$\sim Q$ "defeated"

assignment 2:

P "undefeated"
R "undefeate"
Q "defeated"
$\sim Q$ "undefeated"

P and R are undefeated, but neither Q nor $\sim Q$ is assigned "undefeated" in every assignment, so both are defeated.

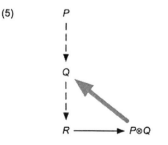

(5)

The reason for making status assignments "partial" is that there are inference graphs for which it is impossible to construct status assignments assigning statuses to every node. One case in which this happens is when we have "self-defeating arguments", i.e., arguments whose conclusions defeat some of the inferences leading to those conclusions. A simple example is inference-graph (5). A partial status assignment must assign "undefeated" to P. If it assigned "undefeated" to Q then it would assign "undefeated" to R and $P \otimes Q$, in which case it would have to assign "defeated" to Q. So it cannot assign "undefeated" to Q. If it assigned "defeated" to Q it would have to assign "defeated" to R and $P \otimes Q$, in which case it would have to assign "undefeated" to Q. So that is not possible either. Thus a partial status assignment cannot assign anything to Q, R, and $P \otimes Q$. Hence there is only one status assignment (i.e., maximal partial status assignment), and it assigns "undefeated" to P and nothing to the other nodes. Accordingly, P is undefeated and the other nodes are defeated. An intuitive example having approximately the same form is shown in inference-graph (6). Here we suppose that people generally tell the truth, and this gives us a reason for believing what they tell us. However, some people suffer from a malady known as "pink-elephant phobia". In the presence of pink elephants, they become strangely disoriented so that their statements about their surroundings cease to be reliable. Now imagine Robert, who tells us that the elephant beside him looks pink. In ordinary circumstances, we would infer that the elephant beside Robert does look pink, and hence probably is pink. However, Robert suffers from pink-elephant phobia. So if it were true that the elephant beside Robert is pink, we could not rely upon his report to conclude that it is. So we should not conclude that it is pink. We may be left wondering why he would say that it is, but we cannot explain his utterance by supposing that the elephant really is pink. So this gives us no reason at all for a judgment about the color of the elephant. On the other hand, it gives us no reason to doubt that Robert did say that the elephant is pink, or that Robert has pink-elephant phobia. Those are perfectly justified beliefs.

(6)

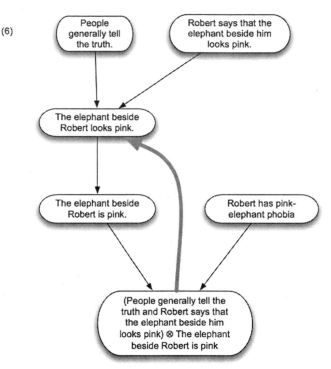

Inference-graphs (5) and (6) constitute intuitive counterexamples to default logic [13] and the stable model semantics [2] because there are no extensions. Hence on those semantics, P has the same status as Q, R, and $P \otimes Q$. It is perhaps more obvious that this is a problem for those semantics if we imagine this self-defeating argument being embedded in a larger inference-graph containing a number of otherwise perfectly ordinary arguments. On these semantics, all of the nodes in all of the arguments would have to have the same status, because there would still be no extensions. But surely the presence of the self-defeating argument should not have the effect of defeating all other (unrelated) arguments.

4 A Problem Case

The multiple-assignment semantics produces the intuitively correct answer for many complicated inference-graphs. For a number of years, I thought that, given the simplifying assumption that all arguments are equally strong, this semantics was correct. But I no longer think so. Here is the problem. Contrast inference-graph (4) with inference-graph (7). Inference-graph (7) involves "odd-length defeat cycles". For an example of inference-graph (7), let A = "Jones says that Smith is unreliable", B = "Smith is unreliable", C = "Smith says that Robinson is unreliable", D = "Robinson is unreliable", E = "Robinson says that Jones is unreliable", F = "Jones is unreliable". Intuitively, this should be another case of collective defeat, with A, C, and E being undefeated and B, D, and F being defeated. The multiple-assignment semantics does yield this result, but it does it in a peculiar way. *A*, *C*, and *E* must be assigned "undefeated", but there is no consistent way to assign defeat-statuses to *B*, *D*, and *F*. Accordingly, there is only one status assignment (maximal partial status assignment), and it leaves *B*, *D*, and *F* unassigned. We get the right answer, but it seems puzzling that we get it in a different way than we do for even-length defeat cycles like that in inference-graph (4). This difference has always bothered me.

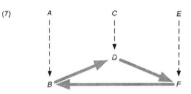

(7)

That we get the right answer in a different way does not show that the semantics is incorrect. As long as otherwise equivalent inference-graphs containing odd-length and even-length defeat cycles always produce the same defeat-statuses throughout the graphs, there is no problem. However, they do not. Contrast inference-graphs (8) and (9). In inference-graph (8), there are two status assignments, one assigning "defeated" to *B* and "undefeated" to *D*, and the other assigning "undefeated" to *B* and "defeated" to *D*. On either status assignment, *P* has an undefeated defeater, so it is defeated on both status assignments, with the result that *Q* is undefeated on both status assignments. Hence *Q* is undefeated simpliciter. However, in inference-graph (9), there is only one status-assignment, and it assigns no status to any of *B*, *D*, *F*, *P*, or *Q*. Thus *Q* is defeated in inference-graph (9), but undefeated in inference-graph (8). This, I take it, is a problem. Although it might not be clear which inference-graph is producing the right answer, the right answer ought to be the same for both inference-graphs. Thus the semantics is getting one of them wrong. It is worth noting in passing that, as far as I know, no currently available semantics for defeasible reasoning handles (8) and (9) correctly. I take this to show that we need a different semantics.

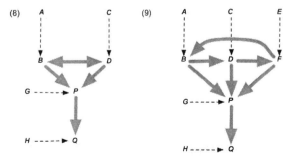

(8)   (9)

5 A Recursive Semantics

The multiple-assignment semantics is based upon the two rules:

(D1)   Initial nodes are undefeated.
(D2)   A non-initial node is undefeated if all the members of its node-basis
       are undefeated and all node-defeaters are defeated.

We have seen that these rules are not true as stated. For example, inference-graph
(4) is a counterexample to rule (D2). Both Q and $\sim Q$ should be defeated, but then
both have undefeated node-bases but no undefeated defeaters. I tried to avoid this
problem by imposing these rules instead on partial-status assignments. But perhaps
we should take seriously the fact that these rules are simply wrong. In inference-
graph (4), in computing the defeat-status of Q, what is crucial is that (a) its node-
basis is undefeated, (b) the node-basis of its defeater is undefeated, and (c) there is
no other defeater for $\sim Q$ besides Q itself. We can capture this by asking whether
$\sim Q$ would be defeated if it were not defeated by Q. We can test this by removing
the mutual defeat-links between Q and $\sim Q$, producing inference-graph (4*). In (4*),
$\sim Q$ is undefeated. The proposal is that this should make Q defeated in (4). Note that
the defeaters we are removing in constructing inference-graph (4*) are those that are
Q-dependent, i.e., those that can be reached by following paths from Q consisting
of inference-links and defeat-links.

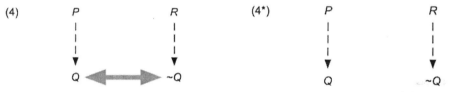

(4)   P   R   (4*)   P   R

        Q ⟷ ~Q   Q   ~Q

Consider another example – inference-graph (10). In computing the defeat-status
of Q, we note that its node-basis is undefeated, and its defeater $P \otimes Q$ is defeated only
by the Q-dependent defeat-link from $R \otimes S$. If we remove the Q-dependent defeat-
links from inference-graph (10) we get inference-graph (10*). In inference-graph
(10*), $P \otimes Q$ is undefeated, so again, the proposal is that this makes Q defeated in
inference-graph (10).

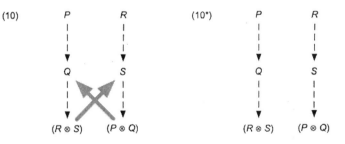

(10)   P   R   (10*)   P   R

           Q   S   Q   S

        (R ⊗ S) (P ⊗ Q)   (R ⊗ S) (P ⊗ Q)

These examples suggest that we might replace rule (D2) by a rule that computes
the defeat-statuses of defeat-links in a modified inference-graph from which we have
removed those defeat-links that make the computation circular. Recall that a defeat-
link or support-link extends from its root to its target. The root of a defeat-link is a
single node, and the root of a support-link is a set of nodes. Let us define:

Definition 9.1. An *inference/defeat-path* from a node φ to a node θ is a sequence of support-links and defeat-links such that (1) φ is or is a member of the root of the first link in the path; (2) θ is the target of the last link in the path; (3) a member of the root of each link after the first member of the path is the target of the preceding link; (4) the path does not contain an internal loop, i.e., no two links in the path have the same target.

Definition 9.2. θ is φ-*dependent* iff there is an inference/defeat-path from φ to φ.

Definition 9.3. A *circular inference/defeat-path* from a node φ to itself is an inference/defeat-path from φ to a defeater for φ.

Definition 9.4. A defeat-link is φ-*critical* iff it is a member of some minimal set of defeat-links such that removing all the defeat-links in the set suffices to cut all the circular inference/defeat-paths from φ to φ.

It will be convenient to modify our understanding of initial nodes. Previously, I took them to be automatically undefeated, and we can still regard that as the default value, but it will also be useful to be able to stipulate that some of the initial nodes in a newly-constructed inference-graph are defeated. The construction I am going to propose builds new inference-graphs as subgraphs of pre-existing inference-graphs by (1) deleting φ-critical links, and (2) making φ-independent nodes initial, i.e., deleting the arguments for them. The latter nodes, being φ-independent, have defeat-statuses that were computable in the original inference-graph without first having to compute a defeat-status for φ. I want to be able to simply stipulate that these newly-initial nodes have the same defeat-statuses in the new inference-graph as they had in the original. This allows us to define:

Definition 9.5. If φ is a node of an inference-graph G, let G_φ be the inference-graph that results from deleting all φ-critical defeat-links from G and making all members of the node-basis of φ and all φ-independent nodes initial-nodes (i.e., deleting their support-links and defeat-links) with stipulated defeat-statuses the same as their defeat-statuses in G.

My proposed semantics now consists of two rules:

(CL1) Initial nodes are undefeated unless they are stipulated to be defeated.

(CL2) A non-initial node φ is undefeated in an inference-graph G iff all members of the node-basis of φ are undefeated in G and any defeater for φ is defeated in G_φ.

On the assumption that arguments cannot be circular, this pair of rules can be applied recursively to compute the defeat-status of any node in a finite inference-graph. The recursion simply steps through arguments, computing the defeat-status of each node φ after the defeat-statuses of the nodes in φ's node-basis are computed. The problem of circular inference/defeat-paths is avoided by removing the φ-critical defeat-links and evaluating node-defeaters in G_φ. I will refer to this new semantics as the *critical-link semantics*, and contrast it with the multiple-assignment semantics.

I believe that the critical-link semantics gets everything right that the multiple-assignment semantics got right. Consider a complex example. Inference-graph (11) illustrates the so called "lottery paradox" [3]. Here P reports a description (e.g., a newspaper report) of a fair lottery with one million tickets. P constitutes a defeasible reason for R, which is the description. That is, the newspaper report gives us a defeasible reason for believing the lottery is fair and has a million tickets. In such a lottery, each ticket has a probability of one in a million of being drawn, so for each i, the statistical syllogism gives us a reason for believing $\sim T_i$ ("ticket i will not be drawn"). The supposed paradox is that although we thusly have a reason for believing of each ticket that it will not be drawn, we can also infer on the basis of R that some ticket will be drawn. Of course, this is not really a paradox, because the inferences are defeasible and this is a case of collective defeat. This results from the fact that for each i, we can infer T_i from (i) the description R (which entails that some ticket will be drawn) and (ii) the conclusions that none of the other tickets will be drawn. This gives us a defeating argument for the defeasible argument to the conclusion that $\sim T_i$, as diagrammed in inference-graph (11). The result is that for each i, there is a status assignment on which $\sim T_i$ is assigned "defeated" and the other $\sim T_j$'s are all assigned "undefeated", and hence none of them are assigned "undefeated" in every status assignment.

(11)

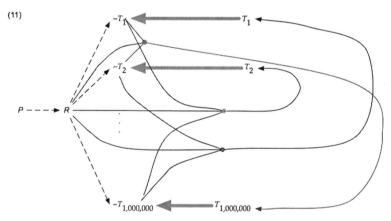

I believe that all (skeptical) semantics for defeasible reasoning get the lottery paradox right. A more interesting example is the "lottery paradox paradox", diagrammed in inference-graph (12). This results from the observation that because R entails that some ticket will be drawn, from the collection of conclusions of the form $\sim T_i$ we can infer $\sim R$, and that is a defeater for the defeasible inference from $\sim P$ to $\sim R$. This is a self-defeating argument. Clearly, the inferences in the lottery paradox should not lead us to disbelieve the newspaper's description of the lottery, so R should be undefeated. Circumscription [5], in its simple non-prioritized form, gets this example wrong, because one way of minimizing abnormalities would be to block the inference from P to R. My own early analysis [8] also gets this wrong. This was the example that led me to the multiple-assignment semantics. The multiple-assignment semantics gets this right. We still have the same status assignments as in inference-graph (11), and $\sim R$ is defeated in all of them because it is inferred from the entire set of $\sim T_i$'s, and one of those is defeated in every status assignment.

(12)

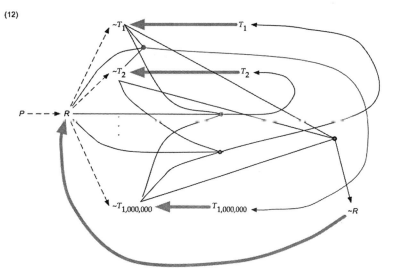

It will be convenient to have a simpler example of an inference-graph with the same general structure as the lottery paradox paradox. For that purpose we can use inference-graph (13). Here P and R should be undefeated, but T_1, T_2, and $\sim R$ should be defeated. In the critical link semantics, to compute the defeat-status of R in inference-graph (13), we construct (13*) by removing the only defeat-link whose removal results in R no longer having an R-dependent defeater. In (13*), the triangle consisting of R, T_1 and T_2 is analogous to inference-graph (4), with the result that T_1 and T_2 are both defeated in inference-graph (13*). They constitute the node-basis for $\sim R$, so $\sim R$ is also defeated in inference-graph (13*). Thus by (CL2), R is undefeated in inference-graph (13). Turning to T_1 and T_2 in inference-graph (13), both have R as their node-basis, and R is undefeated. Thus to compute the defeat-status of T_1 or T_2, we construct inference-graph (13**), and observe that T_1 and T_2 are undefeated there. It then follows by (CL2) that T_1 and T_2 are defeated in inference-graph (13). Then because T_1 and T_2 are defeated, $\sim R$ is defeated in inference-graph (13). So we get the intuitively correct answers throughout.

(13) P (13*) P

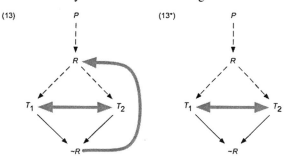

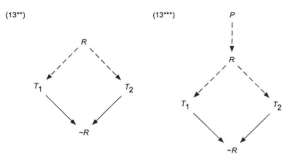

Inference-graph (13) also illustrates why, in constructing G_φ, we remove only the φ-critical defeat-links, and not all of the φ-dependent defeat-links. All of the defeat-links in inference-graph (13) are R-dependent, and if we remove them all we get inference-graph (13***). But in inference-graph (13***), $\sim R$ is undefeated. This would result in R being defeated in inference-graph (13) rather than undefeated. Thus it is crucial to remove only the φ-critical defeat-links rather than all the φ-dependent defeat-links.

6 The Problem Cases

Now let us turn to some cases that the multiple-assignment semantics does not or may not get right. First, consider the pair of inference-graphs that motivated the search for a new semantics. These are inference-graphs (8) and (9). In these inference-graphs, not everyone agrees whether Q should come out defeated or undefeated, but it does seem clear that whatever the right answer is, it should be the same for both inference-graphs. Unfortunately, on the multiple-assignment semantics, Q is undefeated in inference-graph (8) and defeated in inference-graph (9).

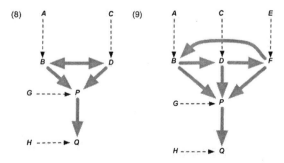

On the critical-link semantics, we compute the defeat-statuses of B and D in inference-graph (8) by constructing inference-graph (8*). B and D are undefeated in inference-graph (8*), so each defeats the other in inference-graph (8), with the result that B and D are defeated in inference-graph (8). There are no P-critical defeat-links in (8), so removing P-critical defeat-links leaves inference-graph (8)

unchanged. *B* and *D* are defeated in inference-graph (8), so it follows that *P* is defeated in inference-graph (8). Then because there are no *Q*-dependent defeat-links in inference-graph (8), *Q* is undefeated.

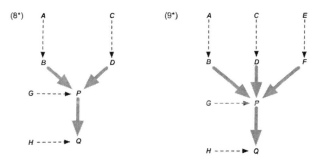

The computation of defeat-statuses in inference-graph (9) works in exactly the same way, via inference-graph (9*), again producing the result that *Q* is undefeated. So on the critical-link semantics, we do not get a divergence between inference-graphs (8) and (9).

Still, we can ask whether the answer we get for inference-graphs (8) and (9) is the correct answer. There is some intuitive reason for thinking so. In inference-graph (8), *B* and *D* are defeated, so they should not have the power to defeat *P*, and hence *P* should defeat *Q*. Similarly, in inference-graph (9), all three of *B*, *D*, and *F* are defeated, and so again, *D* should not have the power to defeat *P*, and hence *P* should defeat *Q*. However, not everyone agrees that this intuitive reasoning is correct. This issue is closely connected with a question that has puzzled theorists since the earliest work on the semantics of defeasible reasoning. The multiple-assignment semantics, as well as default logic, the stable model semantics, circumscription, and almost every familiar semantics for defeasible reasoning and nonmonotonic logic, supports what I have called [8] "presumptive defeat".[2] For example, consider inference-graph (14). On the multiple-assignment semantics, a defeated conclusion like *Q* that is assigned "defeated" in some status assignment and "undefeated" in another retains the ability to defeat. That is because, in the assignment in which it is undefeated, the defeatee is defeated, and hence not undefeated in all status-assignments. In the case of inference-graph (14) this has the consequence that *S* is assigned "defeated" in those status-assignments in which *Q* is assigned "defeated", but *S* is assigned "undefeated" and ∼*S* is assigned "defeated" in those status-assignments in which *Q* is assigned "undefeated". Touretzky, Horty, and Thomason [14] called this "ambiguity propagation", and Makinson and Schlechta [4] called such arguments "Zombie arguments" (they are dead, but they can still get you). However, the critical-link semantics precludes presumptive defeat. It entails that *Q*, ∼*Q*, and hence ∼*S*, are all defeated, and *S* is undefeated. Is this the right answer?

---

[2] The only semantics I know about that does not support presumptive defeat are certain versions of Nute's [6] defeasible logic. See also Covington, Nute, and Vellino [1], and Nute [7].

(14)

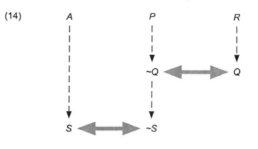

Consider an example. You are sitting with Keith and Alvin, and the following conversation ensues:

Keith: I heard on the news this morning that it is going to rain this afternoon.
Alvin: Nonsense! I was sitting right beside you listening to the same weather report, and the announcer clearly said that it is going to be a sunny day in Tucson.
Keith: You idiot, you must have cotton in your ears! It was perfectly clear that he said it is going ro rain.
Alvin: You never pay attention. No one in his right mind could have thought he said it was going to rain. He said it would be sunny.
. . .

At that point, you wander off shaking your head, still wondering what the weather is going to be. Then it occurs to you that it is about time for the noon News, so you turn on the radio and hear the announcer say, "This just in from the National Weather Service. It is going to rain in Tucson this afternoon." Surely, that settles the matter. You will believe, with complete justification, that it is going to rain. The earlier conversation between Keith and Alvin does not defeat your judgment on the basis of the noon broadcast. This example has the form of inference-graph (14) if we let:

S = "It is going to rain in Tucson this afternoon"
Q = "The morning news said that S"
P = "Alvin says that Q"
R = "Keith says that $\sim Q$"
A = "The noon news says that S"

This seems to me to be a fairly compelling example of the failure of presumptive defeat. Formally, presumptive defeat arises for the multiple-assignment semantics from the fact that if a node P is defeated in one assignment and undefeated in another, then P-dependent nodes will also have different defeat-statuses in the different assignments unless one of their inference-ancestors is defeated absolutely (i.e., in all status assignments). A similar problem arises for inference-nodes P that cannot be assigned defeat-statuses in any assignments. This occurs, for example, in cases of self-defeat or when there are odd-length defeat cycles. In this case, no P-dependent node can be assigned a defeat-status either unless one of its inference-ancestors is defeated absolutely. For example, consider once more the sad case of Robert, the pink-elephant-phobic (inference-graph (6)). We observed that Robert's statement that the elephant beside him is pink does not give us a good reason for believing that it really is pink. Now suppose that Robert is accompanied by Herbert, who is also standing beside the elephant. While Robert is blathering about pink-elephants, Herbert turns to you and says, "I read in the newspaper this morning that the President is going to visit China." From this you infer that he did read that in the newspaper, and hence the President is probably going to visit China. Suppose, however, that Herbert also suffers from pink-elephant phobia. Does that make any difference? It does not seem so, because as we observed, Robert's statement gives us no reason to think the elephant is pink, and so no reason to distrust Herbert's statement. This scenario is diagrammed in inference-graph (15). However, on the multiple-assignment semantics,

> The elephant beside Robert and Herbert is pink

has no status assignment, and hence neither does

> (People generally tell the truth and Herbert says that he read in the newspaper this morning that the President is going to visit China)⊗ Herbert read in the newspaper this morning that the President is going to visit China

or

> Herbert read in the newspaper this morning that the President is going to visit China

or

> The president is going to visit China.

This seems clearly wrong. On the other hand, on the critical-link semantics,

> The elephant beside Robert and Herbert looks pink

is defeated, and hence so is

> The elephant beside Robert and Herbert is pink

and so is

> (People generally tell the truth and Herbert says that he read in the newspaper this morning that the President is going to visit China) ⊗ Herbert read in the newspaper this morning that the President is going to visit China.

Accordingly,

> Herbert read in the newspaper this morning that the President is going to visit China

and

> The president is going to visit China

are undefeated, which is the intuitively correct result.

(15)

The upshot is that the critical-link semantics agrees with the multiple-assignment semantics on simple cases in which the latter seems to give the right answer, but the critical-link semantics also seems to get right a number of cases that the multiple-assignment semantics gets wrong. The test of a semantics for defeasible reasoning is that it agrees with our intuitions about clear cases. So we have reasonably strong inductive reasons for thinking that the critical-link semantics properly characterizes the semantics of defeasible reasoning.

7 Computing Defeat-Statuses

Principles (CL1) and (CL2) provide a recursive characterization of defeat-status relative to an inference-graph. However, this characterization does not lend itself well to implementation because it requires the construction of modified inference-graphs, which would be computationally expensive. The objective of this section is to produce an equivalent recursive characterization that appeals only to the given inference-graph.

A defeat-link is φ-critical iff it is a member of a minimal set such that removing all the defeat-links in the set suffices to cut all the circular inference/defeat-paths from φ to φ. A necessary condition for a defeat-link L to be φ-critical is that it lie on such a circular path. In general, there can be diverging and reconverging paths with several "parallel" defeat-links, as in figure 16. In figure 16, removing the defeat-link D_3 suffices to cut both circular paths. But the set D_1, D_2 of parallel defeat-links is also a minimal set of defeat-links such that the removal of all the links in the set suffices to cut all the circular inference/defeat-paths from φ to φ. Thus in figure 16, all of the defeat-links are φ-critical. However, lying on a circular inference/defeat-path is not a sufficient condition for being φ-critical. A defeat-link on a circular inference/defeat-path from φ to φ fails to be φ-critical when there is a path around it consisting entirely of support-links, as diagrammed in figure 17. In this case, you must remove D_3 to cut both paths, but once you have done that, removing D_1 is a gratuitous additional deletion. So D_1 is not contained in a minimal set of deletions sufficient for cutting all the circular inference/defeat-paths from φ to φ, and hence D_1 is not φ-critical. This phenomenon is also illustrated by inference-graph (13), and we saw that it is crucial to the computation of degrees of justification in that inference-graph that such defeat-links not be regarded as φ-critical. It turns out that this is the only way a defeat-link on a circular inference/defeat-path can fail to be φ-critical, as will now be proven.   Let us say that a node α *precedes* a node β on

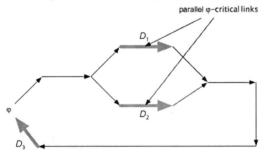

Fig. 9.16 Parallel φ-critical defeat-links

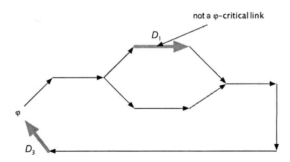

Fig. 9.17 Defeat link that is not φ-critical

an inference/defeat-path iff α and β both lie on the path and either $\alpha = \beta$ or the path contains a subpath originating on α and terminating on β. *Node-ancestors* of a node are nodes that can be reached by following support-links backwards. It will be convenient to define:

Definition 9.6. A defeat-link L is *bypassed* on an inference/defeat-path μ in G iff there is a node α preceding the root of L on μ and a node β preceded by the target of L on μ such that $\alpha = \beta$ or α is a node-ancestor of β in G.

Definition 9.7. μ is a *φ-circular-path* in G iff μ is a circular inference/defeat-path in G from φ to φ and no defeat-link in G is bypassed on μ.

Lemma 9.1. *If μ_1 and μ_2 are φ-circular-paths and every defeat-link in μ_1 occurs in μ_2, then μ_1 and μ_2 contain the same defeat-links and they occur in the same order.*

Proof. Proof: Suppose the defeat-links in μ_1 are $\delta_1, \ldots, \delta_n$, occurring in that order. Suppose μ_1 and μ_2 differ first at the ith defeat-link. Then μ_1 and μ_2 look as in figure 18. But every defeat-link in μ_1 occurs in μ_2, so δ_i must occur later in μ_2. But then the path from δ_{i-1} to δ_i in μ_1 is a bypass around δ_i^* in μ_2, which is impossible if it is a φ-circular-path.$\square$

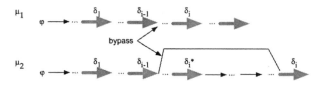

Fig. 9.18 Paths must agree

Lemma 9.2. *Every defeat-link in a φ-circular-path is φ-critical.*

Proof. Suppose δ is a defeat-link on the φ-circular-path μ. Let D be the set of all defeaters in the inference-graph other than those on μ. If deleting all members of D is sufficient to cut all φ-circular-paths not containing δ, then select a minimal subset D_0 of D whose deletion is sufficient to cut all φ-circular-paths not containing δ. Adding δ to D_0 gives us a set of defeat-links whose deletion is sufficient to cut all φ-circular-paths. Furthermore, it is minimal, because adding δ cannot cut any paths not containing δ, and all members of D_0 are required to cut those paths. Thus δ is a member of a minimal set of defeat-links the deletion of which is sufficient to to cut all φ-circular-paths, i.e., δ is φ-critical. Thus if δ is not φ-critical, there is a φ-circular-path ν not containing δ and not cut by cutting all defeat-links not in μ. That is only possible if every defeat-link in ν is in μ. But then by the previous lemma, μ and ν must contain the same defeat-links, so contrary to supposition, δ is in ν. Thus the supposition that δ is not φ-critical is inconsistent with the supposition that it lies on a φ-circular-path. $\square$

Lemma 9.3. *If a defeat-link does not occur on any φ-circular-path then it is not φ-critical.*

Proof. For every circular inference/defeat-path μ from φ to φ there is a φ-circular-path ν such that every defeat-link in ν is in μ. ν results from removing bypassed defeat-links and support-links in μ and replacing them by their bypasses. It follows that any set of deletions of defeat-links that will cut all φ-circular-paths will also cut every circular inference/defeat-path from φ to φ. Conversely, φ-circular-paths are also circular-paths from φ to φ, so any set of deletions that cuts all circular-paths from φ to φ will also cut all φ-circular-paths. So the φ-circular-paths and the circular-paths from φ to φ have the same sets of deletions of defeat-links sufficient to cut them, and hence the same minimal sets of deletions. If a defeat-link δ does not occur on any φ-circular-path, then it is irrelevant to cutting all the φ-circular-paths, and hence it is not in any minimal set of deletions sufficient to cut all circular-paths from φ to φ, i.e., it is not φ-critical. $\square$

Theorem 4 follows immediately from lemmas 2 and 3:

Theorem 9.4. *A defeat-link is φ-critical in G iff it lies on a φ-circular-path in G.*

A further simplification results from observing that, for the purpose of deciding whether a defeat-link is φ-critical, all we have to know about φ-circular-paths is what defeat-links occur in them. It makes no difference what support-links they contain. So let us define:

Definition 9.8. A φ-defeat-loop is a sequence μ of defeat-links for which there is a φ-circular-path ν such that the same defeat-links occur in μ and ν and in the same order.

In other words, to construct a φ-defeat-loop from a φ-circular-path we simply remove all the support-links. We have the following very simple characterization of φ-defeat-loops:

Theorem 9.5. *A sequence $\langle \delta_1, \ldots, \delta_n \rangle$ of defeat-links is a φ-defeat-loop iff (1) φ is a node-ancestor of the root of δ_1, but not of the root of any δ_k for $k > 1$, (2) φ is the target of δ_n, and (3) for each $k < n$, the target of δ_k is equal to or an ancestor of the root of δ_{k+1}, but not of the root of δ_{k+j} for $j > 1$.*

The significance of φ-defeat-loops is that by omitting the support-links we make them easier to process, but we still have the simple theorem:

Theorem 9.6. *A defeat-link is φ-critical in G iff it lies on a φ-defeat-loop in G.*

In simple cases, G_φ will be an inference-graph in which no node ψ has a ψ-critical defeat-link. But in more complex cases, like inference-graph (13), we have to repeat the construction, constructing first G_φ, and then $(G_\varphi)_\psi$. Let us define recursively:

Definition 9.9. $G_{\langle \varphi_1, \ldots, \varphi_n \rangle} = \left(G_{\langle \varphi_2, \ldots, \varphi_n \rangle} \right)_{\varphi_1}$

As formulated, the recursive semantics requires us to construct the inference-graphs $G_{\langle \varphi_1, \ldots, \varphi_n \rangle}$. To reformulate the semantics so as to avoid this, let us define recursively:

Definition 9.10.

A defeat-link δ of G is $\langle \varphi_1, \ldots, \varphi_n \rangle$-*critical* in G iff (1) δ lies on a φ_1-defeat-loop μ in G containing no $\langle \varphi_2, \ldots, \varphi_n \rangle$-critical defeat-links.

A defeat-link δ of G is *hereditarily-$\langle \varphi_1, \ldots, \varphi_n \rangle$-critical* in G iff either δ is $\langle \varphi_1, \ldots, \varphi_n \rangle$-critical in G or δ is hereditarily-$\langle \varphi_2, \ldots, \varphi_n \rangle$ in G.

A defeater (i.e., a node) of G is *hereditarily-$\langle \varphi_1, \ldots, \varphi_n \rangle$-critical* in G iff it is the root of a hereditarily-$\langle \varphi_1, \ldots, \varphi_n \rangle$-critical defeat-link in G.

Obviously:

Theorem 9.7. δ *is hereditarily-*$\langle \varphi_1, \ldots, \varphi_n \rangle$*-critical in* G *iff* δ *is* φ_1*-critical in* $G_{\langle \varphi_2,\ldots,\varphi_n \rangle}$ *or* φ_2*-critical in* $G_{\langle \varphi_3,\ldots,\varphi_n \rangle}$ *or* ... *or* φ_n*-critical in* G.

Note that a defeat-link that is φ_i-critical in $G_{\langle \varphi_{i+1},\ldots,\varphi_n \rangle}$ does not exist in $G_{\langle \varphi_{j+1},\ldots,\varphi_n \rangle}$ for $j < i$, so:

Theorem 9.8. δ *is* φ_1*-critical in* $G_{\langle \varphi_2,\ldots,\varphi_n \rangle}$ *iff* δ *is* $\langle \varphi_1, \ldots, \varphi_n \rangle$*-critical in* G.

Furthermore, a defeat-link still exists in $G_{\langle \varphi_3,\ldots,\varphi_n \rangle}$ (i.e., has not been removed) iff it is not $\langle \varphi_1, \ldots, \varphi_n \rangle$-critical in G.

   Where $\theta, \varphi_2, \ldots, \varphi_n$ are nodes of an inference-graph G, define:

Definition 9.11.

   θ is $\langle \varphi \rangle$-*independent* of ψ in G iff there is no inference/defeat-path in G from φ to θ.

   θ is $\langle \varphi_1, \ldots, \varphi_n \rangle$-*independent* in G iff every inference/defeat-path in G from φ_1 to θ contains a hereditarily-$\langle \varphi_2, \ldots, \varphi_n \rangle$-critical defeat-link.

Theorem 9.9. θ *is* $\langle \varphi_1, \ldots, \varphi_n \rangle$*-independent in* G *iff* θ *is* φ_1*-independent in* $G_{\langle \varphi_2,\ldots,\varphi_n \rangle}$.

Let us define recursively:

Definition 9.12.

(a) If ψ is initial in G then ψ is $\langle \varphi_1, \ldots, \varphi_n \rangle$-*undefeated* in G iff ψ is undefeated in G;
(b) If ψ is $\langle \varphi_1, \ldots, \varphi_n \rangle$-independent in G then ψ is $\langle \varphi_1, \ldots, \varphi_n \rangle$-undefeated in G iff ψ is $\langle \varphi_2, \ldots, \varphi_n \rangle$-undefeated in G;
(c) Otherwise, ψ is $\langle \varphi_1, \ldots, \varphi_n \rangle$-undefeated in G iff (1) all members of the node-basis of ψ are $\langle \varphi_1, \ldots, \varphi_n \rangle$-undefeated in G, (2) all defeaters for ψ that are $\langle \varphi_1, \ldots, \varphi_n \rangle$-independent of ψ in G and are not hereditarily-$\langle \varphi_1, \ldots, \varphi_n \rangle$-critical in G (i.e., still exist in $G_{\langle \varphi_3,\ldots,\varphi_n \rangle}$) are $\langle \varphi_1, \ldots, \varphi_n \rangle$-defeated in G, and (3) all defeaters for ψ that are $\langle \varphi_1, \ldots, \varphi_n \rangle$-dependent of ψ in G and are not hereditarily-$\langle \varphi_1, \ldots, \varphi_n \rangle$-critical in G (i.e., still exist in $G_{\langle \varphi_3,\ldots,\varphi_n \rangle}$) are $\langle \psi, \varphi_1, \ldots, \varphi_n \rangle$-defeated in G,

   The reason this is a recursive definition is that we always reach an n at which there are no more $\langle \varphi_1, \ldots, \varphi_n \rangle$-dependent defeaters, and then the values of all nodes are computed recursively in terms of the values assigned to initial nodes.

   It is now trivial to prove by induction on n that:

Theorem 9.10. ψ *is undefeated in* $G_{\langle \varphi_1,\ldots,\varphi_n \rangle}$ *iff* ψ *is* $\langle \varphi_1, \ldots, \varphi_n \rangle$*-undefeated in* G.

   Thus we have a recursive definition of the defeat-status of a node that computes defeat-statuses entirely by reference to the given inference-graph rather than by building a sequence of modified inference-graphs in accordance with the original analysis. This is easily implemented with two pages of LISP code.

8 Conclusions

In an environment of real-world complexity, it is impossible to know enough about the world to confine one's reasoning to deductively valid inferences. One has to reason defeasibly, drawing conclusions that are made reasonable by one's evidence, but be prepared to change one's mind in the face of new evidence. The question then arises how defeasible reasoning ought to work. In particular, given a set of defeasible arguments some of which support defeaters for others, how is it determined which conclusions ought to be believed? Most semantics for defeasible reasoning agree with regard to simple cases, and produce intuitively congenial answers. But there are some complex cases that all existing semantics seem to get wrong. This chapter proposes a new semantics, based on the concept of a critical link, that arguably gets those cases right. Furthermore, the semantics is recursive and easily implemented.

References

1. M. A. Covington, D. Nute, and A. Vellino. *Prolog Programming in Depth*. Prentice-Hall, Englewood Cliffs, New Jersey, second edition, 1997.
2. P. M. Dung. On the acceptability of arguments and its fundamental role in nonmonotonic reasoning, logic programming, and n-person games. *Artificial Intelligence*, 77(2):321–357, 1995.
3. H. E. Kyburg, Jr. *Probability and the Logic of Rational Belief*. Wesleyan University Press, Middletown, Conneticut, 1961.
4. D. Makinson and K. Schlechta. Floating conclusions and zombie paths: Two deep difficulties in the "directly skeptical" approach to inheritance nets. *Artificial Intelligence*, 48(2):199–209, 1991.
5. J. McCarthy. Applications of circumscription to formalizing common sense knowledge. *Artificial Intelligence*, 28(1):89–116, 1986.
6. D. Nute. Basic defeasible logic. In L. F. del Cerro and M. Penttonen, editors, *Intensional Logics for Programming*, pages 125–154. Oxford University Press, USA, 1992.
7. D. Nute. Norms, priorities, and defeasibility. In P. McNamara and H. Prakken, editors, *Norms, Logics and Information Systems*, pages 201–218. IOS Press, Amsterdam, 1999.
8. J. Pollock. Defeasible reasoning. *Cognitive Science*, 11(4):481–518, 1987.
9. J. Pollock. Justification and defeat. *Artificial Intelligence*, 67(2):377–408, 1994.
10. J. Pollock. *Cognitive Carpentry: A Blueprint for How to Build a Person*. MIT Press, 1995.
11. J. Pollock. Perceiving and reasoning about a changing world. *Computational Intelligence*, 14(4):498–562, 1998.
12. J. Pollock and I. Oved. Vision, knowledge, and the mystery link. *Philosophical Perspectives 19*, pages 309–351, 2005.
13. R. Reiter. A Logic for Default Reasoning. *Artificial Intelligence*, 13(1,2):81–132, 1980.
14. D. S. Touretzky, J. F. Horty, and R. H. Thomason. A clash of intuitions: the current state of nonmonotonic multiple inheritance systems. In *Proceedings IJCAI*, pages 476–482, 1987.

Chapter 10
Assumption-Based Argumentation

Phan Minh Dung, Robert A. Kowalski and Francesca Toni

1 Introduction

Assumption-Based Argumentation (ABA) [4, 3, 27, 11, 12, 20, 22] was developed, starting in the 90s, as a computational framework to reconcile and generalise most existing approaches to default reasoning [24, 25, 4, 3, 27, 26]. ABA was inspired by Dung's preferred extension semantics for logic programming [9, 7], with its dialectical interpretation of the acceptability of negation-as-failure assumptions based on the notion of "no-evidence-to-the-contrary" [9, 7], by the Kakas, Kowalski and Toni interpretation of the preferred extension semantics in argumentation-theoretic terms [24, 25], and by Dung's abstract argumentation (AA) [6, 8].

Because ABA is an instance of AA, all semantic notions for determining the "acceptability" of arguments in AA also apply to arguments in ABA. Moreover, like AA, ABA is a general-purpose argumentation framework that can be instantiated to support various applications and specialised frameworks, including: most default reasoning frameworks [4, 3, 27, 26] and problems in legal reasoning [27, 13], game-theory [8], practical reasoning and decision-theory [33, 29, 15, 28, 14]. However, whereas in AA arguments and attacks between arguments are abstract and primitive, in ABA arguments are deductions (using *inference rules* in an underlying logic) supported by *assumptions*. An attack by one argument against another is a deduction by the first argument of the *contrary* of an assumption supporting the second argument.

Differently from a number of existing approaches to non-abstract argumentation (e.g. argumentation based on classical logic [2] and DeLP [23]) ABA does not have explicit rebuttals and does not impose the restriction that arguments have consistent and minimal supports. However, to a large extent, rebuttals can be obtained "for

Phan Minh Dung
Asian Institute of Technology, Thailand, e-mail: dung@cs.ait.ac.th

Robert A. Kowalski, Francesca Toni
Imperial College London, UK, e-mail: {rak,ft}@doc.ic.ac.uk

I. Rahwan, G. R. Simari (eds.), *Argumentation in Artificial Intelligence*,
DOI 10.1007/978-0-387-98197-0_10, © Springer Science+Business Media, LLC 2009

free" [27, 11, 33]. Moreover, ABA arguments are guaranteed to be "relevant" and largely consistent [34].

ABA is equipped with a computational machinery (in the form of *dispute derivations* [11, 12, 19, 20, 22]) to determine the acceptability of claims by building and exploring a dialectical structure of a proponent's argument for a claim, an opponent's counterarguments attacking the argument, the proponent's arguments attacking all the opponents' counterarguments, and so on. This computation style, which has its roots in logic programming, has several advantages over other computational mechanisms for argumentation. The advantages are due mainly to the fine level of granularity afforded by interleaving the construction of arguments and determining their "acceptability".

The chapter is organised as follows. In Sections 2 and 3 we define the ABA notions of argument and attack (respectively). In Section 4 we define "acceptability" of sets of arguments, focusing on *admissible* and *grounded* sets of arguments. In Section 5 we present the computational machinery for ABA. In Section 6 we outline some applications of ABA. In Section 7 we conclude.

2 Arguments in ABA

ABA frameworks [3, 11, 12] can be defined for any *logic* specified by means of *inference rules*, by identifying sentences in the underlying *language* that can be treated as *assumptions* (see Section 3 for a formal definition of ABA frameworks). Intuitively, *arguments* are "deductions" of a conclusion (or claim) supported by a set of assumptions.

The inference rules may be domain-specific or domain-independent, and may represent, for example, causal information, argument schemes, or laws and regulations. Assumptions are sentences in the language that are open to challenge, for example uncertain beliefs ("it will rain"), unsupported beliefs ("I believe X"), or decisions ("perform action A"). Typically, assumptions can occur as premises of inference rules, but not as conclusions. ABA frameworks, such as logic programming and default logic, that have this feature are said to be *flat* [3]. We will focus solely on flat ABA frameworks. Examples of non-flat frameworks can be found in [3].

As an example, consider the following simplification of the argument scheme from expert opinion [38]:

Major premise: Source E is an expert about A.

Minor premise: E asserts that A is true.

Conclusion: A may plausibly be taken as true.

This can be represented in ABA by a (domain-independent) inference rule: [1]

---

[1] In this chapter, we use inference rule schemata, with variables starting with capital letters, to stand for the set of all instances obtained by instantiating the variables so that the resulting premises and conclusions are sentences of the underlying language. For simplicity, we omit the formal definition of the language underlying our examples.

$h(A) \leftarrow e(E,A), a(E,A), arguably(A)$

with conclusion $h(A)$ ("A holds") and premises $e(E,A)$ ("E is an expert about A"), $a(E,A)$ ("E asserts A"), and an assumption $arguably(A)$. This assumption can be read in several ways, as "there is no reason to doubt that A holds" or " the complement of A cannot be shown to hold" or "the defeasible rule – that a conclusion A holds if a person E who is an expert in A asserts that A is the case – should not apply". The inference rule can be understood as the representation of this defeasible rule as a strict (unchallangable) rule with an extra, defeasible condition – $arguably(A)$ – that is open to challenge. This transformation of defeasible rules into strict rules with defeasible conditions is borrowed from Theorist [31]. Within ABA, defeasible conditions are always assumptions. Different representations of assumptions correspond to different frameworks for defeasible reasoning. For example, in logic programming $arguably(A)$ could be replaced by $not \neg h(A)$ (here not stands for negation as failure), and in default logic it could become $M h(A)$. Note that Verheij [37] also uses assumptions to represent defeasibility of rules. However, his approach amounts to treating every defeasible rule as an assumption.

In ABA, attacks are always directed at the assumptions in inference rules. The transformation of defeasible rules into strict rules with defeasible conditions is also used to reduce rebuttal attacks to undercutting attacks, as we will see in Section 3.

Note that, here and in all the examples given in this chapter, we represent conditionals as inference rules. However, as discussed in [11], this is equivalent to representing them as object language implications together with modus ponens and and-introduction as more general inference rules. Representing conditionals as inference rules is useful for default reasoning because it inhibits the automatic application of modus tollens to object language implications. However, the ABA approach applies to any logic specified by means of inference rules, and is not restricted in the way illustrated in our examples in this chapter.

Suppose we wish to apply the inference rule above to the concrete situation in which a professor of computer science (cs), say jo, advises that a software product sw meets a customer's requirements ($reqs$) for speed (s) and usability (u). Suppose, moreover, that professors are normally regarded as experts within (w) their field. This situation can be represented by the additional inference rules:

$reqs(sw) \leftarrow h(ok(sw,s)), h(ok(sw,u));$
$a(jo,ok(sw,s)) \leftarrow; \quad a(jo,ok(sw,u)) \leftarrow; \quad prof(jo,cs) \leftarrow;$
$w(cs,ok(sw,s)) \leftarrow; \quad w(cs,ok(sw,u)) \leftarrow;$
$e(X,A) \leftarrow prof(X,S), w(S,A), c\_prof(X,S)$

Note that all these inference rules except the last are problem-dependent. Note also that, in general, inference rules may have empty premises.

The potential assumptions in the language underlying all these inference rules are (instances of) the formulae $arguably(A)$ and $c\_prof(X,S)$ ("X is a credible professor in S"). Given these inference rules and pool of assumptions, there is an argument with assumptions $\{arguably(ok(sw,s)), arguably(ok(sw,u)), c\_prof(jo,cs)\}$ supporting the conclusion (claim) $reqs(sw)$.

In the remainder, for simplicity we drop the assumptions $arguably(A)$ and replace the inference rule representing the scheme from expert opinion simply by

$h(A) \leftarrow e(E,A), a(E,A)$. With this simplification, there is an argument for $reqs(sw)$ supported by $\{c\_prof(jo,cs)\}$.

Informally, an argument is a deduction of a conclusion (claim) c from a set of assumptions S represented as a tree, with c at the root and S at the leaves. Nodes in this tree are connected by the inference rules, with sentences matching the conclusion of an inference rule connected as parent nodes to sentences matching the premises of the inference rule as children nodes. The leaves are either assumptions or the special extra-logical symbol τ, standing for an empty set of premises. Formally:

Definition 10.1. Given a deductive system $(\mathcal{L}, \mathcal{R})$, with language $\mathcal{L}$ and set of inference rules $\mathcal{R}$, and a set of assumptions $\mathcal{A} \subseteq \mathcal{L}$, an *argument* for $c \in \mathcal{L}$ (the *conclusion* or *claim*) *supported by* $S \subseteq \mathcal{A}$ is a tree with nodes labelled by sentences in $\mathcal{L}$ or by the symbol τ, such that

- the root is labelled by c
- for every node N

    - if N is a leaf then N is labelled either by an assumption or by τ;
    - if N is not a leaf and l_N is the label of N, then there is an inference rule
      $l_N \leftarrow b_1, \ldots, b_m$ $(m \geq 0)$ and
      either $m = 0$ and the child of N is τ
      or $m > 0$ and N has m children, labelled by $b_1, \ldots, b_m$ (respectively)

- S is the set of all assumptions labelling the leaves.

Throughout this chapter, we will often use the following notation

- an argument for (claim) c supported by (set of assumptions) S is denoted by $S \vdash c$

in situations where we focus only on the claim c and support S of an argument. Note that our definition of argument allows for one-node arguments. These arguments consist solely of a single assumption, say α, and are denoted by $\{\alpha\} \vdash \alpha$.

A portion of the argument $\{c\_prof(jo,cs)\} \vdash reqs(sw)$ is given in Fig. 10.1. Here, for simplicity, we omit the right-most sub-tree with root $h(ok(sw,u))$, as this is a copy of the left-most sub-tree with root $h(ok(sw,s))$ but with s replaced by u throughout.

Arguments, represented as trees, display the structural relationships between claims and assumptions, justified by the inference rules. The generation of arguments can be performed by means of a proof procedure, which searches the space of applications of inference rules. This search can be performed in the forward direction, from assumptions to conclusions, in the backward direction, from conclusions to assumptions, or even "middle-out". Our definition of tight arguments in [11] corresponds to the backward generation of arguments represented as trees. Backward generation of arguments is an important feature of dispute derivations, presented in Section 5.2.

Unlike several other authors, e.g. those of [2] (see also Chapter 7) and [23] (see also Chapter 8), we do not impose the restriction that the support of an argument be minimal. For example, consider the ABA representation of the scheme from expert opinion, and suppose that our professor of computer science, *jo*, is also an engineer (*eng*). Suppose, moreover, that engineers are normally regarded as experts in computer science. These additional "suppositions" can be represented by the inference rules

$$eng(jo) \leftarrow; \quad e(X,A) \leftarrow eng(X), w(cs,A), c\_eng(X)$$

with (instances of) the formula $c\_eng(X)$ ("X is a credible engineer") as additional assumptions. There are now three, different arguments for the claim *reqs(sw)*:

$$\{c\_prof(jo,cs)\} \vdash reqs(sw), \{c\_eng(jo)\} \vdash reqs(sw), \text{ and}$$
$$\{c\_prof(jo,cs), c\_eng(jo)\} \vdash reqs(sw).$$

Only the first two arguments have minimal support. However, all three arguments, including the third, "non-minimal" argument, are *relevant*, in the sense that their assumptions contribute to deducing the conclusion. Minimality is one way to ensure relevance, but comes at a computational cost. ABA arguments are guaranteed to be relevant without insisting on minimality. Note that the arguments of Chapter 9, defined as inference graphs, are also constructed to ensure relevance.

Some authors (e.g. again [2] and [23]) impose the restriction that arguments have *consistent* support [2]. We will see later, in Sections 3 and 4, that the problems arising for logics including a notion of (in)consistency can be dealt in ABA by reducing (in)consistency to the notion of attack and by employing a semantics that insists that sets of acceptable arguments do not attack themselves.

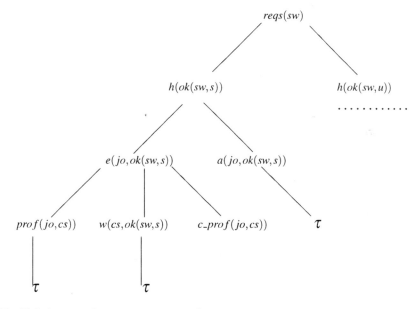

Fig. 10.1 An example argument represented as a tree

---

[2] Note that these authors define arguments with respect to an underlying logic with an explicit negation and hence a notion of consistency, such that inconsistency implies every sentence in the language. The logic underlying an ABA framework need not have an explicit negation and notion of inconsistency.

3 Attacks in ABA

In ABA, the notion of attack between arguments is defined in terms of the *contrary* of assumptions: one argument $S_1 \vdash c_1$ *attacks* another (or the same) argument $S_2 \vdash c_2$ if and only if c_1 is the contrary of an assumption in S_2.

In general, the contrary of an assumption is a sentence representing a challenge against the assumption. For example, the contrary of the assumption "it will rain" might be "the sky is clear". The contrary of the assumption "perform action A" might be "perform action B" (where the actions A and B are mutually exclusive). The contrary of the assumption "I believe X" might be "there is evidence against X". The contrary of an assumption can also represent critical questions addressed to an argument scheme. For example, the argument scheme from expert opinion in Section 2 can be challenged by such critical questions as [38]:

CQ1: How credible is E as an expert source?

CQ2: Is E an expert in the field that A is in?

CQ3: Does E's testimony imply A?

CQ4: Is E reliable?

CQ5: Is A consistent with the testimony of other experts?

CQ6: Is A supported by evidence?

For simplicity, we focus here solely on CQ1, because modelling the other questions would require introducing additional assumptions to our earlier representation of the scheme. [3] Providing negative answers to CQ1 can be understood as proving the contrary $\neg c\_prof(jo, cs)$, $\neg c\_eng(jo, cs)$ of the assumptions $c\_prof(jo, cs)$, $c\_eng(jo, cs)$ respectively.

Contraries may be other assumptions or may be defined by inference rules, e.g.
$$\neg c\_eng(E, cs) \leftarrow \neg prog(E); \quad \neg prog(E) \leftarrow theo(E)$$
where *prog* stands for "programmer" and *theo* stands for "theoretician". The first rule can be used to challenge the assumption that an engineer is a credible expert in computer science by arguing that the engineer is not a programmer. The second rule can be used to show that an engineer is not a programmer by assuming that he/she is a theoretician (here $theo(E)$ is an additional assumption). Given this representation, the argument $\{c\_eng(jo, cs)\} \vdash reqs(sw)$ is attacked by the argument $\{theo(jo)\} \vdash \neg c\_eng(jo, cs)$.

Definition 10.2. Given a notion of contrary of assumptions [4],

- *an argument $S_1 \vdash c_1$ attacks an argument $S_2 \vdash c_2$ if and only if the conclusion c_1 of the first argument is the contrary of one of the assumptions in the support S_2 of the second argument;*
- *a set of arguments Arg_1 attacks a set of arguments Arg_2 if an argument in Arg_1 attacks an argument in Arg_2.*

---

[3] For example, providing negative answers to CQ5 and CQ6 for A can understood as proving the contrary of the assumption *arguably*(A) introduced at the beginning of Section 2 but ignored afterwards.

[4] See definition 10.3 for the formal notion of contrary.

This notion of attack between arguments depends only on attacking ("undercutting") assumptions. In many other approaches, however, such as those of Pollock [30] and Prakken and Sartor [32], an argument can attack ("rebut") another argument by deducing the negation of its conclusion. We reduce such "rebuttal" attacks to "undercutting" attacks, as described in [27, 11, 33, 34]. For example, consider the inference rules

$$prog(X) \leftarrow works\_for(X, micro), nor(X); \quad works\_for(jo, micro) \leftarrow$$

where *micro* is the name of some company, $nor(X)$ stands for "X is normal", and the first inference rule represents the defeasible rule that "normally individuals working at *micro* are programmers". From these and the earlier inference rule for $\neg prog$, we can construct both an argument for $prog(jo)$ supported by $\{nor(jo)\}$ and an argument for $\neg prog(jo)$ supported by $\{theo(jo)\}$. These arguments "rebut" one another but neither one undercuts the other. However, let us set the contrary of assumption $theo(X)$ to $prog(X)$ and the contrary of assumption $nor(X)$ to $\neg prog(X)$. Then, the effect of the rebuttals is obtained by undercutting the assumptions (supporting the arguments for $prog(jo)$ and $\neg prog(jo)$).

Note that an alternative approach to accommodate rebuttals could be to introduce an explicit additional notion of rebuttal attack as done in [10] for logic programming with two kinds of negation.

To complete our earlier definition of argument and attack we need a definition of ABA framework:

Definition 10.3. An ABA framework is a tuple $\langle \mathcal{L}, \mathcal{R}, \mathcal{A}, ^{-} \rangle$ where

- $(\mathcal{L}, \mathcal{R})$ is a deductive system, with a language $\mathcal{L}$ and a set of inference rules $\mathcal{R}$,
- $\mathcal{A} \subseteq \mathcal{L}$ is a (non-empty) set, whose elements are referred to as *assumptions*,
- $^{-}$ is a total mapping from $\mathcal{A}$ into $\mathcal{L}$, where $\overline{\alpha}$ is the *contrary* of α.

4 Acceptability of arguments in ABA

ABA can be used to determine whether a given claim is to be "accepted" by a rational agent. The claim could be, for example, a potential belief to be justified, or a goal to be achieved, represented as a sentence in $\mathcal{L}$. In order to determine the "acceptability" of the claim, the agent needs to find an argument for the claim that can be defended against attacks from other arguments. To defend an argument, other arguments may need to be found and they may need to be defended in turn. As in AA, this informal definition of "acceptability" can be formalised in many ways, using the notion of attack between arguments. In this chapter we focus on the following notions of "acceptable" sets of arguments:

- a set of arguments is *admissible* if and only if it does not attack itself and it attacks every argument that attacks it;
- an admissible set of arguments is *complete* if it contains all arguments that it *defends*, where a set of arguments *Arg* defends an argument *arg* if *Arg* attacks all arguments that attack $\{arg\}$;

- the least (with respect to set inclusion) complete set of arguments is *grounded*.

As for AA (see [8] and Chapter 2), in ABA, given a proposed conclusion c, there always exists a grounded set of arguments, and this can be constructed bottom-up [3, 12].

Consider again our formulation of the scheme for expert opinion. The set consisting of the two arguments

$arg_1 = \{c\_eng(jo, cs)\} \vdash reqs(sw)$

$arg_2 = \{nor(jo)\} \vdash prog(jo)$

is admissible, and as a consequence so is the claim $reqs(sw)$. Indeed, this set does not attack itself and it attacks the argument

$arg_3 = \{theo(jo)\} \vdash \neg prog(jo)$.

However, the set $\{arg_1, arg_2\}$ is not (a subset of) the grounded set of arguments. But the set $\{arg_4\}$ is grounded, where

$arg_4 = \{c\_prof(jo, cs)\} \vdash reqs(sw)$.

The notion of admissibility is *credulous*, in that there can be alternative, conflicting admissible sets. In the example above, $\{arg_3\}$ is also admissible, but in conflict with the admissible $\{arg_1, arg_2\}$.

In some applications, it is more appropriate to adopt a *sceptical* notion of "acceptability". The notion of grounded set of arguments is sceptical in the sense that no argument in the grounded set is attacked by an admissible set of arguments. Other notions of credulous and sceptical "acceptable" set of arguments can be employed within ABA [3, 27, 12].

Note that the notions of "acceptable" *sets of arguments* given here are more structured than the corresponding notions of "acceptable" *sets of assumptions* given in [3, 27, 11, 12]. The correspondence between "acceptability" of arguments and "acceptability" of assumptions, given in [12], is as follows:

- If a set of assumptions S is admissible/grounded then the union of all arguments supported by any subset of S is admissible/grounded;
- If a set of arguments S is admissible/grounded then the union of all sets of assumptions supporting the arguments in S is admissible/grounded.

Note that, if the underlying logic has explicit negation and inconsistency, and we apply the transformation outlined in Section 3 (to reduce rebuttals to our undercutting attacks), then an argument has an inconsistent support if and only if it attacks itself. Thus, in such a case, no argument belonging to an "acceptable" set may possibly contain an argument with an inconsistent support [34].

5 Computation of "acceptability"

The notion of "acceptability" of sets of arguments provides a non-constructive specification. In this section we show how to turn the specification into a constructive proof procedure. As argued in [6, 8], at a conceptual level, a proof procedure for argumentation consists of two tasks, one for generating arguments and one for determining the "acceptability" of the generated arguments. We have already briefly discussed the computation of arguments in Section 2. Below, we first demonstrate how to determine the "acceptability" of arguments that are already constructed, in the spirit of AA, by means of *dispute trees* [11, 12]. Then, we discuss how *dispute derivations* [11, 12, 20, 22], which interleave constructing arguments and determining their "acceptability", can be viewed as generating "approximations" to "acceptable" *dispute trees*.

Dispute derivations are inspired by SLDNF, the "EK" procedure of [17, 9, 7], and the "KT" procedure of [36, 26] for logic programming with negation as failure. Like SLDNF and EK, dispute derivations interleave two kinds of derivations (one for "proving" and one for "disproving"). Like EK, they accumulate defence assumptions and use them for filtering. Like KT, they accumulate culprit assumptions and use them for filtering.

5.1 Dispute trees

Dispute trees can be seen as a way of representing a winning strategy for a *proponent* to win a dispute against an *opponent*. The proponent starts by putting forward an initial argument (supporting a claim whose "acceptability" is under dispute), and then the proponent and the opponent alternate in attacking each other's previously presented arguments. The proponent wins if he/she has a counter-attack against every attacking argument by the opponent.

Definition 10.4. A *dispute tree* for an initial argument a is a (possibly infinite) tree $\mathcal{T}$ such that

1. Every node of $\mathcal{T}$ is labelled by an argument and is assigned the status of *proponent* node or *opponent* node, but not both.
2. The root is a proponent node labelled by a.
3. For every proponent node N labelled by an argument b, and for every argument c attacking b, there exists a child of N, which is an opponent node labelled by c.
4. For every opponent node N labelled by an argument b, there exists exactly one child of N which is a proponent node labelled by an argument attacking b.
5. There are no other nodes in $\mathcal{T}$ except those given by 1-4 above.

The set of all arguments belonging to the proponent nodes in $\mathcal{T}$ is called the *defence set* of $\mathcal{T}$.

Note that a branch in a dispute tree may be finite or infinite. A finite branch represents a winning sequence of arguments (within the overall dispute) that ends with an argument by the proponent that the opponent is unable to attack. An infinite branch represents a winning sequence of arguments in which the proponent counter-attacks every attack of the opponent, ad infinitum. Note that our notion of dispute tree intuitively corresponds to the notion of winning strategy in Chapter 6.

Fig. 10.2 illustrates (our notion of) dispute tree for an extension of our running example, augmented with the following rules

$$\neg c\_prof(X,S) \leftarrow ret(X), inact(X); \quad \neg c\_prof(X,S) \leftarrow admin(X), inact(X);$$
$$act(X) \leftarrow pub(X); \quad ret(jo) \leftarrow; \quad admin(jo) \leftarrow; \quad pub(jo) \leftarrow$$

Here $inact(X)$ is an assumption with $\overline{inact(X)} = act(X)$. These additions express that professors cannot be assumed to be credible ($\neg c\_prof$) if they are retired (ret) or cover administrative roles ($admin$) and can be assumed to be inactive ($inact$). $inact$ cannot be assumed if its contrary (act) can be shown, and this is so for professors with recent publications (pub). The resulting, overall ABA framework is summarised in Fig. 10.3. Note that the tree in Fig. 10.2 has an infinite (left-most) branch with

$\{nor(jo)\} \vdash prog(jo)$ child of $\{theo(jo)\} \vdash \neg prog(jo)$ and
$\{theo(jo)\} \vdash \neg prog(jo)$ child of $\{nor(jo)\} \vdash prog(jo)$

ad infinitum. Note also that our intention is to label the opponent nodes in the middle and right-most branches by two different arguments, but both denoted by $\{inact(jo)\} \vdash \neg c\_prof(jo,cs)$. The two arguments differ with respect to the inference rules used to obtain them (the first and second inference rule for $\neg c\_prof$ in Fig. 10.3, respectively) and thus have different representations as argument trees (as in Definition 10.1).

The definition of dispute tree incorporates the requirement that the proponent must counter-attack every attack, but it does not incorporate the requirement that the proponent does not attack itself. This further requirement is incorporated in the definition of *admissible* and *grounded* dispute trees:

Definition 10.5. A dispute tree $\mathcal{T}$ is

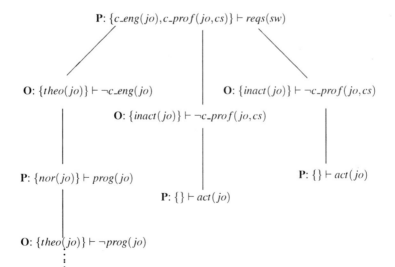

Fig. 10.2 A dispute tree for argument $\{c\_eng(jo), c\_prof(jo,cs)\} \vdash reqs(sw)$, with respect to the ABA framework in Fig. 10.3.

- *admissible* if and only if no argument labels both a proponent and an opponent node. [5]
- *grounded* if and only if it is finite.

Note that, by theorem 3.1 in [12], any grounded dispute tree is admissible. The relationship between admissible/grounded dispute tree and admissible/grounded sets of arguments is as follows:

1. the defence set of an admissible dispute tree is admissible;
2. the defence set of a grounded dispute tree is a subset of the grounded set of arguments;
3. if an argument a belongs to an admissible set of arguments A then there exists an admissible dispute tree for a with defence set A' such that $A' \subseteq A$ and A' is admissible;
4. if an argument a belongs to the grounded set of arguments A (and the set of all arguments supported by assumptions for the given ABA framework is finite) then there exists a grounded dispute tree for a with defence set A' such that $A' \subseteq A$ and A' is admissible.

Results 1. and 3. are proven in [12] (theorem 3.2). Results 2. and 4. follow directly from theorem 3.7 in [26].

Note that the dispute tree in Fig. 10.2 is admissible but not grounded (since it has an infinite branch). However, the tree with root $\{c\_prof(jo,cs)\} \vdash reqs(sw)$ (arg_4 in Section 4) and the two right-most subtrees in Fig. 10.2 is grounded.

We can obtain finite trees from infinite admissible dispute trees by using "filtering" to avoid re-defending assumptions that are in the process of being "defended" or that have already successfully been "defended". For example, for the tree in Fig. 10.2, only the (proponent) child of argument $\{theo(jo)\} \vdash \neg prog(jo)$ needs to be constructed. Indeed, since this argument is already being "defended", the remainder of the (infinite) branch can be ignored.

$\mathcal{R}:$ $reqs(sw) \leftarrow h(ok(sw,s)), h(ok(sw,u));$ $\quad h(A) \leftarrow e(E,A), a(E,A);$
$\quad\quad e(X,A) \leftarrow eng(X), w(cs,A), c\_eng(X);$ $\quad e(X,A) \leftarrow prof(X,S), w(S,A), c\_prof(X,S);$
$\quad\quad a(jo, ok(sw,s)) \leftarrow;$ $\quad a(jo, ok(sw,u));$ $\quad eng(jo) \leftarrow;$ $\quad prof(jo,cs) \leftarrow;$
$\quad\quad w(cs, ok(sw,s)) \leftarrow;$ $\quad w(cs, ok(sw,u)) \leftarrow;$
$\quad\quad \neg c\_eng(E,cs) \leftarrow \neg prog(E);$ $\quad \neg prog(X) \leftarrow theo(X);$
$\quad\quad prog(X) \leftarrow works\_for(X, micro), nor(X);$ $\quad\quad works\_for(bob, micro) \leftarrow;$
$\quad\quad \neg c\_prof(X,S) \leftarrow ret(X), inact(X);$ $\quad ret(jo) \leftarrow;$
$\quad\quad \neg c\_prof(X,S) \leftarrow admin(X), inact(X);$ $\quad admin(jo) \leftarrow;$
$\quad\quad act(X) \leftarrow pub(X);$ $\quad pub(jo) \leftarrow$
$\mathcal{A}:$ $c\_eng(X);$ $\quad c\_prof(X,S);$ $\quad theo(X);$ $\quad nor(X);$ $\quad inact(X)$
$\overline{}:$ $\overline{c\_eng(X)} = \neg c\_eng(X);$ $\overline{c\_prof(X,S)} = \neg c\_prof(X,S);$
$\quad\quad \overline{theo(X)} = prog(X);$ $\overline{nor(X)} = \neg prog(X);$ $\overline{inact(X)} = act(X)$

Fig. 10.3 ABA framework for the running example.

---

[5] Note that admissible dispute trees are similar to the complete argument trees of [2]. We use the term "argument tree" for arguments.

5.2 Dispute derivations

Dispute derivations compute ("approximations of) dispute trees top-down, starting by constructing an argument supporting a given claim. While doing so, they perform several kinds of "filtering" exploiting the fact that different arguments may share the same supporting assumptions. Assumptions that are already under attack in the dispute are saved in appropriate data structures (the *defence assumptions* and *culprits*), in order to avoid re-computation. The assumptions used by the proponent (defence assumptions) are kept separate from the assumptions used by the opponent and attacked by the proponent (culprits). The defence assumptions and culprits for the dispute tree in Fig. 10.2 are $\{c\_eng(jo), c\_prof(jo), nor(jo)\}$ and $\{theo(jo), inact(jo)\}$ respectively.

Dispute derivations employ the following forms of filtering:

1. of defence assumptions by defence assumptions, e.g. performed on the defence assumption $theo(jo)$ in the left-most branch of the dispute tree in Fig. 10.2 (this is analogous to the filtering of arguments we discussed earlier);
2. of culprits by defence assumptions and of defence assumptions by culprits, to guarantee that no argument labels both a proponent and opponent node in the tree and thus attacks itself (see Definition 10.5);
3. of culprits by culprits, for reasons of efficiency; e.g., if the dispute tree in Fig. 10.2 is generated left-to-right, the leaf in the right-most branch does not need to be generated, as the culprit $inact(jo)$ has already been attacked in the middle branch.

The first form of filtering is employed only for computing admissible sets, whereas the other two forms are employed for computing grounded as well as admissible sets.

Dispute derivations are defined in such a way that, by suitably tuning parameters, they can interleave the construction of arguments and determining "acceptability". This interleaving may be very beneficial, in general, as it allows

- abandoning, during their construction, "potential arguments" that cannot be expanded into an actual argument in an "acceptable" set of proponent's arguments,
- avoiding the expansion of the opponent's "potential arguments" into actual arguments when a culprit has already been identified and defeated.

Informally speaking, a *potential argument* of a conclusion c from a set of premises P can be represented as a tree, with c at the root and P at the leaves. As in the case of "actual" arguments (as in Definition 10.1), nodes in the tree are connected by inference rules. However, whereas the leaves of an argument tree are only assumptions or τ, the leaves of a potential argument can also be non-assumption sentences in $\mathcal{L} - \mathcal{A}$. Dispute derivations successively *expand* potential arguments, using inference rules backwards to replace a non-assumption premise, e.g. p, that matches the conclusion of an inference rule, e.g. $p \leftarrow Q$, by the premises of the rule, Q. In this case, we also say that p is *expanded to* Q.

Fig. 10.1 without the dots is an example of a potential argument for $reqs(sw)$, supported by assumption $c\_prof(jo,cs)$ and non-assumption $h(ok(sw,u))$. Fig. 10.4 shows another example of a potential argument. In general there may be one, many or no actual arguments that can be obtained from a potential argument. For example, the potential argument in Fig. 10.1 may give rise to two actual arguments (supported by $\{c\_prof(jo,cs)\}$ and $\{c\_prof(jo,cs), c\_eng(jo)\}$ respectively), whereas the potential argument in Fig. 10.4 gives rise to exactly one actual argument (supported by $\{inact(jo)\}$). However, if no inference rules were given for ret, then no actual argument could be generated from the potential argument in Fig. 10.4.

The benefits of interleaving mentioned earlier can be illustrated as follows:

- A proponent's potential argument is abandoned if it is supported by assumptions that would make the proponent's defence of the claim unacceptable. For example, in Fig. 10.1, if the assumption $c\_prof(jo,cs)$ is "defeated" before $h(ok(sw,u))$ is expanded, then the entire potential argument can be abandoned.
- An opponent's potential argument does not need to be expanded into an actual argument if a culprit can be selected and defeated already in this potential argument. For example, by choosing as culprit and "defeating" the assumption $inact(jo)$ in the potential argument in Fig. 10.4, the proponent "defeats" *any* argument that can be obtained by expanding the non-assumption $ret(jo)$.

However, when a potential argument cannot be expanded into an actual argument, defeating a culprit in the potential argument is wasteful. Nonetheless, dispute derivations employ a *selection function* which, given a potential or actual argument, selects an assumption to attack or a non-assumption to expand. As a special case, the selection function can be *patient* [11, 20], always selecting non-assumptions in preference to assumptions, in which case arguments will be fully constructed before they are attacked. Even in such a case, dispute derivations still benefit from filtering.

Informally, a *dispute derivation* is a sequence of transitions steps from one state of a dispute to another. In each such state, the proponent maintains a set $\mathcal{P}$ of (sentences supporting) potential arguments, representing a *single* way to defend the initial claim, and the opponent maintains a set $\mathcal{O}$ of potential arguments, representing *all* ways to attack the assumptions in $\mathcal{P}$. In addition, the state of the dispute contains the set D of all defence assumptions and the set C of all culprits already encountered in the dispute. The sets D and C are used to filter potential arguments, as we discussed earlier.

A step in a dispute derivation represents either a move by the proponent or a move by the opponent.

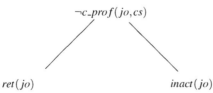

Fig. 10.4 A potential argument for $\neg c\_prof(jo,cs)$, supported by assumption $inact(jo)$ and non-assumption $ret(jo)$.

A *move by the proponent* either expands one of his/her potential arguments in $\mathcal{P}$, or it selects an assumption in one of the opponent's potential arguments in $\mathcal{O}$ and decides whether or not to attack it. In the first case, it expands the potential argument in only *one* way, and adds any new assumptions resulting from the expansion to D, checking that they are distinct from any assumptions in the culprit set C (filtering defence assumptions by culprits). In the second case, either the proponent ignores the assumption, as a non-culprit, or he/she adds the assumption to C (bearing in mind that, in order to defeat the opponent, he/she needs to counter-attack only one assumption in each of the opponent's attacking arguments). In this latter case, he/she checks that the assumption is distinct from any assumptions in D (filtering culprits by defence assumptions) and checks that it is distinct from any culprit already in C (filtering culprits by culprits). If the selected culprit is not already in C, the proponent adds the contrary of the assumption as the conclusion of a new, one-node potential argument to $\mathcal{P}$ (to construct a counter-attack).

A *move by the opponent*, similarly, either expands one of his/her potential arguments in $\mathcal{O}$, or it selects an assumption to attack in one of the proponent's potential arguments in $\mathcal{P}$. In the first case, it expands a non-assumption premise of the selected potential argument in *all* possible ways, replacing the selected potential argument in $\mathcal{O}$ by all the new potential arguments. In the second case, the opponent does not have the proponent's dilemma of deciding whether or not to attack the assumption, because the opponent needs to generate all attacks against the proponent. Thus, he/she adds the contrary of the assumption as the conclusion of a new, one-node potential argument to $\mathcal{O}$. [6]

A *successful dispute derivation* represents a single way for the proponent to support and defend a claim, but all the ways that the opponent can try to attack the proponent's arguments. Thus, although the proponent and opponent can attack one another before their arguments are fully completed, for a dispute derivation to be successful, all of proponent's arguments must be actual arguments. In contrast, the opponent's defeated arguments may be only potential. In this sense, dispute derivations compute only "approximations" of dispute trees. However, for every successful dispute derivation, there exists a dispute tree that can be obtained by expanding the opponent's potential arguments and dropping the potential arguments that cannot be expanded, as well as any of the proponent's unnecessary counter-attacks [22].

We give an informal dispute derivation for the running example:

$\mathcal{P}$:   I want to determine the "acceptability" of claim $reqs(sw)$ ($D = \{\}$ and $C = \{\}$ initially).

$\mathcal{P}$:   I generate a potential argument for $reqs(sw)$ supported by $\{h(ok(sw,s)),$ $h(ok(sw,u))\}$, and then expand it (through several steps) to one supported by $\{c\_prof(jo,cs), h(ok(sw,u))\}$ ($c\_prof(jo,cs)$ is added to D).

$\mathcal{O}$:   I attack the assumption $c\_prof(jo,cs)$ in this potential argument by looking for arguments for its contrary $\neg c\_prof(jo,cs)$.

---

[6] If computing admissibility, however, the opponent would not attack assumptions that already belong to D (filtering defence assumptions by defence assumptions).

$\mathcal{O}$:   I generate two potential arguments for $\neg c\_prof(jo,cs)$, supported by $\{ret(jo),$ $inact(jo)\}$ and $\{admin(jo), inact(jo)\}$ respectively.

$\mathcal{P}$:   I choose $inact(jo)$ as culprit in the first potential argument by $\mathcal{O}$ ($inact(jo)$ is added to C), and generate (through several steps) an argument for its contrary $act(jo)$, supported by the empty set.

$\mathcal{O}$:   There is no point for me to expand this potential argument then. But I still have the attacking argument for $\neg c\_prof(jo,cs)$, supported by $\{admin(jo),$ $inact(jo)\}$.

$\mathcal{P}$:   I again choose $inact(jo)$ as culprit, which I have already defeated ($inact(jo) \in C$).

$\mathcal{P}$:   There is no attacking argument that I still need to deal with: let me go back to expand the argument for $reqs(sw)$.

$\mathcal{P}$:   I need to expand $h(ok(sw,u))$, I can do so and generate (through several steps) an argument for $reqs(sw)$ supported by $\{c\_prof(jo,cs), c\_eng(jo)\}$ ($c\_eng(jo)$ is added to D).

$\mathcal{O}$:   I can attack this argument by generating (through several steps) an argument for the contrary $\neg c\_eng(jo)$ of $c\_eng(jo)$: this argument is supported by assumption $theo(jo)$.

$\mathcal{P}$:   I can attack this argument by generating (through several steps) a potential argument for the contrary of $theo(jo)$.

$\ldots$

This dispute corresponds to the top-down and right-to-left construction of (an approximation of) the dispute tree in Fig. 10.2. The dispute ends successfully for computing admissible sets of arguments, but does not terminate for computing grounded sets of arguments. Note that dispute derivations are defined in terms of several parameters: the selection function, the choice of "player" at any specific step in the derivation, the choice of potential arguments for the proponent/opponent to expand etc (see [20, 22]). Concrete choices for some of these parameters (e.g. the choice of the proponent's arguments) correspond to concrete search strategies for finding dispute derivations and computing dispute trees. Concrete choices for other parameters (e.g. the choice of "player") determine how the dispute tree is constructed in a linear manner.

Several notions of dispute derivations have been proposed, differing in the notion of "acceptability" and in the presentation of the computed set of "acceptable" arguments. More specifically, the dispute derivations of [11, 20, 22] compute admissible sets of arguments whereas the dispute derivations of [12] compute grounded and ideal (another notion of sceptical "acceptability") sets of arguments. Moreover, the dispute derivations of [11, 12] compute the union of all sets of assumptions supporting the "acceptable" sets of arguments for the given claim, whereas the dispute derivations of [20, 22] also return explicitly the computed set of "acceptable" arguments and the attacking (potential) arguments, as well as an indication of the attack relationships amongst these arguments.

6 Applications

In this section, we illustrate recent applications of ABA for dispute resolution (Section 6.1, adapted from [20]) and decision-making (Section 6.2, adapted from [15]). For simplicity, the description of these applications is kept short here. For more detail see [13] (for dispute resolution applied to contracts) and [33, 16, 29] (for decision-making in service-oriented architectures). We also show how ABA can be used to model the stable marriage problem (Section 6.3, building upon [8]).

6.1 ABA for dispute resolution

Consider the following situation, inspired by a real-life court case on contract dispute. A judge is tasked with resolving a disagreement between a software house and a customer refusing to pay for a product developed by the software house. Suppose that this product is the software sw in the running example of Fig. 10.3. The judge uses information agreed upon by both parties, and evaluates the claim by the software house that payment should be made to them.

All parties agree that payment should be made if the product is delivered on time (del) and is a good product ($goodProd$). They also agree that a product is not good ($badProd$) if it is late ($lateProd$) or does not meet its requirements. As before, we assume that these requirements are speed and usability. There is also the indisputable fact that the software was indeed delivered ($del(sw)$). This situation can be modelled by extending the framework of Fig. 10.3 with inference rules

$payment(sw) \leftarrow del(sw), goodProd(sw);$ $badProd(sw) \leftarrow lateProd(sw);$
$badProd(sw) \leftarrow \neg reqs(sw);$ $del(sw) \leftarrow$

and assumptions $goodProd(sw), \neg reqs(sw)$, with contraries:

$\overline{goodProduct(sw)} = badProduct(sw);$ $\overline{\neg reqs(sw)} = reqs(sw)$

Given the expert opinions of jo (see Section 2), the claim that payment should be made is grounded (and thus admissible).

6.2 ABA for decision-making

We use a concrete "home-buying" example, in which a buyer is looking for a property and has a number of goals including "structural" features of the property, such as its location and the number of rooms, and "contractual" features, such as the price, the completion date for the sale, etc. The buyer needs to decide both on a property, taking into account the features of the properties ($\mathcal{R}_i$ below), and general "norms" about structural properties ($\mathcal{R}_n$ below). The buyer also needs to decide and agree on a contract, taking into account norms about contractual issues ($\mathcal{R}_c$ below). A simple example of buyer is given by the ABA framework $\langle \mathcal{L}, \mathcal{R}, \mathcal{A}, \bar{\ } \rangle$ with:

- $\mathcal{R} = \mathcal{R}_i \cup \mathcal{R}_n \cup \mathcal{R}_c$ and
   $\mathcal{R}_i$: $number\_of\_rooms = 5 \leftarrow house_1$;
     $number\_of\_rooms = 4 \leftarrow house_2$; $price = £400K \leftarrow house_2$
   $\mathcal{R}_n$: $safe \leftarrow council\_approval, a_1$; $\neg safe \leftarrow weak\_foundations, a_2$;
     $council\_approval \leftarrow completion\_certificate, a_3$
   $\mathcal{R}_c$: $seller\_moves\_abroad \leftarrow house_2$;
     $quick\_completion \leftarrow seller\_moves\_abroad$
- $\mathcal{A} = \mathcal{A}_d \cup \mathcal{A}_u \cup \mathcal{A}_c$ and
   $\mathcal{A}_d = \{house_1, house_2\}$; $\mathcal{A}_c = \{a_1, a_2, a_3\}$; $\mathcal{A}_u = \{\neg council\_approval\}$
- $\overline{house_1} = house_2$, $\overline{house_2} = house_1$,
   $\overline{a_1} = \neg safe$, $\overline{a_2} = safe$, $\overline{a_3} = \neg council\_approval$,
   $\overline{\neg council\_approval} = council\_approval$.

Here, there are two properties for sale, $house_1$ and $house_2$. The first has 5 rooms, the second has 4 rooms and costs £400K ($\mathcal{R}_i$). The buyer believes that a property approved by the council is normally safe, a completion certificate normally indicates council approval, and a property with weak foundations is normally unsafe ($\mathcal{R}_n$). The buyer also believes that the seller of the second property is moving overseas, and this means that the seller aims at a quick completion of the sale ($\mathcal{R}_c$). Some of the assumptions in the example have a defeasible nature ($\mathcal{A}_c$), others amount to mutually exclusive decisions ($\mathcal{A}_d$) and finally others correspond to genuine uncertainties of the buyer ($\mathcal{A}_u$).

This example combines default reasoning, epistemic reasoning and practical reasoning. An example of "pure" practical reasoning in ABA applied to a problem described in [1] can be found in [35].

6.3 ABA for the stable marriage problem

Given two sets M, W of n men and n women respectively, the stable marriage problem (SMP) is the problem of pairing the men and women in M and W in such a way that no two people of opposite sex prefer to be with each other rather than with the person they are paired with. The SMP can be viewed as a problem of finding *stable extensions* in an abstract argumentation framework [8].

Here we show that the problem can be naturally represented in an ABA framework $\langle \mathcal{L}, \mathcal{R}, \mathcal{A}, ^{-} \rangle$ with:

- $\mathcal{A} = \{pair(A,B) \mid A \in M, B \in W\}$
- $\overline{pair(A,B)} = contrary\_pair(A,B)$
- $\mathcal{R}$ consists of inference rules
   $contrary\_pair(A,B) \leftarrow prefers(A,D,B), pair(A,D)$;
   $contrary\_pair(A,B) \leftarrow prefers(B,E,A), pair(E,B)$
   together with a set P of inference rules of the form $prefer(X,Y,Z) \leftarrow$ such that for each person A and for each two different people of the opposite sex

B and C, either $prefer(A,B,C) \leftarrow$ or $prefer(A,C,B) \leftarrow$ belongs to P, where $prefer(X,Y,Z)$ stands for X prefers Y to Z.

The standard formulation of the stable marriage problem combines the rules, assumptions and contraries of this framework with the notion that a set of arguments/assumptions is "acceptable" if and only if it is stable, where

- A set of arguments/assumptions is *stable* if and only if it does not attack itself, but attacks all arguments/assumptions not in the set.

In SMP, the semantics of stable sets forces solutions to be total, pairing all men and women in the sets M and W. The semantics of admissible sets is more flexible. It does not impose totality, and it can be used when the sets M and W have different cardinalities. Consider for example the situation in which two men, a and b, and two women, c and d have the following preferences:

$prefer(a,d,c) \leftarrow$; $prefer(b,c,d) \leftarrow$; $prefer(c,a,b) \leftarrow$; $prefer(d,b,a) \leftarrow$

Although there is no stable solution in which all people are paired with their highest preference, there exist two alternative stable solutions: $\{pair(a,c), pair(b,d)\}$ and $\{pair(a,d), pair(b,c)\}$. However, suppose a third woman, e, enters the scene, turns the heads of a and b, and expresses a preference for a over b, in effect adding to P:

$prefer(a,e,d) \leftarrow$; $prefer(a,e,c) \leftarrow$;

$prefer(b,e,c) \leftarrow$; $prefer(b,e,d) \leftarrow$; $prefer(e,a,b) \leftarrow$

This destroys both stable solutions of the earlier SMP, but has a single maximally admissible solution: $\{pair(a,e), pair(b,c)\}$.

Thus, by using admissibility we can drop the requirement that the number of men and women is the same. Similarly, we can drop the requirement that preferences are total, namely all preferences between pairs of the opposite sex are given.

7 Conclusions

In this chapter, we have reviewed assumption-based argumentation (ABA), focusing on relationships with other approaches to argumentation, computation, and applications. In contrast with a number of other approaches, ABA makes use of undercutting as the only way in which one argument can attack another. The effect of rebuttal attacks is obtained in ABA by adding appropriate assumptions to rules and by attacking those assumptions instead. The extent to which such undercutting is an adequate replacement for rebuttals has been explored elsewhere [34], but merits further investigation. Also, again in contrast with some other approaches, we do not insist that the support of an argument in ABA be minimal and consistent. Instead of insisting on minimality, we guarantee that the support of an argument is relevant, as a side-effect of representing arguments as deduction trees. Instead of insisting that the support of an argument is consistent, we obtain a similar effect by imposing the restriction that "acceptable" sets of arguments do not attack themselves.

ABA is an instance of abstract argumentation (AA), and consequently it inherits its various notions of "acceptable" sets of arguments. ABA also shares with AA the computational machinery of dispute trees, in which a proponent and an opponent alternate in attacking each other's arguments. However, ABA also admits the computation of dispute derivations, in which the proponent and opponent can attack and defeat each other's potential arguments before they are completed. We believe that this feature of dispute derivations is both computationally attractive and psychologically plausible when viewed as a model of human argumentation.

The computational complexity of ABA has been investigated for several of its instances [5] (see also Chapter 5). The computational machinery of dispute derivations and dispute trees is the basis of the CaSAPI argumentation system [7] [19, 20, 22].

Although ABA was originally developed for default reasoning, it has recently been used for several other applications, including dispute resolution and decision-making. ABA is currently being used in the ARGUGRID project [8] to support service selection and composition of services in the Grid and Service-Oriented Architectures. ABA is also being used for several applications in multi-agent systems [21, 18] and e-procurement [29].

Acknowledgement This work was partially funded by the Sixth Framework IST programme of the EC, under the 035200 ARGUGRID project.

References

1. T. Bench-Capon and H. Prakken. Justifying actions by accruing arguments. In *Proc. COMMA'06*, pages 247–258. IOS Press, 2006.
2. P. Besnard and A. Hunter. *Elements of Argumentation*. MIT Press, 2008.
3. A. Bondarenko, P. Dung, R. Kowalski, and F. Toni. An abstract, argumentation-theoretic approach to default reasoning. *Artificial Intelligence*, 93(1-2):63–101, 1997.
4. A. Bondarenko, F. Toni, and R. Kowalski. An assumption-based framework for non-monotonic reasoning. In *Proc. LPRNR'93*, pages 171–189. MIT Press, 1993.
5. Y. Dimopoulos, B. Nebel, and F. Toni. On the computational complexity of assumption-based argumentation for default reasoning. *Artificial Intelligence*, 141:57–78, 2002.
6. P. M. Dung. On the acceptability of arguments and its fundamental role in non-monotonic reasoning and logic programming. In *Proc. IJCAI'93*, pages 852–859. Morgan Kaufmann, 1993.
7. P. M. Dung. An argumentation theoretic foundation of logic programming. *Journal of Logic Programming*, 22:151–177, 1995.
8. P. M. Dung. On the acceptability of arguments and its fundamental role in non-monotonic reasoning, logic programming and n-person games. *Artificial Intelligence*, 77:321–357, 1995.
9. P. M. Dung. Negations as hypotheses: An abductive foundation for logic programming. In *Proc. ICLP*, pages 3–17. MIT Press, 1991.
10. P. M. Dung. An argumentation semantics for logic programming with explicit negation. In *Proc. ICLP*, pages 616–630. MIT Press, 1993.
11. P. M. Dung., R. Kowalski, and F. Toni. Dialectic proof procedures for assumption-based, admissible argumentation. *Artificial Intelligence*, 170:114–159, 2006.
12. P. M. Dung, P. Mancarella, and F. Toni. Computing ideal sceptical argumentation. *Artificial Intelligence*, 171(10-15):642–674, 2007.
13. P. M. Dung and P. M. Thang. Towards an argument-based model of legal doctrines in common law of contracts. In *Proc. CLIMA IX*, 2008.

---

[7] http://www.doc.ic.ac.uk/~dg00/casapi.html

[8] www.argugrid.eu

14. P. M. Dung, P. M. Thang, and N. D. Hung. Argument-based decision making and negotiation in e-business: Contracting a land lease for a computer assembly plant. In *Proc. CLIMA IX*, 2008.
15. P. M. Dung, P. M. Thang, and F. Toni. Towards argumentation-based contract negotiation. In *Proc. COMMA'08*. IOS Press, 2008.
16. P. M. Dung, P. M. Thang, F. Toni, N. D. Hung, P.-A. Matt, J. McGinnis, and M. Morge. Towards argumentation-based contract negotiation. *ARGUGRID Deliverable D.4.1*, 2008.
17. K. Eshghi and R. Kowalski. Abduction compared with negation as failure. In *Proc. ICLP*. MIT Press, 1989.
18. D. Gaertner, J. Rodriguez, and F. Toni. Agreeing on institutional goals for multi-agent societies. In *Proc. COIN*, pages 94–113, 2008.
19. D. Gaertner and F. Toni. CaSAPI: A system for credulous and sceptical argumentation. In *Proc. ArgNMR*, 2007.
20. D. Gaertner and F. Toni. Computing arguments and attacks in assumption-based argumentation. *IEEE Intelligent Systems*, 22(6):24–33, 2007.
21. D. Gaertner and F. Toni. Preferences and assumption-based argumentation for conflict-free normative agents. In *Proc. ArgMAS'07*. Springer, 2007.
22. D. Gaertner and F. Toni. Hybrid argumentation and its computational properties. In *Proc. COMMA'08*. IOS Press, 2008.
23. A. Garcia and G. Simari. Defeasible logic programming: An argumentative approach. *Journal of Theory and Practice of Logic Programming*, 4(1-2):95–138, 2004.
24. A. C. Kakas, R. A. Kowalski, and F. Toni. Abductive logic programming. *Journal of Logic and Computation*, 2(6):719–770, 1993.
25. A. C. Kakas, R. A. Kowalski, and F. Toni. The role of abduction in logic programming. In *Handbook of Logic in Artificial Intelligence and Logic Programming*, volume 5, pages 235–324. OUP, 1998.
26. A. C. Kakas and F. Toni. Computing argumentation in logic programming. *Journal of Logic and Computation*, 9:515–562, 1999.
27. R. A. Kowalski and F. Toni. Abstract argumentation. *Journal of Artificial Intelligence and Law*, 4(3-4):275–296, 1996.
28. P.-A. Matt and F. Toni. Basic influence diagrams and the liberal stable semantics. In *Proc. COMMA'08*. IOS Press, 2008.
29. P.-A. Matt, F. Toni, T. Stournaras, and D. Dimitrelos. Argumentation-based agents for eprocurement. In *Proc. AAMAS 2008*, 2008.
30. J. Pollock. Defeasible reasoning. *Cognitive Science*, 11(4):481–518, 1987.
31. D. Poole. A logical framework for default reasoning. *Artificial Intelligence*, 36(1):27–47, 1988.
32. H. Prakken and G. Sartor. The role of logic in computational models of legal argument: a critical survey. In *Computational Logic: Logic Programming and Beyond – Essays in Honour of Robert A. Kowalski*, pages 342–381. Springer, 2002.
33. F. Toni. Assumption-based argumentation for selection and composition of services. In *Proc. CLIMA VIII*, 2007.
34. F. Toni. Assumption-based argumentation for closed and consistent defeasible reasoning. In *Proc. JSAI 2007*, pages 390–402. Springer, 2008.
35. F. Toni. Assumption-based argumentation for epistemic and practical reasoning. In *Computable Models of the Law*, pages 185–202. Springer, 2008.
36. F. Toni and A. Kakas. Computing the acceptability semantics. In *Proc. LPNMR'95*, pages 401–415. Springer, 1995.
37. B. Verheij. DefLog: on the Logical Interpretation of Prima Facie Justified Assumptions. *Journal of Logic and Computation*, 13(3):319–346, 2003.
38. D. Walton, C. Reed, and F. Macagno. *Argumentation Schemes*. Cambridge Univ. Press, 2008.

Chapter 11
The Toulmin Argument Model in Artificial Intelligence
Or: how semi-formal, defeasible argumentation schemes creep into logic

Bart Verheij

1 Toulmin's 'The Uses of Argument'

In 1958, Toulmin published *The Uses of Argument*. Although this anti-formalistic monograph initially received mixed reviews (see section 2 of [20] for Toulmin's own recounting of the reception of his book), it has become a classical text on argumentation, and the number of references to the book (when writing these words[1] — by a nice numerological coincidence — 1958) continues to grow (see [7] and the special issue of *Argumentation* 2005; Vol. 19, No. 3). Also the field of Artificial Intelligence has discovered Toulmin's work. Especially four of Toulmin's themes have found follow-up in Artificial Intelligence. First, argument analysis involves half a dozen distinct elements, not just two. Second, many, if not most, arguments are substantial, even defeasible. Third, standards of good reasoning and argument assessment are non-universal. Fourth, logic is to be regarded as generalised jurisprudence. Using these central themes as a starting point, this chapter provides an introduction to Toulmin's argument model and its connections with Artificial Intelligence research. No attempt is made to give a comprehensive history of the reception of Toulmin's ideas in Artificial Intelligence; instead a personal choice is made of representative steps in AI-oriented argumentation research.

When Toulmin wrote his book, he was worried. He saw the influence of the successes of formal logic on the philosophical academia of the time, and was afraid that as a consequence seeing formal logic's limitations would be inhibited. He wrote *The Uses of Argument* to fight the — in his opinion mistaken — idea of formal logic as a universal science of good reasoning. In the updated edition of *The Uses of Argument* [19], he describes his original aim as follows:

> to criticize the assumption, made by most Anglo-American academic philosophers, that any significant argument can be put in formal terms: not just as a syllogism, since for Aristotle himself any inference can be called a 'syllogism' or 'linking of statements', but a rigidly demonstrative deduction of the kind to be found in Euclidean geometry. ([19], vii)

Bart Verheij
Artificial Intelligence, University of Groningen

[1] Source: Google Scholar citation count, April 1, 2008.

I. Rahwan, G. R. Simari (eds.), *Argumentation in Artificial Intelligence*,
DOI 10.1007/978-0-387-98197-0_11, © Springer Science+Business Media, LLC 2009

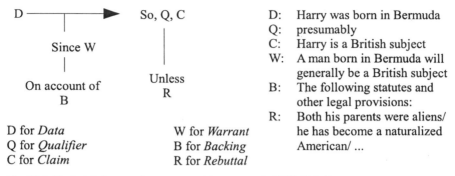

D for *Data*   W for *Warrant*
Q for *Qualifier*   B for *Backing*
C for *Claim*   R for *Rebuttal*

Fig. 11.1 Toulmin's layout of arguments with an example ([18], 104–5)

In short: Toulmin wanted to argue that there are other arguments than formal ones. It is also clear from this quote that Toulmin's goals were first and foremost aimed at his fellow philosophers. In the Preface to the 2003 edition, Toulmin says it thus:

> In no way had I set out to expound a theory of rhetoric or argumentation: my concern was with twentieth-century epistemology, not informal logic. ([19], vii)

Let us look closer at some of Toulmin's points.

1.1 Argument analysis involves half a dozen distinct elements, not just two

Toulmin is perhaps most often read because of his argument diagram (Figure 1). Whereas a formal logical analysis uses the dichotomy of premises and conclusions when analyzing arguments, Toulmin distinguishes six different kinds of elements: Data, Claim, Qualifier, Warrant, Backing and Rebuttal. Before explaining the roles of these elements, let us look at Toulmin's famous example of Harry, who may or may not be a British subject.

When someone claims that Harry is a British subject, it is natural to ask, so says Toulmin: What have you got to go on? An answer to that question can provide the data on which the claim rests, here: Harry was born in Bermuda. But having datum and claim is not enough. A further important question needs to be answered. Toulmin phrases it thus: How do you get there? In other words, why do you think that the datum gives support for your claim? An answer to this question must take the form of a rule-like general statement, the warrant underlying the step from datum to claim. In the example, the warrant is that a man born in Bermuda will generally be a British subject. As the example shows, warrants need not express universal generalizations. Here the warrant is not that *each* man born in Bermuda is a British subject, but merely that a man born in Bermuda will *generally* be a British subject. As a result, on the basis of datum and warrant a claim needs to be qualified. Here the claim becomes that *presumably* Harry is a British subject. When datum, qualified claim and warrant have been made explicit, a further question needs to be asked: Why do you think that the warrant holds? An answer will be provided by the backing of the warrant. In the example, Toulmin refers to the existence of statutes and other legal provisions (without specifying them) that can provide the backing for the warrant that who is born in Bermuda will generally be British subjects. The sixth and final kind of element to be distinguished is that of conditions of exception or rebuttal (101/93)[2]. Conditions of rebuttal indicate 'circumstances in which the general authority of the warrant would have to be set aside' or 'exceptional circumstances which might be capable of defeating or rebutting the warranted conclusion' (101/94). In the example, Harry's parents could be aliens or he could have become a naturalized American. Toulmin refers to Hart and Ross as predecessors for his discussion of rebuttal. Hart coined the term 'defeasibility' (see also [9]) and used it in legal and philosophical settings (contract, free will, responsibility), while Ross emphasized that moral rules must have exceptions (142/131–2).

Here is Toulmin's defence of the difference between a datum and the negation of a rebuttal, which predates discussions about the relation between rule conditions and exceptions:

> [T]he fact that Harry was born in Bermuda and the fact that his parents were not aliens are both of them directly relevant to the question of his present nationality; but they are relevant in different ways. The one fact is a datum, which by itself establishes a presumption of British nationality; the other fact, by setting aside one possible rebuttal, tends to confirm the presumption thereby created. (102/95)

Summarizing, Toulmin distinguishes six kinds of elements in arguments:

> *Claim*: The Claim is the original assertion that we are committed to and must justify when challenged (97/90). It is the starting point of the argument.
> *Datum*: The Datum provides the basis of the claim in response to the question: What have you got to go on? (97–8/90)
> *Warrant*: The Warrant provides the connection between datum and claim. A warrant expresses that '[d]ata such as D entitle[s] one to draw conclusions, or make claims, such as C'. Warrants are 'general, hypothetical statements, which can act as bridges, and authorise the sort of step to which our particular argument commits'. They are 'rules, principles, inference-licences or what you will, instead of additional items of information'. (98/91)
> *Qualifier*: The Qualifier indicates the strength of the step from datum to claim, as conferred by the warrant (101/94)
> *Backing*: The Backing shows why a warrant holds. Backing occurs when not a particular claim is challenged, but the range of arguments legitimized by a warrant (103–4/95–6).
> *Rebuttal*: A Rebuttal can indicate 'circumstances in which the general authority of the warrant would have to be set aside' or 'exceptional circumstances which might be capable of defeating or rebutting the warranted conclusion' (101/94).

1.2 Many, if not most, arguments are substantial, even defeasible

Let us consider another of Toulmin's example arguments:

> (1) Anne is one of Jack's sisters;
>   All Jack's sisters have red hair;
>   So, Anne has red hair. (123/115)

This example is a variant of the paradigmatic example of a syllogism: 'Socrates is a man. All men are mortal. So, Socrates is mortal'. Anyone accustomed to the

---

[2] Page numbers before the slash refer to the original 1958 edition of *The Uses of Argument* [18], those after the slash to the updated 2003 edition [19]

standard logical treatment of syllogisms will recognize the following logical form
underlying this type of syllogistic argument:

(2) $P(t)$
    $(\forall x)\,(P(x) \rightarrow Q(x))$
    _____

    $Q(t)$

In this logical analysis, argument (1) has two premises and one conclusion. Moreover, the two premises have clearly distinctive roles, one often referred to as the
minor premise ($P(t)$), the other the major premise (($\forall x$) ($P(x) \rightarrow Q(x)$)).

If we look at example (1) and its logical analysis (2) — an analysis to which Toulmin does not object for *this* type of argument[3] — one may ask: Why the richness of
primitives in his scheme? Shouldn't we apply Occam's razor and be satisfied with
the good-old dichotomy of premises and conclusions instead of Toulmin's six-fold
scheme?

Toulmin's answer is: no, we shouldn't be satisfied. A central place in the defence
of his position is the claim that syllogistic arguments of the logical form in (2)
are atypical, even rare (147–150/136–139; also: 125–6/116–7). They have special
characteristics that do not hold for other kinds of arguments. Toulmin discusses the
following five characteristics of (2)-fitting arguments:

1. They are *unequivocal in their consequences.*
However, there are also arguments (e.g., the Harry example; Figure 1) that only allow drawing a conclusion tentatively. Hence the need for qualifiers.
2. They are *formally valid.*
Toulmin speaks of a formally valid argument when the argument's conclusion can be
achieved by 'shuffling' the premises and their constituent parts (118/110). Arguments of
the form 'D; W. So C' can in this way be phrased as formally valid, but arguments of the
form 'D; B. So C' normally cannot. Toulmin refers to the Harry example (Figure 1) to make
his point (123/114).
3. They are expressed in terms of *'logical words'.*
Toulmin says it thus: 'The acceptable, logical words include 'all', 'some', 'or', and a few
others: these are firmly herded away from the non-logical goats, i.e. the generality of nouns,
adjectives and the like, and unruly connectives and quantifiers such as 'most', 'few', 'but'.'
(149/138)
4. They are *warrant-using.*
But, says Toulmin, there are also warrant-establishing arguments, as they for instance occur
in scientific papers (120–1/112–3). Toulmin refers to Ryle, who contrasted warrant-using
and warrant-establishing arguments by the analogy of taking a journey along a railway already built and the building of a fresh railway. Toulmin connects warrant-using arguments
to the term 'deduction', and warrant-establishing arguments to 'induction'.
5. They are *analytic.*
Toulmin calls an argument analytic if and only if the backing for the warrant authorising
it includes, explicitly or implicitly, the information conveyed in the conclusion itself. For
instance, the universal statement that all of Jack's sisters have red hair, in a way includes
that Anne, who is one of Jack's sisters, has red hair (123–127/114–118). Arguments that are
not analytic are substantial.

---

[3] The class of analytic arguments, for which both 'D. W. So, C' and 'D. B. So, C' can be expressed
in the formally valid way (2) (123/114).

It is because of the accidental concurrence of these five properties in (2)-arguments that the idea has come about that *all* arguments have them, and must have them; and this is an unfortunate fact of history, says Toulmin.

In the connection of analytic versus substantial arguments, Toulmin distinguishes two variants of the Anne argument (1) (124/115):

> (1, backing version)
> Anne is one of Jack's sisters;
> Each one of Jack's sisters has (been checked individually to have) red hair;
> So, Anne has red hair.
> (1, warrant version)
> Anne is one of Jack's sisters;
> Any sister of Jack's will (i.e. may be taken to) have red hair;
> So, Anne has red hair.

Note the different phrasing of the general statement used in the first and the second variant. In the former, it is formulated as a backing, here taking the form of an empirical fact about Jack's sisters, thereby encompassing the instance of sister Anne having red hair (at a certain moment). In the latter, it is formulated as a warrant, i.e., an inference-licensing general statement ('may be taken to'). The former can be used as a backing for the second.

Under which circumstances is (1, backing version) a genuinely analytic argument defending the claim that Anne has red hair? Well, says Toulmin, 'only if at this very moment I have all of Jack's sisters in sight. .... The thing to do now is use one's eyes, not hunt up a chain of reasoning' (126/117). The 'So' in the argument could be just as well replaced by 'In other words' or 'That is to say'.

In all other situations (which is: most), the conclusion will not be given with datum and backing, hence the argument will be a substantial one. Toulmin continues: 'If the purpose of an argument is to establish conclusions about which we are not entirely confident by relating them back to other information about which we have greater assurance, it begins to be a little doubtful whether any genuine, practical argument could ever be properly analytic.'

Here is how Toulmin extends the Anne example, making it fit his own format:

Datum:	Anne is one of Jack's sisters.
Claim:	Anne has red hair.
Warrant:	Any sister of Jack's will (i.e. may be taken to) have red hair.
Backing:	All his sisters have previously been observed to have red hair.
Qualifier:	Presumably
Rebuttal:	Anne has dyed/gone white/lost her hair ...

Note how Toulmin has added a qualifier and rebuttals, even though the backing assumes that all sisters have been checked. But Toulmin says rightly that normally an argument like this occurs later than at the time of establishing the warrant by the backing; hence making it non-demonstrative/subject to exceptions/defeasible/..., hence substantial, and not analytic (in Toulmin's sense). Checking hair colour today is not a guarantee for hair colour tomorrow.

Toulmin mentions one field in which arguments seem to be safe: mathematics. But then again: 'As a model argument for formal logicians to analyse, it [i.e., a solution to a mathematical problem] may be seducingly elegant, but it could hardly be less representative' (127/118).

1.3 Standards of good reasoning and argument assessment are not universal, but context-dependent

According to Toulmin, our standards for the assessment of real arguments are not universal, but depend on a context. In a section, where he discusses this issue, he uses the term 'possibility' as an illustration (36/34): whereas in mathematics 'possibility' has to do with the absence of demonstrable contradiction, in most cases 'possibility' is based on a stronger standard. His example statement is 'Dwight D. Eisenhower will be selected to represent the U.S.A. in the Davis Cup match against Australia'. This statement involves no contradiction, while still (now former, then actual) President Eisenhower will not be considered a possible team member. In other words, 'possibility' is judged using different standards, some more formal ('absence of contradiction'), others more substantial ('being a top-level tennis player').

The example is however an example of different standards for the possible, not of different standards for the assessment of arguments, his ultimate aim. Here is a succinct phrasing of his position:

> It is unnecessary, we argued, to freeze statements into timeless propositions before admitting them into logic: utterances are made at particular times and in particular situations, and they have to be understood and assessed with one eye on this context. The same, we can now argue, is true of the relations holding between statements, at any rate in the majority of practical arguments. The exercise of the rational judgement is itself an activity carried out in a particular context and essentially dependent on it: the arguments we encounter are set out at a given time and in a given situation, and when we come to assess them they have to be judged against this background. So the practical critic of arguments, as of morals, is in no position to adopt the mathematician's Olympian posture. (182–3/168–9; the quote appears in a section entitled "Logic as a System of Eternal Truths")

According to Toulmin, the differences between standards of reasoning are reflected in the backings that are accepted to establish warrants. For instance, he considers the following three warrants (103–4/96):

> A whale will be a mammal.
> A Bermudan will be a Briton.
> A Saudi Arabian will be a Muslim.

Each of these warrants gives in a similar way the inferential connection between certain types of data and certain kinds of claims. The first allows inferring that a *particular* whale is a mammal, the second that a *particular* Bermudan is a Briton, the third that a *particular* Saudi Arabian is a Muslim (all these inferences, of course, subject to qualification and rebuttal). The different standards become visible when information about the corresponding backings is inserted:

> A whale will be (i.e. *is classifiable as*) a mammal
> A Bermudan will be (*in the eyes of the law*) a Briton
> A Saudi Arabian will be (*found to be*) a Muslim

Toulmin explains (104/96):

> One warrant is defended by relating it to a system of taxonomical classification, another by appealing to the statutes governing the nationality of people born in the British colonies, the third by referring to the statistics which record how religious beliefs are distributed among people of different nationalities.

For Toulmin, the establishment of standards of argument assessment, hence of good reasoning, is an empirical question, cf. the following excerpt:

> Accepting the need to begin by collecting for study the actual forms of argument current in any field, our starting-point will be confessedly empirical: we shall study ray-tracing techniques because they are used to make optical inferences, presumptive conclusions and 'defeasibility' as an essential feature of many legal arguments, axiomatic systems because they reflect the pattern of our arguments in geometry, dynamics and elsewhere. (257/237)[4]

Toulmin goes one step further. Our standards of good reasoning are not only to be established empirically, they are also to be considered historically: they change over time and can be improved upon:

> To think up new and better methods of arguing in any field is to make a major advance, not just in logic, but in the substantive field itself: great logical innovations are part and parcel of great scientific, moral, political or legal innovations. [...] We must study the ways of arguing which have established themselves in any sphere, accepting them as historical facts; knowing that they may be superseded, but only as the result of a revolutionary advance in our methods of thought. (257/237)

Because of his views that standards of good reasoning and argument assessment are non-universal and depend on field, even context, Toulmin has been said to revive Aristotle's Topics (Toulmin 2003, viii).

1.4 Logic is generalised jurisprudence

Toulmin discusses the relation of logic with a number of research areas (3–8/3–8). When logic is regarded as *psychology*, it deals with the laws of thought, distinguishing between what is normal and abnormal, thereby perhaps even allowing a kind of "psychopathology of cognition" (5/5). In logic as psychology, the goal is at heart descriptive: to formulate generalisations about thinkers thinking. But logic can also be seen as a kind of *sociology*. Then it is not individual thinkers that are at issue, but the focus is on general habits and practices. Here Toulmin refers to Dewey, who explains the passage from the customary to the mandatory: inferential habits can turn into inferential norms. Logic can also be regarded as a kind of *technology*, i.e., as providing a set of recipes for rationality or the rules of a craft. Here he speaks of logic as an art, like medicine. In this analogy, logic aims at the formulation of maxims, 'tips', that remind thinkers how they should think. And then there is logic as *mathematics*. There the goal of logic becomes to find truths about logical relations. There is no connection with thinking and logic becomes an objective science.

---

[4] Toulmin here considers the study of defeasibility an empirical question, to be performed by looking at the law! Toulmin has predicted history, by foreseeing what actually has happened and still is happening in the field of AI & law.

Finally Toulmin comes to the metaphor that he prefers and uses as the basis for his work: to view logic as *jurisprudence*:

> Logic is concerned with the soundness of the claims we make-with the solidity of the grounds we produce to support them, the firmness of the backing we provide for them-or, to change the metaphor, with the sort of case we present in defence of our claims. (7/7)

The jurisprudence metaphor emphasises the critical, procedural function of logic, thereby fundamentally changing the perspective on logic. It helps to change logic from an 'idealised logic' to a 'working logic' (cf. the title of the fourth essay in *The Uses of Argument*). At the end of his book he says that jurisprudence should not be seen as merely an analogy, but, more strongly, as providing an example to follow, as being a kind of 'best practice':

> Jurisprudence is one subject which has always embraced a part of logic within its scope, and what we called to begin with 'the jurisprudential analogy' can be seen in retrospect to amount to something more than a mere analogy. If the same as has long been done for legal arguments were done for arguments of other types, logic would make great strides forward. (255/235)

2 The reception and refinement of Toulmin's ideas in AI

The reception of Toulmin's ideas is marked by historical happenstance. It was already mentioned that his original audience, primarily the positivist, logic-oriented philosophers of knowledge of the time, was on the whole critical. For Toulmin's main messages to be appreciated a fresh crowd was needed. It was found in a radical movement in academic research and education refocusing on the analysis and assessment of real-life argument. This movement, referred to by names such as speech communication, informal logic and argumentation theory, started to blossom from the 1970s, continuing so to the present day (see [22]). One thing that Toulmin and this movement shared was the relativising, at times antagonistic, attitude towards logic as a formal science. The swing had swung back to exploring the possibilities of more formal approaches in the 1990s, when Toulmin's project of treating logic as a generalised jurisprudence was almost literally taken up in the field of Artificial Intelligence and Law (see Feteris' [4] for a related development in argumentation theory). Successful attempts were made to formalize styles of legal reasoning in a way that respected actual legal reasoning. The approach taken in this field was rooted in an independent development in Artificial Intelligence, where so-called nonmonotonic logics were studied from the 1980s. In that line of research, formal logical systems were studied that allowed for the retraction of conclusions when new information, indicating exceptional or contradictory circumstances, became available. Also in the 1990s, the study of nonmonotonic logics evolved towards what might be called argumentation logics. More generally, attention was reallocated to implemented systems and an agent-oriented perspective.

The following does not give a fully representative, historical account of AI work taking up Toulmin's ideas. A personal choice of relevant research has been made in order to highlight how Toulmin's points of view have been adopted and refined in Artificial Intelligence.

2.1 Reiter's default rules

An early strand of research in Artificial Intelligence, in which a number of Toulmin's key positions are visible, is Reiter's work on the logic of default reasoning [15]. Reiter's formalism is built around the concept of a default: an expression $\alpha : M\beta_1, ..., M\beta_n / \gamma$, in which α, β_1, ..., β_n, and γ are sentences of first-order logic. Defaults are a kind of generalized rules of inference. The sentence α is the default's prerequisite, playing the role of what Toulmin refers to as the datum. The sentence γ is the default's consequent, comparable to Toulmin's notion of a claim. The sentences β_i are called the default's justifications. A default expresses that its consequent follows given its prerequisite, but only when its justifications can consistently be assumed.

Reiter does not refer to Toulmin in his highly influential 1980 paper, nor in his other work. Being thoroughly embedded in the fertile logic-based AI community of the time, Reiter does not refer to less formal work. Still, in Reiter's work two important ideas defended by Toulmin recur in a formal version. The first is the idea of defeasibility. As said, Reiter's defaults are a kind of generalized rules of inference, but of a defeasible kind. For instance, the default $p : M\neg e / q$ expresses that q follows from p unless $\neg e$ cannot be assumed consistently. Reiter's formal definitions are such that, given only p, it follows that q, while if both p and e are given q does not follow. Reiter's justifications are hence closely related to Toulmin's rebuttals, but as opposites: in our example the opposite e of the default's justification $\neg e$ is a kind of rebuttal in Toulmin's sense. This holds more generally: opposites of justifications can be thought of as formal versions of Toulmin's rebuttals.

There is a second way in which Reiter's work formally explicates one of Toulmin's prime concerns: defaults are contingent rules of inference, in the sense that they are not fixed in the logical system, as is the case for the natural deduction rules of first-order logic. Concretely, in Reiter's approach, defaults are part of the theory from which consequences can be drawn, side by side with the other, factual, information. One can therefore say that Toulmin's creed that standards of reasoning are field-dependent has found a place in Reiter's work. There is one important limitation however. Although Reiter's defaults can be used to construct arguments — in what Toulmin refers to as warrant-using arguments —, they cannot be argued about. In other words, there is no counterpart of warrant-establishing arguments. A default can for instance not have a default as its conclusion. Since Reiter's defaults are givens, it is not possible to give reasons for why they hold. Whereas in Toulmin's model warrants do not stand by themselves, but can be given support by backings, this has no counterpart for Reiter's defaults. (See section 2.7 for an approach to warrant-establishing arguments.)

How did Reiter extend or refine Toulmin? The first way is obvious: Reiter has given a precise explication of a part of Toulmin's notions, which is a direct consequence of the fact that Reiter's approach is formally specified, whereas Toulmin's only exists in the form of an informal philosophical essay. Reiter has shown that it is possible to give a formal elaboration of rebuttals and of warrants.

The other way is perhaps more important, as it concerns a genuine extension of what Toulmin had in mind: Reiter's logical formalism proposes a way of determining which consequences follow from given information. The key formal notion is that of an extension of a default theory (consisting of a set of factual assumptions and a set of defaults), which can be thought of as a possible set of consequences of the theory. Essentially, a set of sentences S is an extension of a default theory if S is equal to the set of consequences of the factual information that one obtains by applying a subset of the defaults, namely those defaults the justifications of which are consistent with S. (Note that S occurs in the definiens and in the definiendum.) Let me show how and to what extent Reiter's system can formalize Toulmin's Harry-example. We will leave out the qualifier and the backing as these have no obvious counterpart in Reiter's work. The core of a formalization of the Harry example is the default $d(x) : M\neg r_1(x), M\neg r_2(x) \,/\, c(x)$ and its instance $d(t) : M\neg r_1(t), M\neg r_2(t) \,/\, c(t)$. The following code is used:

t	Harry
$d(t)$	Harry was born in Bermuda
$c(t)$	Harry is a British subject
$r_1(t)$	Both his parents were aliens
$r_2(t)$	He has become a naturalized American

The default expresses that it follows that Harry is a British subject given that he is born in Bermuda, as long as it can be consistently assumed that his parents are *not* aliens and he has *not* become a naturalized American. Note that the default is a kind of hybrid of the example's warrant and rebuttals and that the default's list of justifications is not open-ended (in contrast with Toulmin's list of rebuttals).

Now consider two sets of sentences: S_1, the first-order closure of $d(t)$, $c(t)$ and S_2, the closure of $d(t)$, $r_1(t)$. Then S_1 is the unique extension of the theory consisting of the default and the factual information $d(t)$, while S_2 is the unique extension of the theory consisting of the default and the factual information $d(t)$ and $r_1(t)$. (Analogous facts hold when the other rebuttal $r_2(t)$ is used.) These facts can be interpreted as saying that, given the warrant encoded by the default, the claim follows from the data, but only when there is no rebuttal.

Three ways in which this formal version refines Toulmin's treatment seem noteworthy. First, here there is a distinction between 'generic' warrants and 'specific' warrants. The former is for Toulmin a pleonasm, while he does not consider the latter. Here the distinction is clear: on the one hand there is the generic inference license that a man born in Bermuda will generally be a British subject, on the other the specific inference license that if Harry was born in Bermuda, he is a British subject. Second, whereas Toulmin only treats single, unstructured sentences, Reiter's formal system inherits the elegant additional structuring of first-order sentences. For instance, disjunction and conjunction are directly inherited. Third and finally, Reiter's version specifies what happens when there is more than one default. Especially, his version incorporates naturally the situations that a sentential element (datum, rebuttal, ...) of one instance of Toulmin's model can be the claim of another. It has sometimes been charged against Toulmin that his model does not allow such recursiveness.

2.2 Pollock's undercutting and rebutting defeaters

Pollock's work on the philosophy and AI of argumentation has rightly achieved recognition in today's argumentation research. He can be regarded as being the first who combined theoretical, computational and practical considerations in his design of an 'artificial person', OSCAR (see, e.g., [12]). In this high ambition, he has had no followers. Pollock's work started with roots close to Toulmin's original audience, namely philosophers of knowledge. Gradually he began using methods from the field of Artificial Intelligence, where his ideas have gained most attention. Pollock does not seem to have been directly influenced by Toulmin. In his [11], where Pollock connects philosophical approaches to defeasibility with AI approaches, he cites work on defeasibility by Chisholm (going back to 1957, hence a year before Toulmin's *The Uses of Argument*) and himself (going back to 1967).

Here are some of Pollock's definitions [11]:

> P is a *prima facie reason* for S to believe Q if and only if P is a reason for S to believe Q and there is an R such that R is logically consistent with P but (P & R) is not a reason for S to believe Q. R is a *defeater* for P as a prima facie reason for Q if and only if P is a reason for S to believe Q and R is logically consistent with P but (P & R) is not a reason for S to believe Q.

So prima facie reasons are reasons that sometimes lead to their conclusion, but not always, namely not when there is a defeater. There is a close connection with non-monotonic consequence relations: when P is a prima facie reason for Q, and R is a defeater for P as a reason, then Q follows from P, but not from P & R. Pollock goes on to distinguish between two kinds of defeaters:

> R is a *rebutting defeater* for P as a prima facie reason for Q if and only if R is a defeater and R is a reason for believing ∼Q. R is an *undercutting defeater* for P as a prima facie reason for S to believe Q if and only if R is a defeater and R is a reason for denying that P wouldn't be true unless Q were true.

Undercutting defeaters only attack the inferential connection between reason and conclusion, whereas a defeater is rebutting if it is also a reason for the opposite of the conclusion. Pollock remarks that 'P wouldn't be true unless Q were true' is a kind of conditional, different from the material conditional of logic, but having learnt from an initial analysis, which he no longer finds convincing, he maintains that it is otherwise not clear how to analyze this conditional ([11], 485).[5]

Pollock's finding that there are different kinds of defeaters has been recognized as an important contribution both for the theory and for the practical analysis of arguments. Nothing of the sort can be found in Toulmin's *The Uses of Argument*.[6] (See section 2.7 for more on different conceptions of a rebuttal.)

---

[5] As far as I know, Pollock's later work (e.g., his [12]) does not contain a new analysis of this conditional. See section 2.7 for an approach addressing this.

[6] Pollock's work contributes significantly to several other aspects of argumentation (e.g., argument evaluation, semi-formal rules of inference and software implementation). See also Verheij's discussion [26], 104–110.

2.3 Prakken, Sartor & Hage on reasoning with legal rules

Toulmin's idea that logic should be regarded as a generalised form of jurisprudence (section 1.4), was taken up seriously in the 1990s in the field of Artificial Intelligence and Law. The work by Prakken, Sartor and Hage on reasoning with legal rules [13, 6] is representative.[7]

Influenced by logic-based knowledge representation (see, e.g., chapter 10 of [16]), Prakken & Sartor and Hage use an adapted first-order language as the basis of their formalism. For instance, here is a formal version of the rule that someone has legal capacity unless he can be shown to be a minor ([13], 340):

r_1: $\sim x$ is a minor $\Rightarrow x$ has legal capacity

Here r_1 is the name of the rule, which can be used to refer to it, and 'x is a minor' and 'x has legal capacity' are unary predicates. The tilde represents so-called weak negation, which here means that the rule's antecedent is fulfilled when it cannot be shown that x is a minor. If ordinary negation were used, the fulfilment of the antecedent would require something stronger, namely that it can be shown that x is not a minor.

In the system of Prakken & Sartor, arguments are built by applying Modus ponens to rules. There are two ways in which arguments can attack each other. First, an argument can attack a weakly negated assumption in the antecedent of a rule used in the attacked argument. Second, two arguments can have opposite conclusions. Information about rule priorities (expressed using the rules names) is then used to compare the arguments. Argument evaluation is defined in terms of winning strategies in dialogue games: an argument is called justified when it can be successfully defended against an opponent's counterarguments.

Hage's approach [6], in several ways similar to Prakken & Sartor's, is more ambitious and philosophically radical.[8] For Hage, rules are first-and-foremost to be thought of as things with properties. As a result, a rule is formalized as a structured term. A rule's properties are then formalized using predicates. For instance, the fact that the rule that thieves are punishable, is valid is formalized as

Valid(rule(theftl, thief(x), punishable(x))).

Here 'theft1' is the name of the rule, 'thief(x)' the rule's antecedent and 'punishable(x)' its consequent. Hage's work takes the possibilities of a knowledge representation approach to the modelling of legal reasoning to its limits. For instance, there are dedicated predicates to express reasons, rule validity, rule applicability and the weighing of reasons.

How does the work by Prakken, Sartor & Hage relate to Toulmin's views? First, they have provided an operationalisation of Toulmin's idea of law-inspired logic, by formalizing aspects of legal reasoning. Second, they have refined Toulmin's treatment of argument. Notably, Prakken & Sartor have modelled specific kinds of rebuttal, namely by the attack of weakly negated assumptions and on the basis of

---

[7] Some other important AI & Law work concerning argumentation is for instance [1, 2, 5, 10].

[8] Hage's philosophical and formal theory of rules and reasons Reason-Based Logic was initiated by Hage and further developed in cooperation with Verheij.

rule priorities, and embedded them in an argumentative dialogue. Hage has added a further kind of rebuttal, namely by the weighing of reasons. Also, Hage has distinguished the validity of a rule from its applicability. The former can be regarded as an expression of a warrant in Toulmin's sense, and since in Hage's system rule validity can depend on other information, it is natural to model Toulmin's backings as reasons for the validity of a rule. And perhaps most importantly: Prakken & Sartor and Hage (and other AI & law researchers) have worked on the embedding of defeasible argumentation in a genuine procedural, dialogical setting (see also section 2.5). A further refinement of Toulmin's view is given by Verheij and colleagues [28], who show how two kinds of warrants (viz. legal rules and legal principles) with apparent logical differences, can be seen as extremes of a spectrum.

2.4 Dung's admissible sets

Dung's paper [3] has supplied an abstract mathematical foundation for formal work on argumentation. Following earlier mathematically flavoured work (e.g., [17, 29, 30]), his abstraction of only looking at the attack relation between arguments has helped organize the field, e.g., by showing how several formal systems of nonmonotonic reasoning can be viewed from the perspective of argument attack. A set of (unstructured) arguments with an attack relation is called an argumentation framework.

Dung has studied the mathematics of three types of subsets of the set of arguments of an argumentation framework: stable, preferred and grounded extensions. A set of arguments is a *stable extension* if it attacks all arguments not in the set. A set of arguments is a *preferred extension* if it is a maximal set of arguments without internal conflicts and attacking all arguments attacking the set. The *grounded extension* (there is only one) is the result of an inductive process: starting from the empty set, consecutively arguments are added that are only attacked by arguments already defended against.

Stable extensions can be regarded as an 'ideal' interpretation of an argumentation framework. When an extension is stable, all conflicts between arguments can be regarded as solved. It turns out that sometimes there are distinct ways of resolving the conflicts (e.g., when two arguments attack each other, each argument by itself is a stable extension) and that sometimes there is no way (e.g., when an argument is self-attacking). Preferred extensions are a generalization of stable extensions, as all stable extensions are also preferred. However, an argumentation framework always has a preferred extension (perhaps several). Preferred extensions can be regarded as showing how as many conflicts as possible can be resolved by counterattack. The grounded extension exists always and is a subset of all preferred and stable extensions.

Dung's work shows that the mathematics of argument attack is non-trivial and interesting. Thereby he has significantly extended our understanding of Toulmin's concept of rebuttal.

2.5 *Walton's argumentation schemes*

Toulmin's proposal that the maxims provided by a standard formal logical system (such as first order predicate logic) are not the only criteria for good reasoning and argument assessment, posed a new problem: if there are other, more field- and context-dependent standards of reasoning, what are they? For, though many recognized the shortcomings of formal logic for practical argument assessment, few were happy with the possible relativistic implication that anything goes. A good way to avoid the trap of uncontrolled relativism is to provide a systematic specification of standards of good reasoning.

One approach in this direction, which is especially close to Toulmin's conception of warrants, can be found in Walton's work on argumentation schemes (e.g., [31]). Argumentation schemes can be thought of as a semi-formal generalization of the rules of inference found in formal logic. Argument from expert opinion is an example ([31], 65):

> E is an expert in domain D.
> E asserts that A is known to be true.
> A is within D.
> Therefore, A may (plausibly) be taken to be true.

As Walton's argumentation schemes are context-dependent, not universal; defeasible, not strict; and concrete, not abstract, there is a strong analogy with Toulmin's warrants. There are two important differences though. First, Walton's argumentation schemes are structured, whereas Toulmin's warrants are not. Walton's argumentation schemes have premises, consisting of one or more sentences (often with informal variables), and a conclusion;[9] Toulmin's warrants are expressed as rule-like statements, such as 'A man born in Bermuda will generally be a British subject'.[10] By giving generic inference licenses more structure, as in Walton's work, the question arises whether they become formal enough to give rise to a kind of 'concrete logic'. Verheij [24] argues that it is a matter of choice, perhaps: taste, whether one draws the border between form and content on either side of argumentation schemes. To indicate the somewhat ambiguous status of argumentation schemes, the term 'semi-formal' may be most appropriate.

Second, Walton's argumentation schemes have associated critical questions. Critical questions help evaluating applications of an argumentation scheme. As a result, they play an important role in the evaluation of practical arguments. For instance, Walton lists the following critical questions for the scheme 'Argument from expert opinion' ([31], 65):

> 1. Is E a genuine expert in D?
> 2. Did E really assert A?

---

[9] Sometimes Walton's schemes take another form, e.g., small chains of argument steps or small dialogues; see Verheij's [24] for a format for the systematic specification of argumentation schemes inspired by knowledge engineering technology.

[10] Occasionally, a bit more structure is made explicit. For instance, when Toulmin phrases a warrant in an 'if ... then ...' form (e.g., 'If anything is red, it will not also be black', 98/91), thereby making an antecedent and consequent recognizable.

3. Is A relevant to domain D?
4. Is A consistent with what other experts in D say?
5. Is A consistent with known evidence in D?

Critical questions are related to argument attack, as they point to circumstances in which application of the scheme is problematic (e.g., [24]). For instance, the question 'Is E a genuine expert in D?' questions whether the element 'E is an expert in domain D' in the premises of the scheme really holds. Some critical questions are like Toulmin's notion of rebuttal. For instance, the question 'Is A consistent with what other experts in D say?' points to a rebuttal 'A is <u>not</u> consistent with what other experts in D say', which, if accepted, can raise doubt whether the conclusion can justifiably be drawn. In general, four types of critical questions can be distinguished [24]:

> 1. Critical questions concerning the *conclusion* of an argumentation scheme. Are there other reasons, based on other argumentation schemes for or against the scheme's conclusion?
> 2. Critical questions concerning the elements of the *premises* of an argumentation scheme. Is E an expert in domain D? Did E assert that A is known to be true? Is A within D?
> 3. Critical questions based on the *exceptions* of an argumentation scheme. Is A consistent with what other experts in D say? Is A consistent with known evidence in D?
> 4. Critical questions based on the *conditions of use* of an argumentation scheme. Do experts with respect to facts like A provide reliable information concerning the truth of A?

The critical questions associated with an argumentation scheme point to the dialogical setting of argumentation. Toulmin mentions the dialogical and procedural setting of argumentation (as, e.g., when discussing the jurisprudence metaphor for logic), but the discussion is not elaborate. Much work on the relation between argumentation and dialogue has been done. There is for instance the pragma-dialectical school (e.g., [21]), but also Walton's conception of argumentation is embedded in a procedural, dialogical setting. For instance, Walton [32] expresses a view on how to determine the relevance of an argument in a dialogue. There are six issues to take into account: the dialogue type[11], the stage the dialogue is in, the dialogue's goal, the type of argument, which is determined by the argumentation scheme underlying the argument, the prior sequence of argumentation, and the institutional and social setting.

In conclusion, Walton's work has played a significant role in two developments in AI with respect to Toulmin's main themes. First, the study of argumentation schemes by Walton and others has made a start with the systematic specification of context-dependent, defeasible, concrete standards of argument assessment, as sought for by Toulmin. And, second, the idea of considering argumentation from a procedural, dialogue perspective has been elaborated upon.

2.6 Reed & Rowe's argument analysis software

Further steps towards the realization of Toulmin's goals have been made by the recent advent of software-support of argumentative tasks, often using argument diagrams [8, 26]. In this connection, Reed & Rowe's work on the Araucaria tool [14] is

---

[11] See also Walton & Krabbe's [33], a treatment of dialogue types that is especially influential in research in AI and multi-agent systems.

especially relevant for the achievement of Toulmin's goals, as they have presented Araucaria specifically as a software tool for argument analysis. Araucaria uses an argument diagramming format, in which the recursive tree-structure of reasons supporting conclusions is depicted. It is also possible to indicate statements that are in conflict. Araucaria's standard diagramming format[12] is different from Toulmin's in several ways, but especially by not graphically distinguishing warrants from data. In an interestingly different way, however, Araucaria's standard format does include the idea of context-dependent types of reasoning as argued for by Toulmin, namely by its incorporation of Walton-style argumentation schemes (cf. section 2.5). Argumentation schemes can be used in Araucaria to label argumentative steps. For instance, a concrete argument 'There is smoke. Therefore, there is fire' could be labelled as an instance of the scheme 'Argument from sign', thereby giving access two critical questions, such as 'Are there other events that would more reliably account for the sign?'. By this possibility, Reed & Rowe's Araucaria is a useful step towards software-supported argument assessment. The tool provides a significant extension of Toulmin's aim to change logic from an 'idealised logic' to a 'working logic'.

2.7 Verheij's formal reconstruction of Toulmin's scheme

Already the examples in this chapter show a wide variety of approaches to — what might be called — semi-formal defeasible argumentation; and this is just the tip of the iceberg. By this embarrassment of riches, the question arises whether there are fundamental differences, e.g., between explicitly Toulmin-oriented approaches and other; or is the similarity of subject matter strong enough to allow for a synthesis of approaches? Looking for answers, I have attempted to reconstruct Toulmin's scheme using modern formal tools [25]. I used the abstract argumentation logic DefLog [23]. DefLog uses two connectives $\times$ and $\leadsto$: the first for expressing the defeat of a prima facie justified statement ('negation-as-defeat', the semantics of which falls outside the scope of this chapter), the second for expressing a conditional relation between statements ('primitive implication', validating Modus Ponens, but lacking a so-called introduction rule).[13] Toulmin's notion of a qualifier has been left out of the reconstruction.

The key to the translation of Toulmin's scheme into DefLog is to explicitly express that a datum leads to a claim; in DefLog: $D \leadsto C$. DefLog's primitive implication can be thought of as expressing a specific inference license. It is an explicit expression of what Toulmin refers to as a 'logical gulf' (9/9) that seems to exist between a reason and the state of affairs it supports. In this way, the licensing of concrete argument steps is removed from the logic, i.e., the fixed formalized background specifying general argument validity, and shifted to the contingent information. In this way, it becomes possible to express substantial arguments about concrete inferential bridges.

---

[12] In later versions, two alternative formats are provided: Toulmin's and Wigmore's.

[13] DefLog is formally an extension of Dung's abstract argumentation framework (section 2.4), as Dung's attack between two arguments A and B can be expressed as $A \leadsto \times B$. DefLog analogues of Dung's stable and preferred semantics are defined and proven to coincide with Dung's when DefLog's language is restricted to Dung's.

In particular, the role of a warrant can now be expressed as a reason for such a conditional statement: $W \rightsquigarrow (D \rightsquigarrow C)$. To formally show that a datum and claim are specific, whereas a warrant is to be thought of as a generic inference license, we can use variables and their instances: $W \rightsquigarrow (D(t) \rightsquigarrow C(t))$. This clarifies the distinctions between the following three:

(1) A man born in Bermuda will generally be a British subject.
(2) If *Person* was born in Bermuda, then generally *Person* is a British subject.
(3) If Harry was born in Bermuda, then generally he is a British subject.

The first is the ordinary language expression of a warrant as a rule-like statement (formally: W). The third is a conditional sentence (formally: $D(t) \rightsquigarrow C(t)$), instantiating the second, which is a scheme of conditional sentences (formally: $D(x) \rightsquigarrow C(x)$, where x is a variable, that can be instantiated by the concrete term t). Note that only (1) and (3) can occur in actual texts, whereas (2) is — by its use of a variable *Person* — an abstraction. One could say however that (1) and (2) imply each other: a warrant corresponds to a scheme of argumentative steps from datum to claim. Given this analysis of warrants and their relation to datum and claim, backings are simply reasons for warrants: $B \rightsquigarrow W$.

Rebuttals are an ambiguous concept in Toulmin's treatment. He associates rebuttals with 'circumstances in which the general authority of the warrant would have to be set aside' (101/94), 'exceptional circumstances which might be capable of defeating or rebutting the warranted conclusion' (101/94) and with the (non)applicability of a warrant (102/95). It turns out that these three can be distinguished, and, given the present analysis of the warrant-datum-claim part of Toulmin's scheme, even extended to five kinds of rebuttals, as there are five different statements that can be argued against: the datum D, the claim C, the warrant W, the conditional $D(t) \rightsquigarrow C(t)$, expressing the inferential bridge from datum to claim, and the conditional $W \rightsquigarrow (D(t) \rightsquigarrow C(t))$, which expresses the application of the warrant in the concrete situation (see [25] for a more extensive explanation). A rebuttal of the latter conditional coincides conceptually with an undercutting defeater in the sense of Pollock's. Note that the analysis suggests an answer to Pollock's open issue of how to analyze the conditional 'P wouldn't be true unless Q were true' (section 2.2). If U undercuts P as a reason for Q, we would write $U \rightsquigarrow \times(P \rightsquigarrow Q)$.

In this analysis, there is a natural extension of Toulmin's concept of warrant: just as it is necessary to specify which data imply claims (by Toulmin's warrants), it is necessary to specify which rebuttals block the application of warrants. Informally: it is a matter of substance, not logic, which statements are rebuttals. It must be *shown* by argument whether some statement is a rebuttal. In the law, for instance, not only legal rules (a kind of warrants) find backing in statutes, but also exceptions to rules. In the present analysis, dealing with 'rebuttal warrants' is a matter of course, since there is an explicit expression that R is a rebuttal.[14]

A side effect of the reconstruction is that arguments modelled according to Toulmin's scheme can be formally evaluated. For instance, assuming that datum and

---

[14] When R is a rebuttal in the sense of a Pollockian undercutter, this requires a sentence of the form $R \rightsquigarrow \times(W \rightsquigarrow (D \rightsquigarrow C))$, expressing that, if R holds, the warrant W is not applicable.

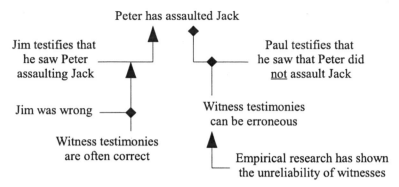

Fig. 11.2 An entangled dialectical argument

warrant hold, but not a rebuttal, the claim follows; when also a rebuttal is assumed, the claim does not follow.[15] A rebuttal of a rebuttal can be shown to reinstate a claim. Verheij [24] extends the approach to include Walton's argumentation schemes.

The result of the formal reconstruction of Toulmin's scheme showed some extensions, while retaining the original flavour. Figure 2 (using a diagramming format used in [27]) illustrates the basic relations between statements as distinguished here: Claims can have reasons for and against them (Jim's testimony supporting the assault by Jack, and Paul's attacking it), and the inferential bridges (the conditionals connecting reasons with their conclusions, here drawn as arrows) can be argued about just like other statements. The resulting argument structures are *dialectical*, by their incorporation of pros and cons, and *entangled* by their allowing the support and attack of inferential bridges.

3 Concluding remarks

It has been shown that central points of view argued for by Toulmin (1958), in particular the defeasibility of argumentation, the substantial, instead of formal, nature of standards of argument assessment, and the richer set of building blocks for argument analysis, are very much alive. Also Toulmin's 'research program' of treating logic as generalised jurisprudence has been taken up (with or without reference to him) and proven to be fertile.

There have also been refinements and extensions. It is now known that defeasible argumentation has interesting (and intricate) formal properties. There exist formal systems for the evaluation of defeasible arguments. Toulmin's argument diagram and its associated set of building blocks for argument analysis have been made precise and become refined, e.g., by distinguishing between kinds of argument attack. Not only is there now a wealth of studies of domain-bound, concrete forms of ar-

---

[15] Formally: using $W \rightsquigarrow (D \rightsquigarrow C)$, $R \rightsquigarrow \times (W \rightsquigarrow (D \rightsquigarrow C))$, two sentences expressing that W is a warrant and R a rebuttal blocking its application, respectively, as background, and then assuming W, and D, one finds a unique dialectical interpretation, in which C holds, whereas adding R to the assumptions leads to a unique dialectical interpretation in which C does not hold.

gumentation, also methods for their systematic investigation have been proposed. Defeasible argumentation has been embedded in procedural models of dialogue. Toulmin's wish to develop logic into a practical tool has found a modern guise in the form of argumentation-support software, aiming at argument analysis and production.

Notwithstanding recent progress, there is ample room for innovative research. Some possible directions of future research are the continuing systematisation and specification of argumentation schemes; the further organisation of the wealth of evaluation paradigms for defeasible argumentation ('semantics'); the prolongation of research aiming at practically useful software tools, especially when supported by user studies or commercial success; the implementation of software agents capable of argumentative behaviour; and the coupling of empirical work on reasoning and argumentation to the findings in AI.

Toulmin ends his introduction in a modest, but hopeful mood:

> The studies which follow are, as I have said, only essays. If our analysis of arguments is to be really effective and true-to-life it will need, very likely, to make use of notions and distinctions that are not even hinted at here. But of one thing I am confident: that by treating logic as generalised jurisprudence and testing our ideas against our actual practice of argument-assessment, rather than against a philosopher's ideal, we shall eventually build up a picture very different from the traditional one. The most I can hope for is that some of the pieces whose shape I have here outlined will keep a place in the finished mosaic. (10/10)

As evidenced by the research discussed in this chapter, the present state of the art in AI-inspired argumentation research shows that Toulmin's hope has been fulfilled.

Acknowledgements The author would like to thank David Hitchcock, Douglas Walton and James Freeman for comments on a prepublication version of this text.

References

1. K. D. Ashley. *Modeling legal argument. Reasoning with cases and hypotheticals.* The MIT Press, Cambridge (Massachusetts), 1990.
2. T. J. M. Bench-Capon. Persuasion in practical argument using value-based argumentation frameworks. *Journal of Logic and Computation*, 13(3):429–448, 2003.
3. P. M. Dung. On the acceptability of arguments and its fundamental role in nonmonotonic reasoning, logic programming and n-person games. *Artificial Intelligence*, 77:321–357, 1995.
4. E. T. Feteris. *Fundamentals of legal argumentation. A Survey of Theories on the Justification of Judicial Decisions.* Kluwer Academic Publishers, Dordrecht, 1999.
5. T. F. Gordon. *The Pleadings Game. An Artificial Intelligence Model of Procedural Justice.* Kluwer Academic Publishers, Dordrecht, 1995.
6. J. C. Hage. A theory of legal reasoning and a logic to match. *Artificial Intelligence and Law*, 4:199–273, 1996.
7. D. L. Hitchcock and B. Verheij, editors. *Arguing on the Toulmin Model. New Essays in Argument Analysis and Evaluation (Argumentation Library, Volume 10).* Springer-Verlag, Dordrecht, 2006.
8. P. A. Kirschner, S. J. Buckingham Shum, and C. S. Carr. *Visualizing Argumentation: Software Tools for Collaborative and Educational Sense-Making.* Springer-Verlag, London, 2002.

9. R. P. Loui. Hart's critics on defeasible concepts and ascriptivism. In *The Fifth International Conference on Artificial Intelligence and Law. Proceedings of the Conference*, pages 21–30. ACM, New York (New York), 1995.

10. R. P. Loui and J. Norman. Rationales and argument moves. *Artificial Intelligence and Law*, 3:159–189, 1995.

11. J. L. Pollock. Defeasible reasoning. *Cognitive Science*, 11:481–518, 1987.

12. J. L. Pollock. *Cognitive Carpentry: A Blueprint for How to Build a Person*. The MIT Press, Cambridge (Massachusetts), 1995.

13. H. Prakken and G. Sartor. A dialectical model of assessing conflicting arguments in legal reasoning. *Artificial Intelligence and Law*, 4:331–368, 1996.

14. C. Reed and G. Rowe. Araucaria: Software for argument analysis, diagramming and representation. *International Journal of AI Tools*, 13(4):961–980, 2004.

15. R. Reiter. A logic for default reasoning. *Artificial Intelligence*, 13:81–132, 1980.

16. S. J. Russell and P. Norvig. *Artificial Intelligence. A Modern Approach*. Prentice Hall, Upper Saddle River (New Jersey), 2003.

17. G. R. Simari and R. P. Loui. A mathematical treatment of defeasible reasoning and its applications. *Artificial Intelligence*, 53:125–157, 1992.

18. S. E. Toulmin. *The Uses of Argument*. Cambridge University Press, Cambridge, 1958.

19. S. E. Toulmin. *The Uses of Argument. Updated Edition*. Cambridge University Press, Cambridge, 2003.

20. S. E. Toulmin. Reasoning in theory and practice. In D. L. Hitchcock and B. Verheij, editors, *Arguing on the Toulmin Model. New Essays in Argument Analysis and Evaluation (Argumentation Library, Volume 10).*, pages 25–30. Springer-Verlag, Dordrecht, 2006.

21. F. H. van Eemeren, R. Grootendorst, S. Jackson, and S. Jacobs. *Reconstructing Argumentative Dialogue*. The University of Alabama Press, Tuscaloosa (Alabama), 1993.

22. F. H. van Eemeren, R. Grootendorst, and F. Snoeck Henkemans. *Fundamentals of Argumentation Theory. A Handbook of Historical Backgrounds and Contemporary Developments*. Lawrence Erlbaum Associates, Mahwah (New Jersey), 1996.

23. B. Verheij. DefLog: on the logical interpretation of prima facie justified assumptions. *Journal of Logic and Computation*, 13(3):319–346, 2003.

24. B. Verheij. Dialectical argumentation with argumentation schemes: An approach to legal logic. *Artificial Intelligence and Law*, 11(1-2):167–195, 2003.

25. B. Verheij. Evaluating arguments based on toulmin's scheme. *Argumentation*, 19(3):347–371, 2005.

26. B. Verheij. *Virtual arguments. On the design of argument assistants for lawyers and other arguers*. TMC Asser Press, The Hague, 2005.

27. B. Verheij. Argumentation support software: Boxes-and-arrows and beyond. *Law, Probability and Risk*, 6:187–208, 2007.

28. B. Verheij, J. C. Hage, and H. J. van den Herik. An integrated view on rules and principles. *Artificial Intelligence and Law*, 6(1):3–26, 1998.

29. G. A. W. Vreeswijk. *Studies in defeasible argumentation*. 1993.

30. G. A. W. Vreeswijk. Abstract argumentation systems. *Artificial Intelligence*, 90:225–279, 1997.

31. D. N. Walton. *Argument Schemes for Presumptive Reasoning*. Lawrence Erlbaum Associates, Mahwah (New Jersey), 1996.

32. D. N. Walton. *The New Dialectic: Conversational Contexts of Argument*. University of Toronto Press, Toronto, 1998.

33. D. N. Walton and E. Krabbe. *Commitment in Dialogue. Basic Concepts of Interpersonal Reasoning*. State University of New York Press, Albany (New York), 1995.

Chapter 12
Proof Burdens and Standards

Thomas F. Gordon and Douglas Walton

1 Introduction

This chapter explains the role of proof burdens and standards in argumentation, illustrates them using legal procedures, and surveys the history of research on computational models of these concepts. It also presents an original computational model which aims to integrate the features of these prior systems.

The 'mainstream' conception of argumentation in the field of artificial intelligence is monological [6] and relational [14]. Argumentation is viewed as taking place against the background of an inconsistent knowledge base, where the knowledge base is a set of propositions represented in some formal logic. Argumentation in this conception is a method for deducing warranted propositions from an inconsistent knowledge base. Which statements are warranted depends on attack relations among the arguments [10] which can be constructed from the knowledge base.

The notions of *proof standards* and *burden of proof* become relevant only when argumentation is viewed as a dialogical process for making *justified* decisions. The input to the process is an initial claim or issue. The goal of the process is to clarify and decide the issues, and produce a justification of the decision which can withstand a critical evaluation by a particular *audience*. The role of the audience could be played by the respondent or a neutral-third party, depending on the type of dialogue. The output of this process consists of: 1) a set of claims, 2) the decision to accept or reject each claim, 3) a theory of the generalizations of the domain and the facts of the particular case, and 4) a *proof* justifying the decision of each issue, showing how the decision is supported by the theory.

Notice that a theory or knowledge-base is part of the *output* of argumentation dialogues, not, as in the relational conception, its input. This is because, as has been

Thomas F. Gordon
Fraunhofer FOKUS, Berlin, Germany, e-mail: thomas.gordon@fokus.fraunhofer.de

Douglas Walton
University of Windsor, Windsor, Canada, e-mail: dwalton@uwindsor.ca

I. Rahwan, G. R. Simari (eds.), *Argumentation in Artificial Intelligence,*
DOI 10.1007/978-0-387-98197-0_12, ⓒ Springer Science+Business Media, LLC 2009

repeatedly recognized [31, 33, 21], the generalizations (rules) of some domain and the particular facts of a problem or case are dependent on one another and need to be constructed together, in an iterative process. For example, one of the founders of the field of computer science and law, Jon Bing, wrote in 1982:

> Legal reasoning is not primarily deductive, but rather a modeling process of shaping an understanding of the facts, based on evidence, and an interpretation of the legal sources, to a construct a theory for some legal conclusion. [7]

The concept of proof in argumentation is weaker than it is in mathematics. The proof need not demonstrate that a proposition is *necessarily* true, given a set of axioms assumed to be true. Rather, as in law, a proof in argumentation is a structure which demonstrates to a particular audience that a proposition statisfies its applicable proof standard. Since expressive logics are undecidable or intractable, the theory constructed during the dialogue cannot usually serve as a proof. A *burden of proof* is not discharged if the audience must solve a hard problem to construct the proof for themselves from the theory.

There are several kinds of proof burdens. The distinctions between them can only be understood with a deeper analysis of particular argumentation processes. There are many kinds of argumentation processes, each regulated by its own procedural rules, usually called 'protocols' in AI. Walton has developed a typology of dialogue types, classifying persuasion dialogues, negotiation, and deliberation, among other types [37].

For our purpose of illustrating different kinds of proof burdens, it is sufficient to use a simplified description of civil procedure, roughly based on the law of California [34]. A civil case begins by the plaintiff filing a *complaint*, stating a claim against the defendant. The complaint is the first step in the pleadings phase of the case. It contains, in addition to the claim, assertions about the facts of the case which the plaintiff contends are sufficient, if true, to prove the defendant has breached some obligation legally entitling the plaintiff to some remedy or compensation. The defendant then has several options for responding to the complaint. For the sake of brevity we will mention just one, filing an *answer* in which the factual allegations are each denied or conceded and asserting additional facts, called an *affirmative defense*, which may be useful for defeating or undercutting later arguments put forward by the plaintiff. The final step in the pleadings phase gives the plaintiff an opportunity to file a *reply* in which he concedes or denies the additional facts alleged by the defendant in his answer. The next phase of the process provides the parties various methods to *discover* evidence, for example by interviewing witnesses under oath, called *taking depositions*. At the *trial*, this evidence is presented to the judge, and possibly a jury, and further evidence is produced by examining and cross-examining witnesses during the trial. At the end of the trial, the evidence is passed on to the *trier-of-fact*, either the judge or the jury, if there is one. If there is a jury, the judge first instructs the jury about the relevant law, since the jury is only responsible for finding the facts. After the jury has completed its deliberations, it reports its *verdict* to the judge, who then enters his *judgment* upon the verdict. The judgment may be appealed by the losing party, but we will end our exposition of legal procedure here.

Our account of legal burdens of proof below is based in part on [30]. The first kind of burden of proof is called the *burden of claiming*. A person who feels he has a right to some legal remedy has the burden of initiating the proceeding by filing a complaint, which must allege facts sufficient to prove the *operative facts* of legal rules entitling him to some remedy. The second type of burden of proof is called the *burden of questioning* or contesting. During pleading, any allegations of fact by either party are implicitly conceded unless they are denied. The third type of burden is called the *burden of production*. It is the burden to discover and bring forward evidence supporting the contested factual allegations in the pleadings. The fourth type of burden of proof is the *burden of persuasion*. In a civil proceeding, this burden becomes operative only at the end of the trial, when the evidence and arguments are put to the jury to decided the factual issues. In a civil proceeding, the plaintiff has the burden of persuasion for all operative facts of his complaint and the defendant has the burden of persuasion for all affirmative defenses, i.e. exceptions. In criminal cases this is different. The prosecution has the burden of persuasion for all facts of the case, whether or not they are the operative facts of the elements of the alleged crime, or defenses, such as self-defense in a murder case. The fifth type of burden is called the *tactical burden of proof*. During the trial, arguments are put forward by both parties, pro and con the various claims at issue. At a finer level of granularity, the argumentation phase can be broken down conceptually into a sequence of stages, where each stage consists of all the arguments which have been put forward by both parties so far in the proceeding. The parties take turns putting forward arguments, by introducing new evidence. The next stage is constructed by adding the arguments put forward during this turn to all the previous arguments. The tactical burden arises from considering whether the arguments of a stage would be sufficient to meet the burden of persuasion with regard to some issue, if hypothetically the trial were to end at the stage and the issues where immediately put to the jury. The tactical burden of proof is the only burden of proof which, strictly speaking, can shift back and forth between the parties during the proceeding.

How does the burden of persuasion operate? Essentially the jury has the task of *weighing* the arguments pro and con each proposition at issue. If the pro arguments are not deemed to sufficiently outweigh the con arguments, then the jury must reject the alleged fact by deciding that the alleged fact is not true. Because of the way the burden of persuasion is allocated, this amounts to accepting the default truth value of the proposition at issue.

When do pro arguments 'sufficiently' outweigh con arguments to meet the burden of persuasion? This leads us to our final topic, *proof standards*. The question is how to aggregate or 'accrue' [24] arguments pro and con some claim. In the legal domain, four proof standards for factual issues exist, at least in common law jurisdictions. The *scintilla of evidence* proof standard is met if there is "any evidence at all in a case, even a *scintilla*, tending to support a material issue ..." [8, p. 1207] The *preponderance of evidence* proof standard is met by "evidence which as a whole shows that the fact sought to be proved ... is more credible and convincing to the mind." [8, p. 1064]. The *clear and convincing evidence* proof standard is the "measure or degree of proof which will produce in mind of trier of facts a firm belief or conviction as to allegations sought to be established; it is intermediate, being more than preponderance, but not to extent of such certainty as is required beyond reasonable doubt ... " [8, p. 227]. Finally, the *beyond reasonable doubt* standard is the strongest legal proof standard, applicable in criminal cases. It requires evidence which leaves the trier of fact "fully satisfied, entirely convinced, ... to a moral certainty" [8, p. 147].

In our view proof standards cannot and should not be interpreted probabilistically. The first and most important reason is that probability theory is applicable only if statistical knowledge about prior and conditional probabilities is available. Presuming the existence of such statistical information would defeat the whole purpose of argumentation about factual issues, which is to provide methods for making justified decisions when knowledge of the domain is lacking. Another argument against interpreting proof standards probabilistically is more technical. Arguments for and against some proposition are rarely independent. What is needed is some way to accrue arguments which does not depend on the assumption that the arguments or evidence are independent.

Prakken has identified three principles any formal account of accrual must satisfy [24]: 1) Combining several arguments pro or con some proposition can not only strengthen one's position, but also weaken it. 2) Once several arguments have been accrued, the individual arguments, considered separately, should have no impact on the acceptability of the proposition at issue, and 3) Finally, any argument which is 'flawed' may not take part in the aggregation process. The models of proof standards presented in the section are designed to respect these principals.

2 Formal Model

Our goal in this section is to define an abstract formal model of argumentation as a theory and proof construction process for making justified decisions. Inspired by Dung's model of abstract argumentation frameworks, the model shall be as abstract and simple as possible while being sufficient for capturing the distinctions between the various types of proof burdens and proof standards identified in the introduction and meeting other known requirements. It is not intended to be a comprehensive formal model of argumentation. We will also take care to abstract from the details of the legal domain and, in particular, the law of civil procedure.

We begin with the concept of an argument. Unlike Dung, we cannot leave this concept fully abstract, since our aim is to model burden of proof and proof standards. The proponent of an argument has the burden of production for its ordinary premises; while the respondent has the burden of production for any exceptions. Moreover, since the task of proof standards is to aggregate arguments pro and con some proposition at issue, the model must represent not only the premises of arguments, and distinctions between types of premises, but also their conclusions. These considerations lead us to the following definition of argument.

Definition 12.1 (argument). Let $\mathcal{L}$ be a propositional language. An **argument** is a tuple $\langle P, E, c \rangle$ where $P \subset \mathcal{L}$ are its **premises**, $E \subset \mathcal{L}$ are its **exceptions** and $c \in \mathcal{L}$

is its **conclusion**. For simplicity, c and all members of P and E must be literals, i.e. either an atomic proposition or a negated atomic proposition. Let p be a literal. If p is c, then the argument is an argument **pro** p. If p is the complement of c, then the argument is an argument **con** p.

Since all conclusions of arguments are literals according to this definition, the *axioms* of the theory constructed during argumentation consist only of literals. Other propositions of the theory can be derived from these axioms using the inference rules of classical logic and the argumentation schemes of the domain.

To model the distinctions between the various kinds of burden of proof, we must model argumentation as a process, consisting of several phases. It is sufficient to distinguish three phases, the opening, argumentation and closing phases of the process. Since typically argumentation takes place in dialogues, we will use the term 'dialogue' as the generic name for argumentation processes.

Definition 12.2 (dialogue). A **dialogue** is a tuple $\langle O, A, C \rangle$, where O, A and C, the **opening**, **argumentation**, and **closing** phases of the dialogue, respectively, are each sequences of **stages**. A stage is a tuple $\langle arguments, status \rangle$, where *arguments* is a set of arguments and *status* is a function mapping the conclusions of the arguments in *arguments* to their **dialectical status** in the stage, where the status is a member of $\{claimed, questioned\}$. In every chain of arguments, $a_1, \ldots a_n$, constructable from *arguments* by linking the conclusion of an argument to a premise of another argument, a conclusion of an argument a_i may not be a premise of an argument a_j, if $j < i$. A set of arguments which violates this condition is said to contain a *cycle* and a set of arguments which complies with this condition is called *cycle-free*.

Notice that the cycles defined here are not the same as cycles in a Dung argumentation framework. Whereas the links (arcs) between arguments in the directed graph induced by a Dung argumentation framework model the attack relation, the links in the directed graph induced by arguments in our system model the premise and conclusion relations. Notice that, in our system, arguments both pro and con some proposition can be included in a set of arguments without causing a cycle.

Constraining the arguments of a stage to be cycle-free is intended to simplify the evaluation of arguments. The set of arguments is intended to model the current state of the proof being constructed by the parties in the dialogue, not a 'pool of information' for constructing proofs. Intuitively, proofs should not contain cycles.

Next we need a structure for evaluating arguments, to assess the acceptability of propositions at issue. As in value-based argumentation frameworks [4, 5] arguments are evaluated with respect to an *audience*, such as the trier-of-fact (judge or jury) in legal trials.

Definition 12.3 (audience). An *audience* is a structure $\langle assumptions, weight \rangle$, where *assumptions* $\subset \mathcal{L}$ is a consistent set of literals assumed to be acceptable by the audience and *weight* is a partial function mapping arguments to real numbers in the range $0.0 \ldots 1.0$, representing the relative weights assigned by the audience to the arguments.

Whereas in value-based argumentation frameworks the audience is defined by a partial-order on a set of values, which is then used to constrain the attack relation on arguments in a Dung argumentation framework, the audience in our system models the relative strength of arguments for this audience. Intuitively, a stronger argument does not necessarily attack a weaker argument. Both arguments could be arguments pro the same proposition, for example. Thus, these two conceptions of an audience are not directly comparable.

An argument evaluation structure associates an audience with a stage of dialogue and assigns proof standards to propositions, providing a basis for evaluating the acceptability of propositions to this audience.

Definition 12.4 (argument evaluation structure). An **argument evaluation structure** is a tuple $\langle stage, audience, standard \rangle$, where *stage* is a stage in a dialogue, *audience* is an audience and *standard* is a total function mapping propositions in $\mathcal{L}$ to their applicable proof standards in the dialogue. A **proof standard** is a function mapping tuples of the form $\langle issue, stage, audience \rangle$ to the Boolean values *true* and *false*, where *issue* is a proposition in $\mathcal{L}$, *stage* is a stage and *audience* is an audience.

Given an argument evaluation structure, the acceptability of a proposition can be defined as follows.

Definition 12.5 (acceptability). A literal p is **acceptable** in an argument evaluation structure $\langle stage, audience, standard \rangle$ if and only if $standard(p, stage, audience)$ is *true*.

The argument evaluation structure is the component of this formal model which is most like a Dung abstract argumentation framework. The role of the attack relation in abstract argumentation frameworks is played by competing pro and con arguments aggregated by proof standards, using the relative weights assigned the arguments by an audience.

Obviously much of the work of argument evaluation has been delegated to the proof standards. We cannot say anything about the computational properties of acceptability in an argument evaluation structure until these standards have been defined. All the proof standards make use of the concept of argument applicability, so let us define this concept first.

Definition 12.6 (argument applicability). Let $\langle stage, audience, standard \rangle$ be an argument evaluation structure. An argument $\langle P, E, c \rangle$ is **applicable** in this argument evaluation structure if and only if

- the argument is a member of the arguments of the *stage*,
- every proposition $p \in P$, the premises, is an assumption of the *audience* or, if neither p nor $\overline{p}$ is an assumption, is acceptable in the argument evaluation structure and
- no proposition $p \in E$, the exceptions, is an assumption of the *audience* or, if neither p nor $\overline{p}$ is an assumption, is acceptable in the argument evaluation structure.

Now we are ready to define the proof standards, beginning with scintilla of the evidence. A proposition satisfies the scintilla standard, in our model, if it is supported by at least one applicable pro argument.

Definition 12.7 (scintilla of evidence). Let $\langle stage, audience, standard \rangle$ be an argument evaluation structure and let p be a literal in $\mathcal{L}$. $scintilla(p, stage, audience) = true$ if and only if there is at least one applicable argument pro p in $stage$.

Scintilla is the weakest of the proof standards we will define and is the only one which can be met by complementary literals in the same argument evaluation structure. That is, if p is an atomic proposition, both p and $\neg p$ can be acceptable in an argument evaluation structure using the scintilla of evidence standard. This would be the case if p has an applicable con argument, as well as an applicable pro argument.

Let us now turn our attention to the three most important legal proof standards: preponderance of the evidence, clear and convincing evidence and beyond reasonable doubt. Intuitively, preponderance is satisfied if the pro arguments outweigh the con arguments, by however much. The issue we have to face when formalizing preponderance is how to aggregate the weights of a set of arguments for the purpose of this comparison. The clear and convincing evidence standard requires more proof than the preponderance standard: not only must the pro arguments outweigh the con arguments, the weight of the pro arguments and the difference in weight of the pro and con arguments both must exceed some thresholds. Finally, the beyond a reasonable doubt standard goes further. Not only must the arguments be clear and convincing, but, as the name of the standard suggests, the weight of the con arguments must be below the threshold of 'reasonable doubt'.

Definition 12.8 (preponderance of the evidence). Let $\langle stage, audience, standard \rangle$ be an argument evaluation structure and let p be a literal in $\mathcal{L}$. $preponderance$ $(p, stage, audience) = true$ if and only if

- there is at least one applicable argument pro p in $stage$ and
- the maximum weight assigned by the audience to the applicable arguments pro p is greater than the maximum weight of the applicable arguments con p.

The preponderance of the evidence standard was called the *best argument* standard in [18].

Definition 12.9 (clear and convincing evidence). Let $\langle stage, audience, standard \rangle$ be an argument evaluation structure and let p be a literal in $\mathcal{L}$. $clear\text{-}and\text{-}convincing$ $(p, stage, audience) = true$ if and only if

- the preponderance of the evidence standard is met,
- the maximum weight of the applicable pro arguments exceeds some threshold α, and
- the difference between the maximum weight of the applicable pro arguments and the maximum weight of the applicable con arguments exceeds some threshold β.

Definition 12.10 (beyond reasonable doubt). Let $\langle stage, audience, standard \rangle$ be an argument evaluation structure $\langle stage, audience, standard \rangle$ and let p be a literal in $\mathcal{L}$. beyond-reasonable-doubt($p, stage, audience$) = $true$ if and only if

- the clear and convincing evidence standard is met and
- the maximum weight of the applicable con arguments is less than some threshold γ.

We assume the α, β and γ thresholds used by the clear and convincing evidence and beyond a reasonable doubt standards are set by the applicable protocol of the dialogue.

At first glance, using maximum weights to aggregate pro and con arguments might seem unintuitive. One might be inclined to compare the *sums* of the weights of the applicable pro and con arguments. However, since arguments cannot be assumed to be independent, summing weights would risk taking the same information or reasons into account multiple times. When several weak arguments can be combined to make a stronger argument, this can be achieved by joining their premises together into a single argument, as discussed further next. We leave it up to the audience to judge the effect of any possible interdependencies among the premises on the weight of the argument. Both alternatives, summing weights or taking their maximum weight, have the property of taking all arguments into account.

Assuming arguments are stated in their strongest form, aggregating arguments using their maximum weight satisfies all three of Prakken's principles of accrual [24]: 1) Aggregated arguments can be evaluated by the audience to be stronger or weaker than the arguments considered separately; 2) Once several arguments have been accrued, the individual arguments, considered separately, have no effect on the acceptability of the proposition at issue; and 3) Any argument which is 'flawed' does not take part in the aggregation process.

By 'stating arguments in their strongest form' we mean the following. Let p and q be two propositions which, when they are true, are evidence pro a third proposition, r. This can be expressed as either two *convergent* arguments or as a *linked* argument [38]. The convergent arguments would be:

a_1: r since p.
a_2: r since q.

The linked form of this argument 'accrues' p and q into a single argument:

a_3: r since p and q.

If the linked argument, a_3, is more persuasive, that is if the party putting forward this argument estimates it would be given more weight by the audience than either a_1 or a_2, then we assume a_3 will be put forward.

To illustrate this more concretely, let's return to Prakken's example about jogging when it is both hot and rainy. The strongest arguments con jogging are the convergent arguments:

a_4:   not jogging since hot.

a_5:   not jogging since rainy.

The strongest argument pro jogging is the following linked argument:

a_6:   jogging since hot and rainy.

Returning to Prakken's three principles of accrual: 1) The audience can decide whether to give a_6 greater or lesser weight than each of the arguments a_4 and a_5; 2) If the accrued argument, a_6, is given greater weight, then a_6 will defeat both a_4 and a_5, rendering them ineffective, using any of the proofs standards which aggregate arguments by weight; and 3) Inapplicable arguments are not be taken into consideration using any proof standard.

In [18] one further proof standard was defined, called *dialectical validity*. For the sake of completeness we include its definitions here.

Definition 12.11 (dialectical validity). Let $\langle stage, audience, standard \rangle$ be an argument evaluation structure $\langle stage, audience, standard \rangle$ and let p be a literal in $\mathcal{L}$. *dialectical-validity*$(p, stage, audience,) = true$ if and only if there is at least one applicable argument pro p in *stage* and no argument con p in *stage* is applicable.

The dialectical validity standard is suitable for aggregating arguments from general rules and exceptions, where any applicable exception is enough to override the general rule.

One of the requirements identified in the introduction is that checking proofs should be an easy task. In more computational terms, using our formal model, the issue is whether the acceptability of a proposition in an argument evaluation structure is tractably decidable. We conjecture that this is the case, but will not try to prove this formally here. The reasons for this conjecture are many. The argument evaluation structure has been designed in part to achieve this goal, by making several restrictions: 1) The language is propositional, not first-order; 2) premises, exceptions and conclusions of arguments must be literals; and 3) the set of arguments of a stage is finite and, by definition, acyclic. Of course the computational complexity of acceptability also depends on the complexity of the proof standards applied.

Now we are ready to turn to modeling the various kinds of burden of proof. The burdens of claiming and questioning must be met during the opening phase of the dialogue. The burden of production and the tactical burden of proof are relevant only during the argumentation phase. Finally, the burden of persuasion comes into play in the closing phase, but is also used hypothetically to estimate the tactical burden of proof during the argumentation phase.

The purpose of the opening stage of a dialogue is to frame the issues. Arguments put forward in the argumentation stage must be relevant to the issues raised in the opening stage. Depending on the protocol of the dialogue, a proposition claimed in the opening stage may be deemed conceded unless it is questioned, requiring the audience to assume it is true, following the principal of "silence implies consent."

Definition 12.12 (burdens of claiming and questioning). Let $s_1, \ldots, s_n$ be the stages of the opening phase of a dialogue. Let $\langle arguments_n, status_n \rangle$ be the last stage,

s_n, of the opening phase. A party has met the **burden of claiming** a proposition p if and only if $status_n(p) \in \{claimed, questioned\}$, that is, if and only if $status_n(p)$ is defined. The **burden of questioning** a proposition p has been met if and only if $status_n(p) = questioned$.

Notice that a questioned proposition satisfies the burden of claiming, since it is assumed that only propositions which have been claimed in an earlier stage are questioned.

This simple model defines only minimal requirements for raising issues in the opening phase of a dialogue. The argumentation protocol of a dialogue may state additional requirements. For example, according to the law of civil procedure in California, the plaintiff must state a *cause of action*: the facts claimed must be sufficient to give the plaintiff a right to judicial relief, as a matter of law.

The burden of production is relevant only during the argumentation phase of a dialogue. The burden of production for some proposition is satisfied if it is acceptable at the end of the argumentation phase using the the weakest proof standard, scintilla of the evidence. The party who puts forward an argument has the burden of production for its premises. Similarly, the respondent to an argument has the burden of production for each exception.

The audience used to assess the burden of production depends on the protocol of the particular dialogue. In civil proceedings in California, the judge is the audience during the argumentation phase, i.e. the trial.

Definition 12.13 (burden of production). Let $s_1, \ldots, s_n$ be the stages of the argumentation phase of a dialogue. Let $\langle arguments_n, status_n \rangle$ be the last stage, s_n, of the argumentation phase. Let *audience* be the relevant audience for assessing the burden of production, depending on the protocol of the dialogue. Let *AES* be the argument evaluation structure $\langle s_n, audience, standard \rangle$, where *standard* is a function mapping every proposition to the scintilla of evidence proof standard. The **burden of production** for a proposition p has been met if and only if p is acceptable in *AES*.

Even though the weakest proof standard, scintillia of the evidence, is used to test whether the burden of production has been met, an arbitrary, or silly, argument would not be sufficient, since only applicable arguments are taken into consideration by all proof standards. A silly argument can be defeated by questioning or attacking its premises. Arguments can be undercut in our system by first revealing, if necessary, an implicit premise about the applicability of the warrant underlying the argument to this case and then attacking this premise [18].

Since arguments put forward to met the burden of production can be defeated by further arguments, the burden of production may be met at some stage, s_i, of a dialogue, but not met at some later stage, s_j, where $j > i$. If the burden of production is not met at the end of the argumentation phase, the audience in the closing phase may be required, depending on the dialogue type, to assume that the proposition is false. In this case, the burden of persuasion for this proposition becomes irrelevant.

The burden of persuasion plays a role only in the closing phase of the dialogue. The burden of persuasion is met only if at the end of the closing phase the proposition at issue is acceptable to the audience. The way proof standards are assigned to propositions depends on the type of dialogue and is regulated by the argumentation protocol. In legal proceedings in California, the proof standards are assigned by the judge, since this is a question of law, not fact. In civil proceedings, the usual proof standard is preponderance of the evidence. In criminal proceedings, the proof standard is beyond reasonable doubt.

Definition 12.14 (burden of persuasion). Let $s_1, \ldots, s_n$ be the stages of the closing phase of a dialogue. Let $\langle arguments_n, status_n \rangle$ be the last stage, s_n, of the closing phase. Let *audience* be the relevant audience for assessing the burden of persuasion, depending on the dialogue type and its protocol. Let *AES* be the argument evaluation structure $\langle s_n, audience, standard \rangle$, where *standard* is a function mapping every proposition to its applicable proof standard for this type of dialogue. The **burden of persuasion** for a proposition p has been met if and only if p is acceptable in *AES*.

In some cases, the party which has the burden of production in the argumentation phase may not have the burden of persuasion in the closing phase. This is the case, for example, in criminal law proceedings. The defendant, as usual, has the burden of production for exceptions, such as self-defense in murder cases, but once this burden has been met, the burden of persuasion is passed to the prosecution. If any evidence of self-defense has been brought forward, satisfying the burden of production, the prosecution has the burden of persuading the trier of fact, beyond a reasonable doubt, that the defendant did not act in self-defense.

This can be achieved in our model by making the exception an ordinary premise after the burden of production has been met in the argumentation phase. For example, let $\langle P, E, c \rangle$ be an argument and e be a proposition in E, meaning "self defense". After the burden of production for e has been met, the other side can be given the burden of persuasion by removing e from E and adding $\neg e$ to P. It may seem odd to modify the argument in this way, but keep in mind the arguments of a stage do not represent the speech acts of the parties, but rather the state of the proof being constructed collaboratively by all parties, according the protocol of the dialogue type. The stage must be modified in some way to reflect this change, and modifying the arguments of the stage is one way to accomplish this.

One kind of burden of proof remains to be defined formally, the tactical burden of proof. The tactical burden is the only one which can shift back and forth between the parties. It is relevant only during the argumentation phase of the dialogue. We defined the burden of persuasion first, even though it is applicable only in the later closing stage, because the tactical burden of proof requires the burden of persuasion to be estimated. At each stage of the argumentation phase, a party must decide whether stronger arguments might be necessary to persuade the audience. In some dialogue types, the audience may reveal its assumptions and evaluations (weight assignments) during the argumentation phase, at least provisionally. This will be the case, for example, in two-party dialogues where the audience to be persuaded is the same as the respondent. In legal proceedings this is not the case, since the respondent is the defendant and the audience is the judge or jury. In such cases it will be necessary to make assumptions about the audience.

Definition 12.15 (tactical burden of proof). Let $s_1, \ldots, s_n$ be the stages of the argumentation phase of a dialogue. Assume *audience* is the audience which will assess the burden of persuasion in the closing phase. Assume *standard* is the function which will be used in the closing phase to assign a proof standard to each proposition. For each stage s_i in $s_1, \ldots, s_n$, let AES_i be the argument evaluation structure $\langle s_i, audience, standard \rangle$. The **tactical burden of proof** for a proposition p is met at stage s_i if and only if p is acceptable in AES_i.

Both sides in a dialogue can have a tactical burden. Intuitively, a party has a tactical burden of proof for a proposition p at some stage s_i only if p is not acceptable in s_i and the party has an interest in proving p, either because proving p is relevant for proving some claim of the party or disproving some claim of the other party, given the arguments which have been put forward. A fuller, more complete account of the tactical burden of proof would require the parties, their claims and the concept of relevance to be modeled.

This completes our formal model of proof standards and burden of proof. Again, we do not claim this is a comprehensive dialogical model of argumentation. Many important elements of argumentation have been abstracted out for the sake of brevity, such as the parties, argumentation schemes and their critical questions, dialogue types, argumentation protocols and commitment stores. Our aim here was to define the simplest, most abstract possible model which is sufficient for distinguishing the various kinds of proof standards and burdens of proof which have been discussed in the computational models of argument literature. Of course, we cannot prove that we have achieved this goal. We leave it up to others in the field to try to develop a simpler model with this scope.

In the introduction we formulated our view of argumentation as a kind of process for making justified decisions, where the input to the process is an initial claim or issue and the output consists of a set of claims, the decision to accept or reject each claim, a theory and a proof. Unlike assumption-based instantiations of Dung's model of abstract argumentation frameworks [9], in which a theory or knowledge base is presumed as part of the input, in our model a theory and a proof are constructed together during argumentation and are part of the output. The theory constructed is the deductive closure, in classical propositional logic, of the set of all propositions which have been assumed by the audience or, if neither the proposition or its complement has been assumed, are acceptable in the final stage of the closing phase of the dialogue. The proof constructed is represented by the argument evaluation structure of the final stage.

3 Survey of Prior Research

Early work in the field of Artificial Intelligence and Law recognized the utility of defeasible rules, subject to exceptions, as a tool for allocating the burden of proof and developed nonmonotonic logics for reasoning with such rules [13, 35]. But different proof standards or kinds of proof burdens were not yet distinguished in these models.

In the Pleadings Game [14], inspired by legal proceedings, argumentation was modeled as dialogical process consisting of several phases, in which theories and arguments are constructed dynamically by the parties during the process. The Pleadings Game modeled the burdens of claiming, questioning and production, but it did not explicitly use this terminology. Proof standards and the burden of persuasion, were not modeled, as they do not play a role in the opening phase.

To our knowledge, the first effort to develop a computational model of proof standards was by Freeman and Farley in 1996 [12]. They modeled argumentation as a dialectical process during which an acyclic argument graph is constructed by putting forward pro and con arguments constructed ('invented') from a propositional rule-base. The model of proof standards comes into play when evaluating the arguments in the graph. An argument is *defendable* if each premise satisfies its proof standard. Five proof standards were defined (scintilla of evidence, preponderance, dialectical validity, beyond a reasonable doubt and beyond a doubt). The relative weights of arguments were not assigned by an audience, but rather computed from certainty factors assigned to premises and the kind of argumentation scheme used to construct the argument, using the weakest premise principle [32]. The model of argumentation developed in this paper has borrowed much from Freeman and Farley, but there are some important differences. By restricting the arguments which can be put forward to those which can be constructed from a static rule-base and model of the facts, provided as input to the dialectical process, Freeman and Farley's model is more of a relational model of argumentation than a theory construction model. The relative strength of arguments is determined by the rules and facts, rather than by the intersubjective judgment of an audience. Only the burden of persuasion has been modeled by this work. Finally, no attempt was made to model proof burdens other than the burden of persuasion in this work.

The Zeno system [17] was inspired by Freeman and Farley's work. Zeno's model of the structure of argument graphs was based on Kunz and Rittel's [22] concept of issue-based information systems (IBIS). Zeno supported arguments about both factual issues and issues about which action to take to solve some problem or achieve some goal (practical reasoning). For factual issues, three proof standards were modeled (scintilla of evidence, preponderance of the evidence and beyond reasonable doubt). For issues about actions, two further proof standards were provided (no better alternative and best choice). The relative strength of arguments in Zeno was computed from qualitative constraints (equations and inequalities) over propositions. The qualitative constraints were issues which could be argued about. Only the burden of persuasion was modeled in Zeno. As in Freeman and Farley's work, Zeno did not explicitly model an audience. On the contrary, in Zeno it was assumed the parties would argue about the evaluation of their own arguments, by putting forward and arguing about constraints.

Prakken formulated the three principles of argument accrual [24] explained in the introduction, which our model has been designed to satisfy. He compared automatic and manual approaches to accrual. In the manual approach, arguments are accrued by changing their representation in the model. In the automatic approach, arguments are accrued by the argument evaluation process, without having to modify the representation of the arguments. Prakken illustrated this approach with a novel system, using a rule-based instantiation of Dung's model of an abstract argumentation framework, in which the conclusions of rules are labeled with the set of their premises. The attack relation of the argumentation framework is defined so that an argument A does not attack an argument B if the set of premises of the conclusion of the argument A is a subset of the (accrued) set of premises of the argument B. This leads to a bottom-up inference process which, Prakken notes, is similar to Reason-Based Logic [20]: first all arguments pro and con some leaf proposition are combined into two competing sets of accruals; next the conflict between these accruals is resolved; and finally the process iterates moving up the tree, with only the winning defeasible conclusion being used. The way arguments are evaluated in our model has much in common with the bottom-up inference approach taken by both Reason-Based Logic and Prakken's system. Nonetheless, our approach to the accrual problem is manual, not automatic, as responsibility for accruing arguments is allocated to the parties who put them forward in dialogues. But unlike Bayesian Networks, which require a complete conditional probabilities table to be provided as input to the process, our approach does not require all possible arguments to be formulated. Accruing arguments when possible to strengthen one's case is part of the burden of proof allocated to the parties. Prakken points out that there is a trade-off between automatic and manual approaches to accrual: in the former unwanted inferences must be expressly blocked while in the latter accruals must be expressly formulated. So neither approach is clearly superior.

In 2006, Prakken and Sartor published the first formal account of the distinctions between the burden of production, the burden of persuasion and the tactical burden of proof [28]. Their model is based on an interpretation of presumptions as default rules, formalized using an extended version of their Inference System (IS) defeasible logic [27], called the Litigation Inference System (LIS) [23], which includes as part of the input, together with the defeasible rules, an assignment of the burden of persuasion for literals to either the plaintiff or defendant in the proceeding. Prakken and Sartor's model of the distinctions between these three proof burdens is more concrete than our model, as it is limited to arguments constructed from defeasible rules. Our model abstracts away the process of constructing arguments and can be instantiated with models of various argumentation schemes, for example for arguments from cases as well as defeasible rules.[1] Prakken and Sartor did not attempt to model the burdens of claiming or questioning or support the use of various proof standards.

Continuing work began with Reed and Walton in 2005 on dialogues about the burden of proof [26], Prakken and Sartor in 2007 presented a model of arguments about the allocation of the burden of persuasion [29]. They note that 'the argumen-

---

[1] We have done some research recently on constructing arguments automatically from formal models of ontologies, rules, and cases, in a way which is well integrated with the model of argument presented here [16].

tation games we define in this paper are not intended as a model of actual legal dialogue but as a proof theory for a nonmonotonic logic. ... All we claim is that our games draw the correct defeasible inferences from a given body of information and an associated allocation of the burden of persuasion. It remains to be seen how the present logical model can be integrated with dialogical and procedural models of legal argument". Clearly, their work is a relational model of argumentation, not a theory construction model. In their conclusion, Prakken and Sartor express concern that their system "lacks an extension-based semantics in the style of [10]" and note, citing [23], that this "raises questions about the adequacy of 'mainstream' nonmonotonic logics for representing legal reasoning".[2]

The idea of using audiences in our model was inspired by work by Bench-Capon, Doutre and Dunne [5]. Bench-Capon's focus is on modeling practical reasoning, i.e. the process of making decisions about which action to take in order to achieve goals which promote an agent's values. Since different agents can have different values, as well as different priority orderings on their set of values, arguments about action can only be evaluated against the values of a particular agent, or 'audience'. Bench-Capon contrasted practical reasoning with argumentation about "what is true in a situation", i.e. the facts of a case, and appears to consider audiences to be relevant only for the former. As illustrated by legal trials, however, audiences can be important in argumentation dialogues about factual issues as well, since different persons will judge the probative weight of evidence, such as witness testimony, differently. Our model of an audience is more abstract, since it orders arguments by their strength, regardless of the kind of argumentation scheme which has been applied to construct the argument. Formally, Bench-Capon's model is an extension of Dung's concept of an abstract argumentation framework. Although a formal dialogue game is defined, the game serves as a proof theory for a relational model of argument. The input to the system is a Value-Based Argumentation Framework (VAF) consisting of a set of arguments, an attack relation over these arguments, a set of values, and a mapping from arguments to values. An audience is defined to be a binary relation over these values, modeling the preference ordering over these values of the audience. The output of the dialogue game is the set of arguments which are objectively or subjectively acceptable. Arguments which are objectively acceptable are, or should be, acceptable by all (rational) audiences. Conversely, arguments which are subjectively acceptable are acceptable to a particular, given audience. Bench-Capon compares the distinction between objective and subjective acceptability with the concept of credulous and skeptical inference familiar from nonmonotonic logic and Dung argumentation frameworks. The distinction between objective and subjective acceptability, like the distinction between credulous and skeptical inference, possibly can be viewed as a simple two-level model of proof standards, but it is questionable that this distinction is of much use outside of the procedural context of dialogues in which the allocation of the burden of proof matters, and such dialogues were outside the scope of this work.

---

[2] But see [36] for a defense of nonmonotonic logic for legal reasoning, even when the burden of persuasion is divided among the parties.

Atkinson and Bench-Capon recently modeled a variety of proof standards using Dung-style argumentation frameworks [2]. This paper also recognizes the need for audiences in dialogues about factual issues, as well as teleological issues about values promoted by alternative courses of action. The basic idea of this paper elaborates on the idea discussed above, of using the distinction between various kinds of acceptability in Dung argumentation frameworks to define proof standards. The scintilla of evidence standard is modeled as membership in some preferred extension (credulous acceptability). Preponderance of the evidence corresponds to membership in all preferred extensions (skeptical acceptability). And, finally, beyond reasonable doubt corresponds to membership in the grounded extension, if there is one. Ways of modeling proof standards between preponderance of the evidence and beyond reasonable doubt, such as the clear and convincing evidence standard, are proposed which make use of an assignment of 'probabilities', i.e. weights, to arguments. However this idea is discarded with the argument that this information is not usually available. In our model this information is provided by the intersubjective judgment of the audience. Later in their paper, Atkinson and Bench-Capon suggest the use of audiences to derive preferences over arguments, starting with Bench-Capon's value-based argumentation frameworks for arguing about teleological issues. This idea is extended to arguments about factual issues by ordering evidence, for example by ordering witness testimony using information about witness credibility.

An advantage of Bench-Capon and Atkinson's line of research is that it elaborates rationality constraints on an audience's assignment of strengths to arguments, using for example its value preferences or its assessment of the relative credibility of witnesses. Although our model leaves the weights assigned by audiences to arguments completely unconstrained, it has the advantage of being more general, applying to arguments from any argumentation scheme. Perhaps it is possible to combine the benefits of these two approaches. This may be an interesting topic for future research.

A disadvantage of modeling proof standards using Dung argumentation frameworks is the computational complexity of testing whether the proof standard has been met. We have argued that, intuitively, to satisfy a burden of proof, the party with the burden must present the proof in a form which is easy to check. The other party shouldn't have to solve an undecidable or intractable problem to check the proof. As discussed previously, in Section 2, this criterion could be satisfied for the proposed scintilla of evidence proof standard, modeled as credulous acceptability, by requiring the proponent to produce an admissible set of arguments. The admissible set could serve as a representation of the proof, since checking whether the set is admissible and whether an argument is a member of this set are both tractable problems. But it is not clear what structures could serve as proofs for the models proposed by Atkinson and Bench-Capon for the stricter proof standards. A related issue is whether or not such proofs could be presented in a form which is comprehensible to human users, using for example some kind of argument mapping or other visualization technique. Existing argument mapping methods have been developed for presenting proofs (argument graphs) of the kind we have presented in this paper

[3, 11, 1, 15]. While Dung argumentation frameworks are often displayed as graphs, these graphs do not represent proofs of the acceptability of any of the arguments in the graph.

Prakken recently published a formal model which explicates the role of judges in deciding issues regarding the admissibility of evidence and the allocation of the burdens of production and persuasion [25]. Interestingly, dialogues are divided into two, rather than tree phases, in the model, called the *pleadings phase* and the *decision phase*. The pleadings phases encompasses the opening and argumentation phases of our model. The decision phase corresponds to our closing phase. The judge plays a role in the decision phase comparable to the audience in the closing phase of our model, but arguments are evaluated by having the judge put forward further arguments, which are then evaluated using Prakken's LIS nonmonotonic logic [23], discussed above. Arguments are not weighed and proof standards are not part of the model.

Prakken and Sartor's chapter on a "Logical Analysis of Burdens of Proof" in [30] highly influenced our model of the distinctions among the various kinds of proof burdens. The main difference between our systems is that they use Dung's abstract argumentation framework to evaluate the arguments at each stage of the dialogue. We have already expressed our reservations about this approach, which does not take into consideration that a burden of proof entails an obligation to put forward the proof in a form which can be tractably checked. In their conclusion they point out that their use of a nonmonotonic logic for evaluating arguments in a stage could be replaced by any formalism "which accepts as input a description of an evidential problem and produces as output a fallible assessment whether a claim has been proven". This is one way looking at we have done here, by replacing their nonmonotonic logic with a structure designed to make argument evaluation tractable for a variety of common proof standards. Proof standards are not given much attention in their chapter, except to suggest that they could be handled using some mechanism for ordering arguments by their strength. Finally, although they recognize the role of the finder-of-fact, they did not explictly model audiences or their impact on assessing proof burdens. For example, the evalution of the tactical burden of proof in their model does not require a party to estimate an audience's assessment of the weight of arguments. Rather, this information appears to be assumed as input to the dialogue, available as common knowledge to both parties.

The model of argumentation developed in this paper is most closely related to the Carneades system, which consists of both a mathematical model of argumentation and software tools for supporting argumentation tasks based on this model.[3] Carneades is work in progress and thus prior publications about the system differ in their details. For example, the version of the model in [19] gave the term 'presumption' a technical meaning which is confusing for those familar with the concept of a presumption in the legal domain. This was pointed out by Prakken and Sartor [28] and corrected when Prakken joined us for the next version of Carneades [18]. Similarly, the use of weights to order arguments in [19] was replaced by a partial order in

---

[3] http://carneades.berlios.de

[18], but now we have come full circle, by again using numeric weights. The initial models of the preponderance of the evidence and beyond reasonable doubt proof standards of [19] were removed from the [18] version, since we had our doubts about their adequacy as models of these legal standards. We feel confident enough about the models of these legal standards in this paper to want to publish them in order to obtain critical feedback. Aside from improved models of various proof standards, the main contribution of the new version presented here is that it more clearly and explicitly models argumentation as a theory and argument construction process, consisting of a sequence of stages divided into opening, argumentation and closing phases. Although we had already suggested in [18] how to use Carneades to model the distinction between the burden of production and the burden of persuasion, the version in this article models these distinctions more explicitly and extends the model to cover the burdens of claiming and questioning in the opening phase and the tactical burden of proof. This version also introduces an explicit model of audiences. Previous versions had used the concept of an argumentation *context* to model argument strengths or priorities, with no reference to an audience.

4 Concluding Remarks

Viewing argumentation as dialogical process for making justified decisions raises a number of issues which have no place in relational, monological accounts of argumentation, proof burdens and standards among them. Thus it should come as no surprise that the concept of *proof* has thus far received little attention in mainstream accounts of argumentation in artificial intelligence. An argument may be acceptable in a Dung-style argumentation framework, or a proposition may be warranted by a default theory in some nonmonotonic logic, but what mathematical structures are adequate as models of proofs of these or other inference relations? We have argued that checking a proof should be an easy, tractable problem. Argumentation frameworks and default theories do not, in general, meet this requirement. And other, less computational requirements could also be formulated, such as transparency and comprehensibility for the intended class of audiences.

Another distinction between relational and dialogical conceptions of argumentation concerns their input/out relations. Whereas in relational accounts an argumentation framework or default theory is provided as input and the task is to derive acceptable arguments or warranted propositions, argumentation dialogues begin with a claim or issue and construct, as part of their output, theories and proofs. Argumentation dialogues includes synthetic as well as analytic tasks.

Abstract argumentation frameworks, which focus on attack relations among arguments, are not well-suited to modeling proof standards, at least not the familiar proof standards from the legal domain. The intuitive idea of legal proof standards since Roman times, symbolized by the scales of the goddess Justitia, involves the weighing of arguments or evidence pro and con some claim. This simple idea cannot be directly represented using abstract argumentation frameworks. Attempts to model proof standards as variations of credulous and skeptical acceptability in an argumentation framework are not very promising, since they largely leave open the question of how to represent proofs in an understandable form which can be easily checked.

Research to date on modeling proof standards and burdens calls into question the common research strategy in the field of computational models of argumentation which presumes that valid dialogical models of argumentation as a process can be constructed on the foundation of relational models of argument as a nonmonotonic inference relation. We recommend a research strategy which begins with a task and requirements analysis of argumentation dialogues in a variety of application domains.

Acknowledgements We'd like to thank Trevor Bench-Capon and Henry Prakken for their helpful comments on various drafts of this article.

References

1. T. Anderson, D. Schum, and W. Twining. *Analysis of Evidence*. Cambridge University Press, 2nd edition, 2005.
2. K. Atkinson and T. Bench-Capon. Argumentation and standards of proof. In *ICAIL '07: Proceedings of the 11th International Conference on Artificial Intelligence and Law*, pages 107–116, New York, NY, USA, 2007. ACM.
3. M. C. Beardsley. *Practical Logic*. Prentice Hall, New York, 1950.
4. T. Bench-Capon. Persuasion in practical argument using value-based argumentation frameworks. *Journal of Logic and Computation*, 13(3):429–448, 2003.
5. T. J. Bench-Capon, S. Doutre, and P. E. Dunne. Audiences in argumentation frameworks. *Artificial Intelligence*, 171(42-71), 2007.
6. P. Besnard and A. Hunter. *Elements of Argumentation*. MIT Press, 2008.
7. J. Bing. Uncertainty, decisions and information systems. In C. Ciampi, editor, *Artificial Intelligence and Legal Information Systems*. North-Holland, 1982.
8. H. C. Black. *Black's Law Dictionary*. West Publishing Co., 1979.
9. A. Bondarenko, P. M. Dung, R. A. Kowalski, and F. Toni. An abstract, argumentation-theoretic approach to default reasoning. *Artificial Intelligence*, 93(1-2):63–101, 1997.
10. P. M. Dung. On the acceptability of arguments and its fundamental role in nonmonotonic reasoning, logic programming and n-person games. *Artificial Intelligence*, 77(2):321–357, 1995.
11. J. B. Freeman. *Dialectics and the Macrostructure of Arguments: A Theory of Argument Structure*. Walter de Gruyter, Berlin / New York, 1991.
12. K. Freeman and A. M. Farley. A model of argumentation and its application to legal reasoning. *Artificial Intelligence and Law*, 4(3-4):163–197, 1996.
13. T. F. Gordon. Some problems with Prolog as a knowledge representation language for legal expert systems. In C. Arnold, editor, *Yearbook of Law, Computers and Technology*, pages 52–67. Leicester Polytechnic Press, Leicester, England, 1987.
14. T. F. Gordon. *The Pleadings Game; An Artificial Intelligence Model of Procedural Justice*. Springer, New York, 1995. Book version of 1993 Ph.D. Thesis; University of Darmstadt.
15. T. F. Gordon. Visualizing Carneades argument graphs. *Law, Probability and Risk*, 6(1-4):109–117, 2007.
16. T. F. Gordon. Hybrid reasoning with argumentation schemes. In *Proceedings of the 8th Workshop on Computational Models of Natural Argument (CMNA 08)*, pages 16–25, Patras, Greece, July 2008. The 18th European Conference on Artificial Intelligence (ECAI 2008).

17. T. F. Gordon and N. Karacapilidis. The Zeno argumentation framework. In *Proceedings of the Sixth International Conference on Artificial Intelligence and Law*, pages 10–18, Melbourne, Australia, 1997. ACM Press.

18. T. F. Gordon, H. Prakken, and D. Walton. The Carneades model of argument and burden of proof. *Artificial Intelligence*, 171(10-11):875–896, 2007.

19. T. F. Gordon and D. Walton. The Carneades argumentation framework — using presumptions and exceptions to model critical questions. In P. E. Dunne and T. J. Bench-Capon, editors, *Computational Models of Argument. Proceedings of COMMA 2006*, pages 195–207, Amsterdam, September 2006. IOS Press.

20. J. Hage. A theory of legal reasoning and a logic to match. *Artificial Intelligence and Law*, 4(3-4):199–273, 1996.

21. H. L. A. Hart. *Essays in Jurisprudence and Philosophy*. Oxford University Press, 1983.

22. W. Kunz and H. W. Rittel. Issues as elements of information systems. Technical report, Institut für Grundlagen der Planung, Universität Stuttgart, 1970. also: Center for Planning and Development Research, Institute of Urban and Regional Development Research. Working Paper 131, University of California, Berkeley.

23. H. Prakken. Modeling defeasibility in law: Logic or Procedure? *Fundamenta Informaticae*, 48:253–271, 2001.

24. H. Prakken. A study of accrual of arguments, with applications to evidential reasoning. In *Proceedings of the Tenth International Conference on Artificial Intelligence and Law*, pages 85–94, New York, 2005. ACM Press.

25. H. Prakken. A formal model of adjudication. In S. Rahman, editor, *Argumentation, Logic and Law*. Springer Verlag, Dordrecht, 2008.

26. H. Prakken, C. Reed, and D. Walton. Dialogues about the burden of proof. In *Proceedings of the Tenth International Conference on Artificial Intelligence and Law*, pages 85–94, Bologna, 2005. ACM Press.

27. H. Prakken and G. Sartor. A dialectical model of assessing conflicting argument in legal reasoning. *Artificial Intelligence and Law*, 4(3-4):331–368, 1996.

28. H. Prakken and G. Sartor. Presumptions and burden of proof. In T. van Engers, editor, *Legal Knowledge and Information Systems. JURIX 2006: The Nineteenth Annual Conference*, pages 21–30, Amsterdam, 2006. IOS Press.

29. H. Prakken and G. Sartor. Formalizing arguments about the burden of persuasion. In *Proceedings of the 11th International Conference on Artificial Intelligence and Law*, pages 97–106, New York, 2007. Stanford University, ACM Press.

30. H. Prakken and G. Sartor. A logical analysis of burdens of proof. In H. Kaptein, H. Prakken, and B. Verheij, editors, *Legal Evidence and Proof: Statistics, Stories, Logic*, Applied Legal Philosophy Series. Ashgate Publishing, 223–253, 2009.

31. J. Rawls. Outline of a decision procedure for ethics. *Philosophical Review*, 177–197, 1951.

32. N. Rescher. *Dialectics: A Controversy-Oriented Approach to the Theory of Knowledge*. State University of New York Press, 1977.

33. H. W. Rittel and M. M. Webber. Dilemmas in a general theory of planning. *Policy Science*, 4:155–169, 1973.

34. M. Rosenberg, J. B. Weinstein, H. Smit, and H. L. Korn. *Elements of Civil Procedure*. Foundation Press, 1976.

35. G. Sartor. Defeasibility in legal reasoning. In *Informatics and the Foundations of Legal Reasoning*, Law and philosophy library, pages 119–157. Kluwer Academic Publishers, Dordrecht, 1995.

36. K. Satoh, S. Tojo, and Y. Suzuki. Formalizing a switch of burden of proof by logic programming. In *Proceedings of the First International Workshop on Juris-Informatics (JURISIN 2007)*, pages 76–85, Miyazaki, Japan, 2007.

37. D. Walton. The new dialectic: A method of evaluating an argument used for some purpose in a given case. *ProtoSociology*, 13:70–91, 1999.

38. D. Walton. *Fundamentals of Critical Argumentation*. Cambridge University Press, Cambridge, UK, 2006.

Part III
Argumentation in Multi-Agent Systems

Chapter 13
Dialogue Games for Agent Argumentation

Peter McBurney and Simon Parsons

1 Introduction

The rise of the Internet and the growth of distributed computing have led to a major paradigm shift in software engineering and computer science. Until recently, the notion of *computation* has been variously construed as numerical calculation, as information processing, or as intelligent symbol analysis, but increasingly, it is now viewed as distributed cognition and interaction between intelligent entities [60]. This new view has major implications for the conceptualization, design, engineering and control of software systems, most profoundly expressed in the concept of systems of intelligent software agents, or multi-agent systems [99]. Agents are software entities with control over their own execution; the design of such agents, and of multi-agent systems of them, presents major research and software engineering challenges to computer scientists.

One key challenge is the design of means of communication between intelligent agents. Considerable research effort has been expended on the design of artificial languages for agent communications, such as DARPA's *Knowledge Query and Manipulation Language (KQML)* [33] and the Foundation for Intelligent Physical Agents' (now IEEE FIPA) *Agent Communications Language (FIPA ACL)* [35]. These languages, and languages like them, have been designed to be widely applicable. As well as being a strength, this feature can also be a weakness: agents participating in conversations have too many choices of what to utter at each turn, and thus agent dialogues may endure a state-space explosion.

Allowing sufficient flexibility of expression while avoiding state-space explosion had led agent communications researchers to the study of formal dialogue games; these are rule-governed interactions between two or more players (or agents), where

Department of Computer Science, University of Liverpool, UK
e-mail: mcburney@liverpool.ac.uk
Department of Computer and Information Science, Brooklyn College, New York, USA
e-mail: parsons@sci.brooklyn.cuny.edu

I. Rahwan, G. R. Simari (eds.), *Argumentation in Artificial Intelligence,*
DOI 10.1007/978-0-387-98197-0_13, © Springer Science+Business Media, LLC 2009

each player "moves" by making utterances, according to a defined set of rules. Although their study dates to at least the time of Aristotle [5], dialogue games have found recent application in philosophy, computational linguistics and Artificial Intelligence (AI). In philosophy, dialogue games have been used to study fallacious reasoning [41, 62] and to develop a game-theoretic semantics for various logics, e.g., intuitionistic and for classical logics [59]. In linguistics, they have been used to explain sequences of human utterances [57], with subsequent application to machine-based natural language processing and generation [49], and to human-computer interaction [9]. Within computer science and AI, they have been applied to modeling complex human reasoning, for example in legal domains [81], and to requirements specification for complex software systems [34]. Dialogue games differ from the games of economic game theory in that payoffs for winning or losing a game are not considered, and, indeed, the notions of *winning* and *losing* are not always applicable to dialogue games. They also differ from the abstract games recently used as a semantics for interactive computation [1], since these latter games do not share the rich rule structure of dialogue games, nor are these latter intended to themselves have a semantic interpretation involving the co-ordination of actions among a group of agents.

This chapter considers the application of formal dialogue games for agent communication and interaction using argumentation. We begin, in the next subsection, with a brief overview of an influential typology of human dialogues, which have proven useful in classifying agent interactions. Because the design of artificial languages for communication between software agents shares much with the study of natural human languages, we structure this chapter according to the standard division within linguistic theory between syntax, semantics and pragmatics; we do this despite this division being imprecise and contested within linguistics (e.g., [58]). Very broadly (following [58]), we may view: *syntax* as being concerned with the surface form and combinatorial properties of utterances, words and their components; *semantics* as being concerned with the truth or falsity of utterances; and *pragmatics* as being concerned with those aspects of the meaning of utterances other than their truth or falsity.[1] Section 2 thus presents a model of a formal dialogue game protocol, focusing primarily on the syntax of such dialogues. We follow this in Section 3 with a discussion of the semantics and the pragmatics of agent dialogues. Section 4 then presents an illustrative example, taken from [68], while Section 5 considers protocol design and assessment. The chapter ends with a brief conclusion in Section 6.

1.1 Types of dialogues

An influential model of human dialogues is the typology of primary dialogue types of argumentation theorists Douglas Walton and Erik Krabbe [96]. This categorization is based upon the information the participants have at the commencement of a

---

[1] Note that the word *semantics* is used differently here than in the study of argumentation frameworks, as in Chapter 2 of this volume.

dialogue (of relevance to the topic of discussion), their individual goals for the dialogue, and the goals they share. **Information-Seeking Dialogues** are those where one participant seeks the answer to some question(s) from another participant, who is believed by the first to know the answer(s). In **Inquiry Dialogues** the participants collaborate to answer some question or questions whose answers are not known to any one participant. **Persuasion Dialogues** involve one participant seeking to persuade another to accept a proposition he or she does not currently endorse. In **Negotiation Dialogues**, the participants bargain over the division of some scarce resource. If a negotiation dialogue terminates with an agreement, then the resource has been divided in a manner acceptable to all participants. Participants of **Deliberation Dialogues** collaborate to decide what action or course of action should be adopted in some situation. Here, participants share a responsibility to decide the course of action, or, at least, they share a willingness to discuss whether they have such a shared responsibility. Participants may have only partial or conflicting information, and conflicting preferences. As with negotiation dialogues, if a deliberation dialogue terminates with an agreement, then the participants have decided on a mutually-acceptable course of action. In **Eristic Dialogues**, participants quarrel verbally as a substitute for physical fighting, aiming to vent perceived grievances.

Several comments are important to make here. The first is that although Walton and Krabbe talk about the *goal* of a dialogue and the *goal* of a dialogue type,[2] only participants can have goals since only they are sentient. Participants may believe that a dialogue interaction they enter has an ostensible purpose, but their own goals or the goals of the other participants may not be consistent with this purpose. For example, participants may enter a negotiation dialogue in order to reach an agreement (a *deal*) over the allocation of some resource; or they may enter it to prevent any such agreement being reached, or to delay agreement [24], or to prove that no such agreement is possible, or to gather information from the other participants, or even to signal something to some third party, not in the dialogue. Participants in dialogues may also seek to hide their true goals from the other participants [25, 64]. Instead of dialogue goals it makes sense only to speak of participant goals and dialogue outcomes [74].

Secondly, most actual dialogue occurrences — both human and agent — involve mixtures of these dialogue types. A purchase transaction, for example, may commence with a request from a potential buyer for information from a seller, proceed to a persuasion dialogue, where the seller seeks to persuade the potential buyer of the importance of some feature of the product, and then transition to a negotiation, where each party offers to give up something he or she desires in return for something else. The two parties may or may not be aware of the different nature of their discussions at each phase, or of the transitions between phases. Instances of individual dialogue types contained entirely within other dialogue types are said to be *embedded* [96]. Several formalisms have been suggested for computational representation of combinations of dialogue: first, the *Dialogue Frames* of Reed [84], which enable iterated, sequential and embedded dialogues to be represented; sec-

---

[2] as do others, e.g., [80].

ond, the *Agent Dialogue Frameworks* of McBurney and Parsons, based on PDL [66], which permit iterated, sequential, parallel and embedded dialogues to be represented; and third, the more abstract $\mathcal{RASA}$ frameworks of Miller and McBurney [73], which permit iterated, sequential, parallel and embedded combinations of any types of agent interaction protocols. All these formalisms are neutral with regard to the modeling of the primary dialogue types themselves, allowing the primary types to be represented in any convenient form, and allowing for types other than the six of the Walton and Krabbe typology to be included. Walton and Krabbe do not claim their typology is comprehensive, and some recent research has explored other types and sub-types, e.g., [14].

Researchers in multi-agent systems and in argumentation have articulated dialogue game protocols for many of the types in the Walton and Krabbe typology. For example, the two-party protocol of Amgoud, Maudet and Parsons [3], which is based on MacKenzie's philosophical dialogue game *DC* [62], supports persuasion, inquiry and information-seeking dialogues; a subsequent extension of this protocol with additional locutions supports negotiation dialogues [4]. Information-seeking dialogues have been considered by Hulstijn [49], and analyzed by Cogan, Parsons and McBurney [14]; indeed this latter work, which examines the pre- and post-conditions of dialogues over beliefs in fine detail, identifies several new types of dialogues not explicitly included in the Walton and Krabbe typology. A study of different persuasion protocols can be found in the review paper by Prakken [80]; other protocols for persuasion dialogues include the PADUA protocol for arguments from experience by Wardeh, Bench-Capon and Coenen [97] and a protocol for arguments over access to information by Doutre and colleagues [22, 23, 78].

Protocols for multi-agent inquiry dialogues have been proposed and studied by McBurney and Parsons [65], who consider the circumstances under which an inquiry dialogue may converge to the truth, and by Black and Hunter [11], whose agent reasoning architecture enables generative inquiry dialogues, i.e., those where new proposals may emerge for consideration and possible endorsement by the agents participating. For dialogues over beliefs (information-seeking, inquiry and persuasion dialogues), Parsons and Sklar consider the question of convergence of beliefs of agents engaged in repeated dialogues with one another [77]. In addition to [4] cited above, protocols for negotiation dialogues include those of Sadri, Toni and Torroni [87], McBurney, van Eijk, Parsons and Amgoud [63], and Karunatillake [54]. Regarding dialogues over action which are not negotiations: McBurney, Hitchcock and Parsons [64] and Tang and Parsons [92] have presented protocols for deliberation dialogues; Atkinson, Bench-Capon and McBurney have given a representation for proposals for actions and a dialogue game protocol to discuss these proposals [6]; and Atkinson, Girle, McBurney and Parsons have presented a dialogue game protocol for dialogues over commands [7]. Finally, the dialogue-game protocols presented in the work of Dignum, Dunin-Kęplicz and Verbrugge [20, 21] are intended to enable agents to form teams and to agree joint intentions, respectively.

2 Syntax

The syntax of a language concerns the surface form of words and phrases, and how these may be combined. Accordingly, defining the syntax of an agent dialogue game protocol usually involves the specification of the possible utterances which agents can make (the locutions) and the rules which govern the order in which utterances can be made. Since the work of Hamblin [41], it has become standard to talk of speakers in a dialogue incurring *commitments*: a speaker who asserts a statement as being true, for example, may be committed to justifying this assertion when challenged by another participant, or else allowed (or even forced) to retract the assertion. Although such dialogical commitments may be viewed as aspects of the semantics (the meaning) of utterances, the rules regarding commitments are typically included in the specification of dialogue syntax because these rules often influence the order of utterances. The various commitments of the participants are usually tracked in a publicly-readable database, called a *commitment store*.

Within the agents communications community, it has become standard to view utterances as composed of two layers: an inner layer comprising the topics of discussion, and an outer (or wrapper) layer, comprising the locutions. An utterance can thus be seen as an instantiated locution, with one variable of instantiation being the topic. This structure, adopted for both *KQML* and *FIPA ACL*, provides great flexibility, since agents encoded appropriately may use the same wrappers to undertake dialogues over different topics.

We now present a generic framework for specification of a dialogue game protocol in terms of its key components, adapted from [66].[3] We first assume that the topics of discussion between the agents (the inner layer) can be represented in some logical language, whose well-formed formulae are denoted by the lower-case Roman letters, p, q, r, etc. A dialogue game specification then comprises the following elements, each of which concern the wrapper layer of communications:

Commencement Rules: Rules which define the circumstances under which the dialogue commences.

Locutions: Rules which indicate what utterances are permitted. Typically, legal locutions permit participants to assert propositions, permit others to question or contest prior assertions, and permit those asserting propositions which are subsequently questioned or contested to justify their assertions. Justifications may involve the presentation of a proof of the proposition or an argument for it. The dialogue game rules may also permit participants to utter propositions to which they assign differing degrees of commitment, for example: one may merely *propose* a proposition, a speech act which entails less commitment than would an *assertion* of the same proposition.

Rules for Combination of Locutions: Rules which define the dialogical contexts under which particular locutions are permitted or not, or obligatory or not. For

---

[3] We are also informed by [80]; note, however, that work defines a mathematical model for analyzing multi-party dialogues, rather than defining a framework for specification of dialogue protocols for agent communications.

instance, it may not be permitted for a participant to assert a proposition p and subsequently the proposition $\neg p$ in the same dialogue, without in the interim having retracted the former assertion.

Commitments: Rules which define the circumstances under which participants incur dialogical commitments by their utterances, and thus alter the contents of the participants' associated commitment stores. For example, a question posed by one agent to another may impose a commitment on the second to provide a response; until provided, this commitment remains undischarged.

Rules for Combination of Commitments: Rules which define how commitments are combined or manipulated when utterances incurring conflicting or complementary commitments are made. For example, the rules may allow a speaker to assert the truth of a proposition and then to assert its negation, with the commitment store holding only the most recent asserted proposition, or the store may hold the earlier proposition until explicitly retracted. These rules become particularly important when multiple dialogues are involved, as when one dialogue is embedded within another; in such a case, the commitments incurred in the inner dialogue may take priority over those of the outer dialogue, or vice versa [66].

Rules for Speaker Order: Rules which define the order in which speakers may make utterances. It may be that any speaker may speak at any time, as in *FIPA ACL*, or that there are rules regarding turn-taking.

Termination Rules: Rules that define the circumstances under which the dialogue ends.

It is worth noting here that more than one notion of *commitment* is present in the literature on dialogue games. For example, Hamblin treats commitments in a purely dialogical sense: *"A speaker who is obliged to maintain consistency needs to keep a store of statements representing his previous commitments, and require of each new statement he makes that it may be added without inconsistency to this store. The store represents a kind of persona of beliefs; it need not correspond with his real beliefs . . ."* [41, p. 257]. In contrast, Walton and Krabbe [96, Chapter 1] treat commitments as obligations to (execute, incur or maintain) a course of action, which they term action commitments. These actions may be utterances in a dialogue, as when a speaker is forced to defend a proposition he has asserted against attack from others; so Walton and Krabbe also consider propositional commitment as a special case of action commitment [96, p. 23]. As with Hamblin's treatment, such dialogical commitments to propositions may not necessarily represent a participant's true beliefs. In contrast, Singh's social semantics [90], requires participants in an interaction to express publicly their beliefs and intentions, and these expressions are called *social commitments*. These include both expressions of belief in some propositions and expressions of intent to execute or incur some future actions.[4] Our primary motivation is the use of dialogue games as the basis for interaction protocols between autonomous agents. Because such agents will typically enter into these interactions

---

[4] It is worth noting that all these notions of *commitment* differ from that commonly used in discussion of agent's internal states, namely the idea of the persistence of a belief or an intention [99, p. 205].

in order to achieve some wider objectives, and not just for the enjoyment of the interaction itself, we believe it is reasonable to define commitments in terms of future actions or propositions external to the dialogue. In a commercial negotiation dialogue, for instance, the utterance of an offer may express a willingness by the speaker to undertake a subsequent transaction on the terms contained in the offer. For this reason, we can view commitments as semantic mappings between locutions and subsets of some set of statements expressing actions or beliefs external to the dialogue.

3 Semantics and Pragmatics

3.1 Purposes of Semantics

We begin this section by discussing the concept of semantics for agent communications languages and dialogue protocols. These languages and protocols are clearly media for communication (between software entities and/or their human principals) and so researchers have naturally looked to theories developed in human linguistics to understand them. But, unlike human languages, agent communications languages and dialogue protocols are also *formal* constructs, usually defined explicitly and often computationally; thus, understanding their properties can also usefully draw on notions from logic and mathematics. Moreover, because these communications languages and dialogue protocols are usually intended to be used by autonomous software entities, they are also programming languages, since software agents will use them to construct sequences of utterances — commands — with which to interact with one another. The theory of programming language semantics is therefore also relevant to their study.

It is thus important to keep in mind the different functions which a semantics for an agent communications language or dialogue protocol may be required to serve:

- To provide a shared understanding to participants in a communicative interaction of the meaning of individual utterances, of sequences of utterances, and of dialogues.
- To provide a shared understanding to designers of agent protocols and to the (possibly distinct) designers of agents using those protocols of the meaning of individual utterances, of sequences of utterances, and of dialogues.
- To provide a means by which the properties of individual agent communications languages and protocols may be studied formally and with rigor.
- To provide a means by which different agent communications languages and protocols may be compared with one another formally and with rigor.
- To provide a means by which languages and protocols may be readily implemented in production systems.
- To help ensure that implementation of agent communications in open, distributed agent systems is undertaken uniformly.

Different types of semantics may serve these various purposes to varying degrees, and so it may be useful to develop more than one semantics for a communications language or protocol. [5] In addition, an articulation of semantics could be undertaken at one or more different levels: for each individual utterance, or speech act; for specified short sequences of utterances,[6] such as a question-and-answer sequence; for complete sequences of utterances, or *dialogues*; and for dialogue *protocols*. Most current published work on agent dialogue protocols presents a semantics defined in terms of individual utterances. In the terms defined below, these semantics are most often axiomatic or operational, and are much less often denotational.

3.2 Types of Semantics

We have inherited two conflicting notions of semantics, one deriving from linguistics and the other from mathematical logic. As linguists normally understand these terms, the syntax of a language is *"the formal relation of signs to one another"* and the semantics of the language *"the relations of signs to the objects to which the signs are applicable"* (Morris [75], cited in [58, p. 1]). Thus, it makes sense to speak of the *truth* of a sign (or of an utterance in a language using such signs), since this indicates that the sign has a relationship to external objects in the world. Within mathematics and mathematical logic, a different understanding of semantics has arisen, beginning with Pieri [79] and Hilbert [43] and first articulated formally by Tarski [94]. In this tradition, a semantics for a formal language is a relationship between that language and a space $\mathcal{M}$ of mathematical structures, called *models*. A statement S in the language specifies a subset $\mathcal{M}(S)$ of $\mathcal{M}$. Such a statement is said to be *true* in a particular model M_0 if $M_0 \in \mathcal{M}(S)$. A statement is said to be logically true if it is true in every model, i.e., if $\mathcal{M}(S) = \mathcal{M}$.[7] These two notions of semantics — one linguistic, one mathematical — collide.[8] In particular, in the mathematical framework, benefit may be gained from defining different semantic mathematical structures for the one language; Tarski himself, for instance, defined topological [93] and discrete lattice [71] semantics for propositional logic. The benefits of this are that different semantic frameworks may enable different properties of the language to be studied and may provide different insights. Insight may also be gained by comparing the structures with each other, a subject known as *model theory* or *metamathematics* [48]. But, defining and comparing alternative structures

---

[5] Traditional mathematical communications theory, due to Shannon and Weaver [89], explicitly ignores the semantics of messages, and so provides little guidance to designers, developers or users of agent communications languages and protocols.

[6] These are known as *conversations* in the agent communications literature, e.g., [39].

[7] Note that Tarski only applied his framework to formal, or mathematical, languages, and was skeptical about its applicability to natural language [94, pp. 163–165].

[8] Their first skirmish was the argument between Hilbert and Frege over the meaning of Hilbert's axioms for geometry: Frege took what we are calling a linguistic approach, Hilbert a model-theoretic approach; see [95, pp. 408–412] and [46, pp. 7–10].

in this way makes no sense in the linguistic understanding of semantics: how could a language admit more than one set of relationships to *the truth*?

Agent communications languages and dialogue protocols straddle this divide. Because they are formal languages, insight into their properties can be gained by defining semantic relationships to mathematical structures, and studying these structures. However, because they are also intended as media for communication, just as natural language is, each agent using a particular communications language or protocol will wish to ensure that all users share a common understanding of utterances.[9] To verify that agents have the same understanding — the same semantics — for a communications language ultimately requires some form of inspection of their internal states or, equivalently, their program code. This is a challenging, and perhaps conceptually impossible, undertaking since a sufficiently-clever agent can always simulate insincerely any required internal state.[10] Rather, in this chapter, our use of semantic frameworks differs from that in linguistics: first, as in model theory, semantic structures are a means to understand the properties of a formal agent communications language, and, second, because our focus is on computer systems, these structures are a means to support the engineering of multi-agent systems software and to aid uniformity of implementation when software engineering is undertaken by different development teams.

It is therefore helpful to consider several different types of semantic frameworks for formal languages. In doing so, we draw on the summary of the literature on programming language semantics presented by van Eijk in [29, Section 1.2.2]; however, we make no claims that the typology is comprehensive. One type of semantics defines each locution of a communications language in terms of the pre-conditions which must exist before the locution can be uttered, and possibly also the post-conditions which apply following its utterance, in a STRIPS-like fashion [32]. This is called an **axiomatic** semantics [29, 72]. For agent communications languages and dialogue protocols we distinguish between public and private axiomatic approaches. In **public** axiomatic approaches, the pre-conditions and post-conditions all describe states or conditions of the dialogue which can be observed by all participants. In **private** axiomatic approaches, at least some of the pre- or post-conditions describe states or conditions which are internal to one or more of the participants, and thus not directly observable by the others. For example, the semantic language, *SL*, for the locutions of the Agent Communications Language, *FIPA ACL*, of the Foundation for Intelligent Physical Agents (FIPA), is a private axiomatic semantics of the speech acts of the language, defined in terms of the beliefs, desires and intentions of the participating agents [35]. For example, the *inform* locution in the *FIPA ACL* language, allows one agent, say agent A, to tell another agent, say B, some proposition p. The *FIPA ACL* semantics of *inform* only permits agent A to do this if [35, p. 10]: (a) agent A believes p to be true, (b) agent A intends that agent B believes p to be true, and (c) agent A believes that agent B does not already have a belief about

---

[9] Friedrich Dürrenmatt's novel, *Die Panne*, shows what tragic consequences may follow when participants assign very different meanings to the same conversation [28].

[10] For more on this, see [98].

the truth of p.[11] Similarly, the semantics defined for many dialogue game protocols for agent interaction, e.g., [3], are also private axiomatic semantics. In contrast, the semantics provided for dialogue games used for modeling legal reasoning in [10] is a public axiomatic semantics.

A second type of semantics, an **operational semantics**, considers the dialogue locutions as computational instructions which operate successively on the states of some abstract machine. Under this approach, the participating agents and their shared dialogue are viewed conceptually as parts of a large abstract or virtual computer, whose overall state may be altered by the utterance of valid locutions or by internal decision processes of the participants; it is as if these locutions or decisions were commands in some computer programme language acting on the virtual machine.[12] The utterances and agent decision-mechanisms are thus seen as state transition operators, and the operational semantics defines these transitions precisely [29]. This approach to the semantics of agent communications languages makes explicit any link between the internal decision mechanisms of the participating agents and their public utterances to one another. The semantics therefore enables the relationships between the mental states of the participants and the public state of the dialogue to be seen explicitly, and shows how these relationships change as a result of utterances and internal agent decisions. Thus, an operational semantics will typically make assumptions about the internal decision-mechanisms of the agents participating in the interaction; the actual agents engaged in a communicative interaction may not necessarily use the decision-process or realize the mental states assumed. Operational semantics have recently been defined for some agent communications languages, for example, in [30, 44] and for some dialogue protocols, e.g., information-passing interactions [19], negotiation dialogue protocols [54, 63], and a general argumentation protocol [68].

Third, in **denotational semantics**, each element of the language syntax is assigned a relationship to an abstract mathematical entity, its denotation. The possible worlds, or Kripkean, semantics defined for modal logic syntax is an example of such a semantics for a logical language [56]. However, two decades before Kripke's work, a denotational semantics mapping logical formulae to subsets of a topological space was given for the modal logic system S4 [91]. For argumentation systems, three denotational semantics have been provided for the ICRF's Logic of Argumentation LA [55]. In the first of these, Ambler [2] articulated a category-theoretic semantics [61] for LA, by extending to arguments the Curry-Howard isomorphism, which connects proofs in a deductive logic to the morphisms of a free cartesian closed category. In this semantics, propositions (i.e., premises or claims) correspond to objects in a particular enriched category, and arguments linking propositions to morphisms between the associated objects. A second denotational semantics for LA, due to Parsons [76], connects argumentation systems to qualitative probabilistic networks (QPNs). In this semantics, propositions correspond to nodes in a QPN, and arguments linking propositions to edges between the associated nodes. Das [17]

---

[11] Note that condition (a) enforces sincerity on the speaker, which is not necessarily desirable. Also, condition (c) precludes the use of *inform* in authentication dialogues.

[12] This virtual machine is purely a conceptual construct and does not need to exist in reality.

articulated a third denotational semantics for logics of argumentation, based on a Kripkean possible-worlds structure. In this semantics, different arguments are assumed classified according to the degree of support they provide for propositions; these differential degrees of support are translated into separate hyper-relations over the accessibility relations of the Kripke structure.[13]

Perhaps the first example of a denotational semantics for a dialogue protocol was the possible-worlds semantics for question-response interactions defined by Hamblin in 1956 [40]. Although possible-worlds and category-theoretic denotational semantics have a long subsequent history in mathematical linguistics, only recently have denotational semantics been defined for agent dialogue protocols. In [67], McBurney and Parsons articulated a category-theoretic semantics, called a *Trace Semantics*, for a broad class of deliberation dialogue protocols. In this semantics, articulation of proposals for action by participants correspond to the creation of objects in certain categories, while participant preferences between these proposals correspond to the existence of arrows (morphisms) between the corresponding objects. Thus, the semantics is constructed jointly and incrementally by the dialogue participants as the dialogue proceeds, in a manner similar to the natural language semantics of Discourse Representation Theory [53] (which uses possible worlds), or the argumentation graph of Gordon's Pleadings Game [38]. A similar denotational semantics, constructed jointly and incrementally by the participants, is outlined by Atkinson and colleagues in [6], for a dialogue protocol for arguments over proposals for action. In this semantics, the mathematical entities constructed are topoi and maps between them, rather than simply categories.[14]

For the denotational semantics approach to be useful, we must be able to derive the semantic mapping of a compound statement in the language from the semantic mappings of its elements, a property called *compositionality*. This property is not always present; for example, it may be absent if the language contains compound statements with infinite combinations of elements or if compound statements have denotations which differ from the composition of those of their elements, as in Hintikka's Independence-Friendly (IF) Logic [47]. In these cases, a specific type of denotational semantics, **game-theoretic semantics**, has sometimes proven useful [45]. In this semantics, each well-formed statement in the language is associated with a conceptual game between two players, a protagonist and an antagonist. A statement in the language is considered to be *true* when and only when a winning strategy exists for the protagonist in the associated game; a winning strategy for a player is a rule giving that player moves for the game such that executing these moves guarantees the player can win the game, no matter what moves are made by the opposing player. Game semantics have been articulated for propositional and predicate logics [59], linear logic [1], and for probability theory [18], among others.

---

[13] This semantics may be viewed as a form of quantification over possible worlds, of which a more general formalism is that developed subsequently (and independently) by van Eijk and his colleagues to compare network topologies [31].

[14] Topoi are generalizations of the category of sets, and incorporate a categorial analogue of the notion of set membership [37].

What value do these different types of semantics have? Axiomatic semantics show the pre- and post-conditions of individual utterances in a communications interaction. They may also be used to show the pre- and post-conditions of sequences of utterances, or even entire dialogues [14, 74]. Thus, they provide a set of rules to regulate participation in rule-governed interactions. Operational semantics, by showing the state transitions effected by utterances, may be used to identify dialogue states which are not reachable or from which no legal utterance may be made. These semantics can be used, therefore, to demonstrate that termination of dialogues between participants using a particular protocol is or is not possible. Operational semantics also identify which internal agent decision-mechanisms are needed by agents in order to issue and comprehend received utterances. Properties of dialogue protocols may also be demonstrated using denotational semantics. In [67], we used the Deliberation Trace Semantics to generalize a result of Harsanyi [42] regarding the pareto-optimality of deals achieved using Zeuthen's Monotonic Concession Protocol (MCP) [100]. Game semantics have also been used to study the properties of formal argumentation systems and dialogue protocols, such as their computational complexity [26], or the extent of truth-convergence under an inquiry dialogue protocol [65], and to identify acceptable sets of arguments in argument frameworks [13, 51].

3.3 Pragmatics

Following Levinson [58], we view the study of language pragmatics as dealing with those aspects of linguistic meaning not covered by considerations of truth and falsity. Chief among these aspects are the desires and intentions of speakers, and these are usually communicated by means of speech acts, non-propositional utterances intended to or perceived to change the state of the world. Examples of speech acts are utterances in which a speaker proposes that some action be undertaken, or promises to undertake it, or commands another to perform it. Modern speech act theory was initially due to Austin [8] and Searle [88], who classified spoken utterances by their intended and actual effects on the world (including the internal mental states of those hearing the utterances), and developed pre-conditions for those effects to be realized. Drawing on this theory, Bretier, Cohen, Levesque, Perrault and Sadek were able to present pre- and post-conditions for agent utterances in terms of the mental states of the participants [12, 15, 16]. This work formed the basis for the axiomatic Semantic Language *SL* of the *FIPA Agent Communications Language ACL* mentioned above [35]. One of the criticisms made of *FIPA ACL* is that the language does not support argumentation [70]; accordingly, McBurney and Parsons [68] extended this language by defining five additional locutions to enable agents to assert, question, challenge, justify and retract statements with one another. A set of locution-combination rules are given (although any such rules are absent from the specification of *FIPA ACL* itself), along with an axiomatic semantics in the style of

SL and an operational semantics. This protocol is discussed in the next Section, as an example of these ideas.

Long before Austin and Searle, Reinach [85] had noted that speech acts typically require endorsement, or *uptake*, from the hearer before changing the state of the world; a speaker may promise a hearer to perform some action, but the speaker is only obligated to act once the promise is accepted by the hearer. Speech acts are thus essentially social activities and cannot, normally, be executed by a lone reasoner: their natural home is a multi-party dialogue. This observation is particularly true for those speech acts for which the speaker does not have power of retraction or revocation. In [69], McBurney and Parsons presented an analysis of the differences in meaning between, for instance, *commands* and *promises*. Once uptaken (i.e., once in effect), a command may only be revoked by the original speaker, whereas a promise may only be revoked by the agent to which the promise was made, not the speaker.

However, capturing such differences in the syntax of utterances can be difficult. For example, the syntactical form of the two utterances:

I command you to wash the car.

I promise you to wash the car.

is identical, but the illocutionary force, the effects on the world, the nature of the obligation incurred, the identity of the agent with revocation powers, and even the identity of the agent intended by the speaker to perform the action are different. Although formal agent communications languages should be less ambiguous than natural language, an interpretation of the syntax of utterances is required for elimination of any ambiguity in meaning. McBurney and Parsons [69] dealt with this problem by modifying the denotational trace semantics of [67] to map action-utterances to tuples in a partitioned tuple space [36]. The different dialogical powers that participating agents have of issuance, endorsement and revocation for particular types of utterance then correspond to different permissions to write, copy and delete (respectively) tuples from associated sub-spaces of the tuple space.

4 Example

As an example of the ideas in this chapter, we present the *Fatio* protocol of [68]. This protocol comprises five locutions which may be added to the 22 locutions of *FIPA ACL*, in order to enable communicating agents to engage in rational argument: *assert, question, challenge, justify* and *retract*. These five locutions are subject to six locution-combination rules, which together encode a particular dialectical argumentation theory. Because these locutions are intended to be complementary to *FIPA ACL*, there are no locutions for commencing or terminating a dialogue.[15] For reasons of space, we only give examples of two of the five legal locutions of *Fatio*:

---

[15] It would be easy to take these from another protocol, such as [63].

F1: assert(P_i, ϕ):   A speaker P_i asserts a statement $\phi \in \mathcal{C}$ (a belief, an intention, a social connection, an external commitment, etc). In doing so, P_i creates a dialectical obligation within the dialogue to provide justification for ϕ if required subsequently by another participant.

F3: challenge(P_j, P_i, ϕ):   A speaker P_j challenges a prior utterance of *assert(P_i, ϕ)* by another participant P_i, and seeks a justification for ϕ. In contrast to a question, with this locution, P_j also creates a dialectical obligation on himself to provide a justification for not asserting ϕ, for example an argument against ϕ, if questioned or challenged. Thus, *challenge(P_j, P_i, ϕ)* is a stronger utterance than *question(P_j, P_i, ϕ)*.

For illustration, we present two of the six *Fatio* locution-combination rules. Here, $\Phi \vdash^+ \phi$ indicates that Φ is an argument in support of ϕ.

CR2:   The utterances *question(P_j, P_i, ϕ)* and *challenge(P_j, P_i, ϕ)* may be made at any time following an utterance of *assert(P_i, ϕ)*. Similarly, the utterances *question(P_j, P_i, Φ)* and *challenge(P_j, P_i, Φ)* may be made at any time following an utterance of *justify($P_i, \Phi \vdash^+ \phi$)*.

CR3:   Immediately following an utterance of *question(P_j, P_i, ϕ)* or *challenge(P_j, P_i, ϕ)*, the speaker P_i of *assert(P_i, ϕ)* must reply with *justify($P_i, \Phi \vdash^+ \phi$)*, for some $\Phi \in \mathcal{A}$.

In [68], both an axiomatic and an operational semantics for this protocol are articulated. The axiomatic semantics is defined in terms of the beliefs, desires and intentions of the participating agents consistent with the axiomatic semantics *SL* of *FIPA ACL*. For example, the semantics of the locution *assert(.)* is defined as follows, with $B_i\phi$ indicating that "Agent i believes that ϕ is true", and $D_i\phi$ that "Agent i desires that ϕ be true."

- *assert(P_i, ϕ)*
  Pre-conditions: A speaker P_i desires that each participant $P_j (j \neq i)$, believes that P_i believes the proposition $\phi \in \mathcal{C}$.
  $((P_i, \phi, +) \notin DOS(P_i)) \wedge (\forall j \neq i)(D_i B_j B_i \phi)$.
  Post-conditions: Each participant $P_k (k \neq i)$, believes that participant P_i desires that each participant $P_j (j \neq i)$, believe that P_i believes ϕ.
  $(P_i, \phi, +) \in DOS(P_i) \wedge (\forall k \neq i)(\forall j \neq i)(B_k D_i B_j B_i \phi)$.
  Dialectical Obligations: $(P_i, \phi, +)$ is added to $DOS(P_i)$, the Dialectical Obligations Store of speaker P_i.

Similarly, the operational semantics for *Fatio* defined in [68] articulates the state-transition effected by an *assert(.)* utterance (here labeled **F1**) on the mental states of, firstly, the agent who uttered it and, secondly, on any agent who heard it.

TR2: $\langle P_i, \mathbf{D1}, \text{utter-assert}(\phi) \rangle \xrightarrow{\mathbf{F1}} \langle P_i, \mathbf{D5}, \text{listen} \rangle$

TR3: $\langle P_i, \mathbf{D1}, \text{utter-assert}(\phi) \rangle \xrightarrow{\mathbf{F1}} \langle P_j, \mathbf{D5}, \text{do-mech}(D2) \rangle$

These excerpts from the semantics of *Fatio* are intended simply for illustration. Full details are given with the protocol definition [68].

5 Protocol design and assessment

The science and software engineering of agent communications and interactions is still in its infancy. Accordingly, designers of multi-agent dialogue game protocols still have little guidance for design questions such as: How many locutions should there be? What types of locutions should be included, e.g., assertions, questions, etc? What are the appropriate rules for the combination of locutions? When should behavior be forbidden, e.g., repeated utterance of one locution? Under what conditions should dialogues be made to terminate? When are dialogues conducted according to a particular protocol guaranteed to terminate? What are the properties of a proposed protocol?

Similarly, the immaturity of the discipline means that software developers and their agents still lack answers to questions such as: How may different protocols be compared and differences measured? Which protocols are to be preferred under which circumstances? In other words, what are their advantages and disadvantages? How should a system developer (or an agent) choose between two protocols which both support the same type of dialogue, for example, two negotiation protocols? When are dialogue game protocols preferable to other forms of agent interaction, such as auction mechanisms or general agent communications languages, such as *FIPA ACL*?

Some work has been undertaken which would assist with such questions. For example, McBurney, Parsons and Wooldridge [70], proposed thirteen desirable properties of agent interaction protocols using dialogue games, and then applied these properties to assess several dialogue game protocols and *FIPA ACL*; all were found wanting, to a greater or lesser extent. From an empirical perspective, Karunatillake [54] undertook an evaluation of various negotiation protocols. This work used simulation studies to compare performance in negotiation interactions for agents using protocols with and using protocols without argumentation, in order to identify the circumstances under which argumentation-based negotiation was beneficial. From a theoretical perspective, Johnson, McBurney and Parsons [52] defined various measures of protocol equivalence, both syntactical and semantic, and showed the relationship of these measures to one another. Knowing that two protocols are equivalent allows inference about their properties (such as termination), and about their compliance with a given specification, such as that laid down as the standard for interacting within some electronic institution [86].

6 Conclusion

In this chapter we have given a brief introduction to the theory of dialogue game protocols for agent interaction and argument, a subject which has become important with the rise of multi-agent systems. We have focused on the syntax and the semantics of these protocols because these topics are important, not only for analysis of protocols, but also for the software engineering specification, design and implementation of agent interaction systems. In only a chapter, there are many topics we do not have space to discuss, for example: the computational complexity of decision-making involved in making utterances, and in deciding whether or not these comply with a protocol, e.g., [27]; strategic issues over what utterances an agent should make and when, under a given protocol [82, 83]; properties of specific protocols, e.g. [3, 11, 87]; experiences arising from implementation [23]; and allowing agents to choose protocols themselves, even at run-time [50, 74]. As can be seen, there are many avenues to explore in this rich and exciting subject.

Acknowledgements We are grateful for partial financial support received from the EC *Information Society Technologies* (IST) programme, through project ASPIC (IST-FP6-002307). This work was also partially supported by the US Army Research Laboratory and the UK Ministry of Defence under Agreement Number W911NF-06-3-0001. The views and conclusions contained in this document are those of the authors and should not be interpreted as representing the official policies, either expressed or implied, of the US Army Research Laboratory, the US Government, the UK Ministry of Defense, or the UK Government. The US and UK Governments are authorized to reproduce and distribute reprints for Government purposes notwithstanding any copyright notation hereon.

References

1. S. Abramsky. Semantics of interaction: an introduction to game semantics. In A. M. Pitts and P. Dybjer, editors, *Semantics and Logics of Computation*, pages 1–31. Cambridge University Press, Cambridge, UK, 1997.
2. S. J. Ambler. A categorical approach to the semantics of argumentation. *Mathematical Structures in Computer Science*, 6:167–188, 1996.
3. L. Amgoud, N. Maudet, and S. Parsons. Modelling dialogues using argumentation. In E. Durfee, editor, *Proceedings of the Fourth International Conference on Multi-Agent Systems (ICMAS 2000)*, pages 31–38, Boston, MA, USA, 2000. IEEE Press.
4. L. Amgoud, S. Parsons, and N. Maudet. Arguments, dialogue, and negotiation. In W. Horn, editor, *Proceedings of the Fourteenth European Conference on Artificial Intelligence (ECAI 2000)*, pages 338–342, Berlin, Germany, 2000. IOS Press.
5. Aristotle. *Topics*. Clarendon Press, Oxford, UK, 1928. (W. D. Ross, Editor).
6. K. Atkinson, T. Bench-Capon, and P. McBurney. A dialogue game protocol for multi-agent argument for proposals over action. *Autonomous Agents and Multi-Agent Systems*, 11(2):153–171, 2005.
7. K. Atkinson, R. Girle, P. McBurney, and S. Parsons. Command dialogues. In I. Rahwan and P. Moraitis, editors, *Proceedings of the Fifth International Workshop on Argumentation in Multi-Agent Systems (ArgMAS 2008)*, Lisbon, Portugal, 2008. AAMAS 2008.
8. J. L. Austin. *How To Do Things with Words*. Oxford University Press, Oxford, UK, 1962.
9. T. J. M. Bench-Capon, P. E. Dunne, and P. H. Leng. Interacting with knowledge-based systems through dialogue games. In *Proceedings of the Eleventh International Conference on Expert Systems and Applications*, pages 123–140, Avignon, 1991.
10. T. J. M. Bench-Capon, T. Geldard, and P. H. Leng. A method for the computational modelling of dialectical argument with dialogue games. *Artificial Intelligence and Law*, 8:233–254, 2000.
11. E. Black and A. Hunter. A generative inquiry dialogue system. In M. Huhns, O. Shehory, E. H. Durfee, and M. Yokoo, editors, *Proceedings of the Sixth International Joint Conference on Autonomous Agents and Multi-Agent Systems (AAMAS 2007)*, Honolulu, Hawaii, USA, 2007. IFAAMAS, ACM Press.

12. P. Bretier and D. Sadek. A rational agent as the kernel of a cooperative spoken dialogue system: Implementing a logical theory of interaction. In J. P. M. *et al.*, editor, *Intelligent Agents III*, Lecture Notes in Artificial Intelligence 1193, pages 189–204. Springer, Berlin, Germany, 1997.

13. C. Cayrol, S. Doutre, and J. Mengin. On decision problems related to the preferred semantics for argumentation frameworks. *Journal of Logic and Computation*, 13(3):377–403, 2003.

14. E. Cogan, S. Parsons, and P. McBurney. New types of inter-agent dialogs. In S. P. *et al.*, editor, *Argumentation in Multi-Agent Systems: Second International Workshop (ArgMAS 2005)*, Lecture Notes in Computer Science 4049, pages 154–168. Springer, Berlin, Germany, 2006.

15. P. R. Cohen and H. J. Levesque. Rational interaction as the basis for communication. In P. R. C. *et al.*, editor, *Intentions in Communication*, pages 221–255. MIT Press, Cambridge, MA, USA, 1990.

16. P. R. Cohen and C. R. Perrault. Elements of a plan-based theory of speech acts. *Cognitive Science*, 3:177–212, 1979.

17. S. Das. How much does an agent believe: An extension of modal epistemic logic. In A. Hunter and S. Parsons, editors, *Applications of Uncertainty Formalisms*, Lecture Notes in Artificial Intelligence 1455, pages 415–426. Springer, Berlin, Germany, 1998.

18. A. P. Dawid and V. G. Vovk. Prequential probability: principles and properties. *Bernoulli*, 5:125–162, 1999.

19. F. S. de Boer, R. Eijk, W. v. Hoek, and J.-J. C. Meyer. A fully abstract model for the exchange of information in multi-agent systems. *Theoretical Computer Science*, 290(3):1753–1773, 2003.

20. F. Dignum, B. Dunin-Kęplicz, and R. Verbrugge. Agent theory for team formation by dialogue. In C. Castelfranchi and Y. Lespérance, editors, *Intelligent Agents VII*, Lecture Notes in Artificial Intelligence 1986, pages 150–166, Berlin, Germany, 2000. Springer.

21. F. Dignum, B. Dunin-Kęplicz, and R. Verbrugge. Creating collective intention through dialogue. *Logic Journal of the IGPL*, 9(2):305–319, 2001.

22. S. Doutre, P. McBurney, and M. Wooldridge. Law-governed Linda as a semantics for agent interaction protocols. In F. D. *et al.*, editor, *Proceedings of the Fourth International Joint Conference on Autonomous Agents and Multi-Agent Systems (AAMAS 2005)*, pages 1257–1258, New York City, NY, USA, 2005. ACM Press.

23. S. Doutre, P. McBurney, M. Wooldridge, and W. Barden. Information-seeking agent dialogs with permissions and arguments. Technical Report ULCS-05-010, Department of Computer Science, University of Liverpool, Liverpool, UK, 2005.

24. P. E. Dunne. Prevarication in dispute protocols. In G. Sartor, editor, *Proceedings of the Ninth International Conference on AI and Law (ICAIL-03)*, pages 12–21, New York, NY, USA, 2003. ACM Press.

25. P. E. Dunne. Suspicion of hidden agenda in persuasive argument. In P. E. Dunne and T. J. M. Bench-Capon, editors, *Computational Models of Argument: Proceedings of COMMA 2006*, pages 329–340, Amsterdam, The Netherlands, 2006. IOS Press.

26. P. E. Dunne and T. J. M. Bench-Capon. Two party immediate response disputes: Properties and efficiency. *Artificial Intelligence*, 149(2):221–250, 2003.

27. P. E. Dunne and P. McBurney. Optimal utterances in dialogue protocols. In J. S. R. *et al.*, editor, *Proceedings of the Second International Joint Conference on Autonomous Agents and Multi-Agent Systems (AAMAS 2003)*, pages 608–615, New York City, NY, USA, 2003. ACM Press.

28. F. Dürrenmatt. *A Dangerous Game*. Jonathan Cape, London, UK, 1960. (Translation by R. and C. Winston of *Die Panne*, published in German in 1956.).

29. R. Eijk. *Programming Languages for Agent Communications*. PhD thesis, Department of Computer Science, Utrecht University, Utrecht, The Netherlands, 2000.

30. R. Eijk, F. S. de Boer, W. v. Hoek, and J.-J. C. Meyer. Operational semantics for agent communications. In F. Dignum and M. Greaves, editors, *Issues in Agent Communications*, Lecture Notes in Artificial Intelligence 1916, pages 80–95. Springer, Berlin, Germany, 2000.

31. R. Eijk, F. S. de Boer, W. v. Hoek, and J.-J. C. Meyer. Modal logic with bounded quantification over worlds. *Journal of Logic and Computation*, 11(5):701–715, 2001.

32. R. E. Fikes and N. J. Nilsson. STRIPS: A new approach to the application of theorem proving to problem solving. *Artificial Intelligence*, 2:189–208, 1971.

33. T. Finin, Y. Labrou, and J. Mayfield. KQML as an agent communication language. In J. Bradshaw, editor, *Software Agents*, pages 291–316. MIT Press, Cambridge, USA, 1997.

34. A. Finkelstein and H. Fuks. Multi-party specification. In *Proceedings of the Fifth International Workshop on Software Specification and Design*, Pittsburgh, PA, USA, 1989. ACM Sigsoft Engineering Notes.

35. FIPA. Communicative Act Library Specification. Standard SC00037J, IEEE Foundation for Intelligent Physical Agents, 3 December 2002.

36. D. Gelernter. Generative communication in Linda. *ACM Transactions on Programming Languages and Systems*, 7(1):80–112, 1985.

37. R. Goldblatt. *Topoi: The Categorial Analysis of Logic*. North-Holland, Amsterdam, The Netherlands, 1979.

38. T. F. Gordon. The Pleadings Game: An exercise in computational dialectics. *Artificial Intelligence and Law*, 2:239–292, 1994.

39. M. Greaves, H. Holmback, and J. Bradshaw. What is a conversation policy? In F. Dignum and M. Greaves, editors, *Issues in Agent Communication*, Lecture Notes in Artificial Intelligence 1916, pages 118–131. Springer, Berlin, Germany, 2000.

40. C. L. Hamblin. *Language and the Theory of Information*. Ph.D. thesis, Logic and Scientific Method Programme, University of London, London, UK, 1957.

41. C. L. Hamblin. *Fallacies*. Methuen, London, UK, 1970.

42. J. C. Harsanyi. Approaches to the bargaining problem before and after the theory of games: a critical discussion of Zeuthen's, Hicks' and Nash's theories. *Econometrica*, 24:144–157, 1956.

43. D. Hilbert. Grundlagen der Geometrie. In *Festschrift zur Feier der Enthüllung des Gauss-Weber-Denkmals in Göttingen*, pages 3–92. Teubner, Leipzig, Germany, 1899.

44. K. V. Hindriks, F. S. de Boer, W. Hoek, and J.-J. C. Meyer. Formal semantics for an abstract agent progamming language. In M. P. S. *et al.*, editor, *Intelligent Agents IV*, Lecture Notes in Artificial Intelligence 1365, pages 215–229. Springer, Berlin, Germany, 1998.

45. J. Hintikka. Language-games for quantifiers. *Americal Philosophical Quarterly Monograph Series 2: Studies in Logical Theory*, pages 46–72, 1968. Blackwell, Oxford, UK.

46. J. Hintikka. On the development of the model-theoretic viewpoint in logical theory. *Synthese*, 77(1):1–36, 1988.

47. J. Hintikka and G. Sandu. Game-theoretical semantics. In J. Benthem and A. Meulen, editors, *Handbook of Logic and Language*, pages 361–410. Elsevier, Amsterdam, The Netherlands, 1997.

48. W. Hodges. *A Shorter Model Theory*. Cambridge University Press, Cambridge, UK, 1997.

49. J. Hulstijn. *Dialogue Models for Inquiry and Transaction*. PhD thesis, Universiteit Twente, Enschede, The Netherlands, 2000.

50. J. Hulstijn, M. Dastani, and L. Torre. Negotiation protocols and dialogue games. In *Proceedings of the Belgian-Dutch AI Conference (BNAIC-2000), ADDRESS =*, 2000.

51. H. Jakobovits and D. Vermeir. Dialectic semantics for argumentation frameworks. In *Proceedings of the Seventh International Conference on Artificial Intelligence and Law (ICAIL-99)*, pages 63–72, New York, NY, USA, 1999. ACM Press.

52. M. W. Johnson, P. McBurney, and S. Parsons. When are two protocols the same? In M.-P. Huget, editor, *Communication in Multi-Agent Systems: Agent Communication Languages and Conversation Policies*, Lecture Notes in Artificial Intelligence 2650, pages 253–268. Springer, Berlin, Germany, 2003.

53. H. Kamp and U. Reyle. *From Discourse to Logic: Introduction to Modeltheoretic Semantics of Natural Language, Formal Logic and Discourse Representation Theory*. Kluwer, Dordrecht, 1993.

54. N. C. Karunatillake. *Argumentation-Based Negotiation in a Social Context*. Ph.D. thesis, School of Electronics and Computer Science, University of Southampton, UK, 2006.

55. P. Krause, S. Ambler, M. Elvang-Gørannson, and J. Fox. A logic of argumentation for reasoning under uncertainty. *Computational Intelligence*, 11 (1):113–131, 1995.

56. S. Kripke. A completeness proof in modal logic. *Journal of Symbolic Logic*, 24:1–14, 1959.
57. J. A. Levin and J. A. Moore. Dialogue-games: metacommunications structures for natural language interaction. *Cognitive Science*, 1(4):395–420, 1978.
58. S. C. Levinson. *Pragmatics*. Cambridge University Press, Cambridge, UK, 1983.
59. P. Lorenzen and K. Lorenz. *Dialogische Logik*. Wissenschaftliche Buchgesellschaft, Darmstadt, Germany, 1978.
60. M. Luck, P. McBurney, O. Shehory, and S. Willmott. *Agent Technology: Computing as Interaction. A Roadmap for Agent Based Computing*. AgentLink III, the European Co-ordination Action for Agent-Based Computing, Southampton, UK, 2005.
61. S. Mac Lane. *Categories for the Working Mathematician*. Springer, New York, USA, 1971.
62. J. D. MacKenzie. Question-begging in non-cumulative systems. *Journal of Philosophical Logic*, 8:117–133, 1979.
63. P. McBurney, R. Eijk, S. Parsons, and L. Amgoud. A dialogue-game protocol for agent purchase negotiations. *Journal of Autonomous Agents and Multi-Agent Systems*, 7(3):235–273, 2003.
64. P. McBurney, D. Hitchcock, and S. Parsons. The eightfold way of deliberation dialogue. *International Journal of Intelligent Systems*, 22(1):95–132, 2007.
65. P. McBurney and S. Parsons. Representing epistemic uncertainty by means of dialectical argumentation. *Annals of Mathematics and Artificial Intelligence*, 32(1–4):125–169, 2001.
66. P. McBurney and S. Parsons. Games that agents play: A formal framework for dialogues between autonomous agents. *Journal of Logic, Language and Information*, 11(3):315–334, 2002.
67. P. McBurney and S. Parsons. A denotational semantics for deliberation dialogues. In I. Rahwan, P. Moraitis, and C. Reed, editors, *Argumentation in Multi-Agent Systems*, Lecture Notes in Artificial Intelligence 3366, pages 162–175. Springer, Berlin, 2005.
68. P. McBurney and S. Parsons. Locutions for argumentation in agent interaction protocols. In R. M. van Eijk *et al.*, editor, *Developments in Agent Communication*, Lecture Notes in Artificial Intelligence 3396, pages 209–225. Springer, Berlin, Germany, 2005.
69. P. McBurney and S. Parsons. Retraction and revocation in agent deliberation dialogs. *Argumentation*, 21(3):269–289, 2007.
70. P. McBurney, S. Parsons, and M. Wooldridge. Desiderata for agent argumentation protocols. In C. Castelfranchi and W. L. Johnson, editors, *Proceedings of the First International Joint Conference on Autonomous Agents and Multi-Agent Systems (AAMAS 2002)*, pages 402–409, New York City, NY, USA, 2002. ACM Press.
71. J. C. C. McKinsey and A. Tarski. Some theorems about the Sentential Calculus of Lewis and Heyting. *Journal of Symbolic Logic*, 13(1):1–15, 1948.
72. B. Meyer. *Introduction to the Theory of Programming Languages*. International Series in Computer Science. Prentice Hall, New York City, NY, USA, 1990.
73. T. Miller and P. McBurney. Using constraints and process algebra for specification of first-class agent interaction protocols. In G. O. *et al.*, editor, *Engineering Societies in the Agents World VII*, Lecture Notes in Artificial Intelligence 4457, pages 245–264, Berlin, Germany, 2007. Springer.
74. T. Miller and P. McBurney. Annotation and matching of first-class agent interaction protocols. In L. P. *et al.*, editor, *Seventh International Joint Conference on Autonomous Agents and Multi-Agent Systems (AAMAS 2008)*, Estoril, Portugal, 2008.
75. C. W. Morris. Foundations of the theory of signs. In O. Neurath, R. Carnap, and C. Morris, editors, *International Encyclopedia of Unified Science*, pages 77–138. Chicago University Press, Chicago, IL, USA, 1938.
76. S. Parsons. Normative argumentation and qualitative probability. In D. M. G. *et al.*, editor, *Qualitative and Quantitative Practical Reasoning*, Lecture Notes in Artificial Intelligence 1244, pages 466–480, Berlin, Germany, 1997. Springer.
77. S. Parsons and E. Sklar. How agents alter their beliefs after an argumentation-based dialogue. In S. P. *et al.*, editor, *Argumentation in Multi-Agent Systems: Second International Workshop (ArgMAS 2005)*, Lecture Notes in Computer Science 4049, pages 297–312. Springer, Berlin, Germany, 2006.

78. L. Perrussel, S. Doutre, J.-M. Thevenin, and P. McBurney. *Argumentation in Multi-Agent Systems*, chapter A persuasion dialog for gaining access to information, pages 63–79. Lecture Notes in Artificial Intelligence 4946. Springer, Berlin, Germany, 2008.

79. M. Pieri. Sui principi che reggiono la geometria di posizione. *Atti della Reale Accademia delle scienze di Torino*, 30:54–108, 1895.

80. H. Prakken. Formal systems for persuasion dialogue. *The Knowledge Engineering Review*, 21(2):163–188, 2006.

81. H. Prakken and G. Sartor. Modelling reasoning with precedents in a formal dialogue game. *Artificial Intelligence and Law*, 6:231–287, 1998.

82. I. Rahwan, S. D. Ramchurn, N. R. Jennings, P. McBurney, S. Parsons, and E. Sonenberg. Argumentation-based negotiation. *Knowledge Engineering Review*, 18(4):343–375, 2003.

83. I. Rahwan, E. Sonenberg, N. R. Jennings, and P. McBurney. STRATUM: a methodology for designing automated negotiation strategies. *Applied Artificial Intelligence*, 21(6):489–527, 2007.

84. C. Reed. Dialogue frames in agent communications. In Y. Demazeau, editor, *Proceedings of the Third International Conference on Multi-Agent Systems (ICMAS-98)*, pages 246–253. IEEE Press, 1998.

85. A. Reinach. Die apriorischen Grundlagen des bürgerlichen Rechtes. *Jahrbuch für Philosophie und phänomenologische Forschung*, 1:685–847, 1913.

86. J. A. Rodríguez, F. J. Martin, P. Noriega, P. Garcia, and C. Sierra. Towards a test-bed for trading agents in electronic auction markets. *AI Communications*, 11(1):5–19, 1998.

87. F. Sadri, F. Toni, and P. Torroni. Logic agents, dialogues and negotiation: an abductive approach. In M. Schroeder and K. Stathis, editors, *Proceedings of the Symposium on Information Agents for E-Commerce (AISB-2001)*, York, UK, 2001. AISB.

88. J. Searle. *Speech Acts: An Essay in the Philosophy of Language*. Cambridge University Press, Cambridge, UK, 1969.

89. C. E. Shannon. The mathematical theory of communication. In C. E. Shannon and W. Weaver, editors, *The Mathematical Theory of Communication*, pages 29–125. University of Illinois Press, Chicago, IL, USA, 1963.

90. M. P. Singh. A social semantics for agent communication languages. In F. Dignum and M. Greaves, editors, *Issues in Agent Communication*, Lecture Notes in Artificial Intelligence 1916, pages 31–45. Springer-Verlag: Heidelberg, Germany, 2000.

91. T. C. Tang. Algebraic postulates and a geometric interpretation for the Lewis calculus of strict implication. *Bulletin of the American Mathematical Society*, 44:737–744, 1938.

92. Y. Tang and S. Parsons. Argumentation-based dialogues for deliberation. In F. D. *et al.*, editor, *Proceedings of the Fourth International Joint Conference on Autonomous Agents and Multi-Agent Systems (AAMAS 2005)*, pages 552–559, New York City, NY, USA, 2005. ACM Press.

93. A. Tarski. Der Aussagenkalkül und die Topologie. *Fundamenta Mathematicae*, 31:103–134, 1938.

94. A. Tarski. The concept of truth in formalized languages. In *Logic, Semantics, Metamathematics*, pages 152–278. Clarendon Press, Oxford, UK, 1956. (Translated by J. H. Woodger).

95. R. Torretti. *The Philosophy of Physics*. Cambridge University Press, Cambridge, UK, 1999.

96. D. N. Walton and E. C. W. Krabbe. *Commitment in Dialogue: Basic Concepts of Interpersonal Reasoning*. SUNY Press, Albany, NY, USA, 1995.

97. M. Wardeh, T. J. M. Bench-Capon, and F. Coenen. Arguments from experience: The PADUA protocol. In P. B. *et al.*, editor, *Computational Models of Argument: Proceedings of COMMA 2008*, pages 405–416, Amsterdam, The Netherlands, 2008. IOS Press.

98. M. J. Wooldridge. Semantic issues in the verification of agent communication languages. *Journal of Autonomous Agents and Multi-Agent Systems*, 3(1):9–31, 2000.

99. M. J. Wooldridge. *Introduction to Multiagent Systems*. John Wiley and Sons, New York, NY, USA, 2002.

100. F. Zeuthen. *Problems of Monopoly and Economic Warfare*. Routledge and Sons, London, UK, 1930.

Chapter 14
Models of Persuasion Dialogue

Henry Prakken

1 Introduction

This chapter[1] reviews formal dialogue systems for persuasion. In persuasion dialogues two or more participants try to resolve a conflict of opinion, each trying to persuade the other participants to adopt their point of view. Dialogue systems for persuasion regulate how such dialogues can be conducted and what their outcome is. Good dialogue systems ensure that conflicts of view can be resolved in a fair and effective way [6]. The term 'persuasion dialogue' was coined by Walton [13] as part of his influential classification of dialogues into six types according to their goal. While *persuasion* aims to resolve a difference of opinion, *negotiation* tries to resolve a conflict of interest by reaching a deal, *information seeking* aims at transferring information, *deliberation* wants to reach a decision on a course of action, *inquiry* is aimed at "growth of knowledge and agreement" and *quarrel* is the verbal substitute of a fight. This classification leaves room for shifts of dialogues of one type to another. In particular, other types of dialogues can shift to persuasion when a conflict of opinion arises. For example, in information-seeking a conflict of opinion could arise on the credibility of a source of information, in deliberation the participants may disagree about likely effects of plans or actions and in negotiation they may disagree about the reasons why a proposal is in one's interest.

The formal study of dialogue systems for persuasion was initiated by Hamblin [5]. Initially, the topic was studied only within philosophical logic and argumentation theory [15, 7], but later several fields of computer science also became interested in this topic. In general AI the embedding of nonmonotonic logic in models of persuasion dialogue was seen as a way to deal with resource-bounded reasoning [6, 2], while in AI & Law persuasion was seen as an appropriate model of legal

---

Henry Prakken

Department of Information and Computing Sciences, Utrecht University, and Faculty of Law, University of Groningen, e-mail: henry@cs.uu.nl

[1] This chapter is a revised and updated version of [11].

procedures [4]. In intelligent tutoring, systems for teaching argumentation skills have been founded on models of persuasion dialogue [16]. Finally, in the field of multi-agent systems dialogue systems have been incorporated into models of rational agent interaction [8].

To delineate the scope of this chapter, it is useful to discuss what is the subject matter of dialogue systems. According to Carlson [3] dialogue systems define the principles of coherent dialogue, that is, the conditions under which an utterance is appropriate. The leading principle here is that an utterance is appropriate if it furthers the goal of the dialogue. For persuasion this means that an utterance should contribute to the resolution of the conflict of opinion that triggered the persuasion. Thus according to Carlson the principles governing the use of utterances should not be defined at the level of individual speech acts but at the level of the dialogue in which the utterance is made. Carlson therefore proposes a game-theoretic approach to dialogues, in which speech acts are viewed as moves in a game and rules for their appropriateness are formulated as rules of the game. Most work on formal dialogue systems for persuasion follows this approach and therefore this chapter will assume a game format of dialogue systems. It should be noted that the term *dialogue system* as used in this chapter only covers the rules of the game, i.e., which moves are allowed; it does not cover principles for playing the game well, i.e., strategies and heuristics for the individual players. The latter are instead aspects of agent models.

Below in Section 2 an example persuasion dialogue will be presented, which will be used for illustration throughout the paper. Then in Section 3 a formal framework for specifying dialogue game systems is proposed, which in Section 4 is instantiated for persuasion dialogues and in Section 5 is used for discussing and comparing three systems proposed in the literature.

2 An example persuasion dialogue

The following example persuasion dialogue exhibits some typical features of persuasion and will be used in this chapter to illustrate different degrees of expressiveness and strictness of the various persuasion systems.

Paul : My car is safe. (*making a claim*)
Olga : Why is your car safe? (*asking grounds for a claim*)
Paul : Since it has an airbag, (*offering grounds for a claim*)
Olga : That is true, (*conceding a claim*) but this does not make your car safe. (*stating a counterclaim*)
Paul : Why does that not make my care safe? (*asking grounds for a claim*)
Olga : Since the newspapers recently reported on airbags expanding without cause. (*stating a counterargument by providing grounds for the counterclaim*)
Paul : Yes, that is what the newspapers say (*conceding a claim*) but that does not prove anything, since newspaper reports are very unreliable sources of technological information. (*undercutting a counterargument*)

Olga: Still your car is still not safe, since its maximum speed is very high. (*alternative counterargument*)
Paul: OK, I was wrong that my car is safe.

This dialogue illustrates several features of persuasion dialogues.

- Participants in a persuasion dialogue not only exchange arguments and counterarguments but also express various propositional attitudes, such as claiming, challenging, conceding or retracting a proposition.
- As for arguments and counterarguments it illustrates the following features.

  - An argument is sometimes attacked by constructing an argument for the opposite conclusion (as in Olga's two counterarguments) but sometimes by saying that in the given circumstances the premises of the argument do not support its conclusion (as in Paul's counterargument). This is Pollock's well-known distinction between rebutting and undercutting counterarguments [9].
  - Counterarguments are sometimes stated at once (as in Paul's undercutter and Olga's last move) and are sometimes introduced by making a counterclaim (as in Olga's second and third move).
  - Natural-language arguments sometimes leave elements implicit. For example, Paul's second move arguably leaves a commonsense generalisation 'Cars with airbags usually are safe' implicit.

- As for the structure of dialogues, the example illustrates the following features.

  - The participants may return to earlier choices and move alternative replies: in her last move Olga states an alternative counterargument after she sees that Paul had a strong counterattack on her first counterargument. Note that she could also have moved the alternative counterargument immediately after her first, to leave Paul with two attacks to counter.
  - The participants may postpone their replies, sometimes even indefinitely: with her second argument why Paul's car is not safe, Olga postpones her reply to Paul's counterattack on her first argument for this claim; if Paul fails to successfully attack her second argument, such a reply might become superfluous.

3 Elements of dialogue systems

In this section a formal framework for specifying dialogue systems is proposed. To summarise, dialogue systems have a *dialogue goal* and at least two *participants*, who can have various *roles*. Dialogue systems have two languages, a a *communication language* wrapped around a *topic language*. Sometimes, dialogues take place in a *context* of fixed and undisputable knowledge, such as the relevant laws in a legal dispute. The heart of a dialogue system is formed by a *protocol*, specifying the allowed moves at each point in a dialogue, the *effect rules*, specifying the effects of utterances on the participants' commitments, and the *outcome rules*, defining the outcome of a dialogue. Two kinds of protocol rules are sometimes separately defined, viz. *turntaking* and *termination* rules.

Let us now specify these elements more formally. The definitions below of dialogues, protocols and strategies are based on Chapter 12 of [1] as adapted in [10]. As for notation, the complement $\overline{\varphi}$ of a formula φ is $\neg\varphi$ if φ is a positive formula and ψ if φ is a negative formula $\neg\psi$.

Definition 14.1. (Dialogue systems) A *dialogue system* consists of the following elements.

- A *topic language* $\mathcal{L}_t$, closed under classical negation.
- A *communication language* $\mathcal{L}_c$, consisting of a set of *speech acts* with a *content*. The set of *dialogues*, denoted by $M^{\leq\infty}$, is the set of all sequences from $\mathcal{L}_c$, and the set of *finite dialogues*, denoted by $M^{<\infty}$, is the set of all finite sequences from $\mathcal{L}_c$. For any dialogue $d = m_1,\ldots,m_n,\ldots$, the subsequence $m_1,\ldots,m_i$ is denoted with d_i.
- A *dialogue purpose*.
- A set $\mathcal{A}$ of *participants* (or 'players') and a set $\mathcal{R}$ of *roles*, defined as disjoint subsets of $\mathcal{A}$. A participant a may or may not have a, possibly inconsistent, *belief base* $\Sigma_a \subseteq Pow(\mathcal{L}_t)$, which may or may not change during a dialogue. Furthermore, each participant has a, possibly empty set of *commitments* $C_a \subseteq \mathcal{L}_t$, which usually changes during a dialogue.
- A *context* $K \subseteq \mathcal{L}_t$, containing the knowledge that is presupposed and must be respected during a dialogue. The context is assumed consistent and remains the same throughout a dialogue.
- A *logic L* for $\mathcal{L}_t$, which may or may not be monotonic and which may or may not be argument-based.
- A set of *effect rules C* for $\mathcal{L}_c$, specifying for each utterance $\varphi \in \mathcal{L}_c$ its effects on the commitments of the participants. These rules are specified as functions

  - $C_a : M^{<\infty} \longrightarrow Pow(\mathcal{L}_t)$

  Changes in commitments are completely determined by the last move in a dialogue and the commitments just before making that move:

  - If $d = d'$ then $C_a(d,m) = C_a(d',m)$

- A *protocol Pr* for $\mathcal{L}_c$, specifying the allowed (or 'legal') moves at each stage of a dialogue. Formally, A *protocol* on $\mathcal{L}_c$ is a function Pr with domain the context plus a nonempty subset D of $M^{<\infty}$ taking subsets of $\mathcal{L}_c$ as values. That is:

  - $Pr : Pow(\mathcal{L}_t) \times D \longrightarrow Pow(\mathcal{L}_c)$

  such that $D \subseteq M^{<\infty}$. The elements of D are called the *legal finite dialogues*. The elements of $Pr(d)$ are called the moves allowed after d. If d is a legal dialogue and $Pr(d) = \varnothing$, then d is said to be a *terminated* dialogue. Pr must satisfy the following condition: for all finite dialogues d and moves m, $d \in D$ and $m \in Pr(d)$ iff $d,m \in D$.

It is useful (although not strictly necessary) to explicitly distinguish elements of a protocol that regulate turntaking and termination:

- A *turntaking* function is a function $T : D \times Pow(\mathcal{L}_t) \longrightarrow Pow(\mathcal{A})$. A *turn* of a dialogue is defined as a maximal sequence of moves in the dialogue in which the same player is to move. Note that T can designate more than one player as to-move next.
- *Termination* is above defined as the case where no move is legal. Accordingly, an explicit definition of termination should specify the conditions under which Pr returns the empty set.

- *Outcome rules* O^K, defining the outcome of a dialogue given a context. For instance, in negotiation the outcome is an allocation of resources, in deliberation it is a decision on a course of action, and in persuasion dialogue it is a winner and a loser of the persuasion dialogue. The outcome must be defined for terminated dialogues and may be defined for nonterminated ones; in the latter case the outcome rules capture an 'anytime' outcome notion.

Note that no relations are assumed between a participant's commitments and belief base. Commitments are an agent's publicly declared points of view about a proposition, which need not coincide with the agent's internal beliefs.

Definition 14.2. (Some protocol types)

- A protocol has a *public semantics* if the set of legal moves is always independent from the agents' belief bases.
- A protocol is *context-independent* if the set of legal moves and the outcome is always independent of the context, so if $Pr(K,d) = Pr(\varnothing,d)$ and $O^K(d) = O^\varnothing(d)$ for all K and d.
- A protocol Pr is *fully deterministic* if Pr always returns a singleton or the empty set. It is *deterministic in* $\mathcal{L}_c$ if the set of moves returned by Pr at most differ in their content but not in their speech act type.
- A protocol is *unique-move* if the turn shifts after each move; it is *multiple-move* otherwise.

Paul and Olga (ct'd): The protocol in our running example is multiple-move.

Dialogue participants can have strategies and heuristics for playing the dialogue game in ways that promote their individual dialogue goal. The notion of a *strategy* for a participant a can be defined in the game-theoretical sense, as a function from the set of all finite legal dialogues in which a is to move into $\mathcal{L}_c$. A strategy for a is a *winning strategy* if every dialogue played in accord with the strategy a realises his dialogue goal (for instance, winning in persuasion). *Heuristics* generalise strategies in two ways: they may leave the choice for some dialogues undefined and they may specify more than one move as a choice option. More formally:

Definition 14.3. (strategies and heuristics) Let D_a, a subset of D, be the set of all dialogues where a is to move, and let D'_a be a subset of D_a. Then a strategy and a heuristic for a are defined as functions s_a and h_a as follows.

- $s_a : D_a \longrightarrow \mathcal{L}_c$
- $h_a : D'_a \longrightarrow Pow(\mathcal{L}_c)$

4 Persuasion

Let us now become more precise about persuasion. Walton & Krabbe [14] define persuasion dialogues as dialogues with as goal to resolve a conflict of points of view between at least two participants. A *point of view* with respect to a proposition can be positive (for), negative (against) or doubtful. The participants aim to persuade the other participant(s) to accept their point of view. According to Walton & Krabbe a conflict is resolved if all parties share the same point of view on the proposition that is at issue. They distinguish *disputes* as a subtype of persuasion dialogues where two parties disagree about a single proposition φ, such that at the start of the dialogue one party has a positive (φ) and the other party a negative ($\neg\varphi$) point of view towards the proposition.

Dialogue systems for persuasion can be formally defined as a particular class of instantiations of the general framework.

Definition 14.4. (dialogue systems for persuasion) A *dialogue system for persuasion* is a dialogue system with at least the following instantiations of Definition 14.1.

- The *dialogue purpose* is resolution of a conflict of opinion about one or more propositions, called the *topics* $T \subseteq \mathcal{L}_t$. This dialogue purpose gives rise to the following participant roles and outcome rules.
- The participants can have the following *roles*. To start with, $prop(t) \subseteq \mathcal{A}$, the *proponents* of topic t, is the (nonempty) set of all participants with a positive point of view towards t. Likewise, $opp(t) \subseteq \mathcal{A}$, the *opponents* of t, is the (nonempty) set of all participants with a doubtful point of view toward a topic t. Together, the proponents and opponents of t are called the *adversaries* with respect to t. For any t, the sets $prop(t)$ and $opp(t)$ are disjoint but do not necessarily jointly exhaust $\mathcal{A}$. The remaining participants, if any, are the *third parties* with respect to t, assumed to be neutral towards t.

  Note that this allows that a participant is a proponent of both t and $\neg t$ or has a positive attitude towards t and a doubtful attitude towards a topic t' that is logically equivalent to t. Since protocols can deal with such situations in various ways, this should not be excluded by definition.
- The *Outcome rules* of systems for persuasion dialogues define for a dialogue d, context K and topic t the *winners* and *losers* of d with respect to topic d. More precisely, O consists of two partial functions w and l:

  - $w : D \times Pow(\mathcal{L}_t) \times \mathcal{L}_t \longrightarrow Pow(\mathcal{A})$
  - $l : D \times Pow(\mathcal{L}_t) \times \mathcal{L}_t \longrightarrow Pow(\mathcal{A})$

  such that they are defined at least for all terminated dialogues but only for those t that are a topic of d. These functions will be written as $w_t^K(d)$ and $l_t^K(d)$ or, if there is no danger for confusion, as $w_t(d)$ and $l_t(d)$. They further satisfy the following conditions for arbitrary but fixed context K:

- $w_t(d) \cap l_t(d) = \varnothing$
- $w_t(d) = \varnothing$ iff $l_t(d) = \varnothing$
- if $|A| = 2$, then $w_t(d)$ and $l_t(d)$ are at most singletons

- Next, to make sense of the notions of proponent and opponent, their commitments at the start of a dialogue should not conflict with their points of view.

    - If $a \in prop(t)$ then $\bar{t} \notin C_a(\varnothing)$
    - If $a \in opp(t)$ then $t \notin C_a(\varnothing)$

- Finally, in persuasion at most one side in a dialogue gives up, i.e.,

    - $w_t(d) \subseteq prop(t)$ or $w_t(d) \subseteq opp(t)$; and
    - If $a \in w_t(d)$ then
        · if $a \in prop(t)$ then $t \in C_a(d)$
        · if $a \in opp(t)$ then $t \notin C_a(d)$

These conditions ensure that a winner did not change its point of view. Note that they make that two-person persuasion dialogues are zero-sum games. Perhaps this is the main feature that sets persuasion apart from information seeking, deliberation and inquiry.

Note that the two last winning conditions of the last bullet lack their only-if part. This is to allow for a distinction between so-called *pure persuasion* and *conflict resolution*. The outcome of pure persuasion dialogues is fully determined by the participants' points of view and commitments:

Definition 14.5. (types of persuasion systems)

- A dialogue system is for *pure persuasion* iff for any terminated dialogue d it holds that $a \in w_t(d)$ iff

    - either $a \in prop(t)$ and $t \in C_{a'}(d)$ for all $a' \in prop(d) \cup opp(d)$
    - or $a \in opp(t)$ and $t \notin C_{a'}(d)$ for all $a' \in prop(d) \cup opp(d)$

- Otherwise, it is for *conflict resolution*.

In addition, pure persuasion dialogues are assumed to terminate as soon as the right-hand-side conjuncts of one of these two winning conditions hold.

Paul and Olga (ct'd): In our running example, if the dialogue is regulated by a protocol for pure persuasion, it terminates after Paul's retraction.

In conflict resolution dialogues the outcome is not fully determined by the participant's points of view and commitments. In other words, in such dialogues it is possible that, for instance, a proponent of φ loses the dialogue about φ even if at termination he is still committed to φ. A typical example is legal procedure, where a third party can determine the outcome of the case. For instance, a crime suspect can be convicted even if he maintains his innocence throughout the case.

If the system has an anytime outcome notion, then another distinction can be made [6]: a protocol is *immediate-response* if the turn shifts just in case the speaker is the 'current' winner and if it then shifts to a 'current' loser.

As for the communication language and effect rules, some common elements can be found throughout the literature. Below are the most common speech acts, with their informal meaning and the various names they have been given in the literature.[2]

- *claim* φ (assert, statement, ...). The speaker asserts that φ is the case.
- *why* φ (challenge, deny, question, ...) The speaker challenges that φ is the case and asks for reasons why it would be the case.
- *concede* φ (accept, admit, ...). The speaker admits that φ is the case.
- *retract* φ (withdraw, no commitment, ..) The speaker declares that he is not committed (any more) to φ. Retractions are 'really' retractions if the speaker is committed to the retracted proposition, otherwise it is a mere declaration of non-commitment (for example, in reply to a question).
- φ *since S* (argue, argument, ...) The speaker provides reasons why φ is the case. Some protocols do not have this move but instead require that reasons be provided by a *claim* φ or *claim S* move in reply to a *why* ψ move (where S is a set of propositions). Also, in some systems the reasons provided for φ can have structure, for example, of a proof three or a deduction.
- *question* φ The speaker asks the hearers' opinion on whether φ is the case.

Paul and Olga (ct'd): In this communication language our example from Section 2 can be more formally displayed as follows:

P_1: *claim* safe	O_2: *why* safe
P_3: safe *since* airbag	O_4: *concede* airbag
	O_5: *claim* $\neg$ safe
P_6: *why* $\neg$ safe	O_7: $\neg$ safe *since* newspaper
P_8: *concede* newspaper	
P_9: so what *since* $\neg$ newspapers reliable	O_{10}: $\neg$ safe *since* high max. speed
P_{11}: *retract* safe	

Most dialogue systems have a notion of typical replies to certain speech acts, although usually this is left implicit in the replies that are allowed by the protocol rules. In most systems these typical replies are as displayed in Table 14.1.

Paul and Olga (ct'd): With this table our running example can be displayed as in Figure 14.1, where the boxes stand for moves and the links for reply relations.

The reply notion induces another distinction between dialogue protocols.

Definition 14.6. A dialogue protocol is *unique-reply* if at most one reply to a move is allowed throughout a dialogue; otherwise it is *multiple-reply*.

Paul and Olga (ct'd): The protocol governing our running example is multiple-reply, as illustrated by the various branches in Figure 14.1.

---

[2] To make this chapter more uniform, the present terminology will be used even if the original publication of a system uses different terms.

Table 14.1 Locutions and typical replies

Locutions	Replies
claim φ	*why* φ, *claim* $\overline{\varphi}$, *concede* φ
why φ	φ *since S* (alternatively: *claim S*), *retract* φ
concede φ	
retract φ	
φ *since S*	*why* ψ ($\psi \in S$), *concede* ψ ($\psi \in S$), φ' *since S'*
question φ	*claim* φ, *claim* $\overline{\varphi}$, *retract* φ

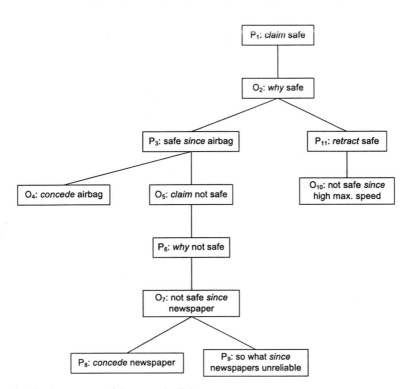

Fig. 14.1 Reply structure of the example dialogue

As for the commitment rules, the following ones are generally accepted in the literature. (Below *pl* denotes the speaker of the move; effects on the other parties' commitments are only specified when a change is effected.)

- If $pl(m) = claim(\varphi)$ then $C_{pl}(d,m) = C_{pl}(d) \cup \{\varphi\}$
- If $pl(m) = why(\varphi)$ then $C_{pl}(d,m) = C_{pl}(d)$
- If $pl(m) = concede(\varphi)$ then $C_{pl}(d,m) = C_{pl}(d) \cup \{\varphi\}$
- If $pl(m) = retract(\varphi)$ then $C_{pl}(d,m) = C_{pl}(d) - \{\varphi\}$
- If $pl(m) = \varphi$ *since S* then $C_{pl}(d,m) \supseteq C_{pl}(d) \cup prem(A)$

The rule for *since* uses $\supseteq$ since such a move may commit to more than just the premises of the moved argument. For instance, in [10] the move also commits to φ, since arguments can also be moved as counterarguments instead of as replies to challenges of a claim. And in some systems that allow incomplete arguments, such as [14], the move also commits the speaker to the material implication $S \rightarrow \varphi$.

Paul and Olga (ct'd): According to these rules, the commitment sets of Paul and Olga at the end of the example dialogue are

- $C_P(d_{11}) \supseteq \{$airbag, newspaper, $\neg$ newspapers reliable$\}$
- $C_O(d_{11}) \supseteq \{\neg$ safe, airbag, newspaper, high max. speed$\}$

5 Three systems

Now three persuasion protocols from the literature will be discussed. The first is primarily based on commitments, the second defines protocols as finite state machines, while the third exploits an explicit reply structure on the communication language.

5.1 Walton and Krabbe (1995)

The first system to be discussed is Walton & Krabbe's dialogue system PPD for "permissive persuasion dialogues" [14]. In PPD, dialogues have no context. The players are called White (W) and Black (B). They are assumed to declare zero or more "assertions" and "concessions" in an implicit preparatory phase of a dialogue. Each participant is proponent of his own and opponent of the other participant's initial assertions. B must have declared at least one assertion, and W starts a dialogue. The communication language consists of challenges, (tree-structured) arguments, concessions, questions, resolution demands ("resolve"), and two retraction locutions, one for assertion-type and one for concession-type commitments. It has no explicit reply structure but the protocol reflects the reply structure of Table 14.1 above.

The logical language is that of propositional logic and the logic consists of an incomplete set of deductively valid inference rules: they are incomplete to reflect that for natural language no complete logic exists. Although an argument may thus be incomplete, its mover becomes committed to the material implication *premises* $\rightarrow$ *conclusion*, which is then open for discussion.

The commitment rules are standard but Walton & Krabbe distinguish between several kinds of commitments for each participant, viz. *assertions*, *concessions* and *dark-side* commitments. Initial assertions and premises of arguments are placed in the assertions while conceded propositions are placed in the concessions. Only assertions can be challenged. Dark-side commitments are hidden or veiled commitments of an agent, of which they are often unaware. This makes them hard to model computationally, for which reason they will be ignored below.

The protocol is driven by two main factors: the contents of the commitment sets and the content of the last turn. W starts and in their first turn both W and B either concede or challenge each initial assertion of the other party. Then each turn must reply to all moves in the other player's last turn except concessions and retractions; in particular, for *since* moves each premise must be conceded or challenged, including the hidden premise of incomplete arguments. Multiple replies are allowed, such as alternative arguments for the same assertion. Counterarguments are not allowed. In sum, the PPD protocol is nondeterministic, multi-move and multi-reply but postponement of replies is not allowed. Dark-side commitments prevent the protocol from having a public semantics.

Most protocol rules refer to the participants' commitments. To start with, challenges, concessions and retractions always concern commitments. Second, a speaker cannot challenge or concede his own commitments, and *question* φ and φ *since S* may not be used if the listener is committed to φ. Furthermore, if a participant has inconsistent commitments, the other participant can demand resolution of the inconsistency by using the *resolve* speech act. Also, if a participant's commitments logically imply an assertion of the other participant but do not contain that assertion, then the initial participant must either concede the assertion or retract one of the implying commitments. Retractions must be successful in that the retracted proposition is not still implied by the speaker's commitments. Finally, the commitments determine the outcome of a dialogue: dialogues terminate after a predetermined number of turns, and the outcome of terminated dialogues is defined as for pure persuasion.

Table 14.2 contains an example dialogue.[3] The first column numbers the turns, and the second contains the moves made in each turn. The other columns contain the assertions and concessions of W and B: the first row contains the initial commitments and the other rows indicate changes in these sets: $+\varphi$ means that φ is added and $-\varphi$ that it is deleted. If the dialogue terminates here, there is no winner, since neither player has conceded any of the other player's assertions or retracted any of his own.

Several points are worth noting about this example. Firstly, B in his first turn moves a complex argument, where the second argument supports a premise of the first: for this reason i is not added to B's assertions. Next, in his second turn, W first concedes j and then asserts j as a premise of an argument; only after the second move has W incurred a burden to defend j if challenged. However, B in his second turn cannot challenge j since B is itself committed to j: if B wants to challenge j, he must first retract j. Note further that after B concedes $f \wedge j \rightarrow a$ in his second turn, his commitments logically imply a, which is an assertion of W. Therefore B must in the same turn either concede a or retract one of the implying commitments. B opts for the latter, retracting f. Next consider B's second move of his second turn: remarkably, B becomes committed to a tautology but W still has the right to challenge it at his third turn. Finally, the example illustrates that the protocol only partly enforces relevance of moves. For instance, at any point a participant could have moved *question* φ for any φ not in the commitments of the listener.

Paul and Olga (ct'd): Let us finally reconstruct our running example in PPD. To start with, Paul's initial claim must now be modelled as an initial assertion in the

---

[3] In this section the dialogue participants will be denoted with W and B, except if they have proponent/opponent roles throughout the dialogues, in which case they are called P and O.

Table 14.2 An example PPD dialogue

Turn	Moves	A_W	C_W	A_B	C_B
		$\{a\}$	$\{b,c\}$	$\{d,e\}$	$\{f,g\}$
W_1	why d concede e		$+e$		
B_1	why a d since h,i, i since j,k			$+h, h \wedge i \to d$, $j,k, j \wedge k \to i$	
W_2	concede j concede k why $j \wedge k \to i$ concede $h \wedge i \to d$ why h a since f,j	$+f, j, f \wedge j \to a$	$+j$ $+k$ $+h \wedge i \to d$		
B_2	h since $l, l \to h$ $j \wedge k \to i$ since m concede $f \wedge j \to a$ retract$_C$ f			$+l, l \to k$, $l \wedge (l \to k) \to k$ $+m, m \to (j \wedge k \to i)$	$+f \wedge j \to a$ $-f$

preparatory phase. Since arguments can be incomplete, they can be modelled as in the example's original version. Two features of PPD make a straightforward modelling of the example impossible. The first is that PPD requires that every claim or argument is replied to in the next turn and the second is that explicit counterarguments are not allowed. To deal with the latter, it must be assumed that Olga has also declared an initial assertion, viz. that Paul's car is not safe.

$(P_0$: *claim* safe O_0: *claim* $\neg$ safe)
                             O_1: *why* safe
P_2: safe *since* airbag
P_3: *why* $\neg$ safe O_4: *concede* airbag
                             O_5: $\neg$ safe *since* newspaper

Here a problem arises, since Olga now has to either concede or challenge Paul's hidden premise airbag $\to$ safe. If Olga concedes it, she is forced to also concede Paul's initial claim, since it is now implied by Olga's commitments. If, on the other hand, Olga challenges the hidden premise, then at his next turn Paul must provide an argument for it, which he does not do in our original example. Similar problems arise with the rest of the example. Let us now, to proceed with the example, ignore this 'completeness' requirement of turns.

P_6: *concede* newspaper

Here another problem arises, since PPD does not allow Paul to move his undercutting counterargument against O_5. The only way to attack O_5 is by challenging its unstated premise (newspaper $\to \neg$ safe).

In sum, two features of PPD prevent a fully natural modelling of our example: the monotonic nature of the underlying logic and the requirement to reply to each claim or argument of the other participant.

5.2 Parsons, Wooldridge & Amgoud (2003)

In a series of papers Parsons, Wooldridge & Amgoud have developed an approach to specifying dialogue systems for various types of dialogues. Here the persuasion system of [8] will be discussed.

The system is for dialogues on a single topic between two players called White (W) and Black (B). Dialogues have no context but each participant has a, possibly inconsistent, belief base Σ. The communication language consists of claims, challenges, and concessions; it has no explicit reply structure but the protocol largely conforms to Table 14.1. Claims can concern both individual propositions and sets of propositions. The logical language is propositional. Its logic is an argument-based nonmonotonic logic in which arguments are classical proofs from consistent premises and counterarguments negate a premise of their target. Conflict relations between arguments are resolved with a preference relation on the premises such that arguments are as good as their least preferred premises. Argument acceptability is defined with grounded semantics. In dialogues, arguments cannot be moved as such but only implicitly as *claim S* replies to challenges of another claim φ, such that S is consistent and $S \vdash \varphi$. Finally, the commitment rules are standard and commitments are only used to enlarge the player's belief base with the other player's commitments; they do not constrain move legality nor determine the dialogue's outcome.

An important feature of the system is that the players are assumed to adopt an assertion and an acceptance attitude, which they must respect throughout the dialogue. The attitudes are defined relative to their internal belief base (which remains constant throughout a dialogue) plus both players' commitment sets (which may vary during a dialogue). The following assertion attitudes are distinguished: a *confident* agent can assert any proposition for which he can construct an argument, a *careful* agent can do so only if he can construct such an argument and cannot construct a stronger counterargument, and a *thoughtful* agent can do so only if he can construct an acceptable argument for the proposition. The corresponding acceptance attitudes also exist: a *credulous* agent accepts a proposition if he can construct an argument for it, a *cautious* agent does so only if in addition he cannot construct a stronger counterargument and a *skeptical* agent does so only if he can construct an acceptable argument for the proposition.

It can be debated whether such the requirement to respect these attitudes must be part of a protocol or of a participant's heuristics. According to one approach, a dialogue protocol should only enforce coherence of dialogues [14, 10]; according to another approach, it should also enforce rationality and trustworthiness of the agents engaged in a dialogue [8]. The second approach allows protocol rules to refer to an agent's internal belief base and therefore such protocols do not have a public semantics. The first approach does not allow such protocol rules and instead regards assertion and acceptance attitudes as an aspect of agent design.

The formal definition of the persuasion protocol is as follows.

Definition 14.7. (PWA persuasion protocol) A move is legal iff it does not repeat a move of the same player, and satisfies the following procedure:

1. W claims φ.
2. B concedes φ if its acceptance attitude allows, if not B asserts $\neg\varphi$ if its assertion attitude allows it, or otherwise challenges φ.
3. If B claims $\neg\varphi$, then goto 2 with the roles of the players reversed and $\neg\varphi$ in place of φ.
4. If B has challenged, then:
   a. W claims S, an argument for φ;
   b. Goto 2 for each $s \in S$ in turn.
5. B concedes φ if its acceptance attitude allows, or the dialogue terminates.

Dialogues *terminate* as specified in condition 5, or when the move required by the procedure cannot be made, or when the player-to-move has conceded all claims made by the hearer.

No win and loss functions are defined, but the possible outcomes are defined in terms of the propositions claimed by one player and conceded by the other.

This protocol is unique-move except that if one element of a *claim S* move is conceded, another element may be replied-to next. Also, it is unique-reply except that each element of a *claim S* move can be separately challenged or conceded. The protocol is deterministic in $\mathcal{L}_c$ but not fully deterministic, since if a player can construct more than one argument for a challenged claim, he has a choice.

Let us first consider some simple dialogues that fit this protocol.

Example 14.1. First, let $\Sigma_W = \{p\}$ and $\Sigma_B = \varnothing$. Then the only legal dialogue is:

W_1: *claim p*, B_1: *concede p*

B_1 is B's only legal move, whatever its acceptance attitude, since after W_1, B must reason from $\Sigma_B \cup C_W(d_1) = \{p\}$ so that B can construct the trivial argument $(\{p\}, p)$. Here the dialogue terminates.

This example illustrates that since the players must reason with the commitments of the other player, they can learn from each other. However, the next example illustrates that the same feature sometimes makes them learn too easily.

Example 14.2. Assume $\Sigma_W = \{q, q \to p\}$ and $\Sigma_B = \{\neg q\}$, where all formulas are of the same preference level.

W_1: *claim p*

Now whatever her acceptance attitude, B has to concede p since she can construct the trivial argument $(\{p\}, p)$ for p while she can construct no argument for $\neg p$. Yet B has an attacker for W's only argument for p, namely, $(\{\neg q\}, \neg q)$, which attacks $(\{q, q \to p\}, p)$ and is not weaker than its target. So even though p is not acceptable on the basis of the agents' joint knowledge, W_1 can win a dialogue about p.

This example thus illustrates that if the players must reason with the other player's commitments, one player can sometimes 'force' an opinion onto the other player by simply making a claim. A simple solution to this problem is to restrict the information with which agent reason to their own beliefs and commitments. A more refined option is to assume that the agents have knowledge about the reliability of information sources and to let them use it in the acceptance policies.

Paul and Olga (ct'd): Finally, our running example can be modelled in this approach as follows. Let us give Paul and Olga the following beliefs:

$$\Sigma_W = \{\text{airbag, airbag} \rightarrow \text{safe}, \neg(\text{newspaper} \rightarrow \neg \text{safe})\}$$
$$\Sigma_B = \{\text{newspaper, newspaper} \rightarrow \neg \text{safe}\}$$

(Note that Paul's undercutter must now be formalised as the negation of Olga's material implication.) Assume that all these propositions are equally preferred. We must also make some assumptions on the players' assertion and acceptance attitudes. Let us first assume that Paul is thoughtful and skeptical while Olga is careful and cautious, and that they only reason with their own beliefs and commitments.

P_1: *claim* safe O_2: *claim* $\neg$ safe

Olga could not challenge Paul's main claim as in the example's original version, since she can construct an argument for '$\neg safe$', while she cannot construct an argument for 'safe'. So she had to make a counterclaim. Now since players may not repeat moves, Paul cannot make the remove required by the protocol and his assertion attitude, namely, claiming 'safe', so the dialogue terminates without agreement.

Let us now assume that the players must also reason with each others commitments. Then the dialogue evolves as follows:

P_1: *claim* safe O_2: *concede* safe

Olga has to concede, since she can use Paul's commitment to construct the trivial argument ($\{\text{safe}\}$, safe), while her own argument for '$\neg$ safe' is not stronger. So here the dialogue terminates with agreement on 'safe', even though this proposition is not acceptable on the basis of the players' joint beliefs.

So far, neither of the players could develop their arguments. To change this, assume now that Olga is also thoughtful and skeptical, and that the players reason with each others commitments. Then:

P_1: *claim* safe O_2: *why* safe

Olga could not concede, nor could she state her argument for $\neg$ safe since it is not preferred over its attacker ($\{\text{safe}\}$,safe). So she had to challenge.

P_3: *claim* $\{\text{airbag, airbag} \rightarrow \text{safe}\}$

Now Olga can create a (trivial) argument for 'airbag' by using Paul's commitments, but she can also create an argument for its negation by using her own beliefs. Neither is acceptable, so she must challenge. Likewise for the second premise, so:

O_4: *why* airbag
P_5: *claim* $\{\text{airbag}\}$ O_6: *why* airbag $\rightarrow$ safe
P_7: *claim* $\{\text{airbag} \rightarrow \text{safe}\}$

Here the nonrepetition rule makes the dialogue terminate without agreement. Note that only Paul could develop his arguments. To give Olga a chance to develop her arguments, let us make her careful and skeptical while the players still reason with each others commitments. Then:

P_1: *claim* safe O_2: *claim* $\neg$ safe

In the new dialogue state Paul's argument for 'safe' is not acceptable any more, since it is not preferred over its attacker ($\{\neg$ safe$\}$, $\neg$ safe). So he must challenge.

P_3: *why* $\neg$ safe O_4: *claim* $\{$newspaper, newspaper $\rightarrow$ $\neg$ safe $\}$

Although Paul can construct an argument for Olga's first premise, namely, ($\{\neg$(newspaper $\rightarrow$ $\neg$ safe'$\}$, safe), it is not acceptable since it is not preferred over its attacker based on Olga's second premise. So he must challenge.

P_5: *why* newspaper O_6: *claim* $\{$newspaper$\}$

Olga had to reply with a (trivial) argument for her first premise, after which Paul cannot repeat his challenge, so he has to go to the second premise of O_4. Based on his beliefs and Olga's commitments he can construct (trivial) arguments both for and against it and neither of these is acceptable. So he must again challenge.

P_7: *why* newspaper $\rightarrow$ $\neg$ safe O_8: *claim* $\{$newspaper $\rightarrow$ $\neg$ safe$\}$

Here the nonrepetition rule again makes the dialogue terminate without agreement. In this dialogue only Olga could develop her arguments (although she could not state her second counterargument).

In conclusion, the PWA persuasion protocol leaves little room for choice and exploring alternatives, and induces one-sided dialogues in that at most one side can develop their arguments for a certain issue. Also, the examples suggest that if a claim is accepted, it is accepted in the first 'round' of moves (but this should be formally verified). On the other hand, the strictness of the protocol induces short dialogues which are guaranteed to terminate, which promotes efficiency. Also, thanks to the strong assumptions on the logic and the participants' beliefs and reasoning behaviour, PWA have been able to prove several interesting properties of their protocols. Finally, without the requirement to respect the assertion and acceptance attitudes the protocol would be much more liberal while still enforcing some coherence.

5.3 Prakken (2005)

In [10] I proposed a formal framework for systems for two-party persuasion dialogues and instantiated it with some example protocols. The participants have proponent and opponent role, and their beliefs are irrelevant to the protocols, so that these have a public semantics. Dialogues have no context. The framework abstracts from the communication language except for an explicit reply structure. It also abstracts from the logical language and the logic, except that the logic is assumed to be argument-based and to conform to grounded semantics and that arguments are trees of deductive and/or defeasible inferences, as in e.g. [9].

A main motivation of the framework is to ensure focus of dialogues while yet allowing for freedom to move alternative replies and to postpone replies. This is achieved with two main features of the framework. Firstly, $\mathcal{L}_c$ has an explicit reply structure, where each move either *attacks* or *surrenders to* its target. An example $\mathcal{L}_c$ of this format is displayed in Table 14.3. Secondly, winning is defined for each dia-

Table 14.3 An example L_c in Prakken's framework

Acts	Attacks	Surrenders
claim φ	*why* φ	*concede* φ
φ *since S*	*why* $\psi(\psi \in S)$	*concede* ψ ($\psi \in S$)
	φ' *since S'* (φ' *since S' defeats* φ *since S*)	*concede* φ
why φ	φ *since S*	*retract* φ
concede φ		
retract φ		

logue, whether terminated or not, and it is defined in terms of a notion of *dialogical status* of moves. The *dialogical status* of a move is recursively defined as follows, exploiting the tree structure of dialogues generated by the reply structure on $\mathcal{L}_c$. A move is *in* if it is surrendered or else if all its attacking replies are *out*. (This implies that a move without replies is *in*). And a move is *out* if it has a reply that is *in*. Then a dialogue is (currently) won by the proponent if its initial move is *in* while it is (currently) won by the opponent otherwise.

Together, these two features of the framework support a notion of relevance that ensures focus while yet leaving a degree of freedom: a move is *relevant* just in case making its target *out* would make the speaker the current winner. Termination is defined as the situation that a player is to move but has no legal moves. Various results are proven about the relation between being the current winner of a dialogue and what is defeasibly implied by the arguments exchanged during the dialogue.

As for dialogue structure, the framework allows for all kinds of protocols. The instantiations of [10] are all multi-move and multi-reply; one of them has the communication language of Table 14.3 and is constrained by the requirement that each move be relevant. This makes the protocol immediate-response, which implies that each turn consists of zero or more surrenders followed by one attacker. Within these limits postponement of replies is allowed, sometimes even indefinitely.

Let us next discuss some examples, assuming that the protocol is further instantiated with Prakken & Sartor's argument-based version of prioritised extended logic programming [12]. This logic uses grounded semantics and supports arguments about rule priorities. (The examples below should speak for themselves so no formal definitions about the logic will be given. Note that since the rules are logic-programming rules, they do not satisfy contraposition or modus tollens. Rule connectives are tagged with a rule name, which is needed to express rule priorities in the object language). Consider two agents with the following belief bases:

$$\Sigma_P = \{p, p \Rightarrow_{r_1} q, q \Rightarrow_{r_2} r, p \wedge s \Rightarrow_{r_3} r_2 > r_4\}$$
$$\Sigma_O = \{t, t \Rightarrow_{r_4} \neg r\}.$$

Then the following is legal in [10]'s so-called relevant protocol (with each move its target is indicated between square brackets):

$P_1[-]$: *claim r* $O_2[P_1]$: *why r*
$P_3[O_2]$: *r since q, q $\Rightarrow$ r* $O_4[P_3]$: *why q*
$P_5[O_4]$: *q since p, p $\Rightarrow$ q* $O_6[P_5]$: *concede p $\Rightarrow$ q*
                                          $O_7[P_5]$: *why p*

(Note that unlike in [8] but like in [14], arguments can be stepwise built in several moves.) Here P has several allowed moves, viz. retracting any of his argument premises or his claim, or giving an argument for p. All these moves are relevant but if P makes any retraction then an argument for p ceases to be relevant, since it cannot make P the current winner. Moreover, if P retracts r as a reply to P_1 then the dialogue terminates with a win for O.

O could at all points after P_3 have moved her argument against r. For instance:

$$O_7[P_3]: \neg r \text{ since } t, t \Rightarrow \neg r$$

$P_8[O_7]$: $r_2 > r_4$ *since* $p, s, p \wedge s \Rightarrow r_1 > r_4$

P_8 is a priority argument which makes P_3 strictly defeat O_7 (note that the fact that s is not in P's own belief base does not make the move illegal). At this point, P_1 is *in*; O has various allowed moves, viz. challenging or conceding any (further) premise of P's arguments, moving a counterargument to P_5 or a second counterargument to P_3, and conceding P's initial claim.

This example shows that the participants have much more freedom in this system than in the one of [8], since they are not bound by assertion and acceptance attitudes and the protocol is structurally less strict. The downside of this is that dialogues can be much longer, that the participants can lie and that they can prevent losing by simply continuing to attack the other participant.

Another drawback of the present approach is that not all natural-language dialogues have an explicit reply structure. For example, often one player tries to extract seemingly irrelevant concessions from the other player with the aim to lure her into a contradiction, as in as in the following witness cross-examination dialogue:

> *Witness*: Suspect was at home with me that day.
> *Prosecutor*: Are you a student?
> *Witness*: Yes.
> *Prosecutor*: Was that day during summer holiday?
> *Witness*: Yes.
> *Prosecutor*: Aren't all students away during summer holiday?

In [14] such dialogues can be modelled with the *question* locution but at the price of decreased coherence and focus.

Paul and Olga (ct'd): Let us finally model our running example in this protocol. Figure 14.2 displays the dialogue tree, where moves within solid boxes are *in* and moves within dotted boxes are *out*.

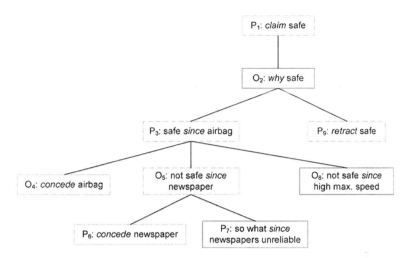

Fig. 14.2 The example dialogue in Prakken's approach

As can be easily checked, this formalisation captures all aspects of the example's original version, except that arguments have to be complete and that counter-arguments cannot be introduced by a counterclaim. (But other instantiations of the framework may be possible without these limitations.)

6 Conclusion

In this chapter a formal framework for dialogue systems for persuasion was proposed, which was then used to critically discuss three systems from the literature. Concluding, we can say that the formal study of persuasion dialogue has resulted in a number of interesting dialogue systems, some of which have been applied in insightful case studies or applications. On the other hand, there is still much room for refining or extending the various sytems with, for example, more refined communication languages or with different modes of reasoning, such as probabilistic, case-based or coherence-based reasoning. Also, the integration of persuasion with other types of dialogues should be studied. Another important research issue is the study of strategies and heuristics for individual participants and how these interact with the protocols to yield certain properties of dialogues. One aspect of such studies is the development of quality measures for dialogues as to how well they satisfy certain desirable properties. More generally, a formal metatheory of systems, their interrelations and their combinations with agent models is still in its early stages.

Perhaps the main challenge in tackling all these issues is how to reconcile the need for flexibility and expressiveness with the aim to enforce coherent dialogues. The answer to this challenge may well vary with the nature of the context and application domain, and a precise description of the grounds for such variations would provide important insights in how dialogue systems for persuasion can be applied.

References

1. J. Barwise and L. Moss. *Vicious Circles*. Number 60 in CSLI Lecture Notes. CSLI Publications, Stanford, CA, 1996.
2. G. Brewka. Dynamic argument systems: a formal model of argumentation processes based on situation calculus. *Journal of Logic and Computation*, 11:257–282, 2001.
3. L. Carlson. *Dialogue Games: an Approach to Discourse Analysis*. Reidel Publishing Company, Dordrecht, 1983.
4. T. Gordon. The Pleadings Game: an exercise in computational dialectics. *Artificial Intelligence and Law*, 2:239–292, 1994.
5. C. Hamblin. *Fallacies*. Methuen, London, 1970.
6. R. Loui. Process and policy: resource-bounded non-demonstrative reasoning. *Computational Intelligence*, 14:1–38, 1998.
7. J. Mackenzie. Question-begging in non-cumulative systems. *Journal of Philosophical Logic*, 8:117–133, 1979.
8. S. Parsons, M. Wooldridge, and L. Amgoud. Properties and complexity of some formal inter-agent dialogues. *Journal of Logic and Computation*, 13, 2003. 347-376.
9. J. Pollock. *Cognitive Carpentry. A Blueprint for How to Build a Person*. MIT Press, Cambridge, MA, 1995.
10. H. Prakken. Coherence and flexibility in dialogue games for argumentation. *Journal of Logic and Computation*, 15:1009–1040, 2005.
11. H. Prakken. Formal systems for persuasion dialogue. *The Knowledge Engineering Review*, 21:163–188, 2006.
12. H. Prakken and G. Sartor. Argument-based extended logic programming with defeasible priorities. *Journal of Applied Non-classical Logics*, 7:25–75, 1997.
13. D. Walton. *Logical dialogue-games and fallacies*. University Press of America, Inc., Lanham, MD., 1984.
14. D. Walton and E. Krabbe. *Commitment in Dialogue. Basic Concepts of Interpersonal Reasoning*. State University of New York Press, Albany, NY, 1995.
15. J. Woods and D. Walton. Arresting circles in formal dialogues. *Journal of Philosophical Logic*, 7:73–90, 1978.
16. T. Yuan, D. Moore, and A. Grierson. A human-computer dialogue system for educational debate: A computational dialectics approach. *International Journal of Artificial Intelligence in Education*, 18:3–26, 2008.

Chapter 15
Argumentation for Decision Making

Leila Amgoud

1 Introduction

Decision making, often viewed as a form of reasoning toward action, has raised the interest of many scholars including economists, psychologists, and computer scientists for a long time. Any decision problem amounts to selecting the "best" or sufficiently "good" action(s) that are feasible among different alternatives, given some available information about the current state of the world and the consequences of potential actions. Available information may be incomplete or pervaded with uncertainty. Besides, the goodness of an action is judged by estimating how much its possible consequences fit the preferences of the decision maker. This agent is assumed to behave in a *rational* way [29], at least in the sense that his decisions should be as much as possible consistent with his preferences.

Classical decision theory, as developed mainly by economists, has focused on making clear what is a rational decision maker. Thus, they have looked for principles for comparing different alternatives. The inputs of this approach are a set of candidate actions, and a function that assesses the value of their consequences when the actions are performed in a given state, together with complete or partial information about the current state of the world. In other words, such an approach distinguishes between knowledge and preferences, which are respectively encoded in practice by a distribution function assessing the plausibility of the different states of the world, and by a utility function encoding preferences by estimating how good a consequence is. The output is a preference relation between actions encoded by the associated principle. Note that such an approach aims at rank-ordering a group of candidate actions rather than focusing on a candidate action individually. Moreover, the candidate actions are supposed to be feasible. What is worth noticing is that in such an approach, the principles that are defined for comparing pairs of alternatives are given in terms of analytical expressions that summarize the whole decision

Institut de Recherche en Informatique de Toulouse, IRIT-UPS
118 route de Narbonne, 31062 Toulouse, Cedex, France, e-mail: amgoud@irit.fr

I. Rahwan, G. R. Simari (eds.), *Argumentation in Artificial Intelligence,*
DOI 10.1007/978-0-387-98197-0_15, © Springer Science+Business Media, LLC 2009

process. It is then hard for a person who is not familiar with the abstract decision methodology, to understand why a proposed alternative is good, or better than another. It is thus important to have an approach in which one can better understand the underpinnings of the evaluation. *Argumentation* is the most appropriate way to advocate a choice thanks to its explanatory power.

Argumentation has been introduced in decision making analysis by several researchers only in the last few years (e.g. [15, 20, 23]). Indeed, in everyday life, decision is often based on arguments and counter-arguments. Argumentation can be also useful for explaining a choice already made. Recently, in [1], a decision model in which some decision criteria were articulated in terms of a two-steps argumentation process has been proposed. At the first step, called *inference* step, the model uses a Dung style system in which arguments in favor/against each option are built, then evaluated using a given acceptability semantics. At the second step, called *comparison* step, pairs of alternatives are compared using a given criterion. This criterion is generally based on the "accepted" arguments computed at the inference step. The model returns thus, an ordering on the set of options, which may be either partial or total depending on the decision criterion that is encoded. This approach presents a great advantage since not only the best alternative is provided to the user but also the reasons justifying this recommendation. In what follows, we will develop that argument-based model for decision making.

2 A general framework for argumentative decision making

Solving a decision problem amounts to defining a pre-ordering, usually a complete one, on a set $\mathcal{D}$ of possible *options* (or candidate decisions), on the basis of the different consequences of each decision. Let us illustrate this problem through a simple example borrowed from [20].

Example 15.1 (Having or not a surgery). The example is about having a surgery (sg) or not ($\neg sg$), knowing that the patient has colonic polyps. The knowledge base contains the following information:

- having a surgery has side-effects,
- not having surgery avoids having side-effects,
- when having a cancer, having a surgery avoids loss of life,
- if a patient has cancer and has no surgery, the patient would lose his life,
- the patient has colonic polyps,
- having colonic polyps may lead to cancer.

In addition to the above knowledge, the patient has also some goals like: "no side effects" and "to not lose his life". Obviously it is more important for him to not lose his life than to not have side effects.

Let $\mathcal{L}$ denote a logical language. From $\mathcal{L}$, a finite set $\mathcal{D} = \{d_1, \ldots, d_n\}$ of n options is identified. An option d_i may be a conjunction of other options in $\mathcal{D}$. Let us, for instance, assume that an agent wants a drink and has to choose between tea, milk or both. Thus, there are three options: d_1 : tea, d_2 : milk and d_3 : tea and milk. In Example 15.1, the set $\mathcal{D}$ contains two options: $d_1 : sg$ and $d_2 : \neg sg$.

Argumentation is used in this chapter for ordering the set $\mathcal{D}$. An argumentation-based decision process can be decomposed into the following steps:

1. Constructing arguments in *favor/against* statements (beliefs or decisions)
2. Evaluating the strength of each argument
3. Determining the different conflicts among arguments
4. Evaluating the acceptability of arguments
5. Comparing decisions on the basis of relevant "accepted" arguments

Note that the first four steps globally correspond to an "inference problem" in which one looks for accepted arguments, and consequently warranted beliefs. At this step, one only knows what is the quality of arguments in favor/against candidate decisions, but the "best" candidate decision is not determined yet. The last step answers this question once a *decision principle* is chosen.

2.1 Types of arguments

As shown in Example 15.1, decisions are made on the basis of available knowledge and the preferences of the decision maker. Thus, two categories of arguments are distinguished: i) *epistemic arguments* justifying beliefs and are themselves based only on beliefs, and ii) *practical arguments* justifying options and are built from both beliefs and preferences/goals. Note that a practical argument may highlight either a positive feature of a candidate decision, supporting thus that decision, or a negative one, attacking thus the decision.

Example 15.2 (Example 15.1 cont.). In this example, α = ["the patient has colonic polyps", and "having colonic polyps may lead to cancer"] is considered as an argument for believing that the patient may have cancer. This epistemic argument involves only beliefs. While δ_1 = ["the patient may have a cancer", "when having a cancer, having a surgery avoids loss of life"] is an argument for having a surgery. This is a practical argument since it supports the option "having a surgery". Note that such argument involves both beliefs and preferences. Similarly, δ_2 = ["not having surgery avoids having side-effects"] is a practical argument in favor of "not having a surgery". However, the two practical arguments δ_3 = ["having a surgery has side-effects"] and δ_4 = ["the patient has colonic polyps", and "having colonic polyps may lead to cancer", "if a patient has cancer and has no surgery, the patient would lose his life"] are respectively against surgery and no surgery since they point out negative consequences of the two options.

In what follows, $\mathcal{A}_e$ denotes a set of epistemic arguments, and $\mathcal{A}_p$ denotes a set of practical arguments such that $\mathcal{A}_e \cap \mathcal{A}_p = \varnothing$. Let $\mathcal{A} = \mathcal{A}_e \cup \mathcal{A}_p$ (i.e. $\mathcal{A}$ will contain all those arguments). The structure and origin of the arguments are assumed to be unknown. Epistemic arguments will be denoted by variables $\alpha_1, \alpha_2, \ldots$, while practical arguments will be referred to by variables $\delta_1, \delta_2, \ldots$ When no distinction is necessary between arguments, we will use the variables $a, b, c, \ldots$

Example 15.3 (Example 15.1 cont.). $\mathcal{A}_e = \{\alpha\}$ while $\mathcal{A}_p = \{\delta_1, \delta_2, \delta_3, \delta_4\}$.

Let us now define two functions that relate each option to the arguments supporting it and to the arguments against it.

- $\mathcal{F}_p : \mathcal{D} \rightarrow 2^{\mathcal{A}_p}$ is a function that returns the arguments *in favor* of a candidate decision. Such arguments are said pro the option.
- $\mathcal{F}_c : \mathcal{D} \rightarrow 2^{\mathcal{A}_p}$ is a function that returns the arguments *against* a candidate decision. Such arguments are said cons the option.

The two functions satisfy the following requirements:

- $\forall d \in \mathcal{D}, \nexists \delta \in \mathcal{A}_p$ s.t. $\delta \in \mathcal{F}_p(d)$ and $\delta \in \mathcal{F}_c(d)$. This means that an argument is either in favor of an option or against that option. It cannot be both.
- If $\delta \in \mathcal{F}_p(d)$ and $\delta \in \mathcal{F}_p(d')$ (resp. if $\delta \in \mathcal{F}_c(d)$ and $\delta \in \mathcal{F}_c(d')$), then $d = d'$. This means that an argument refers only to one option.
- Let $\mathcal{D} = \{d_1, \ldots, d_n\}$. $\mathcal{A}_p = (\bigcup \mathcal{F}_p(d_i)) \cup (\bigcup \mathcal{F}_c(d_i))$, with $i = 1, \ldots, n$. This means that the available practical arguments concern options of the set $\mathcal{D}$.

When $\delta \in \mathcal{F}_x(d)$ with $x \in \{p, c\}$, we say that d is the *conclusion* of δ, and we write $\text{Conc}(\delta) = d$.

Example 15.4 (Example 15.1 cont.). The two options of the set $\mathcal{D} = \{sg, \neg sg\}$ are supported/attacked by the following arguments: $\mathcal{F}_p(sg) = \{\delta_1\}$, $\mathcal{F}_c(sg) = \{\delta_3\}$, $\mathcal{F}_p(\neg sg) = \{\delta_2\}$, and $\mathcal{F}_c(\neg sg) = \{\delta_4\}$.

2.2 Comparing arguments

As pointed out by several researchers (e.g. [14, 18]), arguments may have forces of various strengths. These forces play two key roles: i) they may be used in order to refine the notion of acceptability of epistemic or practical arguments, ii) they allow the comparison of practical arguments in order to rank-order candidate decisions. Generally, the strength of an epistemic argument reflects the quality, such as the certainty level, of the pieces of information involved in it. Whereas the strength of a practical argument reflects both the quality of knowledge used in the argument, as well as how important it is to fulfill the preferences to which the argument refers.

In our particular application, three preference relations between arguments are defined. The first one, denoted by $\geq_e$, is a (partial or total) *preorder*[1] on the set $\mathcal{A}_e$. The second relation, denoted by $\geq_p$, is a (partial or total) preorder on the set $\mathcal{A}_p$.

---

[1] A preorder is a binary relation that is *reflexive* and *transitive*

Finally, a third relation, denoted by $\geq_m$ (m stands for mixed relation), captures the idea that any epistemic argument is stronger than any practical argument. The role of epistemic arguments in a decision problem is to validate or to undermine the beliefs on which practical arguments are built. Indeed, decisions should be made under "certain" information. Thus, $\forall \alpha \in \mathcal{A}_e$, $\forall \delta \in \mathcal{A}_p$, $(\alpha, \delta) \in \geq_m$ and $(\delta, \alpha) \notin \geq_m$.

Note that $(a, b) \in \geq_x$, with $x \in \{e, p, m\}$, means that a is *at least as good as* b. At some places, we will also write $a \geq_x b$. In what follows, $>_x$ denotes the strict relation associated with $\geq_x$. It is defined as follows: $(a, b) \in >_x$ iff $(a, b) \in \geq_x$ and $(b, a) \notin \geq_x$. When $(a, b) \in \geq_x$ and $(b, a) \in \geq_x$, we say that a and b are *indifferent*, and we write $a \approx_x b$. When $(a, b) \notin \geq_x$ and $(b, a) \notin \geq_x$, the two arguments are said *incomparable*.

Example 15.5 (Example 15.1 cont.). $\geq_e = \{(\alpha, \alpha)\}$ and $\geq_m = \{(\alpha, \delta_1), (\alpha, \delta_2)\}$. Now, regarding $\geq_p$, one may, for instance, assume that δ_1 is stronger than δ_2 since the goal satisfied by δ_1 (namely, not loss of life) is more important than the one satisfied by δ_2 (not having side effects). Thus, $\geq_p = \{(\delta_1, \delta_1), (\delta_2, \delta_2), (\delta_1, \delta_2)\}$. This example will be detailed in a next section.

2.3 Attacks among arguments

Since knowledge may be inconsistent, the arguments may be conflicting too. Indeed, epistemic arguments may attack each others. Such conflicts are captured by the binary relation $\mathcal{R}_e \subseteq \mathcal{A}_e \times \mathcal{A}_e$. This relation is assumed abstract and its origin is not specified. Epistemic arguments may also attack practical arguments when they challenge their knowledge part. The idea is that an epistemic argument may undermine the beliefs part of a practical argument. However, practical arguments are not allowed to attack epistemic ones. This avoids wishful thinking. This relation, denoted by $\mathcal{R}_m$, contains pairs (α, δ) where $\alpha \in \mathcal{A}_e$ and $\delta \in \mathcal{A}_p$.

We assume that practical arguments do not conflict. The idea is that each practical argument points out some advantage or some weakness of a candidate decision, and it is crucial in a decision problem to list all those arguments for each candidate decision, provided that they are accepted w.r.t. the current epistemic state, i.e built from warranted beliefs. According to the attitude of the decision maker in face of uncertain or inconsistent knowledge, these lists associated with the candidate decisions may be taken into account in different manners, thus leading to different orderings of the decisions. This is why all accepted arguments should be kept, whatever their strengths, for preserving all relevant information in the decision process. Otherwise, getting rid of some of those accepted arguments (w.r.t. knowledge), for instance because they would be weaker than others, may prevent us to have a complete view of the decision problem and then may even lead us to recommend decisions that would be wrong w.r.t. some decision principles (agreeing with the presumed decision maker's attitude). This point will be made more concrete in a next section. Thus, the relation $\mathcal{R}_p \subseteq \mathcal{A}_p \times \mathcal{A}_p$ is equal to the empty set ($\mathcal{R}_p = \varnothing$).

Each preference relation $\geq_x$ (with $x \in \{e, p, m\}$) is combined with the conflict relation $\mathcal{R}_x$ into a unique relation between arguments, denoted by Def_x and called *defeat* relation, in the same way as in ([4], Definition 3.3, page 204).

Definition 15.1 (Defeat relation). Let $\mathcal{A}$ be a set of arguments, and a, $b \in \mathcal{A}$. $(a, b) \in \text{Def}_x$ iff $(a, b) \in \mathcal{R}_x$, and $(b, a) \notin >_x$.

Let Def_e, Def_p and Def_m denote the three defeat relations corresponding to the three attack relations. In case of Def_m, the second bullet of Definition 15.1 is always true since epistemic arguments are strictly preferred (in the sense of $\geq_m$) to any practical arguments. Thus, $\text{Def}_m = \mathcal{R}_m$ (i.e. the defeat relation is exactly the attack relation $\mathcal{R}_m$). The relation Def_p is the same as $\mathcal{R}_p$, thus it is empty. However, the relation Def_e coincides with its corresponding attack relation $\mathcal{R}_e$ in case all the arguments of the set $\mathcal{A}_e$ are incomparable.

2.4 Extensions of arguments

Now that the sets of arguments and the defeat relations are identified, we can define the decision system.

Definition 15.2 (Decision system). Let $\mathcal{D}$ be a set of options. A *decision system* for ordering $\mathcal{D}$ is a triple $\text{AF} = (\mathcal{D}, \mathcal{A}, \text{Def})$ where $\mathcal{A} = \mathcal{A}_e \cup \mathcal{A}_p{}^2$ and $\text{Def} = \text{Def}_e \cup \text{Def}_p \cup \text{Def}_m{}^3$.

Note that a Dung style argumentation system is associated to a decision system $\text{AF} = (\mathcal{D}, \mathcal{A}, \text{Def})$, namely the system $(\mathcal{A}, \text{Def})$. This latter can be seen as the union of two distinct argumentation systems: $\text{AF}_e = (\mathcal{A}_e, \text{Def}_e)$, called *epistemic system*, and $\text{AF}_p = (\mathcal{A}_p, \text{Def}_p)$, called *practical system*. The two systems are related to each other by the defeat relation Def_m.

Due to Dung's acceptability semantics defined in [17] or their extensions defined in [8], it is possible to identify among all the conflicting arguments, which ones will be kept for ordering the options. Recall that an acceptability semantics amounts to define sets of arguments that satisfy a consistency requirement and must defend all their elements. In what follows, $\mathcal{E}_1, \ldots, \mathcal{E}_x$ denote the different extensions of the system $(\mathcal{A}, \text{Def})$ under a given semantics. Using these extensions, a status is assigned to each argument of AF as follows.

Definition 15.3 (Argument status). Let $\text{AF} = (\mathcal{D}, \mathcal{A}, \text{Def})$ be a decision system, and $\mathcal{E}_1, \ldots, \mathcal{E}_x$ its extensions under a given semantics. Let $a \in \mathcal{A}$.

- a is *skeptically accepted* iff $a \in \mathcal{E}_i$, $\forall \mathcal{E}_{i=1,\ldots,x}$, $\mathcal{E}_i \neq \varnothing$.
- a is *credulously accepted* iff $\exists \mathcal{E}_i$ such that $a \in \mathcal{E}_i$ and $\exists \mathcal{E}_j$ such that $a \notin \mathcal{E}_j$.

---

[2] Recall that options are related to their supporting and attacking arguments by the functions $\mathcal{F}_p$ and $\mathcal{F}_c$ respectively.

[3] Since the relation Def_p is empty, then $\text{Def} = \text{Def}_e \cup \text{Def}_m$.

- a is *rejected* iff $\nexists \mathcal{E}_i$ such that $a \in \mathcal{E}_i$.

A consequence of Definition 15.3 is the following one.

Property 15.1. Each argument has exactly one status.

Let $\text{Acc}(x,y)$ be a function that returns the skeptically accepted arguments of decision system x under semantics y ($y \in \{ad,st,pr\}$ with ad (resp. st and pr) stands for admissible (resp. stable and preferred) semantics). This set may contain both epistemic and practical arguments. Such arguments are very important in argumentation process since they support the conclusions to be inferred from a knowledge base or the options that will be chosen. Indeed, for ordering the candidate decisions, only skeptically accepted practical arguments are used. The following result shows the links between the sets of accepted arguments under different semantics.

Property 15.2. Let $\text{AF} = (\mathcal{D},\mathcal{A},\text{Def})$ be a decision system.

- $\text{Acc}(\text{AF},ad) = \varnothing$.
- If AF has no stable extensions, then $\text{Acc}(\text{AF},st)=\varnothing$ and $\text{Acc}(\text{AF},st)\subseteq\text{Acc}(\text{AF},pr)$.
- If AF has stable extensions, then $\text{Acc}(\text{AF},pr) \subseteq \text{Acc}(\text{AF},st)$.

From the above property, one concludes that in a decision problem, it is not interesting to use admissible semantics. The reason is that no argument is accepted. Consequently, argumentation will not help at all for ordering the different candidate decisions. Let us illustrate this issue through the following simple example.

Example 15.6. Let us consider the decision system $\text{AF} = (\mathcal{D},\mathcal{A}_e \cup \mathcal{A}_p,\text{Def})$ where $\mathcal{D} = \{d_1,d_2\}$, $\mathcal{A}_e = \{\alpha_1,\alpha_2,\alpha_3\}$, $\mathcal{A}_p = \{\delta\}$ and $\text{Def} = \{(\alpha_1,\alpha_2),(\alpha_2,\alpha_1),(\alpha_1,\alpha_3),(\alpha_2,\alpha_3),(\alpha_3,\delta)\}$. We assume that $\mathcal{F}_p(d_1) = \delta$ whereas $\mathcal{F}_p(d_2) = \mathcal{F}_c(d_2) = \varnothing$. The admissible extensions of this system are: $\mathcal{E}_1 = \{\}$, $\mathcal{E}_2 = \{\alpha_1\}$, $\mathcal{E}_3 = \{\alpha_2\}$, $\mathcal{E}_4 = \{\alpha_1,\delta\}$ and $\mathcal{E}_5 = \{\alpha_2,\delta\}$. Under admissible semantics, the practical argument δ is not skeptically accepted. Thus, the two options d_1 and d_2 may be equally preferred since the first one has an argument but not an accepted one, and the second has no argument at all. However, the same decision system has two preferred extensions: $\mathcal{E}_4$ and $\mathcal{E}_5$. Under preferred semantics, the set $\text{Acc}(\text{AF},pr)$ contains the argument δ (i.e. $\text{Acc}(\text{AF},pr) = \{\delta\}$). Thus, it is natural to prefer option d_1 to d_2.

Consequently, in the following, we will use stable semantics if the system has stable extensions, otherwise preferred semantics will be considered for computing the set $\text{Acc}(\text{AF},y)$.

Since the defeat relation Def_p is empty, it is trivial that the practical system AF_p has exactly one preferred/stable extension which is the set $\mathcal{A}_p$ itself.

Property 15.3. The practical system $\text{AF}_p = (\mathcal{A}_p,\text{Def}_p)$ has a unique preferred/stable extension, which is the set $\mathcal{A}_p$.

It is important to notice that the epistemic system AF_e in its side is very general and does not necessarily present particular properties like for instance the existence of stable/preferred extensions. In what follows, we will show that the result of the decision system depends broadly on the outcome of this epistemic system. The first result states that the epistemic arguments of each admissible extension of AF constitute an admissible extension of the epistemic system AF_e.

Theorem 15.1. *Let* $AF = (\mathcal{D}, \mathcal{A}_e \cup \mathcal{A}_p, Def_e \cup Def_p \cup Def_m)$ *be a decision system,* $\mathcal{E}_1, \ldots, \mathcal{E}_n$ *its admissible extensions, and* $AF_e = (\mathcal{A}_e, Def_e)$ *its epistemic system.*

- $\forall \mathcal{E}_i$, *the set* $\mathcal{E}_i \cap \mathcal{A}_e$ *is an admissible extension of* AF_e.
- $\forall \mathcal{E}'$ *such that* $\mathcal{E}'$ *is an admissible extension of* AF_e, $\exists \mathcal{E}_i$ *such that* $\mathcal{E}' \subseteq \mathcal{E}_i \cap \mathcal{A}_e$.

It is easy to show that when Def_m is empty, i.e. no epistemic argument defeats a practical one, then the extensions of AF (under a given semantics) are exactly the different extensions of AF_e (under the same semantics) augmented by the set AF_p.

Theorem 15.2. *Let* $AF = (\mathcal{D}, \mathcal{A}_e \cup \mathcal{A}_p, Def_e \cup Def_p \cup Def_m)$ *be a decision system. Let* $\mathcal{E}_1, \ldots, \mathcal{E}_n$ *be the extensions of* AF_e *under a given semantics. If* $Def_m = \varnothing$ *then* $\forall \mathcal{E}_i$ *with* $i = 1, \ldots, n$, *then the set* $\mathcal{E}_i \cup \mathcal{A}_p$ *is an extension of* AF.

Finally, it can be shown that if the empty set is the only admissible extension of the decision system AF, then the empty set is also the only admissible extension of the corresponding epistemic system AF_e. Moreover, each practical argument is attacked by at least one epistemic argument.

Theorem 15.3. *Let* $AF = (\mathcal{D}, \mathcal{A}_e \cup \mathcal{A}_p, Def_e \cup Def_p \cup Def_m)$ *be a decision system. The only admissible extension of AF is the empty set iff:*

1. The only admissible extension of AF_e *is the empty set, and*
2. $\forall \delta \in \mathcal{A}_p$, $\exists \alpha \in \mathcal{A}_e$ *such that* $(\alpha, \delta) \in Def_m$.

At this step, we have only defined the accepted arguments among all the existing ones. However, nothing is yet said about which option to prefer. In the next section, we will study different ways of comparing pairs of options on the basis of skeptically accepted practical arguments.

2.5 Ordering options

Comparing candidate decisions, i.e. defining a preference relation $\succeq$ on the set $\mathcal{D}$ of options, is a key step in a decision process. In an argumentation-based approach, the definition of this relation is based on the sets of "accepted" arguments pros or cons associated with candidate decisions. Thus, the input of this relation is no longer $\mathcal{A}_d$, but the set $Acc(AF, y) \cap \mathcal{A}_d$, where $Acc(AF, y)$ is the set of skeptically accepted arguments of the decision system $(\mathcal{D}, \mathcal{A}, Def)$ under stable or preferred semantics. In what follows, we will use the notation $Acc(AF)$ for short. Note that in a decision system, when the defeat relation Def_m is empty, the epistemic arguments become useless for the decision problem, i.e. for ordering options. Thus, only the practical system AF_p is needed.

Depending on what sets are considered and how they are handled, one can roughly distinguish between three categories of principles:

Unipolar principles: are those that only refer to either the arguments pros or the arguments cons.

Bipolar principles: are those that take into account both types of arguments at the same time.

Non-polar principles: are those where arguments pros and arguments cons a given choice are aggregated into a unique *meta-argument*. It results that the negative and positive polarities disappear in the aggregation.

Whatever the category is, a relation $\succeq$ should suitably satisfy the following minimal requirements:

1. **Transitivity**: The relation should be *transitive* (as usually required in decision theory).
2. **Completeness**: Since one looks for the "best" candidate decision, it should then be possible to compare any pair of choices. Thus, the relation should be *complete*.

2.5.1 Unipolar principles

In this section we present basic principles for comparing decisions on the basis of only arguments pros. Similar ideas apply to arguments cons. We start by presenting those principles that do not involve the strength of arguments, then their respective refinements when strength is taken into account. A first natural criterion consists of preferring the decision that has more arguments pros.

Definition 15.4 (Counting arguments pros). Let $AF = (\mathcal{D}, \mathcal{A}, \text{Def})$ be a decision system and $\text{Acc}(AF)$ its accepted arguments. Let $d_1, d_2 \in \mathcal{D}$.

$$d_1 \succeq d_2 \text{ iff } |\mathcal{F}_p(d_1) \cap \text{Acc}(AF)| \geq |\mathcal{F}_p(d_2) \cap \text{Acc}(AF)|.$$

Property 15.4. This relation is a *complete* preorder.

Note that when the decision system has no accepted arguments (i.e. $\text{Acc}(AF) = \varnothing$), all the options in $\mathcal{D}$ are equally preferred w.r.t. the relation $\succeq$. It is also worth mentioning that with such a principle, one may prefer a decision d, which has three arguments pointing all to the same positive consequence, to decision d', which is supported by two arguments pointing to different consequences.

When the strength of arguments is taken into account in the decision process, one may think of preferring a choice that has a dominant argument, i.e. an argument pros that is preferred w.r.t. the relation $\geq_p \subseteq \mathcal{A}_p \times \mathcal{A}_p$ to any argument pros the other choices. This principle is called *promotion focus* principle in [2].

Definition 15.5. Let $\mathtt{AF} = (\mathcal{D}, \mathcal{A}, \mathtt{Def})$ be a decision system and $\mathtt{Acc(AF)}$ its accepted arguments. Let $d_1, d_2 \in \mathcal{D}$.

$$d_1 \succeq d_2 \text{ iff } \exists \delta \in \mathcal{F}_p(d_1) \cap \mathtt{Acc(AF)} \text{ such that } \forall \delta' \in \mathcal{F}_p(d_2) \cap \mathtt{Acc(AF)}, \delta \geq_p \delta'.$$

With this criterion, if the decision system has no accepted arguments, then all the options in $\mathcal{D}$ are equally preferred. The above definition relies heavily on the relation $\geq_p$ that compares practical arguments. Thus, the properties of this criterion depends on those of $\geq_p$. Namely, it can be checked that the above criterion works properly only if $\geq_p$ is a complete preorder.

Property 15.5. If the relation $\geq_p$ is a complete preorder, then $\succeq$ is also a complete preorder.

Note that the above relation may be found to be too restrictive, since when the strongest arguments in favor of d_1 and d_2 have equivalent strengths (i.e. are indifferent), d_1 and d_2 are also seen as equivalent. However, we can refine the above definition by ignoring the strongest arguments with equal strengths, by means of the following *strict preorder*.

Definition 15.6. Let $\mathtt{AF} = (\mathcal{D}, \mathcal{A}, \mathtt{Def})$ be a decision system and $\mathtt{Acc(AF)}$ its accepted arguments. Let $d_1, d_2 \in \mathcal{D}$, and $\geq_p$ be a complete preorder. Let $(\delta_1, ..., \delta_r)$, $(\delta'_1, ..., \delta'_s)$ such that $\forall \delta_{i=1,...,r}, \delta_i \in \mathcal{F}_p(d_1) \cap \mathtt{Acc(AF)}$, and $\forall \delta'_{j=1,...,s}, \delta'_j \in \mathcal{F}_p(d_2) \cap \mathtt{Acc(AF)}$. Each of these vectors is assumed to be decreasingly ordered w.r.t $\geq_p$ (e.g. $\delta_1 \geq_p ... \geq_p \delta_r$). Let $v = \min(r, s)$. $d_1 \succeq d_2$ iff:

- $\delta_1 >_p \delta'_1$, or
- $\exists k \leq v$ such that $\delta_k >_p \delta'_k$ and $\forall j < k, \delta_j \approx_p \delta'_j$, or
- $r > v$ and $\forall j \leq v, \delta_j \approx_p \delta'_j$.

Till now, we have only discussed decision principles based on arguments pros. However, the counterpart principles when arguments cons are considered can also be defined. Thus, the counterpart principle of the one defined in Definition 15.4 is the following complete preorder:

Definition 15.7 (Counting arguments cons). Let $\mathtt{AF} = (\mathcal{D}, \mathcal{A}, \mathtt{Def})$ be a decision system and $\mathtt{Acc(AF)}$ its accepted arguments. Let $d_1, d_2 \in \mathcal{D}$.

$$d_1 \succeq d_2 \text{ iff } |\mathcal{F}_c(d_1) \cap \mathtt{Acc(AF)}| \leq |\mathcal{F}_c(d_2) \cap \mathtt{Acc(AF)}|.$$

The principles that take into account the strengths of arguments have also their counterparts when handling arguments cons. The *prevention focus* principle prefers a decision when all its cons are weaker than at least one argument against the other decision. Formally:

Definition 15.8. Let $\mathtt{AF} = (\mathcal{D}, \mathcal{A}, \mathtt{Def})$ be a decision system and $\mathtt{Acc(AF)}$ its accepted arguments. Let $d_1, d_2 \in \mathcal{D}$.

$$d_1 \succeq d_2 \text{ iff } \exists \delta \in \mathcal{F}_c(d_2) \cap \mathtt{Acc(AF)} \text{ such that } \forall \delta' \in \mathcal{F}_c(d_1) \cap \mathtt{Acc(AF)}, \delta \geq_p \delta'.$$

As in the case of arguments pros, when the relation $\geq_p$ is a complete preorder, the above relation is also a complete preorder, and can be refined into the following strict one.

Definition 15.9. Let $\texttt{AF} = (\mathcal{D}, \mathcal{A}, \texttt{Def})$ be a decision system and $\texttt{Acc(AF)}$ its accepted arguments. Let $d_1, d_2 \in \mathcal{D}$.

Let $(\delta_1, \ldots, \delta_r)$, $(\delta'_1, \ldots, \delta'_s)$ such that $\forall \delta_{i=1,\ldots,r}$, $\delta_i \in \mathcal{F}_c(d_1) \cap \texttt{Acc(AF)}$, and $\forall \delta'_{j=1,\ldots,s}$, $\delta'_j \in \mathcal{F}_c(d_2) \cap \texttt{Acc(AF)}$. Each of these vectors is assumed to be decreasingly ordered w.r.t $\geq_p$ (e.g. $\delta_1 \geq_p \ldots \geq_p \delta_r$). Let $v = \min(r, s)$. $d_1 \succ d_2$ iff:

- $\delta'_1 >_p \delta_1$, or
- $\exists k \leq v$ such that $\delta'_k >_p \delta_k$ and $\forall j < k, \delta_j \approx_p \delta'_j$, or
- $v < s$ and $\forall j \leq v, \delta_j \approx_p \delta'_j$.

2.5.2 Bipolar principles

Let's now define some principles where both types of arguments (pros and cons) are taken into account when comparing decisions. Generally speaking, we can conjunctively combine the principles dealing with arguments pros with their counterpart handling arguments cons. For instance, the principles given in Definition 15.4 and Definition 15.7 can be combined as follows:

Definition 15.10. Let $\texttt{AF} = (\mathcal{D}, \mathcal{A}, \texttt{Def})$ be a decision system and $\texttt{Acc(AF)}$ its accepted arguments. Let $d_1, d_2 \in \mathcal{D}$. $d_1 \succeq d_2$ iff

- $|\mathcal{F}_p(d_1) \cap \texttt{Acc(AF)}| \geq |\mathcal{F}_p(d_2) \cap \texttt{Acc(AF)}|$, and
- $|\mathcal{F}_c(d_1) \cap \texttt{Acc(AF)}| \leq |\mathcal{F}_c(d_2) \cap \texttt{Acc(AF)}|$.

However, note that unfortunately this is no longer a complete preorder. Similarly, the principles given respectively in Definition 15.5 and Definition 15.8 can be combined into the following one:

Definition 15.11. Let $\texttt{AF} = (\mathcal{D}, \mathcal{A}, \texttt{Def})$ be a decision system and $\texttt{Acc(AF)}$ its accepted arguments. Let $d_1, d_2 \in \mathcal{D}$. $d_1 \succeq d_2$ iff:

- $\exists \delta \in \mathcal{F}_p(d_1) \cap \texttt{Acc(AF)}$ such that $\forall \delta' \in \mathcal{F}_p(d_2) \cap \texttt{Acc(AF)}, \delta \geq_p \delta'$, and
- $\nexists \delta \in \mathcal{F}_c(d_1) \cap \texttt{Acc(AF)}$ such that $\forall \delta' \in \mathcal{F}_c(d_2) \cap \texttt{Acc(AF)}, \delta \geq_p \delta'$.

This means that one prefers a decision that has at least one supporting argument which is better than any supporting argument of the other decision, and also that has not a very strong argument against it. Note that the above definition can be also refined in the same spirit as Definitions 15.6 and 15.9.

Another family of bipolar decision principles applies the *Franklin principle* which is a natural extension to the bipolar case of the idea underlying Definition 15.6. This principle consists, when comparing pros and cons a decision, of ignoring pairs of arguments pros and cons which have the same strength. After such a simplification, one can apply any of the above bipolar principles. In what follows, we will define formally the Franklin simplification.

Definition 15.12 (Franklin simplification). Let $\text{AF} = (\mathcal{D}, \mathcal{A}, \text{Def})$ be a decision system and $\text{Acc}(\text{AF})$ its accepted arguments. Let $d \in \mathcal{D}$.

Let $P = (\delta_1, \ldots, \delta_r)$, $C = (\delta'_1, \ldots, \delta'_m)$ such that $\forall \delta_i, \delta_i \in \mathcal{F}_p(d) \cap \text{Acc}(\text{AF})$ and $\forall \delta'_j, \delta'_j \in \mathcal{F}_c(d) \cap \text{Acc}(\text{AF})$. Each of these vectors is assumed to be decreasingly ordered w.r.t $\geq_p$ (e.g. $\delta_1 \geq_p \ldots \geq_p \delta_r$). The *result of the simplification* is $P' = (\delta_{j+1}, \ldots, \delta_r)$, $C' = (\delta'_{j+1}, \ldots, \delta'_m)$ s.t.

- $\forall\, 1 \leq i \leq j,\ \delta_i \approx_p \delta'_i$ and ($\delta_{j+1} >_p \delta'_{j+1}$ or $\delta'_{j+1} >_p \delta_{j+1}$)
- If $j = r$ (resp. $j = m$), then $P' = \varnothing$ (resp. $C' = \varnothing$).

2.5.3 Non-polar principles

In some applications, the arguments in favor of and against a decision are aggregated into a unique *meta-argument* having a unique strength. Thus, comparing two decisions amounts to compare the resulting meta-arguments. Such a view is well in agreement with current practice in multiple criteria decision making, where each decision is evaluated according to different criteria using the same scale (with a positive and a negative part), and an aggregation function is used to obtain a global evaluation of each decision.

Definition 15.13 (Aggregation criterion). Let $\text{AF} = (\mathcal{D}, \mathcal{A}, \text{Def})$ be a decision system and $\text{Acc}(\text{AF})$ its accepted arguments. Let $d_1, d_2 \in \mathcal{D}$. Let $(\delta_1, \ldots, \delta_n)^4$ and $(\delta'_1, \ldots, \delta'_m)^5$ (resp. $(\gamma_1, \ldots, \gamma_l)^6$ and $(\gamma'_1, \ldots, \gamma'_k)^7$) the vectors of the arguments pros and cons the decision d_1 (resp. d_2).
$d_1 \succeq d_2$ iff $h(\delta_1, \ldots, \delta_n, \delta'_1, \ldots, \delta'_m) \geq_p h(\gamma_1, \ldots, \gamma_l, \gamma'_1, \ldots, \gamma'_k)$, where h is an *aggregation function*.

A simple example of this aggregation attitude is computing the difference of the number of arguments pros and cons.

Definition 15.14. Let $\text{AF} = (\mathcal{D}, \mathcal{A}, \text{Def})$ be a decision system and $\text{Acc}(\text{AF})$ its accepted arguments. Let $d_1, d_2 \in \mathcal{D}$. $d_1 \succeq d_2$ iff $|\mathcal{F}_p(d_1) \cap \text{Acc}(\text{AF})| - |\mathcal{F}_c(d_1) \cap \text{Acc}(\text{AF})| \geq |\mathcal{F}_p(d_2) \cap \text{Acc}(\text{AF})| - |\mathcal{F}_c(d_2) \cap \text{Acc}(\text{AF})|$.

This has the advantage to be again a complete preorder, while taking into account both pros and cons arguments.

3 A typology of formal practical arguments

This section presents a systematic study of practical arguments. Epistemic arguments will not be discussed here because they have been much studied in the litera-

---

[4] Each $\delta_i \in \mathcal{F}_p(d_1) \cap \text{Acc}(\text{AF})$.

[5] Each $\delta'_i \in \mathcal{F}_c(d_1) \cap \text{Acc}(\text{AF})$.

[6] Each $\gamma_i \in \mathcal{F}_p(d_2) \cap \text{Acc}(\text{AF})$.

[7] Each $\gamma'_i \in \mathcal{F}_c(d_2) \cap \text{Acc}(\text{AF})$.

ture (eg. [3, 9, 26]), and their handling does not make new problems in the general setting of Section 2, even in the decision process perspective of this chapter. Moreover, they only play a role when the knowledge base is inconsistent. Before presenting the different types of practical arguments, we start first by introducing the logical language as well as the different bases needed in a decision making problem.

3.1 Logical representation of knowledge and preference

This section introduces the representation setting of knowledge and preference which are here distinct, as it is in classical decision theory. Moreover, preferences are supposed to be handled in a *bipolar* way meaning that what the decision maker is really looking for may be more restrictive than what it is just willing to avoid. In what follows, a vocabulary $\mathcal{P}$ of propositional variables contains two kinds of variables: *decision variables*, denoted by $v_1, \ldots, v_n$, and *state variables*. Decision variable are controllable, that is their value can be fixed by the decision maker. Making a decision then amounts to fixing the truth value of every decision variable. On the contrary, state variables are fixed by nature, and their value is a matter of knowledge by the decision maker. He has no control on them (although he may express preferences about their values).

1. $\mathcal{D}$ is a set of formulas built from decision variables. Elements of $\mathcal{D}$ represent the different *alternatives*, or candidate *decisions*. Let us consider the example of an agent who wants to know whether she should take her umbrella, her raincoat or both. In this case, there are two decision variables: *umb* (for umbrella) and *rac* (for raincoat). Assume that this agent hesitates between the three following options: i) d_1 : *umb* (i.e. to take only her umbrella), ii) d_2 : *rac* (i.e. to take only her raincoat), or iii) d_3 : *umb* $\wedge$ *rac* (i.e. to take both). Thus, $\mathcal{D} = \{d_1, d_2, d_3\}$. Note that elements of $\mathcal{D}$ are not necessarily mutually exclusive. In the example, if the agent chooses the option d_3 then the two other options are satisfied.

2. $\mathcal{G}$ is a set of propositional formulas built from state variables. It gathers the *goals* of an agent (the decision maker). A goal represents what the agent wants to achieve, and has thus a positive flavor. This means that if $g \in \mathcal{G}$, the decision maker wants that the chosen decision leads to a state of affairs where g is true. This base may be *inconsistent*. In this case it would be for sure impossible to satisfy all the goals, which would induce the simultaneous existence of practical arguments pros and cons. In general $\mathcal{G}$ contains several goals. Clearly, an agent should try to satisfy all goals in its goal base $\mathcal{G}$ if possible. This means that $\mathcal{G}$ may be thought as a conjunction. However, the two goal bases $\mathcal{G} = \{g_1, g_2\}$ and $\mathcal{G}' = \{g_1 \wedge g_2\}$ although they are logically equivalent, will not be handled in the same way in an argumentative perspective, since in the second case there is no way to consider intermediary objectives such as here satisfying g_1, or satisfying g_2 only, in case it turns out that it is impossible to satisfy $g_1 \wedge g_2$. This means that our approach is syntax-dependent.

3. The set $\mathcal{R}$ contains propositional formulas built from state variables. It gathers the *rejections* of an agent. A rejection represents what the agent wants to avoid. Clearly rejections express negative preferences. The set $\{\neg r | r \in \mathcal{R}\}$ describing what is acceptable for the agent is assumed to be *consistent*, since acceptable alternatives should satisfy $\neg r$ due to the rejection of r, and at least there should remain some possible worlds that are not rejected. There are at least two reasons for separately considering a set of goals and a set of rejections. First, since agents naturally express themselves in terms of what they are looking for (i.e. their goals), and in terms of what they want to avoid (i.e. their rejections), it is better to consider goals and rejections separately in order to articulate arguments referring to them in a way easily understandable for the agents. Moreover, recent cognitive psychology studies [13] have confirmed the cognitive validity of this distinction between goals and rejections. Second, if r is a rejection, this does not necessarily mean that $\neg r$ is a goal, and thus rejections cannot be equivalently restated as goals. For instance, in case of choosing a medical drug, one may have as a goal the immediate availability of the drug, and as a rejection its availability only after at least two days. In such a case, if the candidate decision guarantees the availability only after one day, this decision will for sure avoid the rejection without satisfying the goal. Another simple example is the case of an agent who wants to get a cup of either coffee or tea, and wants to avoid getting no drink. If the agent obtains a glass of water, again he would avoid its rejection, without being completely satisfied. We can imagine different forms of consistency between the goals and the rejections. A minimal requirement is to have $\mathcal{G} \cap \mathcal{R} = \varnothing$.

4. The set $\mathcal{K}$ represents the *background knowledge* that is not necessarily assumed to be *consistent*. The argumentation framework for inference presented in Section 2 will handle such inconsistency, namely with the epistemic system. Elements of $\mathcal{K}$ are propositional formulas built from the alphabet $\mathcal{P}$, and assumed to be put in a clausal form. The base $\mathcal{K}$ contains basically two kinds of clauses: i) those not involving any element from $\mathcal{D}$ which encode pieces of knowledge or factual information (possibly involving goals) about how the world is; ii) those involving one negation of a formula d of the set $\mathcal{D}$, and which states what follows when decision d is applied.

Thus, the decision problem we consider will be always encoded with the four above sets of formulas (with the restrictions stated above). Moreover, we may suppose that each of the three bases $\mathcal{K}$, $\mathcal{G}$, and $\mathcal{R}$ are stratified. Having $\mathcal{K}$ stratified would mean that we consider that some pieces of knowledge are fully certain, while others are less certain (maybe distinguishing between several levels of partial certainty such as "almost certain", "rather certain", etc.). Clearly, formulas that are not certain at all cannot be in $\mathcal{K}$. Similarly, having $\mathcal{G}$ (resp. $\mathcal{R}$) stratified means that some goals (resp. rejections) are imperative, while some others are less important (one may have more than two levels of importance). Completely unimportant goals (resp. rejections) do not appear in any stratum of $\mathcal{G}$ (resp. $\mathcal{R}$). It is worth pointing out that we assume that candidate decisions are all considered as *a priori* equally potentially suitable, and thus there is no need to have $\mathcal{D}$ stratified.

Definition 15.15 (Decision theory). A *decision theory* (or a *theory* for short) is a tuple $\mathcal{T} = \langle \mathcal{D}, \mathcal{K}, \mathcal{G}, \mathcal{R} \rangle$.

3.2 A typology of formal practical arguments

Each candidate decision may have arguments in its favor (called pros), and arguments against it (called cons). In the following, an argument is associated with an alternative, and always either refers to a goal or to a rejection. Arguments pros point out the "existence of good consequences" or the "absence of bad consequences" for a candidate decision. A good consequence means that applying decision d will lead to the satisfaction of a goal, or to the avoidance of a rejection. Similarly, a bad consequence means that the application of d leads for sure to miss a goal, or to reach a rejected situation. We can distinguish between practical arguments referring to a goal, and those arguments referring to rejections. When focusing on the base $\mathcal{G}$, an argument pro corresponds to the guaranteed satisfaction of a goal when there exists a consistent subset S of $\mathcal{K}$ such that $S \cup \{d\} \vdash g$.

Definition 15.16 (Positive arguments pro). Let $\mathcal{T}$ be a theory. A *positively expressed argument in favor of* an option d is a tuple $\delta = \langle S, d, g \rangle$ s.t:

1. $S \subseteq \mathcal{K}, d \in \mathcal{D}, g \in \mathcal{G}, S \cup \{d\}$ is consistent
2. $S \cup \{d\} \vdash g$, and S is minimal for set inclusion among subsets of $\mathcal{K}$ satisfying the above criteria (arguments of Type PP).

S is called the *support* of the argument, and d is its *conclusion*.

In what follows, Supp denotes a function that returns the support S of an argument, Conc denotes a function that returns the conclusion d of the argument, and Result denotes a function that returns the consequence of the decision. The consequence may be either a goal as in the previous definition, or a rejection as we can see in the next definitions of argument types. The above definition deserves several comments: 1) The consistency of $S \cup \{d\}$ means that d is applicable in the context S, in other words that we cannot prove from S that d is impossible. This means that impossible alternatives w.r.t. $\mathcal{K}$ have been already taken out when defining the set $\mathcal{D}$. In the particular case where the base $\mathcal{K}$ would be consistent, then condition 1, namely $S \cup \{d\}$ is consistent, is equivalent to $\mathcal{K} \cup \{d\}$ is consistent. But, in the case where $\mathcal{K}$ is inconsistent, independently from the existence of a PP argument, it may happen that for another consistent subset S' of $\mathcal{K}$, $S' \vdash \neg d$. This would mean that there is some doubt about the feasibility of d, and then constitute an epistemic argument against d. In the general framework proposed in section 2, such an argument will overrule decision d since epistemic arguments take precedence over any practical argument (provided that this epistemic argument is not itself killed by another epistemic argument).
2) Note that argument of type PP are reminiscent of the practical syllogism recalled in the introduction. Indeed, it emphasizes that a candidate decision might be chosen

if it leads to the satisfaction of a goal. However, this is only a clue for choosing the decision since this last may have arguments against, which would weaken it, or there may exist other candidate decisions with stronger arguments. Moreover, due to the nature of the practical syllogism, it is worth noticing that practical arguments have an *abductive* form, contrarily to epistemic arguments that are defined in a deductive way, as revealed by their formal respective definitions.

Another type of arguments pros refers to rejections. It amounts to avoid a rejection for sure, i.e. $S \cup \{d\} \vdash \neg r$ (where S is a consistent subset of $\mathcal{K}$).

Definition 15.17 (Negative arguments pros). Let $\mathcal{T}$ be a theory. A *negatively expressed argument in favor of* an option is a tuple $\delta = \langle S, d, r \rangle$ s.t:

1. $S \subseteq \mathcal{K}$, $d \in \mathcal{D}$, $r \in \mathcal{R}$, $S \cup \{d\}$ is consistent
2. $S \cup \{d\} \vdash \neg r$ and S is minimal for set inclusion among subsets of $\mathcal{K}$ satisfying the above criteria (arguments of Type NP).

Arguments cons highlight the existence of bad consequences for a given candidate decision. Negatively expressed arguments cons are defined by exhibiting a rejection that is necessarily satisfied. Formally:

Definition 15.18 (Negative arguments cons). Let $\mathcal{T}$ be a theory. A *negatively expressed argument against* an option d is a tuple $\delta = \langle S, d, r \rangle$ s.t:

1. $S \subseteq \mathcal{K}$, $d \in \mathcal{D}$, $r \in \mathcal{R}$, $S \cup \{d\}$ is consistent,
2. $S \cup \{d\} \vdash r$ and S is minimal for set inclusion among subsets of $\mathcal{K}$ satisfying the above criteria (arguments of Type NC).

Lastly, the absence of positive consequences can also be seen as an argument against (cons) an alternative.

Definition 15.19 (Positive arguments cons). Let $\mathcal{T}$ be a theory. A *positively expressed argument against* an option d is a tuple $\delta = \langle S, d, g \rangle$ s.t:

1. $S \subseteq \mathcal{K}$, $d \in \mathcal{D}$, $g \in \mathcal{G}$, $S \cup \{d\}$ is consistent,
2. $S \cup \{d\} \vdash \neg g$ and S is minimal for set inclusion among subsets of $\mathcal{K}$ satisfying the above criteria (arguments of Type PC).

Let us illustrate the previous definitions on an example.

Example 15.7. Two decisions are possible, organizing a show (d), or not ($\neg d$). Thus $\mathcal{D} = \{d, \neg d\}$. The knowledge base $\mathcal{K}$ contains the following pieces of knowledge: if a show is organized and it rains then small money loss ($\neg d \lor \neg r \lor sml$); if a show is organized and it does not rain then benefit ($\neg d \lor r \lor b$); small money loss entails money loss ($\neg sml \lor ml$); if benefit there is no money loss ($\neg b \lor \neg ml$); small money loss is not large money loss ($\neg sml \lor \neg lml$); large money loss is money loss ($\neg lml \lor ml$); there are clouds (c); if there are clouds then it may rain ($\neg c \lor r$). All these pieces of knowledge are in the stratum of level n, except the last one which is in a stratum with a lower level due to uncertainty. Consider now the cases of two organizers (O_1 and O_2) having different preferences. O_1 does not want any loss $\mathcal{R} = \{ml\}$, and would like benefit $\mathcal{G} = \{b\}$. O_2 does not want large money loss $\mathcal{R} = \{lml\}$, and would like benefit $\mathcal{G} = \{b\}$. In such case, it is expected that O_1 prefers $\neg d$ to d, since there is a NC argument against d and no argument for $\neg d$. For O_2, there is no longer any NC argument against d. He might even prefer d to $\neg d$, if he is optimistic and he considers that there is a possibility that it does not rain (leading to a potential PP argument under the hypothesis to have $\neg r$ in $\mathcal{K}$.

Due to the asymmetry in the human mind between what is rejected and what is desired, the former being usually considered as stronger than the latter, one may assume that NC arguments are stronger than PC arguments, and conversely PP arguments are stronger than NP arguments.

4 Related work

Some works have been done on arguing for decision. Quite early, in [22] Brewka and Gordon have outlined a logical approach to decision (for negotiation purposes), which suggests the use of defeasible consequence relation for handling prioritized rules, and which also exhibits arguments for each choice. However, arguments are not formally defined. In the framework proposed by Fox and Parsons in [20], no explicit distinction is made between knowledge and goals. However, in their examples, values (belonging to a linearly ordered scale) are assigned to formulas which represent goals. These values provide an empirical basis for comparing arguments using a symbolic combination of strengths of beliefs and goals values. This symbolic combination is performed through dictionaries corresponding to different kinds of scales that may be used. In this work, only one type of arguments is considered in the style of arguments in favor of beliefs. In [10], Bonet and Geffner have also proposed an approach to qualitative decision, inspired from Tan and Pearl [27], based on "action rules" that link a situation and an action with the satisfaction of a *positive* or a *negative* goal. However in contrast with the previous two works and the work presented in this paper, this approach does not refer to any model in argumentative inference.

Other researchers in AI, working on practical reasoning, starting with the generic question "what is the right thing to do for an agent in a given situation" [24, 25], have proposed a two steps process to answer this question. The first step, often called deliberation [29], consists of identifying the goals of the agent. In the second step, they look for ways of achieving those goals, i.e. for plans, and thus for intermediary goals and sub-plans. Such an approach raises issues such as: how are goals generated ? are actions feasible ? do actions have undesirable consequences ? are sub-plans compatible ? are there alternative plans for achieving a given goal, etc. In [12], it has been argued that this can be done by representing the cognitive states, namely agent's beliefs, desires and intentions (thus the so-called *BDI* architecture). This requires a rich knowledge/preference representation setting, which contrasts with the classical decision setting that directly uses an uncertainty distribution (a probability distribution in the case of expected utility), and a utility (value) function. Besides, the deliberation step is merely an inference problem since it amounts to finding a set of desires that are justified on the basis of the current state of the world and of conditional desires. Checking if a plan is feasible and does not lead to bad consequences is still a matter of inference. A decision problem only occurs when several plans or sub-plans are possible, and one of them has to be chosen. This latter issue may be viewed as a classical decision problem. What is worth noticing in most works on practical reasoning is the use of argument schemes for providing reasons for choosing or discarding an action (e.g. [19, 21]). For instance, an action may be considered as potentially useful on the basis of the *practical syllogism* [28]:

- G is a goal for agent X
- Doing action A is sufficient for agent X to carry out goal G
- Then, agent X ought to do action A

The above syllogism is in essence already an argument in favor of doing action A. However, this does not mean that the action is warranted, since other arguments (called counter-arguments) may be built or provided against the action. Those counter-arguments refer to critical questions identified in [28] for the above syllogism. In particular, relevant questions are "Are there alternative ways of realizing G?", "Is doing A feasible?", "Has agent X other goals than G?", "Are there other consequences of doing A which should be taken into account?". Recently in [6, 7], the above syllogism has been extended to explicitly take into account the reference to ethical values in arguments.

5 Conclusion

The chapter has proposed an abstract argumentation-based framework for decision making. The main idea behind this work is how to define a complete preorder on a set of candidate decisions on the basis of arguments. The framework distinguishes between two types of arguments: epistemic arguments that support beliefs and practical arguments that justify candidate decisions. Each practical argument concerns only one candidate decision, and may be either in favor of that decision or against it. The framework follows two main steps: i) an inference step in which arguments are evaluated using acceptability semantics. This step amounts to return among the practical arguments, those which are warranted in the current state of information, i.e. the "accepted" arguments. ii) A pure decision step in which candidate decisions are compared on the basis of accepted practical arguments. For the second step of the process, we have proposed three families of principles for comparing pairs of choices. An axiomatic study and a cognitive validation of these principles are worth developing, in particular in connection with [11, 16]. The proposed approach is very general and includes as particular cases already studied argumentation-based decision systems. Moreover it has been shown in [5] that the approach is suitable for multiple criteria decision making as well as decision making under uncertainty. In particular, the approach has been shown to fully agree with qualitative decision making under uncertainty, and to distinguish between pessimistic and optimistic attitude of the decision maker.

Although our model is quite general, it may be still worth extending along different lines. First, the use of default knowledge could be developed. Second, our approach does not take into account rules that recommend or disqualify decisions in given contexts. Such rules should incorporate modalities for distinguishing between strong and weak recommendations. Moreover, they are fired by classical argumentative inference. This contrasts with our approach where the only arguments pertaining to decisions have an abductive structure. Recommendation rules may also turn to be inconsistent with other pieces of knowledge in practical arguments pros or cons w.r.t. a decision. Lastly, agents may base their decision on two types of information, namely generic knowledge and a repertory of concrete reported cases. Then, past observations recorded in the repertory may be the basis of a new form of arguments by exemplification of cases where a decision has succeeded or failed. This would amount to relate argumentation and case-based decision.

References

1. L. Amgoud. A general argumentation framework for inference and decision making. In *21st Conference on Uncertainty in Artificial Intelligence, UAI'2005*, pages 26–33, 2005.
2. L. Amgoud, J-F. Bonnefon, and H. Prade. An argumentation-based approach to multiple criteria decision. In *Proceedings of the 8th European Conference on Symbolic and Quantitative Approaches to Reasoning with Uncertainty (ECSQARU'05)*, pages 269–280, 2005.
3. L. Amgoud and C. Cayrol. Inferring from inconsistency in preference-based argumentation frameworks. *In International Journal of Automated Reasoning*, 29, N2:125–169, 2002.
4. L. Amgoud and C. Cayrol. A reasoning model based on the production of acceptable arguments. *In Annals of Mathematics and Artificial Intelligence*, 34:197–216, 2002.
5. L. Amgoud and H. Prade. Explaining qualitative decision under uncertainty by argumentation. In *Proceedings of the 21st National Conference on Artificial Intelligence (AAAI'06)*, pages 219–224, 2006.
6. K. Atkinson. Value-based argumentation for democratic decision support. In *Proceedings of the First International Conference on Computational Models of Natural Argument (COMMA'06)*, pages 47–58, 2006.
7. K. Atkinson, T. Bench-Capon, and P. McBurney. Justifying practical reasoning. In *Proceedings of the Fourth Workshop on Computational Models of Natural Argument (CMNA'04)*, pages 87–90, 2004.
8. P. Baroni, M. Giacomin, and G. Guida. Scc-recursiveness: a general schema for argumentation semantics. *In Artificial Intelligence*, 168 (1-2):162–210, 2005.
9. Ph. Besnard and A. Hunter. A logic-based theory of deductive arguments. *In Artificial Intelligence*, 128:203–235, 2001.
10. B. Bonet and H. Geffner. Arguing for decisions: A qualitative model of decision making. In *Proceedings of the 12th Conference on Uncertainty in Artificial Intelligence (UAI'96)*, pages 98–105, 1996.
11. J.-F. Bonnefon and H. Fargier. Comparing sets of positive and negative arguments: Empirical assessment of seven qualitative rules. In *Proceedings of the 17th European Conference on Artificial Intelligence (ECAI'06)*, pages 16–20, 2006.
12. M. Bratman. *Intentions, plans, and practical reason.* Harvard University Press, Massachusetts, 1987.

13. J.T. Cacioppo, W.L. Gardner, and G.G. Bernston. Beyond bipolar conceptualizations and measures: The case of attitudes and evaluative space. *In Personality and Social Psychology Review*, 1:3–25, 1997.

14. C. Cayrol, V. Royer, and C. Saurel. Management of preferences in assumption-based reasoning. *In Lecture Notes in Computer Science*, 682:13–22, 1993.

15. Y. Dimopoulos, P. Moraitis, and A. Tsoukias. Argumentation based modeling of decision aiding for autonomous agents. In *IEEE-WIC-ACM International Conference on Intelligent Agent Technology*, pages 99–105, 2004.

16. D. Dubois and H. Fargier. Qualitative decision making with bipolar information. In *Proceedings of the 10th International Conference on Principles of Knowledge Representation and Reasoning (KR'06)*, pages 175–186, 2006.

17. P. M. Dung. On the acceptability of arguments and its fundamental role in nonmonotonic reasoning, logic programming and *n*-person games. *In Artificial Intelligence*, 77:321–357, 1995.

18. M. Elvang-Goransson, J. Fox, and P. Krause. Dialectic reasoning with inconsistent information. In *Proceedings of 9th Conference on Uncertainty in Artificial Intelligence (UAI'93)*, pages 114 – 121, 1993.

19. J. Fox and S. Das. *Safe and Sound. Artificial Intelligence in Hazardous Applications*. AAAI Press, The MIT Press, 2000.

20. J. Fox and S. Parsons. On using arguments for reasoning about actions and values. In *Proceedings of the AAAI Spring Symposium on Qualitative Preferences in Deliberation and Practical Reasoning, Stanford*, 1997.

21. R. Girle, D. Hitchcock, P. McBurney, and B. Verheij. *Decision support for practical reasoning*. C. Reed and T. Norman (Editors): Argumentation Machines: New Frontiers in Argument and Computation. Argumentation Library. Dordrecht, The Netherlands: Kluwer Academic, 2003.

22. T. Gordon and G. Brewka. How to buy a porsche: An approach to defeasible decision making (preliminary report). In *In the workshop of Comutational Dialectics*, 1994.

23. T. F. Gordon and N. I. Karacapilidis. The Zeno Argumentation Framework. *Kunstliche Intelligenz*, 13(3):20–29, 1999.

24. J. Pollock. The logical foundations of goal-regression planning in autonomous agents. *In Artificial Intelligence*, 106(2):267–334, 1998.

25. J. Raz. Practical reasoning. *Oxford, Oxford University Press*, 1978.

26. G. R. Simari and R. P. Loui. A mathematical treatment of defeasible reasoning and its implementation. *In Artificial Intelligence and Law*, 53:125–157, 1992.

27. S. W. Tan and J. Pearl. Qualitative decision theory. In *Proceedings of the 11th National Conference on Artificial Intelligence (AAAI'94)*, pages 928–933, 1994.

28. D. Walton. *Argument schemes for presumptive reasoning*, volume 29. Lawrence Erlbaum Associates, Mahwah, NJ, USA, 1996.

29. M. J. Wooldridge. *Reasoning about rational agents*. MIT Press, Cambridge Massachusetts, London England, 2000.

Chapter 16
Argumentation and Game Theory

Iyad Rahwan and Kate Larson

1 What Game Theory Can Do for Argumentation

In a large class of multi-agent systems, agents are *self-interested* in the sense that each agent is interested only in furthering its individual goals, which may or may not coincide with others' goals. When such agents engage in argument, they would be expected to argue *strategically* in such a way that makes it more likely for their argumentative goals to be achieved. What we mean by arguing strategically is that instead of making arbitrary arguments, an agent would carefully choose its argumentative moves in order to further its own objectives.

The mathematical study of strategic interaction is *Game Theory*, which was pioneered by von Neuman and Morgenstern [13]. A setting of strategic interaction is modelled as a *game*, which consists of a set of players, a set of actions available to them, and a rule that determines the outcome given players' chosen actions. In an argumentation scenario, the set of actions are typically the set of argumentative moves (e.g. asserting a claim or challenging a claim), and the outcome rule is the criterion by which arguments are evaluated (e.g. a judge's attitude or a social norm).

Generally, game theory can be used to achieve two goals:

1. undertake precise analysis of interaction in particular strategic settings, with a view to predicting the outcome;
2. design rules of the game in such a way that self-interested agents behave in some desirable manner (e.g. tell the truth); this is called *mechanism design*;

Both these approaches are quite useful for the study of argumentation in multi-agent systems. On one hand, an agent may use game theory to analyse a given argumentative situation in order to choose the best strategy. On the other hand, we

Iyad Rahwan
British University in Dubai, UAE & University of Edinburgh, UK, e-mail: irahwan@acm.org

Kate Larson
University of Waterloo, Canada e-mail: klarson@cs.uwaterloo.ca

I. Rahwan, G. R. Simari (eds.), *Argumentation in Artificial Intelligence,*   321
DOI 10.1007/978-0-387-98197-0_16, © Springer Science+Business Media, LLC 2009

may use mechanism design to design the rules (e.g. argumentation protocol) in such a way as to promote good argumentative behaviour. In this chapter, we will discuss some early developments in these directions.

In the next section, we motivate the usefulness of game theory in argumentation using a novel game. After providing a brief background on game theory in Section 3, we introduce our Argumentation Mechanism Design approach in Section 4 and present some preliminary results in Section 5. Finally, we discuss related work in Section 6 and conclude in Section 7

2 The "Argumentative Battle of the Sexes" Game

Consider the following situation involving the couple Alice (A) and Brian (B), who want to decide on an activity for the day.[1] Brian thinks they should go to a soccer match (argument α_1) while Alice thinks they should attend the ballet (argument α_2). There is time for only one activity, however (hence α_1 and α_2 defeat one another). Moreover, while Alice prefers the ballet to the soccer, she would still rather go to a soccer match than stay at home. Likewise, Brian prefers the soccer match to the ballet, but also prefers the ballet to staying home. Formally, we can write $u_A(ballet) > u_A(soccer) > u_A(home)$ and $u_B(soccer) > u_B(ballet) > u_B(home)$.

Alice has a strong argument which she may use against going to the soccer, namely by claiming that she is too sick to be outdoors (argument α_3). Brian simply cannot attack this argument (without compromising his marriage at least). Likewise, Brian has an irrefutable argument against the ballet; he could claim that his ex-wife will be there too (argument α_4). Alice cannot stand her! Using Dung's abstract argumentation model [1], which is described in detail in Chapter 2, the argumentative structure of this situation can be modelled as shown in Figure 16.1(a).

Alice can choose to say nothing, utter argument α_2 or α_3 or both. Similarly, Brian can choose to say nothing, utter argument α_1 or α_4 or both. For the sake of the example, we will suppose that Alice and Brian use the grounded semantics as the argumentative foundation of their marriage! The question we are interested in here is: *What will Alice and Bob say?* or at least: *What are they likely to say?*

The strategic encounter, on the other hand, can be modelled as shown in the table in Figure 16.1(b). Each cell corresponds to a strategy profile in which Alice and Brian reveal a particular set of arguments. The numbers in the cells correspond to the utilities they obtain once the grounded extension is calculated on their revealed arguments. For example, if Alice utters $\{\alpha_2\}$ while Brian utters $\{\alpha_1, \alpha_4\}$, we end up with a sub-graph of Figure 16.1(a) in which α_3 is missing. The grounded extension of this argument graph admits arguments $\{\alpha_1, \alpha_4\}$. This corresponds to a situation where Brian wins and the couple head to the soccer. Thus, he gets the highest utility of 2, while Alice gets her second-preferred outcome with utility 1. This representation, shown in Figure 16.1(b), is known as a *normal form game*.

---

[1] We call this the *argumentative battle of the sexes* game. It is similar, but not identical to the well-known "Battle of the Sexes" game.

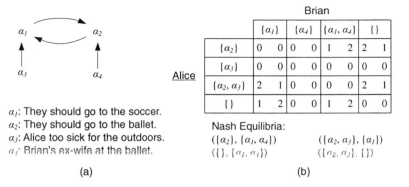

α_1: They should go to the soccer.
α_2: They should go to the ballet.
α_3: Alice too sick for the outdoors.
α_4: Brian's ex-wife at the ballet.

(a)

Brian

	$\{\alpha_1\}$		$\{\alpha_4\}$		$\{\alpha_1, \alpha_4\}$		$\{\}$	
$\{\alpha_2\}$	0	0	0	0	1	2	2	1
$\{\alpha_3\}$	0	0	0	0	0	0	0	0
$\{\alpha_2, \alpha_3\}$	2	1	0	0	0	0	2	1
$\{\}$	1	2	0	0	1	2	0	0

Nash Equilibria:
$(\{\alpha_2\}, \{\alpha_1, \alpha_4\})$ $(\{\alpha_2, \alpha_3\}, \{\alpha_1\})$
$(\{\}, \{\alpha_1, \alpha_4\})$ $(\{\alpha_2, \alpha_3\}, \{\})$

(b)

Fig. 16.1 Simple argumentative scenario and its normal form game representation. The outcome is decided using grounded semantics.

The normal-form game can be used to deduce a number of things about this particular scenario. First, it is never in either Alice or Brian's best interest to utter their irrefutable argument (α_3 or α_4) without also stating their preferred activity (α_1 or α_2), since by announcing their preferred activity then they may possibly attend some event (either ballet or soccer) while if one of them only announces their irrefutable argument then both agents are certain to stay at home (the least preferred outcome for both Alice and Brian). That is, $\{\alpha_3\}$ is *weakly dominated* by $\{\alpha_2, \alpha_3\}$ (and $\{\alpha_2\}$) and α_4 is weakly dominated by $\{\alpha_1, \alpha_4\}$ (and $\{\alpha_1\}$).

Given a game, we are interested in finding the Nash equilibria of the game. A Nash equilibrium is a strategy profile (a listing of one strategy for each agent) where no agent wants to change its strategy, assuming that the other agents do not change. The Nash equilibria are the *stable* outcomes of the game. Consider the strategy profile in which Alice says that she is sick and suggests the ballet (i.e. she utters $\{\alpha_2, \alpha_3\}$) and Brian simply suggests the soccer match (i.e. he utters $\{\alpha_1\}$). This outcome is a Nash equilibrium. On one hand, given that Alice states $\{\alpha_2, \alpha_3\}$, Brian has no incentive to deviate to any other strategy. If he mentions his ex-wife's attendance at the ballet (uttering $\{\alpha_4\}$ or $\{\alpha_1, \alpha_4\}$), he shoots himself in the foot and ends up spending the day at home. And if he stays quiet (uttering $\{\}$), he cannot influence the outcome anyway. On the other hand, assuming that Brian announces $\{\alpha_1\}$ then Alice is best-off stating $\{\alpha_2, \alpha_3\}$ since by doing so, she gets the outcome that she prefers (the ballet). In fact, we list four Nash equilibria in Figure 16.1(b).[2]

The analysis that we just concluded does not allow us to identify a *single* outcome for the example. However, it does identify some interesting strategic phenomena. In particular, it shows that it is never in Alice and Brian's interest for them both to use their irrefutable arguments. For example, if Brian is confident that Alice will state

---

[2] A reader familiar with game theory will note that we only list the pure strategy Nash equilibria. In addition to these four equilibria, there are three mixed equilibria in which players randomize their strategies.

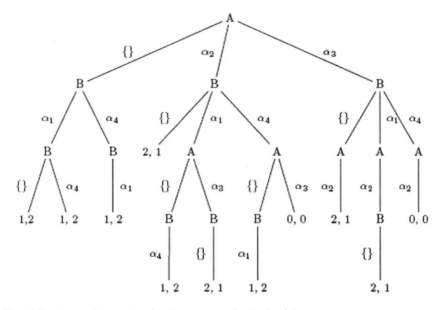

Fig. 16.2 A (pruned) game tree for the argumentative battle of the sexes game.

that she is too sick (α_3) then Brian should not bring up his argument against the ballet.

While the above analysis did not allow us to identify a single outcome of the scenario, at least we were able to rule out so many unstable outcomes. Indeed, in some situations, there is a single Nash equilibrium, which makes predicting the outcome easier.

So far, we used a normal-form representation to model the argument game. While this representation is useful for many purposes due to its simplicity, it fails to capture the *dynamic* aspect of argumentation: the fact that argumentative moves are normally made interactively over multiple time steps. The appropriate tool to model such dynamics are extensive-form games, which we discuss next.

An extensive-form game with perfect information explicitly captures the fact that agents may take turns when choosing actions (for example, declaring arguments). A game tree is used to represent the game. Each node in the tree is associated with an agent whose turn it is to take an action. A path in the tree represents the sequence of actions taken, and leafs nodes are the final outcomes, given the actions on the path to the leaf node. In these games we assume that the actions that each agent takes are fully observable by all the other agents.

We can model the interaction between Alice and Brian using an extensive-form game, if we assume that Alice and Brian take turns uttering arguments. We will assume that i) an agent can only make one argument at a time, ii) agents can not repeat arguments, and iii) if at some step an agent decides not to make an argument, then they are not allowed to make any more arguments in the future. We will also assume, for the sake of the example, that Alice gets to make the first argument. Figure 16.2 shows the game tree for the argumentative battle of the sexes game. Most of the paths which result in an outcome where both agents will get zero have been pruned from the tree. These paths are not played in equilibrium, and their removal allows us to focus on the relevant parts of the tree.

Since Alice gets to make the first move, she has to decide whether to offer no arguments at all $\{\}$, suggest that they go to the ballet (α_2), or present her counter-argument to the soccer match before the soccer match is even brought up (α_3). Based on the argument uttered by Alice, Brian then gets to make a decision. If Alice had made no argument, then as long as Brian announces α_1 (and possibly also α_4) then they will go to the soccer match. Brian will receive utility of two and Alice will receive utility of one (the subtree on the left). If Alice suggested going to the ballet (α_2) then Brian is best off immediately raising his counter-argument to the ballet (α_4). This is because Alice's best counter-argument is then to say nothing, which allows Brian to then present soccer (α_1) as an alternative. This results in Brian getting his favorite outcome (soccer) since Alice's only other option would be to raise argument α_3, resulting in them both staying at home (the least preferred outcome). If instead, Brian had not made an argument or had uttered α_1, then Alice would have been able to to raise her counter-argument, resulting in them both going to the ballet. Finally, if Alice first announces her counter-argument to soccer (α_3) then Brian will end up announcing, at most, argument α_1 since raising the counter-argument to the ballet (α_4) will result in them both staying at home. This means that the outcome will be that both Alice and Brian will go to the ballet. Alice uses this reasoning in order to determine what her initial action should be. She will realize that if she makes no argument, or initially suggests the ballet (α_2) then Brian will be able to take actions so that they end up going to the soccer match. However, if Alice starts with her counter-argument to the soccer match (α_3) then she can force Brian into a situation where he is best off not making his counter-argument to the ballet, and so they will both end up going to the ballet, Alice's preferred outcome. Therefore, in equilibrium, Alice will state her objection to soccer (α_3) first, which will force Brian to either make no argument or make (already defeated) argument α_1, which then allows Alice to counter with the ballet proposal (α_2). This equilibrium is called a *subgame perfect equilibrium* and is a refinement of the Nash equilibria.

We note that by going first, Alice had an advantage over Brian since by carefully choosing her first argument she could force the outcome that she wanted. If Brian had gone first, then he would have been best off first announcing α_4, his counter-argument to the ballet. This would have allowed him to get the outcome that he preferred, that is, the soccer match. Thus in the extensive-form game analysis of argumentation, the *order* in which agents make arguments is critical in the analysis and in the outcome.

A number of researchers have proposed using extensive-form games of perfect information to model argumentation. For example, Procaccia and Rosenschein [10] proposed a *game-based argumentation framework* where they extend Dung's abstract argumentation framework by mapping argumentation frameworks into extensive-form games of perfect information. A similar approach has recently been proposed by Riveret et al [12], giving an extensive-form game characterisation of Prakken's dialectical framework [8]. In both cases, the authors show how standard backward induction techniques can be used to eliminate dominated strategies and characterise Nash equilibrium strategies.

3 Technical Background

Before we present a precise formal mapping of abstract argumentation into game theory, in this section, we give a brief background on key game-theoretic concepts. Readers who lack background in game theory may consult a more comprehensive introduction to the field, such as [5].

3.1 Game Theory

The field of game theory studies strategic interactions of self-interested agents. We assume that there is a set of self-interested agents, denoted by I. We let $\theta_i \in \Theta_i$ denote the *type* of agent i which is drawn from some set of possible types Θ_i. The type represents the private information and preferences of the agent. An agent's preferences are over *outcomes* $o \in \mathcal{O}$, where $\mathcal{O}$ is the set of all possible outcomes. We assume that an agent's preferences can be expressed by a utility function $u_i(o, \theta_i)$ which depends on both the outcome, o, and the agent's type, θ_i. Agent i prefers outcome o_1 to o_2 when $u_i(o_1, \theta_i) > u_i(o_2, \theta_i)$.

When agents interact, we say that they are playing *strategies*. A strategy for agent i, $s_i(\theta_i)$, is a plan that describes what actions the agent will take for every decision that the agent might be called upon to make, for each possible piece of information that the agent may have at each time it is called to act. That is, a strategy can be thought as a complete contingency plan for an agent. We let Σ_i denote the set of all possible strategies for agent i, and thus $s_i(\theta_i) \in \Sigma_i$. When it is clear from the context, we will drop the θ_i in order to simplify the notation. We let *strategy profile* $s = (s_1(\theta_1), \ldots, s_I(\theta_I))$ denote the outcome that results when each agent i is playing strategy $s_i(\theta_i)$. As a notational convenience we define

$$s_{-i}(\theta_{-i}) = (s_1(\theta_i), \ldots, s_{i-1}(\theta_{i-1}), s_{i+1}(\theta_{i+1}), \ldots, s_I(\theta_I))$$

and thus $s = (s_i, s_{-i})$. We then interpret $u_i((s_i, s_{-i}), \theta_i)$ to be the utility of agent i with type θ_i when all agents play strategies specified by strategy profile $(s_i(\theta_i), s_{-i}(\theta_{-i}))$.

Similarly, we also define:

$$\theta_{-i} = (\theta_1, \ldots, \theta_{i-1}, \theta_{i+1}, \ldots, \theta_I)$$

Since the agents are all self-interested, they will try to choose strategies which maximize their own utility. Since the strategies of other agents also play a role in determining the outcome, the agents must take this into account. The *solution concepts* in game theory determine the outcomes that will arise if all agents are rational and strategic. The most well known solution concept is the *Nash equilibrium*. A Nash equilibrium is a strategy profile in which each agent is following a strategy which maximizes its own utility, given its type and the strategies of the other agents.

Definition 16.1 (Nash Equilibrium). A strategy profile $s^* = (s_1^*, \ldots, s_I^*)$ is a *Nash equilibrium* if no agent has incentive to change its strategy, given that no other agent changes. Formally,

$$\forall i, \forall s_i', u_i(s_i^*, s_{-i}^*, \theta_i) \geq u_i(s_i', s_{-i}^*, \theta_i).$$

Although the Nash equilibrium is a fundamental concept in game theory, it does have several weaknesses. First, there may be multiple Nash equilibria and so agents may be uncertain as to which equilibrium they should play. Second, the Nash equilibrium implicitly assumes that agents have perfect information about all other agents, including the other agents' preferences.

A stronger solution concept in game theory is the *dominant-strategy equilibrium*. A strategy s_i is said to be *dominant* if by playing it, the utility of agent i is maximized no matter what strategies the other agents play.

Definition 16.2 (Dominant Strategy). A strategy s_i^* is *dominant* if

$$\forall s_{-i}, \forall s_i', u_i(s_i^*, s_{-i}, \theta_i) \geq u_i(s_i', s_{-i}, \theta_i).$$

Sometimes, we will refer to a strategy satisfying the above definition as *weakly dominant*. If the inequality is strict (i.e. $>$ instead of $\geq$), we say that the strategy is *strictly dominant*.

A dominant-strategy equilibrium is a strategy profile where each agent is playing a dominant strategy. This is a very robust solution concept since it makes no assumptions about what information the agents have available to them, nor does it assume that all agents know that all other agents are being rational (i.e. trying to maximize their own utility). However, there are many strategic settings where no agent has a dominant strategy.

A third solution concept is the *Bayes-Nash equilibrium*. We include it for the sake of completeness. In the Bayes-Nash equilibrium the assumption made for the Nash equilibrium, that all agents know the preferences of others, is relaxed. Instead, we assume that there is some common prior $F((\Theta_1, \ldots, \Theta_I))$, such that the agents' types are distributed according to F. Then, in equilibrium, each agent chooses the strategy that maximizes it's expected utility given the strategies other agents are playing and the prior F.

Definition 16.3 (Bayes-Nash Equilibrium). A strategy profile $s^* = (s_i^*, s_{-i}^*)$ is a Bayes-Nash equilibrium if

$$E_{\theta_{-i}}[u_i((s_i^*(\theta_i), s_{-i}^*(\cdot)), \theta_i)] \geq E_{\theta_{-i}}[u_i((s_i'(\theta_i), s_{-i}^*(\cdot)), \theta_i)] \; \forall \theta_i, \forall s_i'.$$

3.2 Mechanism Design

The problem that mechanism design studies is how to ensure that a desirable system-wide outcome or decision is made when there is a group of self-interested agents who have preferences over the outcomes. In particular, we often want the outcome to depend on the preferences of the agents. This is captured by a *social choice function*.

Definition 16.4 (Social Choice Function). A *social choice function* is a rule f : $\Theta_1 \times \ldots \times \Theta_I \to \mathcal{O}$, that selects some outcome $f(\theta) \in \mathcal{O}$, given agent types $\theta = (\theta_1, \ldots, \theta_I)$.

The challenge, however, is that the types of the agents (the $\theta_i's$) are private and known only to the agents themselves. Thus, in order to select an outcome with the social choice function, one has to rely on the agents to reveal their types. However, for a given social choice function, an agent may find that it is better off if it does not reveal its type truthfully, since by lying it may be able to cause the social choice function to choose an outcome that it prefers. Instead of trusting the agents to be truthful, we use a *mechanism* to try to reach the correct outcome.

A mechanism $\mathcal{M} = (\Sigma, g(\cdot))$ defines the set of allowable strategies that agents can chose, with $\Sigma = \Sigma_1 \times \cdots \times \Sigma_I$ where Σ_i is the strategy set for agent i, and an outcome function $g(s)$ which specifies an outcome o for each possible strategy profile $s = (s_1, \ldots, s_I) \in \Sigma$. This defines a game in which agent i is free to select any strategy in Σ_i, and, in particular, will try to select a strategy which will lead to an outcome that maximizes its own utility. We say that a mechanism *implements* social choice function f if the outcome induced by the mechanism is the same outcome that the social choice function would have returned if the true types of the agents were known.

Definition 16.5 (Implementation). A mechanism $\mathcal{M} = (\Sigma, g(\cdot))$ *implements* social choice function f if there exists an equilibrium s^* such that

$$\forall \theta \in \Theta, \; g(s^*(\theta)) = f(\theta).$$

While the definition of a mechanism puts no restrictions on the strategy spaces of the agents, an important class of mechanisms are the *direct-revelation mechanisms* (or simply *direct mechanisms*).

Definition 16.6 (Direct-Revelation Mechanism). A *direct-revelation mechanism* is a mechanism in which $\Sigma_i = \Theta_i$ for all i, and $g(\theta) = f(\theta)$ for all $\theta \in \Theta$.

In words, a direct mechanism is one where the strategies of the agents are to announce a type, θ_i' to the mechanism. While it is not necessary that $\theta_i' = \theta_i$, the important *Revelation Principle* (see below for more details) states that if a social choice function, $f(\cdot)$, can be implemented, then it can be implemented by a direct mechanism where every agent reveals its true type [5]. In such a situation, we say that the social choice function is *incentive compatible*.

Definition 16.7 (Incentive Compatible). The social choice function $f(\cdot)$ is *incentive compatible* (or *truthfully implementable*) if the direct mechanism $\mathcal{M} = (\Theta, g(\cdot))$ has an equilibrium s^* such that $s_i^*(\theta_i) = \theta_i$.

If the equilibrium concept is the dominant-strategy equilibrium, then the social choice function is *strategy-proof*. In this chapter we will on occasion call a mechanism incentive-compatible or strategy-proof. This means that the social choice function that the mechanism implements is incentive-compatible or strategy-proof.

3.3 The Revelation Principle

Determining whether a particular social choice function can be implemented, and in particular, finding a mechanism which implements a social choice function appears to be a daunting task. In the definition of a mechanism, the strategy spaces of the agents are unrestricted, leading to an infinitely large space of possible mechanisms. However, the *Revelation Principle* states that we can limit our search to a special class of mechanisms [5, Ch 14].

Theorem 16.1 (Revelation Principle). *If there exists some mechanism that implements social choice function f in dominant strategies, then there exists a direct mechanism that implements f in dominant strategies and is truthful.*

The intuitive idea behind the Revelation Principle is fairly straightforward. Suppose that you have a, possibly very complex, mechanism, $\mathcal{M}$, which implements some social choice function, f. That is, given agent types $\theta = (\theta_1, \dots, \theta_I)$ there exists an equilibrium $s^*(\theta)$ such that $g(s^*(\theta)) = f(\theta)$. Then, the Revelation Principle states that it is possible to create a new mechanism, $\mathcal{M}'$, which, when given θ, will then execute $s^*(\theta)$ on behalf of the agents and then select outcome $g(s^*(\theta))$. Thus, each agent is best off revealing θ_i, resulting in $\mathcal{M}'$ being a truthful, direct mechanism for implementing social choice function f.

The Revelation Principle is a powerful tool when it comes to studying implementation. Instead of searching through the entire space of mechanisms to check whether one implements a particular social choice function, the Revelation Principle states that we can restrict our search to the class of truthful, direct mechanisms. If we can not find a mechanism in this space which implements the social choice function of interest, then there does not exist any mechanism which will do so.

It should be noted that while the Revelation Principle is a powerful analysis tool, it does not imply we should only design direct mechanisms. Some reasons why one rarely sees direct mechanisms in the "real world" include (among others);

- they can place a high computational burden on the mechanism since it is required to execute agents' strategies,
- agents' strategies may be computationally difficult to determine, and
- agents may not be willing to reveal their true types because of privacy concerns.

4 Argumentation Mechanism Design

Mechanism design (MD) is a sub-field of game theory concerned with the following question: *what game rules guarantee a desirable social outcome when each self-interested agent selects the best strategy for itself?* In other words, while game theory is concerned with a given strategic situation modelled as a game, mechanism design is concerned with designing the game itself. As such, one might actually call it *reverse game theory*.

In this section we define the mechanism design problem for abstract argumentation. We dub this new approach 'Argumentation Mechanism Design' (ArgMD).

Let $AF = \langle A, \mathcal{R} \rangle$ be an argumentation framework with a set of arguments A and a binary defeat relation $\mathcal{R}$. We define a mechanism with respect to AF and semantics $\mathcal{S}$, and we assume that there is a set of I self-interested agents. We define an agent's type to be its set of arguments.

Definition 16.8 (Agent Type). Given an argumentation framework $\langle A, \mathcal{R} \rangle$, the *type* of agent i, $A_i \subseteq A$, is the set of arguments that the agent is capable of putting forward.

There are two things to note about this definition. Firstly, an agent's type can be seen as a reflection of its expertise or domain knowledge. For example, medical experts may only be able to comment on certain aspects of forensics in a legal case, while a defendant's family and friends may be able to comment on his/her character. Also, such expertise may overlap, so agent types are not necessarily disjoint. For example, two medical doctors might have some identical argument, and so on.

The second thing to note about the definition is that agent types do not include the defeat relation. In other words, we implicitly assume that the notion of defeat is common to all agents. That is, given two arguments, no agent would dispute whether one attacks another. This is a reasonable assumption in systems where agents use the same logic to express arguments or at least multiple logics for which the notion of defeat is accepted by everyone (e.g. conflict between a proposition and its negation). Disagreement over the defeat relation itself requires a form of hierarchical (meta) argumentation [7], which is a powerful concept, but is beyond the scope of the present chapter.

Given the agents' types (argument sets) a social choice function f maps a type profile into a subset of arguments;

$$f : 2^A \times \ldots \times 2^A \to 2^A$$

While our definition of an argumentation mechanism will allow for generic social choice functions which map type profiles into subsets of arguments, we will be particularly interested in *argument acceptability* social choice functions. We denote by $Acc(\langle \mathcal{A}, \mathcal{R} \rangle, \mathcal{S}) \subseteq \mathcal{A}$ the set of acceptable arguments according to semantics $\mathcal{S}$.[3]

Definition 16.9 (Argument Acceptability Social Choice Functions). Given an argumentation framework $\langle \mathcal{A}, \mathcal{R} \rangle$ with semantics $\mathcal{S}$, and given an agent type profile $(\mathcal{A}_1, \ldots, \mathcal{A}_I)$, the *argument acceptability social choice function* f is defined as the set of acceptable arguments given the semantics $\mathcal{S}$. That is,

$$f(\mathcal{A}_1, \ldots, \mathcal{A}_I) = Acc(\langle \mathcal{A}_1 \cup \ldots \cup \mathcal{A}_I, \mathcal{R} \rangle, \mathcal{S}).$$

As is standard in the mechanism design literature, we assume that agents have preferences over the outcomes $o \in 2^{\mathcal{A}}$, and we represent these preferences using utility functions where $u_i(o, \mathcal{A}_i)$ denotes agent i's utility for outcome o when its type is argument set $\mathcal{A}_i$.

Agents may not have incentive to reveal their true type because they may be able to influence the final argument status assignment by lying, and thus obtain higher utility. There are two ways that an agent can lie in our model. On one hand, an agent might create new arguments that it does not have in its argument set. In the rest of the chapter we will assume that there is an *external verifier* that is capable of checking whether it is possible for a particular agent to actually make a particular argument. Informally, this means that presented arguments, while still possibly defeasible, must at least be based on some sort of demonstrable 'plausible evidence.' If an agent is caught making up arguments then it will be removed from the mechanism. For example, in a court of law, any act of perjury by a witness is punished, at the very least, by completely discrediting all evidence produced by the witness. Moreover, in a court of law, arguments presented without any plausible evidence are normally discarded (e.g. "*I did not kill him, since I was abducted by aliens at the time of the crime!*"). For all intents and purposes this assumption (also made by Glazer and Rubinstein [2]) removes the incentive for an agent to make up facts.

A more insidious form of manipulation occurs when an agent decides to *hide* some of its arguments. By refusing to reveal certain arguments, an agent might be able to break defeat chains in the argument framework, thus changing the final set of acceptable arguments. For example, a witness may hide evidence that implicates the defendant if the evidence also undermines the witness's own character. This type of lie is almost impossible to detect in practice, and it is this form of strategic behaviour that we will be the most interested in.

As mentioned earlier, a strategy of an agent specifies a complete plan that describes what action the agent takes for every decision that a player might be called upon to take, for every piece of information that the player might have at each time that it is called upon to act. In our model, the actions available to an agent involve announcing sets of arguments. Thus a strategy $s_i \in \Sigma_i$ for agent i would specify for

---

[3] Here, we assume that $\mathcal{S}$ specifies both the classical semantics used (e.g. grounded, preferred, stable) as well as the acceptance attitude used (e.g. sceptical or credulous).

each possible subset of arguments that could define its type, what set of arguments to reveal. For example, a strategy might specify that an agent should reveal only half of its arguments without waiting to see what other agents are going to do, while another strategy might specify that an agent should wait and see what arguments are revealed by others, before deciding how to respond. In particular, beyond specifying that agents are not allowed to make up arguments, we place no restrictions on the allowable strategy spaces, when we initially define an argumentation mechanism. Later, when we talk about *direct* argumentation mechanisms we will further restrict the strategy space.

We are now ready to define our argumentation mechanism. We first define a generic mechanism, and then specify a direct argumentation mechanism, which due to the Revelation Principle, is the type of mechanism we will study in the rest of the chapter.

Definition 16.10 (Argumentation Mechanism). Given an argumentation framework $AF = \langle \mathcal{A}, \mathcal{R} \rangle$ and semantics $\mathcal{S}$, an *argumentation mechanism* is defined as

$$\mathcal{M}^{\mathcal{S}}_{AF} = (\Sigma_1, \ldots, \Sigma_I, g(\cdot))$$

where Σ_i is an argumentation strategy space of agent i and $g : \Sigma_1 \times \ldots \times \Sigma_I \to 2^{\mathcal{A}}$.

Note that in the above definition, the notion of dialogue strategy is broadly construed and would depend on the protocol used. In a *direct* mechanism, however, the strategy spaces of the agents are restricted so that they can only reveal a subset of arguments.

Definition 16.11 (Direct Argumentation Mechanism). Given an argumentation framework $AF = \langle \mathcal{A}, \mathcal{R} \rangle$ and semantics $\mathcal{S}$, a *direct argumentation mechanism* is defined as

$$\mathcal{M}^{\mathcal{S}}_{AF} = (\Sigma_1, \ldots, \Sigma_I, g(\cdot))$$

where $\Sigma_i = 2^{\mathcal{A}}$ and $g : \Sigma_1 \times \ldots \Sigma_I \to 2^{\mathcal{A}}$.

In Table 16.1, we summarise the mapping of multi-agent abstract argumentation as an instance of a mechanism design problem.

MD Concept	ArgMD Instantiation
Agent type $\theta_i \in \Theta_i$	Agent's arguments $\theta_i = \mathcal{A}_i \subseteq \mathcal{A}$
Outcome $o \in \mathcal{O}$	Accepted arguments $Acc(.) \subseteq \mathcal{A}$
Utility $u_i(o, \theta_i)$	Preferences over $2^{\mathcal{A}}$ (what arguments end up being accepted)
Social choice function $f : \Theta_1 \times \ldots \times \Theta_I \to \mathcal{O}$	$f(\mathcal{A}_1, \ldots, \mathcal{A}_I) = Acc(\langle \mathcal{A}_1 \cup \ldots \cup \mathcal{A}_I, \mathcal{R} \rangle, \mathcal{S})$. by some argument acceptability criterion
Mechanism $\mathcal{M} = (\Sigma, g(\cdot))$ where $\Sigma = \Sigma_1 \times \cdots \times \Sigma_I$ and $g : \Sigma \to \mathcal{O}$	Σ_i is an argumentation strategy, $g : \Sigma \to 2^{\mathcal{A}}$
Direct mechanism: $\Sigma_i = \Theta_i$	$\Sigma_i = 2^{\mathcal{A}}$ (every agent reveals a set of arguments)
Truth revelation	Revealing $\mathcal{A}_i$

Table 16.1 Abstract argumentation as a mechanism

5 Case Study: Implementing the Grounded Semantics

In this section, we demonstrate the power of our ArgMD approach by showing how it can be used to systematically analyse the strategic incentives imposed by a well-established argument evaluation criterion. In particular, we specify a direct-revelation argumentation mechanism, in which agents' strategies are to reveal sets of arguments, and where the mechanism calculates the outcome using sceptical (grounded) semantics.[4] That is, we look at the grounded semantics as if it was designed as a mechanism and analyse it from that perspective. We show that, in general, this mechanism gives rise to strategic manipulation. We prove, however, that under various conditions, this mechanism turns out to be strategy-proof.

In a direct argumentation mechanism, each agent i's available actions are $\Sigma_i = 2^A$. We will refer to a specific action (i.e. set of declared arguments) as $A_i^\circ \in \Sigma_i$.

We now present a direct mechanism for argumentation based on a sceptical argument evaluation criteria. The mechanism calculates the grounded extension given the union of all arguments revealed by agents.

Definition 16.12 (Grounded Direct Argumentation Mechanism). A *grounded direct argumentation mechanism* for argumentation framework $\langle A, \mathcal{R} \rangle$ is $\mathcal{M}_{AF}^{grnd} = (\Sigma_1, \ldots, \Sigma_I, g(.))$ where:

- $\Sigma_i \in 2^A$ is the set of strategies available to each agent;
- $g : \Sigma_1 \times \cdots \times \Sigma_I \to 2^A$ is an outcome rule defined as: $g(A_1^\circ, \ldots, A_I^\circ) = Acc(\langle A_1^\circ \cup \cdots \cup A_I^\circ, \mathcal{R} \rangle, \mathcal{S}^{grnd})$ where $\mathcal{S}^{grnd}$ denotes sceptical grounded acceptability semantics.

To simplify our analysis, we will assume below that agents can only lie by hiding arguments, and not by making up arguments. Formally, this means that $\forall i, \Sigma_i \in 2^{A_i}$.

For the sake of illustration, we will consider a particular family of preferences that agents may have. According to these preferences, every agent attempts to maximise the number of arguments in A_i that end up being accepted. We call this preference criteria the *individual acceptability maximising preference*.

Definition 16.13 (Acceptability maximising preferences). An agent i has *individual acceptability maximising preferences* if and only if $\forall o_1, o_2 \in \mathcal{O}$ such that $|o_1 \cap A_i| \geq |o_2 \cap A_i|$, we have $u_i(o_1, A_i) \geq u_i(o_2, A_i)$.

Let us now consider aspects of incentives using mechanism $\mathcal{M}_{AF}^{grnd}$ through an example.

Example 16.1. Consider grounded direct argumentation mechanism with three agents x, y and z with types $A_x = \{\alpha_1, \alpha_4, \alpha_5\}$, $A_y = \{\alpha_2\}$ and $A_z = \{\alpha_3\}$ respectively. And suppose that the defeat relation is defined as follows: $\mathcal{R} = \{(\alpha_1, \alpha_2), (\alpha_2, \alpha_3), (\alpha_3, \alpha_4), (\alpha_3, \alpha_5)\}$. If each agent reveals its true type (i.e. $A_x^\circ = A_x$; $A_y^\circ = A_y$; and

---

[4] In the remainder of the chapter, we will use the term *sceptical* to refer to *sceptical grounded*, since the chapter focuses on the grounded semantics.

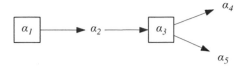
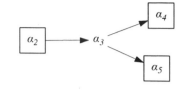

(a) Argument graph in case of full revelation   (b) Argument graph with α_1 withheld

Fig. 16.3 Hiding an argument is beneficial (case of acceptability maximisers)

$\mathcal{A}_z^\circ = \mathcal{A}_z$), then we get the argument graph depicted in Figure 16.3(a). The mechanism outcome rule produces the outcome $o = \{\alpha_1, \alpha_3\}$. If agents have individual acceptability maximising preferences, with utilities equal to the number of arguments accepted, then: $u_x(o, \{\alpha_1, \alpha_4, \alpha_5\}) = 1$; $u_y(o, \{\alpha_3\}) = 1$; and $u_z(o, \{\alpha_2\}) = 0$.

It turns out that the mechanism is susceptible to strategic manipulation, even if we suppose that agents do not lie by making up arguments (i.e., they may only withhold some arguments). In this case, for both agents y and z, revealing their true types weakly dominates revealing nothing at all. However, it turns out that agent x is better off revealing $\{\alpha_4, \alpha_5\}$. By withholding α_1, the resulting argument network becomes as depicted in Figure 16.3(b), for which the output rule produces the outcome $o' = \{\alpha_2, \alpha_4, \alpha_5\}$. This outcome yields utility 2 to agent x, which is better than the truth-revealing strategy.

Remark 16.1. Given an arbitrary argumentation framework AF and agents with acceptability maximising preferences, mechanism $\mathcal{M}_{AF}^{grnd}$ is *not* strategy-proof.

The following theorem provides a full characterisation of strategy-proof mechanisms for sceptical argumentation frameworks for agents with acceptability maximising preferences.

Theorem 16.2. *Let AF be an arbitrary argumentation framework, and let $\mathcal{E}_{\mathcal{GR}}(AF)$ denote its grounded extension. Mechanism $\mathcal{M}_{AF}^{grnd}$ is strategy-proof for agents with acceptability maximising preferences if and only if AF satisfies the following condition: $\forall i \in I, \forall S \subseteq \mathcal{A}_i$ and $\forall A_{-i}$, we have $|\mathcal{A}_i \cap \mathcal{E}_{\mathcal{GR}}(\langle \mathcal{A}_i \cup \mathcal{A}_{-i}, \mathcal{R} \rangle)| \geq |\mathcal{A}_i \cap \mathcal{E}_{\mathcal{GR}}(\langle (\mathcal{A}_i \backslash S) \cup \mathcal{A}_{-i}, \mathcal{R} \rangle)|$.*

Although the above theorem gives us a full characterisation, it is difficult to apply in practice. In particular, the theorem does not give us an indication of how agents (or the mechanism designer) can identify whether the mechanism is strategy-proof for a class of argumentation frameworks by appealing to their graph-theoretic properties. Below, we provide an intuitive, graph-theoretic condition that is sufficient to ensure that $\mathcal{M}_{AF}^{grnd}$ is strategy-proof when agents have focal arguments.

Let $\alpha, \beta \in \mathcal{A}$. We say that α *indirectly defeats* β, written $\alpha \hookrightarrow \beta$, if and only if there is an odd-length path from α to β in the argument graph.

Theorem 16.3. *Suppose agents have individual acceptability maximising preferences. If each agent's type corresponds to a conflict-free set of arguments which does not include (in)direct defeats (formally $\forall i \nexists \alpha_1, \alpha_2 \in \mathcal{A}_i$ such that $\alpha_1 \hookrightarrow \alpha_2$), then $\mathcal{M}_{AF}^{grnd}$ is strategy-proof.*

Note that in the theorem, $\hookrightarrow$ is over all arguments in $\mathcal{A}$. Intuitively, the condition in the theorem states that *all* arguments of every agent must be conflict-free (i.e. consistent), both explicitly and implicitly. Explicit consistency implies that no argument defeats another. Implicit consistency implies that other agents cannot possibly present a set of arguments that reveal an indirect defeat among one's own arguments. More concretely, in Example 16.1 and Figure 16.3, while agent x's argument set $\mathcal{A}_x = \{\alpha_1, \alpha_4, \alpha_5\}$ is conflict-free, when agents y and z presented their own arguments α_2 and α_3, they revealed an implicit conflict in x's arguments. In other words, they showed that x contradicts himself (i.e. committed a *fallacy* of some kind).

In addition to characterising a sufficient graph-theoretic condition for strategy-proofness, Theorem 16.3 is useful for individual agents. As long as the agent knows that it is *not* possible for a path to be created which causes an (in)direct defeat among its arguments (i.e., a fallacy to be revealed), then the agent is best off revealing all its arguments. The agent only needs to know that no argument imaginable can reveal conflicts among its own arguments.

We now ask whether the *sufficient* condition in Theorem 16.3 is also *necessary* for agents to reveal all their arguments truthfully. Example 16.2 shows that this is not the case. In particular, for certain argumentation frameworks, an agent may have truthtelling as a dominant strategy despite the presence of indirect defeats among its own arguments.

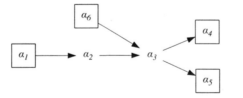

Fig. 16.4 Strategy-proofness despite indirect self-defeat

Example 16.2. Consider the variant of Example 16.1 with the additional argument α_6 and defeat (α_6, α_3). Let the agent types be $\mathcal{A}_x = \{\alpha_1, \alpha_4, \alpha_5, \alpha_6\}$, $\mathcal{A}_y = \{\alpha_2\}$ and $\mathcal{A}_z = \{\alpha_3\}$ respectively. The full argument graph is depicted in Figure 16.4. Under full revelation, the mechanism outcome rule produces the outcome $o = \{\alpha_1, \alpha_4, \alpha_5, \alpha_6\}$.

Note that in Example 16.2, truth revelation is now a dominant strategy for x (since it gets all its arguments accepted) despite the fact that $\alpha_1 \hookrightarrow \alpha_4$ and $\alpha_1 \hookrightarrow \alpha_5$. This hinges on the presence of an argument (namely α_5) that cancels out the negative effect of the (in)direct self-defeat among x's own arguments.

6 Related Work

6.1 Pareto Optimality of Outcomes

A well-known property of the grounded semantics is that it is extremely sceptical, accepting only undefeated arguments and arguments defended by undefeated arguments. An interesting question, then, is whether it is possible to be more inclusive (i.e. being more credulous) in order to produce argumentation outcomes that are more *socially* desirable. For example, consider the simple argument graph in Figure 16.5 and suppose we have two agents with types $\mathcal{A}_1 = \{\alpha_1\}$ and $\mathcal{A}_2 = \{\alpha_2\}$ who both reveal their arguments. The grounded extension (Figure 16.5(a)) is empty here.

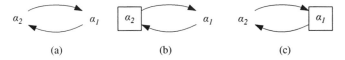

     (a)   (b)   (c)

Fig. 16.5 Preferred extensions 'dominate' the grounded extension

Suppose the judge chooses one of the preferred extensions instead (Figure 16.5(b) or (c)). Clearly, when compared to outcome (a), each preferred extension makes one agent better-off without making the other worse-off. Formally, we say that outcomes (b) and (c) each Pareto dominates outcome (a). An outcome that is not Pareto dominated is called *Pareto optimal*.

Recently, Rahwan and Larson [11] presented an extensive analysis of Pareto optimality in abstract argumentation, and established correspondence results between different semantics on one hand and the Pareto optimal outcomes on the other.

6.2 Glazer and Rubinstein's Model

Another game-theoretic analysis of argumentation was presented by Glazer and Rubinstein [2]. The authors explore the mechanism design problem of constructing rules of debate that maximise the probability that a listener reaches the right conclusion given arguments presented by two debaters. They study a very restricted setting, in which the world state is described by a vector $\omega = (w_1, \ldots, w_5)$, where each 'aspect' w_i has two possible values: 1 and 2. If $w_i = j$ for $j \in \{1,2\}$, we say that aspect w_i supports outcome O_j. Presenting an argument amounts to revealing the value of some w_i. The setting is modelled as an extensive-form game and analysed. In particular, the authors investigate various combinations of *procedural rules* (stating in which order and what sorts of arguments each debater is allowed to state) and *persuasion rules* (stating how the outcome is chosen by the listener). In terms of procedural rules, the authors explore: (1) *one-speaker debate* in whichone debater chooses two arguments to reveal; (2) *simultaneous debate* in which the two debaters simultaneously reveal one argument each; and (3) *sequential debate* in which one debater reveals one argument followed by one argument by the other. Our mechanism is closer to the simultaneous debate, but is much more general as it enables the simultaneous revelation of an arbitrary number of arguments. Glazer and Rubinstein investigate a variety of persuasion rules. For example, in one-speaker debate, one rule analysed by the authors states that 'a speaker wins if and only if he presents two arguments from $\{a_1, a_2, a_3\}$ or $\{a_4, a_5\}$.' In a sequential debate, one persuasion rule states that 'if debater D_1 argues for aspect a_3, then debater D_2 wins if and only if he counter argues with aspect a_4.' These kinds of rules are arbitrary and do not follow an intuitive notion of persuasion (e.g. like scepticism). The sceptical mechanism presented in this chapter provides a more natural criterion for argument evaluation, supplemented by a strong solution concept that ensures all agents have incentive to reveal their arguments, and thus for the listener to reach the correct outcome. Moreover, our framework for argumentation mechanism design is more general in that it can be used to model a variety of more complex argumentation settings.

6.3 Game Semantics

It is worth contrasting our work with work on so-called *game semantics* for logic, which was pioneered by logicians such as Paul Lorenzen [4] and Jaakko Hintikka [3]. Although many specific instantiations of this notion have been presented in the literature, the general idea is as follows. Given some specific logic, the truth value of a formula is determined through a special-purpose, multi-stage dialogue game between two players, the *verifier* and *falsifier*. The formula is considered true precisely when the verifier has a winning strategy, while it will be false whenever the falsifier has the winning strategy. Similar ideas have been used to implement dialectical proof-theories for defeasible reasoning (e.g. by Prakken and Sartor [9]).

In a related development, Matt and Toni recently proposed a game-theoretic approach to characterise argument strength [6]. Thus, the acceptability of each argument is rated between 0 and 1 by using a two-person zero-sum game with imperfect information between a proponent and an opponent.

There is a fundamental difference between the aims of game semantics and our ArgMD approach. In game semantics, the goal is to interpret (i.e., characterise the truth value of) a specific formula by appealing to a notion of a winning strategy. As such, each player is carefully endowed with a specific set of formulae to enable the game to characterise semantics correctly (e.g. the verifier may own all the disjunctions in the formula, while the falsifier is given all the conjunctions).

In contrast, ArgMD is about designing rules for argumentation among self-interested players who may have incentives to manipulate the outcome given a variety of possible individual preferences (specified in arbitrary instantiations of a utility function). Our interest is in conditions that guarantee truth-revelation given different classes of preferences. Game semantics have no similar notion of strategic manipulation by hiding information. Moreover, our framework allows an arbitrary number of players (as opposed to two agents).

6.4 Argumentation and Cooperative Games

Another notable early link between argumentation and *cooperative game theory* has been proposed by Dung in his seminal paper [1]. Let $A = \{a_1, \ldots, a_{|A|}\}$ be a set of agents. A cooperative game is defined by specifying a value to $V(C)$ to each coalition $C \subseteq A$ of agents. An outcome of the game is a vector $\mathbf{u} = (u_{a_1}, \ldots, u_{a_{|A|}}) \in \mathbb{R}^{|A|}$ specifying a vector of utilities, one per agent.

Outcome $\mathbf{u}$ dominates outcome $\mathbf{u}'$ if there is a (nonempty) coalition $K \subseteq A$ in which agents get more utility (as a whole) in $\mathbf{u}$ than in $\mathbf{u}'$. An outcome is said to be *stable* if no outcome dominates it (i.e. if no subset of agents has *incentive* to leave their own coalition and be all individually better off). A *solution* of the cooperative game is a set of outcomes S satisfying the following conditions:

1. No $s \in S$ is dominated by an $s' \in S$.
2. Every $s \notin S$ is dominated by some $s' \in S$.

Dung argued that an *n*-person game can be seen as an argumentation framework $\langle \mathcal{A}, \mathcal{R} \rangle$ in which the set of arguments $\mathcal{A}$ is the set of all possible outcomes of the cooperative game, and the defeat relation is defined as $\mathcal{R} = \{(\mathbf{u}, \mathbf{u}') \mid \mathbf{u} \text{ dominates } \mathbf{u}'\}$. Dung shows that with this characterisation, the set of solutions to the cooperative game corresponds to the set of stable extensions of an abstract argumentation framework. This enabled Dung to describe the well-known *stable marriage problem* as a problem of finding a stable extension.

Another important notion in cooperative game theory is that of the *core*: the set of (feasible) outcomes which are not dominated by any other outcome. Dung showed that the core corresponds to $\mathcal{F}(\varnothing)$ where $\mathcal{F}$ is the characteristic function of the corresponding argumentation framework.

7 Conclusion

In this chapter, our aim was to demonstrate the importance of game theory as a tool for analysing strategic argumentation. We showed how normal form games and extensive-form games can be used to analyse equilibrium strategies in strategic argumentation. We then introduced Argumentation Mechanism Design (ArgMD) as a new framework for designing and analysing argument evaluation criteria. With ArgMD, designing new argument acceptance criteria becomes akin to designing auction protocols in strategic multi-agent settings. The goal is to design rules that ensure, under precise conditions, that agents have no incentive to manipulate the outcome. We believe this approach will become increasingly important before argumentation can be applied in open agent systems.

References

1. P. M. Dung. On the acceptability of arguments and its fundamental role in nonmonotonic reasoning, logic programming and n-person games. *Artificial Intelligence*, 77(2):321–358, 1995.
2. J. Glazer and A. Rubinstein. Debates and decisions: On a rationale of argumentation rules. *Games and Economic Behavior*, 36:158–173, 2001.
3. J. Hintikka and G. Sandu. Game-theoretical semantics. In J. van Benthem and A. ter Meulen, editors, *Handbook of Logic and Language*, pages 361–410. Elsevier, Amsterdam, The Netherlands, 1997.
4. P. Lorenzen. Ein dialogisches konstruktivitätskriterium. In *Infinitistic Methods*, pages 193–200. Pergamon Press, Oxford, UK, 1961.
5. A. Mas-Colell, M. D. Whinston, and J. R. Green. *Microeconomic Theory*. Oxford University Press, New York NY, USA, 1995.
6. P.-A. Matt and F. Toni. A game-theoretic measure of argument strength for abstract argumentation. In S. Hölldobler, C. Lutz, and H. Wansing, editors, *Logics in Artificial Intelligence, 11th European Conference, JELIA 2008*, volume 5293 of *Lecture Notes in Computer Science*, pages 285–297. 2008.
7. S. Modgil. Hierarchical argumentation. In *Proceedings of the 10th European Conference on Logics in Artificial Intelligence. Liverpool, UK*, 2006.
8. H. Prakken. Coherence and flexibility in dialogue games for argumentation. *Journal of Logic and Computation*, 15(6):1009–1040, 2005.
9. H. Prakken and G. Sartor. Argument-based logic programming with defeasible priorities. *Journal of Applied Non-classical Logics*, 7:25–75, 1997.
10. A. D. Procaccia and J. S. Rosenschein. Extensive-form argumentation games. In *Proceedings of the Third European Workshop on Multi-Agent Systems (EUMAS-05), Brussels, Belgium*, pages 312–322, 2005.
11. I. Rahwan and K. Larson. Pareto optimality in abstract argumentation. In D. Fox and C. Gomes, editors, *Proceedings of the 23rd AAAI Conference on Artificial Intelligence (AAAI-2008)*, Menlo Park CA, USA, 2008.
12. R. Riveret, H. Prakken, A. Rotolo, and G. Sartor. Heuristics in argumentation: A game-theoretical investigation. In P. Besnard, S. Doutre, and A. Hunter, editors, *Proceedings of the 2nd International Conference on Computational Models of Argument (COMMA)*, pages 324–335. IOS Press, Amsterdam, The Netherlands, 2008.
13. J. von Neuman and O. Morgenstern. *The Theory of Games and Economic Behaviour*. Princeton University Press, Princeton NJ, USA, 1944.

Chapter 17
Belief Revision and Argumentation Theory

Marcelo A. Falappa, Gabriele Kern-Isberner and Guillermo R. Simari

1 Introduction

Belief revision is the process of changing beliefs to adapt the epistemic state of an agent to a new piece of information. The logical formalization of belief revision is a topic of research in philosophy, logic, and in computer science, in areas such as databases or artificial intelligence. On the other hand, *argumentation* is concerned primarily with the evaluation of claims based on premises in order to reach conclusions. Both provide basic and substantial techniques for the art of reasoning, as it is performed by human beings in everyday life situations and which goes far beyond logical deduction. Reasoning, in this sense, makes possible to deal successfully with problems in uncertain, dynamic environments and has been promoting the development of human societies. The interest of computer scientists in both domains has increased considerably over the past years, as agent systems are to be endowed with similar capabilities. In an agent environment, belief revision describes the way in which an agent is supposed to change her beliefs when new information arrives, or changes in the world are observed; argumentation deals with strategies agents employ for their own reasoning, or to change the beliefs of other agents, by providing reasons for such change.

In this chapter, we will elaborate on the relationships between argumentation and belief revision, first recalling important work done by others and ourselves concern-

Marcelo A. Falappa
CONICET (National Council of Technical and Scientific Research) – Department of Computer Science and Engineering – Universidad Nacional del Sur – Bahía Blanca, Argentina, e-mail: mfalappa@cs.uns.edu.ar

Gabriele Kern-Isberner
Department of Computer Science – University of Dortmund – Dortmund, Germany – e-mail: gabriele.kern-isberner@cs.uni-dortmund.de

Guillermo R. Simari
Department of Computer Science and Engineering – Universidad Nacional del Sur – Bahía Blanca, Argentina, e-mail: grs@cs.uns.edu.ar

I. Rahwan, G. R. Simari (eds.), *Argumentation in Artificial Intelligence*,
DOI 10.1007/978-0-387-98197-0_17, © Springer Science+Business Media, LLC 2009

ing the links between both areas. Based on such insights, we will develop a conceptual view on this topic, which is based on the understanding of argumentation and belief revision being complementary disciplines for the broad picture sketched above. Each needs the other's support if we want to model successful decision making in a real world application. We will also discuss how one area may contribute to the other, enriching the respective framework.

2 Basic facts on argumentation and belief revision

An *argument A* for α is a set of interrelated pieces of knowledge supporting α from evidence. Abstract approaches to argumentation such as [13] make use of argumentation frameworks $\langle \mathbf{A}, \mathbf{R} \rangle$ with is a finite set $\mathbf{A}$ of arguments and an attack relation $\mathbf{R}$ among arguments. The main issue of such argumentation frameworks is the selection of acceptable sets of arguments called *extensions* on the basis of which argumentation semantics can be defined. We assume that the reader is familiar with the basic concepts from argumentation theory such as conflict, attack, non-attack, defeat, evaluation of arguments, etc.

In classical belief revision frameworks, a fixed finite language $\mathcal{L}$ with a complete set of boolean connectives is usually used. Formulae in $\mathcal{L}$ are be denoted by lower case Greek characters $\alpha, \beta, \delta, \ldots$, while sets of formulae from $\mathcal{L}$ will be denoted by upper case letters $A, B, C, \ldots$. The underlying logic contains a consequence operator Cn ($Cn : 2^{\mathcal{L}} \Rightarrow 2^{\mathcal{L}}$) and it is assumed to be *supraclassical* (*i.e.*, include classical propositional calculus), *compact* ($Cn(A) = Cn(B)$ for some finite subset B of A) and to satisfy the *deduction theorem* ($\alpha \rightarrow \beta \in Cn(A)$ if and only if $\beta \in Cn(A \cup \{\alpha\})$). Sometimes, the relation $\vdash$ is used as an alternative notation of the consequence operator: $A \vdash \alpha$ if and only if $\alpha \in Cn(A)$.

There are many different frameworks for belief revision with their respective epistemic models. The epistemic model is the formalism in which beliefs are represented and in which different kinds of operators can be defined. The basic representation of epistemic states is through belief sets (sets of sentences closed under logical consequence) or belief bases (sets of sentences not necessarily closed). Operators may be presented in two ways: by giving an explicit construction (algorithm) for the operator, or by giving a set of rationality postulates to be satisfied. Rationality postulates determine constraints that the operators should satisfy. They treat the operators as black boxes by describing their response behavior to inputs in basic cases, but not the internal mechanisms used.

The distinction between belief sets and belief bases is similar to the distinction between the coherence approach and the foundational approach to belief revision. The *coherence approach* focuses on logical relations among beliefs rather than on inferential relations, that is, no belief is more fundamental than others [11]. Beliefs provide each other with mutual support; therefore, a belief set represents the limit case of this approach. On the other hand, the *foundational approach* divides beliefs into two classes: explicit beliefs and those beliefs justified by the explicit beliefs.

The explicit beliefs can be seen as "self-justified beliefs" whereas the other beliefs are considered as derived, justified or supported beliefs. The foundational approach provides explanation of beliefs by requiring that each belief is supportable by means of non-circular arguments from explicit or basic beliefs [11]. Since a belief α may be justified by several independent beliefs, if some of the justifications for α are removed, α may be retained because it is supported by other beliefs. Belief base revision provides a good example of the foundational approach.

The AGM paradigm [1] has been extensively studied during the last three decades and it is the most influential model of belief revision so far, serving as a frame of reference for improvements, extensions or criticisms of the original proposal. The AGM model is conceived as an idealistic theory of rational change in which epistemic states are represented by belief sets and the epistemic input is represented by a sentence. AGM theory studies the changes at the *knowledge level* whereas some others approaches studies the changes at the *symbol level*. The distinction about knowledge and symbol level was proposed by Allen Newell [43]. According to Newell, the knowledge level lies above the symbol level where all of the knowledge in the system is represented. Some belief bases with different symbol representations may represent the same knowledge. Suppose that p and q are logically independent propositions. Then, $K_1 = \{p, q\}$ and $K_2 = \{p, p \rightarrow q\}$ are different belief bases. Since their closure is the same $Cn(K_1) = Cn(K_2) = Cn(\{p, q\})$ they represent the same beliefs at the knowledge level. Although they are statically equivalent (they represent the same beliefs), they could be dynamically different: changes of K_1 can be different from changes of K_2 because p and q are totally independent in K_1 but interrelated in K_2 by the sentence $p \rightarrow q$.

Suppose that the set K represents the beliefs of an agent. The AGM theory defines three basic types of change operations for K:

- **Expansions**: the result of expanding K by a sentence α is a larger set which infers α;
- **Contractions**: the result of contracting K by α is a smaller set which does not infer α;
- **Revisions**: the result of revising K by α is a set that neither extends nor is part of the set K. In general, if K infers $\neg\alpha$ then α is consistently inferred from the revision of K by α.

In the classical AGM framework and all coherence approaches, the internal structure of beliefs is ignored and the focus is on belief sets. Given a belief set $\mathbf{K}$[1] and a sentence α, the expansion of $\mathbf{K}$ by α is denoted by $\mathbf{K}+\alpha$ and is defined as $\mathbf{K}+\alpha = Cn(\mathbf{K} \cup \{\alpha\})$.

Suppose that $\div$ is a contraction operator. The contraction of $\mathbf{K}$ by α is denoted as $\mathbf{K} \div \alpha$. The basic postulates for contraction are [1, 20] the following:

- **Closure**: $\mathbf{K} \div \alpha = Cn(\mathbf{K} \div \alpha)$.
- **Inclusion**: $\mathbf{K} \div \alpha \subseteq \mathbf{K}$.

---

[1] Belief sets (*i.e.*, logically closed sets of sentences) are typically denoted by Latin letters in boldface.

- **Success**: If $\nvdash \alpha$ then $\alpha \notin K \div \alpha$.
- **Vacuity**: If $\alpha \notin K$ then $K \div \alpha = K$.
- **Recovery**: $K \subseteq (K \div \alpha) + \alpha$.
- **Extensionality**: If $\vdash \alpha \leftrightarrow \beta$ then $K \div \alpha = K \div \beta$.

Recovery is one of the most controversial postulates of the AGM theory: it says that a sequence of first contracting by a sentence α, and then expanding by the same sentence α leaves the belief state unchanged. In other words, so much is retained in a belief set that everything can be recovered by reinstatement of the contracted sentence.

Revision operators can be defined through *Levi identity* [38, 20] from contraction operators; in order to revise a belief set **K** with respect to a sentence α, we contract with respect to $\neg \alpha$ and then expand the new epistemic state with respect to α. That is, the revision of **K** by α, noted by $K*\alpha$, is defined as $K*\alpha = (K \div \neg \alpha) + \alpha$. There is a set of basic postulates for revision that correspond to the above postulates for contraction. One of the most important (though not indisputable) properties is *success* ($\alpha \in K*\alpha$) which specifies that the new information has primacy over the beliefs of an agent.

2.1 Changes on belief sets

Partial meet contractions cover exactly the basic AGM-contractions. They are based on the concept of remainder sets.

Definition 17.1. [2] Let K be a set of sentences and α a sentence. Then $K \perp \alpha$ is the set of all H such that $H \subseteq K$, $H \nvdash \alpha$ and if $H \subset K' \subseteq K, H \neq K'$, then $K' \vdash \alpha$. The set $K \perp \alpha$ is called the *remainder set* of K with respect to α, and its elements are called the α-remainders of K.

In order to define a partial meet contraction operator, a selection function is needed. This function makes a selection among the α-remainders, choosing those candidate sets for contraction which are preferred.

Definition 17.2. Let K be a set of sentences. A *selection function for K* is a function γ defined on $\{K \perp \alpha | \alpha \in \mathcal{L}\}$ such that for any sentence $\alpha \in \mathcal{L}$, it holds that:
1) If $K \perp \alpha \neq \varnothing$, then $\gamma(K \perp \alpha)$ is a non-empty subset of $K \perp \alpha$.
2) If $K \perp \alpha = \varnothing$, then $\gamma(K \perp \alpha) = K$.

Definition 17.3. Given a set of sentences K, a sentence α and a selection function γ for K, the *partial meet contraction* of K by α, denoted by $K \div_\gamma \alpha$, is defined as $K \div_\gamma \alpha = \cap \gamma(K \perp \alpha)$. That is, $K \div_\gamma \alpha$ is equal to the intersection of the α-remainders of K selected by γ. If γ selects a single element, then the induced contraction is called *maxichoice contraction*. If γ selects all elements of the remainder set, then the induced contraction is called *full meet contraction*.

Representation theorems (also called *axiomatic characterizations*) characterize an operation in terms of axioms or postulates. They are widely used in belief revision in order to show an interrelation between constructions and postulates. The following is a representation theorem for partial meet contractions.

Theorem 17.1. *[1, 20] Let* **K** *be a belief set and* $\div$ *be a contraction operator for* **K**. *Then* $\div$ *is a* partial meet contraction *for* **K** *if and only if* $\div$ *satisfies* closure, inclusion, success, vacuity, recovery *and* extensionality.

Partial meet revisions are defined from partial meet contractions using Levi identity. On the other hand, partial meet contractions on belief sets can be defined from partial meet revisions using the *Harper identity* [20]: $\mathbf{K} \div \alpha = \mathbf{K} \cap (\mathbf{K} * \neg \alpha)$. A representation theorem for partial meet revisions on belief sets can be found in [1].

2.2 Changes on belief bases

Following the seminal work of the AGM trio, almost all works on belief revision employed models in which epistemic states are represented by theories or belief sets, that is, set of sentences closed under logical consequence. However, it was observed by Alchourrón and Makinson [2] that "the intuitive processes of contraction and revision, contrary to casual impressions, are never really applied to theories as a whole, but rather to more or less clearly identified bases for them". Perhaps inspired by this observation, operations on belief bases have been investigated, among other, by Hansson [26, 29, 30], Fuhrmann [17], and Nayak [42].

Fuhrmann [17] defined a contraction operator $-$ on a belief base K and then studied the properties of its related contraction operator $\div$ on belief sets $\mathbf{K} = Cn(K)$ defined as $\mathbf{K} \div \alpha = Cn(K - \alpha)$. That is, the definition of $\mathbf{K} \div \alpha$ actually depends on K and α. Fuhrmann proposed a set of postulates for the operator $-$ on belief bases based on the basic postulates on belief sets proposed by Gärdenfors, showing that recovery does not hold on belief bases.

Hansson proposed an alternative approach, studying the changes on belief bases and not on their associated belief sets. He proposed an alternative contraction, called *kernel contraction*. Kernel contractions [31] are based on a selection among the sentences that imply the information to be retracted and they are a natural non-relational generalization of *safe contractions* [3].

Definition 17.4. [31] Let K be a set of sentences and α a sentence. Then $K \perp\!\!\!\perp \alpha$ is the set of all X such that $X \subseteq K$, $X \vdash \alpha$, and if $K' \subset X$, then $K' \nvdash \alpha$. The set $K \perp\!\!\!\perp \alpha$ is called the *kernel set*, and its elements are called the *α-kernels of K*.

In order to retract some information α from K, some sentences in each α-kernel must be erased. This is done by incision functions.

Definition 17.5. [31] Let K be a set of sentences. An *incision function for K* is a function σ defined on $\{K \perp\!\!\!\perp \alpha | \alpha \in \mathcal{L}\}$ such that for any sentence $\alpha \in \mathcal{L}$, the following statements hold:

1) $\sigma(K\!\perp\!\!\perp\!\alpha) \subseteq \cup(K\!\perp\!\!\perp\!\alpha)$.

2) If $X \in K\!\perp\!\!\perp\!\alpha$ and $X \neq \varnothing$ then $(X \cap \sigma(K\!\perp\!\!\perp\!\alpha)) \neq \varnothing$.

In the limit case when $K\!\perp\!\!\perp\!\alpha = \varnothing$ then $\sigma(K\!\perp\!\!\perp\!\alpha) = \varnothing$.

So, incision functions cut into each α-kernel, removing at least one sentence. Since all α-kernels are minimal subsets implying α, from the resulting sets it is no longer possible to derive α. Hence, incision functions may be used to derive (kernel) contraction operations.

Definition 17.6. [31]   Given a set of sentences K, a sentence α and an incision function σ for K, the *kernel contraction* of K by α, denoted by $K\div_\sigma\alpha$, is defined as: $K\div_\sigma\alpha = K \setminus \sigma(K\!\perp\!\!\perp\!\alpha)$.

That is, $K\div_\sigma\alpha$ can be obtained by erasing from K the sentences cut out by σ.

In the following, we recall a set of postulates for contraction that can be considered on every arbitrary set of sentences K:

- **Inclusion**: $K\div\alpha \subseteq K$.
- **Success**: If $\alpha \notin Cn(\varnothing)$ then $\alpha \notin Cn(K\div\alpha)$.
- **Vacuity**: If $\alpha \notin Cn(K)$ then $K\div\alpha = K$.
- **Core-Retainment** [27]: If $\beta \in K$ and $\beta \notin K\div\alpha$ then there is a set K' such that $K' \subseteq K$ such that $\alpha \notin Cn(K')$ but $\alpha \in Cn(K' \cup \{\beta\})$.
- **Uniformity** [28]: If it holds for all subsets K' of K that $\alpha \in Cn(K')$ if and only if $\beta \in Cn(K')$ then $K\div\alpha = K\div\beta$.
- **Relative Closure** [27]: $K \cap Cn(K\div\alpha) \subseteq K\div\alpha$.

The following is a representation theorem for kernel contractions on belief bases.
Theorem 17.2. *[31] Let K a belief base and $\div$ be a contraction operator for K. Then $\div$ is a kernel contraction for K if and only if $\div$ satisfies* inclusion, success, core-retainment *and* uniformity.

Smooth kernel contractions are kernel contractions that satisfy relative closure. Hansson showed that smooth kernel contractions and partial meet contractions are equivalent on belief sets. That is, smooth kernel contractions and partial meet contractions are just two different ways to construct the same class of operations on belief sets. However, kernel contractions are more general than partial meet contractions on belief bases. More relations about partial meet and kernel contractions can be found in [14]. The textbook [32] gives a good overview on axiomatic work in general (belief) base revision.

2.3 Alternative approaches and iterated revision

There are other approaches to belief change realizing AGM change operations, for instance, *Grove's sphere system* [23], *epistemic entrenchment* [22], and *safe contraction* [3]. Grove's sphere system is very similar to the sphere semantics for counterfactuals proposed by Lewis [39]. Concentric spheres allow the ordering of possible worlds according to some notion of similarity or the like. Then, the result of revising by α can be semantically described by the set of α-models that are closest to the **K**-models. Epistemic entrenchment allows that a revision can be based on a relation $\leq$ among sentences that when forced to choose between two beliefs, an agent will give up the less entrenched one. Gärdenfors and Makinson [22] proposed an epistemic entrenchment relation from which it is possible to define AGM contractions.

Belief updating [33] is a change operation of a different kind. Whereas in belief revision, both the old beliefs and the new information refer to the same situation, in updating the new information is about a current, possibly changed situation. Recent work relates update to actions [37]. Much current work in belief revision focuses on iterated revision that deals with changing epistemic relations such as epistemic entrenchment [7]. For a recent paper that considers iterated belief (base) revision in a broad epistemic framework, *cf.* [36].

3 Related work

Before entering into the discussion on the backgrounds of belief revision and argumentation theories, and possible connections in between, we will give an overview over work addressing this broad topic.

3.1 Truth Maintenance Systems [1979–1986]

Doyle [10] presents initially the *truth maintenance system*, or TMS, which is a knowledge representation method for representing both beliefs and their *justifications*. The aim of such systems is to restore consistency when a new justification has been added. A TMS associates a special data structure, called a *node*, with each problem solver datum which includes database entries, inference rules, and procedures. It records justifications, *i.e.*, arguments, for potential inferred beliefs, so as to compute the current set of beliefs by manipulating the status of nodes representing beliefs and evaluating justifications that represent reasons to believe. The truth maintenance process starts when a new justification for a node is added, and runs through basic steps of argumentation, such as evaluating the justifications to determine the status of nodes and checking justifications and contradictions, while avoiding circular relations among justifications and nodes.

A different type of truth maintenance systems was proposed by de Kleer's *assumption-based truth maintenance systems (ATMS)*[8]. Instead of evaluating justifications in a global process, ATMS label each datum with the corresponding sets of assumptions, representing the contexts under which it holds. These assumption sets are computed by the ATMS from the justifications that are supplied by the problem solver. The idea is that the assumptions provide contexts from which beliefs can be derived and hence may serve as arguments. The assumptions are primitive data, and all other data can be derived from them. There is no necessity that the overall database be consistent; it is easy to refer to contexts, and moving to different points in the search space requires very little effort.

3.2 Inconsistencies from multiple sources [1995]

Benferhat *et al.* [4] present an article primarily oriented towards the treatment of inconsistency caused by the use of multiple sources of information. Knowledge bases are stratified, namely each formula in the knowledge base is associated with its level of certainty corresponding to the layer to which it belongs.

The authors investigate two classes of approaches to deal with inconsistency in knowledge bases: coherence theories and foundation theories. The first insists on revising the knowledge base and restoring consistency, while the latter accepts inconsistency and copes with it. Coherence theories propose to give up some formulas of the knowledge base in order to get one or several consistent subbases, and to apply classical entailment on these consistent subbases to deduce plausible conclusions of the knowledge base. Foundation theories proceed differently since they retain all available information but each plausible conclusion inferred from the knowledge base is justified by some strong argumentative reason for believing in it.

The claim of the paper is that it does not always make sense to revise an inconsistent knowledge base, in particular, if the information comes from multiple sources. It is not even necessary to restore consistency in order to make sensible inferences from an inconsistent knowledge base, since inference based on argumentation can derive conclusions and reasons to believe them, independently of the consistency of the knowledge base.

3.3 Belief revision and epistemology [2000]

Pollock and Gillies [46] studied the dynamics of a belief revision system considering relations among beliefs in a "derivational approach" trying to derive a theory of belief revision from a more concrete epistemological theory. According to them, one of the goals of belief revision is to generate a knowledge base in which each piece of information is justified (by perception) or warranted by arguments containing previously held beliefs.

The difficulty is that the set of justified beliefs can exhibit all kinds of logical incoherencies because it represents an intermediate stage in reasoning. Therefore, the authors propose a theory of belief revision concerned with warrant rather than justification. The set of warranted propositions already takes account of all possible inferences, so there is only one way to acquire new warranted propositions: through perception. However, perception adds a percept to the inference-graph, not a belief, so the effect of perception on warrant cannot be represented as the addition of a proposition to a belief state.

3.4 Deductive explanations and belief revision [2002]

Falappa *et al.* [16] present a kind of non-prioritized revision operator based on the use of explanations. The idea is that an agent, before incorporating information which is inconsistent with its knowledge, requests an explanation supporting it. The authors build on the classical distinction between the *explanandum*, which is the final conclusion, and the *explanans*, represented by a set of sentences supporting the conclusion. The structure of an explanation is very similar to the structure of a deductive argument; the main difference is that every belief of an explanation is undefeasible (in a moment of time) whereas some beliefs of an argument may be defeasible or tentatively inferred.

In this framework, every explanation contains rules and factual knowledge. If the sentences in the explanans are better or more plausible than the sentences in the original belief base, then the explanation is incorporated. Therefore, not beliefs, but explanations (and hence arguments) supporting a belief are used for the change process. The authors considered both kernel and partial meet revision by a set of sentences and gave representation theorems for them. These operators may partially accept the new information, so they are non-prioritized.

3.5 Data-oriented Belief Revision [2006]

Paglieri and Castelfranchi [45] join argumentation and belief revision in the same conceptual framework by following Toulmin's layout of argumentation, which is intended to be used to analyze the rationality of arguments typically found in court-rooms. The connection to belief revision is made by considering argumentation as "persuasion to believe", hence argumentation is supposed to initiate successful revision processes. The authors propose *Data-oriented Belief Revision (DBR)* as an alternative to the AGM approach. Two basic informational categories, data and beliefs, are put forward in their approach, to account for the distinction between pieces of information that are simply gathered and stored by the agent (*data*), and pieces of information that the agent considers (possibly up to a certain degree) truthful representations of states of the world (*beliefs*). The beliefs are a subset of the data: an agent might well be aware of a datum that he does not believe (*i.e.*, he does not consider reliable enough). Data structures are conceived as networks of nodes (data), linked together by the relations of support, contrast and union. Data are selected (or rejected) as beliefs on the basis of their properties, described by *relevance, credibility, importance*, and *likeability*.

According to Paglieri and Castelfranchi [45], the Toulmin's layout schema is liable of immediate implementation in DBR, since it uses a specific data structure. The union of data and warrant supports the claim, and the warrant is in turn supported by its backing and contrasted by the rebuttal, *i.e.*, supports of the rebuttal make the warrant less reliable.

3.6 Merging Dung argumentation systems [2007]

Coste-Marquis *et al.* [6] proposed a general framework for merging Dung's style argumentation systems. They presented a framework for deriving reasonable information from a collection of Dung argumentation systems. Their approach consists in merging such systems assuming that all agents do not share the same sets of arguments. No assumption is made concerning the meaning of the attack relations, so that such relations may differ not only because agents have different points of view on the way arguments interact but more generally may disagree on what an interaction is.

Every argumentation system is expanded to a partial argumentation system, and such partial systems are built over the same set of arguments. *Merging* is used on the expanded systems as a way to solve the possible conflicts between them, and a set of argumentation systems which are as close as possible to the whole profile is generated. Finally, the last step consists in selecting the acceptable arguments at the group levels from the set of argumentation systems.

3.7 Prioritized revision by arguments [2008]

Rotstein *et al.* [47] introduce an abstract theory that captures the dynamics of an argumentation framework through the application of belief revision concepts. They define a *dynamic abstract argumentation theory* including dialectical constraints, and then present argument revision techniques to describe the fluctuation of the set of active arguments (the ones considered by the inference process of the theory). Expansion, contraction, and revision operators are realized in this framework, where the revision can be expressed in terms of the other two, leading to an identity similar to the one defined by Isaac Levi [38]. Their abstract theory allows the introduction of an argument ensuring it can be believed afterwards. The expansion operator is quite straightforward, but the definition of the contraction operator allows a wide range of possibilities from affecting unrestrictedly any number of arguments in the system to keeping this perturbation to a minimum, following the minimal change principle of the AGM theory. Contraction may also have an indirect impact on the attack relation among arguments.

In a second paper, Moguillansky *et al.* [41] proposed an instantiation of these change operators to *Defeasible Logic Programming, DeLP* [19]. In particular, a *warrant-prioritized argument revision operator (WPA)* is defined that implements successful change. To be more precise, when a program is revised by an argument ⟨A, α⟩ (where A is an argument for α), the revised program will be such that A is an undefeated argument, and α will therefore be warranted. The main issue underlying WPA revision lies in the selection of arguments and the incisions that have to be made over them. An argument selection criterion determines which arguments should not be present and once this selection is made, incisions (in the form of deletion of rules) will make those arguments "disappear" following some minimal change principle.

3.8 Adding arguments to Dung systems [2008]

Cayrol *et al.* [5] proposed a Dung-style abstract argumentation system that allows the addition of a new argument which may interact with previous arguments. An argumentation framework ⟨**A, R**⟩ is identified with an associated attack graph 𝒢. The revision process produces a new framework represented by a graph 𝒢′ and a new set of extensions. By considering how the set of extensions is modified under the revision process, the authors propose a typology of different revisions including *decisive revision*, when there is only one acceptable set of arguments in the revised framework, and *expansive revision*, when the revision simply adds the new argument to the existing extensions.

3.9 Relating reinstatement and recovery [2008]

Boella *et al.* [24] try to show a direct relation between argumentation and belief revision on the level of abstract properties. Like Paglieri and Castelfranchi [45], the authors also consider argumentation as persuasion to believe, and persuasion should be related to belief revision. They establish a link between *reinstatement* and *recovery*. *Reinstatement* plays an important role in argumentation; it refers to the situation that an argument that is not acceptable because of the existence of an attacking argument become acceptable again when an attacker to the attacking argument exists. *Recovery* reflects the central idea of minimal change in AGM belief revision; according to it, expansion by α should recover what was lost when α was contracted.

More recently, Boella *et al.* [25] present the application of a belief revision machinery to argumentation in a multi-agent system. The authors define an argument base revision that gives priority to the last introduced argument. As they are interested particularly in the persuasive power of argumentation, they express appealingness of arguments in terms of belief revision.

4 A conceptual view on Argumentation and Belief Revision

An investigation of the multifaceted relationships between argumentation and belief revision makes it necessary to consider cross-links between different aspects on either side, while at the same time taking the whole context of reasoning into account. The works sketched in section 3 have contributed to clarify this broad picture, in one way or another. In this chapter, we will add some pieces and links to the complex scenario.

4.1 The big picture

In order to obtain a clear view on possible connections between argumentation and belief revision, we start with making the basic steps of reasoning, as it was sketched in the introduction, more precise, pointing out the way from receiving (new) information to coming up with adequate plausible beliefs on which a decision can be based. We hereby assume that the current epistemic state is given and represented within some chosen framework.

- *Receiving new information:* The new information I may come in very different shapes and forms. In the simplest scenario, I is a propositional fact. This is the scope of the basic AGM theory, assuming the epistemic state of the agent to be given by a belief set, *i.e.*, a deductively closed set of (propositional) formulas. But I might be much more complex. It can be equipped with a degree of plausibility, or have the form of a rule or even a complete argument, or consist of a set of such entities.
- *Evaluating new information:* For the further processing of I, it is crucial for the agent to know its origin, as this knowledge will influence decisively her willingness to adopt I. For instance, if I is based on an observation made by the agent herself, she will usually be convinced of it being true. However, if I is conveyed to her by another agent, be it as part of the official news, in personal communication or found as written material, the agent will require some justification for I. In any case, as a mandatory step for rational, critical thinking, she will evaluate both I and a possibly given justification on the basis of her own beliefs and decide if I is to be incorporated into her stock of beliefs or not.
- *Changing beliefs:* If the agent has decided to adopt I in the previous step, she employs strategies to incorporate I consistently into her beliefs. For this, she has to use belief revision techniques that allows her to change her epistemic state accordingly.
- *Inference:* From her new epistemic state, the agent derives (most) plausible beliefs that guide her behavior.

This scenario can also be applied in parts if I is not a new information but a query to which the agent is expected to reply. In most of such cases, the change step would be obsolete, and evaluation and inference would collapse. However, if I is a conditional query "Suppose α holds, would you believe β?", whatever α and β are, reasoning would include a hypothetical change process that the current epistemic state of the agent must undergo.

From this embedding into a complex reasoning process, the complementary characters of argumentation and belief revision become obvious: while argumentation can make substantial contributions to the evaluation step, belief revision theory should be employed in the belief change part. But this is not the end of the story. Evaluation might include hypothetical change processes, considering what would happen if the new information were to be believed, and belief change implicitly relies on logical links between pieces of information which can be represented by arguments. In the end, both from argumentation processes and from belief revision processes, plausible beliefs can be obtained, but both areas focus only on parts of the dynamic reasoning process while at the same time providing general and versatile frameworks. Revision operators can not only be applied to beliefs, but also to intentions, preferences, theories, ontologies, law codes, etc. Argumentation can be used for *negotiation* (when the agents have conflicting interests and they try to make the best out of a deal for themselves), *inquiry* (when the agents have general ignorance in some subject and they try to find a proof or destroy one), *deliberation* (when the agents collaborate to decide what course of action to take) or *information seeking* (when the agents have personal ignorance on some subject and every agent seeks the answer to some questions from other agents). This is a much more general view than considering argumentation as persuasion to believe, as has been proposed in [45, 25].

These contemplations result in a most complex, highly interrelated view on argumentation and belief revision. Consequently, discussing links between both fields must reflect this complexity, taking into regard that proposed frameworks on either side might only implement some but not all aspects of the corresponding field. In particular, the famous AGM theory [1] in belief revision is more concerned with judging the results of change in a very abstract way than with the change process itself; moreover, argumentative evaluation of justifications to believe the given information in the sense described above is not at all a topic of AGM. That is why *success* is one of the basic postulates of the AGM theory according to which the agent is forced to believe the new information. Here, it is implicitly assumed that evaluation has been done beforehand. Hence, a comparison between AGM and some approach that makes use of a sophisticated argumentative evaluation of information to select beliefs, as has been developed *e.g.* in [45], is very likely to shed a bad light on AGM. AGM is no more on argumentative reasons for belief than is Dung's framework [13] on change processes. Both are highly abstract, declarative approaches to the respective field, hence (necessarily) over-simplifying in some respects but nevertheless extremely valuable as reference points.

Therefore, an investigation of the connections between belief revision and argumentation theory that is to do justice to both areas must go beneath the surface of abstract frameworks. It must study methods and the rationale underlying these methods, as well as purposes and intentions guiding the application of techniques.

We will first identify characteristic and prototypic concepts on either side and find basic correspondences as well as crucial differences. Afterwards, we will investigate how either domain may enrich the other domain's framework.

4.2 Comparing belief revision and argumentation

At first glance, the differences between argumentation and belief revision prevail. To begin with representational issues, the syntactic and semantic foundations of both areas have not much in common. In standard belief revision, logical formulas are used for knowledge representation, and the result of change processes are logical formulas. In more advanced frameworks, epistemic states are changed in which some qualitative relation allows for ranking worlds or sentences with respect to entrenchment, plausibility, and the like. In order to verify the results of the change processes, classical logical semantics is used. On the contrary, argumentation theory focuses on the interactions of arguments as pieces of information that may attack one another, and a relation between arguments may give priority to one argument or another. The arguments themselves, however, are very heterogeneous. In most approaches, they are quite complex *argument structures* built up by some kind of rules, using standard or non-standard derivation to implement reasoning. However, they might as well be abstract objects as in Dung's framework [13] without any internal structure. A special semantics makes precise what good arguments are, and there are several such semantics possible, implemented by preferred, stable, and grounded extensions.

As to the common grounds, both disciplines aim at resolving conflicts which are usually based on logical grounds, *i.e.*, on contradictions, and make use of preference relations to achieve this aim. However, belief revision theory provides a highly declarative framework for that, based on postulates, whereas argumentation theory is more concerned with practical, justification-based techniques.

For a direct comparison of argumentation and belief revision, it is tempting to take the standard AGM approach [1], as no other work has influenced the development of belief revision theory in a similar way. And the AGM postulates offer a clear framework that makes fundamental views explicit. However, one of the most basic assumptions of the standard AGM theory, namely its focus on deductively closed sets of formulas as representing belief sets, does not fit at all to argumentation theory, as it abstracts from the basic steps of reasoning, blurring the distinction between what is explicitly given or serves as assumptions, and what is justified belief. Hence, works on belief base revision (*e.g.* [32, 14]), or on iterated epistemic change (*e.g.* [7, 34, 35, 9]) offer a much richer base for comparison, since they allow one to take deeper insights into change processes.

Belief revision methods and most argumentation frameworks can be used directly for reasoning, although this is not their principal concern. The connection between belief revision and nonmonotonic inference has been made clear by [40] and further developed for iterative change operations in [36]; this is the BRDI view on belief revision, as Dubois [12] calls it. As to argumentation, those approaches that are based on rules or use some sort of derivation provide logical chains that establish links between what is presupposed and what is concluded. Also with respect to that aspect, belief revision theories remain on an abstract level, describing by axioms *what* good inferences are, while argumentation is more concerned with *how* and *why* conclusions are drawn, making reasons for belief apparent.

These considerations make obvious that belief revision and argumentation theory are basically complementary areas of research. In the following, we will discuss how they may complement each other.

4.3 Argumentation in Belief Revision

In this subsection we study how argumentation concepts and techniques can be used in belief revision theory. Among the works relating argumentation and belief revision, many of them add belief revision capabilities to an argumentation system. However, there are some papers that propose to use an "argumentative machinery" for a belief revision process, like e.g. [46, 45] (see also section 3). The first approach to use argumentation in belief revision is *justification-based truth maintenance systems (TMS's)* proposed by Doyle [10] (*cf.* section 3.1). Doyle studies the interactions between justifications when a new justification has been added, to find out which conclusions can be justified. He does not consider retraction of justifications. *Assumption-based truth maintenance systems (ATMS)* [8] are more concerned with managing assumptions instead of implementing change processes. As in DBR [45], we have data and beliefs: a data is believed in some contexts represented by assumptions sets. As in [4], there is no necessity that the overall database be consistent; it is easy to refer to contexts and move to different points in the search space representing the proper context. Both types of truth maintenance systems work on belief bases and are very early approaches to belief revision, dating before AGM theory.

In [16], we combine the ATMS idea with base revision and propose a system that uses argumentative structures in the form of explanations for nonprioritized revisions of belief bases K. Different from standard approaches to belief revision, the new information not only consists of a proposition α but of reasons to believe a proposition, *i.e.*, of rules and prerequisites A from which α can be deductively derived. So, A can be considered an explanans for the explanandum α. In order to integrate an argumentative evaluation of the new information into the revision process, we defined *partial acceptance revision operators* in the following way: i) the epistemic input is the set of sentences A as explanans for the explanandum α, ii) A is initially accepted, that is, A is joined to K (possibly producing an inconsistent intermediate state), iii) all possible inconsistencies of $K \cup A$ are removed, returning a consistent revised belief base $K \circ A$. This operator is an operator of *external revision*. The name "external" indicates that the revision process takes place outside of the original set.

Whether α is accepted or not depends on the evaluation of its explanans A with respect to the current belief base. The acceptance of the explanans forces the acceptance of the explanandum in the revised set, since explanation here is based on classical deduction. However, there is an important remark to be made regarding the degree of acceptance of the explanans and the explanandum. While the explanans can be explicitly included in the revised set, the explanandum may be inferred from it without actually being included. So, the distinction between explicitly given information (as data in [45]) and inferred beliefs is respected and can be implemented only when working with belief bases instead of belief sets.

The main difference between the process of revision by a set of sentences and the process of argumentation is significant: in revision, external beliefs are compared with internal beliefs and, after a selection process, some sentences are discarded, other ones are accepted. In argumentation, the process is more procedural: we have an argument, attack this by counterarguments, defend it by counterarguments to counterarguments, and so on. Nevertheless, the rationale behind partial acceptance revision operators matches the intentions leading argumentation in that not the new information itself, but reasons to believe it, are evaluated.

4.4 Belief Revision in Argumentation

Belief revision theory offers nice methods to implement dynamical features in an argumentation framework. The papers by Rotstein, Moguillansky et al. [47, 41] and Boella et al. [25] are among the most comprehensive approaches to address such a revision theory for argument systems (cf. section 3). Several different ways of applying belief revision in argumentation may be distinguished:

- Changing by adding or deleting an argument.
- Changing by adding or deleting a set of arguments.
- Changing the attack (and/or defeat) relation among arguments.
- Changing the status of beliefs (as conclusions of arguments).
- Changing the type of an argument (from strict to defeasible, or vice versa).

The distinction between the two first ways is similar to the distinction among single change (as in AGM model) and multiple change (as in *multiple contraction* [18, 44]). Adding or removing an argument or a set of arguments may trigger a change in the justified conclusions. The consideration of such changes may lead to a base revision theory which deals with changes of argumentative bases, and in which deduction is replaced by an argumentation process. The method of kernel contraction making use of incision functions to eliminate base elements (cf. section 2) is of particular interest here; first steps towards this direction can be found in [41].

Changing the attack and/or defeat relation among arguments may lead to a completely different behavior of the system, the understanding and the control of which constitutes substantially new challenges for belief revision theory. Boella et al. [25] have proposed an approach that changes the attack relation in a dictatorial way in favor of the new information. More sophisticated change processes are conceivable, taking ideas from the methods for epistemic belief change (or iterated belief change) that deal with modifying relations on possible worlds (*cf. e.g.* [7, 35]). Although arguments are very different from possible worlds, those works might be considered as approaches to realize minimal change processes for general relations. However, before applying those techniques from epistemic belief revision to argumentative attack or defeat relations, a careful investigation has to be done concerning conceptual differences between both frameworks.

Changing the status of beliefs may be a consequence of previous changes to the argument system. In classical, Dung-style argument systems, the criterion to be a justified belief is based on extensions. Cayrol *et al.* [5] have studied how extensions change when new arguments are added. In argumentation frameworks where argumentation is based on conclusions (*e.g.* DeLP [19]), the addition of an argument may change the status of a claim from unwarranted to warranted and vice versa. This touches basic concerns of the reasoning aspect of belief revision, and investigations on the level of belief revision postulates might be very useful. The link between reinstatement (in argumentation) and recovery (in belief revision) proposed in [24] is in this line of research.

Finally, changing the type of an argument from strict to defeasible, or vice versa, addresses novel issues in belief revision. Such modifications are not dealt with properly by chaining retraction and addition of arguments, as the old and the new argument are linked by a syntactic or semantic relation which gets lost when these operations are carried out independently. The basic idea is that inconsistencies that arise when new information has to be incorporated into the stock of beliefs can be eliminated not only by removing arguments (resp. beliefs), but by weakening strict beliefs to defeasible rules (resp. conditionals). The procedure of *dynamic classification* of generic rules has been frequently used in the evolution of humanity's knowledge. The possibility of changing the status of beliefs from undefeasible to defeasible induces revision operations of a new quality, with important consequences for argumentation, as arguments are formed very often by defeasible beliefs. In [16], we have introduced a new type of base revision that implements such a dynamic classification of beliefs and is likewise interesting for argumentation and belief revision theory. We proposed a framework in which defeasible conditionals can be generated by revising belief structures composed of defeasible rules and undefeasible knowledge. The approach preserves consistency in the undefeasible knowledge and it provides a mechanism to dynamically qualify the beliefs as undefeasible or defeasible, providing a more complete set of epistemic attitudes and extending the inference power of knowledge based systems. As a particular case, Falappa *et al.* [15] propose to extend the application of this non-prioritized revision operator to *Defeasible Logic Programming (DeLP)* [19].

4.5 Possible future work

To alleviate orientation within the complex picture and promote further work, we will take up some of our ideas and suggestions developed above and propose a list of possible important topics for future work on the connection between argumentation and belief revision.

- *Development of new change operators for argumentative systems:* this point may include non-prioritized revision as well as symmetrical revision operators. Non-prioritized revision means revision in which the new information (argument) could be accepted, partially accepted or rejected. Symmetric revision means merging of argumentative systems.
- *Elaborating a set of postulates or properties for changes of argumentative systems:* this may include postulates for expansions, contractions, revisions as well as postulates for consolidations (for instance, changes for cleaning blocking defeaters) or merging the beliefs of several argumentative systems.
- *Finding representation theorems for changes on argumentative systems:* representation theorems establish links between constructive approaches to revision that propose mechanisms and algorithms for change, and black box approaches that specify the properties that a change operator should have to show equivalence.
- *Epistemic entrenchment and defeat:* epistemic entrenchment relations among beliefs may be derived from attack/defeat relations among arguments and vice versa. Basically, warranted beliefs should be more entrenched than non-warranted beliefs.
- *Argumentation and epistemic revision:* interesting new views that alleviate the combination of belief revision and argumentation might arise from studying change operators within the broader framework of iterated revision. In particular, it would be interesting to find parallels in changing relational structures on either side.

5 Conclusion

In this chapter, we discuss the relationships between argumentation and belief revision, first recalling important work done, then analyzing the current state of the art and proposing some tentative future research lines.

We developed a conceptual view on argumentation and belief revision based on the understanding of both areas as being complementary disciplines in the art of reasoning. While argumentation seems to be more appropriate for the evaluation of (rule-based) information, belief revision proves to be useful for the handling of dynamic beliefs. Hence they should not be regarded as competitive alternatives that may replace each other. Just to the contrary – combining argumentation and belief revision allows the modelling of reasoning processes in greater variety and complexity than each of the areas can. Moreover, their diverseness makes it possible that each of argumentation and belief revision provides enriching aspects for the respective other discipline beyond any differences. We pointed out various starting points for work in this direction, and proposed future lines of research along the borderline between argumentation and revision.

Acknowledgements This research was funded by Consejo Nacional de Investigaciones Científicas y Técnicas (CONICET), Agencia Nacional de Promocion Científica y Tecnológica (ANPCyT), Universidad Nacional del Sur (UNS), Ministerio de Ciencia y Tecnología (MinCyT) [Argentina] and Fundação para a Ciência e a Tecnologia (FCT) [Portugal].

References

1. C. Alchourrón, P. Gärdenfors, and D. Makinson. On the Logic of Theory Change: Partial Meet Contraction and Revision Functions. *The Journal of Symbolic Logic*, 50:510–530, 1985.
2. C. Alchourrón and D. Makinson. On the Logic of Theory Change: Contraction Functions and their Associated Revision Functions. *Theoria*, 48:14–37, 1982.
3. C. Alchourrón and D. Makinson. On the Logic of Theory Change: Safe Contraction. *Studia Logica*, 44:405–422, 1985.
4. S. Benferhat, D. Dubois, and H. Prade. How to infer from inconsistent beliefs without revising. In *Proceedings of IJCAI'95*, pages 1449–1455, 1995.
5. C. Cayrol, F. D. de Saint Cyr, and M. C. Lagasquie Schiex. Revision of an Argumentation System. In *Proceedings of KR 2008*, pages 124–134, 2008.
6. S. Coste-Marquis, C. Devred, S. Konieczny, M.-C. Lagasquie-Schiex, and P. Marquis. On the Merging of Dung's Argumentation Systems. *Artificial Intelligence*, 171:730–753, 2007.
7. A. Darwiche and J. Pearl. On the Logic of Iterated Belief Revision. *Artificial Intelligence*, 89:1–29, 1997.
8. J. de Kleer. An Assumption-based TMS. *Artificial Intelligence*, 28(2):127–162, 1986.
9. J. Delgrande, D. Dubois, and J. Lang. Iterated Revision and Prioritized Merging. In *Proceedings of KR 2006*, pages 210–220. AAAI Press, 2006.
10. J. Doyle. A Truth Maintenance System. *Artificial Intelligence*, 12:231–272, 1979.
11. J. Doyle. Reason Maintenance and Belief Revision: Foundations versus Coherence Theories. In *Belief Revision* [21], pages 29–51.
12. D. Dubois. Three Scenarios for the Revision of Epistemic States. In Besnard and Hanks, editors, *Proceedings of NMR 2006*, pages 296–305, San Francisco, CA., 2006. Morgan Kaufmann.
13. P. M. Dung. On the Acceptability of Arguments and its Fundamental Role in Nonmonotonic Reasoning, Logic Programming and n-Person Games. *Artificial Intelligence*, 77:321–357, 1995.
14. M. A. Falappa, E. L. Fermé, and G. Kern-Isberner. On the Logic of Theory Change: Relations between Incision and Selection Functions. In *Proceedings of ECAI 2006*, pages 402–406, 2006.
15. M. A. Falappa, A. J. García, and G. R. Simari. Belief Dynamics and Defeasible Argumentation in Rational Agents. In *Proceedings of NMR 2004, section Belief Change*, pages 164–170, 2004.
16. M. A. Falappa, G. Kern-Isberner, and G. R. Simari. Belief Revision, Explanations and Defeasible Reasoning. *Artificial Intelligence Journal*, 141:1–28, 2002.
17. A. Fuhrmann. Theory Contraction through Base Contraction. *The Journal of Philosophical Logic*, 20:175–203, 1991.

18. A. Fuhrmann and S. O. Hansson. A Survey of Multiple Contractions. *The Journal of Logic, Language and Information*, 3:39–76, 1994.
19. A. J. García and G. R. Simari. Defeasible Logic Programming: an Argumentative Approach. *Theory and Practice of Logic Programming*, 4(1):95–138, 2004.
20. P. Gärdenfors. *Knowledge in Flux: Modelling the Dynamics of Epistemic States*. The MIT Press, Bradford Books, Cambridge, Massachusetts, 1988.
21. P. Gärdenfors. *Belief Revision*. Gärdenfors, Cambridge University Press, 1992.
22. P. Gärdenfors and D. Makinson. Revisions of Knowledge Systems using Epistemic Entrenchment. *Second Conference on Theoretical Aspects of Reasoning About Knowledge*, pages 83–95, 1988.
23. A. Grove. Two Modellings for Theory Change. *The Journal of Philosophical Logic*, 17:157–170, 1988.
24. G. Guido Boella, C. d. Costa Perera, A. Tettamanzi, and L. van der Torre. Dung Argumentation and AGM Belief Revision. In *Fifth International Workshop on Argumentation in Multi-Agent Systems, ArgMAS 2008*, 2008.
25. G. Guido Boella, C. d. Costa Perera, A. Tettamanzi, and L. van der Torre. Making others believe what they want. *Artificial Intelligence in Theory and Practice II*, pages 215–224, 2008.
26. S. O. Hansson. New Operators for Theory Change. *Theoria*, 55:114–132, 1989.
27. S. O. Hansson. Belief Contraction without Recovery. *Studia Logica*, 50:251–260, 1991.
28. S. O. Hansson. A Dyadic Representation of Belief. In *Belief Revision* [21], pages 89–121.
29. S. O. Hansson. In Defense of Base Contraction. *Synthese*, 91:239–245, 1992.
30. S. O. Hansson. Theory Contraction and Base Contraction Unified. *The Journal of Symbolic Logic*, 58(2), 1993.
31. S. O. Hansson. Kernel Contraction. *The Journal of Symbolic Logic*, 59:845–859, 1994.
32. S. O. Hansson. *A Textbook of Belief Dymanics: Theory Change and Database Updating*. Kluwer Academic Publishers, 1999.
33. H. Katsuno and A. Mendelzon. On the Difference between Updating a Knowledge Database and Revising it. In *Belief Revision* [21], pages 183–203.
34. G. Kern-Isberner. Postulates for Conditional Belief Revision. In *Proceedings of IJCAI'99*, pages 186–191. Morgan Kaufmann, 1999.
35. G. Kern-Isberner. A Thorough Axiomatization of a Principle of Conditional Preservation in Belief Revision. *Annals of Mathematics and Artificial Intelligence*, 40(1-2):127–164, 2004.
36. G. Kern-Isberner. Linking Iterated Belief Change Operations to Nonmonotonic Reasoning. In G. Brewka and J. Lang, editors, *Proceedings of KR 2008*, pages 166–176, Menlo Park, CA, 2008. AAAI Press.
37. J. Lang. Belief Update Revisited. In *Proceedings of IJCAI 2007*, pages 2517–2522, 2007.
38. I. Levi. Subjunctives, Dispositions, and Chances. *Synthese*, 34:423–455, 1977.
39. D. Lewis. *Counterfactuals*. Harvard University Press, Cambridge, Massachusetts, 1973.
40. D. Makinson and P. Gärdenfors. Relations between the Logic of Theory Change and Nonmonotonic Logic. *Lecture Notes in Computer Science*, 465:183–205, 1991.
41. M. O. Moguillansky, N. D. Rotstein, M. A. Falappa, A. J. García, and G. R. Simari. Argument Theory Change: Revision Upon Warrant. In *Proceedings of The Twenty-Third Conference on Artificial Intelligence, AAAI 2008*, pages 132–137, 2008.
42. A. Nayak. Foundational Belief Change. *Journal of Philosophical Logic*, 23:495–533, 1994.
43. A. Newell. The Knowledge Level. *Readings from the AI Magazine*, pages 357–377, 1988.
44. R. Niederée. Multiple Contraction: a further case against Gärdenfors' Principle of Recovery. *Lecture Notes in Computer Science*, 465:322–334, 1991.
45. F. Paglieri and C. Castelfranchi. *The Toulmin Test: Framing Argumentation within Belief Revision Theories*, pages 359–377. Berlin, Springer, 2006.
46. J. L. Pollock and A. S. Gillies. Belief Revision and Epistemology. *Synthese*, 122(1–2):69–92, 2000.
47. N. D. Rotstein, M. O. Moguillansky, M. A. Falappa, A. J. García, and G. R. Simari. Argument Theory Change: Revision upon Warrant. In *Proceedings of The Computational Models of Argument, COMMA 2008*, pages 336–347, 2008.

Part IV
Applications

Chapter 18
Argumentation in Legal Reasoning

Trevor Bench-Capon, Henry Prakken and Giovanni Sartor

1 Introduction

A popular view of what Artificial Intelligence can do for lawyers is that it can do no more than deduce the consequences from a precisely stated set of facts and legal rules. This immediately makes many lawyers sceptical about the usefulness of such systems: this mechanical approach seems to leave out most of what is important in legal reasoning. A case does not appear as a set of facts, but rather as a story told by a client. For example, a man may come to his lawyer saying that he had developed an innovative product while working for Company A. Now Company B has made him an offer of a job, to develop a similar product for them. Can he do this? The lawyer firstly must interpret this story, in the context, so that it can be made to fit the framework of applicable law. Several interpretations may be possible. In our example it could be seen as being governed by his contract of employment, or as an issue in Trade Secrets law. Next the legal issues must be identified and the pros and cons of the various interpretations considered with respect to them. Does his contract include a non-disclosure agreement? If so, what are its terms? Was he the sole developer of the product? Did Company A support its development? Does the product use commonly known techniques? Did Company A take measures to protect the secret? Some of these will favour the client, some the Company. Each interpretation will require further facts to be obtained. For example, do the facts support a claim that the employee was the sole developer of the product? Was development work carried

Trevor Bench-Capon
Department of Computer Science, University of Liverpool, UK e-mail: tbc@liverpool.ac.uk

Henry Prakken
Department of Information and Computing Sciences, Utrecht University, and Faculty of Law, University of Groningen, The Netherlands e-mail: henry@cs.uu.nl

Giovanni Sartor
European University Institute, Law Department, Florence, and CIRSFID, University of Bologna, Italy e-mail: giovanni.sartor@eui.eu

I. Rahwan, G. R. Simari (eds.), *Argumentation in Artificial Intelligence,*
DOI 10.1007/978-0-387-98197-0_18, © Springer Science+Business Media, LLC 2009

out in his spare time? What is the precise nature of the agreements entered into? Once an interpretation has been selected, the argument must be organised into the form considered most likely to persuade, both to advocate the client's position and to rebut anticipated objections. Some precedents may point to one result and others to another. In that case, further arguments may be produced to suggest following the favourable precedent and ignoring the unfavourable one. Or the rhetorical presentation of the facts may prompt one interpretation rather than the other. Surely all this requires the skill, experience and judgement of a human being? Granted that this is true, much effort has been made to design computer programs that will help people in these tasks, and it is the purpose of this chapter to describe the progress that has been made in modelling and supporting this kind of sophisticated legal reasoning.

We will review[1] systems that can store conflicting interpretations and that can propose alternative solutions to a case based on these interpretations. We will also describe systems that can use legal precedents to generate arguments by drawing analogies to or distinguishing precedents. We will discuss systems that can argue why a rule should not be applied to a case even though all its conditions are met. Then there are systems that can act as a mediator between disputing parties by structuring and recording their arguments and responses. Finally we look at systems that suggest mechanisms and tactics for forming arguments.

Much of the work described here is still research: the implemented systems are prototypes rather than finished systems, and much work has not yet reached the stage of a computer program but is stated as a formal theory. Our aim is therefore to give a flavour (certainly not a complete survey) of the variety of research that is going on and the applications that might result in the not too distant future. Also for this reason we will informally paraphrase example inputs and outputs of systems rather than displaying them in their actual, machine-readable format; moreover, because of space limitations the examples have to be kept simple.

2 Early systems for legal argumentation

In this section we briefly discuss some early landmark systems for legal argumentation. All of them concern the construction of arguments and counterarguments.

2.1 Conflicting interpretations

Systems to address conflicting interpretations of legal concepts go back to the very beginnings of AI and Law. Thorne McCarty (e.g. [25, 27]) took as his key problem a landmark Supreme Court Case in US tax law which turned on differing interpretations of the concept of ownership, and set himself the ambitious goal of reproducing,

---

[1] This chapter is a revised and updated version of [6].

in his TAXMAN system, both the majority and the dissenting opinions expressing these interpretations. This required highly sophisticated reasoning, constructing competing theories and reasoning about the deep structure of legal concepts to map the specific situation onto paradigmatic cases. Although some aspects of the system were prototyped, the aim was perhaps too ambitious to result in a working system, certainly given the then current state of the art. This was not McCarty's goal, however: his motivation was to gain insight into legal reasoning through a computational model. McCarty's main contribution was the recognition that legal argument involves theory construction as well as reasoning with established knowledge. McCarty [26] summarises his position as follows: "The task for a lawyer or a judge in a "hard case" is to construct a theory of the disputed rules that produces the desired legal result, and then to persuade the relevant audience that this theory is preferable to any theories offered by an opponent" (p. 285). Note also the emphasis on persuasion, indicating that we should expect to see argumentation rather than proof. Both the importance of theory construction and the centrality of persuasive argument are still very much part of current thinking in AI and Law.

Another early system was developed by Anne Gardner [15] in the field of offer and acceptance in American contract law. The task of the system was "to spot issues": given an input case, it had to determine which legal questions arising in the case were easy and which were hard, and to solve the easy ones. The system was essentially rule based, and this simpler approach offered more possibilities for practical exploitation than did McCarty's system. One set of rules was derived from the Restatement of Contract Law, a set of 385 principles abstracting from thousands of contract cases. These rules were intended to be coherent, and to yield a single answer if applicable. This set of rules was supplemented by a set of interpretation rules derived from case law, common sense and expert opinion, intended to link these other rules to the facts of the case. Gardner's main idea was that easy questions were those where a single answer resulted from applying these two rule sets, and hard questions, or issues, were either those where no answer could be produced, because no interpretation rule linked the facts to the substantive rules, or where conflicting answers were produced by the facts matching with several rules. Some of the issues were resolved by the program with a heuristic that gives priority to rules derived from case law over restatement and commonsense rules. The rationale of this heuristic is that if a precedent conflicts with a rule from another source, this is usually because that rule was set aside for some reason by the court. The remaining issues were left to the user for resolution.

Consider the following example, which is a very much simplified and adapted version of Gardner's own main example[2]. The main restatement rule is

R1: An offer and an acceptance constitute a contract

Suppose further that there are the following commonsense (C) and expert (E) rules on the interpretation of the concepts of offer and acceptance:

---

[2] We in particular abstract from Gardner's refined method for representing knowledge about (speech act) events.

C1: A statement "Will supply ..." in reply to a request for offer is an offer.

C2: A statement "Will you supply ..." is a request for offer.

C3: A statement "I accept ..." is an acceptance.

E1: A statement "I accept" followed by terms that do not match the terms of the offer is not an acceptance.

Suppose that Buyer sent a telegram to Seller with "Will you supply carload salt at $2.40 per cwt?" to which Seller replied with "Will supply carload at $2.40, terms cash on delivery", after which Buyer replied with her standard "Purchase Order" indicating "I accept your offer of 12 July" but which also contained a standard provision "payment not due until 30 days following delivery".

Applying the rules to these events, the "offer" antecedent of R1 can be established by C1 combined with C2, since there are no conflicting rules on this issue. However, with respect to the "acceptance" antecedent of R1 two conflicting rules apply, viz. C3 and E1. Since we have no way of giving precedence to C3 or E1, the case will be a hard one, as there are two conflicting notions of "acceptance". If the case is tried and E1 is held to have precedence, E1 will now be a precedent rule, and any subsequent case in which this conflict arises will be easy, since, as a precedent rule, E1 will have priority over C3.

2.2 Reasoning with precedents

The systems described in the last section do recognise the importance of precedent cases as a source of legal knowledge, but they make use of them by extracting the rationale of the case and encoding it as a rule. To be applicable to a new case, however, the rule extracted may need to be analogised or transformed to match the new facts. Nor is extracting the rationale straightforward: judges often leave their reasoning implicit and in reconstructing the rationale a judge could have had in mind there may be several candidate rationales, and they can be expressed at a variety of levels of abstraction. These problems occur especially in so-called 'factor-based' domains, i.e., domains where problems are solved by considering a variety of factors that plead for or against a solution. In such domains a rationale of a case often just expresses the resolution of a particular set of factors in a specific case. A main source of conflict in such domains is that a new case often will not exactly match a precedent but will share some features with it, lack some of its other features, and/or have some additional features. Moreover, cases are more than simple rationales: matters such as the context and the procedural setting can influence the way the case should be used. In consequence, some researchers have attempted to avoid using rules and rationales altogether, instead representing the input, often interpreted as a set of factors, and the decisions of cases, and defining separate argument moves for interpreting the relation between the input and decision (e.g. [23, 1], both to be discussed below). This approach is particularly associated with researchers in US, where the common law tradition places a greater stress on precedent cases and their particular features than is the case with the civil law jurisdictions of Europe. None the less cases are also used in civil law jurisdictions and the reasoning techniques are similar.

The most influential system of this sort is HYPO [2], developed by Edwina Rissland and Kevin Ashley in the domain of US Trade Secrets Law, which can be seen as a factor-based domain. In HYPO cases are represented according to a number of dimensions. A dimension is some aspect of the case relevant to the decision, for example, the security measures taken by the plaintiff. One end of the dimension represents the most favourable position for the plaintiff (e.g. specific non-disclosure agreements), while the other end represents the position most favourable to the defendant (e.g. no security measures at all). Typically a case will lie somewhere between the two extremes and will be more or less favourable accordingly. HYPO then uses these dimensions to construct three-ply arguments. First one party (say the plaintiff) cites a precedent case decided for that side and offers the dimensions it shares with the current case as a reason to decide the current case for that side. In the second ply the other party responds either by citing a counter example, a case decided for the other side which shares a different set of dimensions with the current case, or distinguishing the precedent by pointing to features which make the precedent more, or the current case less, favourable to the original side. In the third ply the original party attempts to rebut the arguments of the second ply, by distinguishing the counter examples, or by citing additional precedents to emphasise the strengths or discount the weaknesses in the original argument.

Subsequently Ashley went on, with Vincent Aleven, to develop CATO (most fully reported in [1]), a system designed to help law students to learn to reason with precedents. CATO simplifies HYPO in some respects but extends it in others. In CATO the notion of dimensions is simplified to a notion of factors. A factor can be seen as a specific point of the dimension: it is simply present or absent from a case, rather than present to some degree, and it always favours either the plaintiff or defendant. A new feature of CATO is that these factors are organised into a hierarchy of increasingly abstract factors, so that several different factors can be seen as meaning that the same abstract factor is present. One such abstract factor is that the defendant used questionable means to obtain the information, and two more specific factors indicating the presence of this factor are that the defendant deceived the plaintiff and that he bribed an employee of the plaintiff: both these factors favour the plaintiff. The hierarchy allows for argument moves that interpret the relation between a case's input and its decision, such as emphasising or downplaying distinctions. To give an example of downplaying, if in the precedent defendant used deception while in the new case instead defendant bribed an employee, then a distinction made by the defendant at this point can be downplayed by saying that in both cases the defendant used questionable means to obtain the information. To give an example of emphasising a distinction, if in the new case defendant bribed an employee of plaintiff while in the precedent no factor indicating questionable means was present, then the plaintiff can emphasise the distinction "unlike the precedent, defendant bribed an employee of plaintiff" by adding "and therefore, unlike the precedent defendant used questionable means to obtain the information".

Perhaps the most elaborate representation of cases was produced in Karl Brant-ing's Grebe system in the domain of industrial injury, where cases were represented as semantic networks [13]. The program matched portions of the network for the new case with parts of the networks of precedents, to identify appropriate analogies.

Of all this work, HYPO in particular was highly influential, both in the explicit stress it put on reasoning with cases as constructing arguments, and in providing a dialectical structure in which these arguments could be expressed, anticipating much other work on dialectical procedures.

3 Logical accounts of reasoning under disagreement

The systems discussed in the previous section were (proposals for) implemented systems, based on informal accounts of some underlying theory of reasoning. Other AI & Law research aims at specifying theories of reasoning in a formal way, in order to make general reasoning techniques from nonmonotonic logic and formal argumentation available for implementations.

The first AI & Law proposals in this vein, for example, [16, 30], can be regarded as formal counterparts of Gardner's ideas on issue spotting. Recall that Gardner allows for the presence in the knowledge base of conflicting rules governing the interpretation of legal concepts and that she defines an issue as a problem to which either no rules apply at all, or conflicting rules apply. Now in logical terms an issue can be defined as a proposition such that either there is no argument about this proposition or there are both arguments for the proposition and for its negation.

Some more recent work in this research strand has utilised a very abstract AI framework for representing systems of arguments and their relations developed by Dung [14]. For Dung, the notion of argument is entirely abstract: all that can be said of an argument is which other arguments it attacks, and which it is attacked by. Given a set of arguments and the attack relations between them, it is possible to determine which arguments are acceptable: an argument which is not attacked will be acceptable, but if an argument has attackers it is acceptable only if it can be defended, against these attackers, by acceptable arguments which in turn attack those attackers. This framework has proved a fruitful tool for understanding non-monotonic logics and their computational properties. Dung's framework has also been made use of in AI & Law. It was first applied to the legal domain by Prakken & Sartor [35], who defined a logic for reasoning with conflicting rules as an instan-tiation of Dung's framework. (See below and Chapter 8 of this book) Bench-Capon [3] has explored the potential of the fully abstract version of the framework to rep-resent a body of case law. he uses preferred semantics, where arguments can defend themselves: in case of mutual attack this gives rise to multiple sets of acceptable arguments, which can explain differences in the application of law in different juris-dictions, or at different times in terms of social choices. Dung's framework has also been extended to include a more formal consideration of social values (see Chapter 3 of this book).

3.1 Reasoning about conflicting rules

Generally speaking, the proposed systems discussed so far attempt to identify conflicting interpretations and arguments, but do not attempt to resolve them, leaving it to the user to choose which argument will be accepted. As we saw above, Gardner's system went somewhat further in that it gave priority to rules derived from case law over restatement and commonsense rules. Thus her system was able to solve some of the cases to which conflicting rules apply. This relates to much logical work in Artificial Intelligence devoted to the resolution of rule conflicts in so-called commonsense reasoning. If we have a rule that birds can fly and another that ostriches cannot fly, we do not want to let the user decide whether Cyril the ostrich can fly or not: we want the system to say that he cannot, since an ostrich is a specific kind of bird. Naturally attempts have been made to apply these ideas to law.

One approach was to identify general principles used in legal systems to establish which of two conflicting rules should be given priority. These principles included preferring the more specific rule (as in the case of the ostrich above, or where a law expresses an exception to a general provision), preferring the more recent rule, or preferring the rule deriving from the higher legislative authority (for instance, 'federal law precedes state law'). To this end the logics discussed above were extended with the means to express priority relations between rules in terms of these principles so that rule conflicts would be resolved. Researchers soon realised, however, that general priority principles can only solve a minority of cases. Firstly, as for the specificity principle, whether one rule is more specific than another often depends on substantive legal issues such as the goals of the legislator, so that the specificity principle cannot be applied without an intelligent appreciation of the particular issue. Secondly, general priority principles usually only apply to rules from regulations and not to, for instance, case rationales or interpretation rules derived from cases. Accordingly, in many cases the priority of one rule over another can be a matter of debate, especially when the rules that conflict are unwritten rules put forward in the context of a case. For these reasons models of legal argument should allow for arguments about which rule is to be preferred.

As an example of arguments about conflicting case rationales, consider three cases discussed by, amongst others, [10, 7, 32] and [8] concerning the hunting of wild animals. In all three cases, the plaintiff (P) was chasing wild animals, and the defendant (D) interrupted the chase, preventing P from capturing those animals. The issue to be decided is whether or not P has a legal remedy (a right to be compensated for the loss of the game) against D. In the first case, *Pierson v Post*, P was hunting a fox on open land in the traditional manner using horse and hound, when D killed and carried off the fox. In this case P was held to have no right to the fox because he had gained no possession of it. In the second case, *Keeble v Hickeringill*, P owned a pond and made his living by luring wild ducks there with decoys, shooting them, and selling them for food. Out of malice, D used guns to scare the ducks away from the pond. Here P won. In the third case, *Young v Hitchens*, both parties were commercial fisherman. While P was closing his nets, D sped into the gap, spread his own net and caught the fish. In this case D won. The rules we are concerned with here are the rationales of these cases:

R1 *Pierson*: If the animal has not been caught, the defendant wins
R2 *Keeble*: If the plaintiff is pursuing his livelihood, the plaintiff wins
R3 *Young*:   If the defendant is in competition with the plaintiff and the animal is not caught, the defendant wins.

Note that R1 applies in all cases and R2 in both *Keeble* and *Young*. In order to explain the outcomes of the cases we need to be able to argue that R3 > R2 > R1. To start with, note that if, as in HYPO, we only look at the factual similarities and differences, none of the three precedents can be used to explain the outcome of one of the other precedents. For instance, if we regard *Young* as the current case, then both *Pierson* and *Keeble* can be distinguished. A way of arguing for the desired priorities, first mooted in [10], is to refer to the purpose of the rules, in terms of the social values promoted by following the rules.

The logic of [35] provides the means to formalise such arguments. Consider another case in which only plaintiff was pursuing his livelihood and in which the animal was not caught. In the following (imaginary) dispute the parties reinterpret the precedents in terms of the values promoted by their outcomes, in order to find a controlling precedent (we leave several details implicit for reasons of brevity; a detailed formalisation method can be found in [32]; see also [8].

Plaintiff: I was pursuing my livelihood, so (by *Keeble*) I win
Defendant: You had not yet caught the animal, so (by *Pierson*) I win
Plaintiff: following *Keeble* promotes economic activity, which is why *Keeble* takes precedence over *Pierson*, so I win.
Defendant: following *Pierson* protects legal certainty, which is why *Keeble* does not take precedence over *Pierson*, so you do not win.
Plaintiff: but promoting economic activity is more important than protecting legal certainty since economic development, not legal certainty is the basis of this country's prosperity. Therefore, I am right that *Keeble* takes precedence over *Pierson*, so I still win.

This dispute contains priority debates at two levels: first the parties argue about which case rationale should take precedence (by referring to values advanced by following the rationale), and then they argue about which of the conflicting preference rules for the rationales takes precedence (by referring to the relative order of the values). In general, a priority debate could be taken to any level and will be highly dependent on the context and jurisdiction. Various logics proposed in the AI & Law literature are able to formalise such priority debates, such as [17, 35, 19] and [21].

3.2 Other arguments about rules

Besides priority debates in case of conflicting rules, these logics can also model debates about certain properties of rules, such as their legal validity or their applicability to a legal case. The most fully developed logical theory about what it takes to apply a rule is reason-based logic, developed jointly by Jaap Hage and Bart Verheij (e.g. [19, 45]). They claim that applying a legal rule involves much more than subsuming a case under the rule's conditions. Their account of rule application can be briefly summarised as follows. First in three preliminary steps it must be determined whether the rule's conditions are satisfied, whether the rule is legally valid, and whether the rule's applicability is not excluded in the given case by, for instance, a statutory exception. If these questions are answered positively (and all three are open to debate), it must finally be determined that the rule can be applied, i.e., that no conflicting rules or principles apply. On all four questions reason-based logic allows reasons for and against to be provided and then weighed against each other to obtain an answer.

Consider by way of illustration a recent Dutch case (HR 7-12-1990, *NJ* 1991, 593) in which a male nurse aged 37 married a wealthy woman aged 97 whom he had been nursing for several years, and killed her five weeks after the marriage. When the woman's matrimonial estate was divided, the issue arose whether the nurse could retain his share. According to the relevant statutes on Dutch matrimonial law the nurse was entitled to his share since he had been the woman's husband. However, the court refused to apply these statutes, on the grounds that applying it would be manifestly unjust. Let us assume that this was in turn based on the legal principle that no one shall profit form his own wrongdoing (the court did not explicitly state this). In reason-based logic this case could be formalised as follows (again the full details are suppressed for reasons of brevity).

Claimant: Statutory rule R is a valid rule of Dutch law since it was enacted according to the Dutch constitution and never repealed. All its conditions are satisfied in my case, and so it should be applied to my case. The rule entitles me to my late wife's share in the matrimonial estate. Therefore, I am entitled to my wife's share in the matrimonial estate.
Defendant: Applying rule R would allow you to profit from your own wrongdoing: therefore rule R should not be applied in this case.
Court: The reason against applying this rule is stronger than that for applying the rule, and so the rule does not apply.

Of course, in the great majority of cases the validity or applicability of a statute rule is not at issue but instead silently presumed by the parties (recall the difference between arguments and proofs described in the introduction). The new logical techniques alluded to above can also deal with such presumptions, and they can be incorporated in reason-based logic.

Reason-based logic also has a mechanism for 'accruing' different reasons for conclusions into sets and for weighing these sets against similar sets for conflicting conclusions. Thus it captures that having more reasons for a conclusions may strengthen one's position. Prakken [33] formalises a similar mechanism for accruing arguments in the context of Dung's framework. Prakken also proposes three principles that any model of accrual should satisfy. In Chapter 12 of this book Gordon and Walton show that the Carneades logic of [18] has an accrual mechanism that satisfies these principles.

One way to argue about the priority of arguments is to claim that the argument is preferred if it is grounded in the better or more coherent legal theory[3]. While there has been considerable progress in seeing how theories can be constructed on the basis of a body of past cases, evaluation of the resulting theories in terms of their coherence is more problematic, since coherence is a difficult notion to define precisely[4]. Bench-Capon & Sartor [8] describe some features of a theory which could be used in evaluation, such as simplicity of a theory or the number of precedent cases explained by the theory. As an (admittedly somewhat simplistic) example of the last criterion, consider again the three cases on hunting animals, and imagine two theories that explain the case decisions in terms of the values of promotion of economic activity and protection of legal certainty. A theory that gives precedence to promoting economic activity over protecting legal certainty explains all three precedents while a theory with the reverse value preference fails to explain *Keeble*. The first theory is therefore on this criterion the more coherent one. However, how several coherence criteria are to be combined is a matter for further research. For an attempt to give a metric for coherence, see [7]. Coherence is also discussed in [20], where coherence is treated mainly in terms of respecting *a fortiori* arguments.

4 Dialogue and mediation systems

Implicit in the notion of argument is that there are two parties with opposing views. Already in HYPO there is the dialectical structure of point, counter point and rebuttal, and most logics for argumentation discussed above also have this dialectical flavour. It is therefore a natural step to make this dialogical structure explicit, and to build systems to conduct or mediate dialogues between the opposed parties. Such dialogue systems also provide the opportunity to model the procedure under which a dispute is conducted, and the context in which information is introduced to a dispute. Taking a procedural point of view forces us to think about matters such as burden of proof, admissibility of evidence, agreed and contested points, and the role of a neutral third party to arbitrate the dispute.

One of the first such systems in AI & Law was Tom Gordon's Pleadings Game, which embodies an idealised model of civil pleadings in common law systems [17]. The objective of the system is to extend the issue-spotting task of Gardner's pro-

---

[3] There is, of course, a debate in legal theory as to how we can provide an epistemology of law, and coherence is only one position. Coherence is discussed here as it is the position which has received most attention in AI & Law

[4] For fuller discussions of coherence, see [29] and [28, Ch. 2]

gram to a dialogical setting. It is to allow two human parties to state the arguments and facts that they believe to be relevant, so that they can determine where they agree and where they disagree. The residual disagreements will go on to form the issues when the case is tried. The system plays two roles in this process: it acts as a referee to ensure that the proper procedure is followed, and records the facts and arguments that are presented and what points are disputed, so as to identify the issues that require resolution. The Pleadings Game has a built-in proof mechanism for an argumentation logic, which is applied to check the logical well-formedness of the arguments stated by the user, and to compute which of the stated arguments prevail, on the basis of the priority arguments also stated by the user and a built-in specificity checker. The main addition to Gardner's system is that in the Pleadings Game not only the content of the arguments is relevant but also the attitudes of the parties expressed towards the arguments and their premises.

Let us illustrate this with the following simplified dispute, based on the example that we used in section 2.1 to illustrate Gardner's system.

Plaintiff: I claim (1) we have a contract
Defendant: I deny 1
Plaintiff: We have a valid contract since (2) I made an offer and (3) you accepted it, so we have a contract.
Defendant: I concede 2 but I deny 3.
Plaintiff: (4) you said "I accept...", so by C3 you accepted my offer.
Defendant: I concede 4 and C3, but (5) my statement "I accept ..." was followed by terms that do not match the terms of your offer. So by E1 (which takes priority over C3) I (6) did not accept you offer.
Plaintiff: I concede Ei and that Ei takes priority over C3 but I deny 5.
Defendant: (7) you required payment upon delivery while (8) I offered payment 30 days following delivery, so there is a mismatch between our terms.
Plaintiff: I concede (7) and the argument but I deny (8).

At this point, there is one argument for the conclusion that a contract was created, based on the premises 2, 4 and C3 (note that plaintiff left R1 implicit and defendant silently agreed with this). The intermediate conclusion (3) of this argument that there was an acceptance is defeated by a counterargument based on premises 7, 8 and E1. So according to a purely logical analysis of the dispute the case is easy, having as outcome that no contract exists between the parties. This agrees with Gardner's treatment of the example. However, in the Pleadings Game it also matters that the plaintiff has denied defendant's claim (8). This is a factual issue making the case hard, and which has to be decided in court.

The Pleadings Game was fully implemented, but purely as an experimental system: in particular the arguments had to be presented in a complicated logical syntax so that they could be handled by the underlying proof mechanism. The trade-off between ease of use and the ability of the system to process the information it receives remains a difficult problem for such systems.

Following Gordon's work, a number of other systems for dialogue were produced. Arno Lodder's Dialaw [22] is a two-player dialogue game that combines the notion of propositional commitment [48] with Hage and Verheij's Reason Based Logic. The players can use locutions for claiming a proposition and for challenging, conceding and retracting a claimed proposition. Arguments are constructed implicitly, by making a new claim in reply to a challenge. Arguments can also be about the procedural correctness of dialogue moves. Each dialogue begins with a claim of one player, and then the turn usually switches after each move. When the commitments of one player logically imply a claim of the other player, the first player must either concede it or retract one of the implying commitments. A dialogue terminates if no disagreement remains, i.e., if no commitment of one player is not also a commitment of the other. The first player wins if at termination he is still committed to his initial claim, the second player wins otherwise.

Bench-Capon's TDG [5] is intended to produce more natural dialogues than the "stilted" ones produced by systems such as the Pleadings Game and Dialaw. To this end, its speech acts are based on Toulmin's well-known argument scheme [44]. In this scheme, a *claim* is supported by *data*, which support is *warranted* by an inference licence, which is *backed* by grounds for its acceptance; finally, a claim can be attacked with a *rebuttal*, which itself is a claim and thus the starting point of a counterargument. Arguments can be chained by regarding data also as claims, for which data can in turn be provided. TDG has speech acts for asking for and providing these elements of an argument; a dialogue starts with a claim and then the protocol supports a dialogue which constructs a Toulmin structure whilst subjecting it to a top-down critical examination.

In [34] Prakken proposes a dialogue game model for "adjudication dialogues", by adding a neutral third party who adjudicates the conflict between two adversaries. The main feature of the model is a division into an argumentation phase, where the adversaries plea their case and the adjudicator has a largely mediating role, and a decision phase, where the adjudicator decides the dispute on the basis of the claims, arguments and evidence put forward in the argumentation phase. The model allows for explicit decisions on admissibility of evidence and burden of proof by the adjudicator in the argumentation phase. Adjudication is modelled as putting forward arguments, in particular undercutting and priority arguments, in the decision phase.

Such a dialogue game model of adjudication paves the way for formal models of burden of proof and presumption. Research on legal argumentation has recently addressed these issues, which has required models going beyond existing 'standard' non-monotonic logics. In [31] the logic of [35] is adapted to make the acceptability of an argument dependent on how such a burden is distributed over the parties, while in the original system it is always allocated to one side. In [36] Prakken & Sartor extend the resulting logic with the means to explicitly represent and reason about distributions of the burden of proof. They also claim that if such a logic is embedded in a dialogue model for adjudication, a precise distinction can be made between three kinds of burdens of proof often distinguished in the law, namely, the burden of production, the burden of persuasion and the tactical burden of proof. The resulting combination of logic and dialogue game is applied to presumptions in

[37]: by developing the idea that legal presumptions can be modelled as defeasible rule, they provide ways of representing how a legal presumption can be defeated by evidence to the contrary and how the burden of proof can be allocated with regard to the disproval of presumed facts. In related work, Gordon, Prakken & Walton [18] have provided a logical model of reasoning under standards of proof within the Carneades logic. In Chapter 12 of this volume, Gordon and Walton extend it with definitions of these three and some further notions of burden of proof and compare their account with the work of Prakken & Sartor.

5 Tactics for dispute

Once arguments are placed in a dialogical setting, it becomes apparent that at various points of the dialogue, the parties will have a choice of moves by which to attack their opponent or defend their own arguments. Questions then arise as to which moves are available to construct, attack and defend arguments, and whether there are principles to guide the choice of move. In fact, the implemented dialogue systems of the previous section do not address these questions, because they are intended to act as a mediator between two human players. The responsibility of the system is thus limited to enforcing the rules of the game, while strategy and tactics are the responsibility of the human users.

In their work on the CABARET system, Skalak & Rissland [43] attempted to identify arguments that could be made in a dispute using rules and cases. They begin by identifying a number of forms of argument, and then describe argument strategies to be used according to the context of the dispute. For example, if the current case matches with most but not all the features of some statutory rule that one wishes to use, the rule must be broadened so as to make the rule applicable to the case. Or if a rule is applicable to the case under consideration but would be unfavourable, that rule needs to be discredited. They then identify the moves that can be made to realise the strategies, depending on the disposition of the precedent, and whether the precedent does or does not establish the desired consequent. One move to broaden a rule is to find a precedent that also lacked the missing features but in which the conclusion of the rule was nevertheless drawn. To discredit a rule one can try to find a precedent case in which it was not followed even though all its conditions were satisfied in the case. Finally they identify a number of primitive operations in terms of which the moves can be realised. These operations include all moves that can be made in HYPO with cases. All of this is then brought together in a decision tree which suggests which strategy should be adopted, which moves need to be used to fulfill it and which primitives will enable the required moves.

Loui & Norman [23] take this approach a step further in their formal model of the use of rationales in disputes. They allow for a position under attack to be first restated, in order to make the attack more effective. For example if an argument using a rationale *if P then Q* is to be attacked, it may be helpful to restate this as if *P then R and if R then Q*, and to provide a counter example to *if P then R*. They provide a number of other examples of rationales and tactics for attacking them.

CABARET, by distinguishing different kinds of building materials, and providing different moves and attacks appropriate to each kind, can produce its elegant classification of strategies. The central idea of distinguishing different kinds of premises and different ways of dealing with them is explicitly addressed by work on argument schemes, which we discuss in the next section.

Finally, in [41] and [40] strategic aspects of legal argument are modelled with game-theoretic methods. A game-theoretical analysis of legal argumentation requires a method of determining the payoffs the parties will receive as a consequence of the arguments they present in a dispute (combined with the choices of the other parties) as well as the identification of the equilibrium strategies the parties should pursue (namely what strategies of the two parties are such that each one of them represents a best response to the strategy of the other). The first aspect has been addressed in [41], while the second has been considered in [40].

6 Argument schemes

In a logical proof we have a set of premises and a conclusion which is said to follow from them. The premises are considered to be entirely homogeneous. Many of the systems discussed so far likewise make no distinctions among their premises. In arguments expressed in natural language in contrast we can typically see the premises as playing different roles in the argument. By identifying these roles, we can present the arguments in a more readily understandable fashion, and also identify the various different ways in which the argument may be attacked. Structuring the argument in this way produces an argument scheme. Analysing legal reasoning in terms of argument schemes produces a taxonomy of arguments, which may provide useful guidance for building implemented argumentation systems, analogous to the guidance provided by domain ontologies for building knowledge-based systems (cf. e.g. [28]).

One argument scheme that has been widely used in AI and Law is that devised by Toulmin [44] (see the description of TDG in Section 4)). This has been mainly used to present arguments to users, as in PLAID [9] and SPLIT UP [52], but it has also been used as the basis of a dialogue game, Bench-Capon's TDG, in which the moves of the game relate to providing various elements of the scheme.

While Toulmin attempts to supply a general scheme for arguments, others have attempted to classify arguments in terms of various specific schemes [47]. One of the schemes discussed by Walton (pp. 61–63) is the scheme of arguments from the position to know:

Person *W* says that *p*
Person *W* is in the position to know about *p*
Therefore, p

Walton also discusses two special versions of this scheme for witness and expert testimonies. Clearly, these schemes are very relevant for evidential legal reasoning. Another scheme discussed by Walton (pp. 75–77) is the scheme from good (or bad) consequences:

> If *A* is brought about, then good (bad) consequences will (may plausibly) occur. *Therefore,* *A* should (not) be brought about.

One instantiation is adapted from a recent discussion in Dutch privacy law whether email addresses are personal data.

> If the term "personal data" of the Dutch Data Protection Act is interpreted to include email addresses, then legal measures against spam become possible, which is good. *Therefore,* the term "personal data" of the Dutch Data Protection Act should be interpreted to include email addresses.

Argument schemes are not classified according to their logical form but according to their content. Many argument schemes in fact express epistemological principles (such as the scheme from the position to know) or principles of practical reasoning (such as the scheme from consequences). Accordingly, different domains may have different sets of such principles. Each argument scheme comes with a customised set of critical questions that have to be answered when assessing whether their application in a specific case is warranted. Thus with argument schemes it becomes clear that the different premises are each associated with their own particular types of attack, in contrast to the purely logical systems in which attacks are uniform. Some of these questions pertain to acceptability of the premises, such as "is *W* in the position to know about *p*?" or "is the possibility to use legal means against spam really good?". Other critical questions point at exceptional circumstances in which the scheme may not apply, such as "is *W* sincere?" or "are there better ways to bring about these good consequences?". Clearly, the possibility to ask such critical questions makes argument schemes defeasible, since negative answers to such critical questions are in fact counterarguments, such as "Person *W* is not sincere since he is a relative of the suspect and relatives of suspects tend to protect the suspect". Another reason why argument schemes are defeasible is that they may be contradicted by conflicting applications of the same or another scheme. For instance, a positive instance of the scheme from consequences can be attacked by a negative instance of the same scheme, such as by "interpreting email addresses as personal data also has bad consequences, since the legal system will be flooded with litigation, so the term "personal data" should not be interpreted to include email addresses". Or one person in a position to know (say an eyewitness) may have said that the suspect was at the crime scene while another eyewitness may have said that the suspect was not at the crime scene.

Originally only Toulmin's argumentation scheme was paid explicit attention in AI & Law, although implicit appeal to other argumentation schemes can be seen in many of the systems discussed above. For example, HYPO identifies the two ways in which the citation of a precedent may be attacked, and reason-based logic identifies ways to reason about the application of legal rules. More recently explicit argumentation schemes have been used. For example, [4] use an extended version of the scheme from consequences to link legal arguments and social values, and this approach has been applied to the representation of a particular case by [51]. [50] presented a set of particular argumentation schemes designed to capture the cased based reasoning used in CATO. [12] modelled several schemes for reasoning about evidence, and this work has subsequently been developed by [11]. In Carneades [18] a generalised notion of argument schemes is applied to legal cases; Carneades is further described in chapter 12 of this volume.

7 Systems to structure argument

Arguments can often be rather complex, so that understanding the web of relationships becomes difficult. There is clear potential for computers to provide a means of addressing this problem. The idea of providing a visual means of structuring legal arguments is not new to the legal field: as early as the 1930s John Henry Wigmore [49] produced a graphical notation for depicting legal arguments and their relations of support and attack, so as to make sense of a mass of evidence. In this way the relationships between the evidence and the point to be proven, and the ways in which the chain of reasoning could be attacked could be clearly seen.

In Wigmore's days the only way to draw such graphs was with pencil and paper, which perhaps explains why his method was forgotten until Schum & Tillers [42] saw the potential of the computer for supporting the drawing and manipulation of such graphs. They proposed a software system MarshalPlan for visualising preliminary fact investigation based on Wigmore's diagrams. Some other systems within AI & Law that provide support for the graphical structuring of argumentation are Verheij's ArguMed system [46] and Loui's Room 5 system [24], which replaces ArguMed's (and MarshalPlan's) graph structures with encapsulated text boxes, to avoid "pointer spaghetti". The Araucaria system [38] combines an ArguMed-like graphical notation with means to label the arguments as instances of predefined argumentation schemes, which are stored in a database together with their critical questions. The Avers system [11] in turn combines an Araucaria-like approach with the means to visualise crime scenarios as abductive reasoning. An overview of various argument visualisation tools and their legal applications is given in [39].

Argument structuring systems have uses in areas where the clear presentation of the argument is of prime importance. They could be used in preliminary fact investigation (see MarshalPlan or Avers), in teaching (many argument structuring systems outside the legal domain have been developed especially for teaching), for case management or for mediation in online dispute resolution. In all these cases, the usefulness of such systems might be increased by integrating them with documentary sources. For instance, when supporting preliminary fact investigation, the structured evidential arguments could be linked to police documents containing the available evidence. Or when used for case management, the structured arguments could be linked to the case files. Or when a structuring system is used for teaching the analysis of a case decision, the structured arguments could be linked to the corresponding fragment in the case decisions in the casebook used by the students. Work on argumentation schemes can further augment the usefulness of such systems. When constructing arguments, argument schemes provide a repertoire of forms of argument to be considered, and a template prompting for the pieces that are needed; when attacking arguments they provide a set of critical questions that can identify potential weaknesses in the opponents case. Araucaria and Avers provide examples of research systems pointing in this direction.

8 Concluding remarks

In this chapter we have given an overview of the ways in which argumentation has been addressed in legal applications. Legal reasoning has many distinctive features, which include: any proposed set of rules inevitably contain gaps and conflicts; many of its concepts are imprecisely defined meaning that interpretation is required; precedent cases play an important role; procedural issues can influence the status of arguments; much legal argumentation is adversarial and dialectic in nature; the facts of a case need to be selected and characterised; many decisions express a preference for particular values and purposes; and all its conclusions are defeasible, subject often to formal appeal. All of these features mean that deduction cannot provide an adequate model of legal reasoning and instead argumentation must take centre stage to allow for these contextual, procedural and interpretative elements. For this reason developments in computational models of argumentation have been readily taken up by the AI & Law community. Equally, however, the legal AI community has contributed much to computational models of argumentation: a considerable amount of the work described in this book has its origins in work motivated by legal applications, and more than half the chapters have authors who have published in specialist AI & Law venues.

The legal domain can thus act both a motivation and a test-bed for developments in argumentation, and we look forward to much fruitful future interaction between the two areas.

References

1. V. Aleven. *Teaching Case-Based Argumentation Through a Model and Examples.* PhD Dissertation University of Pittsburgh, 1997.
2. K. Ashley. *Modeling Legal Argument: Reasoning with Cases and Hypotheticals.* MIT Press, Cambridge, MA, 1990.
3. T. Bench-Capon. Representation of case law as an argumentation framework. In T. Bench-Capon, A. Daskalopulu & R. Winkels, editors, *Legal Knowledge and Information Systems. JU-RIX 2002: The Fifteenth Annual Conference*, pages 53–62, Amsterdam etc, 2002. IOS Press.
4. T. Bench-Capon, K. Atkinson, and A. Chorley. Persuasion and value in legal argument. *Journal of Logic and Computation*, 15:1075–1097, 2005.

5. T. Bench-Capon, T. Geldard, and P. Leng. A method for the computational modelling of dialectical argument with dialogue games. *Artificial Intelligence and Law*, 8:233–254, 2000.

6. T. Bench-Capon and H. Prakken. Argumentation. In A. Lodder and A. Oskamp, editors, *Information Technology and Lawyers: Advanced technology in the legal domain, from challenges to daily routine*, pages 61–80. Springer, Berlin, 2006.

7. T. Bench-Capon and G. Sartor. A quantitative approach to theory coherence. In B. Verheij, A. Lodder, R.Loui & A. Muntjewerff, editors, *Legal Knowledge and Information Systems. JURIX 2001: The Fourteenth Annual Conference*, pages 53–62, Amsterdam etc, 2001. IOS Press.

8. T. Bench-Capon and G. Sartor. A model of legal reasoning with cases incorporating theories and values. *Artificial Intelligence*, 150:97–143, 2003.

9. T. Bench-Capon and G. Staniford. PLAID - proactive legal assistance. In *Proceedings of the Fifth International Conference on Artificial Intelligence and Law*, pages 81–88, New York, 1995. ACM Press.

10. D. Berman and C. Hafner. Representing teleological structure in case-based legal reasoning: the missing link. In *Proceedings of the Fourth International Conference on Artificial Intelligence and Law*, pages 50–59, New York, 1993. ACM Press.

11. F. Bex, S. v. d. Braak, H. v. Oostendorp, H. Prakken, B. Verheij, and G. Vreeswijk. Sensemaking software for crime investigation: how to combine stories and arguments? *Law, Probability and Risk*, 6:145–168, 2007.

12. F. Bex, H. Prakken, C. Reed, and D. Walton. Towards a formal account of reasoning about evidence: argumentation schemes and generalisations. *Artificial Intelligence and Law*, 12:125–165, 2003.

13. L. Branting. *Reasoning with Rules and Precedents: A Computational Model of Legal Analysis*. Kluwer Academic Publishers, Dordrecht/Boston/London, 1999.

14. P. Dung. On the acceptability of arguments and its fundamental role in nonmonotonic reasoning, logic programming, and n–person games. *Artificial Intelligence*, 77:321–357, 1995.

15. A. Gardner. *Artificial Intelligence Approach to Legal Reasoning*. MIT Press, Cambridge, MA, 1987.

16. T. Gordon. An abductive theory of legal issues. *International Journal of Man-Machine Studies*, 35:95–118, 1991.

17. T. Gordon. *The Pleadings Game. An Artificial Intelligence Model of Procedural Justice*. Kluwer Academic Publishers, Dordrecht/Boston/London, 1995.

18. T. Gordon, H. Prakken, and D. Walton. The Carneades model of argument and burden of proof. *Artificial Intelligence*, 171:875–896, 2007.

19. J. Hage. A theory of legal reasoning and a logic to match. *Artificial Intelligence and Law*, 4:199–273, 1996.

20. J. Hage. Formalizing legal coherence. In *Proceedings of the Eighth International Conference on Artificial Intelligence and Law*, pages 22–31, New York, 2001. ACM Press.

21. R. Kowalski and F. Toni. Abstract argumentation. *Artificial Intelligence and Law*, 4:275–296, 1996.

22. A. Lodder. *DiaLaw. On Legal Justification and Dialogical Models of Argumentation*. Kluwer Academic Publishers, Dordrecht/Boston/London, 1999.

23. R. Loui and J. Norman. Rationales and argument moves. *Artificial Intelligence and Law*, 3:159–189, 1995.

24. R. Loui, J. Norman, J. Alpeter, D. Pinkard, D. Craven, J. Linsday, and M. Foltz. Progress on Room 5: A testbed for public interactive semi-formal legal argumentation. In *Proceedings of the Sixth International Conference on Artificial Intelligence and Law*, pages 207–214, New York, 1997. ACM Press.

25. L. McCarty. Reflections on TAXMAN: An experiment in artificial intelligence and legal reasoning. *Harvard Law Review*, 90:89–116, 1977.

26. L. McCarty. An implementation of Eisner v. Macomber. In *Proceedings of the Fifth International Conference on Artificial Intelligence and Law*, pages 276–286, New York, 1995. ACM Press.

27. L. McCarty and N. Sridharan. The representation of an evolving system of legal concepts: II. Prototypes and deformations. In *Proceedings of the Seventh International Joint Conference on Artificial Intelligence*, pages 246–253, 1981.
28. L. Mommers. *Applied Legal Epistemology*. Doctoral dissertation Leiden University, 2002.
29. A. Peczenik. Jumps and logic in the law. *Artificial Intelligence and Law*, 4:297–329, 1996.
30. H. Prakken. A logical framework for modelling legal argument. In *Proceedings of the Fourth International Conference on Artificial Intelligence and Law*, pages 1–9, New York, 1993. ACM Press.
31. H. Prakken. Modelling defeasibility in law: logic or procedure? *Fundamenta Informaticae*, 48:253–271, 2001.
32. H. Prakken. An exercise in formalising teleological case-based reasoning. *Artificial Intelligence and Law*, 10.113–133, 2002.
33. H. Prakken. A study of accrual of arguments, with applications to evidential reasoning. In *Proceedings of the Tenth International Conference on Artificial Intelligence and Law*, pages 85–94, New York, 2005. ACM Press.
34. H. Prakken. A formal model of adjudication dialogues. *Artificial Intelligence and Law*, 16:305–328, 2008.
35. H. Prakken and G. Sartor. A dialectical model of assessing conflicting arguments in legal reasoning. *Artificial Intelligence and Law*, 4:331–368, 1996.
36. H. Prakken and G. Sartor. Formalising arguments about the burden of persuasion. In *Proceedings of the Eleventh International Conference on Artificial Intelligence and Law*, pages 97–106, New York, 2007. ACM Press.
37. H. Prakken and G. Sartor. More on presumptions and burdens of proof. In G. Sartor, editor, *Legal Knowledge and Information Systems. JURIX 2008: The Twentyfirst Annual Conference.* pages 176–185, Amsterdam etc., 2008. IOS Press.
38. C. Reed and G. Rowe. Araucaria: Software for argument analysis, diagramming and representation. *International Journal of AI Tools*, 13:961–980, 2004.
39. C. Reed, D. Walton, and F. Macagno. Argument diagramming in logic, law and artificial intelligence. *The Knowledge Engineering Review*, 22:87–109, 2007.
40. R. Riveret, H. Prakken, A. Rotolo, and G. Sartor. Heuristics in argumentation: a game-theoretical investigation. In P. Besnard, S. Doutre, and A. Hunter, editors, *Computational Models of Argument. Proceedings of COMMA 2008*, pages 324–335, Amsterdam etc, 2008. IOS Press.
41. R. Riveret, A. Rotolo, G. Sartor, H. Prakken, and B. Roth. Success chances in argument games: a probabilistic approach to legal disputes. In A. Lodder and L. Mommers, editors, *Legal Knowledge and Information Systems. JURIX 2007: The Twentieth Annual Conference*, pages 99–108. IOS Press, Amsterdam etc., 2007.
42. D. Schum and P. Tillers. Marshaling evidence for adversary litigation. *Cardozo Law Review*, 13:657–704, 1991.
43. D. Skalak and E. Rissland. Arguments and cases. an inevitable intertwining. *Artificial Intelligence and Law*, 1:3–44, 1992.
44. S. Toulmin. *The Uses of Argument*. Cambridge University Press, Cambridge, 1958.
45. B. Verheij. *Rules, reasons, arguments: formal studies of argumentation and defeat*. Doctoral dissertation University of Maastricht, 1996.
46. B. Verheij. Automated argument assistance for lawyers. In *Proceedings of the Seventh International Conference on Artificial Intelligence and Law*, pages 43–52, New York, 1999. ACM Press.
47. D. Walton. *Argumentation Schemes for Presumptive Reasoning*. Lawrence Erlbaum Associates, Mahwah, NJ, 1996.
48. D. Walton and E. Krabbe. *Commitment in Dialogue. Basic Concepts of Interpersonal Reasoning*. State University of New York Press, Albany, NY, 1995.
49. J. Wigmore. *The Principles of Judicial Proof*. Little, Brown and Company, Boston, 2nd edition, 1931.

50. A. Wyner and T. Bench-Capon. Argument schemes for legal case-based reasoning. In A. Lodder and L. Mommers, editors, *Legal Knowledge and Information Systems. JURIX 2007: The Twentieth Annual Conference*, pages 139–149. IOS Press, Amsterdam etc., 2007.

51. A. Wyner, T. Bench-Capon, and K. Atkinson. Arguments, values and baseballs: Representation of Popov v. Hayashi. In A. Lodder and L. Mommers, editors, *Legal Knowledge and Information Systems. JURIX 2007: The Twentieth Annual Conference*, pages 151–160. IOS Press, Amsterdam etc., 2007.

52. J. Zeleznikow and A. Stranieri. The split-up system. In *Proceedings of the Fifth International Conference on Artificial Intelligence and Law*, pages 185–195, New York, 1995. ACM Press.

Chapter 19
The Argument Interchange Format

Iyad Rahwan and Chris Reed

1 Introduction

While significant progress has been made in understanding the theoretical properties of different argumentation logics and in specifying argumentation dialogues, there remain major barriers to the development and practical deployment of argumentation systems. One of these barriers is the lack of a shared, agreed notation or "interchange format" for argumentation and arguments. In the last years a number of different argument mark-up languages have been proposed in the context of tools developed for argument visualisation and construction (see [10] for a review). Thus, for example, the Assurance and Safety Case Environment (ASCE)[1] is a graphical and narrative authoring tool for developing and managing assurance cases, safety cases and other complex project documentation. ASCE relies on an ontology for *arguments about safety* based on *claims*, *arguments* and *evidence* [8]. Another mark-up language was developed for Compendium,[2] a semantic hypertext concept mapping tool. The Compendium argument ontology enables construction of networks, in which nodes represent *issues*, *positions* and *arguments*.

The analysis and study of human argument has also prompted the development of specialised argument mark-up languages and tools. Two particularly relevant developments in this direction are *ClaiMaker* [5] and AML [18]. *ClaiMaker* and related technologies [5] provide a set of tools for individuals or distributed communities to publish and contest ideas and arguments, as is required in contested domains such as research literatures, intelligence analysis, or public debate. This system is based on the *ScholOnto* ontology [4], which can express a number of basic reasoning

Iyad Rahwan
British University in Dubai, UAE & University of Edinburgh, UK, e-mail: irahwan@acm.org

Chris Reed
University of Dundee, UK e-mail: chris@computing.dundee.ac.uk

[1] http://www.adelard.co.uk/software/asce/
[2] http://www.compendiuminstitute.org/tools/compendium.htm

I. Rahwan, G. R. Simari (eds.), *Argumentation in Artificial Intelligence*,
DOI 10.1007/978-0-387-98197-0_19, © Springer Science+Business Media, LLC 2009

schemes (causality, support) and relationships between concepts found in scholarly discourse (e.g. similarity of ideas, taxonomies of concepts, etc.). The argument-markup language (AML) used by the Araucaria system [18] is an XML-based language designed for the markup of analysed human argument. The syntax of AML is specified in a Document Type Definition (DTD) which imposes structural constraints on the form of valid AML documents. AML was primarily produced for use in the Araucaria tool, though has more recently been adopted elsewhere.

These various attempts at providing argument mark-up languages share two major limitations. Firstly, each particular language is designed for use with a specific tool (usually for the purpose of facilitating argument visualisation) rather than for facilitating inter-operability of arguments among a variety of tools. As a consequence, the semantics of arguments specified using these languages is tightly coupled with particular schemes to be interpreted in a specific tool and according to a specific underlying theory. Thus, for example, arguments in the Compendium concept mapping tool are to be interpreted in relation to a rigorous theory of issue-based information systems. Clearly, in order to enable true interoperability of arguments and argument structures we need an argument description language that can be extended beyond a particular argumentation theory, enabling us to accommodate a variety of argumentation theories and schemes. Another limitation of the above argument mark-up languages is that they are primarily aimed at enabling users to structure arguments through diagrammatic linkage of natural language sentences. Hence, these mark-up languages are not designed to process formal logical statements such as those used within multi-agent systems. For example, AML imposes structural limitations on well formed arguments, but provides no semantic model. Such a semantic model is an important requirement in order to enable the automatic processing of argument structures by heterogeneous software agents.

In order to address these limitations, a group of researchers interested in 'argument and computation' gathered for a workshop[3] whose aim was to sketch an *Argumentation Interchange Format (AIF)* which consolidates –where possible– the work in argumentation mark-up languages and multi-agent system frameworks by focusing on two main aims:

- to facilitate the development of (closed or open) multi-agent systems capable of argumentation-based reasoning and interaction using a shared formalism;
- to facilitate data interchange among tools for argument manipulation and argument visualization.

This article describes and analyzes the main components of the draft specification for AIF. It must be remarked that AIF as it stands represents a consensus 'abstract model' established by researchers across fields of argumentation, artificial intelligence and multi-agent systems. In its current form, this specification is intended as a starting point for further discussion and elaboration by the community, rather than an attempt at a definitive, all encompassing model. In order to demonstrate the power of the proposed approach, we describe use cases which show how AIF fits

---

[3] AgentLink Technical Forum Group meeting, Budapest, Hungary, September 2005.

into some argument-based tools and applications. We also illustrate a number of concrete realisations or 'reifications' of the proposed abstract model.

2 The Core AIF

In this section, we briefly describe the first AIF draft specification, as reported in more detail elsewhere [6] and subsequently formalised in [16, 14].

The core AIF has two types of nodes: *information nodes* (or *I-nodes*) and *scheme nodes* (or *S-nodes*). These are represented by two disjoint sets, $\mathcal{N}_I \subset \mathcal{N}$ and $\mathcal{N}_S \subset \mathcal{N}$, respectively. Information nodes are used to represent *propositional* information contained in an argument, such as a claim, premise, data, etc. S-nodes capture the application of *schemes* (i.e. patterns of reasoning). Such schemes may be domain-independent patterns of reasoning, which resemble rules of inference in deductive logics but broadened to include non-deductive inference. The schemes themselves belong to a class, $\mathcal{S}$, and are classified into the types: *rule of inference scheme*, *conflict scheme*, and *preference scheme*. We denote these using the disjoint sets $\mathcal{S}^R$, $\mathcal{S}^C$ and $\mathcal{S}^P$, respectively. The predicate (uses : $\mathcal{N}_S \times \mathcal{S}$) is used to express the fact that a particular scheme node uses (or instantiates) a particular scheme. The AIF thus provides an ontology for expressing schemes and instances of schemes, and constrains the latter to the domain of the former via the function uses, i.e., $\forall n \in \mathcal{N}_S, \exists s \in \mathcal{S}$ such that uses(n, s).

The present ontology has three different types of scheme nodes: *rule of inference application nodes* (or *RA-nodes*), *preference application nodes* (or *PA-nodes*) and *conflict application nodes* (or *CA-nodes*). These are represented as three disjoint sets: $\mathcal{N}_S^{RA} \subseteq \mathcal{N}_S$, $\mathcal{N}_S^{PA} \subseteq \mathcal{N}_S$, and $\mathcal{N}_S^{CA} \subseteq \mathcal{N}_S$, respectively. The word 'application' on each of these types was introduced in the AIF as a reminder that these nodes function as instances, not classes, of possibly generic inference rules. Intuitively, $\mathcal{N}_S^{RA}$ captures nodes that represent (possibly non-deductive) rules of inference, $\mathcal{N}_S^{CA}$ captures applications of criteria (declarative specifications) defining conflict (e.g. among a proposition and its negation, etc.), and $\mathcal{N}_S^{PA}$ are applications of (possibly abstract) criteria of preference among evaluated nodes.

The AIF specification does not type its edges. The (informal) semantics of edges can be inferred from the types of nodes they connect. One of the restrictions is that no outgoing edge from an I-node can be linked directly to another I-node. This ensures that the type of any relationship between two pieces of information must be specified explicitly via an intermediate S-node.

Definition 19.1. (Argument Network) An *argument network* Φ is a graph consisting of:

- a set $\mathcal{N} = \mathcal{N}_I \cup \mathcal{N}_S$ of vertices (or *nodes*); and
- a binary relation $\xrightarrow{edge}$: $\mathcal{N} \times \mathcal{N}$ representing edges.

where $\nexists(i, j) \in \xrightarrow{edge}$ where both $i \in \mathcal{N}_I$ and $j \in \mathcal{N}_I$

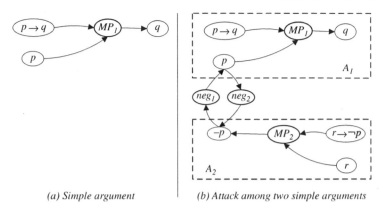

(a) Simple argument | (b) Attack among two simple arguments

Fig. 19.1 Examples of simple arguments; S-Nodes denoted with a thicker border

A *simple* argument can be represented by linking premises to a conclusion.

Definition 19.2. (Simple Argument) A *simple argument*, in network Φ and schemes $\mathcal{S}$, is a tuple $\langle P, \tau, c \rangle$ where:

- $P \subseteq \mathcal{N}_I$ is a set of nodes denoting premises;
- $\tau \in \mathcal{N}_S^{RA}$ is a rule of inference application node;
- $c \in \mathcal{N}_I$ is a node denoting the conclusion;

such that $\tau \xrightarrow{edge} c$, uses$(\tau, s)$ where $s \in \mathcal{S}$, and $\forall p \in P$ we have $p \xrightarrow{edge} \tau$.

Following is a description of a simple argument in propositional logic, depicted in Figure 19.1(a).

Example 19.1. **(Simple Argument)**

The tuple $A_1 = \langle \{p, p \rightarrow q\}, MP_1, q \rangle$ is a simple argument in propositional language $\mathcal{L}$, where p, $(p \rightarrow q) \in \mathcal{N}_I$ are nodes representing premises, and $q \in \mathcal{N}_I$ is a node representing the conclusion. In between them, the node $MP_1 \in \mathcal{N}_S^{RA}$ is a rule of inference application node (i.e., RA-node) that uses the *modus ponens* natural deduction scheme, which can be formally written as follows: uses$(MP_1, \forall A, B \in \mathcal{L} \frac{A \quad A \rightarrow B}{B})$.

An attack or conflict from one information or scheme node to another information or scheme node is captured through a CA-node, which captures the type of conflict. The attacker is linked to the CA-node, and the CA-node is subsequently linked to the attacked node. Note that since edges are directed, each CA-node captures attack in one direction. Symmetric attack would require two CA-nodes, one in each direction. The following example describes a conflict between two simple arguments (see Figure 19.1(b)).

Example 19.2. **(Simple Arguments in Conflict)**

Recall the simple argument $A_1 = \langle \{p, p \rightarrow q\}, MP_1, q \rangle$. And consider another simple argument $A_2 = \langle \{r, r \rightarrow \neg p\}, MP_2, \neg p \rangle$. Argument A_2 undermines A_1 by supporting the negation of the latter's premise. This (symmetric) propositional conflict is captured through two CA-nodes: neg_1 and neg_2, both of which insantiate a conflict scheme based on propositional contraries.

3 An Extended AIF in RDF

In this section, we present a brief description of an implementation of an extended AIF ontology which may be used as a seed for a variety of Semantic Web argument annotation tools. The ontology is described in detail in a recent joint paper with other colleagues [16]. It enables the annotation of arguments using RDF, and is based on the AIF, extended with Walton's account of argumentation schemes [22].

3.1 Representing Argument Schemes

Recall that schemes are *forms* of argument, representing stereotypical ways of drawing inferences from particular patterns of premises to conclusions. We consider the set of schemes $\mathcal{S}$ as themselves nodes in the argument network. And we introduce a new class of nodes, called *forms* (or *F-nodes*), captured in the set $\mathcal{N}_F \subseteq \mathcal{N}$. Two distinct types of forms are presented: *premise descriptors* and *conclusion descriptors*, denoted by $\mathcal{N}_F^{Prem} \subseteq \mathcal{N}_F$ and $\mathcal{N}_F^{Conc} \subseteq \mathcal{N}_F$, respectively. As can be seen in Figure 19.2, we can now explicitly link each node in the actual argument (the four unshaded nodes at the bottom right) to the form node it instantiates (the four shaded nodes at the top right).[4] Notice that here, we expressed the predicate 'uses' with the edge $\xrightarrow{fulfilsScheme}: \mathcal{N}_S \times \mathcal{S}$.

Since each critical question corresponds either to a presumption or an exception, we provide explicit descriptions of the presumptions and exceptions associated with each scheme. To express the scheme's presumptions, we add a new type of F-node called *presumption*, represented by the set $\mathcal{N}_F^{Pres} \subseteq \mathcal{N}_F$, and linked to the scheme via a new edge type, $\xrightarrow{hasPresumption}: \mathcal{S} \times \mathcal{N}_F^{Pres}$. This is shown in the three (shaded) presumption nodes at the bottom left of Figure 19.2. As for representing exceptions, the AIF offers a more expressive possibility. In just the same way that stereotypical patterns of the passage of deductive, inductive and presumptive inference can be captured as rule of inference schemes, so too can the stereotypical ways of characterising conflict be captured as conflict schemes. Conflict, like inference, has some patterns that are reminiscent of deduction in their absolutism (such as the conflict between a proposition and its complement), as well as others that are reminiscent

---

[4] To improve readability, we will start using typed edges. All typed edges will take the form $\xrightarrow{type}$, where *type* is the type of edge, and $\xrightarrow{type} \subseteq \xrightarrow{edge}$.

of non-deductive inference in their heuristic nature (such as the conflict between two courses of action with incompatible resource allocations). Thus, exceptions can most accurately be presented as conflict scheme descriptions (see top left of Figure 19.2).

Finally, in Walton's account of schemes, some presumptions may be implicitly or explicitly *entailed* by a premise. While the truth of a premise may be questioned directly, questioning associated with the underlying presumptions can be more specific, capturing the nuances expressed in Walton's characterisation. This relationship, between is captured explicitly using a predicate ($\xrightarrow{entails}: \mathcal{N}_F^{Prem} \times \mathcal{N}_F^{Pres}$).

Definition 19.3. (Presumptive Inference Scheme Description) A *presumptive inference scheme description* is a tuple $\langle PD, \alpha, cd, \Psi, \Gamma, \xrightarrow{entails} \rangle$ where:

- $PD \subseteq \mathcal{N}_F^{Prem}$ is a set of *premise descriptors*;
- $\alpha \in \mathcal{S}^R$ is the scheme;
- $cd \in \mathcal{N}_F^{Conc}$ is a *conclusion descriptor*.
- $\Psi \subseteq \mathcal{N}_F^{Pres}$ is a set of *presumption descriptors*;
- $\Gamma \subseteq \mathcal{S}^C$ is a set of *exceptions*; and
- $\xrightarrow{entails} \subseteq \mathcal{N}_F^{Prem} \times \mathcal{N}_F^{Pres}$

such that:

- $\alpha \xrightarrow{hasConcDesc} cd$;
- $\forall pd \in PD$ we have $\alpha \xrightarrow{hasPremiseDesc} pd$;
- $\forall \psi \in \Psi$ we have $\alpha \xrightarrow{hasPresumption} \psi$;
- $\forall \gamma \in \Gamma$ we have $\alpha \xrightarrow{hasException} \gamma$;

With the description of the scheme in place, we can now show how argument structures can be linked to scheme structures. In particular, we define a presumptive argument, which is an extension of the definition of a simple argument.

Definition 19.4. (Presumptive Argument) A *presumptive argument* based on presumptive inference scheme description $\langle PD, \alpha, cd, \Psi, \Gamma, \xrightarrow{entails} \rangle$ is a tuple $\langle P, \tau, c \rangle$ where:

- $P \subseteq \mathcal{N}_I$ is a set of nodes denoting premises;
- $\tau \in \mathcal{N}_S^{RA}$ is a rule of inference application node;
- $c \in \mathcal{N}_I$ is a node denoting the conclusion;

such that:

- $\tau \xrightarrow{edge} c$; $\forall p \in P$ we have $p \xrightarrow{edge} \tau$;
- $\tau \xrightarrow{fulfilsScheme} \alpha$; $c \xrightarrow{fulfilsConclusionDesc} cd$; and
- $\xrightarrow{fulfilsPremiseDesc} \subseteq P \times PD$ corresponds to a one-to-one correspondence from P to PD.

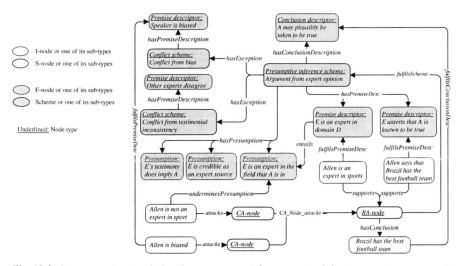

Fig. 19.2 An argument network showing an argument from expert opinion, two counter-arguments undermining a presumption and an exception, and the descriptions of the schemes used by the argument and attackers. *A:* Brazil has the best football team: Allen is a sports expert and he says so; *B:* But Allen is biased, and he is not an expert in sports!

3.2 Implementation in ArgDF

We implemented our extended ontology using RDF and RDFS [2], and call the resulting ontology AIF-RDF. In summary, we view elements of arguments and schemes (e.g. premises, conclusions) as RDF resources, and connect them using binary predicates as described earlier.

ArgDF[5] is a Semantic Web-based system that uses the AIF-RDF ontology. The Sesame RDF repository offers the central features needed by the system, namely: (i) uploading RDF and RDFS single statements or complete files; (ii) deleting RDF statements; (iii) querying the repository using the Semantic Web query language RQL; and (iv) returning RDF query results in a variety of computer processable formats including XML, HTML or RDF.

Creating New Arguments: The system presents the available schemes, and allows the user to choose the scheme to which the argument belongs. Details of the selected scheme are then retrieved from the repository, and the form of the argument is displayed to the user, who then creates the conclusion followed by the premises.

Support/Attack of Existing Expressions: The expressions (i.e. premises or conclusions) in the repository can be displayed, supported or attacked. When a user chooses to support an existing premise through a new argument/scheme, this premise will be both a premise in one argument, and a conclusion in another. Thus, the system enables argument *chaining*. If the user chooses to *attack* an expression, on the other hand, s/he will be redirected to choose an appropriate conflict scheme,

---

[5] ArgDF is a proof-of-concept prototype and can be accessed at: http://www.argdf.org

and create a new argument whose conclusion is linked to the existing conclusion via a conflict application node (as in Example 19.2).

Searching through Arguments: The system enables users to search existing arguments, by specifying text found in the premises or the conclusion, the type of relationship between these two (i.e. support or attack), and the scheme(s) used. For example, one can search for arguments, based on expert opinion, *against* the '*war on Iraq*,' and mentioning '*weapons of mass destruction*' in their premises. An RQL query is generated in the background.

Linking Existing Premises to a New Argument: While creating premises supporting a given conclusion through a new argument, the user can *re-use* existing premises from the system. This premise thus contributes to multiple arguments in a *divergent* structure. This functionality can be useful, for example, in Web-based applications that allow users to use existing Web content (e.g. a news article, a legal document) to support new or existing claims.

Attacking Arguments through Implicit Assumptions: With our account of presumptions and exceptions, it becomes possible to construct an automatic mechanism for *presuming*. ArgDF allows the user to inspect an existing argument, allowing the exploration of the hidden assumptions (i.e. presumptions and exceptions) by which its inference is warranted. This leads the way for possible implicit attacks on the argument through pointing out an exception, or through undermining one of its presumptions (as shown in Figure 19.2). This is exactly the role that Walton envisaged for his critical questions [22]. Thus, ArgDF exploits knowledge about implicit assumptions in order to enable richer interaction between the user and the arguments.

Creation of New Schemes: The user can create new schemes through the interface of ArgDF without having to modify the ontology. This feature enables a variety of user-created schemes to be incorporated, thus offering flexibility not found in any other argument-support system.

4 The AIF in Description Logic

In ArgDF, the actual arguments are specified by instantiating nodes, while actual schemes are created by instantiating the "scheme" class. Then, argument instances (and their constituent parts) are linked to scheme instances (and their part descriptors) in order to show what scheme the argument follows.

From the above, it is clear that ArgDF's reification of the AIF causes some redundancy at the instance level. Both arguments and schemes are described with explicit structure at the instance level. As a result, the property "*fulfilsScheme*" does not capture the fact that a S-node represents an instantiation of some generic *class of arguments* (i.e. scheme). Having such relationship expressed explicitly can enable reasoning about the classification of schemes.

In this section, we present another AIF-based ontology, which captures schemes as classes of arguments explicitly. The AIF model is reified by interpreting schemes as classes and S-nodes as instances of those classes; in this case, the semantics of the *"uses"* edge can be interpreted as *"instance – of"*.

We formalise the new ontology using Description Logics (DLs) [1], a family of logical formalisms that have initially been designed for the representation of conceptual knowledge in Artificial Intelligence. DL knowledge representation languages provide means for expressing knowledge about concepts composing a terminology (TBox), as well as knowledge about concrete facts (i.e. objects instantiating the concepts) which form a world description (ABox). Since Description Logics are provided with a formal syntax and formal model-theoretic semantics, sound and complete reasoning algorithms can be formulated. Our summary here of AIF in OWL-DL draws upon [15].

4.1 The ontology

At the highest level, three concepts are identified: *statements* that can be made (that correspond to AIF I-nodes), *schemes* that describe arguments made up of statements (that correspond to AIF S-nodes) and *authors* of those statements and arguments (formerly just properties in AIF). All these concepts are disjoint.

$$Scheme \sqsubseteq Thing \qquad Statement \sqsubseteq Thing \qquad Author \sqsubseteq Thing$$
$$Author \sqsubseteq \neg Scheme \qquad Author \sqsubseteq \neg Statement \qquad Statement \sqsubseteq \neg Scheme$$

As with the ArgDF reification of AIF, different specialisations of scheme are identified; for example the rule scheme (which describes the class of arguments), conflict scheme, preference scheme etc.

$$RuleScheme \sqsubseteq Scheme \qquad ConflictScheme \sqsubseteq Scheme \qquad PreferenceScheme \sqsubseteq Scheme$$

Each of these schemes can be further classified. For example, a rule scheme may be further specialised to capture deductive or presumptive arguments. The same can be done with different types of conflicts, preferences, and so on.

$$DeductiveArgument \sqsubseteq RuleScheme \qquad LogicalConflict \sqsubseteq ConflictScheme$$
$$InductiveArgument \sqsubseteq RuleScheme \qquad PresumptivePreference \sqsubseteq PreferenceScheme$$
$$PresumptiveArgument \sqsubseteq RuleScheme \qquad LogicalPreference \sqsubseteq PreferenceScheme$$

A number of properties (or *roles* in DL terminology) are defined, which can be used to refer to additional information about instances of the ontology, such as authors of arguments, the creation date of a scheme, and so on. The domains and ranges of these properties are restricted appropriately and described below.

$$\top \sqsubseteq \forall creationDate.Date \qquad \top \sqsubseteq \forall creationDate^-.Scheme$$
$$\top \sqsubseteq \forall argTitle.String \qquad \top \sqsubseteq \forall argTitle^-.RuleScheme$$
$$\top \sqsubseteq \forall authorName.String \qquad \top \sqsubseteq \forall authorName^-.Author$$
$$Scheme \sqsubseteq \forall hasAuthor.Author \qquad Scheme \sqsubseteq= 1creationDate$$
$$RuleScheme \sqsubseteq= 1argTitle$$

To capture the structural relationships between different schemes, their components should first be classified. This is done by classifying their premises, conclusions, assumptions and exceptions into different *classes of statements*. For example, at the highest level, we may classify statements as declarative, comparative or imperative, etc.

$DeclarativeStatement \sqsubseteq Statement$ $ImperativeStatement \sqsubseteq Statement$
$ComparativeStatement \sqsubseteq Statement$ $\ldots$

Actual statement instances have a property that describes their textual content.

$\top \sqsubseteq \forall claimText.String$ $\top \sqsubseteq \forall claimText^{-}.Statement$

When defining a particular RuleScheme (i.e. class of arguments), we capture the relationship between each scheme and its components. Each argument has exactly one conclusion and at least one premise (which are, themselves, instances of class "Statement"). Furthermore, presumptive arguments may have assumptions and exceptions.

$RuleScheme \sqsubseteq \forall hasConclusion.Statement$ $RuleScheme \sqsubseteq \geq 1 hasPremise$
$RuleScheme \sqsubseteq = 1 hasConclusion$ $PresumptiveArgument \sqsubseteq \forall hasAssumption.Statement$
$RuleScheme \sqsubseteq \forall hasPremise.Statement$ $PresumptiveArgument \sqsubseteq \forall hasException.Statement$

4.2 Example

With this in place, it becomes possible to further classify the above statement types to cater for a variety of schemes. For example, to capture the scheme for "Argument from Position to Know," the following classes of declarative statements need to be defined (each class is listed with its property `formDescription`[6] that describes its typical form).

$PositionToHaveKnowledgeStmnt \sqsubseteq DeclarativeStatement$

   `formDescription` : "E is in position to know whether A is true (false)"

$KnowledgeAssertionStmnt \sqsubseteq DeclarativeStatement$

   `formDescription` : "E asserts that A is true(false)"

$KnowledgePositionStmnt \sqsubseteq DeclarativeStatement$

   `formDescription` : "A may plausibly be taken to be true(false)"

$LackOfReliabilityStmnt \sqsubseteq DeclarativeStatement$

   `formDescription` : "E is not a reliable source"

Now it is possible to fully describe the scheme for "Argument from Position to Know." Following are the necessary and sufficient conditions for an instance to be classified as an argument from position to know.

$ArgFromPositionToKnow \equiv (PresumptiveArgument \sqcap \exists hasConclusion.KnowledgePositionStmnt \sqcap$

$\exists hasPremise.PositionToHaveKnowledgeStmnt \sqcap \exists hasPremise.KnowledgeAssertionStmnt)$

$ArgFromPositionToKnow \sqsubseteq \exists hasException.LackOfReliabilityStmnt$

Other argument schemes (e.g. argument from analogy, argument from sign, etc.) can be defined in the same way.

---

[6] formDescription is an annotation property in OWL-DL. Annotation properties are used to add meta-data about classes.

4.3 Representing Conflicts Among Arguments

Conflict among arguments are captured through different specialisations of *ConflictScheme* such as *GeneralConflict* and *ExceptionConflict*.

$$ExceptionConflict \sqsubseteq ConflictScheme \qquad\qquad GeneralConflict \sqsubseteq ConflictScheme$$

GeneralConflict instances capture simple symmetric and asymmetric attacks among arguments while *ExceptionConflict* instances represent exceptions to rules of inference. The definition of *ConflictScheme* and *Statement* classes have been extended to include the appropriate restrictions on properties used to represent attacks among different arguments.

$$ConflictScheme \sqsubseteq \forall confAttacks.(Statement \sqcup RuleScheme) \qquad Statement \sqsubseteq \forall attacks.ConflictScheme$$
$$ConflictScheme \sqsubseteq \forall isAttacked.Statement \qquad\qquad Statement \sqsubseteq \forall confIsAttacked.ConflictScheme$$
$$ConflictScheme \sqsubseteq \forall underminesAssumption.Statement$$

Figures 19.3(a) to 19.3(d) illustrate how instances of *ConflictScheme* and the related properties are used to represent four different types of conflicts among arguments, namely, asymmetric attacks (a), symmetric attacks (b), undermining assumptions (c) and attacking by supporting existing exceptions (d).

In these figures, argument instances are denoted by Arg_n, premises are denoted by PX_n, conclusions by CX, assumptions by $AsmX_n$, exceptions by $ExcpX_n$ and instances of general conflict and exception conflict as GC_n and EC_1 respectively where $X = \{A, B, C, ...\}$ and n represents the set of natural numbers $\{1,2,3,...\}$.

5 Reasoning over Argument Structures

In this section, we describe two ways in which the expressive power of Description Logic and its support for reasoning can be used to enhance user interaction with arguments. The features discussed here were implemented in a pilot system called *Avicenna*, utilizing the DL-compatible Web Ontology Language (OWL) .

5.1 Automatic Classification of Schemes and Arguments

In this section, we describe the general inference pattern behind classification of argument schemes (and their instances). This inference is based on the statement hierarchy and the conditions defined on each scheme. Two examples of this inference are also provided.

Consider two specialisations (sub-classes) of *PresumptiveArgument* : *PresScheme*1 and *PresScheme*2. An instance of the first scheme, *PresScheme*1, might have an instance of *CA* class as its conclusion and premises from classes $(PA_1, PA_2, ..., PA_n)$, where classes *CA* and $(PA_1, PA_2, ..., PA_n)$ are specialisations of the class *Statement*. Similarly, *PresScheme*2 has members of *CB* class as its

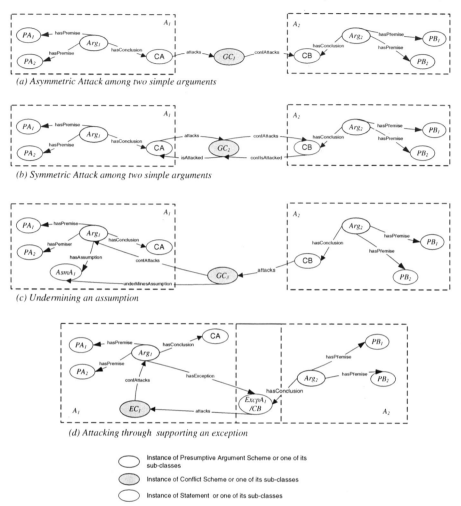

(a) Asymmetric Attack among two simple arguments

(b) Symmetric Attack among two simple arguments

(c) Undermining an assumption

(d) Attacking through supporting an exception

○ Instance of Presumptive Argument Scheme or one of its sub-classes

◔ Instance of Conflict Scheme or one of its sub-classes

○ Instance of Statement or one of its sub-classes

Fig. 19.3 Representation of different types of attack among arguments

conclusion and its premises are from classes $(PB_1, PB_2, ..., PB_m$ where CB and $(PB_1, PB_2, ..., PB_m)$ are specialisations of *Statement* and $m >= n$. Let us assume that a relationship exists between CA and CB, that they are either referring to the same class or else that the latter is a specialisation of the former, i.e., $(CB \equiv CA) \vee (CB \sqsubseteq CA)$.

We also assume a relationship exists among the premises of these two schemes in a way that for every premise class of *PresScheme*1, there is a corresponding premise class in *PresScheme*2 that is either equal to or is a specialisation of the premise class in *PresScheme*1 (the opposite does not hold as we have allowed that *PresScheme*2 could have greater number of premises than *PresScheme*1), i.e. $\forall x \in 1, 2, ...m, \forall y \in 1, 2, ..., n, (PB_x \equiv PA_y) \vee (PB_x \sqsubseteq PA_y)$.

The necessary and sufficient conditions on *PresScheme*1 and *PresScheme*2 are defined as:

$$PresScheme1 \equiv (PresumptiveArgument \sqcap \exists hasConclusion.CA \sqcap \exists hasPremise.PA1 \sqcap \exists hasPremise.PA2 \sqcap$$
$$\exists hasPremise.(...) \sqcap \exists hasPremise.PAn)$$

$$PresScheme2 \equiv (PresumptiveArgument \sqcap \exists hasConclusion.CB \sqcap \exists hasPremise.PB1 \sqcap \exists hasPremise.PB2 \sqcap$$
$$\exists hasPremise.(...) \sqcap \exists hasPremise.PBm)$$

Considering the statement hierarchy and the necessary and sufficient conditions defined on each class, *PresScheme*2 is inferred by the description logic reasoner as the sub-class of *PresScheme*1 in case the number of premises in *PresScheme*2 is greater than number of premises in *PresScheme*1 (i.e. $m > n$). In case the number of premises are the same (i.e $m = n$), and at least one of the premises of *PresScheme*2 is a specialisation of a premise in *PresScheme*1 and/or the conclusion *CB* is a specialisation of *CA*, *PresScheme*2 is also inferred as the sub-class of *PresScheme*1.

Following the above explanation, due to the hierarchy of specialisation among different descriptors of scheme components (statements) as well as the necessary and sufficient conditions defined on each scheme, it is possible to infer the classification hierarchy among schemes.

An interesting example is offered by the specialisation relationship that can be inferred between "Fear Appeal Argument" and "Argument from Negative Consequences".

Scheme 1 *Argument From Negative Consequences*

- Premise: *If A is brought about, bad consequences will plausibly occur.*
- Conclusion: *A should not be brought about.*
- *Critical Questions*

   1. *How strong is the probability or plausibility that these cited consequences will (may, might, must) occur?*
   2. *What evidence, if any, supported the claim that these consequences will (may, might, must) occur if A is brought about?*
   3. *Are there consequences of the opposite value that ought to be taken into account?*

Scheme 2 *Fear Appeal Argument*

- Fearful situation premise: *Here is a situation that is fearful to you.*
- Conditional premise: *If you carry out A, then the negative consequences portrayed in this fearful situation will happen to you.*
- Conclusion: *You should not carry out A.*
- *Critical Questions*

   1. *Should the situation represented really be fearful to me, or is it an irrational fear that is appealed to?*
   2. *If I don't carry out A, will that stop the negative consequences from happening?*

3. If I do carry out A, how likely is it that the negative consequences will happen?

The necessary and sufficient conditions of the "Argument from Negative Consequences" are detailed as:

ArgNegatvieConseq ≡ (*PresumptiveArgument* ⊓
∃*hasConclusion.ForbiddenActionStmnt* ⊓
∃*hasPremise.BadConsequenceStmnt*)

Likewise, for "Fear Appeal Argument":

FearAppealArg ≡ (*PresumptiveArgument* ⊓ ∃*hasConclusion.ForbiddenActionStmnt* ⊓
∃*hasPremise.FearfulSituationStmnt* ⊓ ∃*hasPremise.FearedBadConsequenceStmnt*)

The statements are defined below. Note that the "Feared Bad Consequence" statement is a specialization of "Bad Consequence" statement, since it limits the bad consequence to those portrayed in the fearful situation.

BadConsequenceStmnt ⊑ *DeclarativeStatement*

  formDescription : "If A is brought about, bad consequences will plausibly occur"

ForbiddenActionStmnt ⊑ *DeclarativeStatement*

  formDescription : "A should not be brought about"

FearfulSituationStmnt ⊑ *DeclarativeStatement*

  formDescription : "Here is a situation that is fearful to you"

FearedBadConsequenceStmnt ⊑ *BadConsequenceStmnt*

  formDescription : "If you carry out A, then the negative consequences portrayed
in this fearful situation will happen to you"

As a result of classification of schemes into hierarchies, instances belonging to a certain scheme class will also be inferred to belong to all its super-classes. For example, if the user queries to return all instances of "Argument from Negative Consequences," the instances of all specializations of the scheme, such as all argument instances from "Fear Appeal Arguments" are also returned.

5.2 Inferring Critical Questions

In this section we describe the general inference pattern behind inference of critical questions from an argumentation scheme's super-classes and provide an example.

In the previous section we described an assumption about two specialisations of *PresumptiveArgument*, *PresScheme1* and *PresScheme2* and the fact that *PresScheme2* was inferred to be the sub-class of *PresScheme1*. Each of these schemes might have different assumptions and exceptions defined on their classes. For example, *PresScheme1* has *AsmA1* and *AsmA2* as its assumptions and *ExcA1* as its exception. *PresScheme2* has *AsmB1* and *ExcB1* as its assumption and exception respectively. *AsmA1*, *AsmA2*, *AsmB1*, *ExcA1* and *ExcB1* are specialisations of *Statement* class. The the necessary conditions defined on classes *PresScheme1* and *PresScheme2* are:

PresScheme1 ⊑ ∃*hasAssumption.AsmA1*
PresScheme1 ⊑ ∃*hasAssumption.AsmA2*
PresScheme1 ⊑ ∃*hasException.ExcA1*

*PresScheme2 ⊑ ∃hasAssumption.AsmB*1
*PresScheme2 ⊑ ∃hasException.ExcB*1

Since *PresScheme2* has been inferred by the reasoner as the specialization (sub-class) of *PresScheme*1, a query to the system to return all assumptions and exceptions of *PresScheme2*, is able to return all those explicitly defined on the scheme class (i.e. *AsmB*1 and *ExcB*1) as well as those defined on any of its super-classes (in this case: *AsmA*1, *AsmA*2 and *ExcA*1).

Since the schemes are classified by the reasoner into a hierarchy, if certain assumptions or exceptions are not explicitly stated for a specific scheme but are defined on any of its super-classes, the system is able to infer and add those assumptions and exceptions to instances of that specific scheme class. Since critical questions enable evaluation of an argument, inferring additional questions for each scheme will enhance the analysis process.

Consider the critical questions for "Fear Appeal Argument" and "Argument from Negative Consequences" given in the previous section. These critical questions are represented in the ontology through the following statements:

IrrationalFearAppealStmnt ⊑ DeclarativeStatement

   `formDescription` : "It is an irrational fear that is appealed to"

PreventionOfBadConsequenceStmnt ⊑ DeclarativeStatement

   `formDescription` : "If A is not carried out, this will stop the negative consequences from happening"

OppositeConsequencesStmnt ⊑ DeclarativeStatement

   `formDescription` : "There are consequences of the opposite value that ought to be taken into account"

StrongConsequenceProbabilityStmnt ⊑ DeclarativeStatement

   `formDescription` : "There is a strong probability that the cited consequences will occur"

ConsequenceBackUpEvidenceStmnt ⊑ DeclarativeStatement

   `formDescription` : "There is evidence that supports the claim that these

     consequences will occur if A is brought about."

The necessary conditions on "Argument from Negative Consequences" that define these critical questions are:

ArgNegatvieConseq ⊑ ∃hasException.OppositeConsequencesStmnt

ArgNegatvieConseq ⊑ ∃hasAssumption.StrongConsequenceProbabilityStmnt

ArgNegatvieConseq ⊑ ∃hasAssumption.ConsequenceBackUpEvidenceStmnt

Likewise, the necessary conditions on "Fear Appeal Argument" are:

FearAppealArg ⊑ ∃hasException.IrrationalFearAppealStmnt

FearAppealArg ⊑ ∃hasAssumption.PreventionOfBadConsequenceStmnt

FearAppealArg ⊑ ∃hasAssumption.StrongConsequenceProbabilityStmnt

"Fear Appeal Argument" is classified as a sub-class of "Argument from Negative Consequences." The critical questions 2 and 3 of "Argument from Negative Consequences" have not been explicitly defined on "Fear Appeal Argument", but can be inferred through reasoning.

6 Current Issues and Future Directions

The AIF will come into its own as it demonstrates that it can be used to build bridges between applications, and, perhaps, between theories. Work with the Araucaria diagramming tool [18] has demonstrated (at least in the specific area of linguistic analysis) how carefully designed representation can support analysts working in different traditions, and to a certain extent can help reuse across domains. At the time of writing, Araucaria has in the region of 10,000 users. Some few of these submit analyses using a number of different analytical techniques (Toulmin schema, argumentation schemes, Wigmore charts, etc.) to a centralised corpus. Though there are analysed arguments from an enormous range of domains, one that is particularly interesting is the legal domain. Wigmore charts were designed specifically for analysis of cases and are rarely used in other domains. The Toulmin-schema is rooted in legal analysis though is now much more widely used. Walton's approach to argumentation schemes has generic application, though one that encompasses use in law [23]. These various degrees of specificity to the legal domain counterbalance the number of analysts working in each tradition (relatively few using Wigmore, many more using Walton argumentation schemes). As a result, the part of the corpus that might be said to encompass examples from the legal domain has a theoretically diverse basis. Despite this diversity, that part of the corpus has been successfully used in an unrelated project investigating discourse markers in legal argumentation [13]. What has made this possible is the underlying unifying representation.

This example shows in microcosm what the AIF is trying to do right across computational uses of argument. Though it is still early days, there are a number of systems, tools and techniques that are working, planning or considering implementation to support AIF. We provide a brief overview of a number of them here to give an indication of the range of potential applications, and the types of role that AIF might play.

Argkit and Dungine. Argkit[7] is designed to be a reusable, plug and play code-base for developing and linking together applications that use argument, and particularly those that have a requirement for processing abstract argument [20]. In a compelling demonstration, South has shown how the Dungine component, which performs computations according to Dung acceptability semantics, can be connected to Araucaria to compute acceptability of real arguments on the fly. Though there are theoretical challenges with connecting models of abstract and concrete argumentation, this proof of concept demonstrator shows how the two areas of research might be harmonised. Argkit plans have scheduled integration of AIF as a way to support such integration more broadly across other sources of both concrete and abstract argumentation.

Araucaria. The analysis tool, Araucaria [18], has a large user base, but is now suffering from limitations of its underlying representation and increasingly dated interface and interaction metaphors. A large-scale rewrite is underway, which provides

---

[7] http://www.argkit.org

AIF support: an early alpha is available with reusable code modules for processing AIF resources.

Rationale. Rationale [21] is a highly polished commercial product for argument visualisation in a primarily educational context, which has been recently complemented by a new product from the same company, Austhink Software Pty Ltd[8], providing related functionality targeted at a commercial context. Rationale, in particular, has explored interaction with resources that Araucaria produces and vice versa. From Austhink's commercial point of view, the cost of developing an AIF component (even if low) would need to be offset against value; that value will only be clear when there is a critical mass of other systems and environments that can work with AIF. This is perhaps an inevitable part of the relationship between academic and commercial sides of research in argumentation.

Compendium. Compendium is similar to Rationale in a number of ways in that it is a polished tool with its origins in a research programme but now mature with a wide user-bases supported by the Compendium Institute[9], run by the Open University. Compendium focuses not just on arguments, but on a wide range of semantic types (issues, decisions, etc.). It has been used with other tools, such as Araucaria, which can provide embedded support for building the fine-grained structure of arguments which form components of Compendium maps. Compendium has also made use of Araucaria's argumentation scheme representation, by automatically importing the various "*schemesets*" that capture the definitions of schemes offered by various authors. The import makes those same definitions available as templates to Compendium users[10]. Richer integration with more detailed models of these schemes would be made possible by AIF import along these same lines.

Cohere. Cohere is an ambitious project that aims to bring Compendium-like flexibility in 'sense-making' to a broad online audience. Though it supports a very broad range of semantic relationships between componets, it has a particular focus on those that might be considered argumentative. As a part of its mission to be "an idea management tool"[11], Buckingham Shum states that, "A key priority is to provide Argument Interchange Format compatibility" [3] to provide smooth interoperability with both other tools in the space (such as those listed here) and also to provide Cohere with structured access to additional argument resources.

Carneades. The Carneades system is both a framework for reasoning about arguments and a system that implements that framework. Carneades is sited squarely within an AI & Law context [9], and has already worked to integrate with the Legal Knowledge Interchange Format, LKIF. At its core, however, lies argumentation-based representation and reasoning at both concrete and abstract levels (though, interestingly in regards to the latter not using Dung's popular approach [7]). As a result, the Carneades work is exploring the possibility of using AIF as a mechanism for exporting and importing argument structures from other systems.

---

[8] http://www.austhink.com

[9] http://compendium.open.ac.uk/institute

[10] http://compendium.open.ac.uk/compendium-arg-schemes.html

[11] http://kmi.open.ac.uk/technologies/cohere

ArguGRID. ArguGRID is a large EU project funded under FP7. Though its goals cover a broad spectrum of activity, models of argumentation lie at its centre. The project aims to use argumentation to provide semantically rich processes for negotiating services across grid networks – see e.g. [11]. Drawing heavily upon abstract argumentation models, it needs AIF to develop far enough that it provides strong support for abstract argumentation before AIF can play an important role. In the meantime, AIF remains on the roadmap of development for ArguGRID systems.

AAC. The Arguing Agents Competition is a new collaboration that aims to provide an open, competitive environment in which agents can compete in their ability to argue successfully [24]. It aims to be similar in spirit to the leading example set by the Trading Agent Competition[12]. As the AAC is currently under development, it has been designed to use AIF from the outset. This represents the first significant test case for AIF's suitability for autonomous reasoning (as opposed to human-in-the-loop processing).

InterLoc. Interloc is an online educational environment for structuring pedagogic discourse and debate [17]. Its rich representations of argument, and strongly typed dialogue games are well suited to what AIF can offer. Initial explorations are under way to explore potential uses of AIF in the Interloc project, but there is a significant challenge: Interloc focuses heavily upon the design and execution of a number of sophisticated and intricate dialogue games for structuring interactions online. AIF in its simplest form, presented here, does not support dialogue at all.

6.1 Dialogue in AIF

Though discussed at the initial AgentLink meeting in Budapest, argumentation dialogue was deprioritised against the more basic requirement of being able to represent "monologue": it is first necessary to be able to handle relatively static knowledge structures (such as those represented in abstract argumentation frameworks) before going on to tackle how those structures are updated and modified. The problem is that very many systems and use cases for the AIF involve dialogue.

The first step in introducing dialogue into the AIF is presented in [12], which shows how protocol application steps can be introduced into the AIF framework. [19] goes on to show how both dialogue game descriptions, and the actual dialogues they govern can be represented in a common extension to AIF, called AIF^+. The aim is to allow specifications of dialogue games to be represented in a way that is analogous to argument scheme representations, and to allow instantiated dialogues to be analogous to argument instantiations. The challenge lies in ensuring that the instantiations of dialogues are connected in appropriate ways to instantiations of arguments, according to the rules of the appropriate dialogue game. Both [12] and [19] are, however, rather preliminary, and many issues remain to be resolved.

---

[12] http://www.sics.se/tac

7 Conclusion

The current AIF specification and its reifications mark a starting point. As experience with AIF grows, and different systems and research programmes make call upon it, the specification will inevitably shift to accommodate the broadening demands. Extensions to handle dialogue represent and early example of this broadening – albeit one that has been anticipated from the outset.

Unfortunately, this shifting poses two distinct problems: one in the short term, and one in the longer term. The first problem is one of bootstrapping. With a number of teams working to implement slightly different reifications of the AIF, tracking versions to ensure at least some compatibility is becoming tricky. To some extent, the core of AIF is stabilising, and as reference implementations become available, code reuse will become more common, and compatibility will be improved. The second, related problem, concerns the process of solidification by which the AIF settles into stability. It is important that this solidification not happen too early: the AIF must support the theories and systems that are being developed right across the community. But on the other hand, it must also not happen to late, or we risk fragmentation and a loss of coherence, which is the raison d'être of the specification. Currently, the balance is being successfully struck informally through personal networks and regular communication. If AIF starts to scale, a control system that is less lightweight may be necessary to maintain stability of at least a common core.

Finally, [16] present a vision of a World Wide Argument Web of interconnected arguments and debates, founded upon the AIF. Though it leaves many questions unanswered it does present a challenging goal for development not only of AIF components but also large-scale infrastructure for supporting online argumentation. The WWAW vision has the potential to draw together a number of different initiatives in the space allowing each to find a wider audience and more practical utility than they might individually, which would be a true measure of success for the AIF.

Acknowledgements The authors are grateful to Steve Willmott, Peter McBurney, and AgentLink III for initiating and organising the Technical Forum "Towards a Standard Agent-to-Agent Argumentation Interchange Format," and to all those who contributed to the initial AIF specification that it produced.

References

1. F. Baader, D. Calvanese, D. McGuinness, D. Nardi, and P. Patel-Schneider, editors. *The Description Logic Handbook*. Cambridge University Press, Cambridge, UK, 2003.
2. D. Brickley and R. V. Guha. RDF Vocabulary Description Language 1.0: RDF Schema. W3C Recommendation REC-rdf-schema-20040210, World Wide Web Consortium (W3C), February 2004.
3. S. Buckingham Shum. Cohere: Towards Web 2.0 argumentation. In P. Besnard, S. Doutre, and A. Hunter, editors, *Proceedings of the 2nd International Conference on Computational Models of Argument (COMMA)*, pages 97–108. IOS Press, Amsterdam, The Netherlands, 2008.

4. S. Buckingham Shum, E. Motta, and J. Domingue. ScholOnto: An ontology-based digital library server for research documents and discourse. *International Journal of Digital Libraries*, 3(3):237–248, 2000.
5. S. Buckingham Shum, V. Uren, G. Li, B. Sereno, and C. Mancini. Modelling naturalistic argumentation in research literatures: Representation and interaction design issues. *International Journal of Intelligent Systems, Special Issue on Computational Modelling of Naturalistic Argumentation*, 22(1):17–47, 2007.
6. C. I. Chesñevar, J. McGinnis, S. Modgil, I. Rahwan, C. Reed, G. Simari, M. South, G. Vreeswijk, and S. Willmott. Towards an argument interchange format. *The Knowledge Engineering Review*, 21(4):293–316, 2007.
7. P. M. Dung. On the acceptability of arguments and its fundamental role in nonmonotonic reasoning, logic programming and n-person games. *Artificial Intelligence*, 77(2):321–358, 1995.
8. L. Emmet and G. Cleland. Graphical notations, narratives and persuasion: a pliant systems approach to hypertext tool design. In *HYPERTEXT 2002, Proceedings of the 13th ACM Conference on Hypertext and Hypermedia, June 11-15, 2002, University of Maryland, College Park, MD, USA*, pages 55–64, New York, USA, 2002. ACM Press.
9. T. F. Gordon, H. Prakken, and D. Walton. The Carneades model of argument and burden of proof. *Artificial Intelligence*, 171(10–15):875–896, 2007.
10. P. A. Kirschner, S. J. B. Schum, and C. S. Carr, editors. *Visualizing Argumentation: Software Tools for Collaborative and Educational Sense-Making*. Springer Verlag, London, 2003.
11. P.-A. Matt, F. Toni, T. Stournaras, and D. Dimitrelos. Argumentation-based agents for eprocurement. In *AAMAS '08*, pages 71–74, 2008.
12. S. Modgil and J. McGinnis. Towards characterising argumentation based dialogue in the argument interchange format. In I. Rahwan and P. Moraitis, editors, *Proceedings of the 4th International Workshop on Argumentation in Multi-Agent Systems (ArgMAS)*, volume 5384 of *Lecture Notes in Computer Science*. Springer Verlag, 2008. to appear.
13. M. F. Moens, E. Boiy, R. M. Palau, and C. Reed. Automatic detection of arguments in legal texts. In *Proceedings of the International Conference on AI & Law (ICAIL-2007)*, 2007.
14. I. Rahwan. Mass argumentation and the Semantic Web. *Journal of Web Semantics*, 6(1):29–37, 2008.
15. I. Rahwan and B. Banihashemi. Arguments in OWL: A progress report. In P. Besnard, S. Doutre, and A. Hunter, editors, *Proceedings of the 2nd International Conference on Computational Models of Argument (COMMA)*, pages 297–310, Amsterdam, Nethrelands, 2008. IOS Press.
16. I. Rahwan, F. Zablith, and C. Reed. Laying the foundations for a world wide argument web. *Artificial Intelligence*, 171(10–15):897–921, 2007.
17. A. Ravenscroft. Promoting thinking and conceptual change with digital dialogue games. *Journal of Computer Assisted Learning*, 23(6):453–465, 2007.
18. C. Reed and G. Rowe. Araucaria: Software for argument analysis. *International Journal of AI Tools*, 14(3–4):961–980, 2004.
19. C. Reed, S. Wells, J. Devereux, and G. Rowe. AIF+: Dialogue in the Argument Interchange Format. In P. Besnard, S. Doutre, and A. Hunter, editors, *Proceedings of the 2nd International Conference on Computational Models of Argument (COMMA)*, pages 311–323. IOS Press, Amsterdam, The Netherlands, 2008.
20. M. South, G. Vreeswijk, and J. Fox. Dungine: A Java Dung reasoner. In P. Besnard, S. Doutre, and A. Hunter, editors, *Proceedings of the 2nd International Conference on Computational Models of Argument (COMMA)*, pages 360–368, Amsterdam, Nethrelands, 2008. IOS Press.
21. T. van Gelder. The rationale for rationale. *Law, Probability and Risk*, 6(1–4):23–42, 2007.
22. D. Walton. *Argumentation Schemes for Presumptive Reasoning*. Erlbaum, Mahwah NJ, 1996.
23. D. Walton. *Legal Argumentation and Evidence*. Penn State Press, University Park, PA, 2002.
24. T. Yuan, J. Schulze, J. D. C., and Reed. Towards an arguing agents competition: Building on Argumento. In *Working Notes of the 8th Workshop on Computational Models of Natural Argument (CMNA-2008)*, 2008.

Chapter 20
Empowering Recommendation Technologies Through Argumentation

Carlos Iván Chesñevar, Ana Gabriela Maguitman and María Paula González

1 Introduction and motivations

User support systems have evolved in the last years as specialized tools to assist users in a plethora of computer-mediated tasks by providing guidelines or hints [19]. Recommender systems are a special class of user support tools that act in cooperation with users, complementing their abilities and augmenting their performance by offering proactive or on-demand, context-sensitive support. Recommender systems are mostly based on machine learning and information retrieval algorithms, providing typically suggestions based on *quantitative* evidence (i.e. measures of similarity between objects or users). The inference process which led to such suggestions is mostly unknown (i.e. 'black-box' metaphor). Although the effectiveness of existing recommenders is remarkable, they still have some serious limitations. On the one hand, they are incapable of dealing formally with the defeasible nature of users' preferences in complex environments. Decisions about user preferences are mostly based on heuristics which rely on ranking previous user choices or gathering information from other users with similar interests. On the other hand, they are not equipped with explicit inference capabilities. This is a hindrance for providing explanation facilities which could help the user to assess the analysis underlying the

Carlos Iván Chesñevar
CONICET (National Council of Technical and Scientific Research) – Department of Computer Science and Eng. – Universidad Nacional del Sur – Bahía Blanca, Argentina, e-mail: cic@cs. uns.edu.ar

Ana Gabriela Maguitman
CONICET (National Council of Technical and Scientific Research) – Department of Computer Science and Eng. – Universidad Nacional del Sur – Bahía Blanca, Argentina, e-mail: agm@cs. uns.edu.ar

María Paula González
CONICET (National Council of Technical and Scientific Research) – Department of Computer Science and Eng. – Universidad Nacional del Sur – Bahía Blanca, Argentina
GRIHO Research Group – University of Lleida – Lleida, Spain. e-mail: mpg@cs.uns.edu.ar

I. Rahwan, G. R. Simari (eds.), *Argumentation in Artificial Intelligence*,
DOI 10.1007/978-0-387-98197-0_20, © Springer Science+Business Media, LLC 2009

recommendations provided (i.e., which elements were taken into account in order to come up with a specific suggestion).

In fact, quantitative approaches in AI, as opposed to qualitative approaches, have often been criticized for their inability to obtain conclusions supported by a rationally justified procedure. The quantitative techniques adopted by most existing user support systems suffer also from this limitation. The absence of an underlying formal model makes it hard to provide users with a clear explanation of the factors and procedures that led the system to come up with some particular recommendations. As a result, serious trustworthiness issues may arise, especially in those cases when business interests are involved, or when external manipulation is possible. Logic-based approaches could help to overcome these issues, enhancing recommendation technology by providing a means to formally express constrains and to draw inferences. In this context, frameworks for defeasible argumentation [10, 25] constitute an interesting alternative for empowering recommendation technologies by providing appropriate inference mechanisms for qualitative reasoning. In fact, the argumentation paradigm has proven to be successful in a growing number of real-world applications such as multiagent systems [3, 6], legal reasoning [24], intelligent web-based forms [15], and semantic web [26, 9], among many others.

This chapter presents a generic approach to characterize *argument-based recommender systems, i.e.* user support tools in which recommendations are provided on the basis of arguments. The proposed approach is based on modelling user preference criteria by means of facts, strict rules and defeasible rules encoded in an argumentation formalism. These preference criteria are combined with additional background information and used by the argumentation framework to prioritize potential suggestions, thus enhancing the final results provided to the user. The rest of the chapter is structured as follows. Section 2 presents an overview of current recommender system technologies. Section 3 summarizes the main elements of Defeasible Logic Programming, a general-purpose argumentation formalism based on logic programming used for our proposal. Section 4 discusses our approach to empowering recommendation technologies through argumentation. Section 5 describes a particular application which emerged as an instance of this approach, oriented towards providing suitable decision support in the context of content-based web search. Finally, Section 6 discusses related work and Section 7 presents some conclusions and future research directions.

2 Recommendation Technologies: an overview

Recommendation systems are aimed at helping users to deal with the problem of information overload by facilitating access to relevant items. They attempt to generate a model of the user or user's task and apply diverse heuristics to anticipate what information may be of interest to the user. User support systems operate in association with the user to effectively accomplish a range of tasks. Some of these systems serve the purpose of expanding the user's natural capabilities, for example by acting as intelligence or memory augmentation mechanisms [13]. Some of these systems reduce the user's work by carrying out the routinizable tasks on the user's behalf. Others offer tips on how to refine or complete human generated products (such as electronic documents) by highlighting potential inaccuracies and proposing alternative solutions, thus minimizing the user's cognitive effort. Some aides "think ahead" to anticipate the next steps in a user's task providing the capability for the user to confirm the prediction and ask the system to complete the steps automatically.

Recommender systems are a special class of user support tools that act in cooperation with users, complementing their abilities and augmenting their performance by offering proactive or on demand context-sensitive support. They usually operate by creating a model of the user's preferences or the user's task with the purpose of facilitating access to items (e.g., news, web pages, books, etc.) that the user may find useful. While in many situations the user explicitly posts a request for recommendations in the form of a query, many recommender systems attempt to anticipate the user's needs and are capable of proactively providing assistance. In order to come up with recommendations for user queries, conventional recommender systems rely on *similarity measures* between users or contents, computed on the basis of methods coming either from the information retrieval or the machine learning communities. Recommender systems adopt mainly two different views to help predict information needs. The first approach is known as *user modeling* and relies on the use of a profile or model of the users, which can be created by observing users' behavior (e.g., [20]). The second approach is based on *task modeling*, and recommendations are based on the context in which the user is immersed (e.g., [7]). The context may consist of an electronic document the user is editing, web pages the user has recently visited, etc.

Two main techniques have been used to compute recommendations: *content-based* and *collaborative filtering*. Content-based recommenders [23] are driven by the premise that user's preferences tend to persist through time. These recommenders frequently use machine-learning techniques to generate a profile of the active user. Typically, a model of the active user is stored as a list of rated items. In order to determine if a new item is a potentially good recommendation, content-based recommender systems rely on similarity measures between the new items and the rated items stored as part of the user model. On the other hand, recommender systems based on collaborative filtering [28] are based on the assumption that users' preferences are correlated. These systems maintain a pool of users' profiles associated with items that the users rated in the past. For a given active user, collaborative recommender systems find other similar users whose ratings strongly correlate with the current user. New items not rated by the active user can be presented as suggestions if similar users have rated them highly.

A combination of collaborative-filtering and content-based recommendation gives rise to *hybrid recommender systems* (e.g., [4]). Other combinations can be made resulting on other kinds of hybrid technologies. A survey of hybrid recommender systems can be found in [8]. Additional dimensions of analysis for recommender systems are the content of the suggestion (e.g., news, URLs, people, articles, text, products), the purpose of the suggestion (e.g., sales or information), the event that triggers the search for suggestions (by user's demand or proactively), and the level of intrusiveness (none, low, moderate or high).

2.1 Limitations of current recommendation technologies

Although large amounts of qualitative data is available on the Web in the form of rankings, opinions, and other facts, this data is hardly used by existing recommenders to perform inference. Even quantitative data available on the Web could give rise to highly reliable and traceable suggestions if used by a system with the ability to perform qualitative inference on this data. An important deficiency of current recommendations technologies, therefore, is due to their inability to qualitatively exploit these data. This gives rise to a number of research opportunities for the development of a new generation of recommenders.

- **Exposing underlying assumptions.** Because the evidence used to provide suggestions is not traced or tracked, existing recommenders are unable to expose the underlying assumptions to careful scrutiny by the user. While recommendations in the form of simple pointers or hints may be useful in many situations, it is easy to come up with scenarios in which the user may need further evidence before taking a course of action based on a recommendation.
- **Dealing with the defeasible nature of users' preferences.** Users preferences are dynamic and typically change as time evolves or as new material becomes available for analysis. Because quantitative approaches are not equipped with mechanism to revise previous conclusions, the changing nature of users preferences is poorly dealt with. Modeling the dynamics of users preferences can help to keep the system up-to-date, without disregarding selections and decisions made by the user in the past.
- **Approaching trust and trustworthiness.** Recommendation technologies are increasingly gaining importance in commercial applications. However, most existing systems simply focus on tracking a customer's interests and make suggestions for the future without a contextualized justification. As a result the user is unable to evaluate the reasons that led the system to present certain recommendations. In certain domains (e.g., e-commerce), this is not sufficient, as this lack of justification can be associated with ulterior motives on the recommendation provider's side, leading to lack of confidence or reliability [22]. This emerging area requires a careful investigation of the notion of trust and trustworthiness.
- **Proving rationally compelling arguments.** The absence of a formal model underlying quantitative approaches makes it hard to provide users with a justification of why certain recommendations should be trusted or preferred. In many situations, more than one potential course of action could be proposed by a recommendation tool. However, the convenience of using these support tools is limited if no rational arguments for these suggestions are provided to help the user make a final decision.

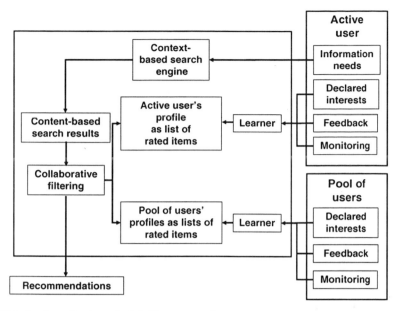

Fig. 20.1 A schematic view of a hybrid recommender system

- **Going beyond the basic collaborative model.** Because trust is to a great degree subjective, quantifying trust by combining measures coming from a pool of credibility assessments may not be entirely realistic. Although the "wisdom of the crowds" [29] is typically useful, it should be combined in a rational manner with information coming from individual users or communities.

A solution to some of these problems can be provided by integrating existing user support technologies with appropriate inferential mechanisms for qualitative reasoning. As we will see in the next sections, the use of argumentation will allow to enhance recommender systems with inference abilities to present reasoned suggestions, which the user will be able to further investigate and accept only if a convincing case can be made by the recommendation tool.

3 Defeasible Logic Programming in a Nutshell

Defeasible logic programming (DeLP)[1] [14] is a general-purpose defeasible argumentation formalism based on logic programming, intended to model inconsistent and potentially contradictory knowledge. A defeasible logic program has the form $\mathcal{P} = (\Pi, \Delta)$, where Π and Δ stand for *strict* and *defeasible* knowledge, respectively. The set Π involves *strict rules* of the form $P \leftarrow Q_1, \ldots, Q_k$ and *facts* (strict rules with empty body), and it is assumed to be *non-contradictory* (i.e., no complementary literals P and $\sim P$ can be inferred, where $\sim P$ denotes the contrary of P). The set Δ involves *defeasible rules* of the form $P \relbar\joinrel\prec Q_1, \ldots, Q_k$, which stand for "$Q_1, \ldots Q_k$ *provide a tentative reason to believe P.*" Rules in DeLP are defined in terms of *literals*. A literal is an atom A or the strict negation ($\sim A$) of an atom. Default negation (denoted not A) is also allowed in the body of defeasible rules (see [14] for details).

Deriving literals in DeLP results in the construction of *arguments*. An argument $\mathcal{A}$ for a literal Q (denoted $\langle \mathcal{A}, Q \rangle$) is a (possibly empty) set of ground defeasible rules that together with the set Π provide a proof for a given literal Q, satisfying the additional constraints of *non-contradiction* (*i.e.*, an argument should not allow the derivation of contradictory literals) and *minimality* (*i.e.*, the set of defeasible information used to derive Q should be minimal).[2] Note that arguments are obtained by a mechanism similar to the usual query-driven SLD derivation from logic programming, performed by backward chaining on *both* strict and defeasible rules; in this context a negated literal $\sim P$ is treated just as a new predicate name no_P. In DeLP, arguments provide tentative support for claims (literals). Clearly, as a program $\mathcal{P}$ represents incomplete and tentative information, an argument $\langle \mathcal{A}, Q \rangle$ may be *attacked* by other arguments also derivable from $\mathcal{P}$. An argument $\langle \mathcal{B}, R \rangle$ is a *counter-argument* for $\langle \mathcal{A}, Q \rangle$ whenever a subargument $\langle \mathcal{A}', Q' \rangle$ (with $\mathcal{A}' \subseteq \mathcal{A}$) in $\langle \mathcal{A}, Q \rangle$ can be identified, such that $\langle \mathcal{B}, R \rangle$ and $\langle \mathcal{A}', Q' \rangle$ cannot be simultaneously accepted since their joint acceptance would allow contradictory conclusions to be inferred from $\Pi \cup \mathcal{A}' \cup \mathcal{B}$. If the attacking argument $\langle \mathcal{B}, R \rangle$ is preferred over $\langle \mathcal{A}', Q' \rangle$, then $\langle \mathcal{B}, R \rangle$ is called a *defeater* for $\langle \mathcal{A}, Q \rangle$. The preference criterion commonly used is *specificity* [14], preferring those arguments which are more direct or more informed, although other criteria could be adopted.

In DeLP the search for defeaters for a given argument $\langle \mathcal{A}, Q \rangle$ prompts a recursive process, resulting in the generation of a *dialectical tree*: the root node of this tree is the original argument at issue, and every children node in the tree is a defeater for its parent. Additional restrictions help to avoid circular situations when computing branches in a dialectical tree, guaranteeing that every dialectical tree is finite (see [14] for details). Nodes in the tree can be marked either as *defeated* (D-nodes) or as *undefeated* (U-nodes). The marking of the dialectical tree is performed as in an AND-OR trees: leaves are always marked as undefeated nodes (as they have no defeaters); inner nodes can be be marked either as undefeated (if and only if every

---

[1] For an in-depth description of Defeasible Logic Programming the reader is referred to Chapter 8 in this book.

[2] This definition of argument was originally introduced by Simari & Loui [30].

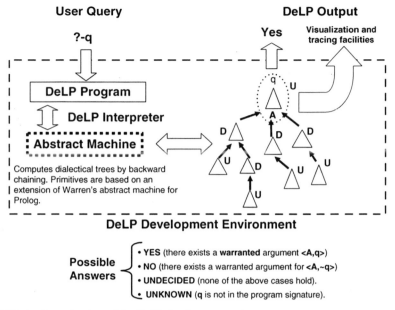

Fig. 20.2 A schematic view of the DeLP development environment

of its children nodes is marked as defeated) or as defeated (whenever at least one of its children has been marked as undefeated). The original argument $\langle \mathcal{A}, Q \rangle$ (the root of tree) is deemed as ultimately acceptable or *warranted* whenever it turns out to be marked as undefeated after applying the above process.

Given a DeLP program $\mathcal{P}$, solving a query Q with respect to $\mathcal{P}$ may result in four possible answers:

- YES (there is at least one warranted argument $\mathcal{A}$ for Q);
- NO (there is at least one warranted argument $\mathcal{A}$ for $\sim Q$);
- UNDECIDED (none of the previous cases hold); and
- UNKNOWN (Q is not present in the program signature).

The emerging semantics is skeptical, computed by DeLP on the basis of the goal-directed construction and marking of dialectical trees, which is performed in a depth-first fashion. Additional facilities (such as visualization of dialectical trees, zoom-in/zoom-out view of arguments, etc.) are integrated in the DeLP environment to facilitate user interaction when solving queries. The DeLP environment is available online at http://lidia.cs.uns.edu.ar/delp_client.

4 Argument-based Recommendation Technologies

We contend that argument-based reasoning can be integrated into recommender systems in order to provide a qualitative perspective in decision making. This can be achieved by integrating inference abilities to offer reasoned suggestions modelled in terms of arguments in favor and against a particular decision. This approach complements existing qualitative techniques by enriching the user's mental model of such computer systems in a natural way: suggestions are statements which are backed by arguments supporting them. Clearly, conflicting suggestions may arise, and it will be necessary to determine which suggestions can be considered as valid according to some rationally justified procedure. The role of argumentation is to provide a sound formal framework as a basis for such analysis.

In this context, our proposal is based on modelling users' preference criteria in terms of a DeLP program built on top of a traditional content-based search engine. Figure 20.3 depicts the basic architecture of a generic argument-based user support system based on DeLP. In such a setting users' preferences and background knowledge can be codified as facts, strict rules and defeasible rules in a DeLP program. These facts and rules can come from different sources. For example, user's preferences could be entered explicitly by the user or could be inferred by the system (e.g., by monitoring the user's behavior). Additional facts and rules could be obtained from other repositories of structured (e.g., databases) and semistructured data (e.g., the web.).

We will distinguish particular subsets in a DeLP program, representing different elements in a user support system. For example, a DeLP program could take the form $\mathcal{P} = \mathcal{P}_{user} \cup \mathcal{P}_{pool} \cup \mathcal{P}_{domain}$, where sets $\mathcal{P}_{user}$ and $\mathcal{P}_{pool}$ represent preferences and behavior of the active user and the pool of users, respectively. In the case of the active user, his/her profile can be encoded as facts and rules in DeLP. In the case of the pool of users, rule induction techniques are in order[3] resulting in defeasible rules characterizing trends and general preference criteria (e.g., *normally if a given user likes X then she also likes Y*). The set $\mathcal{P}_{domain}$ represents the domain (background) knowledge, encoded using facts and rules in DeLP. Either proactively or upon a user's request, an argument-based user support system triggers the search for suggestions. If needed, the collected results could be codified as facts and added to the DeLP program. Finally, a DeLP interpreter is in charge of performing the qualitative analysis on the program and to provide the final suggestions to the user.

Given the program $\mathcal{P}$, a user's request is transformed into suitable DeLP queries, from which different *suggestions* are obtained. For the sake of simplicity, we will assume in our analysis that user suggestions will be DeLP terms associated with a distinguished predicate name *rel* (which stands for *relevant* or *acceptable as a valid suggestion*). Using this formalization, suggestions will be classified into three sets, namely:

- S^w (warranted suggestions): those suggestions s_i for which there exists at least one warranted argument supporting $rel(s_i)$ based on $\mathcal{P}$;

---

[3] An approach for inducing defeasible rules from association rules can be found in [17].

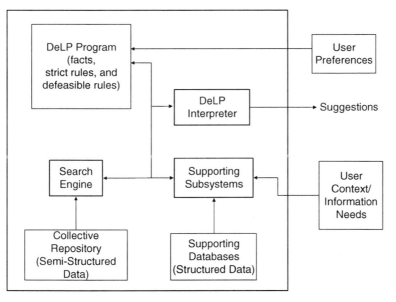

Fig. 20.3 A Generic Argument-Based User Support System based on DeLP

- S^u (undecided suggestions): those suggestions s_i for which there is no warranted argument for $rel(s_i)$, neither there is a warranted argument for $\sim rel(s_i)$ on the basis of $\mathcal{P}$, and
- S^d (defeated suggestions): those suggestions s_i such that there is a warranted argument supporting $\sim rel(s_i)$ on the basis of $\mathcal{P}$.

Given a potential suggestion s_i, the existence of a warranted argument $\langle \mathcal{A}_1, rel(s_i) \rangle$ built on the basis of the DeLP program $\mathcal{P}$ will allow to conclude that s_i should be presented as a final suggestion to the user. If results are presented as a ranked list of suggestions, then warranted suggestions will be more relevant than those which are undecided or defeated. Note that the above classification has a direct correspondence with the doxastic attitudes associated with answers to DeLP queries.

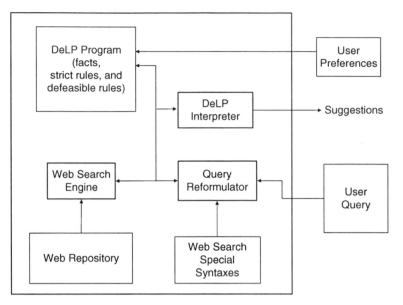

Fig. 20.4 A particular instance of the Generic Argument-Based User Support System for Content-based Search

5 Providing Argument-based User Support for Content-Based Web Search

We will present next a particular instantiation of our approach: an argument-based recommendation tool for content-based search queries [12]. In this context, the intended user support system aims at providing an enriched (content-based) web search engine which categorizes results, where the user's needs correspond to strings to be searched on the web. The underlying search engine may be a conventional search engine (e.g., GOOGLE), or a specialized content-based search engine. Final recommendation results for a query q are prioritized according to domain background knowledge and the user's declared preferences. Figure 4 illustrates the architecture of our argument-based recommender system.

Given a user query q, it will be given as an input to a traditional content-based web search engine, returning a list of search results L. If required, the original query q could be suitably re-formulated in order to improve the quality of the search results to be obtained. In the list L we can assume that s_i is a unique name characterizing a piece of information $info(s_i)$, in which a number of associated features

ALGORITHM Recommend_on_Query
INPUT: Query q, DeLP program $\mathcal{P} = \mathcal{P}_{user} \cup \mathcal{P}_{pool} \cup \mathcal{P}_{domain}$
OUTPUT: List L_{new} {*recommendation results wrt* $\mathcal{P}'$}
   Let $L = [s_1, s_2, \ldots s_k]$ be the output of solving q
   wrt content-based search engine SE
   {L *is the list of (the first k) results obtained from query q via SE* }
   $\mathcal{P}_{search} = \{$facts encoding $info(s_1), info(s_2) \ldots info(s_k)\}$
   {$info(s_i)$ *stands for features associated with result s_i* }
   $\mathcal{P}' := $ **Revise** $(\mathcal{P} \cup \mathcal{P}_{search})$.
   {**Revise** *stands for a belief revision operator to ensure consistency in* $\mathcal{P}'$ }
   Initialize S^w, S^u, and S^d as empty sets.
   {S^w, S^u, *and* S^d *stand for the set of results s_i's which are warranted as*
   relevant, undecided and warranted as non-relevant, respectively }
   FOR EVERY $s_i \in L$
     DO
      Solve query $rel(s_i)$ using DeLP program $\mathcal{P}'$
      IF $rel(s_i)$ is warranted **THEN** add s_i to S^w
      ELSE
        IF $\sim rel(s_i)$ is warranted **THEN** add s_i to S^d
        ELSE add s_i to S^d
   Return Recommendation $L_{new} = [s_1^w, s_2^w, \ldots, s_{j1}^w, s_1^u, s_2^u, \ldots, s_{j2}^u, s_1^d, \ldots, s_{j3}^d]$

Fig. 20.5 High-level algorithm for solving queries with argumentation support in content-based search

(meta-tags, filename, URL, etc.) can be identified. We assume that such features can be identified and extracted from $info(s_i)$ by some specialized tool, as suggested by Hunter [18] in his approach to dealing with structured news reports. Such features will be encoded as a set $\mathcal{P}_{search}$ of new DeLP facts, extending thus the original program $\mathcal{P}$ into a new program $\mathcal{P}'$. A special operator **Revise** deals with possible inconsistencies found in $\mathcal{P}_{search}$ with respect to $\mathcal{P}'$, ensuring $\mathcal{P} \cup \mathcal{P}_{search}$ is not contradictory.[4] Following the algorithm shown in Figure 20.5 we can now analyze L in the context of a new DeLP program $\mathcal{P}'=\mathcal{P} \cup Facts$, where $Facts$ denotes the set corresponding to the collection discussed above and $\mathcal{P}$ corresponds to domain knowledge and the user's preferences about the search domain.[5] For each s_i, the query $rel(s_i)$ will be analyzed in light of the new program $\mathcal{P}'$. Elements in the original list L of content-based search results will be classified into three sets of warranted, undecided, and defeated results. The final output presented to the user will be a sorted list L' in which the elements of L are ordered according to their epistemic status with respect to $\mathcal{P}'$. Figure 20.5 outlines a high level algorithm, which will be exemplified in the case study shown next.

---

[4] For example, contradictory facts may be found on the web. A simple belief revision criterion is to prefer the facts with a newer timestamp over the older ones.
[5] In this particular context, note that $\mathcal{P} = \mathcal{P}_{domain} \cup \mathcal{P}_{user}$.

5.1 A worked example

Example 20.1. Consider a tourist who wants to search for books about London. A content-based query *q* containing the terms *books, about, London* will return thousands of search results. The tourist performing the query may have some implicit knowledge to guide the search, such as:

1. She usually considers as relevant those books about London which are not outdated and are written by authors with good reputation.
2. She trusts a ranked list provided by the website www.rankings.com to assess the quality of a given author. Authors ranked less than 20 are considered trustworthy.[6]
3. According to the tourist's opinion, there is a particular author (John Doyle) which has a good reputation in books about London (independently of web-based rankings).
4. Usually all search results which include the keyword 'London' are of interest, but not those involving 'Jack' and 'London' (as they are assumed to belong to the American writer Jack London, and not the city of London).
5. She usually likes books which are not expensive (not exceeding $ 300), except for those books published by Acme Inc. (in that case, she is willing to pay a higher price).
6. She usually considers non-relevant those books published by Boring Books Ltd.

Such rules and facts can be modelled in terms of a DeLP program $\mathcal{P}$ as shown in Figure 20.7. Note that some rules in $\mathcal{P}$ rely on "built in" predicates computed elsewhere and not provided by the user.

For the sake of example, let us suppose that the original query *"books about London"* returns a list of content-based search results $L=[s_1, s_2, s_3, s_4]$. Note that a traditional content-based search engine would present these results exactly in this order to the user, independently of the user's preferences or background knowledge. However, as discussed before, most of such results will be associated with XML or HTML pages, in which a number of attributes can be identified (e.g. author, date, URL, etc.). Such attributes can be encoded in a collection of DeLP facts as shown in Figure 20.6. We can now analyze s_1, s_2, s_3 and s_4 in the context of the user's preference theory about the search domain by considering the DeLP program $\mathcal{P}'=\mathcal{P}\cup Facts$, where *Facts* denotes the set corresponding to the collection of facts in Figure 20.6. For each s_i, the query $rel(s_i)$ will be analyzed wrt this new program $\mathcal{P}'$.

Consider the case for s_1. The search for an argument for $rel(s_1)$ returns the argument $\langle\mathcal{A}_1, rel(s_1)\rangle$: s_1 should be considered as a relevant item since it corresponds to a book about London written by a good author (John Doyle), and at a reasonable price. In this case we have the argument[7]

---

[6] It must be remarked that the ranked list mentioned in this example is fictitious, although websites such as all-rankings.com (a trademark of Lists & Ranks, S.L., Barcelona, Spain) allow to create such lists, making them available to others users. In this example the number 20 is an arbitrary threshold value, just for illustrative purposes.

[7] For the sake of clarity, semicolons to separate elements in an argument $\mathcal{A} = \{e_1 ; e_2 ; \dots ; e_k \}$.

$\mathcal{A}_1 = \{\ rel(s_1) \rightarrowtail goodauthor(s_1), aboutlondon(s_1), goodprice(s_1)\ ;$
$\quad goodauthor(s_1) \rightarrowtail author(s_1, \text{`john doyle'}), trust(\text{`john doyle'});$
$\quad aboutlondon(s_1) \rightarrowtail keywords(s_1, [\text{`london'}, \text{`history'}]),$
$\quad member(\text{`london'}, [\text{`london'}, \text{`history'}]);$
$\quad goodprice(s_1) \rightarrowtail not\ expensive(s_1)\ \}.$

Search for defeaters for argument $\langle \mathcal{A}_1, rel(s_1) \rangle$ will result in a proper defeater $\langle \mathcal{A}_2, \sim rel(s_1) \rangle$: s_1 is not relevant as it corresponds to an outdated book (more than 20 years old). In this case we have the argument

$\mathcal{A}_2 = \{\ \sim rel(s_1) \rightarrowtail goodauthor(s_1), aboutlondon(s_1), goodprice(s_1), outdated(s_1)\ ;$
$\quad goodauthor(s_1) \rightarrowtail author(s_1, \text{`john doyle'}), trust(\text{`john doyle'});$
$\quad aboutlondon(s_1) \rightarrowtail keywords(s_1, [\text{`london'}, \text{`history'}]),$
$\quad member(\text{`london'}, [\text{`london'}, \text{`history'}]);$
$\quad goodprice(s_1) \rightarrowtail not\ expensive(s_1)\ \}.$

There are no other arguments to consider in the dialectical analysis. The dialectical trees for $\langle \mathcal{A}_1, rel(s_1) \rangle$ and $\langle \mathcal{A}_2, \sim rel(s_1) \rangle$ are shown in Figure 20.8a. As $\sim rel(s_1)$ is warranted, the item s_1 will be considered <u>non-relevant</u>.

Now consider the case for s_2. Let us assume that the author Joe Foo is ranked number 10 in `www.rankings.com`. Following a similar analysis as above, the search for an argument for $rel(s_2)$ returns the argument $\langle \mathcal{B}_1, rel(s_2) \rangle$, where

$\mathcal{B}_1 = \{\ rel(s_2) \rightarrowtail goodauthor(s_2), aboutlondon(s_2), goodprice(s_2)\ ;$
$\quad goodauthor(s_2) \rightarrowtail author(s_2, \text{`joe foo'}), trust(\text{`joe foo'});$
$\quad aboutlondon(s_2) \rightarrowtail keywords(s_2, [\text{`london'}, \text{`jack'}, \text{`stories'}]),$
$\quad member(\text{`london'}, [\text{`london'}, \text{`jack'}, \text{`stories'}]);$
$\quad goodprice(s_2) \rightarrowtail not\ expensive(s_2)\ \}.$

However, an argument $\langle \mathcal{B}_2, \sim rel(s_2) \rangle$ can be found defeating the previous argument: s_2 should not be considered as a relevant item since it seems to correspond to the writer Jack London, and not the city of London:

$\mathcal{B}_2 = \{\ rel(s_2) \rightarrowtail \sim aboutlondon(s_2)\ ;$
$\quad \sim aboutlondon(s_2) \rightarrowtail keywords(s_2, [\text{`london'}, \text{`jack'}, \text{`stories'}]),$
$\quad member(\text{`london'}, [\text{`london'}, \text{`jack'}, \text{`stories'}]),$
$\quad member(\text{`jack'}, [\text{`london'}, \text{`jack'}, \text{`stories'}]);$

Note that there exists a third argument $\langle \mathcal{B}_3, aboutlondon(s_2) \rangle$, where

$\mathcal{B}_3 = \{\ aboutlondon(s_2) \rightarrowtail keywords(s_2, [\text{`london'}, \text{`jack'}, \text{`stories'}]),$
$\quad member(\text{`london'}, [\text{`london'}, \text{`jack'}, \text{`stories'}])\}$

which would also attack $\langle \mathcal{B}_2, \sim rel(s_2) \rangle$. However, such argument is discarded in the dialectical analysis, since it is strictly *less specific* than $\langle \mathcal{B}_2, \sim rel(s_2) \rangle$ and hence cannot be considered as a defeater. There are no more arguments to consider, and consequently (as in the previous case), since $\sim rel(s_2)$ is warranted, the item s_2 can be deemed as <u>non-relevant</u> (see Figure 20.8b).

Now consider the case for s_3. Once again, let us assume that Jena Bar is an author ranked number 5 in 'www.rankings.com'. There is an argument $\langle \mathcal{C}_1, rel(s_3) \rangle$ supporting the conclusion $rel(s_3)$, namely:

$\mathcal{C}_1 = \{$ $rel(s_3) \multimap goodauthor(s_3), aboutlondon(s_3), goodprice(s_3)$;
$goodauthor(s_3) \multimap author(s_3, \text{'jena bar'}), trust(\text{'jena bar'})$;
$aboutlondon(s_3) \multimap keywords(s_3, [\text{'london'}, \text{'tourism'}])$,
$member(\text{'london'}, [\text{'london'}, \text{'tourism'}])$;
$goodprice(s_3) \multimap not\ expensive(s_3)$ $\}$.

However, this argument is defeated by argument $\langle \mathcal{C}_2, expensive(s_3) \rangle$, since the price of this particular book is above \$ 300.

$\mathcal{C}_2 = \{$ $expensive(s_3) \multimap price(s_3, 350), 350 > 300.$ $\}$

Nevertheless, there is a third argument $\langle \mathcal{C}_3, \sim expensive(s_3) \rangle$ which attack the previous one, supporting the claim that this particular book is considered as relevant for the user, as it is published by ACME, which is an exceptional publisher.

$\mathcal{C}_3 = \{$ $\sim expensive(s_3) \multimap price(s_3, 350), 350 > 300, publisher(s_3, acme).$ $\}$

There are no more arguments to consider, and consequently we have computed the dialectical tree for $\langle \mathcal{C}_1, rel(s_3) \rangle$ (see Figure 20.8c). According to the marking criterion introduced in Section 3, the root of the tree turns out to be an undefeated node, and hence $\langle \mathcal{C}_1, rel(s_3) \rangle$ is warranted and considered as a <u>relevant</u> information item.

Finally, let us consider the case for s_4. Let us assume that Tim Burton is an author ranked number 5 in 'www.rankings.com'. As in the case of s_1, there is an argument $\langle \mathcal{D}_1, rel(s_4) \rangle$ supporting the fact that s_4 is a relevant item, since it corresponds to a book about London written by a good author and at a reasonable price.

$\mathcal{D}_1 = \{$ $rel(s_4) \multimap goodauthor(s_4), aboutlondon(s_4), goodprice(s_4)$;
$goodauthor(s_4) \multimap author(s_4, \text{'tim burton'}), trust(\text{'tim burton'})$;
$aboutlondon(s_4) \multimap keywords(s_4, [\text{'london'}, \text{'history'}])$,
$member(\text{'london'}, [\text{'london'}, \text{'history'}])$;
$goodprice(s_4) \multimap not\ expensive(s_4)$ $\}$.

However, it turns out that this book was edited by Boring Books Ltd., so that it should not be considered as relevant. Indeed, there is an argument $\langle \mathcal{D}_2, \sim rel(s_4) \rangle$ defeating the previous one

$\mathcal{D}_2 = \{$ $\sim rel(s_4) \multimap publisher(s_4, \text{'boring books ltd'}).$ $\}$

It must be noted that $\langle \mathcal{D}_2, \sim rel(s_4) \rangle$ is a blocking defeater for $\langle \mathcal{D}_1, rel(s_4) \rangle$, and $\langle \mathcal{D}_1, rel(s_4) \rangle$ is a blocking defeater for $\langle \mathcal{D}_2, \sim rel(s_4) \rangle$, as both arguments cannot be compared by specificity. According to the marking criterion presented before, the conclusion $rel(s_4)$ is deemed as <u>undecided</u>, as neither $\langle \mathcal{D}_1, rel(s_4) \rangle$ nor $\langle \mathcal{D}_2, \sim rel(s_4) \rangle$ are warranted arguments (see Figure 20.8d).

$author(s_1, \text{`John Doyle'}).$
$title(s_1, \text{`Everything about London'}).$
$publisher(s_1, \text{`peterbooks'}).$
$pubyear(s_1, 1960).$
$price(s_1, 20).$
$keywords(s_1, [\text{`london'}, \text{`history'}]).$

$author(s_2, \text{`Joe Foo'}).$
$title(s_2, \text{`American Stories'}).$
$publisher(s_2, \text{`inkhouse'}).$
$pubyear(s_2, 2007).$
$price(s_2, 20).$
$keywords(s_2, [\text{`london'}, \text{`jack'}, \text{`stories'}]).$

$author(s_3, \text{`Jena Bar'}).$
$title(s_3, \text{`London for tourists'}).$
$publisher(s_3, \text{`acme'}).$
$pubyear(s_3, 2007).$
$price(s_3, 250).$
$keywords(s_3, [\text{`london'}, \text{`tourism'}]).$

$author(s_4, \text{`Tim Burton'}).$
$title(s_4, \text{`London History'}).$
$publisher(s_4, \text{`boring books ltd'}).$
$pubyear(s_4, 2007).$
$price(s_4, 20).$
$keywords(s_4, [\text{`london'}, \text{`history'}]).$

Fig. 20.6 Facts encoded from original content-based search results

From the previous analysis, and according to the high-level algorithm in Figure 20.5, we get the sets $S^w = \{s_3\}$, $S^d = \{s_1, s_2\}$, and $S^u = \{s_4\}$. Consequently, the system will return the list $L_{new}=[s_3, s_4, s_1, s_2]$ of final recommendation results, where users' preferences and background knowledge were taken into account, instead of just suggesting the original list of content-based search results L [s_1, s_2, s_3, s_4].

6 Related Work

As explained before, our approach for integrating argumentation in recommendation systems is based on modelling users' preference criteria in terms of a DeLP program built on top of a content-based search engine. Part of our recent research involved a variation of this schema in order to provide assessment on natural language usage using the web as a linguistic corpus [11]. The user preferences consist of a number

$$
\begin{array}{rl}
rel(B) \mathrel{-\!\!\prec} & goodauthor(B), aboutlondon(B), goodprice(B). \\
\sim rel(B) \mathrel{-\!\!\prec} & goodauthor(B), aboutlondon(B), \\
& goodprice(B), outdated(B). \\
\sim rel(B) \mathrel{-\!\!\prec} & \sim aboutlondon(B). \\
\sim rel(B) \mathrel{-\!\!\prec} & publisher(B, \texttt{'boring books ltd'}). \\
goodauthor(B) \mathrel{-\!\!\prec} & author(B,A), trust(A). \\
trust(A) \leftarrow & queryranking(A, \texttt{'www.rankings.com'}, Rank), \\
& Rank < 20. \\
trust(A) \leftarrow & A = \texttt{'John Doyle'}. \\
aboutlondon(B) \mathrel{-\!\!\prec} & keywords(B,K), member(\texttt{'london'},K). \\
\sim aboutlondon(B) \mathrel{-\!\!\prec} & keywords(B,K), member(\texttt{'jack'},K), \\
& member(\texttt{'london'},K). \\
goodprice(B) \mathrel{-\!\!\prec} & \text{not } expensive(B). \\
expensive(B) \mathrel{-\!\!\prec} & price(B,P), P > 300. \\
\sim expensive(B) \mathrel{-\!\!\prec} & price(B,P), P > 300, publisher(B, acme). \\
oudated(B) \leftarrow & pubyear(B,Y), getcurrentyear(CY), \\
& (CY - Y) > 20.
\end{array}
$$

$$
\begin{array}{rl}
getcurrentyear(T) \leftarrow & \text{[Computed elsewhere]} \\
member(String, List) \leftarrow & \text{[Computed elsewhere]} \\
keywords(Book, List) \leftarrow & \text{[Computed elsewhere]}
\end{array}
$$

Fig. 20.7 DeLP program modelling user preferences about books

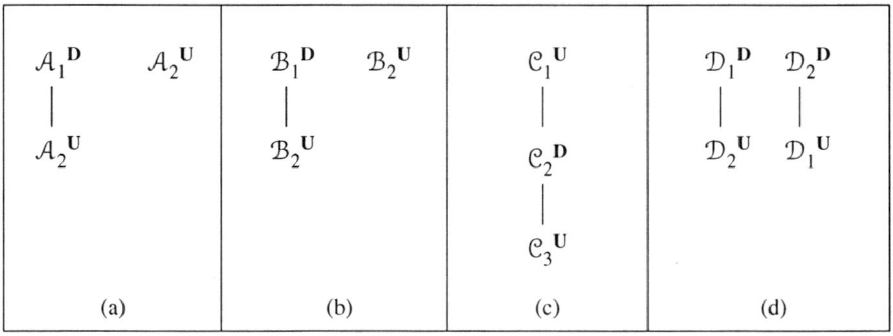

Fig. 20.8 Dialectical trees associated with (a) $\langle \mathcal{A}_1, rel(s_1) \rangle$ and $\langle \mathcal{A}_2, \sim rel(s_1) \rangle$; (b) $\langle \mathcal{B}_1, rel(s_2) \rangle$ and $\langle \mathcal{B}_2, \sim rel(s_2) \rangle$; (c) $\langle \mathcal{C}_1, rel(s_3) \rangle$ and (d) $\langle \mathcal{D}_1, rel(s_4) \rangle$ and $\langle \mathcal{D}_2, \sim rel(s_4) \rangle$

of (possibly defeasible) rules and facts which encode different aspects of adequate language usage, defining the acceptability of different terms on the basis of so-called "usage indices", which are good indicators of the suitability of an expression on the basis of the Web corpus. Argumentation is used to determine if a given expression is ultimately recommendable on the basis of a DeLP program which encodes the user's preferences.

Recommender systems can be seen as a particular instance of decision making systems oriented to assist users in solving computer-mediated tasks. In the last years there have been several efforts towards integrating argumentation in generic decision making systems. In [16] argumentation was applied in the context of modelling Shared Knowledge and Shared Knowledge Awareness when solving tasks collaboratively in a computer-supported collaborative learning (CSCL) environment. While Shared Knowledge (SK) refers to the common knowledge students acquire when they work in a collaborative activity, Shared Knowledge Awareness (SKA) is associated with the consciousness on the Shared Knowledge that a particular student has. In that context, DeLP was used to formalize an automated argumentation system as a support tool for characterizing SK and SKA in CSCL scenarios. Warranted arguments could be seen as suggestions provided by the argumentation system, providing a part of the SK among students, whereas visualization and explanation facilities provided by the argumentation system will help to make explicit the associated SKA.

In [34], an argument-based approach to modelling group decision making is presented, in which argumentation is used to support group decision task generation and identification. In contrast with our approach, the argumentation process is not automated, and the authors use argumentation for agreement among multiple users in a team, whereas we focus on argumentation for eliciting conclusions for a particular user on the basis of available information. In [31] a number of interesting *argument assistance tools* are presented. Even though there is a sound logical framework underlying this approach, the focus is rather restricted to legal reasoning, viewing the application of law as dialectical theory construction and evaluating alternative ways of representing argumentative data. In contrast, our analysis is oriented towards characterizing more generic argument-based user support systems.

Recent research has led to some interesting proposals to combine argumentation and machine learning techniques for rule induction. As discussed in Section 4, such combination lends itself applicable for extending our current approach towards a collaborative filtering setting, where defeasible rules would characterize trends and general preference criteria. Two recent research works are particularly relevant in this direction. In [21], a generic argumentation-based machine learning model (ABML) is proposed. This approach combines machine learning from examples with concepts from the field of argumentation. The idea is to provide expert's arguments, or reasons, for some of the learning examples. An improved argument-based rule learning was developed, which could be naturally integrated in the context of obtaining and justifying new rules which capture the knowledge associated with a pool of users. A different direction is adopted in the PADUA protocol [33], where a novel combination of argumentation and datamining is introduced in order to classify objects in a domain. Classification is the topic of a dialogue game between two agents, based on an argument scheme and critical questions designed to be used by agents whose knowledge of the domain comes from data mining. Each agent has its own set of examples which it can mine to find arguments based on association rules for and against a classification of a new instance. As in the case of ABML, this approach can help improve recommendation technologies in a collaborative setting, allowing agents to perform argument-based reasoning from the database of cases corresponding to knowledge provided by users in the past.

During the last years there has been a growing attention to the development of the Semantic Web [5]. In particular, the integration of Semantic Web languages (such as OWL and RDF Schema) with argumentation has been recently explored with promising results by Iyad Rahwan *et al.*(*e.g.* [27, 26]). Their proposal involves an argumentation ontology (based on Walton's argumentation schemes [32]) which enables the representation of networks of arguments on the Semantic Web. Using a Semantic Web-based system called ARGDF, users can create arguments using different argumentation schemes and can query arguments using a suitable Semantic Web query language. Clearly, such integration can provide a powerful platform for the development of more evolved argument-based recommendation technologies, where arguments presented by others users can be taken into account for making decisions or presenting recommendations.

7 Conclusions. Future Directions

We have introduced a novel approach for enhancing recommendation technologies through the use of qualitative, argument-based analysis. As we have shown in this chapter, the argumentation formalism provided by Defeasible Logic Programming constitutes a powerful tool for carrying out this analysis when dealing with users' complex information needs. We performed some preliminary experiments on the integration of argumentation and recommendation technologies, which only served as a "proof of concept" prototype. We are currently carrying out more through evaluations in order to assess the full applicability of our proposal. Part of our current research in this context is related to combining quantitative and qualitative features in the argumentative analysis through the use of P-DeLP [1, 2], an extension of Defeasible Logic Programming which incorporates the treatment of possibilistic uncertainty at the object language level. In P-DeLP, in contrast to DeLP, arguments are attached with numerical values which determine their strength. Such values (necessity degrees) are assigned to the facts and rules present in the program, and propagated when performing inference via generalized modus ponens. In that respect, P-DeLP would be a natural tool for enhancing our current approach to argument-based recommendation, as such necessity degrees can be associated with rankings or user-assigned values.

We contend that the evolution of recommender systems will result in efficient and reliable content-based search environments, where both quantitative and qualitative analysis will play important roles. We believe our proposal is a realistic and doable approach to help fulfill this long-term goal.

Acknowledgements This research was funded by Agencia Nacional de Promoción Científica y Tecnológica (PICT 2005 - 32373), by CONICET (Argentina), by Projects TIN2006-15662-C02-01 and TIN2008-06596-C02-01 (MEC, Spain), and PGI Projects 24/ZN10, 24/N023 and 24/N020 (SGCyT, Universidad Nacional del Sur, Argentina).

References

1. T. Alsinet, C. Chesñevar, L. Godo, S. Sandri, and G. Simari. Formalizing argumentative reasoning in a possibilistic logic programming setting with fuzzy unification. *International Journal of Approximate Reasoning*, 48(3):711–729, 2008.
2. T. Alsinet, C. Chesñevar, L. Godo, and G. Simari. A logic programming framework for possibilistic argumentation: Formalization and logical properties. *Fuzzy Sets and Systems*, 159(10):1208–1228, 2008.
3. L. Amgoud and M. Serrurier. Agents that argue and explain classifications. *Autonomous Agents and Multi-Agent Systems*, 16(2):187–209, 2008.
4. M. Balabanovic and Y. Shoham. Content-based, collaborative recommendation. *Communications of the ACM*, 40(3):66–72, 1997.
5. T. Berners-Lee, J. Hendler, and O. Lassila. The semantic web. *Scientific American*, May 2001.
6. R. Brena, J. Aguirre, C. Chesñevar, E. Ramírez, and L. Garrido. Knowledge and information distribution leveraged by intelligent agents. *Knowledge and Information Systems*, 12(2):203–227, 2007.
7. J. Budzik, K. Hammond, and L. Birnbaum. Information access in context. *Knowledge based systems*, 14(1–2):37–53, 2001.
8. R. Burke. Hybrid recommender systems: Survey and experiments. *User Modeling and User-Adapted Interaction*, 12(4):331–370, 2002.
9. C. Chesñevar, J. McGinnis, S. Modgil, I. Rahwan, C. Reed, G. Simari, M. South, G. Vreeswijk, and S. Wilmott. Towards an argument interchange format. *Knowledge Engineering Review*, 21(4):293–316, 2006.
10. C. Chesñevar, A. Maguitman, and R. Loui. Logical Models of Argument. *ACM Computing Surveys*, 32(4):337–383, Dec. 2000.
11. C. Chesñevar, A. Maguitman, and M. Sabaté. An argument-based decision support system for assessing natural language usage on the basis of the web corpus. *International Journal of Intelligent Systems (IJIS)*, 21(11):1151–1180, 2006.
12. C. Chesñevar, A. Maguitman, and G. Simari. Argument-Based Critics and Recommenders: A Qualitative Perspective on User Support Systems. *Journal of Data and Knowledge Engineering*, 59(2):293–319, 2006.
13. D. Engelbart. Augmenting human intellect: A conceptual framework. Summary report, Stanford Research Institute, on Contract AF 49(638)-1024, October 1962.
14. A. García and G. Simari. Defeasible Logic Programming: An Argumentative Approach. *Theory and Practice of Logic Programming*, 4(1):95–138, 2004.
15. S. Gómez, C. Chesñevar, and G. Simari. Defeasible reasoning in web-based forms through argumentation. *International Journal of Information Technology and Decision Making (IJITDM)*, 7(1):71–101, Mar. 2008.
16. M. González, C. Chesñevar, C. Collazos, and G. Simari. Modelling shared knowledge and shared knowledge awareness in cscl scenarios through automated argumentation systems. In J. M. Haake, S. F. Ochoa, and A. Cechich, editors, *CRIWG*, volume 4715 of *Lecture Notes in Computer Science*, pages 207–222. Springer, 2007.
17. G. Governatori and A. Stranieri. Towards the application of association rules for defeasible rules discovery. In *Legal Knowledge & Information Systems*, pages 63–75. JURIX, IOS Press, 2001.
18. A. Hunter. Hybrid argumentation systems for structured news reports. *Knowledge Engineering Review*, pages 295–329, 2001.

19. J. Konstan. Introduction to recommender systems: Algorithms and evaluation. *ACM Transactions on Information Systems*, 22(1):1–4, 2004.
20. F. Linton, D. Joy, and H. Schaefer. Building user and expert models by long-term observation of application usage. In *Proceedings of the seventh international conference on User modeling*, pages 129–138. Springer-Verlag New York, Inc., 1999.
21. M. Mozina, J. Zabkar, and I. Bratko. Argument based machine learning. *Artificial Intelligence*, 171(10-15):922–937, 2007.
22. J. O'Donovan and B. Smyth. Trust in recommender systems. In *IUI '05: Proceedings of the 10th international conference on Intelligent user interfaces*, pages 167–174, New York, NY, USA, 2005. ACM.
23. M. Pazzani and D. Billsus. Content-based recommendation systems. In P. Brusilovsky, A. Kobsa and W. Nejdl, editors, *The Adaptive Web, Methods and Strategies of Web Personalization*, volume 4321 of *Lecture Notes in Computer Science*, pages 325–341. Springer, 2007.
24. H. Prakken and G. Sartor. The role of logic in computational models of legal argument: A critical survey. In A. C. Kakas and F. Sadri, editors, *Computational Logic: Logic Programming and Beyond*, volume 2408 of *Lecture Notes in Computer Science*, pages 342–381. Springer, 2002.
25. H. Prakken and G. Vreeswijk. Logical Systems for Defeasible Argumentation. In D. Gabbay and F.Guenther, editors, *Handbook of Philosophical Logic*, pages 219–318. Kluwer, 2002.
26. I. Rahwan. Mass argumentation and the semantic web. *Journal of Web Semantics*, 6(1):29–37, 2008.
27. I. Rahwan, F. Zablith, and C. Reed. Laying the foundations for a world wide argument web. *Artificial Intelligence*, 171(10-15):897–921, 2007.
28. J. Sandvig, B. Mobasher, and R. Burke. A survey of collaborative recommendation and the robustness of model-based algorithms. *IEEE Data Engineering Bulletin*, 31(2):3–13, 2008.
29. R. Schenkel, T. Crecelius, M. Kacimi, T. Neumann, J. Parreira, M. Spaniol, and G. Weikum. Social wisdom for search and recommendation. *IEEE Data Engineering Bulletin*, 31(2):40–49, 2008.
30. G. Simari and R. Loui. A Mathematical Treatment of Defeasible Reasoning and its Implementation. *Artificial Intelligence*, 53:125–157, 1992.
31. B. Verheij. Artificial argument assistants for defeasible argumentation. *Artificial Intelligence*, 150(1-2):291–324, 2003.
32. D. Walton. *Argumentation Schemes for Presumptive Reasoning*. Erlbaum, Mahwah, NJ, 1996.
33. M. Wardeh, T. Bench-Capon, and F. Coenen. Arguments from experience: The padua protocol. In P. Besnard, S. Doutre, and A. Hunter, editors, *COMMA*, volume 172 of *Frontiers in Artificial Intelligence and Applications*, pages 405–416. IOS Press, 2008.
34. P. Zhang, J. Sun, and H. Chen. Frame-based argumentation for group decision task generation and identification. *Decision Support Systems*, 39:643–659, 2005.

Chapter 21
Arguing on the Semantic Grid

Paolo Torroni, Marco Gavanelli and Federico Chesani

1 Introduction

In the last decade, the rapid evolution of Internet technologies has opened new perspectives, created new application areas, provided new social environments for communication and posed new challenges. Among the most influential domains of Internet sciences to date we find Web services, Grid computing, the Web 2.0, and the Semantic Web. These are components of a wider vision, which we call the *Semantic Grid*.

We believe that the Semantic Grid is an interesting domain for Argumentation, for two reasons. First, its new challenges can give motivation to further Argumentation research in ways that have not been explored so far. Second, existing Argumentation theories and technologies can find in the Semantic Grid a natural and convenient application domain.

With this chapter we aim to give a gentle introduction to the Semantic Grid, to Argumentation researchers potentially interested in this new research and application domain. In particular, the next section will be rich in pointers and is mainly intended for "novices" to provide them with a global picture of the main ideas, mainstream technologies and challenges. In addition, we position in this global picture some Argumentation research done, and motivate future work by discussing possible roles that Argumentation can play in Semantic Grid research and applications.

Paolo Torroni
Dipartimento di Elettronica, Informatica e Sistemistica, University of Bologna, Viale Risorgimento 2, 40136 Bologna, Italy, email: paolo.torroni@unibo.it

Marco Gavanelli
Dipartimento di Ingegneria, University of Ferrara, Via Saragat 1, 44100 Ferrara, Italy, email: marco.gavanelli@unife.it

Federico Chesani
Dipartimento di Elettronica, Informatica e Sistemistica, University of Bologna, Viale Risorgimento 2, 40136 Bologna, Italy, email: federico.chesani@unibo.it

I. Rahwan, G. R. Simari (eds.), *Argumentation in Artificial Intelligence,*   423
DOI 10.1007/978-0-387-98197-0_21, © Springer Science+Business Media, LLC 2009

We will not present new argumentation theories and technologies. We will rather refer to other chapters of this book when needed. Moreover, by no means we aim to produce an exhaustive survey of research done across Argumentation and the Semantic Grid. We will instead give some specific examples, so as to adopt a concrete approach when discussing the bigger picture and the challenges that wait for us.

Some readers will agree that the Semantic Grid is a natural arena for Argumentation to apply its results and further its development following the influential themes identified by Bench-Capon and Dunne [2]. These themes are: argumentation's origins in non-classical logics, models of argumentation as dialogue processes, and diagrammatic views of argument structure.

Important motivations that brought argumentation theory into use in AI arose from the issues of *reasoning and explanation under incomplete and uncertain information*. Some fundamental traits of the Web are openness, incompleteness, and peaceful coexistence of contradictory information. These are not to be seen as limitations but rather as an asset, and their presence is one of the main reasons that caused the popularity of the Internet to reach today's levels. The Semantic Grid swarms with new technologies, standards and abstractions, but all of them are faithful to the open nature of the traditional Web.

The possibility to engage in *dialogue processes* was one of the main social drivers of the Web and of the development of the notion of Social Web and community. These are fundamental elements of the Semantic Grid. At a more abstract level, dialogue is a particular form of interaction, and the Semantic Grid, from Grid computing through Web services to Web 2.0 is all about interaction.

Finally, Web communities have become a reference model for new social participation paradigms such as those of eGovernment and eDemocracy. These paradigms rely on applications and user interfaces, aimed to help exchange of concepts and ideas, accessibility, communication and debate. Thus an influential theme of Semantic Grid development is *visualization methods*.

In this chapter, we argue that Argumentation research can contribute to the creation of an "argumentation-enabled Semantic Grid" vision. We give concrete examples of how this can be achieved, and we discuss the main challenges that must be faced. We conclude by discussing some application areas where argumentation-based approaches to the Semantic Grid may be particularly influential.

2 The Semantic Grid: A bird's-eye view

The Semantic Grid is a vision of collaboration and computation on a global scale, which emerges from the synergy of Semantic Web technologies and ideas coming from three different domains of Internet sciences: Web services, Web 2.0, and Grid computing. These domains differ from one another in terms of inspiration, architecture, technologies, resources they target and features they offer, but they also have many areas of intersection. The Semantic Grid vision proposes to build on the technologies developed in these domains and to add meaning to the Grid, to enhance

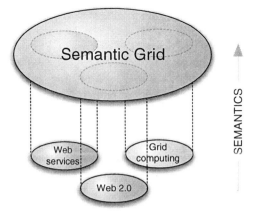

Fig. 21.1 The Semantic Grid

the existing features and offer new ones. In this section we present the main concepts and technologies of each domain, and we discuss the features envisioned by the global picture.

2.1 Semantic Web Technologies

Since its presentation on the pages of a popular scientific magazine [4], the Semantic Web (SW) has appealed to many computer science researchers and outsiders for its features and promises. It has motivated so many research directions, that it has become hard nowadays to clearly identify what the SW is anymore. However, looking back eight years later, it is easy to see how some parts of the original proposal have been dropped or postponed, while the core ideas have resisted and evolved, and the adoption of standards has begun in the information industry.

The SW initiative,[1] in its fundamentals, aimed to overcome the main limitations of the World Wide Web, as it was perceived in 2001. A huge amount of information was available, but machines could not automatically exploit it in full, since its representation only targeted human users. In fact, standard mark-up languages such as HTML—the most common format for Web pages—define how the information should be *presented* to the human users, but do not tell anything about *what* is being presented. This type of information structuring would not help automatic information extraction from Web sites, because the quality of the result highly depends on how frequently a Web site's presentation—i.e., its graphical appearance—changes.

The first step towards the SW consisted in identifying standards supporting interoperability, to overcome problems arising from the heterogeneity of software and hardware. It was decided to build upon UNICODE and XML. Such a choice

---

[1] See the W3C Semantic Web Activity's official Web site, http://www.w3.org/2001/sw/.

sets the same alphabet for SW applications, but it does not suffice to guarantee interoperability, like the French and the English are not guaranteed to interoperate by simply using the same letters.

The introduction of the Resource Description Framework (RDF)[2] represented a step ahead towards Web information structuring. RDF is simple yet effective. The idea is to represent each piece of knowledge by sentences of the form *subject, predicate, object*. Each part of the sentence is an entity identified by a name. The whole sentence—or *triple*—is read as a binary relation between *subject* and *object*, whose name—or *type*—is defined by the *predicate*. The SW consortium adopted an existing naming system standard: the Uniform Resource Identifier (URI).

With the introduction of RDF, the SW initiative met one of its goals: it managed to provide a standard, structured way for representing information. This again did not suffice to capture the *meaning* given to information. The French and the English structure their sentences in a similar way, but they do not necessarily give the same meaning to words. Therefore, standards were developed to define the meaning of terms/entities, which converged into RDF Schema (RDFS)[3] and its successor, Web Ontology Language (OWL),[4] endorsed by the W3C.[5]

OWL enables to formally define *ontologies*, i.e. to specify the features that characterize a concept, and the relations among concepts. One of the main relations linking concepts with one another is *inheritance*, which defines a parent-child hierarchy. Many other relations are supported, and, above all, users can define their own relations, treated by OWL as first-class objects.

Ontologies are usually defined by a *Terminological Box* (TBox), plus an *Assertion Box* (ABox). The TBox is the set of logical axioms, defining the concepts and the relations among them. The ABox is a set of TBox-compliant concept instances. OWL comes in three different flavours (Lite, DL and Full), each one characterized by a different language expressiveness and underlying formal semantics. OWL Lite and DL refer to the family of Description Logics, while OWL Full refers to First Order Logic and Higher Order Logic. To date, a large number of ontologies have been defined for all sorts of general concepts and specific domains. A new research theme is: how to find suitable ontologies from libraries, such as the Protégé[6] and the DAML[7] ontology libraries, or from the Web. There are also many ontology design tools. The most popular one is probably Protégé [18] developed by the Stanford Center for Biomedical Informatics Research.

---

[2] The work of the RDF Core Working Group, completed in 2004, is summarised in the W3C Resource Description Framework official Web site, http://www.w3.org/RDF/.

[3] See the W3C RDF Vocabulary Description Language 1.0: RDF Schema, http://www.w3.org/TR/rdf-schema/.

[4] See the W3C OWL Web Ontology Language Reference, released as a W3C Recommendation on 10 February 2004 http://www.w3.org/TR/owl-ref/.

[5] W3C is the World Wide Web Consortium, see http://www.w3.org/.

[6] See the Protégé Ontology Library on http://protegewiki.stanford.edu/index.php/Protege_Ontology_Library.

[7] See the DAML Ontology Library http://www.daml.org/ontologies/.

The SW architecture has been conceived as a layered cake, in which each layer uses the services offered by the one below, and offers new, richer and more complex services to the one above. The layers above OWL however are still at an early development stage. Recently, great interest is on the Linking Open Data initiative,[8] which aims at making data freely available to everyone and at defining best practices for exposing, sharing, and connecting pieces of data, information, and knowledge on the Semantic Web using URIs and RDF. The interested reader can find more material on the Semantic Web Activity's official Web site.

2.2 Web services

The Service Oriented Architecture (SOA) has recently emerged as a paradigm for structuring complex information systems within a distributed environment. The main idea consists in organizing a system in terms of re-usable components (services) that provide a precise functionality. To maximize re-usability, services are intended to be loosely coupled with one another. Thus the invocation of a service is typically stateless, and the interaction is based on message passing. Complex applications are then built as groups of services that provide the desired behaviour as a whole, by interacting with each other. Developing complex systems amounts to selecting the services and establishing how and in which order they should interact.

A requirement for the feasibility itself of a SOA is service *interoperability*. To this end, the SOA envisages a de-coupling between the description of the service and its real implementation. Each service publishes a set of metadata describing how it can be invoked by a service requester. The content of such information spans from the logical location were the service can be invoked, to the supported communication protocols and the parameter types.

Although several application frameworks support SOA principles and claim to be SOA-oriented, the most common technological implementation of an SOA is based on Web services. Already supported by many industrial vendors, Web services are characterized by a set of standards regulating all the aspects concerning interaction, leaving a great deal of freedom about the implementation of the services. E.g., the Web Service Description Language (WSDL)[9] provides a standard for describing a service in terms of its logical location, its invocation parameters and the interaction protocol, such as SUN's RPC, HTTP, or the Simple Object Access Protocol (SOAP).[10] The Universal Description, Discovery and Integration standard (UDDI)[11] regulates service description publishing and brokering.

---

[8] See the Linking Open Data Web site, http://linkeddata.org and Berners-Lee's report on Linked Data at http://www.w3.org/DesignIssues/LinkedData.html.

[9] See the Web Service Description Language Web site, http://www.w3.org/TR/wsdl20/.

[10] See the W3C's SOAP V1.2 Specifications,http://www.w3.org/TR/soap12-part1/.

[11] Documents produced by the UDDI Specification Technical Committee are available from the following Web site: http://www.oasis-open.org/committees/uddi-spec/.

Let us give an example of Web service. In the scenario illustrated in [24], Sarah is a research scientist who often travels to conferences, and must abide by her department's regulations concerning refunds. A problem is that Sarah is not an expert in such regulations. A traditional solution consists of publishing all relevant information on a public repository, such as a Web site. Every time Sarah needs to travel, she reads the most recent regulations, downloads the relevant forms from the Web, does the necessary paperwork, and delivers the filled-in forms to her administration. However, this solution does not help Sarah using the information properly, it is prone to errors and misunderstandings, and is not highly automated, instead it heavily relies on direct interaction between Sarah and the administration.

A different solution based on SW technologies seems more appropriate: regulations are encoded in a semantically rich, machine-understandable format, and made available via a "department Web service." Using a smartphone with an intelligent agent running in it, Sarah can have all relevant information automatically downloaded from the Web service. Whenever Sarah needs to travel, she queries her smartphone to know if her trip is approved. Because the rules are published in a machine-understandable format and a semantically rich language, the intelligent smartphone agent can understand their meaning, reason from them, and determine whether Sarah's goal can be accomplished given the current regulations.

While the technological implementation of Web services is now well developed, the task of composing services into a complete system is still the focus of intense research activities. Here we find two main approaches: one relying on the idea of *orchestration*, by a central actor, the other one stressing instead the concept of *choreography*, of many cooperating peers. The textual Business Process Execution Language (BPEL),[12] proposed in an industrial setting, supports the definition of a system as a service that coordinates (orchestrates) many other services. Commercially available BPEL engines can be used to execute the BPEL definition of a system. The graphical Web Service-Choreography Description Language (WS-CDL)[13] instead assumes that services are organized like a choreography, where each peer plays a role and the overall system is given by the contribution of all the players.

It is worthwhile mentioning another language whose aim is also to define complex applications. The Business Process Modeling Notation (BPMN),[14] developed in the Business Processes domain, is a high-level, graphical notation for defining a business process in terms of a procedural flow of business activities. BPMN is highly expressive, but its specifications are not executable—although research has mapped fragments of BPMN into BPEL.

Key issues in the Web services context are discovery and interoperability. The Web services' ability of discovering and being discovered, and then effectively interoperate, greatly affects their potential success. The aforementioned UDDI standard

---

[12] See IBM's Business Process Execution Language for Web Services V1.1 Specifications, http://www.ibm.com/developerworks/library/specification/ws-bpel/.

[13] See the W3C's Recommendation for Web Service-Choreography Description Language V1.0, http://www.w3.org/TR/ws-cdl-10/.

[14] See the Object Management Group's Business Process Management Initiative Web site, http://www.bpmn.org/.

was proposed to meet this need. UDDI addresses service discovery using WSDL. However, WSDL descriptions do not contain any metadata about the service semantics, thus UDDI cannot use any information about *what* services provide.

To this end, researchers have studied ways to extend service descriptions with semantic information, by exploiting the results obtained within the Semantic Web Activity. The Semantic Markup for Web Services (OWL-S)[15] and the Web Service Modeling Ontology (WSMO)[16] are the two main proposals. They both rely on SW technologies, in particular on the ontology layer. They extend service descriptions by characterizing the semantics of the input parameters, of the outputs, as well as of the preconditions and the effects related to the service invocation. Semantically enhanced Web services are called *semantic Web services* [17].

2.3 Grid computing

The World Wide Web is mainly about presenting content. It was not designed to provide other types of resources, such as storage space or computing power. Web services enable to invoke a specific service via the Web, but they do not allow user processes to target computing resources of other computers. The Grid started as an idea to overcome these shortcomings, building on two successful distributed schemes for the Internet: peer-to-peer computing and Internet computing.

Nowadays, most of the network traffic in the Internet is due to peer-to-peer. Peer-to-peer applications, such as those mainstream relying on the BitTorrent protocol,[17] and other former file sharing applications such as Napster, GNUtella, and Freenet [7], provide a means to distribute files across a network, by replicating them on many storage devices. The ubiquity of these types of applications paved the way to a new model for mass storage, in which a distributed file system over the network gives a user petabytes of virtual space, transparently distributed across the hard-disks of many users, providing replication, fast distributed access, and increased reliability.

The success of this model was also due to a steady decrease in the cost of home computers. Mainframes and supercomputers became less used, while intensive, number-crunching applications are more and more split into (almost) independent sub-parts and fed to computer clusters. The ubiquity of home computers and extension of the Internet made it possible to target and use new resources, such as idle CPU time of millions of computers. One example is given by the famous SETI@Home project and its quest for extraterrestrial life, which has produced the largest computation in history to date, and by other projects which adopted the same method and gave birth to the new model of Internet computing.

The Grid is, in general, the possibility to publish and use computational resources (as opposed to Web pages) on the Internet. For example, the computer of a European

---

[15] See the DAML Services Web site on DAML-S and OWL-S, http://www.daml.org/services/owl-s/.

[16] See the The ESSI WSMO working group Web site, http://www.wsmo.org/.

[17] See the BitTorrent.org forum, http://www.bittorrent.org/.

user is often idle when its owner is sleeping: there we have a resource—computing power—which could be made available on the Grid, for the benefit of another user who is not sleeping, say an Australian. The Grid concept heavily relies on the idea of reciprocation, thus the amount of accessible resources will depend the amount of shared resources. For instance, the Australian is expected to return the favour at some point, say 12 hours later, as night falls in Oceania. The implementation of the Grid opens a number of issues [11], such as the need to define new standards and protocols, to ensure security and to provide new accounting methods, access rules and policies, but it also offers unprecedented computing power and storage capacity. The organization leading the global standardization effort for Grid computing is a community of users, developers, and vendors, called the Open Grid Forum (OGF).[18]

Besides providing computing resources, research on the Grid is focussed on the concept of *Virtual Organizations* (VOs) [9]. Users that have similar goals but belong to different (physical) organizations might be interested in sharing various types of resources. For example, the members of a project might work in different departments or universities, but they want to share memory and CPU time, but also software, data, experimental results, partial computations that could be reused by other members of the VO. A type of VO could be a Data Grid: as a single virtual data store which is actually distributed. The VO concept is also used in the context of Web services, for example by the ArguGRID project (see Section 3.3).

A notable example of Data Grid was the CombeChem project [22], which also represented a step towards the evolution of the Grid in the direction of adding meaning to data. The project's aim was to build a distributed repository of chemical experimental results. A requirement was that the repository should accept data taken from any sort of chemical experiment, possibly with new types of inputs (instrument sensitivity, substance purity, etc.), unforeseen at the time the repository was being designed. Another requirement, to ensure practical usability and automated processing, was that the input data would have to have a machine-understandable semantics. The adopted solution was to use RDF. Every laboratory can add new information associated with some chemical compound (either new or already present) simply by adding a triple in the (distributed) RDF store. Despite all the limitations of RDF compare to, say, OWL, CombeChem was nevertheless an example showing the practical need of adding semantics to the Grid. The need for semantic information is present at the various levels of the Grid, as it is discussed in the Open Grid Service Architecture (OGSA) documentation produced by the OGF [8].

2.4 Web 2.0

The World Wide Web, originally conceived and developed to enable automatic information sharing between geographically distributed individuals, is being more and more strongly shaped by the idea of community. The so-called Web 2.0 is a

---

[18] See the Open Grid Forum Web site, http://www.ogf.org/.

place where people exchange ideas using Web sites, blogs, chats, and spaces for social networking, such as Orkut, mySpace, Flickr, Blogger, LinkedIn, FaceBook and many others [19]. The mainstream technologies developed in this context are mostly application-driven. They are wikis, blogs, microformats, and social tagging tools. Differently from the areas presented above, the Web 2.0 was not born from a vision but it rather emerged from the grassroots. This is why we would not talk about an architecture for the Web 2.0, but rather about a collection of Web-based applications. According to IBM software architect Steven Watt,[19] the Web 2.0 is best described as a core set of patterns that are observable in applications that share the Web 2.0 label. These patterns are *services* (as an architectural feature), *simplicity*, both for the user and the developer, and *community mechanisms*. Web 2.0 applications are dominated by sites that explicitly seek to create communities and connect people via the artifacts that they share [5]. Differently form Grid computing and Web services, Web 2.0's expansion found its main driver in the people's need to feel a part of a community, in which they can contribute and give their best efforts without expecting any direct return on investment. We could say that the Web 2.0 comes from a view of the Internet as a social experiment, and therefore has a strong social connotation.

The area in which Semantic Web and Web 2.0 meet is sometimes called *Social Semantic Web*. There we find initiatives such as SIOC (Semantically Interlinked Online Communities)[20] and FOAF (Friend Of A Friend).[21]

2.5 Putting it all together

From a historical perspective, Grid computing and SW research have joined forces as researchers in the two communities realised that they had a common goal: fostering collaborative work. Semantic technologies enable machines to share information, and to feed it to applications which have been developed independently from one another. Adding meaning to the Grid amounts to associating semantic information to computing resources, which allows for resource discovery [14], and inherits features of SW services, such as interoperability. SW services gain from the Grid better reliability and scalability, thanks to the replication of data and services. On the other hand, from a technological and business-oriented perspective, XML and Web services are becoming the industrial standard for integrating distributed systems.

Many researchers have recognized the synergy of ideas developed in these different communities. Thus a vision has emerged which draws from all the above and goes under the name of *Semantic Grid*. Among others, De Roure defines the Semantic Grid as an "extension of the current Grid in which information and services

---

[19] See *Mashups—The evolution of the SOA, Part 1: Web 2.0 and foundational concepts* by Steven Watt on the IBM Web site, http://www.ibm.com/developerworks/webservices/library/ws-soa-mashups/.

[20] See the SIOC initiative Web site, http://sioc-project.org.

[21] See the FOAF project Web site, http://foaf-project.org.

Table 21.1 Inspiration, architectures, resources and features of the Grid

	Web 2.0	**Web services**	**Grid computing**
Technologies	wikis, blogs, microformats, social tagging	protocols, standards, implementations, tools	middleware, standards, implementations, tools
Inspiration	social, community	business	e-Sciences
Architecture	Web-based applications	SOA, distributed systems	distributed computing
Resources	social communication	services	storage space, CPU time
Features	freedom of expression, cooperative work, dissemination, exchange	service-level agreement, quality of service, fault tolerance	VOs, performance, transparency, fault tolerance, accessibility

are given well-defined meaning, better enabling computers and people to work in cooperation."[22] Nowadays, the user base of Web 2.0 technologies is limited only by the extension of the Internet. The extent and impact of the Web 2.0 phenomenon cannot be neglected, and we consider technologies oriented to social networking and community to be first-class citizens of the Semantic Grid grand vision.

Table 21.1 gives the global picture. By Semantic Grid, we mean the vision where semantic technologies contribute to achieving, as a whole, enhanced virtual organisations, resource discovery, selection, cooperation, user-oriented communication and creative content browsing.

3 Argumentation and the Semantic Grid

State-of-the-art research has recently identified several areas in the Semantic Grid vision in which argumentation can play a role, either by exploiting Semantic Grid technologies, or by contributing to them.

3.1 Web 2.0 and Semantic Web Technologies for Argumentation

The advent of Web 2.0 has opened up new horizons for participation and expression. Arguments definitely play a role in this picture. Any basic blog and community software supports posting of user comments, replies to comments, etc., and although conversations sometimes tend to drift to eristic dialogues, still there is a large share of information which could represent a valuable asset if it was put in a structured way. Consider for example typical Web 2.0 topics of discussion such as "Monogamy is out of date," "The phrase *war on terrorism* is a misnomer" or "Being a nihilist ain't that bad." The level of discussion could raise significantly if search engines could answer queries such as "what is the support of such a topic," "what are all arguments that attack a given argument," or "what can a given argument be used

---

[22] See the Semantic Grid Community Portal, http://www.semanticgrid.org/.

for," and possibly reason about the results automatically. Technology has not yet reached this stage, but there are tools aimed to facilitate structured Web discussion. They include, for example, TruthMapping.com,[23] which incidentally hosts discussions about the topics above, and Discourse DB, already mentioned in Chapter 19. TruthMapping.com provides an intuitive interface to enable users to engage in structured argumentation dialogues about topics, by identifying arguments, rebuttals, undercuts, and organise them using a simplified structure. Discourse DB[24] is a more specialized forum to discuss politics, and it can export content in RDF.

In this direction also goes work by Rahwan et al. on a World Wide Web of arguments [20]. A standard, semantically rich format is assumed for Web information, as well as for arguments. Arguments can be published on the Web using a well-defined structure, that enables automatic agents to use the published information, without posing excessive difficulty to non-expert human users. The challenge is to take the best balance of usability with automatic agents and simplicity for human users. Automatic agents should be able to understand arguments published by humans as humans understand them. On the other hand, humans should not be burdened by complicated tasks that would refrain them from publishing, in everyday life, arguments in a semantic form.

With a look at a future in which several argumentation-enabled Web applications will interoperate with one another, Rahwan and colleagues [6] propose the Argument Interchange Format (AIF), an ontology to represent arguments, together with RDF encodings and tools for authoring and navigating arguments (see Chapter 19). The AIF ontology was implemented in RDF and RDFS using Protégé (see Section 2.1).

3.2 Argumentation Technology for the Semantic Web

In the same way as SW technologies can help community-oriented argumentation and argumentation-based reasoning, also argumentation technologies can help the development of the SW. Laera et al. have identified a possible role of argumentation technologies in the ontology mapping process [16]. Ontologies, as we have seen earlier on, specify concepts and their relations in a formal way. In a distributed context, agents or Web services that need to interact will refer to some specific ontology, possibly developed by their designer for completing specific tasks. The ontology might be published on the Web, or simply inserted in an agent's knowledge base. When the interacting parties need to communicate, they can either use a common ontology, or they can try to establish a set of correspondences between terms in one ontology and the other. Various methods can be conceived to perform such an *alignment* [21]. The proposal presented in [16] is to provide agents with means to discuss, via argumentation, a mapping that is satisfactory for both parties. In this

---

[23] See TruthMapping.com Web site, http://www.truthmapping.com.

[24] More information on http://discoursedb.org/wiki/DiscourseDB:About.

setting, each agent can have its preferences and interests in the correspondence between terms. For example, one agent might have a very shallow ontology, and might prefer using terminological correspondences, instead of structural correspondences that would make less sense in this case.

The alignment starts with an ontology alignment service [10] that provides the possible matchings, together with a confidence level for each matching and a set of justifications that explain why the mapping was proposed. The agents compare the confidence level with an internal threshold. Mappings that do not reach the threshold are discarded. The arguments are the possible matchings returned by the ontology alignment service based on a Value-based Argumentation Framework (see Chapter 3).

3.3 Arguing Virtual Organizations: ArguGRID

The ArguGRID project, led by Francesca Toni, proposes a vision in which Web services/agents and argumentation technologies may be combined to support decision making and negotiations inside Virtual Organizations (VOs). Some of the main issues addressed by way of argumentation are Web service selection and composition. The project proposes an architecture consisting of a platform [23] using peer-to-peer computing, and VOs made of Web services associated with argumentation-based agents using resources of various kind. Agents are built on top of a middleware, which is the main component of the ArguGRID platform.

ArguGRID agents are responsible for the negotiation of contracts regulating their interaction. Argumentation is used for different tasks: to solve a decision-making problem in the service selection process, to support contract negotiation and agreement about executable workflows, and to help dispute resolution with respect to agreed workflows and contracts. The agents use CaSAPI [12], a general-purpose argumentation tool for Assumption-Based Argumentation (see Chapter 10).

The project focusses on three main applications: Earth Observation, eProcurement, and eBusiness. In first application, the problem is information source heterogeneity and distribution. The role of argumentation is mainly in decision-making and service composition, especially in crisis scenarios such as oil spill or fire detection. The purpose is to produce user-tailored solutions that combine existing services in a workable and effective way. The eProcurement application investigates use cases based on automating decision-making processes and negotiations among a large number of partners. There are specific example cases showing, for instance, how eAuction parameters can be optimised. The last application focusses on the idea of contract. Argumentation is used to negotiate contracts based on a formal framework using goals and preferences and to resolve conflicts. ArguGRID uses a two-level reasoning process. The acceptability of certain beliefs and facts is established at the "object-level," while at the "meta-level" the legal doctrines determine the risk allocation. More information is on the ArguGRID Web site.[25]

3.4 Arguing Semantic Web Services: ArgSCIFF

The research presented by Torroni et al. in [24] proposes a framework that supports dialogic argument exchange between SW services. Interaction among Web services is essentially of a request response kind. This is sometimes not enough informative for human users, who cannot understand the justification of the interaction outputs nor can effectively intervene to modify it. ArgSCIFF aims to making Web service reasoning more visible to potential users by using dialogues for service interaction. Argumentation technology is used to drive the interaction at a high level, where human users can perceive message exchanges and service-request sequences as dialogues that they can understand better than current modalities. ArgSCIFF agents use the SCIFF[26] abductive logic programming framework [1] to implement an argumentation framework in the style of Assumption-Based Argumentation (see Chapter 10). Let us look into ArgSCIFF in more detail.

3.4.1 Argumentation for machine-supported, collaborative problem-solving

Let us consider again the scenario introduced in Section 2.2. The solution based on Web services greatly automates the process, but it is not enough to accommodate interactive, dialogical problem-solving. If Sarah's request is rejected, Sarah cannot interact with the administration staff and find out why. This is true of all client-server based systems which provide definitional answers rather than informed justifications that users could argue with and, possibly, eventually understand and accept. The risk is the creation of a barrier to human adoption of IT solutions.

What ArgSCIFF proposes instead is a third scenario, in which the department's service and Sarah's smartphone agent interact by exchanging arguments in a dialogical fashion. Sarah's smartphone not only posts requests to the department's service and obtains replies but also reasons from such replies. When the replies are negative, the agent challenges them and tries to understand ways to obtain alternative, positive replies. If necessary, the agent can provide fresh information that could inhibit some regulations and activate others. This solution delegates most of the reasoning and interaction to the machine by relying on semantic Web service technology, and it gives Sarah understandable, justified answers and decisions. The whole process is a machine-supported, collaborative problem-solving activity rather than a flat client-server, query-answer interaction.

---

[25] See the ArguGRID project Web site, http://www.argugrid.eu/.

[26] See the SCIFF framework Web site, http://lia.deis.unibo.it/sciff.

3.4.2 Dialogue based Web service interaction

The ArgSCIFF architecture extends the semantic Web service architecture with argumentation technology implemented through *request* and *challenge* methods. The ArgSCIFF argumentation protocol is asymmetric: the requester agent sees a dialogue, and the provider agent sees service requests. Requester and provider interact with each other using SW technologies. From the SW's ontology layer downward, the two semantic Web services will adopt some agreed standard, such as HTTP, SOAP, and RuleML for rule exchange. At the logic level, knowledge is expressed by SCIFF programs. The ArgSCIFF proof procedure instead is used to evaluate queries and replies, according to the abductive semantics defined in [24]. The exchanged messages follow a simple request-reply protocol, but at a high level, the user can see a dialogue, in which the requester service engages, to argue for its own case. From the provider's standpoint, no dialogue occurs. The two different views of the ongoing interaction generate a decoupling, and this decoupling makes it possible to marry stateless Web services with argumentation dialogues.

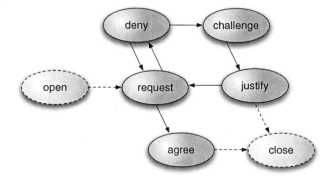

Fig. 21.2 The ArgSCIFF dialogue protocol starts by a *request* and can *challenge* the provider in case of negative answer.

The dialogue protocol starts by a *request*, which can result in an agreement or a denial. In case of denial, the requester can *challenge* the provider, which will answer by justifying his previous answer. Depending on the requester's knowledge and goals, the dialogue can proceed by a new request, or reach an end. The protocol is depicted in Fig. 21.2.

The dialogue protocol's implementation relies on two kinds of knowledge: (1) a domain-independent knowledge that encodes the argumentation protocol and is the same for both requester and provider, and (2) specific, private knowledge, which distinguishes one party from the other. This separation makes the ArgSCIFF able to accommodate other kinds of possible scenarios, in which the domain knowledge will be different, and it supports heterogeneity of policies and negotiation strategies.

3.5 Concluding Remarks

With this brief review we covered only a part of the research pursued at the intersection between Argumentation and the Semantic Grid. There are many other important contributions, such as work by Bentahar et al. [3], who propose to help Web services better interact by giving reasons that support their conclusions and receive counterarguments, and Buckingham Shum's Cohere project [5] mentioned in Chapter 19. Without even attempting to be exhaustive, this short survey suffices to demonstrate an existing interest of various research groups in these topics. We believe that such an interest will grow. In the near future, we expect application-driven development in theories, standardization, and tools and a closer dialogue between the Semantic Grid and the Argumentation communities. In the next, concluding section we give a subjective and speculative view about the future of this exciting new multidisciplinary domain.

4 Future Directions

We believe that the marriage between Argumentation and Semantic Grid will result in an enrichment of the Semantic Grid features. We identify some possible directions and challenges that motivate future research, and discuss Semantic Grid applications in which Argumentation can take a lead.

Argumentation and Grid computing. Some of the main issues in the Grid are accounting, access rules and policies specification, management, and enactment. Argumentation technologies can be used to reason and negotiate about the rights acquired over some resource's access. Moreover, they could help cross-domain reasoning, encompassing user preferences, regulations, and technical constraints. For example, a user could prefer not to give resources to other users that have a certain profile—users that are weapon producers or that are not generous with their own resources. Argumentation could play a role in the procedures that determine resource access by taking such kinds of preferences into account. Semantic technologies, and in particular ontological reasoning, could become more important when these procedures need to determine, e.g., that a "gun" is a kind of "weapon." A challenge here is to provide powerful reasoners that are lightweight, performing, and customizable, so that many different argumentation proof procedures and semantics such as those discussed in Chapter 2 and Chapter 6 can be made available. Another one is to develop suitable policy specification languages that can be used on top of these reasoners.

Argumentation and the Web 2.0. Web social communities nowadays seem to be among the best places to argue. Argumentation-related technologies could play a role in the Web 2.0 by automating tasks that help social communication activities. Some possible scenarios may involve tools to find related discussions and related results of discussions, tools to verify argument backing from specialized corpora, and tools to find arguments from selected communities, which could be used in other contexts as "expert opinions." This should be done in integration with onto-logical reasoners, able to find meaningful links between elements of discussions, whether inside the same topic or across multiple topics. Moreover, research pre-sented in books such as [15] demonstrate the rich potential of state-of-the-art argu-ment mapping and visualization tools. They can also have a great impact in the Web 2.0. We identify, as a challenge, gearing existing tools for Web 2.0 usage, following the patterns of service, simplicity and community seen in Section 2.4. Great effort has to be put into graphical user interfaces and usability.

Argumentation and Web services. ArgSCIFF and ArguGRID have shown the potential impact of argumentation technologies in Web service interaction, selec-tion and VO creation. Service discovery and selection are key aspects of Web ser-vice technologies. Argumentation-enabled Web service search engines could greatly improve these processes and thus have a considerable impact in the Web service domain. An open challenge is the development of standards, necessary for the inte-gration of argumentation technologies in the service-oriented world.

Argumentation and the Semantic Web. Ontological reasoning nowadays fo-cusses on concepts such as subsumption and consistency. In the future, other onto-logical relations could become important, such as for example relations of strength, support, and the trustworthiness and reliability of sources. They could be properly determined by argumentation procedures, and become key elements of distributed ontological reasoning. Here the main challenges that we see are of a theoretical na-ture. Essential steps in this direction must be moved towards integrating Semantic Web languages and logics, such as Description Logics, and argumentation theories, similarly to what authors have done in the past to combine, e.g., Description Logics with Logic Programming to help integrating ontological reasoning with rule-based reasoning [13].

4.1 Challenges

These directions draw a vision in which the Semantic Grid will offer richer services, more links, better interaction, information, and transparency of its processes. To achieve this goal, two challenges must be faced.

The first one is in the **theory**. Much of the potential of argumentation technolo-gies depends on the ways they can be *integrated* with other logics and reasoning frameworks, such as ontological reasoners. Issues of *computational complexity* and *distribution* must be addressed, to propose methods that can be applicable in such a vast and heterogeneous domain.

The second one is in the **tools**. The Web 2.0 has became so popular thanks to the applications. A relatively small part of the argumentation community today works on implementing tools. This is a limitation. To produce an argumentation-enabled Semantic Grid, tools must be developed for argument visualization, ex-change, tagging, and the theory must be followed by automated procedures that are user-friendly and efficient. In particular, the main issues here are about *reasoners*, which must be fast and easy to use on the Web, *user interfaces*, which must be simple and ergonomic, and *standards*, needed to leverage the deployment of Semantic Grid applications.

4.2 Applications

We conclude the chapter by suggesting five areas where argumentation-based approaches to the Semantic Grid may be particularly influential.

Trust and service selection. The proliferation of Web services is an asset. Because it is important to make the best out of it, semantic search engines are now subject of extensive investigation. But do current technologies provide the necessary guarantees to the user? Nowadays, users seek reassurance in reputation-based methods such as customer reviews and feedback forums. This method does not obviously scale up. Along with scalable semantic search methods, we need powerful tools that help service selection based on an increasing amount of information. We see a big role of argumentation-based techniques in supporting qualitative, open, community-oriented trust management.

Contracting and negotiation. Business contracts are synchronization points that enable services to create, evaluate, negotiate, and execute interaction. They can answer some of the challenges posed by the future Semantic Grid requirements, such as quality of service, rights of use, and interoperability at a very large scale. Thus contract specification, generation, update, management, and negotiation methods are and will be subject of increasing research efforts. Here there is an opportunity for argumentation technologies to take a lead in supporting declarative, collaborative Web services contracting, and in integration with Semantic search engine technologies, to play an important role in service selection and composition, negotiation, dispute resolution and legal reasoning.

Human-Web service interaction. A great amount of business resources is devoted to interaction with people. Keeping customers happy can be challenging and expensive. We are moving towards a world of composite services, dynamically created on demand, specialized and tailored to the need of the individual. Traditional resources and interfaces with the user, such as call centers, user manuals, information repositories may soon be not up to the task any more. The knowledge needed to understand a service's behaviour and explain it to a potential customer may grow too fast, and equally fast it may become obsolete. Argumentation theories can provide a solution in the difficult task of selecting relevant, non-contradictory information that can be used for the interactive advertisement of new products or for justifying the behaviour of a Web service to a human user.

E-Sciences. Some pilot projects in the Semantic Grid domain, such as Argu-GRID, consider argumentation as a core technology to manage Virtual Organizations. Argumentation may be particularly influential in enhancing distributed global collaborations, and can play a key role in some application domains, such as oil drilling or pharmaceutical testing, in which costly experiments must not be repeated and each one of them must be exploited scientifically to the full. To take a lead in this direction, research in argumentation will have to push towards cross-domain decision making support, encompassing domain-specific know-how, contract-based reasoning, and normative reasoning, to cite some.

Digital Libraries and Technology Enhanced Learning. The application of ICT to cultural heritage, education, and learning, is catalysing the interest of many research groups. At the time of writing, the European digital library, museum and archive—Europeana—is being launched to provide users direct access to some 2 million digital objects, including film material, photos, paintings, sounds, maps, manuscripts, books, newspapers and archival papers.[27] We think that suitable evolutions of the AIF and new argument exchange, mapping and visualization methods for cross-domain knowledge exploration are directions to pursue. The products of such research will be an invaluable asset for scholars and may determine new trends in the creative exploration of cultural content.

Acknowledgements

This research has been partially supported by the Italian MIUR PRIN 2007 project No 20077WWCR8, "Le Forme di Correlazione tra Italian Style, Flussi di Turismo e Trend di Consumo del Made in Italy," and by the Italian FIRB project TOCAI.IT, "Tecnologie Orientate alla Conoscenza per Aggregazioni di Imprese in Internet."

References

1. M. Alberti, F. Chesani, M. Gavanelli, E. Lamma, P. Mello, and P. Torroni. Verifiable agent interaction in abductive logic programming: the SCIFF framework. *ACM Transactions on Computational Logic*, 9(4):Article 29, 2008.
2. T. J. Bench-Capon and P. E. Dunne. Argumentation in artificial intelligence. *Artificial Intelligence*, 171:897–921, 2007.
3. J. Bentahar, Z. Maamar, D. Benslimane, and P. Thiran. An argumentation framework for communities of Web services. *IEEE Intelligent Systems*, 22(6):75–83, Nov/Dec 2007.
4. T. Berners-Lee, J. A. Hendler, and O. Lassila. The Semantic Web. *Scientific American*, 284(5):34–43, May 2001.
5. S. J. Buckingham Shum. Cohere: Towards Web 2.0 argumentation. In P. Besnard, S. Doutre, and A. Hunter, editors, *Computational Models of Argument*, volume 172 of *Frontiers in Artificial Intelligence and Applications*, pages 97–108. IOS Press, 2008.
6. C. I. Chesnevar, J. McGinnis, S. Modgil, I. Rahwan, C. Reed, G. Simari, M. South, G. Vreeswijk, and S. Willmott. Towards an argument interchange format. *The Knowledge Engineering Review*, 21(4):293–316, 2007.
7. I. Clarke, O. Sandberg, B. Wiley, and T. Hong. Freenet: A distributed anonymous information storage and retrieval system. In *ICSI Workshop on Design Issues in Anonymity and Unobservability*, 1999.
8. O. Corcho, P. Alper, I. Kotsiopoulos, P. Missier, S. Bechhofer, and C. Goble. An overview of S-OGSA: A reference semantic grid architecture. *Web Semantics: Science, Services and Agents on the World Wide Web*, 4:102–115, 2006.

---

[27] See the Europeana Web site, http://www.europeana.eu/portal/.

9. D. De Roure, J. Frey, D. Michaelides, and K. Page. The collaborative semantic grid. In *International Symposium on Collaborative Technologies and Systems (CTS'06)*, pages 411–418, Los Alamitos, CA, USA, 2006. IEEE Computer Society.
10. J. Euzenat and P. Valtchev. Similarity-based ontology alignment in OWL-lite. In R. L. de Màntaras and L. Saitta, editors, *Proceedings of the 16th Eureopean Conference on Artificial Intelligence, ECAI'2004*, pages 333–337, 2004.
11. I. Foster, C. Kesselman, and S. Tuecke. The anatomy of the grid: Enabling scalable virtual organizations. *International Journal of High Performance Computing Applications*, 15:200 – 222, Aug 2001.
12. D. Gaertner and F. Toni. Computing arguments and attacks in assumption-based argumentation. *IEEE Intelligent Systems*, 22(6):24–33, Nov/Dec 2007.
13. B. N. Grosof, I. Horrocks, R. Volz, and S. Decker. Description logic programs: Combining logic programs with description logic. In *Proceedings of the Twelfth International World Wide Web Conference*, pages 48–57, 2003.
14. T. Guan, E. Zaluska, and D. De Roure. A semantic service matching middleware for mobile devices discovering grid services. In S. Wu, L. T. Yang, and T. L. Xu, editors, *Advances in Grid and Pervasive Computing, Third International Conference, GPC 2008, Kunming, China, May 25-28, 2008. Proceedings*, volume 5036 of *Lecture Notes in Computer Science*, pages 422–433. Springer-Verlag, 2008.
15. P. A. Kirschner, S. J. Buckingham Shum, and C. S. Carr, editors. *Visualizing Argumentation*, Computer Supported Cooperative Work, London, UK, 2003. Springer.
16. L. Laera, V. Tamma, J. Euzenat, T. J. Bench-Capon, and T. Payne. Reaching agreement over ontology alignments. In I. Cruz, S. Decker, D. Allemang, C. Preist, D. Schwabe, P. Mika, M. Uschold, and L. Aroyo, editors, *Proceedings of the First international Semantic Web Conference on the Semantic Web (ISWC)*, volume 4273 of *Lecture Notes in Computer Science*, pages 371–384, Berlin, Germany, 2006. Springer-Verlag.
17. S. A. McIlraith, T. C. Son, and H. Zeng. Semantic Web Services. *IEEE Intelligent Systems*, 16(2):46–53, 2001.
18. N. Noy, M. Sintek, S. Decker, M. Crubezy, R. Fergerson, and M. Musen. Creating semantic web contents with Protégé-2000. *IEEE Intelligent Systems*, 16(2):60–71, 2001.
19. T. OReilly. What is Web 2.0: Design patterns and business models for the next generation of software. http://www.oreilly.com/pub/a/oreilly/tim/news/ 2005/09/ 30/what-is-web-20.html, 2005.
20. I. Rahwan, F. Zablith, and C. Reed. Laying the foundations for a world wide argument web. *Artificial Intelligence*, 171:897–921, 2007.
21. P. Shvaiko and J. Euzenat. A survey of schema-based matching approaches. *Journal on data semantics*, 4:146–171, 2005.
22. K. Taylor, J. Essex, J. Frey, H. Mills, G. Hughes, and E. Zaluska. The semantic Grid and chemistry: Experiences with CombeChem. *Web semantics: Science, Services and Agents on the World Wide Web*, 4:84–101, 2006.
23. F. Toni, M. Grammatikou, S. Kafetzoglou, L. Lymberopoulos, S. Papavassiliou, D. Gaertner, M. Morge, S. Bromuri, J. McGinnis, K. Stathis, V. Curcin, M. Ghanem, and L. Guo. The ArguGRID platform: An overview. In J. Altmann, D. Neumann, and T. Fahringer, editors, *Grid Economics and Business Models, 5th International Workshop, GECON 2008, Las Palmas de Gran Canaria, Spain, August 26, 2008. Proceedings*, volume 5206 of *Lecture Notes in Computer Science*, pages 217–225. Springer, 2008.
24. P. Torroni, M. Gavanelli, and F. Chesani. Argumentation in the Semantic Web. *IEEE Intelligent Systems*, 22(6):67–74, Nov/Dec 2007.

Chapter 22
Towards Probabilistic Argumentation

Ingrid Zukerman

1 Introduction

All arguments share certain key similarities: they have a goal and some support for the goal, although the form of the goal and support may vary dramatically. Human argumentation is also typically *enthymematic*, i.e., people produce and expect arguments that omit easily inferable information. In this chapter, we draw on the insights obtained from a decade of research to formulate requirements common to computational systems that interpret human arguments and generate their own arguments. To ground our discussion, we describe how some of these requirements are addressed by two probabilistic argumentation systems developed by the User Modeling and Natural Language (UMNL) Group at Monash University: the argument generation system NAG (*Nice Argument Generator*) [18, 19, 20, 38, 39, 40], and the argument interpretation system BIAS (*Bayesian Interactive Argumentation System*) [7, 8, 34, 35, 36, 37].

The generation and interpretation of arguments have the following aspects in common: (1) both processes are performed in some context (e.g., an existing conversation or situation); (2) they support a goal by means of a "line" of reasoning that links premises with the goal;[1] they should handle (3) uncertainty (as most human beliefs are not absolute), and (4) discrepancies in beliefs and reasoning patterns between the speaker and the addressee; and (5) they should handle different argumentation strategies. In addition, in order to generate or interpret enthymematic arguments, (6) a system must consider the omission of information.

To illustrate some of these aspects, consider the goal "Mr Green possibly did not murder Mr Body" in the context of some background information given about

---

Ingrid Zukerman
Faculty of Information Technology
Monash University
Clayton, VICTORIA 3800, AUSTRALIA
e-mail: ingrid@infotech.monash.edu.au

[1] We will not consider non-factual arguments, such as *ad hominem* attacks or appeals to authority.

I. Rahwan, G. R. Simari (eds.), *Argumentation in Artificial Intelligence,*   443
DOI 10.1007/978-0-387-98197-0_22, © Springer Science+Business Media, LLC 2009

a murder mystery. An argument generation system attempts to connect the goal with beliefs shared by the system and the addressee (to a sufficient extent for the argument to work). It then considers different argumentation strategies, e.g., reasoning-by-cases, premise-to-goal or *reductio-ad-absurdum* [39], and decides which propositions can be omitted from the argument to make it enthymematic. The omitted information could be argument branches that have a small impact on the belief in the goal, or obvious intermediate conclusions.

An argument interpretation system "reverses" the last two steps of this process. The user's argumentation strategy must be inferred in order to identify the premises and the goal of the argument, e.g., the initial "premise" in a *reductio-ad-absurdum* argument is the negation of the goal. In addition, the system incorporates into a user's argument the necessary information to make the argument acceptable in terms of the system's knowledge representation. This step may require including additional argument branches, and adding propositions and relations that bridge gaps (according to the system's knowledge representation) between antecedents and consequents in the user's argument. It is worth noting that the information so included is not necessarily the information omitted by the user. Rather, it is information that the system (addressee) needs in order to make sense of the user's argument.

Let us now discuss the above aspects of argumentation systems in more detail.

1.1 Incorporating context

Context is information that surrounds an interaction, and is shared by the dialogue participants. This information could be situational (e.g., the participants are in the same room and can see the same things); background (conveyed prior to the interaction), which makes the participants partially aware of each others' beliefs; or attentional (i.e., items in the focus of attention). Situational and background context provide an anchor for constructing or interpreting an argument on the basis of established facts. Attentional context influences the selection of propositions during both argument generation and interpretation. For example, given several reasoning paths that connect between an antecedent and a consequent, it is reasonable to prefer the path that uses propositions in the focus of attention. NAG considers attentional and background context during argument generation (Section 2), and BIAS during interpretation (Section 3).

1.2 Reasoning process for supporting a goal

From a procedural point of view, the process of connecting the antecedents and consequents within an argument during argument interpretation can be performed in any order. In contrast, argument construction is traditionally a backwards reasoning process (from goal to premises), as the goal is typically unique, and it is not immediately apparent which premises are the most appropriate to support the goal. In NAG we have implemented a semi-directed process for argument generation by employing an attentional model that postulates intermediate argument milestones, i.e., "islands of attention" (Section 2.1).

In addition, both argument generation and interpretation require a procedure that searches for a "good" argument or interpretation respectively. In NAG we defined a good argument as one that is correct and persuasive (we called such an argument "nice" [18]), and in BIAS we defined a good interpretation as one that reflects the user's intentions and makes sense to the system. If we operationalize these definitions by means of evaluation functions that assess the merit of candidate solutions, both problems can be handled as search problems. Indeed, this is how our argument interpretation system BIAS works (Section 3.1). In contrast, NAG relies on heuristic functions for argument generation (Section 2.1). An interesting avenue of investigation involves adapting the search procedure and evaluation metrics developed for BIAS to argument generation. The main challenge pertains to developing metrics which compare arguments that have different argumentation strategies.

1.3 Handling uncertainty

The human experience is fraught with uncertainty, as the facts in front of us are almost never clear cut. Hence, people and the systems that interact with them must be able to cope with uncertainty. In our research, we have employed Bayesian networks (BNs) as our underlying knowledge representation and reasoning formalism (a brief overview of BNs appears in Appendix B). Nielsen and Parsons [23] also use BNs in argumentation, but they fuse BNs for different agents into a consensus BN — a generalization of the approach described in [20].

We selected BNs because they represent normatively correct reasoning under uncertainty. However, when faced with uncertainty, people generally do not engage in normative probabilistic reasoning [16]. Additionally, Bayesian belief propagation potentially affects all the nodes in a BN. This is generally not the case in human reasoning, where arguments tend to have a localized impact on beliefs.

Next, we outline an approach which handles some differences between BN reasoning patterns and those used by people. Difficulties associated with a Bayesian implementation of localized probabilistic reasoning are discussed in Section 4.

1.4 Handling discrepancies in beliefs and reasoning patterns

When an argument generation system faces discrepancies in beliefs and reasoning patterns with a user, it must decide to what extent it is willing to take advantage of the addressee's "misconceptions" in order to achieve its goal. This extent may range from "none", yielding a normative argument that relies solely on the system's presumably correct beliefs and inferences, to "all the way", yielding a persuasive argument that takes advantage of a user's erroneous beliefs and reasoning patterns. The system operator must therefore set a *disposition* parameter, which determines the extent to which the system is prepared to depart from its beliefs and inferences.

To produce an argument on this basis, an argument generation system requires a model of addressees' beliefs and inference patterns. An extensive discussion of the acquisition of such models is outside the scope of this chapter. In brief, a model of a user's beliefs is normally obtained from previous interactions with the user (say, via argument interpretation). Models of a user's inference patterns, such as those assumed by NAG, are more difficult to obtain. Hence, we also experimented with coarse computational models of certain cognitive fallacies [6], which we used to modulate NAG's normative Bayesian inferences [18] (Nisbett *et al.* [24] show that inference fallacies are situation dependent, hence requiring finer models than those we investigated). These cognitive models, together with the models of users' beliefs and inferences, were used to generate *nice* arguments, which combine normative-ness with persuasiveness [18, 20].[2]

Clearly, inability to entertain a user's discrepant beliefs and inference patterns may reduce the persuasiveness of an argument generation system, but the system would still be able to produce correct arguments. In contrast, inability to consider a user's discrepant beliefs may severely hinder an argument interpretation system. In fact, as indicated above, it is part of the job of an interpretation system to infer a user's beliefs [7]. For instance, the following argument would make sense only if the user believes that the murder did *not* occur at 11 pm: "Since Mr Green probably arrived at the house at 11 pm, he probably did not murder Mr Body". BIAS attributes discrepant beliefs to a user if this leads to a "better" interpretation of the user's argument (Section 3). Owing to the time limitations of the project, reasoning fallacies were not incorporated into BIAS's interpretation process. However, the effect of reasoning fallacies is more subtle than that of discrepant beliefs, hence interpretation performance was still creditable. An interesting avenue for future research is the incorporation of reasoning fallacies into the argument interpretation process.

1.5 Considering different argumentation strategies

The applicability of an argumentation strategy depends on the properties of the argument, e.g., is there one convincing line of reasoning, or are there multiple branches that together prove the goal? Also, concise arguments are usually preferred to longer arguments, and people may have personal preferences for certain strategies. NAG determines whether an argumentation strategy is applicable by checking its *applicability conditions*. These conditions pertain to the beliefs in the premises and

---

[2] Owing to space limitations, the argument generation process described in Section 2 does not consider reasoning fallacies.

goal of a preliminary argument (a Bayesian subnet) [39].[3] For instance, the strategy inference-to-best-explanation is employed when the assertion of the goal G supports a premise Q which is firmly believed, but which would be unexplained (improbable) without supposing the truth of the goal. If more than one strategy is applicable, then that which yields the most concise argument is selected. Owing to the time limitations of the project, BIAS assumes that the user employs a premise-to-goal argumentation strategy. The incorporation of strategy identification into the argument interpretation process is an interesting avenue for future investigation.

1.6 Handling enthymematic arguments

As mentioned above, in order to generate or interpret enthymematic arguments, a system must consider the omission of information. An argument generation system must decide which information may be omitted without significantly affecting the achievement of the argument goal, while ideally an interpretation system should reinstate the information omitted by the user.

NAG generates enthymematic arguments by initially producing a complete argument, and then considering two types of omissions: *semantic suppression*, where it removes easily inferred propositions, and *probabilistic pruning*, where it removes superfluous premises and possibly entire reasoning branches (Section 2.2). When interpreting an argument, it is normally not feasible to reinstate information a conversational partner omitted, as addressees do not have access to such unstated information. All an addressee can do is construct an explanation that makes sense to him or her. BIAS does this as follows. It first includes in an interpretation propositions from its domain knowledge that connect the propositions in a user's argument. It then adds argument branches that improve the coherence of the argument, but were not mentioned by the user (Section 3).

1.7 Summary

Table 22.1 summarizes the above aspects of the generation and interpretation processes. The first column shows the aspect, and the second and third columns propose an approach for handling this aspect during generation and interpretation respectively. As indicated above, some of these requirements are currently not handled by NAG or BIAS. Specifically, NAG employs a hand-coded model of a user's beliefs and inferences, rather than a model acquired while interacting with the user, and uses a coarse model of reasoning fallacies. BIAS does not incorporate reasoning fallacies in its reasoning process, and does not infer an argumentation strategy. In Section 2, we describe NAG's main reasoning process and handling of enthymematic arguments.

---

[3] Owing to space limitations, the procedure for selecting an argumentation strategy is not described in this chapter.

Table 22.1 Aspects of argument generation and interpretation systems

Aspect	Generation	Interpretation
Context	establish shared and discrepant beliefs and create "islands of attention"	
Goal support – reasoning process	goal to premises connect antecedents and consequents connect between "islands of attention"	
Uncertainty	choose an appropriate knowledge representation, e.g., Bayesian networks	
Discrepant beliefs and reasoning patterns	decide how to take advantage of a user's discrepant beliefs and inferences, and reasoning fallacies	postulate a user's discrepant beliefs and inferences, and reasoning fallacies
Argumentation strategy	select a strategy	infer a strategy
Enthymematic arguments	decide which information to omit infer missing information (between antecedent and consequents; entire argument branches)	

In Section 3, we consider these issues for BIAS plus the postulation of discrepant user beliefs. In Section 4, we discuss additional requirements for argumentation systems in light of our experience with NAG and BIAS.

2 NAG – Argument Generation

NAG receives as input a goal proposition to be argued for accompanied by a target range of beliefs for it, and an initial argument context, which comprises the argument goal plus the propositions and concepts mentioned in a preamble to the argument. The system produces an argument that aims to get the belief in the goal proposition within the target range of beliefs. During argument generation, the context is expanded, and the actual premises used in the argument are selected from the set of propositions believed by NAG and the user (sufficiently for the argument to work). Upon completion of this process, the system produces an *Argument Graph* — a subnet of the domain BN which connects a set of premises to the goal proposition. An argumentation strategy is then selected on the basis of the properties of this Argument Graph [39], and superfluous steps and branches are pruned to produce an enthymematic argument for presentation [19]. In this section, we describe the generation of an Argument Graph and the removal of superfluous information.

2.1 Argument Generation Process

A basic argument generation process involves reasoning from the argument goal backwards to premises that are mutually believed by the system and the user. However, human reasoning is influenced by attentional focus. For instance, when thinking of an argument, people are likely to consider propositions that are related to recently mentioned concepts. NAG emulates this process by incorporating attentional context (the propositions in the system's focus of attention) into its argument

---

Algorithm 22.1 Argument Generation

Require: Argument goal, domain knowledge BN, context, target belief range
1: Start with an Argument Graph that contains only the goal.
2: **loop**
3:   Use attentional focus to determine subgoals for investigation.
4:   Expand the Argument Graph around the subgoals identified in Step 3 and the leaf nodes of the Argument Graph.
5:   Analyze the Argument Graph by propagating belief in it.
6:   **if** the Argument Graph achieves a belief in the goal inside the target range **then** go to Step 9.
7:   Expand the context by incorporating the nodes newly connected to the goal and salient nodes.
8: **end loop**
9: Select an argumentation strategy, simplify the Argument Graph, and present the resultant argument.

---

generation process. This is done by identifying "islands of attention" in the domain BN, and expanding the argument around them. After each expansion, the Argument Graph (i.e., the Bayesian subnet that is connected to the goal) is analyzed. If it achieves the argument goal, an argumentation strategy is selected, and the Argument Graph is made enthymematic for presentation. These ideas are implemented in Algorithm 22.1.

The identification of islands of attention is performed in Step 3 of Algorithm 22.1. To this effect, NAG employs a hierarchical Semantic net (SN) built on top of the BN, which captures associative connections between information items. Figure 22.1(a) illustrates such a *semantic-Bayesian network (SN-BN)*: the base of the pyramid contains the BN, which comprises propositions, and the upper layers contain the SN, which is composed of concepts. The context of the argument provides an initial set of salient concepts, which are activated in the SN. We then iteratively spread activation [1] from these salient concepts to determine the focus of attention. During this process, each node in the SN-BN is activated to the degree implied by the activation levels of its neighbors, the strength of association to those neighbors, and its immediately prior activation level (vitiated by a time-decay factor). The spreading activation process ceases when an activation cycle fails to activate a new node. At this point, all items in the SN-BN which achieve a threshold activation level are brought into the span of attention. The argument is then expanded around the BN nodes that reach this threshold and the leaf nodes in the Argument Graph constructed so far (Step 4 in Algorithm 22.1). This expansion process, which may connect previously disconnected Bayesian subnets, yields a new Argument Graph, which is analyzed by performing Bayesian belief propagation. If the resultant belief in the goal is inside the target belief range, then the argument can be presented. Otherwise, the attention-expansion-analysis process is repeated.

Figure 22.1(b) illustrates the steps of Algorithm 22.1. The top-left panel contains the goal proposition (circled diamond) and the propositions mentioned in the preamble. The top-right panel shows the concepts and propositions activated in Step 3 (the diamonds are BN propositions, and the circles are SN concepts). The expansion of the argument is performed around the BN nodes connected to the goal and salient

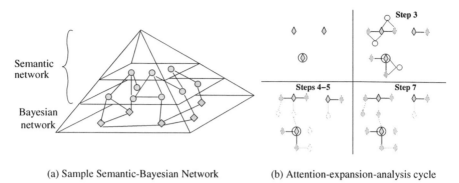

(a) Sample Semantic-Bayesian Network   (b) Attention-expansion-analysis cycle

Fig. 22.1 Argument-generation process

nodes identified in Step 3, yielding the Bayesian subnets illustrated in the bottom-left panel (the expansion of some nodes may not yield additional neighbours). Note that two subnets which were isolated in the top-right panel have become connected after this expansion, yielding a larger Argument Graph. If this graph achieves the argument goal, the argument can be presented. Otherwise, in Step 7 the algorithm expands the context to include the nodes in this Argument Graph and salient nodes in subnets that are detached from this graph (bottom-right panel). The attention-expansion-analysis process is now repeated in light of this context.

It is worth noting that although an argument can be generated by performing backwards reasoning from the goal, the incorporation of attentional focus saves processing time [38]. This is because it allows NAG to concentrate its search on propositions connected to propositions in focus, which are likely to be relevant to the argument.

2.2 Producing an Enthymematic Argument

Algorithm 22.2 generates an enthymematic argument from an Argument Graph by combining probabilistic pruning with semantic suppression.

- **Probabilistic pruning** removes premises that alter the belief in the argument goal to only a small degree, such that removing them does not put the belief in the goal outside the given target belief range. After attempting the removal of a premise, the argument is re-analyzed, and if the belief in the goal is now outside the target range, the removed premise is reinstated.[4] Since this process is iterative, probabilistic pruning may eventually remove an entire reasoning branch.
- **Semantic suppression** checks intermediate conclusions in the Argument Graph to see if they are *easily inferred*, and hence can be left implicit, rather than being explicitly stated. We say that a proposition is easily inferred if it has a high level

---

[4] Probabilistic pruning also has attentional implications, which are discussed in [19].

Algorithm 22.2 Argument Pruning

Require: Argument Graph, presentation ordering $< N_1, \ldots, N_k >$ for the propositions in the graph
1: **for** $i = 1$ to k **do**
2:     **if** N_i is a premise **then**
3:         Invoke ***probabilistic pruning***.
4:         **if** N_i is retained **then** activate it for attentional processing.
5:     **else** [N_i is an intermediate proposition]
6:         Simulate the user's attentional state.
7:         Invoke ***semantic suppression*** to determine whether N_i may be left implicit.
8: **end for**
9: **if** no change was made in the last pass through the Argument Graph or time has run out
    then exit.
10: **else** go to Step 1.

---

of semantic activation, and it is obtained from a probabilistically strong inference (which greatly strengthens the belief in the proposition in question) [20]. NAG determines the strength of an inference by means of partial Bayesian propagation from its antecedents, and obtains the level of activation of a proposition by spreading activation from the (planned) presentation of the preceding propositions in the argument.

Semantic suppression is performed for one intermediate conclusion at a time in a greedy fashion. That is, the first intermediate conclusion that can be left implicit is removed, and an implication is stated from its antecedents to its consequent. For instance, given the reasoning chain $A \rightarrow B \rightarrow C \rightarrow D$, if B can be removed, then C must remain. Semantic suppression fails if the omission of a consequent drives the level of semantic activation of the next consequent (C in our example) below a threshold. In this case, the last removed proposition is reinstated, and the pass through the current ordering continues.

To illustrate the argument pruning process, consider the example in Figure 22.2, which contains an Argument Graph for the proposition [Phobos is building nuclear weapons] (Figure 22.2(a)), and assume that we have selected a premise-to-goal argumentation strategy. Now, if the user believes N_8 and N_9 sufficiently, then N_{10} and N_{11} can be probabilistically pruned respectively. In addition, N_2, N_3, N_4 and N_5 can be semantically suppressed, since they are easily inferred from their antecedents. The resultant argument (hand-generated from NAG's output) appears in Figure 22.2(b).

The application of these argument-pruning techniques assumes a complete presentation order of the nodes in an Argument Graph. Hence, pruning is performed after an argumentation strategy has been selected, and the propositions in the graph have been ordered [19, 39]. The propositions are ordered by applying policies that rely on the probabilistic properties of the inferences in the Argument Graph to group them into sub-arguments, and order the sub-arguments and remaining stand-alone inferences. Attention-based heuristics are then applied to order the antecedents of the sub-arguments and inferences. For instance, the output in Figure 22.2(b) is produced by combining N_6 and N_7 into one sub-argument, and N_8 and N_9 into another sub-argument, and then ordering the antecedents within each sub-argument [19].

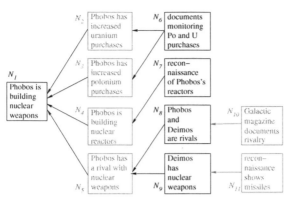

*"Phobos and Deimos are
rivals and Deimos has
nuclear weapons. These
observations indicate
that Phobos is possibly
building nuclear weapons.
Furthermore, documents
monitoring Phobos's
increased purchases of
polonium and uranium, and
reconnaissance of Phobos's
reactors suggest that Phobos
is very probably building
nuclear weapons."*

(a) Sample Argument Graph   (b) Resultant argument

Fig. 22.2 Argument pruning: Phobos-Deimos Example

2.3 Related Research

Our argument generation mechanism uses BNs to reason about an argument, and performs spreading activation to focus the argument. This use of spreading activation resembles Charniak and Goldman's use of a marker passing mechanism to focus attention in a Bayesian plan recognition system [2].

NAG's expansion-analysis cycle resembles the propose-evaluate-modify cycle in [3]. However, NAG uses Bayesian reasoning to determine the impact of an argument on an addressee's beliefs, and it may combine several lines of reasoning to achieve its goal, rather than selecting a single proposition.

Vreeswijk [32] describes IACAS, an interactive system for generating arguments. However, IACAS does not attempt to model the user's attentional processes or tailor the presentation of its arguments to the user. Instead, IACAS shows supporting arguments for the current goal proposition in a sequence until the user is satisfied or chooses a new goal proposition. The chosen sequence of presentation is the order in which IACAS finds its arguments.

Huang and Fiedler's system [15] uses a limited implementation of attentional focus to select which step in a proof should be mentioned next, and Reed and Long's system [28] takes attention (salience) into consideration when deciding how to present arguments. However, unlike NAG, the former system does not generate enthymematic arguments, and the latter does not consider salience while gathering the information necessary to generate an argument. Two systems that can turn an existing fully explicit argument into an enthymematic one are described in [12, 21], but neither of these systems can generate an argument from constituent propositions. A generative system based on the work of Hobbs *et al.* [11] is described in [30]. That system deals with what can be readily inferred, and so deleted, during communication, but the generated discourse is not an argument in support of a proposition.

3 BIAS – Argument Interpretation

BIAS receives as input an argument in the form of probabilistic implications that lead to a goal. For instance, the following text is a gloss of an input argument.

Mr Green's fingerprints were found on the gun, therefore he probably had the means to murder Mr Body. In addition, the Bayesian Times reports that Mr Body seduced Mr Green's girlfriend, therefore he probably had a motive.

Since Mr Green probably had means and motive, he possibly killed Mr Body.

BIAS produces an interpretation for this argument, which takes the form of a sub-net of the domain BN, plus suppositions about a user's beliefs. To avoid difficulties associated with the interpretation of free-form Natural Language statements (Section 4), the antecedents and consequents of the argument are selected from a list of propositions known to the system. The argument is typically enthymematic, as users are not aware of the implications known to BIAS, and hence make their own connections between antecedents and consequents.

We view an interpretation of an argument as a "self-explanation" — an account of the argument that makes sense to the addressee. For BIAS, such an account requires three components: an *Interpretation Graph IG*, a *Supposition Configuration SC*, and *Explanatory Extensions EE*.[5]

- An **Interpretation Graph** is a structure comprising propositions and inferences from the system's domain knowledge that connect between the propositions in the argument. This structure bridges inferential leaps in an enthymematic argument, but the bridges so constructed may not be those intended by the user.
- A **Supposition Configuration** is a set of suppositions attributed to the user (instead of the system's beliefs) to account for the beliefs expressed in the argument. As indicated in Section 1.4, recognizing a user's beliefs that differ from those of the system is an essential part of argument interpretation, which supports the construction of a model of a user's beliefs.
- **Explanatory Extensions** consist of domain propositions that are added to an Interpretation Graph in order to make the inferences in the interpretation more acceptable to people (in early trials of the system, people objected to increases in certainty and to large jumps in belief between the antecedents and the consequent of implications). Contrary to suppositions, the beliefs in Explanatory Extensions are shared by the user and the system.

Thus, Interpretation Graphs and Explanatory Extensions are proposed to handle enthymematic arguments — they could be respectively viewed as the inverse of semantic suppression and probabilistic pruning in argument generation (Section 2.2). Supposition Configurations are posited to better understand a user's reasoning.

---

[5] Argument interpretation requires the identification of the user's argumentation strategy, but BIAS assumes a premise-to-goal strategy.

Algorithm 22.3 Argument Interpretation

Require: User argument, domain knowledge BN

1: **while** there is time **do**
2:     Propose a Supposition Configuration SC_i — this can be an existing Supposition Configuration or a new one.
3:     Propose a new Interpretation Graph IG_{ij} under Supposition Configuration SC_i, such that the nodes in the user argument are connected.
4:     Propose Explanatory Extensions EE_{ij} for Interpretation Graph IG_{ij} under Supposition Configuration SC_i as necessary.
5:     Estimate the probability of interpretation $\{SC_i, IG_{ij}, EE_{ij}\}$.
6:     Retain the top K most probable interpretations.
7: **end while**
8: Present the retained interpretations to the user for validation.

3.1 Argument Interpretation Process

The problem of finding the best interpretation of an argument is exponential, as there are many candidates for each component of an interpretation, and complex interactions between Interpretation Graphs and Supposition Configurations. For example, making a supposition could invalidate an otherwise sound line of reasoning.

In order to generate reasonable interpretations in real time, we apply Algorithm 22.3 — an *anytime* algorithm [5, 14] that iteratively proposes interpretations until time runs out, i.e., until the system has to act upon a preferred interpretation or show the user one or more interpretations for validation [8]. The algorithm proposes an interpretation which consists of a Supposition Configuration, an Interpretation Graph and Explanatory Extensions (Steps 2-4). It then estimates the probability of this interpretation (Step 5), and retains the top K (=4) most probable interpretations (Step 6). The procedure for building Interpretation Graphs is described in [36], and the procedures for postulating Supposition Configurations and generating Explanatory Extensions are described in [8]. Here we outline the general interpretation process and the estimation of the probability of an interpretation.

Figure 22.3(a) depicts a portion of the search tree generated by Algorithm 22.3, with Supposition Configurations in the first level, Interpretation Graphs in the second level, and Explanatory Extensions in the third. Supposition Configurations are generated first due to their effect on Interpretation Graphs, i.e., the beliefs in the domain BN and the suppositions attributed to the user (which are incorporated in the BN) affect the beliefs in the candidate Interpretation Graphs. Specifically, a supposition may block a path in a BN (precluding the propagation of evidence through this path), or unblock a previously blocked path (for a discussion of blocked paths, see [26]). These interactions, which are difficult to predict until an Interpretation Graph is complete, motivate the large number of alternatives considered in the first two levels of the search tree. In contrast, Explanatory Extensions do not seem to have complex interactions with Interpretation Graphs or Supposition Configurations. Hence, they are deterministically generated in the third level of the search

Argument (connected propositions)

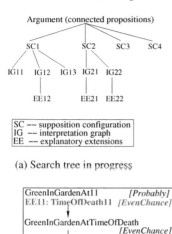

SC — supposition configuration
IG — interpretation graph
EE — explanatory extensions

(a) Search tree in progress

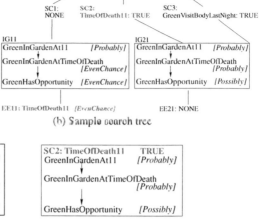

*Mr Green probably being in the garden at 11 implies that
Mr Green possibly had the opportunity to kill Mr Body.*

(b) Sample search tree

GreenInGardenAt11	[Probably]
EE11: TimeOfDeath11	[EvenChance]
GreenInGardenAtTimeOfDeath	[EvenChance]
GreenHasOpportunity	[EvenChance]

*I know this is not quite what you said, but
it is the best I could do given what I believe.*
Since it is probable that Mr Green was in the
garden at 11, and it is even chance that the
time of death was 11, it is even chance that
Mr Green was in the garden at the time of
death, which implies that it is even chance
that he had the opportunity to kill Mr Body.

(c) Interpretation (*SC*1, *IG*11, *EE*11)

SC2: TimeOfDeath11	TRUE
GreenInGardenAt11	[Probably]
GreenInGardenAtTimeOfDeath	[Probably]
GreenHasOpportunity	[Possibly]

*Your argument seems to suppose that the
time of death was 11. Hence, Mr Green
probably being in the garden at 11 implies
that he probably was in the garden at the
time of death, which implies that he
possibly had the opportunity to kill Mr Body.*

(d) Interpretation (*SC*2, *IG*21, *EE*21)

Fig. 22.3 Argument interpretation process

tree, i.e., only one set of Explanatory Extensions is proposed for each interpretation, rather than multiple options (Step 4).

Figure 22.3(b) depicts a portion of the search tree instantiated for the short argument at the root node of this tree: *"Mr Green probably being in the garden at 11 implies that Mr Green possibly had the opportunity to kill Mr Body"*. In this example, the user's belief in the consequent of the argument differs from the belief obtained by BIAS by means of Bayesian propagation from the evidence nodes in the domain BN. As indicated above, BIAS attempts to address this problem by making suppositions about the user's beliefs. The first level of the sample search tree in Figure 22.3(b) contains three Supposition Configurations *SC*1, *SC*2 and *SC*3. *SC*1 posits no beliefs that differ from those in the domain BN, thereby retaining the mismatch between the user's belief in the consequent and BIAS's belief; *SC*2 posits that the user supposes that the time of death is 11; and *SC*3 posits that the user supposes that Mr Green visited Mr Body last night.

The best Interpretation Graph for *SC*1 is *IG*11 (the evaluation of the goodness of an interpretation is described in Section 3.2). Here the belief in the consequent differs from that stated by the user (due to the absence of suppositions), prompting the generation of a preface that acknowledges this fact. In addition, the Interpretation Graph has a large jump in belief (from Probably to EvenChance), which causes BIAS to add the mutually believed proposition TimeOfDeath11[EvenChance] as an Explanatory Extension. The resultant interpretation and its gloss appear in Figure 22.3(c). The best Interpretation Graph for *SC*2 is *IG*21, which matches the beliefs in the user's argument. The resultant interpretation and its gloss appear in Figure 22.3(d). Note that both $(SC1, IG11, EE11)$ and $(SC2, IG21, EE21)$ mention TimeOfDeath11. However, in the first interpretation this proposition is used as an Explanatory Extension (with a belief of EvenChance obtained by Bayesian propagation), while in the second interpretation it is used as a supposition (with a belief of True). Upon completion of this process, BIAS retains the four best interpretations. In this example, the winning interpretation is $\{SC2, IG21, EE21\}$.

3.2 Estimating the Probability of an Interpretation

An interpretation is evaluated by calculating its posterior probability. Our approach, which is inspired by the Minimum Message Length model selection criterion [33], requires the specification of three elements: *background knowledge, model* and *data*. **Background knowledge** is everything known to the system and the user prior to interpreting the argument, e.g., domain knowledge, beliefs shared by the user and the system, and dialogue history; the ***data*** comprise the argument itself; and the ***model*** is the interpretation.

We posit that the best interpretation is that with the highest posterior probability.

$$IntBest = \text{argmax}_{i=1,\ldots,n} \Pr(SC_i, IG_i, EE_i | Argument)$$

where n is the number of candidate interpretations.

After applying Bayes rule, we obtain

$$\Pr(SC_i, IG_i, EE_i | Argument) \propto \Pr(SC_i, IG_i, EE_i) \times \Pr(Argument | SC_i, IG_i, EE_i)$$

The first factor represents the prior probability of the model (interpretation) in light of the background knowledge, and the second factor represents the probability of the data (argument) in light of the model.

- The prior probability of a model reflects how "easy" it is to construct the model from background knowledge. For instance, complex models (i.e., interpretations with larger Interpretation Graphs) usually have a lower prior probability than simpler models. This factor is also known as model complexity.

- The probability of the data in light of the model is the probability that a user uttered an argument (data) when intending a particular interpretation (model). The more similar the data are to the model, the higher the probability of the data given the model. This factor is also known as data fit.

Both the argument and its interpretation contain numerical and structural information. The numerical information in the argument and the interpretation comprises the beliefs in their propositions, which include Supposition Configurations for the interpretation. The structural part of the argument comprises the stated propositions and the relationships between them, while the structural part of the interpretation comprises the Interpretation Graph and Explanatory Extensions. The estimation of the probabilities of structural and numerical information is described in [8, 35, 36]. Here we describe the general principles underlying these calculations.

- **Prior model probability** – we adopt a combinatorial approach to the estimation of the probability of the structure of an interpretation (i.e., we calculate the probability of selecting a k-node Bayesian subnet corresponding to the interpretation from an N-node domain BN[6]). The probability of the numerical information in an interpretation depends on how well it matches the beliefs in the domain BN (background).
- **Data fit** – the probability of the structure of an argument given the structure of an interpretation depends on how well these structures match (this can be encoded as a function of the edit distance between the structures). As above, the probability of the beliefs in an argument given the beliefs in an interpretation depends on how well these beliefs match.

These ideas have a straightforward implementation when an interpretation consists only of an Interpretation Graph. Let us now see how Supposition Configurations and Explanatory Extensions fit into this scheme.

- **Supposition Configurations** – suppositions that are not consistent with the beliefs in the domain BN increase the difference between the beliefs in an interpretation and those in the domain BN. Hence, they reduce the prior probability of the interpretation. At the same time, suppositions are warranted when they substantially reduce the discrepancy between the beliefs in an interpretation and those in the argument (i.e., improve data fit).
- **Explanatory Extensions** – adding such argument branches increases the size of an Interpretation Graph, thereby reducing its structural probability (from a combinatorial perspective). At the same time, Explanatory Extensions have a positive impact, as they satisfy people's expectations for what constitutes an acceptable inference (an inference without increases in certainty or large changes in certainty [8]). To account for the inclusion of Explanatory Extensions in an interpretation, we incorporate these expectations into our background knowledge. Thus, inferences that do not meet these expectations reduce the prior probability of an interpretation. If these expectations are met by adding Explanatory Extensions, the prior probability of the interpretation increases.

---

[6] This approach and its extensions based on dialogue salience are described in [36].

In summary, for all three constructs (Interpretation Graph, Supposition Configuration and Explanatory Extensions), our model selection approach balances prior model probability (in light of background knowledge) and data fit. In general, a simple model has a higher prior probability than a more complex model. However, if the simpler model has a worse data fit or a worse match with background knowledge than the complex model, then the more complex model could have a higher posterior probability. Specifically, the addition of suppositions makes an interpretation (model) more complex, reducing its prior probability, but improves data fit. The addition of Explanatory Extensions has a mixed effect on the prior probability of a model: on one hand, Explanatory Extensions increase the complexity of an interpretation, which reduces its probability; on the other hand, they improve the match between an interpretation and the expectations in the background knowledge, which increases the probability of the interpretation. The winning interpretation is that with the highest posterior probability after these different factors are taken into account.

3.3 Related Research

Our approach offers an abductive account of users' arguments, using BNs as our main reasoning formalism. Such abductive accounts have been provided by several researchers for different discourse interpretation tasks, e.g., [11, 22]. Hobbs *et al.* [11] focused on problems of reference resolution and disambiguation in single sentences. Our work is more similar to the research of Ng and Mooney [22], in that it explains discourse consisting of several propositions. However, Ng and Mooney apply a coherence heuristic to select an explanation for a user's discourse (similar to the approach used in NAG for argument generation), while our selection process is based on an optimization framework that incorporates a user's posited beliefs and people's preferences. Additionally, the above researchers employ a logic-based formalism for the selection of an interpretation, while our approach is probabilistic.

BNs have been used in several intention recognition tasks, e.g., [2, 9, 13]. Charniak and Goldman's system handled complex narratives [2], Gertner *et al.* represented students' solutions of physics problems [9], and Horvitz and Paek used BNs at different levels of an abstraction hierarchy to infer a user's goal in information-seeking interactions [13]. BIAS's generation of Interpretation Graphs most resembles the work described in [2, 9]. However, these systems do not posit discrepant user beliefs or augment their interpretations with additional explanations.

Our work on positing suppositions is related to the research described in [4, 27] on the recognition of flawed plans, in the sense that we also attempt to justify a user's statements. The main difference between BIAS and these systems is that they use a plan-based approach to postulate a user's (erroneous) beliefs, restricting their attention to beliefs within the inferred plans. In contrast, BIAS employs a probabilistic approach, and considers its domain model (and not just the inferred Bayesian subnet) when postulating discrepant beliefs (i.e., suppositions).

4 Discussion

In this section, we outline some challenges for argumentation systems in light of lessons learned from NAG and BIAS: (1) what shall we argue about?, (2) probabilistic and human reasoning, (3) argumentation process, and (4) argumentation interface.

What shall we argue about?

Typically, computer systems know a limited number of propositions and relations between them. To deal with this, an argumentation system can (1) restrict the user to use only the propositions known to the system, (2) ignore the propositions the system doesn't know, or (3) try to learn the import of new propositions. Our experience with BIAS shows that the first solution is frustrating for users, as people did not like having to shoehorn their reasoning into the propositions known to the system. The second solution leads to only a partial understanding of the user's intentions, and hence potentially to a mis-directed discussion. The third solution is clearly the most sound. However, learning new propositions and their relationship with a system's current beliefs is a challenging task that falls under the purview of probabilistic reasoning and human-computer interfaces, as users must define the new propositions in terms amenable to the system's reasoning.

This indicates that a fruitful domain for current argumentation systems is an expert domain, where the system knows all or most of what there is to know, e.g., medical reasoning. Alternatively, one can devise applications of argumentation systems which assist people in argument construction and rational thought, without having to engage in a fully fledged argument with users [29, 31].

Probabilistic and human reasoning

As stated in Section 1, we adopted a Bayesian formalism because of its sound probabilistic reasoning. However, Bayesian belief propagation differs from human reasoning in two main respects: (1) it may affect any node in a BN, while human reasoning has a more localized effect; and (2) it may not represent adequately the user's reasoning process. This may be due to the absence of a model of human reasoning fallacies, beliefs that differ from users' beliefs, and inference patterns that differ from those of users.

One way of modeling localized reasoning in a Bayesian framework involves cutting off the interpretation sub-net from the domain BN. However, such subnets may produce effects that are difficult to justify to people (due to the marginalization of parent nodes and excision of children nodes [17, 26]). An alternative solution involves employing logic-based formalisms or different approaches to reasoning under uncertainty, e.g., subjective logic [25]. However, the former would remove a system's capacity to deal with uncertainty, and the latter have been applied to problems that differ in nature from that considered by NAG and BIAS.

Our Bayesian reasoning framework was augmented with a (rather coarse) model of certain types of human reasoning fallacies for argument generation (Section 1). An interesting avenue for future research consists of developing finer, domain dependent models of human reasoning, and incorporating them into generation and interpretation processes. In Section 3, we described how we incorporated a model of suppositions (user beliefs that differ from those of the system) in our argument interpretation mechanism, and in Section 1 we discussed how an argumentation system may take advantage of such suppositions to generate more persuasive arguments. However, user inference patterns that differ from those of the system pose a more challenging problem. In the context of BNs, this involves modifying links between nodes and updating Conditional Probability Tables. As for the above mentioned "new proposition" problem, this has significant implications with respect to the system's reasoning, and presents non-trivial interface problems. The solution of this problem constitutes an interesting avenue for future investigation.

Argumentation process

Our argument generation process is based on heuristics (Section 2), while our interpretation process relies on a search procedure that uses a probabilistic function to assess the merit of an interpretation (Section 3). Other differences between our implementation of argument generation and interpretation pertain to the consideration of argumentation strategies, and to how to take into account discrepant user beliefs and reasoning patterns (Table 22.1). An interesting avenue of investigation consists of devising uniform processes that can be employed for generation and interpretation [10]; and considering the impact of using a search procedure coupled with an evaluation function, rather than heuristics, for argument generation.

Argumentation interface

People normally argue in Natural Language. However, it is not clear that this is the best medium for effective communication. An interesting alternative involves combining a graphical interface with Natural Language. However, even if the user did not introduce information unknown to the system, such an argumentation interface would have to map Natural Language statements into propositions in the system's domain knowledge. The design of an effective argumentation interface is essential to enable the deployment of practical argumentation systems.

Acknowledgements The author thanks her collaborators on the research described in this chapter: Sarah George, Natalie Jitnah, Kevin Korb, Richard McConachy and Michael Niemann. This research was supported in part by grants A49531227, A49927212 and DP0344013 from the Australian Research Council, and by the ARC Centre for Perceptive and Intelligent Machines in Complex Environments.

References

1. J. R. Anderson. *The Architecture of Cognition*. Harvard University Press, Cambridge, Massachusetts, 1983.
2. E. Charniak and R. Goldman. A Bayesian model of plan recognition. *Artificial Intelligence*, 64(1):53–79, 1993.
3. J. Chu-Carroll and S. Carberry. Response generation in collaborative negotiation. In *Proceedings of the 33rd Annual Meeting of the Association for Computational Linguistics*, pages 136–143, Cambridge, Massachusetts, 1995.
4. J. Chu-Carroll and S. Carberry. Conflict resolution in collaborative planning dialogues. *International Journal of Human Computer Studies*, 6(56):969–1015, 2000.
5. T. Dean and M. Boddy. An analysis of time-dependent planning. In *AAAI88 – Proceedings of the 7th National Conference on Artificial Intelligence*, pages 49–54, St. Paul, Minnesota, 1988.
6. J. Evans. *Bias in human reasoning: Causes and consequences*. Lawrence Erlbaum Associates, Hillsdale, New Jersey, 1989.
7. S. George, I. Zukerman, and M. Niemann. Modeling suppositions in users' arguments. In *UM05 – Proceedings of the 10th International Conference on User Modeling*, pages 19–29, Edinburgh, Scotland, 2005.
8. S. George, I. Zukerman, and M. Niemann. Inferences, suppositions and explanatory extensions in argument interpretation. *User Modeling and User-Adapted Interaction*, 17(5):439–474, 2007.
9. A. Gertner, C. Conati, and K. VanLehn. Procedural help in Andes: Generating hints using a Bayesian network student model. In *AAAI98 – Proceedings of the 15th National Conference on Artificial Intelligence*, pages 106–111, Madison, Wisconsin, 1998.
10. N. Green and S. Carberry. A hybrid reasoning model for indirect answers. In *Proceedings of the 32nd Annual Meeting of the Association for Computational Linguistics*, pages 58–65, Las Cruces, New Mexico, 1994.
11. J. R. Hobbs, M. E. Stickel, D. E. Appelt, and P. Martin. Interpretation as abduction. *Artificial Intelligence*, 63(1-2):69–142, 1993.
12. H. Horacek. How to avoid explaining obvious things (without omitting central information). In *ECAI94 – Proceedings of the 11th European Conference on Artificial Intelligence*, pages 520–524, Amsterdam, The Netherlands, 1994.
13. E. Horvitz and T. Paek. A computational architecture for conversation. In *UM99 – Proceedings of the 7th International Conference on User Modeling*, pages 201–210, Banff, Canada, 1999.
14. E. Horvitz, H. Suermondt, and G. Cooper. Bounded conditioning: flexible inference for decision under scarce resources. In *UAI89 – Proceedings of the 1989 Workshop on Uncertainty in Artificial Intelligence*, pages 182–193, Windsor, Canada, 1989.
15. X. Huang and A. Fiedler. Proof verbalization as an application of NLG. In *IJCAI97 – Proceedings of the 15th International Joint Conference on Artificial Intelligence*, pages 965–970, Nagoya, Japan, 1997.
16. D. Kahneman, P. Slovic, and A. Tversky. *Judgment under Uncertainty: Heuristics and Biases*. Cambridge University Press, 1982.
17. K. Korb and A. Nicholson. *Bayesian Artificial Intelligence*. Chapman & Hall/CRC, 2004.
18. K. B. Korb, R. McConachy, and I. Zukerman. A cognitive model of argumentation. In *Proceedings of the 19th Annual Conference of the Cognitive Science Society*, pages 400–405, Stanford, California, 1997.
19. R. McConachy, K. B. Korb, and I. Zukerman. Deciding what not to say: An attentional-probabilistic approach to argument presentation. In *Proceedings of the 20th Annual Conference of the Cognitive Science Society*, pages 669–674, Madison, Wisconsin, 1998.
20. R. McConachy and I. Zukerman. Towards a dialogue capability in a Bayesian argumentation system. *ETAI 3 – Electronic Transactions of Artificial Intelligence (Section D)*, pages 89–124, 1999.

21. S. Mehl. Forward inferences in text generation. In *ECAI94 – Proceedings of the 11th European Conference on Artificial Intelligence*, pages 525–529, Amsterdam, The Netherlands, 1994.
22. H. Ng and R. Mooney. On the role of coherence in abductive explanation. In *AAAI90 – Proceedings of the 8th National Conference on Artificial Intelligence*, pages 337–342, Boston, Massachusetts, 1990.
23. S. H. Nielsen and S. Parsons. An application of formal argumentation: Fusing Bayesian networks in multi-agent systems. *Artificial Intelligence*, 171:754–775, 2007.
24. R. Nisbett, E. Borgida, R. Crandall, and H. Reed. Popular induction: Information is not necessarily informative. In J. Carroll and J. Payne, editors, *Cognition and social behavior*, pages 113–133. Hillsdale, NJ: LEA, 1976.
25. N. Oren, T. Norman, and A. Preece. Subjective logic and arguing with evidence. *Artificial Intelligence*, 171:838–854, 2007.
26. J. Pearl. *Probabilistic Reasoning in Intelligent Systems*. Morgan Kaufmann Publishers, San Mateo, California, 1988.
27. A. Quilici. Detecting and responding to plan-oriented misconceptions. In A. Kobsa and W. Wahlster, editors, *User Models in Dialog Systems*, pages 108–132. Springer-Verlag, 1989.
28. C. Reed and D. Long. Content ordering in the generation of persuasive discourse. In *IJCAI97 – Proceedings of the 15th International Joint Conference on Artificial Intelligence*, pages 1022–1027, Nagoya, Japan, 1997.
29. G. Rowe and C. Reed. Argument diagramming: The Araucaria project. In A. Okada, S. Buckingham Shum, and A. Sherborne, editors, *Knowledge Cartography*, pages 163–181. Springer, 2008.
30. R. H. Thomason, J. R. Hobbs, and J. D. Moore. Communicative goals. In *Proceedings of ECAI96 Workshop – Gaps and Bridges: New Directions in Planning and NLG*, pages 7–12, Budapest, Hungary, 1996.
31. T. van Gelder. Teaching critical thinking: some lessons from cognitive science. *College Teaching*, 45(1):1–6, 2005.
32. G. Vreeswijk. IACAS: An interactive argumentation system. Technical Report CS 94-03, Department of Computer Science, University of Limburg, 1994.
33. C. Wallace. *Statistical and Inductive Inference by Minimum Message Length*. Springer, Berlin, Germany, 2005.
34. I. Zukerman. An integrated approach for generating arguments and rebuttals and understanding rejoinders. In *UM01 – Proceedings of the 8th International Conference on User Modeling*, pages 84–94, Sonthofen, Germany, 2001.
35. I. Zukerman. Discourse interpretation as model selection – a probabilistic approach. In B. Bouchon-Meunier, C. Marsala, M. Rifqi, and R. Yager, editors, *Uncertainty and Intelligent Information Systems*, pages 61–73. World Scientific, 2008.
36. I. Zukerman and S. George. A probabilistic approach for argument interpretation. *User Modeling and User-Adapted Interaction, Special Issue on Language-Based Interaction*, 15(1-2):5–53, 2005.
37. I. Zukerman, S. George, and M. George. Incorporating a user model into an information theoretic framework for argument interpretation. In *UM03 – Proceedings of the 9th International Conference on User Modeling*, pages 106–116, Johnstown, Pennsylvania, 2003.
38. I. Zukerman, R. McConachy, and K. B. Korb. Bayesian reasoning in an abductive mechanism for argument generation and analysis. In *AAAI98 – Proceedings of the 15th National Conference on Artificial Intelligence*, pages 833–838, Madison, Wisconsin, 1998.
39. I. Zukerman, R. McConachy, and K. B. Korb. Using argumentation strategies in automated argument generation. In *INLG'2000 – Proceedings of the 1st International Conference on Natural Language Generation*, pages 55–62, Mitzpe Ramon, Israel, 2000.
40. I. Zukerman, R. McConachy, K. B. Korb, and D. A. Pickett. Exploratory interaction with a Bayesian argumentation system. In *IJCAI99 – Proceedings of the 16th International Joint Conference on Artificial Intelligence*, pages 1294–1299, Stockholm, Sweden, 1999.

Chapter 23
Argument-Based Machine Learning

Ivan Bratko, Jure Žabkar and Martin Možina

1 Introduction

The most common form of machine learning (ML) is learning from examples, also
called inductive learning . Usually the problem of learning from examples is stated
as: Given examples, find a theory that is consistent with the examples. We say that
such a theory is induced from the examples. Roughly, we say that a theory is consistent with the examples if the examples can be derived from the theory. In the case
of learning from imperfect, noisy data, we may not insist on perfect consistency
between the examples and the theory. In such cases, a shorter and only "approximately" consistent theory may be more appropriate.

Illustrative applications of learning from examples are:

- Given examples of weather situations, learn to predict weather in the future;
- Given examples of past patients, learn to diagnose new patients.

Examples for learning may come from nature, experiments, observations, existing databases, etc. Examples may also come from an expert who may take special
care in preparing a good set of examples. The situation is similar to teaching humans
where good learning examples designed by the teacher are especially valuable. An
expert user of a ML tool may help the learning system by selecting good examples

Ivan Bratko
Faculty of Computer and Information Science, University of Ljubljana, Tržaška 25, Ljubljana,
Slovenia e-mail: ivan.bratko@fri.uni-lj.si

Jure Žabkar
Faculty of Computer and Information Science, University of Ljubljana, Tržaška 25, Ljubljana,
Slovenia e-mail: jure.zabkar@fri.uni-lj.si

Martin Možina
Faculty of Computer and Information Science, University of Ljubljana, Tržaška 25, Ljubljana,
Slovenia e-mail: martin.mozina@fri.uni-lj.si

I. Rahwan, G. R. Simari (eds.), *Argumentation in Artificial Intelligence,*
DOI 10.1007/978-0-387-98197-0_23, © Springer Science+Business Media, LLC 2009

Table 23.1 Learning examples for credit approval

Name	PaysRegularly	Rich	HairColor	CreditApproved
Mrs. Brown	no	yes	blond	yes
Mr. Grey	no	no	grey	no
Miss White	yes	no	blond	yes

from observations in nature, or even by designing his own examples to convey essential information. This point is especially relevant to argument-based ML that will be discussed in this chapter.

To introduce some basic notions and terminology of machine learning, required in this chapter, consider a simple example of learning about credit approval. We will later extend this example to illustrate argument-based ML. Table 23.1 gives some learning data. There are three learning examples in this table, each of them corresponding to a person that made a credit application. Each person is described in terms of three attributes: PaysRegularly, with possible values "yes" and "no", Rich (possible values "yes" and "no"), and HairColor (possible values "blond", "grey"). The right-most column CreditApproved tells for each person whether credit was approved or not. This attribute is called class, that is the attribute whose value we want to learn to predict from the values of the other attributes.

A typical rule learning algorithm will induce the following theory about this domain:

> IF HairColor = blond THEN CreditApproved = yes
> ELSE CreditAproved = no

This is short and consistent with the data. It correctly classifies all three learning examples. We say that the first IF-THEN rule *covers* two examples (Mrs Brown and Miss White), and the ELSE rule covers the third example (Mr Grey). On the other hand, this theory may not make much sense to a financial expert. The theory classifies the learning examples correctly, but for wrong reasons. It does not really correspond to the intended theory.

We will now look at how this may be improved by introducing arguments into the learning examples. We call this approach argument-based machine learning, or ABML for short. With arguments, the learning problem statement changes to:

- Given examples + supporting arguments for some of the examples
- Find a theory that explains the examples using given arguments

To illustrate what we mean by "explaining the examples using given arguments", consider again the data in Table 23.1 and assume that an expert gave an argument for Mrs. Brown: "Mrs. Brown received credit because she is rich". Now consider again the first rule above that all blond people receive credit. This rule correctly classifies Mrs. Brown, but it does not explain this classification in terms of the given argument for Mrs. Brown. The rule does not even mention Mrs. Brown's property in the argument, namely that she is rich. Therefore we say that this rule *covers*

Mrs. Brown, however the rule does not *AB-cover* Mrs. Brown. "AB-cover" stands for "argument based cover". An ABML algorithm has to induce another rule to this effect, namely to explain Mrs. Brown's case in terms of the given argument. An ABML algorithm may achieve this effect by inducing the rule:

IF Rich = yes THEN CreditApproved = yes

This rule explains Mrs. Brown example using the given argument: credit was approved because Rich = yes. We say that this rule AB-covers Mrs. Brown. This example also shows how the given argument guides the learning system to induce a theory that makes more sense to an expert.

The foregoing examples illustrate the idea of using annotated (argumented) examples in machine learning. They also illustrate the advantages of ABML over standard ML from examples. These advantages can be summarised as:

- Reasons (arguments) impose constraints over the space of possible hypotheses, thus reducing search complexity.
- An induced theory should make more sense to an expert as it has to be consistent with the given arguments. So it tends to construct the right reasons for the propositions in question.
- Introducing expert knowledge through arguments about *specific* cases is much easier for experts than work out complete, generally applicable rules or theories.

The examples above also indicate how an existing machine learning method may be enhanced into its AB extension. One way of looking at it is as adding a special declarative bias to the machine learning method. As usual, the method looks for theories that are consistent with the learning data. The added bias that results from the arguments requires an extra condition that the theories have to satisfy. Namely, the acceptable theories are those only that allow proofs of the argumented examples so that the proofs mention the given arguments. In rule learning, this bias can be enforced by insisting that the precondition of the rule that covers the argumented example conjunctively contains the given reason. This also illustrates how the arguments constrain the search space among possible hypotheses, or how the arguments may guide the search.

Although the basic principle of turning a standard ML method into an ABML method may be quite straightforward, all the details of this may be rather complicated. In the next section we will describe through examples how learning in logic (inductive logic programming, ILP) may be extended to argument-based ILP. In Section 3 we describe in detail how a well-known rule learning algorithm CN2 has been extended to its argument-based variant ABCN2. Then we describe the "ABML refinement loop" – a way of using argument based ML for knowledge acquisition from examples in practical applications.

2 Argument based Inductive Logic Programming

Our credit approval example above belongs to attribute-value learning. The data (Table 1) was stated in terms of attribute values for each example, and the induced theory was stated in terms of propositional logic formulas where propositions are attribute-value pairs. Typically in this formalism, examples are explained in terms of the given arguments directly – a rule that predicts a class value directly mentions the argument, so there is just one step inference between the class value and the argument.

"Deeper" explanation of examples in terms of given arguments is possible when the learning is done in first-order logic, as in Inductive Logic Programing (ILP) . Extending the problem of ILP to argument-based ILP (AB-ILP) may be as follows. First, consider the usual ILP problem statement, without arguments. This can be:

- Given positive examples E and negative examples NE, and background knowledge BK
- Find a logic formula H (called a "hypothesis"), such that

$$BK \wedge H \vdash E,$$

and for each negative example N in NE:

$$not(BK \wedge H \vdash N)$$

That is, all positive examples can be derived from hypothesis H and BK, but none of the negative examples can. To illustrate this, consider the credit approval problem of Table 1, this time stated as an ILP problem. This can be done by translating the problem into predicate logic as follows (using the syntax of Prolog):

```
% Background knowledge
pays_regularly( miss_White).
rich(mrs_Brown).
hair_color( mrs_Brown, blond).
hair_color(mr_Grey, grey).
hair_color( miss_White, blond).

% Positive examples
ex( credit_approved( mrs_Brown)).
ex( credit_approved( miss_White)).

% Negative example
nex( credit_approved( mr_Grey)).
```

A typical ILP program will induce from this a definition of the credit_approved predicate, which is equivalent to the typical result of an attribute-value rule learning algorithm. For example, running the ILP program HYPER [2] on this data produces the theory:

```
credit_approved( X)   :-
   hair_color( X, blond).
```

Again, a more sensible result from the expert's point of view can be obtained by turning the usual ILP to argument-based ILP (abbreviated as AB-ILP) and adding the arguments about Mrs. Brown as before (because she is rich).

The above definition of the ILP problem can be extended to AB-ILP problem definition as [3]:

- Given examples E, annotated by arguments (reasons) R, and background knowledge BK
- Find a hypothesis H, such that

$$BK \wedge H \vdash_R E,$$

and for each negative example N in NE:

$$not(BK \wedge H \vdash N)$$

This says that hypothesis H explains the examples w.r.t. BK using reasons R. The notation $\vdash_R$ means: derivation of E mentions reasons R.

If we now add our usual arguments about Mrs Brown, the theory about credit_approved induced by AB-ILP becomes:

```
credit_approved(X):-
    rich(X).

credit_approved(X):-
    pays_regularly(X).
```

The first clause AB-covers Mrs Brown since acccording to this rule, credit_approved(mrs_brown) follows from the fact rich(mrs_brown), that is the given reason.

Now, to illustrate a deeper reason (that requires more than just one inference step), consider the following changes to our learning data whereby we also add to background knowledge the predicate married/2, owns/2, and well-paid/1:

```
% Background knowledge

rich( X)    :- owns( X, castle).

rich( X)    :- well_paid( X).

pays_regularly( miss_White).

owns( mr_Brown, castle).

well_paid( mrs_Bond).

hair_color( mrs_Brown, blond).
hair_color( mr_Grey, grey).
hair_color( miss_White, blond).
hair_color( mr_Bond, blond).
hair_color( mrs_Grey, grey).

married( mrs_Brown, mr_Brown).
```

```
married( mr_Bond, mrs_Bond).
...

% Examples
ex( credit_approved( mrs_Brown)).        % A positive example
ex( credit_approved( miss_White)).
ex( credit_approved( mr_Bond)).

nex( credit_approved( mr_Grey)).         % A negative example
nex( credit_approved( mrs_Grey)).
```

Now Mrs Brown is not described as rich, and the argumented example now is: Mrs Brown received credit because Mr Brown owns a castle. A theory induced from this data and consistent with the argument is:

```
credit_approved(X):-
  married(X,Y),
  rich(Y).

credit_approved(X):-
  pays_regularly(X).
```

Notice that the argument this time did not mention a direct property of Mrs Brown, so that AB-ILP had to induce a two step inference connection between the Mrs Brown example and the argument. The proof of the example with the induced theory and background knowledge indeed mentions the given argument owns(mr_Brown, castle). This proof is:

```
credit_approved( mrs_Brown)  FOLLOWS FROM
    married( mrs_Brown, mr_Brown), AND
    rich( mr_Brown)  WHICH FOLLOWS FROM
        owns( mr_Brown, castle)
```

The induced theory also explains the Mr Bond example:

```
credit_approved( mr_Bond)  FOLLOWS FROM
    married( mr_Bond, mrs_Bond), AND
    rich( mrs_Bond)  WHICH FOLLOWS FROM
        well_paid( mrs_Bond)
```

A preliminary extension of the program HYPER to AB-ILP is described in (I. Bratko, Argumentation Based ILP: Towards AB-HYPER, ASPIC Project working paper, 2005). Examples of learning family relations show that huge speed-up may result from the use of arguments.

3 ABCN2 – an argument-based rule learning algorithm

In this section we describe an algorithm, called ABCN2 , for induction of rules in argument-based framework for machine learning. ABCN2, which stands for "argument based CN2", was introduced in [19] as an extension of the well-known CN2 rule induction algorithm of Clark and Niblett [7].

We will give in this section a formal definition of argumented examples in the form accepted by ABCN2, and present a version of CN2 and its extension into its argument based counterpart ABCN2.

In our implementation of ABCN2, "CN2" stands for a state-of-the-art version of the original Clark and Niblett's CN2 algorithm, in which various improvements were added over the years. Details of these improvements are described in [18], which also gives experimental results comparing the improved CN2 with several other representative ML methods. In these experiments, this improved CN2 (without the use of arguments) performed overall significantly better than the original CN2, and better or comparably to some other popular ML methods.

3.1 Argumented examples

A learning example E in the usual form accepted by CN2 is a pair (A,C), where A is an attribute-value vector, and C is a class value. For instance, the first example in Table 23.1 can be written in this syntax as:

$$((PaysRegularly = no, Rich = yes, HairColor = blond),$$
$$CreditApproved = yes)$$

An attribute can be either discrete, nominal, or continuous. In addition to such examples, ABCN2 also accepts argumented examples. An argumented example AE is a triple of the form:

$$AE = (A, C, Arguments)$$

A is an attribute-value vector and C is a class value. *Arguments* is a set of arguments $Arg_1,\ldots,Arg_n$, where an argument Arg_i has one of the following forms:

$$\text{because } Reasons$$

or

$$\text{despite } Reasons$$

The former specifies a *positive* argument (speaks for the given class value), while the latter specifies a *negative* argument (speaks against the class value). For example, the expert's argument for approving credit to Mrs. Brown (see Table 23.1) can be: Mrs. Brown received credit because she is rich. A negative argument can be: Mrs. Brown received credit despite her not paying regularly. This argumented example would in our syntax be written as:

$$((PaysRegularly = no, Rich = yes, HairColor = blond),$$
$$CreditApproved = yes,$$
$$\{ \text{ because } Rich = yes, \text{ despite } PaysRegularly = no\}).$$

In general, *Reasons* is a conjunction of reasons $r_1, \dots, r_n$,

$$Reasons = r_1 \wedge r_2 \wedge \dots \wedge r_n$$

where each of the reasons r_i can be in one of the possible forms below. In the explanation of these forms below we assume that r_i is a part of a positive argument; for negative arguments, the explanations are exactly the opposite. The possible forms of reasons are:

- $X = x_i$ means that value x_i of attribute X is a reason why example is in the class as given. This is the only allowed form for discrete attributes.
- $X > x_i$ $(or X >= x_i)$ means that the value of attribute X of example being greater than (greater or equal to) x_i is a reason for class value.
- $X > (or X >=)$ "X is high"; similar to $X > x_i$ $(X >= x_i)$, just that in this case we do not know the threshold value x_i and it has to be found by ABCN2 automatically. Such an argument says that the value of X of the example is high enough for the example to be in the class as given.
- The forms $X < x_i, X <= x_i, X <,$ and $X <=$ ("X is low"), are defined analogously as the opposite of $X > x_i$, $(X >= x_i)$, $X >$, and $(X >=)$, respectively.

In CN2, rules have the form:

IF *Complex* THEN *Class*

where *Complex* is the conjunction of simple conditions, called *selectors*. A selector specifies the value of an attribute, for example *HairColor = blond* or a threshold on the attribute value, for example *Salary > 5000*. A rule for our credit approval domain can be:

IF *PaysRegularly = no* AND *HairColor = blond*

THEN *CreditApproved = yes*

The condition part of the rule is satisfied by the attribute values of Mrs. Brown example, so we say that this rule *covers* this example.

Arguments given to an example constrain rules that *AB-cover* this example. Consider again the argumented example "Mrs Brown received credit because she is rich and despite she does not pay regularly". How can these arguments be used in rule learning so as to constrain the form of rules? A rule that handles Mrs Brown has to mention, in its IF-part, the condition "Rich = yes", but must not mention the condition "PaysRegulary = no". In ABCN2, this intuition is formalized through the notions (1) a rule is *consistent* with an argument, and (2) a rule *AB-covers* and example.

A rule R = "IF Complex THEN Class" is *consistent* with an argument "because *Reasons*" if Complex implies all the reasons in Reasons. A rule is consistent with an argument "despite Reasons" if Complex does not imply Reasons. Implication of reasons of special forms like "attribute is high" is defined as follows. A complex

Complex implies a reason r_i of the form "$X >$" (or "$X <$", "$X <=$", "$X >=$"), if Complex contains a selector of the form "$X > x_i$" (or "$X < x_i$", "$X >= x_i$", "$X <= x_i$", respectively) where the threshold x_i can be any possible value of attribute X.

For argumented examples, the definition of a rule *covering* an example needs to be refined. In the standard definition, a rule covers an example if the condition part of the rule is true for this example. In argument based rule learning, this definition is modified to: A rule R *AB-covers* an argumented example E if:

1. All the conditions in R are true for E (the same as *covers* in CN2), and
2. R is consistent with at least one positive argument of E, and
3. R is consistent with all negative arguments of E.

As an illustration of the differences between AB-covering and the usual definition of covering, consider again the Mrs Brown example with the arguments that she received credit because she is rich and despite her not paying regularly. Now consider four rules R1 - R4. All of them cover the Brown example, but not all of them AB-cover this example:

R1: IF *HairColor* = *blond* THEN *CreditApproved* = *yes*
R2: IF *PaysRegularly* = *no* AND *HairColor* = *blond*
    THEN *CreditApproved* = *yes*
R3: IF *PaysRegularly* = *no* AND *Rich* = *yes*
    THEN *CreditApproved* = *yes*
R4: IF *HairColor* = *blond* AND *Rich* = *yes*
    THEN *CreditApproved* = *yes*

All four rules cover the Brown example and have 100% accuracy on the data set from Table 23.1. However, Rule 1 does not AB-cover the example, because it is not consistent with the positive argument. For the same reason, rule 2 does not AB-cover the Brown example, but this rule fails also because it is not consistent with the negative argument (*PaysRegularly* = *no*). Rule 3 also fails due to the negative argument, although it is consistent with the positive argument. The last example AB-covers the Brown example.

3.2 ABCN2 algorithm

The CN2 algorithm [6, 7] consists of a covering algorithm and a search procedure that finds individual rules by performing beam search. The covering algorithm (see Algorithm 23.1) induces a list of rules that cover all the examples in the learning set. Roughly, the covering algorithm starts by finding a rule, then it removes from the set of learning examples those examples that are covered by this rule, and adds the rule to the set of rules. In each iteration, a "best" rule is heuristically constructed by beam search (call to procedure Find_best_rule). This process is repeated until all the examples are removed. This is called a "covering" algorithm because the constructed rules cover all the examples.

Algorithm 23.1 A sketch of the basic CN2 covering algorithm. The algorithm takes a set of examples ES and computes an ordered list of rules RULE_LIST that cover all the examples.

Procedure CN2(Examples ES)

Let RULE_LIST be the empty list.
while ES is not empty **do**
    Let BEST_RULE be *Find_best_rule(ES)*
    Add BEST_RULE to RULE_LIST.
    Remove from ES examples AB-covered by BEST_RULE.
end while
Return RULE_LIST.

Algorithm 23.2 Covering algorithm of ABCN2 algorithm that learns rules from examples ES for given class T.

Procedure ABCN2ForOneClass(Examples ES, Class T)

Let RULE_LIST be the empty list.
Let AES be the set of examples of class T that have arguments; $AES \subseteq ES$
Determine thresholds for "vague" reasons (of form $X >$ and $X <$)
Evaluate arguments (as if they were rules) of examples in AES and **sort** examples in AES according to the evaluations of their best argument.
while AES is not empty **do**
    Let AE1 be the first example in AES.
    Let BEST_RULE be *ABFind_best_rule(ES,AE1,T)*
    Add BEST_RULE to RULE_LIST.
    Remove from AES examples AB-covered by BEST_RULE.
end while
for all RULE in RULE_LIST **do**
    Remove from ES examples AB-covered by RULE.
end for
Add to RULE_LIST the rules returned by *CN2ForOneClass(ES,T)*.
return RULE_LIST

There are two versions of CN2: one induces ordered list of rules, and the other unordered list of rules. Our algorithm in this paper is based on the second version of CN2. In this case, the covering algorithm consists of two procedures, CN2unordered and CN2ForOneClass. The first procedure iteratively calls CN2ForOneClass for all the classes in the domain, while the second induces rules only for the class given. When removing covered examples, only examples of this class are removed [6]. Essentially, CN2ForOneClass is a covering algorithm that covers the examples of the given class.

Now we will extend the CN2 algorithm to ABCN2. The first requirement for ABML is that an induced hypothesis explains the argumented examples using given arguments. In rule learning, this means that for each argumented example, there has to be at least one rule in the set of induced rules that AB-covers this example. This is achieved simply by replacing covering in original CN2 with AB-covering.

Replacing the "covers" relation in CN2 with "AB-covers" in ABCN2 ensures that both argumented and non-argumented examples are AB-covered. However, in addition to simpy AB-covering all the examples, we would also prefer explaining as many as possible non-argumented examples by arguments given for the argumented examples. Therefore, CN2ForOneClass is changed into ABCN2ForOneClass (see Algorithm 23.2). The procedure starts by creating an empty list of rules, and makes a separate set AES of argumented examples only. Then it looks for "vague" reasons in the arguments – reasons of the forms "$X >$", "$X <$", etc., and finds the "best" threshold t for each of such reasons. A "vague" reason $X >$ so becomes $X > t$. Arguments in the examples AES are then evaluated by the rule evaluation function (explained later) as if the arguments were rules of the form "IF argument THEN class". The examples in AES are then sorted according to the "goodness" of their best arguments.

In the while loop, the procedure induces a rule, using ABFind_Best_rule, to cover the first argumented example. ABFind_Best_rule is a modified beam search procedure that accepts examples and an argumented example, where the resulting rule is guaranteed to AB-cover the given argumented example. This rule is added to the rule set, and the procedure removes from AES argumented examples AB-covered by this rule. The removal of all positive examples is not necessary, as each of the argumented examples differently constrains the search and thus prevents ABCN2 from inducing the same rule again. When all argumented examples are covered, all positive examples AB-covered by rules are removed, and the remaining rules are learned using classical CN2ForOneClass to cover the non-argumented examples.

Algorithm 23.3 shows the AB search procedure. The procedure takes a set of examples to learn from, and an argumented example that needs to be AB-covered by the induced rule.

3.3 Rule evaluation and extreme value correction

An evaluation function is used to estimate the quality of a rule. The quality of a rule is a user-defined measure to estimate how well the rule will eventually work in classification. Generally, this measure should reflect the accuracy of the rule when classifying new examples. Several formulas for estimating the probability of correct classification of new cases by a rule have been used in CN2. In [6], Clark and Boswell use Laplace's rule of succession. Džeroski et al. [9] use Cestnik's m-estimate [5].

The problem with all these probability estimates is that rule learning algorithms choose the best hypothesis among many candidate hypotheses. Therefore the example set covered by the best looking rule is not really a random sample, which these formulas assume. Rather, this example set is the best among those that belong to many competing rules. This gives rise to optimistic estimates. This problem, also known as multiple-comparison problem in induction algorithms [14], can be even worse in the case of ABCN2. Rules learned from argumented examples are typically

Algorithm 23.3 Algorithm that finds best rule that AB-covers argumented example E. The "quality" of a complex is evaluated by user-defined evaluation function.

Procedure ABFind_Best_Rule(Examples ES, Example E)

Let T be the class of E
Let the set STAR contain positive arguments of E (written as complexes).
Evaluate complexes in STAR (using quality function).
Let *BEST_CPX* be the best complex from STAR.
Let *SELECTORS* be the set of all possible selectors that are TRUE for E
Let *ARG_REASONS* be the set of all reasons in positive arguments of E (union of reasons).
while STAR is not empty **do**
    {Specialize all complexes in STAR as follows}
    Let *NEWSTAR* be the set
        $\{x \wedge y \,\|\, x \in STAR, y \in SELECTORS\}$
    Remove from *NEWSTAR* all complexes that are not consistent with any of negative arguments of E.
    for every complex C_i in NEWSTAR **do**
        if C_i is statistically significant(ES,T) **and**
           quality(C_i) > quality(BEST_CPX) **then**
           Let *BEST_CPX* be C_i
        end if
    end for
    Let STAR be best N complexes from NEWSTAR; N is a user-defined size of STAR (size of beam in beam search, usually N=5).
    Let ABNEWSTAR be such subset of NEWSTAR
        where complexes in ABNEWSTAR contain only
        conditions from *ARG_REASONS*.
    Let ABSTAR be best N complexes from ABNEWSTAR.
    Let STAR be STAR merged with ABSTAR.
end while
return rule: "**IF** *BEST_CPX* **THEN** T.

selected from less hypotheses than rules induced by standard CN2 algorithm. Thus the accuracy of rules learned from an argumented examples are relatively underestimated in comparison with rules learned by standard CN2.

In [15] we developed a method called EVC (extreme value correction) that accounts for multiple comparisons and corrects otherwise optimistic evaluation measure. All the experiments with ABCN2 mentioned in this chapter were done with this method of rule evaluation. To enable efficient implementation of EVC in ABCN2, a probabilistic coverage and removal strategy was designed in [19].

3.4 Classification with rules

Learned rules are used to predict the class of a new example. In the case where only one rule triggers for this example, classification is simply the class of the rule. In cases where several rules trigger, we need to resolve clashes between opposing rules. In standard CN2 these conflicts are resolved by summing the distributions of covered examples of all the rules to find the most probable class. However, such classification works only in cases where covering rules are sufficiently independent, which is often not true. Moreover, such a classification technique only considers the distribution of covered examples, without considering the rule's quality, which becomes a problem when classifying from rules that were induced from arguments. Rules learned from argumented examples might have relatively small coverage and might become relatively unimportant in such a classification technique. On the other hand, we showed in the previous section how to compute the quality of a rule that accounts for the number of tried hypotheses. To make rules induced from argumented examples competitive, we used in our experiments a simple classification technique based on the quality of rules: we take the best rule (having highest quality) for each class covering the given example, and classify the example in the class predicted by the best rule. Note that this classification can also be used to give probabilistic class predictions by normalizing the qualities of the best rules so that they sum up to 1.

4 ABML refinement loop

Giving arguments to all examples is not likely to be feasible in practice because it would require too much effort by a domain expert who provides arguments. Can we help the expert by suggesting which examples to explain by arguments? We developed a method to automatically find "problematic" examples , that is examples where arguments would be likely to have a significant effect on learning. So the "commentator" of examples (expert) is asked to concentrate on these "problematic" cases. This idea is realized by the following iterative procedure which we call "ABML refinement loop". The loop starts with "plain" examples only (i.e. no argumented examples are initially given). Then it proceeds as follows:

1. *Induce a theory from plain examples, without arguments (using classical CN2).*
2. *Find a critical example that would be useful to be argumented.* This step involves a search for the most problematic example (e.g. outlier) in the learning set. For this task we use a k-fold cross-validation repeated n times (e.g. $n = 4, k = 5$), so that each example is tested n times. The example that is most frequently missclassified in cross-validations is chosen as the most critical example that needs to be argumented. If there are several such examples, then the algorithm picks one at random.
3. *If a critical example was not found (in step 2), then stop the iteration.*
4. *An expert gives arguments to the selected example.* Two things can happen here: in the preferred case the expert finds argumenting this example easy; in the undesired case, the expert finds this to be hard. The second case may be due to different reasons (deciding attributes are not available, the example is indeed an outlier, or argumenting may be hard in the chosen representation of arguments). Each of these cases can be mended in different ways. In the extreme, this example can simply be discarded from the learning set.

5. *Induce rules on the learning set using ABCN2 and new argumented example.*
6. *Return to step 2.*

5 Experiments and applications

In this section we present a number of experiments and applications with ABCN2. These highlight a number of important points which concern the questions:

- Success of learning with arguments, compared with standard learning where examples come without arguments. Success of learning can be measured in terms of classification accuracy, number of examples needed for learning, understandability (or interpretability by the user) of the induced theory.
- How effective is the interactive ABML refinement loop where the system automatically selects critical examples that are to be argumented by the expert. That is, how well does this mechanism guide the expert's attention to important cases and missing information.
- How can a knowledge base be reconstructed from examples with ABML?
- Can relevant arguments be extracted automatically from relevant literature, rather than provided by an expert?

In these experiments, an implementation of ABCN2 within the Orange-toolkit [8] was used. Some other applications, in medicine and law, are described in [19].

5.1 ZOO Data Set

ZOO data set [20] contains descriptions of 101 animals (instances) with 17 attributes: *hair, feathers, eggs, milk, predator, toothed, domestic, backbone, fins, legs, tail, catsize, airborne, aquatic, breathes, venomous, and type*, which is the class attribute. *Type* has seven possible values: *mammal, bird, reptile, fish, amphibian, insect, other*. An advantage of this data set is that a domain expert is not really needed as source of arguments. Just using an encyclopedia, a non-expert is able to provide good arguments to automatically selected critical examples.

The set was split into a learning set (70%) and a test set (30%). Classical CN2, without arguments, induced seven IF-THEN rules. The accuracy of these rules on the learning set was 100%, but the (more important!) accuracy on the test set was about 90%. The refinement loop with identifying critical examples only required three iterations:

1. The first critical example was the tortoise (type *reptile*). A good argument for tortoise to be a reptile is that it has the backbone and it lays eggs (tortoise is a reptile because backbone=yes AND eggs=yes). Now, the rule induced by ABCN2 that AB-covers the tortoise was:

  IF **backbone=yes** AND **eggs=yes** AND aquatic=no AND feathers=no THEN
  type=Reptile

The attribute-value pairs in boldface correspond to the argument.

2. The next critical example was a sea snake (a reptile). When the encyclopedia was consulted to look for an argument about sea snake, it turned out that there was an error in the example set. The example set said that sea snake is a non-breathing reptile, whereas the encyclopedia stated that it is in fact air-breathing. So this critical example just helped to identify and correct a mistake in the data.

3. The next critical example was the newt (amphibian). The argument extracted from the encyclopedia was that the newt is an amphibian because it has the back-bone, is aquatic, and lays eggs.

This resulted in final eight IF-THEN rules with 100% accuracy on both learning set and test set.

This experiment clearly illustrates the effectiveness of the refinement loop based on selecting critical examples. Only two examples had to be argued to achieve perfect rule set. The example also nicely illustrates that it is much easier for a human to give arguments only to an individual example (e.g why tortoise is a reptile), than it would be to articulate general rules that correctly classify the animals. Moreover, the rules learned from arguments are consistent with prior knowledge and thus make more sense to the user.

5.2 Extracting arguments from free text

In ABML applications, arguments are usually provided by domain experts. In [17], an alternative approach was investigated where arguments were automatically extracted from text. This approach eliminates the reliance on an expert who may not be available. One expected advantage of this idea is in that it should be much easier to extract from text specific relations in the form of arguments that concern concrete examples, rather than extracting general theories from text. For the purpose of extracting arguments for ABML from text, we are interested in finding semantic relations between class values and attribute values (taken from the learning data). For example, given the class value *reptile* and the attribute *eggs* we are interested in relations such as "Most reptiles lay eggs" and "Reptiles hatch eggs." In [17], a simple idea was explored that if many sentences reference both a class value and an attribute, then the class value and the attribute are likely to be related. Here, one problem is the lexicalization of the class values and attribute descriptions. The names of attributes and classes should be similar to those used in text. It can be very difficult to find occurrences of the lexicalizations of such concepts in the same sentence and, consequently, to determine whether or not a relation exists. To deal with the variability of natural language, alternative lexical variants were generated using WordNet [10], a lexical database containing semantic relations among words. Variants for all class values and attributes were generated using the following semantic relations in WordNet: synonyms (e.g., breathe $\rightarrow$ respire) and morphological derivations (e.g., predator $\rightarrow$ predators). The arguments were then extracted from text simply by statistical means, depending on whether a class value and an attribute co-occur significantly more frequently or less frequently than it would be statistically expected.

This approach was experimentally applied to the ZOO dataset. Arguments were automatically extracted from Wikipedia. The method was evaluated by 10-times repeated 10-fold cross-validation. In each iteration, all the examples in the learning set were argumented, then a classifier was built from these examples with ABCN2. The induced classifier's accuracy was then estimated on the test set. Using ABCN2 without arguments resulted in 94.5% classification accuracy, while ABCN2 with arguments scored, on average, 96.7%. For comparison, some other standard machine learning methods (as implemented in Orange [8]) scored 90% (SVM), 92.57% (C4.5) and 92.6% (naïve Bayes). The accuracy results in this experiment differ somewhat from those obtained in the experiment with expert-constructed arguments. The main reason for the differences is that in the Wikipedia experiment, accuracy was measured with 10-fold cross validation whereas in the previous section this was done by 70:30% split into learning and test set.

5.3 Construction of sophisticated chess concepts

Today's chess playing programs are extremely good at playing chess, but their use for chess commenting or tutoring is rather limited. Such programs evaluate chess positions numerically, but are then not able to explain a numerical evaluation in terms of concepts that human chess players use when they reason about the position. For example, the program may say that the current position's value is 1.70 in favor of White. Now the beginner chess player would ask "Why"? An answer, which is beyond today's chess programs, might be: "Because Black has a bad bishop"? Typically, the concept of bad bishop is not built into chess programs, although the program's numerical evaluation function may incorporate some features that are related to the concept of bad bishop. Watson [21] gives the following definition as traditional: a bishop that is on the same colour of squares as its own pawns is bad, since its mobility is restricted by its own pawns and it does not defend the squares in front of these pawns. Watson adds some further qualitative comments to this definition (such as which own pawns are particularly important). However, all this is very hard to translate precisely into program code that would reliably recognize bad bishops. An attempt by women grandmaster Jana Krivec and FIDE master Matej Guid at manually formalizing the definition of bad bishop as if-then rules, only resulted in a classifier that had 59% accuracy.

Guid et al. [13, 16] applied ABCN2 to the construction of chess concepts intended for a tutoring chess program. In a case study, the concept of bad bishop was induced with ABCN2. 200 examples of positions that included bishops were prepared for learning. The positions were selected from real chess games. 78 bishops in these positions were bad, and 122 not bad. The set of 200 positions was randomly divided into a 100 position learning set, and the remaining 100 position test set. As an initial set of attributes for learning, the features included in the evaluation function of the well-known chess program Crafty were used. The learning with CN2, without arguments, achieved 72% accuracy on the test set. Then, in the ABML refinement loop, eight critical examples were iteratively identified and equipped by arguments by the chess experts Krivec and Guid. In some cases, the experts were not able to produce meaningful arguments in terms of the existing set of attributes. In such cases they also suggested new attributes which were then added to the attribute set. This illustrates another important point in ABML. The mechanism of selecting and argumenting critical examples may also help an expert to improve the representation for learning. Five new attributes were thus added to the initial set of Crafty's attributes. The final induced classifier by ABCN2 attained 95% accuracy on the test set. So the argumenting of just eight examples resulted in the improved accuracy from the initial 72% to 95%. An interesting question is: How much of this improvement can be attributed to the arguments alone, and how much to the improved set of attributes. To answer this, CN2 was run again on the original, non-argumented learning set, by this time using the extended attribute set. The resulting CN2's accuracy on the test set was 91%. We may interpret this result as that the main improvement in accuracy was due to the improved attribute set, enabled by the ABML refinement loop.

5.4 Japanese Credit Screening Database

Japanese Credit Screening Database [20] contains 125 persons applying for credit described with 10 attributes. The class attribute is whether a person got credit or not. This domain definition also contains imperfect prior knowledge (accuracy 83% on the examples) - it was generated by talking to individuals at a Japanese company that grants credit. This prior knowledge was used in the experiment [19] as a substitute for the domain expert. It was assumed that this "expert" cannot give a complete definition of the target concept, but can only give arguments for certain examples. The data was split to a learning set (70%) and test set (30%). CN2 induced three rules from this data set.

These three rules achieved 84% accuracy on the learning set and 76% accuracy on the test set. Then, in the ABML refinement loop, critical examples were argumented automatically by the "expert" (knowledge base). After 5 iterations, when remaining problematic examples could not be argumented any more, final theory induced by ABCN2 consisted of seven rules. These rules had accuracy 85% on the learning set, and 89% on the test set.

This experiment indicated several points of interest regarding the reconstruction of expert's prior knowledge. Six of the seven final induced rules correspond precisely to complete background knowledge given by experts. This was achieved by asking our "expert" to explain only five examples, which indicates the effectiveness of the ABML refinement loop. This also indicates how effective ABML is as a tool for extracting expert's informal background knowledge. Imagine that we did not have experts' prior knowledge already formalized, and that we wanted to extract it from the expert. The way to do this with interactive use of ABCN2, is to generate questions for the expert by identifying critical examples. Expert's explanations in terms of arguments of the five critical cases would, in our example, be sufficient to completely formalize the expert's prior intuitions. In addition to reconstructing the original expert knowledge base, ABCN2 was able also to improve its classification accuracy.

This experiment also nicely illustrates the difference between induced rules resulting from data only, and actual causal rules that generated the data. Both hypotheses, with and without arguments, have a similar accuracy on the learning set, but to a domain expert the first set of rules would be difficult to understand as they show unfamiliar dependencies. Moreover, the first set of rules scored significantly lower accuracy on the test set, meaning that the first hypothesis merely reflected a spurious relation in the learning set.

A similar learning problem – learning about credit status – occurred within the European 6th framework project ASPIC[1]. Learning about credit status is a part of a larger business-to-business scenario used in ASPIC as the main large-scale demonstration application for argument-based methods. In that experiment we also showed how ABCN2 can be used to improve existing knowledge bases in argumentation based expert systems. The data set consisted of 5000 companies described by 18 attributes (three of them were actually relevant for credit status). We began the experiment with the induction of rules from 2500 examples (learning set) without considering any prior knowledge. The system induced a set of 40 rules. These rules correctly classified 95% of the examples in the test set (the remaining 2500 examples). After adding arguments to two problematic examples, ABCN2 induced six rules only, and the classification accuracy of these rules on the test set was 99.9%. This is a significant improvement in terms of classification accuracy, but even more spectacular is the improvement in terms of the complexity of the induced theories, from the initial 40 rules to 6 only.

6 Conclusions

In this chapter we described an approach to machine learning that, in addition to learning examples as usual, also uses arguments about some of the examples. This approach has been named ABML (argument based machine learning). Advantages of ABML are:

- Expressing expert knowledge in the form of arguments for individual examples is easier for the expert than providing general theories.
- Critical examples whose arguments are expected to improve the learning most, are automatically identified inside the ABML refinement loop.

---

[1] Argument Service Platform with Integrated Components (ASPIC), url: http://www.argumentation.org/

- ABCN2, an argument-based extension of the known CN2 learning algorithm, produces more comprehensible rules than CN2, because ABCN2 uses expert-given arguments that constrain the search among possible hypotheses, thereby suppressing spurious hypotheses.
- In experiments in number of domains, ABCN2 achieved higher classification accuracy than classical CN2. An important practical question is, what happens with ABCN2 accuracy when there are errors in arguments. In [19] it was shown experimentally that, on average, imperfect, or even completely random arguments are unlikely to harm the classification accuracy of ABCN2.

There has been some related work on combining machine learning and argumentation. [1, 4] focused on the use of machine learning to build arguments that can be later used in the argumentation process, most notably in the law domain. Gomez and Chesñevar [11] suggested several ideas on combining argumentation and machine learning. They implemented an approach where they used argumentation to improve the performance of a neural network [12].

The main principles of extending a standard ML technique to its ABML version seem to be quite straightforward. However, when extending attribute-value rule-learning algorithm CN2 to ABCN2, many quite intricate problems had to be solved in the process. One would expect that extending ILP to AB-ILP would be even more beneficial. However, this is largely subject of future work.

7 Acknowledgements

This work was carried out under the auspices of the European Commission's Information Society Technologies (IST) programme, through Project ASPIC (IST-FP6-002307). It was also supported by the Slovenian research agency ARRS.

References

1. Kevin D. Ashley and Edwina L. Rissland. Law, learning and representation. *Artificial Intelligence*, 150:17–58, 2003.
2. *Prolog Programming for Artificial Intelligence* Pearson Education / Addison-Wesley, 2001.
3. Ivan Bratko and Martin Možina. Argumentation and machine learning. In: Deliverable 2.1 for the ASPIC project, 2004.
4. Stefanie Brüninghaus and Kevin D. Ashley. Predicting the outcome of case-based legal arguments. In G. Sartor, editor, *Proceedings of the 9th International Conference on Artificial Intelligence and Law (ICAIL)*, pages 233–242, Edinburgh, United Kingdom, June 2003.
5. B. Cestnik. Estimating probabilities: A crucial task in machine learning. In *Proceedings of the Ninth European Conference on Artificial Intelligence*, pages 147–149, 1990.
6. Peter Clark and Robin Boswell. Rule induction with CN2: Some recent improvements. In *Machine Learning - Proceeding of the Fifth Europen Conference (EWSL-91)*, pages 151–163, Berlin, 1991.
7. Peter Clark and Tim Niblett. The CN2 induction algorithm. *Machine Learning Journal*, 4(3):261–283, 1989.

8. J. Demšar and B. Zupan. Orange: From experimental machine learning to interactive data mining. White Paper [http://www.ailab.si/orange], Faculty of Computer and Information Science, University of Ljubljana, 2004.

9. Sašo Džeroski, Bojan Cestnik, and Igor Petrovski. Using the m-estimate in rule induction. *CIT. J. Comput. Inf. Technol.*, 1:37–46, 1993.

10. C. Fellbaum. *WordNet. An Electronic Lexical Database*. MIT Press, 1998.

11. Sergio A. Gomez and Carlos I. Chesnevar. Integrating defeasible argumentation and machine learning techniques. Technical report, Universidad Nacional del Sur, 2004.

12. Sergio A. Gomez and Carlos I. Chesnevar. Integrating defeasible argumentation with fuzzy art neural networks for pattern classification. *Journal of Computer Science and Technology*, 4(1):45–51, April 2004.

13. Matej Guid, Martin Možina, Jana Krivec, Aleksander Sadikov, and Ivan Bratko. Learning positional features for annotating chess games. *Computers and Games Conference 2008*, Bejing, 2008.

14. David D. Jensen and Paul R. Cohen. Multiple comparisons in induction algorithms. *Machine Learning*, 38(3):309–338, March 2000.

15. Martin Možina, Janez Demšar, Jure Žabkar, and Ivan Bratko. Why is rule learning optimistic and how to correct it. In Johannes Fuernkranz, Tobias Scheffer, and Myra Spiliopoulou, editors, *Proceedings of 17th European Conference on Machine Learning (ECML 2006)*, pages 330–340, Berlin, 2006. Springer-Verlag.

16. Martin Možina, Matej Guid, Jana Krivec, Aleksander Sadikov, and Ivan Bratko. Fighting knowledge acquisition bottleneck with Argument Based Machine Learning *Proc. ECAI'08*, Patras, 2008.

17. Martin Možina, Claudio Giuliano, and Ivan Bratko. Arguments extracted from text in argument based machine learning: a case study. *SAMT Workshop*, Koblenz, 2008.

18. Martin Možina, Jure Žabkar, and Ivan Bratko. D3.4: Implementation of and experiments with ABML and MLBA. ASPIC Deliverable D3.4, 2006.

19. Martin Možina, Jure Žabkar, and Ivan Bratko. Argument based machine learning. *Artificial Intelligence*, 171:922–937, 2007.

20. P. M. Murphy and D. W. Aha. UCI Repository of machine learning databases [http://www.ics.uci.edu/~mlearn/mlrepository.html]. Irvine, CA: University of California, Department of Information and Computer Science, 1994.

21. J. Watson. *Secrets of Modern Chess Strategy*. Gambit Publications, 1999.

Appendix A
Description Logic

Description Logics (DLs)[1] are a family of knowledge representation languages used to represent the terminological knowledge of an application domain. The idea is to define complex concept hierarchies from basic (atomic) concepts, and to define complex roles (or properties) as relationships between concepts.

Table A.1 shows the syntax and semantics of common concept and role constructors. The letters A, B are used for atomic concepts and C, D for concept descriptions. For roles, the letters R and S are used and non-negative integers (in number restrictions) are denoted by n, m and individuals (i.e. instances) by a, b. An *interpretation* $\mathcal{I}$ consists of a non-empty set $\Delta^{\mathcal{I}}$ (the domain of the interpretation) and an interpretation function, which assigns to every atomic concept A a set $A^{\mathcal{I}} \subseteq \Delta^{\mathcal{I}}$ and to every atomic role R a binary relation $R^{\mathcal{I}} \subseteq \Delta^{\mathcal{I}} \times \Delta^{\mathcal{I}}$.

A DL knowledge base consists of a set of *terminological axioms* (often called *TBox*) and a set of *assertion axioms* or assertions (often called *ABox*). A finite set of definitions is called a *terminology* or *TBox* if the definitions are unambiguous, i.e., no atomic concept occurs more than once as left hand side.

Suppose that Person and Female are atomic concepts. Then *Person $\sqcap$ Female* is a concept describing persons that are female. If, in addition, we suppose that *hasChild* is an atomic role, we can form the concept *Person $\sqcap \exists hasChild$*, denoting those persons that have a child. Using the bottom concept, we can also describe those persons without a child by the concept *Person $\sqcap \forall hasChild.\bot$*. These examples show how we can form complex descriptions of concepts to describe classes of objects.

An equality whose left-hand side is an atomic concept is a *definition*. Definitions are used to introduce symbolic names for complex descriptions. For instance, by the axiom *Mother $\equiv$ Woman $\sqcap \exists hasChild.Person$*, we associate to the description on the right-hand side the name *Mother*. Symbolic names may be used as abbreviations in other descriptions. If, for example, we have defined *Father* analogously to *Mother*, we can define *Parent* as *Parent $\equiv$ Mother $\sqcup$ Father*. Table A.2 shows a terminology with concepts concerned with family relationships.

---

[1] See: F. Baader, D. Calvanese, D. McGuinness, D. Nardi and P. Patel-Schneider (Eds.). *The Description Logic Handbook*. Cambridge University Press, Cambridge, UK, 2003.

Name	Syntax	Semantics
Concept & Role Constructors		
Top	$\top$	$\Delta^{\mathcal{J}}$
Bottom	$\bot$	$\varnothing$
Concept Intersection	$C \sqcap D$	$C^{\mathcal{J}} \cap D^{\mathcal{J}}$
Concept Union	$C \sqcup D$	$C^{\mathcal{J}} \cup D^{\mathcal{J}}$
Concept Negation	$\neg C$	$\Delta^{\mathcal{J}} \setminus C^{\mathcal{J}}$
Value Restriction	$\forall R.C$	$\{a \in \Delta^{\mathcal{J}} \mid \forall b.(a,b) \in R^{\mathcal{J}} \to b \in C^{\mathcal{J}}\}$
Existential Quantifier	$\exists R.C$	$\{a \in \Delta^{\mathcal{J}} \mid \exists b.(a,b) \in R^{\mathcal{J}} \wedge b \in C^{\mathcal{J}}\}$
Unqualified	$\geq nR$	$\{a \in \Delta^{\mathcal{J}} \mid \| \{b \in \Delta^{\mathcal{J}} \mid (a,b) \in R^{\mathcal{J}}\} \| \geq n\}$
Number	$\leq nR$	$\{a \in \Delta^{\mathcal{J}} \mid \| \{b \in \Delta^{\mathcal{J}} \mid (a,b) \in R^{\mathcal{J}}\} \| \leq n\}$
Restriction	$= nR$	$\{a \in \Delta^{\mathcal{J}} \mid \| \{b \in \Delta^{\mathcal{J}} \mid (a,b) \in R^{\mathcal{J}}\} \mid = n\}$
Role-value-	$R \subseteq S$	$\{a \in \Delta^{\mathcal{J}} \mid \forall b.(a,b) \in R^{\mathcal{J}} \to (a,b) \in S^{\mathcal{J}}\}$
map	$R = S$	$\{a \in \Delta^{\mathcal{J}} \mid \forall b.(a,b) \in R^{\mathcal{J}} \leftrightarrow (a,b) \in S^{\mathcal{J}}\}$
Nominal	I	$I^{\mathcal{J}} \subseteq \Delta^{\mathcal{J}}$ with $\mid I^{\mathcal{J}} \mid = 1$
Universal Role	U	$\Delta^{\mathcal{J}} \times \Delta^{\mathcal{J}}$
Role Intersection	$R \sqcap S$	$R^{\mathcal{J}} \cap S^{\mathcal{J}}$
Role Union	$R \sqcup S$	$R^{\mathcal{J}} \cup S^{\mathcal{J}}$
Role Complement	$\neg R$	$\Delta^{\mathcal{J}} \times \Delta^{\mathcal{J}} \setminus R^{\mathcal{J}}$
Role Inverse	R^-	$\{(b,a) \in \Delta^{\mathcal{J}} \times \Delta^{\mathcal{J}} \mid (a,b) \in R^{\mathcal{J}}\}$
Transitive Closure	R^+	$\bigcup_{n>1}(R^{\mathcal{J}})^n$
Role Restriction	$R\|c$	$R^{\mathcal{J}} \cap (\Delta^{\mathcal{J}} \times C^{\mathcal{J}})$
Identity	$id(C)$	$\{(d,d) \mid d \in C^{\mathcal{J}}\}$
Teminological Axioms		
Concept Inclusion	$C \sqsubseteq D$	$C^{\mathcal{J}} \subseteq D^{\mathcal{J}}$
Concept Equality	$C \equiv D$	$C^{\mathcal{J}} = D^{\mathcal{J}}$
Role Inclusion	$R \sqsubseteq S$	$R^{\mathcal{J}} \subseteq S^{\mathcal{J}}$
Role Equality	$R \equiv S$	$R^{\mathcal{J}} = S^{\mathcal{J}}$

Table A.1 Some Description Logic Role and Concept Constructors, and Terminological Axioms

The sentence $\top \sqsubseteq \forall hasParent.Person$ expresses that the range of the property *hasParent* is the class *Person* (more technically, if the property *hasParent* holds between any concept and another concept, the latter concept must be of type *Person*).

Name	DL Syntax	Example
Constructor / axiom		
Concept Intersection	$C \sqcap D$	$Woman \equiv Person \sqcap Female$
Concept Union	$C \sqcup D$	$Parent \equiv Mother \sqcup Father$
Concept Negation	$\neg C$	$Man \equiv Person \sqcap \neg Woman$
Existential Quantifier	$\exists R.C$	$Mother \equiv Woman \sqcap \exists hasChild.Person$
Value Restriction	$\forall R.C$	$MotherWithoutSons \equiv Mother \sqcap \forall hasChild.Woman$
MinCardinality	$\geq nR$	$MotherWithAtLeastThreeChildren \equiv Mother \sqcap \geq 3hasChild$
Cardinality	$= nR$	$FatherWithOneChild \equiv Father \sqcap = 1hasChild$
Bottom	$\bot$	$PersonWithoutAChild \equiv Person \sqcap \forall hasChild.\bot$
Transitive Property	$R^+ \sqsubseteq R$	$ancestor^+ \sqsubseteq ancestor$
Role Inverse	$R \equiv S^-$	$hasChild \equiv hasParent^-$
Concept Inclusion	$C \sqsubseteq D$	$Woman \sqsubseteq Person$
Disjoint with	$C \sqsubseteq \neg D$	$Man \sqsubseteq \neg Woman$
Role Inclusion	$R \sqsubseteq S$	$hasDaughter \sqsubseteq hasParent$
Range	$\top \sqsubseteq \forall R.C$	$\top \sqsubseteq \forall hasParent.Person$
Domain	$\top \sqsubseteq \forall R^-.C$	$\top \sqsubseteq \forall hasParent^-.Person$

Table A.2 A terminology (TBox) with concepts about family relationships

Appendix B
Bayesian Networks

Bayesian networks (BNs)[2] popular representation for reasoning under uncertainty, as they integrate a graphical representation of the relationships between propositions with a sound Bayesian foundation.

BNs are directed acyclic graphs where nodes correspond to random variables or propositions. The nodes in a BN are connected by directed arcs, which may be thought of as causal or influence links; the arcs go from "parents" to "children". The structure and connections in a BN specify conditional independence relations between nodes. For instance, given a particular node, its children are independent of its parents. These conditional independence relations allow the joint probability distribution of all the random variables to be specified by exponentially fewer probability values than the full joint distribution.

A *conditional probability distribution* (CPD) is associated with each node in a BN. The CPD gives the probability of each node value for all combinations of the values of its parent nodes. The probability distribution for a node with no parents is its prior distribution. Given these prior probabilities and the CPDs, *belief propagation* is performed to compute posterior probability distributions for all the nodes in a BN. These posterior probabilities represent *beliefs* about the values of the propositions represented by these nodes. The observation of specific values for nodes is called *evidence*. Beliefs in unobserved nodes in a BN can then be updated by performing belief propagation given the evidence nodes. Belief propagation for general BNs is NP-hard. However, on *polytrees* (where there is at most one path between any pair of nodes) belief propagation is linear.

To illustrate these ideas, consider the Earthquake BN in Figure B.1.[3] This BN represents a situation where a burglary or an earthquake may cause an alarm to ring, and John or Mary may call the owner of the house if they hear the alarm (i.e., their

---

[2] For a more comprehensive introduction, see:

– K. Korb and A. Nicholson. *Bayesian Artificial Intelligence*. Chapman & Hall/CRC, 2004.

– J. Pearl. *Probabilistic Reasoning in Intelligent Systems*. Morgan Kaufmann Publishers, San Mateo, California, 1988.

[3] Many sample BNs, together with the application package Netica, may be found in http://www.norsys.com.

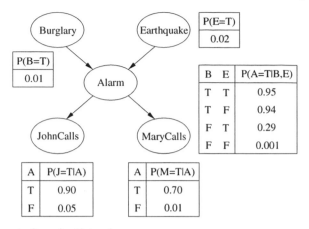

Fig. B.1 Earthquake Bayesian Network

phone call is evidence for the alarm having rang). The joint probability distribution of the propositions in the BN is represented compactly through the conditional independences implied by the structure of the BN. For instance, $\Pr(Burglary=False \wedge Earthquake=True \wedge Alarm=True \wedge JohnCalls=False \wedge MaryCalls=True)$ may be expressed as follows.

$$\Pr(Burglary=False) \times \Pr(Earthquake=True) \times$$
$$\Pr(Alarm=True|Burglary=False, Earthquake=True) \times$$
$$\Pr(JohnCalls=False|Alarm=True) \times \Pr(MaryCalls=True|Alarm=True)$$

This is because *Burglary* and *Earthquake* have no parent nodes, and the structure of the BN implies that *JohnCalls* and *MaryCalls* are conditionally independent of *Burglary* and *Earthquake* given *Alarm*. The probabilities required to calculate this joint probability are obtained from the CPDs, e.g., according to the CPD for *Alarm*, $\Pr(Alarm=True|Burglary=False, Earthquake=True) = 0.29$. If we are interested in a particular variable, say *Alarm*, we obtain its probability by performing belief propagation. For example, we can start by calculating the probability of *Alarm* without any observed evidence (just propagating the prior probabilities), and then obtain an updated probability for *Alarm* after observing that *MaryCalls* is true and *JohnCalls* is false. It is worth noting that all the nodes in this example are Boolean, but belief propagation is applicable to multi-valued nodes.

Index

Printed in the United States
152570LV00001B/19/P

9 780387 981963